Cybersecurity for Decision Makers

This book is aimed at managerial decision makers, practitioners in any field, and the academic community. The chapter authors have integrated theory with evidence-based practice to go beyond merely explaining cybersecurity topics. To accomplish this, the editors drew upon the combined cognitive intelligence of 46 scholars from 11 countries to present the state of the art in cybersecurity. Managers and leaders at all levels in organizations around the globe will find the explanations and suggestions useful for understanding cybersecurity risks as well as formulating strategies to mitigate future problems. Employees will find the examples and caveats both interesting as well as practical for everyday activities at the workplace and in their personal lives. Cybersecurity practitioners in computer science, programming, or espionage will find the literature and statistics fascinating and more than likely a confirmation of their own findings and assumptions. Government policymakers will find the book valuable to inform their new agenda of protecting citizens and infrastructure in any country around the world. Academic scholars, professors, instructors, and students will find the theories, models, frameworks, and discussions relevant and supportive to teaching as well as research.

Cybersecurity for Decision Makers

Edited by
Narasimha Rao Vajjhala
Kenneth David Strang

CRC Press
Taylor & Francis Group
Boca Raton London New York

CRC Press is an imprint of the
Taylor & Francis Group, an **informa** business

Designed cover image: @Shutterstock

First edition published 2023
by CRC Press
6000 Broken Sound Parkway NW, Suite 300, Boca Raton, FL 33487–2742

and by CRC Press
4 Park Square, Milton Park, Abingdon, Oxon, OX14 4RN

CRC Press is an imprint of Taylor & Francis Group, LLC

Library of Congress Cataloging-in-Publication Data
Names: Vajjhala, Narasimha, 1978– editor. | Strang, Kenneth David, 1962– editor.
Title: Cybersecurity for decision makers / edited by Narasimha Rao Vajjhala,
    Kenneth David Strang.
Description: First edition. | Boca Raton : CRC Press, 2023. | Includes
    bibliographical references.
Identifiers: LCCN 2023002036 (print) | LCCN 2023002037 (ebook) | ISBN 9781032334967
    (hardback) | ISBN 9781032334974 (paperback) | ISBN 9781003319887 (ebook)
Subjects: LCSH: Management. | Decision making. | Computer security.
Classification: LCC HD30.23 .C87 2023 (print) | LCC HD30.23 (ebook) |
    DDC 658.4/03—dc23/eng/20230223
LC record available at https://lccn.loc.gov/2023002036
LC ebook record available at https://lccn.loc.gov/2023002037

ISBN: 9781032334967 (hbk)
ISBN: 9781032334974 (pbk)
ISBN: 9781003319887 (ebk)

DOI: 10.1201/9781003319887

Typeset in Times
by Apex CoVantage, LLC

Contents

Foreword

Mikko Hyppönen, Finland

How many of the Fortune 500 companies have been hacked? Answer: 500.

If a company network is large enough, it will always have vulnerabilities, and there will always be hackers checking for opportunities to illegally make money. Each of the Fortune 500 companies has more than 100,000 workstations around the world, which will always include hacked or infected systems.

I often visit our clients, providing management teams and boards with status updates. Occasionally, a member of the team, usually the chief financial officer, will ask me a difficult question. Browsing the annual budget, the CFO will ask why the company is paying so much for information security each year, since they have no IT security problems. I glance around their conference room, complimenting them on its cleanliness. The CFO looks puzzled. I repeat the compliment and add that they could probably lay off the janitor and housekeeping staff, given how clean everything is . . . (that was a joke – most companies have been visited by hackers, but company leaders do not realize this if they had nothing of real value online for the criminals to steal).

Companies do not go bankrupt because they get hacked. I know of only a handful of companies that have been wiped out by a security breach or leak. Companies seem to recover fairly well, even from large-scale attacks. However, their management seldom recovers, and we often see cases where the CEO, CIO, or VP in charge of IT is shown the door after a hacking incident. This is a good reason for decision makers to become more aware of cybersecurity.

Nowadays, almost every company has a massive number of devices online. Not all are computers, though, which makes them harder to protect: IT security staff also need to consider protecting printers, routers, security systems, photocopiers, and videoconferencing systems from hackers.

The general model for protecting a company network is simple: keep cyberattackers out by building walls around the network that are impenetrable to outsiders. Sounds effective and simple – but whenever something sounds simple, it's usually too simple.

If the only principle applied to company network protection is that firewalls, filters, and gateways keep unwanted guests out, defenders will focus all their attention on this. And if the sole focus is keeping attackers out, no one watches the internal network – but that is precisely what they should be watching. This is perhaps where organizations fail most, and the reason is clear: after investing a great deal of money and effort in building walls around a network, nobody wants to assume that this carefully constructed protection will be breached by attackers. However, this is precisely what they should assume.

If a network's guardians anticipate failure from the beginning, their attitude will change. The focus will shift from building walls to monitoring internal network traffic. This way we can detect breaches – so we can respond to them.

This book is an essential starting point to help readers understand the nature and importance of cybersecurity. Read it – then take action.

Mikko Hyppönen is cybersecurity researcher based in Helsinki, Finland. He has written for the New York Times, Wired, and Scientific American and lectured at the universities of Oxford, Stanford, and Cambridge. His latest book is "If It's Smart, It's Vulnerable"

(Wiley 2022).

Preface

This book is aimed at business decision makers, practitioners in any field, and the academic community. The authors have integrated theory with evidence-based practice to go beyond merely explaining cybersecurity topics. To accomplish that, we drew upon the combined cognitive intelligence of 46 scholars from 11 countries to present the state of the art in cybersecurity concerns. Managers and leaders at all levels in organizations around the globe will find the explanations and suggestions useful for understanding cybersecurity risks as well as formulating strategies to mitigate future problems. Employees will find the examples and caveats both interesting as well as practical for everyday activities at the workplace and in their personal lives. Cybersecurity practitioners in computer science, programming, or espionage will find the literature and statistics fascinating and more than likely a confirmation of their assumptions. Government policymakers will find the book valuable to inform their new agenda of protecting citizens and infrastructure in any country around the world. Academic scholars, professors, instructors, and students will find the theories, models, frameworks, and discussions relevant to support teaching as well as research.

The book editors conducted machine learning analytics on the contents to present an evidence-based summary of topic coverage. Figure A is a thematic analysis of the chapter coverage, where the size of the keyword indicates higher frequency and importance within the book. Importance, as an attribute, illustrates that the keywords were significant within the context of the discussion beyond the frequency count, as revealed using machine learning algorithms.

The results of the thematic analysis were used to organize the book contents in terms of dividing the chapters into sections, naming the sections, and sequencing the chapters within the sections. In the evidence-based diagram of Figure A, it is obvious from the large font size that cybersecurity, organizational decision-making, ethical issues, and ethical measures were the central, most important topics discussed. Many authors touched upon those keywords but in the context of specific industries, applications, and disciplines.

FIGURE A Thematic evidence-based keyword topic coverage.

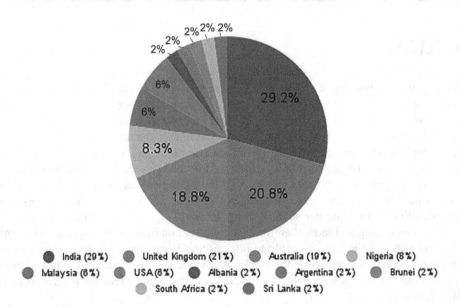

FIGURE B   Demographics of book authors.

As noted earlier, there were 46 authors from 11 countries spread around the world and most of the continental regions. Figure B is a demographic analysis of the authors. Most authors (29%) were from India; then 21% were from the United Kingdom, 19% were from Australia, 8% from Nigeria, 6% in Malaysia, and another 6% from the United States. The remainder of the authors were evenly spread across South Africa (2%), Argentina (2%), Albania (2%), Brunei (2%), and Sri Lanka (2%).

In terms of book metrics, prior to typesetting, there were 34 submissions; 23 chapters were accepted (at the time of writing), bringing the acceptance rate to 68% (0.6765). Prior to typesetting, there were approximately 250,000 words, including references and diagrams.

METHODS AND PROJECT MANAGEMENT

The editors applied project management to control the entire book-writing process. The project management was shared between Vajjhala and Strang. As a result, the current book project finished on schedule, under budget, and within the agreed-upon scope, and the editors assert it has acceptable quality levels. No conflicts of interest were reported by any team member. Both editors received ethical approval from their respective employers, and no specific external funding was received.

A central website was used to communicate the project's key milestones (http://kennethstrang. com/cyber). Easychair software was used to manage the submission and double-blinded peer review process. Every chapter, including the first, underwent a double-blind peer review within the Easy-chair system. At least two reviewers, either an author for another chapter or an external expert, conducted an evaluation using an objective rubric supplied by Strang. Vajjhala served as the managing editor since Strang contributed the first draft of the first chapter as well as developing the evaluation rubric.

Vajjhala conducted most of the administration, including the final proofreading, author management in Easychair, and communication with authors. Strang performed customer relationship management with the other non-author stakeholders. Vajjhala conducted plagiarism checks on all chapters, investigated any high duplication rates beyond 30%, and rejected any chapter with unaccounted-for high duplication rates (to explain, several authors extended earlier papers and declared that in their chapters, so these were accepted at higher duplication rates).

The preface was written as a draft by Strang, including statistical analysis of the keywords, and then extended by Vajjhala. Strang managed the solicitation and decision-making for the foreword author. Taylor and Francis managing editor, Gabriella Williams (Gabby), and her staff were involved at critical milestones for quality assurance and answering production questions.

BOOK CONTENT OVERVIEW

In Chapter 1, "Why Cyberattacks Disrupt Society and How to Mitigate Risk," Kenneth David Strang and Narasimha Rao Vajjhala state that government websites and private and public companies have all been hampered by cybersecurity threats. The authors explain that the effects have been severe, affecting daily communications, e-commerce, and the supply chain. This chapter's main research question revolves around that. The authors reveal how cybersecurity attacks have crippled government as well as private and public company sites around the world. The impacts have been serious, including disrupting the supply chain, e-commerce, and everyday communications. Although technology has continued to advance, so have cyber terrorists! In parallel with cyber terrorism, technology has developed exponentially in the last five years, which researchers have termed Industry 4.0. Policymakers, academics, and managers working with organizations that use Industry 4.0 technologies and applications should find this chapter interesting.

In Chapter 2, "Onto Nature, Forms and Remedies of Cyberbullying on Social Media Platforms: A Brief Philosophical Perspective," Sooraj Kumar Maurya posits that technological advancement was one of many good things that came into being with the dawn of modernity. The author explains that despite all the benefits of technology, cyberbullying has emerged as a serious social danger that harms those comfortable using it. As technology has advanced, cyberbullying is now carried out through various platforms, including mobile phones, chat rooms on the internet, blogs, email, and text messages. The author further explains that many college students are frequently caught up in some form of digital technology for extended periods. Growing social media use among youth offers cause for severe concern. The author argues that the deliberate, repetitive, and occasionally violent use of communication and information technologies to irritate and harm others is morally unacceptable. The author of this chapter highlights how cyberbullying negatively impacts adults and is a growing global concern. Along with this, the author tries to identify precise strategies and treatments to deal with the effects of cyberbullying for the betterment of our children.

In Chapter 3, "Cybersecurity and Human Factors: A Literature Review," Natasha Cecilia Edeh argues that organizations and experts alike have noted that human factors are the "weakest link" in cybersecurity. In most cases, security breaches and incidents that result in significant financial losses in enterprises are caused by intentional and inadvertent human mistakes. The author suggests the use of an interdisciplinary approach to address security challenges has recently undergone a paradigm change. However, there has been little attention paid to and inadequate research done on the topic of human factors and how they might be employed as a cybersecurity solution. The goal of this chapter is to raise awareness of how underutilized human elements in cybersecurity can be used to address problems with cybersecurity. This chapter searched for and examined relevant material on human factors in cybersecurity using a selection procedure. Themes that potentially support the claims that human factors can contribute to organizational security were identified through an analysis of 16 articles.

In Chapter 4, "An Introduction to Cybercrime and Cybersecurity: The Whys and Whos of Cybersecurity," Riddhita Parikh explains that cybercriminals may employ various techniques to harm and profit from the victim. The author states that cybersecurity is the knowledge of numerous procedures that protect the system, networks, and applications against dangerous threats. The author cites recent studies that have found a staggering increase in cybersecurity breaches. The author illustrates examples of cybercrimes linked to banking, credit/debit card fraud, fake social media news, stalking, and bullying. This chapter aims to raise awareness and educate people about cybersecurity to counteract the threat of e-crime. The history of the digital age, its development, the appearance of cybercrimes and e-securities, and the fact that everyone involved in cyberspace must know this information to feel secure and safe online are all covered in this chapter.

In Chapter 5, "Cybersecurity Attack Case Studies, Lessons Learned," D. V. Manjula, Aisshwarya Nallamilli, and Dulkarnine Raseeda state that the frequency of cyberattacks is rising gradually as technology advances. The authors argue that these attacks cause significant damage to businesses. The authors give examples of several cybersecurity measures currently used by organizations, including multi-factor authentication (MFA), virtual private networks (VPNs), firewalls, and other generic security measures. The authors also illustrate several case studies of cybersecurity attacks that will help decision makers in organizations. The chapter's goal is to ensure that organizations learn from previous case studies of cyberattacks and avoid repeating similar attacks. This chapter should help decision makers to develop policies and prepare for potential cyberattacks.

In Chapter 6, "Towards a Cybersecurity Awareness Program for a Non-Technical Audience in Malaysia," Shafiq Ul Rehman and Selvakumar Manickam argue that despite all the advantages the Internet offers, people need to be aware that hackers can exploit online access media to cause significant monetary and material damage to the target audience. The authors state that because cyberattacks affect enterprises, banking, and the public, cybercrime stands apart from traditional crime due to its diversity, flexibility, dynamism, and ability to evolve. The authors point out that cybercriminals have evolved, becoming more sophisticated and intelligent in their methods of operation due to the intricacy involved in how the economy runs due to the integration of online and Internet technology. This chapter identifies scams and online fraud cases in the last few years. Based on their findings, the authors created a cybersecurity awareness program to help beginner Internet and technology users avoid becoming victims of cyberattacks and effectively raise long-lasting awareness.

In Chapter 7, "Raising Awareness Towards Social Engineering Among Adolescents: Psychological and Cybersecurity Perspective," Ruchi Joshi and Shafiq Ul Rehman posit that ever-evolving technologies ensure the rate of human progress keeps advancing and that we achieve new levels of informational access. The authors focus on social engineering, which is the practice of tricking and manipulating individuals to gain access to vulnerable, sensitive, and intimate data. Social engineering has a psychological, emotional, and occasionally emotional impact on the victim. This chapter aims to shed light on how con artists use psychological strategies to prey on their victims' emotional weaknesses. This chapter also aims to show how social pressure and victims' responses to social cues in conformity, compliance, and obedience cause them to fall for social engineering schemes like phishing, pretexting, baiting, and tailgating. The chapter emphasizes the value of educating students about cybersecurity and the function of educational institutions, teachers, and counselors in addition to cybersecurity, legal, and technological specialists. The authors also discuss how social engineering affects people psychologically and the value of mental health experts in offering support.

In Chapter 8, "Intelligent Named Entity-Based Cybercrime Recognition System for Social Media Network Platforms," Kathiravan Pannerselvam, Saranya Rajiakodi, Shanmugavadivu Pichai explore artificial intelligence (AI) as a technology employed to address the problems of current online threats on social media platforms. The authors focus on the role of natural language processing (NLP) in preventing cybercrime and restricting access to malicious social media posts. The authors illustrate social media post analysis (SMPA) – a tool for examining interactions between various individuals and groups on social media sites, including Twitter, Facebook, Instagram, and Reddit. SMPA supports the investigation of revolutionary plans and maintains tabs on terrorist actions. The use of a more accurate identification method in named entity recognition is discussed in this study as an essential notion for mitigating cyberattacks on social media networks. Named entity recognition (NER) uses various techniques, including rule-based NER, machine learning-based NER, and hybrid NER, to recognize and extract meaningful information from unstructured data, such as Facebook and Twitter comments. With the help of random forest and various upgraded recurrent neural networks (RNN) architectures like long short-term memory (LSTM) and bidirectional long short-term memory (BiLSTM), the authors proposed a CyNER system to identify entities like I-Malware, O (others), B-Malware, B-System, I-System, B-Organization, B-Indicator, I-Organization, and I-Vulnerability from a given social media post containing cybersecurity issues. The experimental findings in this chapter demonstrate that the accuracy of the proposed CyNER system is superior to that of BiLSTM and the random forest algorithm.

In Chapter 9, "A Case Study on Zonal Analysis of Cybercrimes Over a Decade in India," Diya C. R., Umme Salma M., and Chaitra R. Beerannavar argue that despite the immense potential of the Internet, cyberspace is also where most crimes are committed. The authors emphasize that cybercrime is one of the critical aspects of cybersecurity, which is crucial to information technology and requires urgent attention. This chapter examines cybercrimes in India as a case study. The key source for the analysis is the data gathered from the National Crime Records Bureau (NCRB) from 2010 to 2020. By splitting geo-locations into seven zones – the central, east, west, north, south, northeast, and union territories – a thorough analysis of cybercrimes across India is conducted in this chapter. The reported cybercrimes in each zone are analyzed to determine which area necessitates immediate implementation of security measures. The top ten states with the highest cybercrime rates are also listed in this chapter. This chapter aims to give a thorough analysis of the crimes and the steps taken to stop them.

In Chapter 10, "Taming the Confluence of Space Systems and Cybersecurity," Syed Shahzad, Keith Joiner, and Felicity Deane emphasize that space systems are essential parts of vital infrastructure, and their removal would have a significant impact on a sizable population, increasingly with safety repercussions. The authors also state that today's digitally connected space infrastructure is vulnerable to sophisticated and destructive cyberattacks in other interconnected cyber systems like banking. The two main categories of these attacks are electronic and cyber. This chapter builds on earlier academic work by making a case for creating engineering, legal, and business frameworks that aim to ensure that space systems are cyber resilient to present and emerging threats. The research on existing space technologies, attack surfaces, and legal frameworks for their protection and regulation is presented in this chapter.

In Chapter 11, "Regulating Cyber-Physical Systems for Safety Consequences," Mark van Zomeren, Keith Joiner, Lily Qiao, and Elena Sitnikova consider using cyber-physical systems (CPS) within the context of large and complex organizations such as nation-state defense organizations and critical civilian infrastructure. The authors build on a literature review identifying the international best practices for the through-life technical assurance of cyber-capable systems. The chapter expands on the idea of CPS by discussing the social effects of complex CPS (CCPS). The necessity to examine not only the information assurance components of CPS but also the continual provision of timely and secure physical outputs of CPS is highlighted in the argument for shifting from traditional cybersecurity to cyber-worthiness. This chapter considers the significance of model-based cyber-worthiness evaluations in the framework of monitoring and informing CPS about threats. This chapter explores how emergent aspects of complex CPS may be addressed via cyber-worthiness assessment and complex systems governance (CSG).

In Chapter 12, "Mapping the State of the Art: Artificial Intelligence for Decision Making in Financial Crime," Borja Álvarez Martínez, Richard Allmendinger, Hadi Akbarzadeh Khorshidi, Theodore Papamarkou, Andre Feitas, Johanne Trippas, Markos Zachariadis, Nicholas Lord, and Katie Benson provide an overview of recent research on the many uses of AI-based solutions to financial crime problems. The authors employ a multidisciplinary, practitioner-oriented approach that focuses widely on solutions for a financial crime without focusing on a particular criminal typology. This chapter is intended to address potential decision makers and relevant stakeholders from both industry and governmental organizations, such as risk or fraud analysts, compliance officers, law enforcement officers, managers in financial institutions, policymakers, and academics with related interests. The aim of the chapter is to enable decision makers to assess the capabilities, drawbacks, and specific techniques favored by researchers when dealing with issues unique to the context of finance. The authors use a chronological approach to describe present methods, new uses, and forthcoming trends, contextualizing artificial intelligence as a useful tool that has not yet been fully utilized.

In Chapter 13, "Understanding and Measuring the Impact of Cyberattacks on Businesses – A Systematic Literature Review," Xiuqin Li, Richard Allmendinger, Elvira Uyarra, and James Mercer examine how cyberattacks impact businesses. The authors identify the gaps in the literature and what future research is needed by systematically evaluating the relevant literature. The COVID-19 epidemic has led to an increase in the number and seriousness of cyberattacks. The authors emphasize that wide-ranging serious corporate damages have resulted from this, including financial losses, reputational damage, decreased productivity, operation disruptions, and complete failure of all business processes. The authors argue that the practice of justifying cybersecurity investment and the future mitigation of cyber hazards would need to be improved by consistent measurement techniques. This chapter's purpose is to contribute to the still-evolving field of cyberattacks from the standpoint of impact measurement. The findings in this chapter provide academics and practitioners with useful information to spot current research trends, influential authors, methodologies, and barriers; identify future research areas; and promote thinking about suitable solutions.

In Chapter 14, "Problems and Ethical issues in Cybersecurity Today: Some Critical Readings," Maximiliano E. Korstanje examines the problems and ethical issues in the context of cybersecurity from a critical philosophical view. This chapter critically examines the problems and conundrums surrounding cybersecurity while providing the groundwork for a fresh perspective on the media industry. The chapter advances the argument that global modernity has produced some decentralized modes of production while centralizing essential knowledge, echoing Jacques Ellul and Max Weber's worries.

In Chapter 15, "An Empirical Investigation of Psychological Factors Affecting Compliance With Information Security Organizational Policies," Tatyana Ryutov emphasizes that technological solutions cannot exclusively ensure the security of a company's IT assets. The author posits that information security should also consider human factors. Information security policies (ISPs) are frequently violated by employees, which poses a severe risk to businesses. So the author emphasizes that it is crucial to advance our understanding of voluntary compliance behavior if we want security measures to work better. By evaluating several user-based risk types, the chapter offers insights on efficiently addressing the issue of ISP non-compliance in enterprises. The author assesses compliance with each of the six main categories of information security policy using decision vignettes, building on a well-supported model of security policy compliance intentions, and comparing model parameters. Practitioners can use the study's findings to strengthen security education and awareness campaigns and improve the protection of organizational assets.

In Chapter 16, "Nexus between Banking Cybersecurity Breaches, Cyber Vulnerabilities, and Kidnap for Ransom in Nigeria – A Comparative Analysis of Kaduna and Abuja Metropolis, Nigeria," Hassan Abdulazeez and Sule Magaji examine the cyberinfrastructure platforms for Nigeria's electronic banking system. The authors state that the simplicity of conducting banking transactions made possible by the system; the decrease in high currency circulation; and the projected consequent impact of lowering crime, such as robberies and corruption, served as the system's central tenets. This chapter looks at how much the system has slowed down, prevented, or even caused the development of additional crimes. This chapter aims to determine the types of crimes that occurred before cyberbanking security-induced systems regarding the nature and scope of crimes after introducing the system. The chapter uses crime statistical data from the police, conducts interviews with law enforcement officials, and tries to conduct a social survey. The chapter findings reveal a considerable disparity between Kaduna and Abuja in mean electronic banking and the rise in abduction. The authors recommend that institutions that use electronic banking platforms ensure their hardware and software are constantly functional and frequently submitted to hackproof/integrity checks.

In Chapter 17, "SME Cybersecurity Misconceptions – A Guide for Decision Makers," Martin Wilson and Sharon McDonald investigate the attitudes of small- to medium-sized businesses (SMEs) toward adopting cybersecurity in the United Kingdom through a survey of 85 small firms. The findings of this chapter imply that misconceptions regarding the degree of risk to businesses, the nature of cyberattacks, and a general lack of knowledge about cybersecurity procedures and technologies commonly influence business owners' decisions when interacting with cybersecurity. The authors consider this information when deciding how to inform SME cybersecurity decision makers best and help those who work with SMEs to strengthen cybersecurity.

In Chapter 18, "Rethinking the Impact of Informal Organizational Rules on Organizational Cybersecurity," Maharazu Kasim emphasizes that information and communication technologies (ICT) firms have benefited from technological advancements. However, organizations still need to be concerned about the numerous cybersecurity challenges that have come with it. Organizations must also consider social measures that go beyond even the most robust technological cybersecurity controls. Organizations use formal rules as one of their defenses against both internal and external threats to their systems. Organizations must focus more on the detrimental effects of their internal cybersecurity. As a result, unofficial regulations are created, which could be harmful to organizational cybersecurity. This chapter examines the formal and informal rules literature and aims to understand how formal and informal organizational norms support or undermine organizational cybersecurity. This chapter's findings show that although formal regulations can support cybersecurity, certain situations can undermine it.

In Chapter 19, "Ethical Aspects of Cybersecurity in E-Commerce," Tanya Kumar and Satveer Kaur show that data emphasize that cybersecurity is one of the necessities of today's business world because businesses use these systems to safeguard their pertinent data against theft and damage. The authors state that the e-commerce ecosystem suffers financial and reputational harm from cyberattacks. The authors explain one of the main concerns in e-commerce – privacy protection. The authors posit that implementing cybersecurity ethics in the best way feasible is needed to ensure privacy protection. The chapter lists several ways of demonstrating ethical behavior, including maintaining confidentiality, privacy concerns, fair policies, avoiding discrimination, respecting intellectual property rights, including copyrights and patents, and giving back to others and society at large. The chapter aims to identify the ethical concerns surrounding cybersecurity in e-commerce and the ethical controls needed to manage cybersecurity as a pertinent ethical issue in the modern digital world.

In Chapter 20, "Cybersecurity in Healthcare," Arijita Banerjee and Sumit Kumar posit that numerous healthcare companies are targets of cybersecurity threats because of the extensive access to electronic health records. The authors explain that due to the rapid development of connected information technology, patients' safety and the reliability of machine learning tools are now at risk, which raises various concerns concerning medical infrastructure. The authors explain that in another three years, it is anticipated that cyber events will have caused $10 trillion in global economic losses. Healthcare businesses must therefore highlight the need for flexible cyber defenses. The authors emphasize that hospital breaches have been linked to a lack of cybersecurity understanding. This chapter aims to safeguard information assets and promote a more robust cybersecurity culture across all nations. The authors emphasize that it is crucial to reform new cybersecurity-related legislation and regulations to obtain a comprehensive solution.

In Chapter 21, "Business Continuity and Disaster Recovery Strategies as Resilience Tools After Cyberattacks in Toxic Entrepreneurship Ecosystems," Lukman Raimi describes how businesses and corporate organizations might respond to unfavorable occurrences and economic turmoil. The author describes business continuity and disaster recovery strategies (BCRS) as resilience measures for dealing with the susceptibility of cyberattacks in unhealthy entrepreneurial environments. The author emphasizes that the use of digital technologies has improved the technical and economic performance of businesses, impacting employee productivity; service delivery effectiveness; customer experience and satisfaction; risk management; the detection of human errors; and the precise use of human, financial, and material resources (HFM) in digital workplaces. The author states that the digital age and its associated technologies have seen an increase in cyberattacks that have disrupted businesses, stolen massive amounts of data, caused financial losses, resulted in rapid bankruptcy, and posed risks to entrepreneurship. The chapter aims to discuss 11 different business continuity and disaster recovery strategies that entrepreneurs and corporate organizations can use to thwart cyberattacks in unhealthy entrepreneurial ecosystems. These strategies are based on the plethora of cybersecurity issues and concerns raised in the literature.

In Chapter 22, "Building Cybersecurity Capacity Through Education, Awareness, and Training," Ruth Shillair, William H. Dutton, Patricia Esteve-Gonzalez, Sadie Creese, and Basie Von Solms offer managers and decision makers advice on how to prioritize scarce resources as they struggle to safeguard stakeholders against evolving internet dangers. The authors discovered a definite effect of cybersecurity education, awareness raising, and training (CEAT) on the vitality of internet use and services at the national level based on a comparative analysis of 80 countries. The Cybersecurity Capacity Maturity Model for Nations, or CMM, was created by the Global Cybersecurity Capacity Centre and included one of the five components of a wider cybersecurity capacity-building model. The education, awareness, and training indicators that make up this aspect of capacity building within the CMM are briefly discussed in this chapter, along with a cross-national analysis of the results of CEAT on internet use. The quantitative analysis in this chapter demonstrates a positive and statistically significant impact of CEAT on the vitality of internet use and services while controlling for contextual variables such as country wealth and the extent of internet use. The authors make recommendations for policy and practice to address the need for more successful programs while acknowledging the immaturity of cybersecurity education, awareness raising, and training in most countries reviewed.

In the last chapter of this book, "Cybersecurity Awareness – Prerequisites for Strategic Decision Makers," Sadiq Nasir investigates the principles of cybersecurity awareness (CSA) for people who make strategic decisions for an organization. The author undertakes a social-technical approach to present ideas that decision makers need to be aware of. Additionally, this chapter looks at the cyber-security-related considerations that must be made by decision makers. The author emphasizes that a strong CSA from the top will support and safeguard the company's good cybersecurity practices.

Acknowledgments

ASSOCIATE PROFESSOR NARASIMHA RAO VAJJHALA, ALBANIA

I want to thank my family members, particularly my mother, Mrs. Rajeswari Vajjhala, for her blessings and for instilling in me the virtues of perseverance and commitment.

A special note of thanks to co-editor Professor Kenneth David Strang for consistently motivating me to continue my research work.

PROFESSOR KENNETH DAVID STRANG, USA

I'm shouting out a thank you to all our chapter co-authors for cooperating with me to ensure this edited book project was completed on time – their names are published within. Obviously, without our chapter co-author's contributions, Rao and I would have had to do much more work, which may have taken more than 20 times as long.

I also think about those people not in the book. I want to extend best wishes and empathy to those emerging scholars who, for one reason or another, were not able to finish their studies in time for publication here. To those colleagues – don't worry: there will be other opportunities in the future for you to share your wonderful research.

My co-editor Dr. Narasimha Rao Vajjhala (Rao) has done almost 100% of the administration for this project, including overseeing the laborious peer review processes and manuscript editing, so he has proven his ability. Rao is on a trajectory to become a global scholar, and I am proud to see him grow as a scholar every year.

Mikko Hyppönen helped us by writing the foreword in a short time over the busy Christmas season. I recruited Mikko and selected him due to his industry expertise and his being based in Helsinki, Finland (explained further subsequently). When you read his foreword, I hope you realize he is correct – cyber hacking is pervasive. My best wishes to other practitioners who were evaluated as possible foreword writers.

Bulcsu Szekely (Bubu) deserves thanks for educating me about contemporary cyber warfare, and he influenced me to select a European foreword writer. Bubu works for a university in Finland, and he has lived through cybersecurity warfare. His rich descriptions of what can happen inspired me to include contemporary content. We avoid politics in scholarship (except if the discipline is political science – which it is not here), but I want to reveal the significance of Bubu's input, as I will summarize in the following.

Finland shares a very long 830-mile (1,340-km) border with Russia, and I probably don't have to spell out all the details of the Ukraine situation and Finland's recent emergency application to join NATO. It is clear to me, as an outsider a continent away, based on what I have researched, that many companies, government departments (including medical facilities), and individuals in Finland have experienced financial damage due to cybersecurity warfare.

Past behavior repeats itself – that is a well-known axiom, and it has been proven true based on psychology research. Russia has a long history of aggressive behavior, including invasions of other countries, often denying being the aggressor. For example, back in 1939, Russia's Red Army shelled its own Soviet village of Mainila and blamed Finland by covertly raising a fake flag as an excuse to initiate a war. There have been numerous well-documented Russian invasions, as briefly enumerated in the following:

- Iran (1941–1946)
- Hungary (1944)
- Romania (1944)
- Bulgaria (1944)

- Czechoslovakia (1944)
- Northern Norway (1944–1946)
- Bornholm, Denmark (1945–1946)
- Germany (1945)
- Austria (1945–1955)
- Manchuria (1945–1946)
- Korea (1945–1948)
- Kuril Islands (1945)
- Czechoslovakia (1968–1989)
- Afghanistan (1979–1989)
- Crimean Peninsula (2014)
- Ukraine (2022+)
  (portions adapted from public data at
       www.ghpage.com/tall-list-of-
   countries-russia-has-invaded-since-
              1941-drops/221973/)

Russia is considered the second most powerful country in the world (after the United States) from a military perspective. By comparison, the United States has not initiated any such hostile military invasions in over 100 years. This may be an oversimplification of history, but as an American, I remember from grade school that many years ago the French were killed along the northern border at a time when the United States was attempting to become independent of the British monarchy rule (note that Canada is still formally under the rule of England).

Interestingly, a political confrontation in 1990 made the history books when a small band of Mohawk Indians, who were US citizens, traveled to Quebec at the invitation of the Kanesatake Mohawk Oka reservation to protest the expansion of a golf course on disputed tribal land. After two months of confrontations, over 100 Quebecois police, backed by 4400 Canadian Army troops, defeated the Mohawks, taking 200 prisoners (including 30 US citizens). One French Quebecois police person, was killed and numerous soldiers on both sides were hospitalized for injuries sustained during the fighting (adapted from public data at www.mentalfloss.com/article/60380/4-times-us-invaded-canada). The Quebec government subsequently bought the land to stop the development of the golf course and to end the fighting! Back to Bubu, this illustrates my cybersecurity experience pales in comparison to his.

Finally, although I have already mentioned this, I want to thank the staff at Taylor & Francis who accepted our proposal for this book and assisted us in making it a reality.

Editor Biographies

 **Narasimha Rao Vajjhala** is working as an associate professor at the Faculty of Engineering and Architecture at the University of New York Tirana in Albania. He had previously worked as the Chair of the Information Systems department at the School of IT and Computing at the American University of Nigeria. He is a senior member of ACM and IEEE. He is the Editor-in-Chief (EiC) for the *International Journal of Risk and Contingency Management* (IJRCM) and the Guest Associate Editor for AI in *Business, Frontiers in Artificial Intelligence* (Scopus Indexed). He is also a member of the Project Management Institute (PMI). He has over 20 years of experience in teaching mainly programming and database-related courses at both graduate and undergraduate levels in Europe and Africa. He has also worked as a consultant in technology firms in Europe and has experience participating in EU-funded projects. He has completed a doctorate in information systems and technology (United States) and holds a master of science in computer science and applications (India) and a master of business administration with a specialization in information systems (Switzerland).

 **Kenneth David Strang** has more than 300 mostly sole-authored scholarly publications. He is a professor who teaches and supervises undergraduate, graduate, and doctoral students across five disciplines: business administration, management information systems, marketing/consumer behavior, supply chain management, and economics/statistics. Ken has a doctorate in project management (operations research), an MBA (strategic management), a BSBA (marketing), and an AAS (IT), all with summa cum laude/honors; plus he is an internationally licensed Project Management Professional (PMI, USA), a Certified Research Professional (IIPMR, USA), a Certified Network Administrator (Novell, USA), a Certified Supply Chain Specialist/ Procurement Professional (IIPMR, USA), and a Fellow Life Management Institute with distinction (LOMA, USA). Dr. Strang has lifetime grant projects valued over $7+ million, and he has won several honors, including a Behavior Energy Climate Change Fellowship from the American Council for an Energy-Efficient Economy, the Emerald Literati award, and the Duke of Edinburgh community service medal, along with several presidential citations.

Contributors

Hassan Abdulazeez is presently a lecturer in the Department of Sociology at Kaduna State University. Hassan obtained his BSc in sociology from Bayero University, Kano, in 1991, MSc in sociology in 2014, and PhD in sociology 2020, with a specialization in criminology and minors in social gerontology and sociology of development, among others, from the University of Abuja, Nigeria. He started his early career with the now-defunct Tate Industries Plc, headquartered in Lagos, between 1993 and 1994, where he served in different departments as a supervisor and assistant manager, respectively. He left the company's services to engage in private business between 1995 and 2018. Due to his zeal to contribute to human and national development through imparting knowledge, He joined Kaduna State University in 2019 as an assistant lecturer, where he lectures in the sociology department. Presently, he is the level coordinator of the Criminology Unit of the department, where he coordinates students' academic and related welfare issues. He is a member of professional bodies such as the Nigeria Society of Criminologists and the Nigerian Anthropological & Sociological Association. His research interests include cybersecurity and cybercrime, and he participates in rights advocacy for vulnerable older adults. He is married with children.

Richard Allmendinger (Member, IEEE) is Professor in Applied Artificial Intelligence at Alliance Manchester Business School, University of Manchester, and Fellow of the Alan Turing Institute, the UK's national institute for data science and artificial intelligence. Richard has a PhD in computer science from UoM. He works in the development and application of decision support systems comprising simulation, optimization, and machine learning tools. Richard's work is primarily funded by EPSRC, ESRC, Innovate UK, and industrial partners.

Banerjee, Arijita received her DNB and MD in physiology. She was attached to various institutes like PGIMS Rohtak and Maulana Azad Medical college, Delhi for residency program. Currently she is working as Assistant Professor in Dr BC Roy Multi-specialty medical research Centre, IIT Kharagpur, India. She is a recipient of various awards and has published articles both on national and international platforms. She is also a lifetime member of American Physiological society and Indian Physiological Society.

Chaitra R. Beerannavar is an assistant professor at the School of Law, Christ (Deemed to be) University, Bangalore, India. Her PhD was awarded on "A Critical Study of Reverse Mergers as a Method of Going Public: A Comparative Study of US, China and India" by the Faculty of Law, Symbiosis International University, Pune, in 2015. She is the recipient of the 16th Dr. D.C. Pavate Memorial Visiting fellowship at the Centre of International Studies/Department of Politics and International Studies, University of Cambridge, UK, 2016. She has participated in various international conferences and published several articles.

Katie Benson is a lecturer in criminology at the University of Manchester. Her research and teaching focuses on financial crime, organized crime, money laundering, and illicit finance.

Diya C. R. is an assistant professor at the School of Law, Christ (Deemed to be) University, Bangalore, India. She received a NET qualification in 2015. She was a practicing lawyer in the High Court of Kerala for 21 years and was guest faculty for law at NUALS, Cochin University of Science and Technology, Cochin, and various MBA colleges for ten years. She joined CHRIST University (Deemed to be University) in 2017. She is presently pursuing a PhD at Christ (Deemed to be University). She has participated in various international conferences and published articles. She has also conducted guest talks at various schools and colleges on cybercrimes and prevention as an awareness program. Her research interests are in cyber law, digital evidence, property law, and constitutional law.

Sadie Creese is Professor of Cybersecurity in the Department of Computer Science at the University of Oxford. She teaches operational aspects of cybersecurity, including threat detection, risk assessment, and security architectures. Sadie is the founding Director of the Global Cybersecurity Capacity Centre (GCSCC) at the Oxford Martin School, where she continues to serve as a director, conducting research into what constitutes national cybersecurity capacity, working with countries and international organizations around the world. She was the founding director of Oxford's cybersecurity network launched in 2008 and now called CyberSecurity@Oxford.

Felicity Deane is an associate professor at the Queensland University of Technology. Felicity has published extensively in areas where economics and the law intersect. She has been researching and teaching the law of the World Trade Organization for over a decade and has extensive knowledge of international trade law and practice. Her first book, *Emissions Trading and WTO Law: A Global Analysis*, examined the impact of trade rules on climate change market-based instruments. Over the past ten years, she has collaborated with industry partners on projects that focus on land use practices in Australia, export markets, and impacts on natural resources. This inspired work for her second book, *Natural Capital, Agriculture, and the Law*. Most recently Felicity has led projects that focus on agriculture, technology, trade, and regulation.

William H. Dutton is an emeritus professor, University of Southern California; an Oxford Martin Fellow, supporting the Global Cybersecurity Capacity Centre at the University of Oxford; Senior Fellow at the Oxford Internet Institute (OII); and Visiting Professor, Media and Communication, University of Leeds. Bill was OII's Founding Director and first Professor of Internet Studies at Oxford before his appointment as the James H. Quello Professor of Media and Information Policy at Michigan State University, where he directed the Quello Center.

Natasha Cecilia Edeh is an education consultant at EZ Career Consultant Pvt Ltd. Edeh focuses on human-centered research that includes open innovation practices, cybersecurity, and human–robot collaboration. Edeh received her master's degree from the American University of Nigeria in 2018.

Sitnikova, Elena is Associate Professor of Cybersecurity and Networking, College of Science and Engineering, Flinders University. A Certified Secure Software Lifecycle Professional, Elena leads cutting-edge research in Critical Infrastructure protection, focusing on intrusion detection for Supervisory Control and Data Acquisition systems cybersecurity and the Industrial Internet of Things. With cyber-attacks increasing globally, she is exploring system antifragility and using artificial intelligence to analyze abnormal data that may affect critical Cyber-Physical Systems.

Patricia Esteve-González is a research fellow at the Global Cybersecurity Capacity Centre. She has a PhD in economics from Universitat Rovira i Virgili (Spain), and her research interests are in applied microeconomic theory, with a special focus on institutions, mechanism design, and competitions. Her published and ongoing research uses theoretical and empirical methodologies in a variety of contexts – public procurement, affirmative action, European integration, and cybersecurity.

Andre Feitas leads the Reasoning & Explainable AI Lab at the Department of Computer Science at the University of Manchester and is a research group leader at the Idiap Research Institute. He is also the AI group leader at the digital Experimental Cancer Medicine Team (Cancer Research UK). His main research interests are enabling the development of AI methods to support abstract, explainable, and flexible inferences.

Keith Joiner was an Air Force aeronautical engineer, project manager, and teacher for 30 years before joining UNSW to teach and research test and evaluation. As a director-general, he was awarded a Conspicuous Service Cross and for drawdown plans in Iraq a US Meritorious Service Medal. His 1999 PhD was in reform of calculus education, and he is actively researching classroom environments, management and teaching of artificial intelligence, interoperability, cybersecurity, and advanced test techniques.

Ruchi Joshi is an assistant professor, researcher, and rehabilitation counselor with experience spanning a decade. She has authored and co-authored work in journals and books of national and international repute. Her research interests lie in child and adolescent counseling, therapy and intervention, the role of artificial intelligence in mental health geriatrics, and gender psychology.

Maharazu Kasim is a doctoral student in the American University of Nigeria. He holds a national diploma in mass communication and a bachelor of science in the same discipline. Later, he joined the American University of Nigeria in 2017, where he read MSc in information systems. As a beginning scholar, Maharazu's research interest is in organizational cybersecurity, especially how human actions could cause outright damage to deployed information systems. Maharazu works with Kaduna State University, Kaduna, Nigeria.

Satveer Kaur is currently working as an assistant professor, School of Management, Maharaja Agrasen University, Baddi, Himachal Pradesh, India. She has done a BCom, MBA (finance and marketing) and PhD (finance). She has nine years of teaching experience as faculty of management with specialization in accounting and finance. She has published many research papers in national and international journals and presented at national and international conferences. She has guided many MBA, BBA, and BCom students in their research work and projects. She has published 11 research papers, 10 book chapters, and 1 book. One PhD has been submitted under her guidance. Currently, three research scholars are pursuing PhDs under her guidance.

Hadi Akbarzadeh Khorshidi is a senior research fellow at the University of Melbourne. He is a chief investigator in the "FinTech and Financial Crimes: Methods, Applications, and Regulations" project funded by Melbourne-Manchester Research Fund scheme. His expertise lies within areas such as optimization, machine learning, artificial intelligence, decision-making, and modeling. He has applied his expertise in cancer research, medical problems, health policy, manufacturing systems, and finance.

Maximiliano E. Korstanje is Senior Lecturer in the Department of Economics at the University of Palermo, Argentina. He is editor-in-chief of the *International Journal of Safety and Security in Tourism* and the *International Journal of Cyber Warfare and Terrorism*. Previously, he was Visiting Fellow at CERS University of Leeds, UK, and the University of La Habana, Cuba.

Tanya Kumar works as an assistant professor at the University School of Business at Chandigarh University, Punjab, India. Her area of specialization is finance and marketing. She has done her doctor of philosophy in commerce. She has published various journal articles, research papers, and book chapters in national and international publications. She has attended various Faculty Development Programs (FDPs), workshops, and webinars. She has also presented her research work in various national and international publications.

Xiuqin Li is Research Associate at the Manchester Institute of Innovation Research (MIOIR) and the Decision and Cognitive Science Research Centre (DCSRC) at Alliance Manchester Business School, University of Manchester (UoM). Xiuqin Li has a PhD in innovation management from UoM. She works in the broad area of innovation in relation to cybersecurity, R&D services, digitalization, and knowledge-intensive business services. Her work is funded by ESRC and Innovate UK.

Nicholas Lord is a professor of criminology in the School of Social Sciences at the University of Manchester, where he is also the Director of the Centre for Digital Trust and Society. Nicholas has research expertise in white-collar, financial, and organized crimes, such as corruption, fraud and illicit finance, and their regulation and control.

Sule Magaji, a professor of financial economics, University of Abuja, was born 18 August 1968 in Hardawa, Misau, L.G.A., of Bauchi State. He obtained a BSc in economics from the University of Maiduguri in 1992, an MSc in banking and finance from Bayero University Kano, in 1996 and a PhD in economics from Usman Danfodio University Sokoto in 2005. He started his academic career as an assistant lecturer at the University of Abuja in 1996 and rose to professor of financial economics in 2011. He holds an e-teaching certificate jointly by the Open University of UK and NUC in 2012 after two years of training. Professor Magaji has held various positions at the University of Abuja, including as Director of Academic Planning, Director of Quality Assurance, and a member of the University of Abuja Management. He also served as Deputy Director of Consultancy Services of the University. He was the pioneer Coordinator of the University's Centre for Entrepreneurship, pioneer HOD Banking and Finance, and HOD Department of Economics, as well as serving as a member of various university committees. During his career, Professor Magaji has supervised 20 PhD and 125 MSc students and served as an external examiner to 15 universities. He has 70 publications in journals, articles, conference proceedings, and monographs to his credit. Some of his conference proceedings include two research papers on entrepreneurship research in Africa presented to a South African business school, which Heineman Publishers published in 2009.

Selvakumar Manickam is an associate professor working in cybersecurity, the Internet of Things, Industry 4.0, and machine learning. He has authored or co-authored almost 200 articles in journals, conference proceedings, and book reviews and has graduated 13 Ph.D. students. He had ten years of industrial experience before joining academia. He is a member of technical forums at national and international levels. He also has experience building IoT, embedded, server, mobile, and web-based applications.

D. V. Manjula is an associate professor in the Department of Computer Science and Engineering at Pragati Engineering College in India. Her research interests span artificial intelligence, machine learning, and cybersecurity. She has published over ten papers in standard indexed journals

Borja Álvarez Martínez is a PGR at the University of Manchester School of Social Sciences, researching arms and dual use goods exports controls from a multi-stakeholder compliance perspective, and has worked and continues to work in technological applications for financial crime. His research interests include international human rights law/humanitarian law, state-corporate regulations and state-corporate crime, domestic implementation of supranational legal frameworks, dual use goods, AI, compliance, and arms exports controls.

Sooraj Kumar Maurya is working as an assistant professor of philosophy and teacher-in-charge, Department of Philosophy, Ramanujan College, University of Delhi, Delhi. He has completed a BA, MA, and DPhil from the Department of Philosophy, University of Allahabad. He has published and presented more than 35 research papers at various international and national journals and conferences. His research interests are social philosophy, political philosophy, and moral philosophy.

Sharon McDonald is a visiting researcher at the Northeast Business Resilience Centre. She holds a PhD in cognitive psychology from Durham University and is a chartered psychologist. She has extensive research experience, previously holding posts at the professorial level. Her research interests include human factors, issues in cybersecurity adoption, user research methods, and contextual studies of information systems in organizations. She has recently taken up a post as Senior User Researcher with the Digital Cabinet office.

James Mercer (Member, ACM) is R&D Director at the Hut Group (THG). Recent work includes self-healing systems; anomaly, attack, and bot detection of e-commerce and cloud systems; distributed systems and multi-data center platform architecture; and a program teaching computer science to STEM graduates. James has a PhD in physics from the Georgia Institute of Technology.

Aisshwarya Nallamilli is a final year B.Tech. student at Pragati Engineering College in India. Her research interests include developing projects in artificial intelligence and cybersecurity.

Sadiq Nasir is an experienced information technology consultant with several years of experience serving private and public sector clients. He has assisted organizations in attaining their strategic objectives through IT consulting, systems integration, capacity development, and IT project management. He is a graduate of a BSc in multimedia technology and design from the University of Kent and holds an MSc in eBusiness from Oxford Brookes, both in the United Kingdom. He is a social innovator and an active voice in the promotion of cybersecurity hygiene and child online safety.

Kathiravan Pannerselvam received MSc and MPhil degrees in computer science from Bharathidasan University in 2011 and 2012, respectively. He is pursuing a PhD in computer science at the Central University of Tamil Nadu. His research interests include natural language processing, machine learning, deep learning, and social media data analytics. He is currently working on knowledge discovery from electronic word of mouth.

Theodore Papamarkou is a reader in the mathematics of data science at the University of Manchester. Prior to his current role, Theodore was a strategic hire in artificial intelligence at the Oak Ridge National Laboratory. His research spans Bayesian deep learning, approximate Monte Carlo methods, and mathematics of data science. By conducting research in these areas, Theodore is interested in addressing questions related to uncertainty quantification for deep learning and to approximate inference with big data or with high-dimensional models.

Riddhita Parikh is working as an assistant professor in psychology at the Faculty of Law, GLS University. Her teaching at the college focuses on domains like core psychology, gender crimes, legal psychology, criminology, and forensic and cyber psychology. She has completed a Ph.D. in the field of clinical psychology, with her research focusing on neurodevelopmental disorders. Her association with teaching field is over ten years. Currently, she is associated with Red Flower Publication, New Delhi, India, as editorial board member and holds lifetime memberships at International Association of Holistic Psychology and Women's International League for Peace and Freedom. So far, she has participated in various workshops, conferences, and seminars specifically pertaining to the field of psychology.

Shanmugavadivu Pichai serves as a professor of computer science and applications at the Gandhigram Rural Institute (Deemed to be University), with 32 years of academic experience and 22 years of research experience. Her research areas include medical image and data analytics, machine vision, parallel computing, software engineering, content-based image retrieval, and AI models. She holds a master's degree in computer applications (REC, Tiruchirapalli, 1990), PhD in digital image restoration (GRI-DU, Gandhigram, 2008), MBA (IGNOU, New Delhi, 2017), and MSc in applied psychology (Bharathiar University, Coimbatore, 2019). She has published more than 150 articles in journals and edited volumes. She is a recipient of funded research projects from UGC, DST, ICMR, and PMMMNMTT of worth Rs. 2.39 Cr.

Li Qiao is a Lecturer in space system engineering in the School of Engineering and Information Technology (SEIT), at the University of New South Wales (UNSW) located at the Australian Defense Force Academy (ADFA) based in Canberra, Australia. Lily obtained her PhD in Guidance Navigation and Control from Nanjing University of Aeronautics and Astronautics in 2011, including a study exchange at the School of Surveying and Spatial Information Systems at the University of New South Wales, Sydney. Her research interests lie in space engineering, systems engineering, and applying computer-based analysis methods, including, but not limited to, space systems. In addition, she focuses on developing computer-based methods to support decision-making for complex systems such as satellite mission design. She has been granted an internal SFRG fund to launch a trade space exploration research group. Lily's teaching crosses the postgraduate and undergraduate. Most of her time, she is teaching at master's levels for the UNSW Canberra Space program. Besides her academic work, Lily serves as the Transactions on Aerospace and Electronic Systems Aerospace chapter chair and student counsellor at the IEEE ACT section. Lily currently serves as Postgraduate Assessment Coordinator in the Postgraduate Education Leadership Group in SEIT, UNSW Canberra. At university, Lily serves as Canberra representative of the Women in Research Network (WiRN).

Lukman Raimi is an assistant professor of entrepreneurship at the Universiti Brunei Darussalam (UBD). His research interests include entrepreneurship, medical entrepreneurship, space tourism entrepreneurship, sustainability issues in entrepreneurship, innovation management, and venture growth strategies. Currently, he is an associate editor of the *Journal of Business and Economic Analysis* (JBEA), Universiti Brunei Darussalam, Brunei; Member, Editorial Board, *Indonesian Journal of Sustainability Accounting & Management Indonesia*; and Member, Editorial Advisory Board, Emerald Emerging Markets Case Studies, Emerald, UK, among others.

Saranya Rajiakodi received her ME from Anna University, Chennai, and her PhD in software engineering from Madurai Kamaraj University (2015), Madurai. Her fields of specialization include cybersecurity, software engineering, machine learning, distributed consensus algorithms, and IoT. She has 11 years of teaching and research experience. Her significant research contributions are integrated quantum flow and hidden Markov chain approach for resisting DDoS attacks and C-Worm, DAG-based distributed ledgers, and IoT-based accident prevention mechanisms. She is a lifetime member of CSI and IAE and subscribed to various professional bodies like IEEE. She has more than 30 reputed research publications. She is currently guiding two PhD research scholars. She currently serves as an assistant professor, Dept. of Computer Science, CUTN.

Dulkarnine Raseeda is a final year B.Tech. student at Pragati Engineering College in India. Her research interests include developing projects in artificial intelligence and cybersecurity.

Shafiq Ul Rehman is an assistant professor, researcher, and cybersecurity consultant. He has authored and co-authored articles in reputed journals and conference proceedings, He has more than ten years of research experience. His current research interests include cybersecurity, Internet of Things, cloud computing, machine learning, and Industry 4.0.

Tatyana Ryutov, PhD, is a computer security expert with extensive experience in conducting research; developing projects and software; engaging in inter-disciplinary collaborations; and teaching, supervising, and mentoring students. She teaches full time at the University of Southern California, Viterbi School of Engineering. Her work focuses on access control, security policies, trusted system design, and biomedical privacy.

Syed Shahzad is a PhD candidate at the Australian Defense Force Academy (ADFA), University of New South Wales, Australia. He has received his postgraduate degrees in computer science from ADFA and finance from St Hugh's College, University of Oxford. He is a cybersecurity practitioner and works in the Australian defense industry. Syed's main research areas are cyber resilience, cybersecurity, and risk management for critical space infrastructure.

Ruth Shillair is an assistant professor at Michigan State University in Media and Information Studies and director of the master's program. Her research covers a range of work, looking to maximize the benefits of technology while minimizing harm. This includes communication strategies to improve cybersecurity practices, ways to increase digital literacy, and policies to reduce the digital divide.

Basie Von Solms is a research professor in the Academy for Computer Science and Software Engineering at the University of Johannesburg in Johannesburg, South Africa. He is an associate director of the Global Cybersecurity Capacity Centre (GCSCC) of the University of Oxford in the United Kingdom. He is also a member of the technical boards of the GCSCC and the Cybersecurity Capacity Centre of South Africa (C3SA).

Kumar, Sumit received his MD in Psychiatry. He was attached to various institutes like JSS Medical College Mysore, KIMS Bhubaneshwar, IHBAS Delhi and Durgapur Steel Plant Hospital, Kolkata. Currently he is working as Associate specialist in Tata Main Hospital, Jamshedpur. Dr Sumit has an interest in consultation liaison psychiatry. He has good number of publications both on national and international platform.

Johanne Trippas is a vice-chancellor's research fellow at RMIT University. She works at the intersection of conversational systems, interactive information retrieval, human–computer interaction, and dialogue analysis. Her work investigates next-generation capabilities for intelligent systems, including spoken conversational search, digital assistants in cockpits, and artificial intelligence to identify cardiac arrests.

Umme Salma M. received BSc and MSc (computer science) degrees from Kuvempu University. She secured the first rank in the MSc in computer science in 2009 and is a gold medalist. She is a recipient of the Maulana Azad National Fellowship from UGC and a Summer Research Fellowship from the Indian Academy of Sciences. She received her PhD from Mangalore University. At present she is working as an assistant professor at Christ (Deemed to be University), Bangalore. She has published many research articles in many reputed journals and conferences. Her areas of interest include data mining and knowledge discovery, machine learning, and swarm intelligence.

Elvira Uyarra is Professor of Innovation Studies at Alliance Manchester Business School (University of Manchester), where she is also Executive Director of the MIOIR. She teaches and conducts research on science and innovation policy and management and on regional innovation. She is Fellow of the Regional Studies Association (RSA) and Chair of the Northwest of England branch of the RSA.

Martin Wilson is a UK police detective inspector seconded into the Northeast Business Resilience Centre (NEBRC). The NEBRC is a not-for-profit, government-supported initiative which seeks to help small businesses improve their cybersecurity. Martin has extensive experience working with the National Cybersecurity Centre (NCSC), academia, and the private sector. He holds an MSc (Distinction) in cybersecurity from the University of Sunderland (2021).

Markos Zachariadis holds the Chair of Financial Technology (FinTech) and is Full Professor of Information Systems at Alliance Manchester Business School (AMBS) at the University of Manchester. He is a member of the World Economic Forum's Global Future Council on Financial & Monetary Systems; Chief Fintech Advisor to the President of the Hellenic Competition Commission, Greece's competition and markets authority; and a FinTech Research Fellow at the Cambridge

Centre for Digital Innovation (CDI), University of Cambridge. Professor Zachariadis's research sits at the cross-section of economics of digital innovation, financial technology studies, and network economics, and he has studied extensively the economic impact of ICT adoption on bank performance, the diffusion of payment networks, and the role of data and standards in payment infrastructures (SWIFT), financial markets (LEI), and digital banking (open banking), among other things.

Mark van Zomeren is a doctoral student at the Australian Defense Force Academy (ADFA), University of New South Wales, Australia. He received his postgraduate degree in systems engineering from the University of New South Wales. He is a systems engineering practitioner and works in the Australian defense industry. Mark's primary research areas are cyber-worthiness and complex systems governance for cyber-physical systems utilized in defense industry and critical infrastructure.

1 Why Cyberattacks Disrupt Society and How to Mitigate Risk

Kenneth David Strang and Narasimha Rao Vajjhala

CONTENTS

INTRODUCTION

Cybersecurity attacks have crippled governments as well as private and public companies around the world (Sawik 2022). The impacts have been serious and costly, including disrupting the supply chain, impeding e-commerce transactions, theft of government classified information and publicly disseminating confidential personal data. The US Federal Bureau of Investigations (FBI, 2021) estimated the total cost of cyber terrorism was $4.2 billion USD by the end of 2021 (data for 2022 were not yet analyzed at the time of writing). The BlueLeaks cyberattack on 271 US anti-terrorism agencies resulted in 270 gigabytes holding 700,000 law enforcement police officers' classified personal data being broadcast on Twitter and stored on a public website for free download (Lee 2020). Prior to the COVID-19 pandemic, there were 1244 data breaches in the US, with over 446.5 million information records stolen, which cost stakeholders over $575 billion (Sawik 2022).

Cyber terrorism is now a major weapon leveraged in war, in addition to traditional nuclear missile and chemical bomb threats. For example, the US government and other countries allege Russia cyberattacked Ukraine several times before and during the 2022 invasion (Blinken 2022). Furthermore, NATO allies claim Russian intelligence agents, as well as Chinese-backed hackers, cyberattacked numerous organizations during 2020–2021 (Lee 2020).

This chapter will highlight some recent cybersecurity incidents for awareness and estimate their impacts on stakeholders. Specific examples of cyber terrorism incidents during 2020–2022 include WhisperGate malware, defacing government website landing pages, deleting important public service databases, and forcing essential e-commerce sites offline at critical periods by casting distributed-denial-of-service (DDOS) network traffic towards centralized servers (Blinken 2022).

DOI: 10.1201/9781003319887-1

Cyber terrorism is driven by technology. Industry 4.0 is a concept coined by researchers to describe modern technology such as the Internet of Things (IoT), cyber-physical systems, and cybersecurity. It is also known as the fourth industrial revolution. Industry 4.0 is a vision of smart factories created with intelligent cyber-physical systems (Thames and Schaefer 2017). Industry 4.0 encompasses the digitalization of all industry components (Rubio, Roman, and Lopez 2018). Industry 4.0 concepts include the Internet of Things, big data analytics, cloud computing, artificial intelligence (AI), and autonomous machines (Sawik 2022). Industry 4.0 can assist businesses in achieving considerable operating efficiencies and increased growth productivity (Thames and Schaefer 2017). For example, in the advanced manufacturing industry, Industry 4.0 applications combine IoT and AI to improve production efficiency and product quality by upgrading industrial processes with high-fidelity and high-value data from machines, workers, and products (Bamunu-arachchi et al. 2020).

Industry 4.0 was intended to help decision makers in public and private organizations. One research question is, did it? Another research question is, did Industry 4.0 instead arm terrorists with better cyber warfare tools? Those research questions are addressed in this chapter. Although technology such as Industry 4.0 has continued to advance, so has cybersecurity and terrorist methodologies (Sawik 2022), so all decision makers remain vulnerable to cyberattack or ransom risks. One interesting difference between cybersecurity terrorist methodologies and traditional terrorism is that the former usually targets the most successful companies or government administrations which stand to lose the greatest amount of money, as contrasted with the latter, where the goal is to kill or wound the greatest number of innocent people. Therefore, decision makers in government and non-government organizations need to be aware of cybersecurity warfare and how to defend against it. This chapter will explain how cyber terrorism is linked to Industry 4.0 and how decision makers can be aware of and defend against new cyber warfare.

PROBLEM RATIONALE AND RESEARCH QUESTIONS

This chapter addresses two key research questions:

RQ1. Why should decision makers be aware of cybersecurity in the context of Industry 4.0, what should this awareness include, and who should be informed?

RQ2. How can organizations using Industry 4.0 applications and environments assess their cybersecurity vulnerabilities, and what benchmarks, indicators, or maturity levels would be relevant?

GLOBAL CYBERATTACK TYPES, SOURCES, MOTIVES, AND IMPACTS

It would be difficult to explain cybersecurity without discussing the ideology of the terrorists and vice versa, as these are recursive and interdependent. In this section, we will start by highlighting some recent cybersecurity attacks and the impacts on stakeholders; then we will follow by explaining the underlying ideologies of the terrorists as well as how decision makers could prevent or mitigate these risks in the future. Where relevant, we will explain how Industry 4.0 technology may have contributed to helping terrorists create cyber warfare. We will turn the tables on terrorists, so to speak, by thinking outside the box, suggesting how future cyber warfare might be circumvented by leveraging technology.

The best way to illustrate the importance of cybersecurity risk management would be to first discuss the extent of recent cybersecurity warfare incidents and impacts. The literature is already saturated with rich descriptions of cyber warfare activities prior to COVID-19, but during and after the pandemic (2020–2022), particularly surrounding the Russian invasion of Ukraine, cyber terrorism incidents increased in intensity. We classify the major cyberattacks into data theft, service disruption, extortion, or a combination of these three, as summarized in Table 1.1 and discussed in more detail within the subsections in the following. Note we do not review every cyberattack – instead

TABLE 1.1

Major Cyberattacks Organized by Type, Hacker Source, and Motive (2020–2022)

Year	Incident	Attack Type	Hacker Source	Central Motive
2020	Blue Leaks Gov	Data theft	US	Expose government corruption
2020	European Medicines Agency	Data theft	Russia + China	Pharma trade secrets
2020	JP Nintendo Giga Leaks	Data theft	Japan	Gaming trade secrets
2020	US Gov Leaks	Data theft	Intelligence spying	Foreign intelligence spying
2020	UK EasyJet Data Breach	Data theft	Russia	Human trafficking cartels
2021	US Ivanti VPN Gov Communication	Data theft	Russia	Foreign intelligence spying
2021	Microsoft Exchange Server breaches	Disruption	Russia	Foreign intelligence spying
2021	US Epik Domain Service	Disruption	US	Expose government corruption
2021	US FBI Email Hack	Disruption	Canada	Disrupt government service
2022	Ukraine Cyberattacks	Disruption	Russia	Disrupt government service
2022	Europe Red Cross Cyberattack	Disruption	Russia suspected	Disrupt nonprofit service
2022	US Anonymous Cyberattack	Disruption	US	Expose government corruption
2022	Russian Invasion of Ukraine	Disruption	Russia	Disrupt nonprofit service
2022	Romania cyberattacks	Disruption	Russia	Disrupt nonprofit service
2020	US Twitter Celebrity Hijacking	Extortion	US	User bitcoin ransom
2020	FI Vastaamo Medical Breach	Extortion	Finland	Patient bitcoin ransom
2021	US Colonial Pipeline Supply Chain	Extortion	Russia	GasOil bitcoin ransom
2021	UK Health Service Executive	Extortion	Russia	Healthcare bitcoin ransom
2021	NZ Waikato District Health Board	Extortion	New Zealand	Healthcare bitcoin ransom
2021	BZ JBS Mea Supply Chain	Extortion	Brazil	Food supply bitcoin ransom
2021	US Kaseya VSA Security	Extortion	Russia	SaaS user bitcoin ransom
2021	SA Transnet Shipping	Extortion	South Africa	Shipping port bitcoin ransom
2021	US National Rifle Association	Extortion	US	Member bitcoin ransom
2022	Costa Rica Cyberattack	Extortion	Russia	Government finance bitcoin ransom
2022	China Shanghai National Police	Extortion	China	Government employee bitcoin ransom

we cover the major global cyberattacks representative of the type, motive, and significance of the impact caused to stakeholders.

DATA THEFT CYBERATTACKS

One of the most recent famous cybersecurity data breaches in 2020 was the BlueLeaks theft of 269.21 gigabytes (GB) by the Anonymous hacker group of 700,000 US law enforcement officers' classified personal data from 271 US "fusion" anti-terrorism agencies (Lee 2020). The 270 GB of police data stolen by Anonymous were distributed on Twitter by the @DDoSecrets account on June 19, 2020, and made available on the website http://hunter.ddosecrets.com, which was apparently owned by an activist group named Distributed Denial of Secrets (Lee 2020; FBI, 2021). According to Lee (2020), the BlueLeaks archive contains more than 16 million rows of data from hundreds of thousands of hacked police databases, personal information of police officers, email and newsletters, descriptions of alleged crimes with geolocation coordinates, internal survey results, website logs, PDFs, Microsoft Office documents, thousands of videos, and millions of images.

"Fusion" sites refers to the National Fusion Center Association (NFCA) consortium, which was formed after 9/11 by US anti-terrorism related agencies to join crime-fighting stakeholders in federal, state, and municipal government, along with private and non-profit associations, in a joint effort to combat terrorism. The NCFA was a well-intended cause, but as BlueLeaks revealed, some participants apparently went off script and allegedly incorrectly classified peaceful citizens as terrorists if they posted certain phrases or if citizens looked like terrorists as judged by certain agency members (Lee 2020).

NFCA centers were criticized as privacy invading, ineffective, and targeted at political groups. In 2012, the US Senate Permanent Subcommittee on Investigations found that after a 13-month review, NFCA centers did not contribute to the identification or prevention of a terrorist plot, and 75% of the 386 unclassified NFCA reports had no connection to terrorism at all (FBI 2021). In 2008, the Department of Homeland Security identified several privacy-related concerns created by NFCA centers, and reports sometimes distributed inaccurate or incomplete information (FBI 2021). Of more concern was that the NFCA documents clearly indicate a pattern of spying on citizens, with surveillance data proving that police can obtain and did obtain end-user data from social media sites including Facebook, Twitter, TikTok, Reddit, Instagram, and Tumblr. Finally, NFCA collected and distributed detailed data from automatic license plate readers from states and borders. It was even more troubling to learn that surveys from law enforcement training programs revealed certain instructors were prejudiced and unprofessional; the teaching was biased, outdated, and discriminatory, with sexual content unrelated to the class; and there was one report of a police instructor admitting to lying in court frequently.

Although the @DDoSecrets Twitter account was banned shortly after the tweet for dissemination of hacked materials, and the ddosecrets website was shut down, some BlueLeaks data can still be found on dark websites and even in some public domains. The exposed data include internal intelligence, suspected terrorist or activist threat interpretations, bulletins, emails, and reports produced by the various 271 NFCA law enforcement agencies between August 1996 and June 2020. While much of the leaked data identified police enforcement officers, the chilling aspect was the nature of citizen misrepresentations. In one case file, a college student was asking for legal advice and pro bono help for peaceful Black Lives Matters assemblies, but she was incorrectly categorized by NFCA agents as an Antifa terrorist. In another case file, apparently Google forwarded suspicious YouTube and Gmail activity based on certain keywords to NFCA agencies – for example, in June 2020 there were comments made about the George Floyd murder video from a user in Michigan which appeared to be a poem from an African American complaining about the police brutality on George Floyd – the writer became a suspect.

Although most of the hacked NFCA websites belonged to traditional organized crime surveillance centers, such as Minnesota's ICEFISHX, other US counter-intelligence agencies were also cyberattacked as part of BlueLeaks, such as NFCA in the Mariana Islands, a US commonwealth in the North Pacific. Other NFCA sites hit by BlueLeaks included the Energy Security Council, a nonprofit where law enforcement collaborates with oil companies, made up of board of director executives from companies like Chevron and Exxon Mobil. Chicagoland Financial Security Group, a "crime watch"–type website that Chicago law enforcement uses to communicate with the financial industry, was also an NFCA site breached. NFCA partner organizations breached included Bank of America, Chase, US Bank, Chicago Hospitality Entertainment and Tourism Security Association (Chicago HEAT), Illinois Hotel & Lodging Association, Law Enforcement and Private Security Los Angeles, Alert Mid-South (Tennessee, Mississippi, Alabama), CAL ORCA (California), Central New York ORCA, and many others. Several of the hacked websites belonged to high-intensity drug trafficking area programs, or HIDTAs, such as Atlanta-Carolinas HIDTA, New Mexico HIDTA, and Puerto Rico-US Virgin Islands HIDTA. The magnitude of BlueLeaks was significant due to volume, data sensitivity, and which organizations were hacked.

Either way you look at BlueLeaks, whether you consider the NFCA enforcement consortium became misguided or the theft of their classified data unethical, the goal of this chapter is not to judge that; instead, the aim is to point out the risk of cyber specialists accessing sensitive data of such a high magnitude. The weak link in the chain was the NFCA website developer Netsential, who apparently was the contractor. Netsential created the application using Microsoft Visual Basic and Microsoft Access Database, which did not have robust security defenses. The Netsential application was easy to hack into, since all 271 NFCA sites used the same program. Therefore, the Anonymous hacker group would likely have had no difficulty regularly downloading law enforcement data from the 1996–2020 period. BlueLeaks could have been prevented if decision makers had required the contractor to add better security and if the server logs were routinely checked for cyberattack signatures.

Interestingly, COVID-19 vaccines were cyberattacked in 2020, in as far as cyber hackers attempted to steal Pfizer copyrighted documents on their products. At the time Pfizer was collaborating with BioNTech, the latter conducted vaccine tests and released the first COVID-19 vaccine in the United Kingdom. According to Dutch newspaper reporter Modderkolk (2021), the European Medicines Agency (EMA) complained of being hacked by a Russian intelligence agency as well as a Chinese espionage group. The Russians gained access to EMA's internal network by exploiting a loophole in the EMA authentication system that allowed them to abuse two-step verification.

The impact of this pharmaceutical industry data breach was not necessarily severe, although allegedly dozens of EMA internal documents and emails appeared on Internet forums, and some of the EMA documents had been tampered with, which makes it likely that this was a disinformation campaign aimed at spreading doubts about admission procedures and safety of the vaccines. Nevertheless, copyrighted scientific materials were at risk, and the credibility of the vaccines could have been lowered, at least in the European Community.

When looking more deeply into the cause of the cyber theft, it appears EMS experienced earlier data breaches from Chinese hackers in the spring of 2020 (Modderkolk 2021). Apparently, the Chinese cyber criminals were successful at least to some degree, and the data theft continued for months. Subsequently, Russian criminals targeted medical organizations in Europe, including the EMA, by using malware buried within emails, called a spearfish; when clicked on, it activated the malware implanted within the EMA email server. The malware made it possible for the Russians to intercept email traffic. Luckily, EMA had secured their internal network with two-step verification, so the hackers didn't gain further access at first, but Russians issued new malware through a zip file which faked a user alert to change their password. Unfortunately, the various firewalls at the EMA didn't flag any suspicious attempts to log in either, so the Russians were able to intercept emails.

In the EMA data breach case, Russian cyber criminals cleverly hid their own IP addresses, and for weeks on end, and certainly for more than a month, they could log in without being noticed. According to sources, they were not so much interested in the technique of the Pfizer/BioNTech and Moderna vaccines but more in which countries were buying them and in what quantities. Eventually, the cyber breach was discovered during an internal audit when a system manager noticed in the log files that a certain EMA employee regularly logged on to the network outside of office hours. This could have been prevented simply by the carrying out the internal audit earlier and periodically.

From the pharmaceutical industry to airlines and tourism, cyber data breach attacks occurred in every discipline and continent during and after the pandemic. In the Europe, while the United Kingdom was still a member of the European Union, cyberattackers stole data from 9,000,000 EasyJet customers, including credit card data of 2208 customers (Calder 2020). The breached data included flight booking information such as home address, phone numbers, and passport or travel document numbers. The credit card data included the security code on the back of the card, thus allowing criminals to easily make online transactions. Although the cyber theft occurred in January 2020, EasyJet publicly announced the loss only four months later in May 2020. According to UK newspapers, EasyJet claimed in April they privately notified customers whose details were stolen, due to the complexity of the cyberattack, which made it difficult to determine the scope and extent of data that had been breached.

A relevant point to make concerning the European Union is that a relatively new law had been formulated to protect people's data privacy. This new law was called the General Data Protection Regulation (GDPR). The GDPR is an important component of EU privacy law to protect human rights law, in particular Article 8(1) of the Charter of Fundamental Rights of the European Union. It also addresses the transfer of personal data outside the European Union. The GDPR requires companies to store personal details securely; otherwise penalties could be levied by governments in additional to private lawsuits from those whose data were stolen.

There were advance warnings of the EasyJet data breach in as far as British Airways had suffered similar data breaches in 2018. The EasyJet cyberattack could possibly have been prevented if the company had encrypted data in storage, which would make the stolen data practicality useless since it would take years and powerful computing power to decode the encryption. However, a weak point in any encryption algorithm is that a private key is needed to decrypt the data, and this key must be stored somewhere – anything which is stored or held by employees becomes a cybersecurity risk.

In 2021, one of the better-known data breaches was the Ivanti Pulse Connect Secure product, which many US government departments use as a virtual private network (VPN) for internet video and communications of a secure nature. There were again rumors that the cyberattacks were perpetrated by a Russian-backed hacker group identified as CVE-2021–22893. The VPN software owner Ivanti worked with a cybersecurity specialist company Mandiant to investigate the attacks and propose risk mitigation workarounds in public white papers intended to help the affected victims, government stakeholders (Perez et al. 2021). The impact of the cyberattack was that hackers were able to log into the systems using spoofed passwords and then download any communication data such as recorded videos, emails, or files. Theoretically, the hackers could reconfigure the VPN to allow a hidden observer to listen in to any conversation by copying and decoding any packets transmitted on the VPN. It was unclear if how much, if any, secure government data were stolen.

Apparently Mandiant detected 12 cyberattack malware programs associated with the exploitation of the Ivanti VPN (Perez et al. 2021). The 12 malware programs were meant to take advantage of or bypass security access authentication and install hacker backdoor security access to Avanti VPN end point devices like routers, switches, and servers. Mandiant debugged the activities of UNC2630 against US Defense Industrial base (DIB) networks. Mandiant also collaborated with the Microsoft Threat Intelligence Center (MSTIC) and relevant government and law enforcement agencies to investigate the threats, as well as to develop risk mitigation for affected VPN network device customers (Perez et al. 2021).

Interestingly, Mandiant observed that the Ivanti VPN devices had been hacked earlier, before 2021, during 2019 and 2020. This was not disclosed earlier and would have assisted in the early detection and mitigation of the cyberattacks (Perez et al. 2021). Apparently, the method of the hackers was to steal credentials from various Ivanti VPN device login flows by tapping into the network and capturing packets with certain headers, which ultimately allowed the hackers to use legitimate account credentials to move laterally into the affected networks. The hackers then added bypass code within the authentication flows in the VPN systems to steal other passwords or to bypass multifactor authentication for certain "backdoor" users the hackers had either inserted or knew about in advance from earlier network traffic surveillance (Perez et al. 2021). At the time of writing, it appears Mandiant has helped stakeholders avoid further cyberattacks on the Ivanti VPN. Again, the lesson learned here was to pay attention to early, possibly unsuccessful, cyberattacks and to immediately fortify processes and initiate cyberattack risk mitigation to prevent future attacks.

Healthcare continued to be on the hacker hitlist in 2022. The International Committee of the Red Cross suffered a cyber data breach on its client information stored in Switzerland on or about January 20. Apparently, the perpetrators have not identified themselves at the time of writing. Nevertheless, we know that the Red Cross made a public appeal to hackers who had stolen their private data, saying they would like to speak directly and confidentially to those responsible for the attack (Dobberstein 2022).

Finally, cyber data hackers hit the video game industry. The biggest incident was called the Nintendo Gigaleak, which consisted of a series of cyber data thefts from the Japanese video game company Nintendo posted in the anonymous public forum 4chan (Robinson 2021). It was named Gigaleak because some of the key data breached contained 3 gigabytes, which is 1/20 the capacity of most smartphones in 2022. The cyber data breach started in March 2018 but became most prominent in 2020 when ten main sets of Nintendo data were stolen and posted on 4chan, ranging from game and console source code to internal documentation and development tools.

The Gigaleak cyber data thefts continued through 2019 and 2020, releasing internal documentation about Nintendo's iQue Player ROMs, early Pokémon designs, Wii, Super Nintendo Entertainment System, and Nintendo 64 consoles with their games including prototype data related to Star Fox and Star Fox 2. In the first week of September 2020, a third, smaller set of information was leaked on 4chan. Later cyber thefts captured documents for two unreleased GameCube models, a backup of the Wii's hardware repository (codenamed "Tako", later "Vegas" by ATi), a block diagram for a portable version of the Wii, Verilog files for near-final versions of the Wii components, and a 2003 ATI proposal for a console that would natively render games at HD video resolutions like the Xbox 360 and PlayStation 3. Another hacker data theft took internal documents for Wii Sports and Wii Sports Resort, source code to the Nintendo DSi boot ROM, DSi apps, and a Game Boy with Game Boy Color ROM. The cyber data thefts continued, netting the hackers demo ROMs for Pokémon Ranger, Pokémon Mystery Dungeon: Blue Rescue Team and Red Rescue Team, Pokémon FireRed and LeafGreen, internal tools for the Nintendo 3DS, and a Famicom Disk System ROM lot containing released as well as unreleased games.

The Gigaleak data theft of Nintendo continued with source code being stolen for Pokémon Sun and Moon, its updated rereleases, as well as an early version of the Wii's home menu. This was followed by data breaches of debug builds for Pokémon Sword dated March 2018 and December 2017. Another set of Gigaleaks in late 2020 contained prototype designs of the Nintendo Switch and a prerelease SDK for the New Super Mario Bros, Nintendo Space World 1997 demos for Pokémon Gold and Silver. Interestingly, it appears the cyber hackers also obtained information on Nintendo's company internal surveillance such as video of a Belgian hacker the company attempted to hire for unknown reasons (Robinson 2021).

The impact of the Gigaleak data theft was constrained to the company Nintendo. However, other gaming companies and casino businesses became nervous about their internal processes being hacked. The Gigaleak data theft could have been prevented, possibly if Nintendo had taken more precautions with employee screening and security vigilance. Apparently, due to the nature of what was stolen and how it was stolen, it looked like an insider job in as far as employees who knew about the unreleased code would be the only logical candidates. This could have included current and former employees. Another possible source was Zammis Clark, a Malwarebytes employee and hacker who in 2019 pleaded guilty to and was sentenced to 15 months in prison for infiltrating Microsoft and Nintendo's servers between March and May 2018 (Robinson 2021). Mr. Clark sent the data he stole to several of his acquaintances, who subsequently began leaking the information on 4chan (Robinson 2021). Nintendo likely knew the material would eventually be leaked but did not act on that hypothesis by asserting copyright or taking legal steps.

SERVICE DISRUPTION CYBERATTACKS

The Russian cyberattacks on Ukraine dominated the global news in early 2022. In retrospect, there was a clear timeline of the Russian attacks, which preceded the physical invasion of Ukraine and continued during the war effort. Even prior to 2022, there was a long history of conflict with Russia since the collapse of the Soviet Union in 1991. The Russian cyberattack weapon Ouroboros malware had been around since 2005, but it was used mostly against large government systems in Ukraine. In 2013 Russian "Operation Armageddon" systematic cyber espionage (which included Snake, Ouroboros, and Turlaof malware) was unleashed against the information systems of government agencies, law enforcement, and defense agencies in Ukraine (FBI 2021). When Russian troops entered Ukraine's Crimea region during February–March 2014, Russian troops tampered with fiber optic cables, cutting the connection between the Crimea peninsula and mainland Ukraine. In parallel, Russia cyberattacked Ukrainian government websites, online news outlets, and social media using targeted DDoS blasts to shut down sites and jam cell phone switching systems. Two groups Russian hacker groups were identified in 2015: APT29 (also known as Cozy Bear or Cozy Duke) and APT28 – also called Sofacy Group, Tsar Team, Pawn Storm, and Fancy Bear (FBI 2021). The acronym APT refers to advanced persistent threat.

The recent Russian cyberattacks on Ukraine began January 14, 2022, by replacing text on 70 government websites with fake disinformation – the sites included the Ministry of Foreign Affairs, the Cabinet of Ministers, and the Security and Defense Council (FBI 2021). A new Belarus hacker group, UNC1151, was identified, and Ukraine Deputy Secretary of the NSDC Serhiy Demedyuk thought that a third-party service company's administration rights were used to carry out the attack. This illustrates a key weakness that can be leveraged by cyber terrorists, the security rights of internet and system maintenance contractors. Decision makers need to be aware of that vulnerability and act.

Across the pond in Seattle, WA, the Microsoft Threat Intelligence Center detected malware had been installed on devices belonging to multiple government, non-profit, and information technology organizations in Ukraine, which became known as DEV-0586 or WhisperGate (FBI 2021). Microsoft explained that WhisperGate was designed to look like a Windows system software recovery feature, but it would destroy files by overwriting the master boot record with a generic message when the device was powered down – when powered back up, the message would be displayed and other files would be overwritten, deleting data.

Later in the Ukraine invasion, the Russian APT Gamaredon (also known as Primitive Bear) attempted to compromise a US government entity stationed in Ukraine. Additionally, the Invisi-Mole threat group also attacked the same systems that the Russian APT Gamaredon had earlier compromised and fingerprinted (FBI 2021). The point here is for decision makers to be prepared for repeated attacks when an incident is detected, as likely there could be undetected malware still on those systems. Although Russia denied responsibility for all cyberattacks, as it denied the physical attacks were an offensive initiative, the European Union and NATO allies had no doubt of who was accountable.

Russia allegedly launched a large distributed-denial-of-service attack on February 15, 2022, which brought down the websites of the Ukraine defense ministry, army, and their two largest banks, PrivatBank and Oschadbank (FBI 2021). Cybersecurity monitoring company NetBlocks reported that the attack intensified over the course of the day, also affecting the mobile apps and ATMs of the banks, and the *New York Times* and FBI described it as the largest assault of its kind in the country's history (FBI 2021). According to the UK government and US National Security Council, the attack was performed by Russian Main Intelligence Directorate (GRU) by transmitting high volumes of communications to Ukraine-based IP addresses and domains (FBI 2021). A third DDoS attack dubbed HermeticWiper malware took down multiple Ukrainian government, military, and bank websites a few days later, as well as deleting data on hundreds of computers belonging to multiple Ukrainian organizations (FBI 2021). The root of this problem was that Symantec, the anti-virus company, had reported malicious activity months earlier in November 2021 by identifying the HermeticWiper signature in a hijacked certificate from a legitimate Cyprus-based company Hermetica Digital Ltd (which was reportedly compiled on 28 December 2021). The problem was decision makers either were not informed about this or did not act on this cyber threat. More so, Symantec had reported malicious wiper attacks against devices in Lithuania, and some organizations were compromised months prior to the 2022 Ukraine invasion. No one acted on that.

We ought to note that Ukraine and its allies were responsive to the Russian cyberattacks. On February 26, the Ukraine minister of digital transformation, Mykhailo Fedorov, announced the creation of an IT army, which included cyber specialists, copywriters, designers, and marketers. After that, Ukraine began cyberattacks to disrupt services on many Russian government websites and at banks. In fact, dozens of Russian stars and officials have been cyberattacked in some manner, and Ukrainian songs have been broadcast on popular Russian television channels, including Prayer for Ukraine (FBI 2021). Back in 2016, Ukraine ought to have known Russia was planning physical and cyberattacks because the Surkov Leaks hack group (likely allies of Ukraine) stole 2337 e-mails and hundreds of attachments from Russian intelligence, which revealed plans dated to 2013–2014 for seizing Crimea from Ukraine and fomenting separatist unrest in Donbas (FBI 2021). Decision makers need to act on cyber warfare advance intelligence.

As the 2022 invasion progressed, the Russian military increased cyber warfare on Ukraine. On March 9, Russian agents managed to install or activate the Quad9 malware-blocking recursive resolver, but it was intercepted by Ukraine, mitigating 4.6 million attacks against computers and phones in Ukraine as well as in Poland. Cybersecurity expert Bill Woodcock of Packet Clearing House claimed that the blocked DNS queries coming from Ukraine clearly demonstrated an increase in phishing and malware attacks against Ukrainians (FBI 2021). The Russian internet service provider BGP (RTComm.ru) hijacked Twitter's 104.244.42.0/24 IPv4 address block for a period of 2 hours 15 minutes on March 28, using it to tweet messages (FBI 2021). What can decision makers do to mitigate that type of attack? Likely they could prepare in advance by letting citizens know what to expect if a war has broken out.

Many other cyberattacks for data theft, service disruption, and extortion likely took place which were not reported publicly, and therefore we were not able to include them in this chapter. On November 13, 2021, a hacker named Pompompurin compromised the FBI's external email system, sending thousands of spam emails warning of a fake cyberattack by cybersecurity researcher and CEO of Night Lion Security and Shadowbyte Vinny Troia, who is falsely labeled in the emails as being a part of the Dark Overlord hacking group (Pannett 2021). Pompompurin sent emails to addresses taken from the American Registry for Internet Numbers database, and it was reported that the hacker used the FBI's public-facing email system, which made the emails appear legitimate. The campaign was likely done to defame Troia. In a later interview with ProPublica, Pompompurin later claimed the hack was done for fun (Pannett 2021). In a blog post, Vinny Troia claimed that the Pompompurin alias belonged to the Canadian hacker Chris Meunier, but later in an interview with ProPublica, Pompompurin denied being Meunier (Pannett 2021). Nevertheless, although it was nonsense, this cyberattack disrupted the FBI's internal operations and cast more doubt on the ability of government to prevent such cyberattacks.

Apparently, hackers stole private data on more than 515,000 vulnerable people from at least 60 Red Cross and Red Crescent societies (Dobberstein 2022). Thus far there is no evidence that the breached data have been leaked, but the Red Cross said that its gravest concern was the risk posed by exposing the data (Dobberstein 2022). Prior to that, during the pandemic, it was understood in global society that ransomware slingers would not target medical organizations because they already had enough on their plates, but obviously that didn't hold for long, because, as noted earlier, the EHS and New Zealand hospitals and others were cyberattacked and now the Red Cross. There are social impacts of cyberattacks even if extortion is not involved. A Red Cross spokesperson stated that when the organization isn't under a cyberattack, it reunites 12 missing people with their families every day. Red Cross claimed that because of the cyberattack, they were obliged to shut down the systems underpinning Restoring Family Links work, affecting the Red Cross and Red Crescent Movement's ability to reunite separated family members (Dobberstein 2022).

Ukraine and the United States were not the only targets of Russian-backed cyber hackers attempting to disrupt government services. Beginning April 29, 2022, until May 1, a series of multiple DDoS attacks were launched against several Romanian government, military, bank, and mass media websites (FBI 2021). Behind the attacks was the pro-Kremlin hacking group Killnet, which resorted to this in response to a declaration made by Florin Cîțu, then president of the Senate of Romania, that Romania would provide Ukraine with military aid. The Russian Federation, which had invaded

Ukraine, publicly spoke against Western military support for Ukraine, stating that it would result in lightning-fast retaliatory strikes – which certainly correlates to what happened to Romania.

In Romania, president of the chamber of deputies of Romania Marcel Ciolacu, Prime Minister Nicolae Ciucă, and Minister of Foreign Affairs Bogdan Aurescu visited Kyiv, Ukraine, to meet with Ukrainian President Volodymyr Zelenskyy; Ukrainian Prime Minister Denys Shmyhal; and the president of the Verkhovna Rada, Ruslan Stefanchuk. In the meeting, Romania reiterated its support for Ukraine and its European integration aspirations, as well as committing to active involvement in the reconstruction of the country. The meeting had been planned since as early as April, with the Romanian delegation initially consisting of President of the Senate Florin Cîțu and President of the Chamber of Deputies Marcel Ciolacu, both visiting Kyiv on April 27 at the invitation of Stefanchuk. Prime Minister Ciucă justified the absence of Cîțu around the fact that there were two state visits separately planned, under condition of the safety measures imposed in Kyiv due to the 2022 Russian invasion of Ukraine. Nevertheless, Florin Cîțu visited Kyiv by himself on April 27, 2022, after which he stated that Romania should do more for Ukraine, supporting it with military equipment.

On April 29, 2022, the websites of the Ministry of National Defence (MApN), the Romanian Border Police, the government of Romania, and CFR Călători were taken down by a DDoS attack. According to the MApN, the cyberattack did not compromise the functioning of its website but rather prevented user access to it. The government stated that IT specialists at the structures at governmental level were collaborating with experts from specialized institutions to restore access and identify the causes. The Romanian Intelligence Service (SRI) stated that the hackers behind the cyberattack used network equipment from outside Romania. The pro-Kremlin hacking group Killnet claimed the attacks through Telegram, asserting that the president of the Romanian Senate, Marcel Ciolacu, issued a statement promising the Ukrainian authorities maximum assistance in supplying lethal weapons to Kyiv. Furthermore, they revealed a list of websites that were taken down through the DDoS attack, and the website of OTP Bank (the Romanian division) was also listed.

In retaliation, Romania's National Cybersecurity Directorate (DNSC) published a list of 266 IP addresses involved in the April 29 DDoS attacks to its official website, but a few days later, the hackers brought down that website, too, although it was later restored. Later the same day, a further DDoS attack took down the website of the Romanian police. The pro-Kremlin hacking group threatened to take down another 300 Romanian websites in a similar manner, including websites of stores, military, government, mass-media, banks, hospitals, educational institutions, and political parties. Some websites using Moldovan (.md) domains were also included in the list. On May 1, 2022, Killnet took down the websites of seven Romanian airports (including those located in Bucharest, Cluj-Napoca, etc.), as well as of the TAROM airline and several news media websites, including Digi24.

It has been suspected that a Romanian resident in the United Kingdom helped Killnet take down Romanian websites, translating content in Romanian to Russian. However, we would point out the Russian cyber hackers could have used Google to translate the website content without UK help. Nevertheless, the UK suspects were put in custody. In retaliation, Killnet threatened to destroy Romania, the United Kingdom, and Moldova if they are not released in 48 hours (FBI 2021). At the time of writing, there have been no further developments observed for this incident.

As cited in the previous section, Russia allegedly conducted several recent cyberattacks against Ukraine. Those attacks included installing WhisperGate malware on approximately 70–80 Ukraine servers running Microsoft Windows server software which manifested in early May 2022. The malware propagated itself and deleted critical operating system files (Blinken 2022). Apparently, Russia used other cyberattack methods to deface government website landing pages, gaining unauthorized access to important public services databases followed by stealing data, and the terrorists forced essential e-commerce sites offline during critical periods by blasting distributed-denial-of-service network traffic packets at centralized servers (Blinken 2022). These were merely the tip of the iceberg in terms of recent cybersecurity attacks. These types of cyberattacks have occurred for over a decade. With every new technological advancement to prevent cyber warfare, a new technique seems to be developed by terrorists.

In the previous year, by February 2021, at least 100 private sector companies in the United States and nine federal US government departments had been cyberattacked by Russian Foreign Intelligence Service spies – approximately 18,000 computer sites had downloaded malicious SolarWinds malware, according to the US press secretary and national security advisor for cyber and emerging technology (Psaki and Neuberger 2021). SolarWinds was the US Texas-based IT software provider targeted, and the company had over 320,000 customers. The key SolarWinds software product targeted was Orion, which is an intranet network performance management and monitoring system. Hackers apparently knew that many US federal and state level government departments used Orion.

Russian cyber terrorism activity began in September 2019 when Russian-based hackers accessed SolarWinds Orion and installed two malicious malware modules they called Sunburst and Supernova into the application programming workflow at the SolarWinds software development office (Psaki and Neuberger 2021). This allowed the malware to be propagated with every build and deployment cycle to 18,000 customer network sites throughout the year. The Russian hackers initiated a proof-of-concept test in February 2021, causing the impacts noted previously. Then the terrorists were clever enough to remove the malware from the SolarWinds software development platform by June 4, 2020, to cover their tracks.

Nevertheless, despite the SolarWinds terrorists covering their tracks, their activity was discovered in the log files of several companies. Luckily the Russian Sunburst malware was detected by FireEye, a cybersecurity company, on December 12, 2020, whereby customers including the US government were notified (Psaki and Neuberger 2021). Consequently, thanks to the prescriptive sleuthing cybersecurity activities by FireEye, the impacted SolarWinds customers were able to secretly remove the Russian Sunburst malware over three days, thus preventing it from manifesting as the terrorists had planned. However, little did customers know that the second malware, Supernova, was still present in the Orion network monitoring software system. SolarWinds became more proactive in following up with customers, which allowed them to detect the Supernova malware a week later. SolarWinds worked with the US government to help customers annihilate Supernova (and Sunburst) on affected computers by January 25, 2021.

Although the SolarWinds Sunburst and Supernova Russian-backed cyberattacks were thwarted by FireEye and the US government, the potential impact was immense. The key intrusion goal for the cyber malware was to gain access to an Orion customer's internal network and customers' nonpublic information, which would allow hackers to see sensitive confidential government and investment company client data. If hackers had gained access to government and investor confidential data, they could have exploited consumers for ransomware demands and sold US secrets to other terrorists (or leveraged the information for a new world war). The US government asserted there were no indications that hackers exploited the vulnerabilities resulting from Sunburst or Supernova in any financial services organization (Psaki and Neuberger 2021).

Nevertheless, there were real hard costs from the SolarWinds Sunburst and Supernova cyberattack attempts. First, there were actual significant labor costs by specialists and end users at all impacted stakeholder companies to perform malware removal. Second, fear spread throughout the private and government end-user community, particularly in the US financial sector, which is where one of the largest economic contributions to the US gross domestic product originates. While not trying to put the US government up on a global pedestal, suffice to say that if Russian hackers almost succeeded with a cyberattack that would likely have destroyed the US economy, this is a serious matter which decision makers need to mitigate against. The United States is certainly not the only rich country – other countries may be secretly under cyberattack in early stages in stealth mode even as this chapter is being written.

SolarWinds was one of many cyber warfare attacks – the total cost of cyber-criminal activities is unknown. According to the US Federal Bureau of Investigations, there were 791,790 complaints of suspected internet crime in 2020 and reported losses exceeding $4.2 billion (FBI 2021). These were the most recent data available at the time of writing. The top three crimes reported by victims in 2020 were phishing scams, non-payment/non-delivery scams, and ransomware extortion for money (FBI 2021). Victims lost the most money to business email compromise scams, romance and confidence schemes, consumer investment scheme fraud, and COVID-19 testing pandemic-related fraud (FBI 2021). In fact, the FBI (2021) processed over 28,500 complaints related to COVID-19, with fraudsters targeting both businesses and individuals. As a lesson learned to prevent future cyber warfare like Sunburst or Supernova, the US government initiated and applied these steps:

1. Check system integrity and audit logs for indicators of unusual activity on a regular basis.
2. Once unusual activity in logs was detected, the system must be immediately taken offline for a thorough investigation, cleaned (if malware is present), security patches installed, tested, and returned to network.
3. Security patches must be installed on schedule as advised by software manufacturers.

We will add a fourth step, which we call cybersecurity risk management. This would involve awareness training for decision makers, administrators, and lead end-users so they could alert security staff of any suspicious network or application-level system behavior. After the Sunburst and Supernova cyberattacks, many companies and government departments became vigilant about cyber warfare. In December 2021, the US government detected vulnerabilities in common web server software called Apache Log4j (DHS 2021). The US Department of Homeland Security's Cybersecurity and Infrastructure Security Agency, the National Security Agency, and others announced a critical remote code execution vulnerability in many versions of Apache's Log4j JavaScript logging utility software. Apparently, this utility was and is widely used by major SaaS cloud-hosted services as well as by numerous well-known software vendors and manufacturers. According to senior cybersecurity professionals at DHS, this vulnerability was among the most serious seen to date, because cyber terrorists could exploit it to deploy ransomware, as well as steal customer and government sensitive data, simultaneously and quickly without staging installations needed over time, as with the SolarWinds incidents.

The Sunburst and Supernova cyberattacks were among several similar data breach incidents during 2020, which had a common theme of exploiting three US-based supply chain e-commerce software vendors: SolarWinds, Microsoft, and VMware (formerly DEC). The Microsoft and VMware cyberattacks were not altogether different in method than those perpetrated on SolarWinds, so they will be briefly discussed here. A key vulnerability was that software updates were being provided via the internet, and access to installed malware to steal documents was facilitated by the federated authentication distributed across the victim servers via single sign-on infrastructure instead of multifactor authentication (Kantchev and Strobel 2021).

In the Microsoft cyberattack, the hackers targeted Microsoft's cloud services by exploiting the "Zerologon" vulnerability in the Microsoft authentication protocol NetLogon, which allowed attackers to access all valid usernames and passwords in each Microsoft network that they breached (Kantchev and Strobel 2021). The Zerologon loophole allowed hackers to access admin credentials necessary to assume the privileges of any legitimate user of the network, which in turn allowed them to gain access to any of the Microsoft Office 365 customer email accounts (Kantchev and Strobel 2021). Another flaw in Microsoft's Outlook Web App may have allowed attackers to bypass multi-factor authentication if that mechanism was activated by customers (Kantchev and Strobel 2021).

The impact of the Microsoft Zerologon cyberattack was that hackers were able to monitor US government emails of any department and at any level which were part of the Microsoft Outlook 365 system in the cloud service. A common pattern we noticed with the Sunburst, Supernova, and similar cyberattacks was that the victims, usually government departments or companies, downloaded software updates automatically from the internet, or administrators initiated downloads periodically – this is the mechanism by which the cyber malware was installed: through software updates downloaded from the internet.

For decision makers, we recommend all software updates, whether on a company server or personal smartphone/laptop, be scanned for malware. If possible, we recommend delaying software updates for a month because even though many vendors claim the updates contain security patches, as history has proven, some updates may contain viruses or malware. That was what caused Solar-Winds customers and clients of several other companies to fall victim to cyberattacks. This also points to the requirement for software vendors to take better proactive action to ensure the software updates they are providing are malware and virus free. If companies need urging to do that, perhaps the government could establish a regulation with severe penalties ordered if a software vendor fails to protect customers against malware or viruses downloaded through online provisioning services.

Another lesson learned from the SolarWinds and the other COVID-19 pandemic cyberattacks was to raise awareness across other industries beyond public administration and the financial sector. In particular, the supply chain represents a significant vulnerability to cyberattacks since there are many third parties involved – with more software touchpoints, interactions, and transactions, this increases exposure to potential cyber malware attacks. Customers of third-party software providers should implement the previous cybersecurity risk management methods, and those third-party providers ought to do likewise. Cybersecurity risk management ought to become part of the due diligence and contractual clauses for purchasing software in the future. This will force providers to be more alert due to the potential they would void contractual terms at a severe financial penalty should a cybersecurity malware attack occur with their product at a customer site.

As part of cybersecurity risk management, all stakeholders should notify one another immediately if they detect any potential indicator that malware may be installed, and this includes adding mandatory terms to procurement contracts. While this zero-trust attitude between vendors and their clients may seem to disrupt a collegial customer relationship management process, it is simply the new normal given the current global status.

EXTORTION CYBERATTACKS

Extortion cyberattacks usually involve a demand for money or some type of asset. Sometimes cyber extortion leverages hacked credentials, such as the Twitter incidents, or in other cases, ransomware is installed on critical servers and then activated to shut down key systems until a demand by the terrorists is met. The Twitter high-profile account hijacking was perhaps the most publicized cyber extortion attempt in 2020 and was a successful scam for hackers – for a little while. Numerous high-profile Twitter accounts were hacked by extortionists on July 15, 2020, in an organized scam to request the public to invest their Bitcoin for only 24 hours to obtain a 200% return for a social good ideology.

The Twitter cyber extortion worked because in three hours almost $115,000 was received from 200 transfers into the account linked to the Bitcoin address cited in the tweets (Ingram and Collier 2020). Another impact from the cyberattack was that affected celebrities and critical government agencies, including US President Joe Biden and the US National Weather Service (NWS), had their Twitter accounts suspended for most of the day. The NWS stated this prevented it from announcing a tornado warning for Illinois (Ingram and Collier 2020), and likely there were many unreported negative impacts. Another unfortunate impact was borne by Twitter, as public confidence plummeted, the value of its shares dropped 4% after the markets closed, and its stock price ended at $36.40, down 38 cents, or 0.87%, at the end of the next day, according to the NYSE public data. Twitter also delayed deploying a new API product due to the cybersecurity incident.

The seriousness of the Twitter cyber extortion can be rationalized by considering the socio-cultural influence of the affected accounts. Many of the extorted Twitter accounts have large social networks of followers. For example, according to Twitter statistics, Bill Gates has around 51 million Twitter followers, Elon Musk has about 37 million, the Apple group account has more than 4.5 million, and other popular corporations such as Uber as well as CashApp (a money transfer service) were compromised in the cyber extortion.

The underlying terrorist motivation was money, Bitcoin in this case, rather than to steal data or disrupt service. The cyberattackers used deception to gain access and then social identity theory (credibility of a celebrity) along with capitalistic greed to entice victims to transfer Bitcoin with the promise of doubling their investment in only 24 hours. The method of access according to Twitter was that suspected cyber extortionists tricked current and former employees into providing their passwords and codes to pass through multifactor authentication. The criminals used the popular professional social media site Linkedin.com to locate current and former Twitter employees. They purchased the graded employer job recruiting version of LinkedIn to gain access to LinkedIn account holder email addresses and phone numbers. Extortionists set up a fake Twitter server that would then allow the criminals to capture the typed-in password and multifactor authentication token. Criminals then contacted the Twitter employees, using email and or phone numbers, pretending to be Twitter administrators, asking them to reset their passwords, while directing them to their fake site to capture the actual password and multifactor authentication token.

The Twitter cyber extortionists were very clever to best the multifactor authentication. In parallel with obtaining the passwords and tokens from Twitter employees using their fake server, within a few seconds, the extortionists accessed the employees' production Twitter accounts, this time using the password and multifactor authentication token just provided by the employer. In this way, the Twitter employees would not have time to act even if they had become suspicious. It was a successful strategy, allowing the extortionists to gain internal access to all Twitter account holders. Of additional concern was that apparently former Twitter employees who had worked in the security function still had some type of privileged access and possession of administrative tools, so they may have also been targeted. The extortionists then selected the Twitter accounts with the largest population of social network followers to send the messages in their scam to obtain Bitcoin.

The duration of the Twitter account holder extortion cyber incident was small, but the potential severity was large. There was potential for this type of cyber extortion to affect political leaders and large investment owners, which could have carried over to influencing government policy or national security. A similar cyber extortion activity occurred in parallel on Google, which seemed to be perpetrated by the same criminal gang. Bitcoin extortion messages also appeared on Google's YouTube, featuring fake videos by celebrities like Apple co-founder Steve Wozniak and 17 others. Mr. Wozniak initiated a lawsuit against Google's parent Alphabet the following week, asserting that the company did not take sufficient steps to remove similar Bitcoin scam videos posted to YouTube that used his and the other plaintiffs' names, fraudulently claiming to back the Bitcoin scam as compared to Twitter reacting almost immediately to the cyber extortion incident (Burnson 2020).

The Twitter account holders were impacted in two ways. First, their credibility may be diminished by their public credentials being used in this way by cyber extortionists, and due to the fact, the entire world now is aware of the incident. Second, Twitter account holders did not have access to their accounts, as noted previously. According to time stamp information, the Twitter cyber extortion began roughly at 3 p.m. EST on July 15, 2020, and continued until around 6 p.m. EST. At that point Twitter appeared to have shut down all suspect celebrity and government accounts to prevent them from being compromised further. At some time overnight or the next day, allegedly, service was restored to users of the compromised Twitter accounts. Insiders stated that hundreds of Twitter accounts had been hijacked by the cyber extortionists, but there has not been a public investigation report to verify this. Although beyond the scope of the current chapter in terms of looking back, Twitter was earlier cyber extorted in 2018 when thousands of businesses, individuals, schools, news agencies, and other places throughout the United States, Canada, and Australia received emailed bomb threats warning that a mercenary had placed a bomb in the receiver's workplace and demanding that a ransom of $20,000 be sent to a Bitcoin address to prevent the bomb from being detonated. The impact of that was many schools and businesses were evacuated for the day after cyber extortion threats. Later it was determined that the cyber extortionist did not profit from the attempt, but the fear and service disruption made a lasting impression on society.

Decision makers could have prevented the Twitter cyber extortion. First, former employee privileges ought to have been revoked if they were not. Second, training ought to have been given to Twitter employees so they would recognize fake websites with similar host domain names. Third, Twitter ought to have been monitoring unusual activity such as a certain employee's account accessing the administrative function to control hundreds of end-user accounts during the same span of three hours. That was a huge red flag missed, especially given that Twitter had been hacked for Bitcoin cyber extortion in 2018. Fourth, Twitter and other social media companies could set up an internal money laundering and criminal activity spotting department, using their own tools to identify suspicious patterns in the account traffic or activity, and then investigate the actions in more detail without falsely accusing anyone but merely verifying if illegal activity is taking place and, if so, passing that on to trained cyber specialists like the FBI. This is already being done in the US financial and insurance industry, driven by the US Securities and Exchange Commission and the Financial Investment Regulation Agency. Their regulatory and compliance concepts could be expanded to encompass social media and other industries targeted by cyber criminals. Furthermore, Industry 4.0 technology such as big data analytics and artificial intelligence is capable of spotting patterns, beyond consumer spending behavior, such as identifying potential cyber-criminal activity. Therefore, Industry 4.0 technology ought to be applied toward identifying and preventing cyberattacks.

Across the world from the United States to Finland, in Scandinavia, cyber extortion was also taking place in 2020. The RandomMan cyber extortion targeted a large Helsinki, Finland-based psychology services organization named Vastaamo. Cyber hackers took data of Vastaamo's 400 employees and approximately 40,000 of its patients (Ralston 2020). Apparently, the stolen data included not only full names but also addresses, contact details, and unique government-issued Finnish identity numbers, along with detailed therapy notes and diagnoses (Ralston 2020).

The RansomMan hacker targeted both the company Vastaamo as well as its patients for extortion. First RansomMan demanded a 40-bitcoin (£403,000) ransom from Vastaamo, and when it was not received, he began publishing some data from the employees and patients on a public forum in Finland. RansomMan threatened to publish the data of 100 people each day onto a dark web Tor file server until the bitcoin ransom was received from Vastaamo. As the company resisted, RansomMan carried out the threat, publishing the personal data of 300 people, including various public figures and police officers, on a public forum. Although the forum was shut down later, the damage was done. RansomMan also made a 10.9-GB TAR file of the stolen Vastaamo data available to the public.

Interestingly, and shortly after the RansomMan demand, informants believe that Vastaamo paid the extortionists but keep the ransom payment private as suggested by police (Ralston 2020). Shortly after, RansomMan took down the public shared data, and the hacker's Tor dark web server disappeared. We could speculate that Vastaamo paid the ransom, but we do not know if the amount was approximately $500,000 USD. In parallel with extorting the company Vastaamo, RansomMan began targeting each patient, demanding, for example, according to a victim statement from an email dated October 24, 2020, "€200 in bitcoin," and if the patient didn't pay within 24 hours, the ransom would rise to €500; otherwise the content of therapist-patient details would be made public (Ralston 2020). According to investigations and Finland court system documents, data suggest that around 36,000 patient reports were stolen, and more than 25,000 victims were contacted by RansomMan for extortion, while police stated between 10 and 20 patients paid the ransom (Ralston 2020). Others tried to pay but failed, and Vastaamo staff sent over 37,000 messages by email, letter, and phone informing victims about the security breach (Ralston 2020).

The method RansomMan used was apparently a security flaw in Vastaamo's patient management system, which the company's co-founder and CEO, Ville Tapio, a trained product developer with an education in marketing, commissioned a team of in-house software developers to create (Ralston 2020). In other words, the exploited system was an in-house product, not commercial software, and would likely not have had project management or development methodologies applied as compared to IBM or a similar large software developer.

The RansomMan cyber extortion could be considered successful for the hacker. Some ransoms were paid, and the hacker has never been caught as of the date of writing. The impact would be money spent by Vastaamo on the ransom paid (if it was), as well as the ransom paid by the patients. Additionally, Vastaamo lost credibility to the public. Vastaamo is a private company that runs 25 therapy centers across Finland and sub-contracts psychotherapy services for Finland's public health system. After the extortion incident, it lost customers of all types. Vastaamo staff resources also suffered internally, as it dismissed CEO Ville Tapio on October 26, 2020 (Ralston 2020) and likely dismissed other staff without making it public. Another impact from the RansomMan extortion was that Vastaamo violated Finland's national data protection authority act in accordance with the European Union's GDPR individual data privacy laws.

The RansomMan cyber extortion could have been avoided. Apparently, there were data breaches at Vastaamo in 2018, as well as in 2019, prior to the 2020 ransom extortion. There were rumors that some staff at Vastaamo knew it was possible their data could be breached due to weaknesses in the patient management system. In fact, Helsinki District Court ordered a temporary seizure of Tapio's assets, worth more than €10 million, on the application of PTK Midco Oy, the holding company behind the investment vehicle that bought Vastaamo in June 2019, in that Tapio concealed the security failings of their patient management system (Ralston 2020). According to records, one major breach at Vastaamo took place on November 25, 2018, when the size of the electronic patient registry (EPR), where all data was stored, was just over 33,000 customers (Ralston 2020). Data logs reveal that the EPR was accessed again in March 2019, but it's not known if this was by the same hackers. It's also not clear exactly what data were taken (Ralston 2020). It has been reported that historic documents referring to Vastaamo's system documentation were accessible via a simple Google search, which would make it easy for a hacker to develop methods to gain access to the patient management system. There are some allegations that Vastaamo employees or former employees may have cooperated with the hackers in some way (Ralston 2020).

Americans certainly remember and suffered from the DarkSide extortion cyberattack on Colonial Pipelines on May 7, 2021. Colonial Pipelines is an American oil pipeline system that originates in Houston, Texas, and carries gasoline as well as jet fuel mainly to the southeastern United States. However, due to the volume of production, any disruption in the oil gas supply chain affects the entire United States. Colonial Pipelines halted all operations to contain the attack and secretly brought the FBI on board to assist. The company paid the $4.4 million USD in Bitcoin ransom to the DarkSide Russian-backed hacker group within several hours of the extortion demand (Mallin and Barr 2021). Apparently, once the ransom was paid, DarkSide hackers made good on their promise and supplied Colonial Pipeline Company with an IT tool to restore their system (Mallin and Barr 2021), although it took more than a day to complete the restoration to bring the systems back online.

The impact of the Russian DarkSide cyberattack went beyond the $4.4 million ransom paid. The Federal Motor Carrier Safety Administration issued a regional emergency declaration for 17 states and Washington, DC, to keep fuel supply lines open during the DarkSide cyberattack that kept Colonial Pipeline systems offline (Mallin and Barr 2021). The DarkSide attack was considered the largest cyberattack on an oil infrastructure company in the history of the United States. Panic buying caused widespread gasoline shortages in a domino effect, and some gas stations went without fuel for several days in May 2021.

Apparently, the primary target of the attack was the billing infrastructure of the company, so Colonial Pipelines oil pumping systems was still able to work, yet they could not track revenue – so for capitalistic reasons, they shut down. According to internal sources in the company, the inability to bill customers was the reason for halting the pipeline operation (Mallin and Barr 2021). Publicly, Colonial Pipeline claimed that it shut down the pipeline as a precaution due to a concern that the hackers might have obtained information allowing them to carry out further attacks on vulnerable parts of the pipeline. The day after the attack, Colonial could not confirm at that time when the pipeline would resume normal functions (Mallin and Barr 2021).

The DarkSide cyber extortion impact spread widely. In response to fuel shortages at Charlotte Douglas International Airport caused by the pipeline shutdown, American Airlines changed flight schedules temporarily (Mallin and Barr 2021). At least two flights (to Honolulu and London) had fuel stops or plane changes added to their schedules for a four-day period. The shortage also required Hartsfield–Jackson Atlanta International Airport to use other fuel suppliers, and there are at least five other airports directly serviced by the pipeline (Mallin and Barr 2021). Fuel shortages began to occur at filling stations amid panic buying as the pipeline shutdown entered its fourth day. Alabama, Florida, Georgia, North Carolina, and South Carolina all reported shortages (Mallin and Barr 2021). Areas from northern South Carolina to southern Virginia were hardest hit, with 71% of filling stations running out of fuel in Charlotte on May 11 and 87% of stations out in Washington, DC, and average fuel prices rose to their highest since 2014, reaching more than $3 a gallon.

The question here is, considering the earlier 2020 data breach, service disruption, and extortion cyberattacks, should Colonial Pipelines have better protected its systems? The company carries gasoline, diesel, and jet fuel from Texas to as far away as New York, which amounts to 45% of all fuel consumed on the East Coast. To some extent, the DarkSide cyber extortion on Colonial Pipelines was mitigated. The FBI investigated the DarkSide hackers and traced the money. The Russian DarkSide attackers also stole nearly 100 gigabytes of data and threatened to release it on the internet if the ransom was not paid (Mallin and Barr 2021), so this makes one wonder exactly what sensitive information or customer details were in that hacked data. On June 7, the US Department of Justice announced that it had recovered 63.7 of the bitcoins (approximately $2.3 million) from the ransom payment (Mallin and Barr 2021). At the time of writing, no more of the remaining $2.1 million USD ransom has been found, and the Russian DarkSide hacker group has not been prosecuted. Furthermore, since DarkSide were Russian backed, and we know there were 100 GB of data stolen, one may wonder what, if any, of that sensitive data have found its way into other hands, perhaps for additional revenue to the hackers.

Across the Atlantic Ocean from Colonial Pipelines, there was another cyber extortion taking place, which was like the Finland Vastaamo patient data ransom incident. On May 14, 2021, the Health Service Executive (HSE) of Ireland was cyberattacked for extortion by a hacker group named WizardSpider, believed to be operating from Saint Petersburg, Russia (O'Loughlin 2021). WizardSpider used the American-made Cobalt Strike Beacon IT diagnosis software to break into HSE's servers, stealing medical information of at least 520 patients, along with corporate documents (O'Loughlin 2021).

The WizardSpider attackers began by sending a malicious email to a workstation on March 16, 2021, which was opened on March 18, and an infected Microsoft Excel file was downloaded, which allowed the attackers access to HSE systems (O'Loughlin 2021). The attackers gained more access over the following weeks. Apparently the HSE antivirus software detected unusual activity on 31 March, but it could not block Conti because HSE's antivirus checking software was set to monitor mode. On May 13, the cybersecurity provider hired by HSE emailed the HSE Security Operations team that there had been unhandled threats on at least 16 systems since May 7; subsequently the HSE Security Operations team restarted servers, but the malware was not removed (O'Loughlin 2021). The WizardSpider cyberattack on HSE was detected only by 4 a.m. on May 14, 2021 (O'Loughlin 2021). By that time, the ransomware virus had affected both national and local systems, involving in all core services, forcing the HSE to take down its IT system to protect it from the further attack and to give the HSE time to consider options (O'Loughlin 2021). The attack occurred during the COVID-19 pandemic, which must have impacted the COVID-19 vaccination program.

The impact of the of the attack was that on 28 May, the HSE confirmed that data relating to 520 patients, including sensitive information, was published online (O'Loughlin 2021). Apparently, the Irish government had not filled a vacant position at the National Cybersecurity Centre, which is responsible for the state's cybersecurity, because the salary was too low to attract candidates (O'Loughlin 2021). If the government had filled that position, perhaps the WizardSpider ransomware attack could have been detected earlier or prevented. Another point was that the method used by WizardSpider hackers was the Conti ransomware cyber virus. This same group was believed to have attacked the Department of Health with a similar cyberattack previously (O'Loughlin 2021). It seems unusual that a repeat occurrence would not have been detected or planned for. Although it was assumed there would be extortion for money, none has been documented yet. On May 28, the HSE confirmed that confidential data relating to 520 patients, including sensitive departmental information, was published online (O'Loughlin 2021). The WizardSpider ransomware cyberattack had a significant impact on hospital appointments across the country, with many appointments cancelled, including all outpatient and radiology services (O'Loughlin 2021). Several hospitals described situations where they could not access electronic systems and records and had to rely on paper records, while other institutions warned of significant disruption, with routine appointments being cancelled, including maternity checkups and scans (O'Loughlin 2021). The chief operations officer of the HSE, Anne O'Connor, said on May 14 that some cancer and stroke services had been affected and that the situation would have been be very serious had it continued (O'Loughlin 2021).

In New Zealand, cyber terrorists attacked the Waikato District Health Board (WDHB) in May 2021, demanding an undisclosed ransom. New Zealand police did not learn the identity of the cyber hackers, but the New Zealand Herald reported that an unidentified group had claimed responsibility for the hack (Russell 2021). The hackers apparently stole confidential patient notes, staff details, and financial information, and the group gave the WDHB seven days to contact them following the cyberattack, but WDHB refused to pay any ransom (Russell 2021). On May 27, senior WDHB executives confirmed that hackers had seized patient and staff details and that files had been sent to several media outlets, including the New Zealand Herald (Russell 2021). Although it was not disclosed, insiders speculated the ransom was in the millions of dollars (Russell 2021).

The impact was that the WDHB hospital computer systems and phone lines remained affected by the ransomware attack for several days (Russell 2021). Apparently, some surgeries were postponed because of the attack, but most went ahead as planned. Two Air New Zealand flights were cancelled after the airline was unable to get a negative COVID-19 certificate for a crew member who was to work on both flights. On May 26, an unidentified doctor claimed that seriously ill cancer patients had to be flown to Australia for treatment due to the disruption and potential data breach caused by the cyberattack. By June 2, the WDHB confirmed that it had made progress in restoring half of its servers over the past four days, and by June 7, radiation therapy had resumed. The DHB also faced a backlog of patients who had their outpatient appointments and other services cancelled because of the cyberattack. Due to the disruption, some patients had to seek treatment at other district health boards (Russell 2021). Could the New Zealand ransomware cyberattack have been prevented? Possibly, because the Ministry of Health had entered negotiations with an IT vendor in 2019 to purchase a more advanced cybersecurity system for the country's district health boards (Russell 2021). However, these negotiations were abandoned since the ministry lacked the budget to purchase the proposed system, and the pandemic had disrupted operations (Russell 2021).

On the other side of the Pacific Ocean from New Zealand, JBS, a Brazil-based meat processing plant, was cyberattacked for extortion by Russia-based REvil hackers on May 30, 2021. JBS supplies approximately one-fifth of meat globally, making it the world's largest producer of beef, chicken, and pork by sales, thereby making the ransomware attack comparable in magnitude to the Colonial Pipeline cyberattack discussed earlier – and both occurred in the same month. Insiders alleged that ransomware attacks had also been made to other food producers, including the Molson Coors beer manufacturer (Fung, Cohen, and Sands 2021). JBS paid the hackers an $11 million USD ransom in Bitcoin (Fung, Cohen and Sands 2021).

The US FBI investigated this cyberattack and apparently others which did not make it to fruition or the media – stakeholders can be grateful for that. At that point, after so many cyberattacks coming from Russia and targeting US-based organizations, the US White House and President Joe Biden confronted Russian President Putin. Allegedly, after a July 9, 2021, phone call between US President Joe Biden and Russian President Vladimir Putin, Biden told the press, "I made it very clear to him that the United States expects when a ransomware operation is coming from his soil even though it's not sponsored by the state, we expect them to act if we give them enough information to act on who that is" – Biden later added that the United States would take the group's servers down if Putin did not (Fung, Cohen and Sands 2021). On July 13, 2021, REvil websites and other infrastructure vanished from the internet – we do not know if any ransom was paid, but we suspect it was not.

Despite the REvil hacker group being stopped, the impact of the extortion attempt impacted all facilities belonging to JBS USA, including JBS's American subsidiary – all those focused on pork and poultry faced disruption due to the attack (Fung, Cohen and Sands 2021). All JBS-owned beef facilities in the United States were rendered temporarily inoperative. Slaughterhouses located in states including Utah, Texas, Wisconsin, and Nebraska were impacted. A notable shutdown was the JBS beef facility in Souderton, Pennsylvania, which is the largest such facility east of Chicago, according to JBS. The beef industry in Australia faced disruption because of the attack, and JBS laid off some 7000 Australian employees on June 2 (Fung, Cohen and Sands 2021).

Another impact was that the US Department of Agriculture was unable to offer wholesale beef and pork prices on June 1 (Fung, Cohen and Sands 2021). Due to predicted shortfalls in meat production and price increases, the USDA encouraged other companies to increase production. JBS had indicated on June 1 that most of its facilities would resume functioning on June 2, but it took longer. The attack heightened awareness of consolidation in the meatpacking industry in the United States and around the world and the corresponding vulnerability to decreased production, should one of the four major meat producers reduce its output (Fung, Cohen and Sands 2021). Again, we see a pattern of Bitcoin facilitating cyber extortion hackers. Perhaps a solution to the cyber problem would be to regulate the Bitcoin industry internationally.

Several managed hosted computer software providers and their customers became victims of a ransomware attack from the Russia-backed REvil group, resurfacing after the JSB incident. On July 2, 2021, the REvil group cyberattacked Kaseya Limited, an American company hosting cloud-based applications, which caused widespread downtime for over 1000 company clients (DOJ 2021). REvil ransomware gang claimed to have encrypted more than 1 million systems during the incident and initially asked for a $70 million ransom payment to release a universal decryptor to unlock all affected systems (DOJ 2021). On July 5, Kaseya said that between 800 and 1500 downstream businesses were impacted in the attack (DOJ 2021). Researchers in the Netherlands identified the first vulnerabilities in the software on April 1. They warned Kaseya and worked together with company experts to solve four of the seven reported vulnerabilities. Despite the efforts, Kaseya could not patch all the bugs in time. The source of the outbreak was identified within hours to be virtual system administrator (VSA) software, a remote monitoring and management software package developed by Kaseya. An authentication bypass vulnerability in the software allowed REvil attackers to compromise VSA and distribute a malicious payload through hosts managed by the software, amplifying the reach of the attack. In response, the company shut down its VSA cloud and SaaS servers and issued a security advisory to any customers, including those with on-premises deployments of VSA.

Initial reports of companies affected by the incident include Norwegian financial software developer Visma, which manages some systems for Swedish supermarket chain Coop. The supermarket chain had to close its 800 stores for almost a week, some in small villages without any other food shop. It did not pay ransom but rebuilt its systems from scratch after waiting for an update from Kaseya. As mentioned in the JBS ransomware attack by REvil, US President Joe Biden put his foot down and basically ordered Russian President Putin to act. As noted, the REvil websites and other infrastructure vanished from the internet. On July 23, 2021, Kaseya announced it had received a universal decryptor tool for the REvil-encrypted files from an unnamed trusted third party and was helping victims restore their files.

On November 8, 2021, the United States Department of Justice (DOJ 2021) unsealed indictments against Ukrainian national Yaroslav Vasinskyi and Russian national Yevgeniy Polyanin. Vasinskyi was charged with conducting ransomware attacks against multiple victims including Kaseya and was arrested in Poland on October 8. Polyanin was charged with conducting ransomware attacks against multiple victims including Texas businesses and government entities. The department worked with the national police of Ukraine for the charges and announced the seizure of $6.1 million tied to ransomware payments. If convicted on all charges, Vasinskyi faces a maximum penalty of 115 years in prison and Polyanin 145 years in prison (DOJ 2021). At last, we see a potential solution to cyberattacks: if the source can be identified as Russia or another country, those governments could be engaged and encouraged to assist in fighting cyber criminals. However, it is unlikely those foreign governments would assist in arresting their own intelligence, that is, if they were possibly guilty of cyber espionage.

Across the Atlantic Ocean in South Africa, another cyberattack was occurring. Transnet, a large container terminal company in the Port of Durban, suffered a ransomware attack on July 22, 2021 (Diphoko 2021). Not much information was released because the South African government was managing the situation and considered it a national security risk to discuss the incident (Diphoko 2021). The extortion ransomware attack caused Transnet to declare force majeure at several key container terminals, including Port of Durban, Ngqura, Port Elizabeth, and Cape Town. Durban handles 60% of the shipping container traffic in the country. The attack was the first time that the operational integrity of the country's critical maritime infrastructure suffered a severe disruption, leading South African's National Institute for Security Studies (ISS) to call its impact unprecedented in South African history (Diphoko 2021).

The ISS speculated that Transnet was also withholding details about the attack because the attack might cause legal liabilities for the company (Diphoko 2021). Bloomberg News stated that the attackers encrypted files on Transnet's computer systems, thereby preventing the company from accessing its own information while leaving instructions on how to start ransom negotiations (Diphoko 2021). The Bloomberg article quotes a source from the cybersecurity firm Crowdstrike Holdings Inc. which states that the ransomware used in the attack was linked to strains known variously as Death Kitty, Hello Kitty, and Five Hands, which likely originated from Russia or Eastern Europe (Diphoko 2021). The timing of the attack, which followed closely after the 2021 South African unrest following former South African President Jacob Zuma's imprisonment, caused speculation that the two events might have been part of a coordinated effort to disrupt economic activity in the country, but ISS stated that the two events were likely unrelated (Diphoko 2021). It remained unclear if the ransom was paid, but we suspect it was.

Back in the United States, shortly after the Capitol riot incident, American domain registry Epik suffered a cyber data breach from the hacker group Anonymous, which seemed to be politically motivated, at an in-kind extortion of degrading Republication Party credibility (Thalen 2021). The breach exposed a wide range of information including personal information of customers, domain history and purchase records, credit card information, internal company emails, and records from the company's WHOIS privacy service (Thalen 2021). More than 15 million unique email addresses were exposed belonging to customers and non-customers whose information had been stolen. The stolen data also included 843,000 transactions from a period of over ten years and almost 1 million invoices. An engineer performing an initial impact assessment for an Epik customer said that Epik's entire primary database, which contained account usernames, passwords, SSH keys, and credit card numbers stored in plaintext, had also been compromised, along with internal memos describing subpoenas and preservation requests related to investigations following the January Capitol attack (Thalen 2021).

The attackers responsible for the Epik data theft identified themselves as members of the hacktivist collective Anonymous. The attackers released an initial 180-gigabyte dataset on September 13, 2021, though the data appeared to have been exfiltrated in late February of the same year. A second release, this time containing bootable disk images, was made on September 29. A third release on October 4 reportedly contained more bootable disk images and documents belonging to the Texas Republican Party, a customer of Epik's (Thalen 2021). The hackers claimed they had obtained "a decade's worth of data," including all customer data and records for all domains ever hosted or registered through the company, as well as poorly encrypted passwords and other sensitive data stored in plaintext. The Distributed Denial of Secrets (DDoSecrets) organization announced later that day that it was working to curate the leaked data for public download and said that it consisted of 180 gigabytes of user, registration, forwarding, and other information (Thalen 2021).

Epik is known for providing services to websites that host far-right, neo-Nazi, and other extremist content – past and present Epik customers include Gab, Parler, 8chan, the Oath Keepers, and the Proud Boys (Thalen 2021). The hack was described as a Rosetta Stone to the far right because it has allowed researchers and journalists to discover links between far-right websites, groups, and individuals (Thalen 2021). Distributed Denial of Secrets co-founder and hacker Emma Best said researchers had been describing the breach as the Panama Papers of hate groups. Anonymous is widely known for its various cyberattacks against several governments and governmental institutions, corporations, and the Church of Scientology. Primarily active in the late 2000s and early 2010s, Anonymous's media profile diminished by 2018, but the group re-emerged in 2020 to support the George Floyd protests and other causes (Thalen 2021).

There were some interesting alleged politics behind this cyberattack. In September 2021, Anonymous asked people to support Operation Jane, an effort by the group to oppose the Texas Heartbeat Act, a six-week abortion ban that went into effect on September 1 (Thalen 2021). On September 4, Epik had begun providing services to a whistleblower website run by the anti-abortion Texas Right to Life organization, which allowed people to anonymously report suspected violators of the bill. The website, which moved to Epik after being denied services by GoDaddy, went offline after Epik told the group it had violated the terms of service by collecting private information about third parties. On September 11, Anonymous hacked the website of the Republican Party of Texas, which is hosted by Epik, to replace it with text about Operation Jane (Thalen 2021).

The impact of the Anonymous cyber hack of Epik included reducing the credibility of those cited earlier, and Epik was subsequently criticized for lax data security practices, in particular failing to properly encrypt sensitive customer data (Thalen 2021). Epik submitted a data-breach notice in the state of Maine, in which it reported that 110,000 people had been affected by the breach and that financial account and credit card data had been exposed. In a statement to the *Washington Post*, an Epik spokesperson said that up to 38,000 credit card numbers had been leaked (Thalen 2021). We will not go into if this cyberattack could have been prevented.

The National Rifle Association (NRA) suffered an extortion attack on October 27, 2021, which was attributed to Russian-backed REvil hacker group going under the public name Grief as a rebrand. REvil had been linked to ransomware attacks on Sinclair Broadcast Group as well as hundreds of financial entities across more than 40 countries (Ropek 2021). Grief published 13 documents stolen from the National Rifle Association in a ransomware scam and threatened to release more NRA documents if the undisclosed ransom was not paid. On October 21, 2021, the FBI hacked and shut down REvil (Ropek 2021).

Prior to the ransomware attack, the NRA had been involved in multiple legal disputes, which may have made it an easier target for cyberattacks, as attention within the organization was pulled away from security. An anonymous person with direct knowledge of the events at the NRA told the media that the NRA had been having issues with its email system in the week prior to the publication of files by Grief, which is a potential indicator of a ransomware attack (Ropek 2021). The leaked files included the minutes from an NRA board meeting that occurred shortly before the release of documents as well as multiple files related to grants. One document appeared to be a late 2019 grant application made to the NRA by David Kopel on behalf of the Independence Institute for $267,000, with $248,500 earmarked as Kopel's salary (Ropek 2021). Kopel has repeatedly filed amicus briefs supporting the NRA in court and has not disclosed a financial connection to the organization (Ropek 2021).

On November 11, Grief published more internal documents which included bank account information of the NRA members as well as information about specific employees including Social Security numbers and home addresses (Ropek 2021). Also, Grief moved the NRA-related documents on its website from a section indicating hacks in progress to a different one indicating that it had been completed. Whether Grief or REvil were successful would be debatable, as was the exact motive or if a ransom was paid.

Now, going down to the Caribbean, a US territory, Costa Rica, experienced a cyber extortion attack by the Russian-backed Conti hackers. Beginning on the night of April 17, 2022, a cyber-attack began against nearly 30 institutions of the government of Costa Rica, including its Ministry of Finance; Ministry of Science, Innovation, Technology and Telecommunications (MICITT); National Meteorological Institute; state internet service provider RACSA; the Costa Rican Social Security Fund (Caja Costarricense de Seguro Social, CCSS); Ministry of Labor and Social Security [es]; Fund for Social Development and Family Allowances; and the Administrative Board of the Municipal Electricity Service of Cartago. The pro-Russian Conti Group claimed the first group of attacks and demanded a US$10 million ransom in exchange for not releasing the information stolen from the Ministry of Finance, which could include sensitive information such as citizens' tax returns and companies operating in Costa Rica (Delfino 2022).

Consequently, the government had to shut down the computer systems used to declare taxes and for the control and management of imports and exports, causing losses to the productive sector on the order of US$30 million per day. Likewise, the web pages of the Ministry of Science, Innovation, Technology and Telecommunications were removed from the network (Delfino 2022). Costa Rica required technical assistance from mainland United States, Israel, Spain, and Microsoft, among others, to deal with the cyberattack. The attack consisted of infections of computer systems with ransomware, defacement of web pages, theft of email files, and attacks on the Social Security human resources portal, as well as on its official Twitter account (Delfino 2022).

On May 6, 2022, the US government through the FBI offered a US$10 million reward for information leading to the identification of a person or persons in a leadership position within the Conti Group and an additional US$5 million for information leading to the capture or conviction, in any country, of individuals who aided or conspired to carry out Conti ransomware attacks. Days after the FBI's announcement, Conti announced that it would begin a shutdown process (Delfino 2022). On May 8, 2022, the new president of Costa Rica, Rodrigo Chaves Robles, decreed a state of national emergency due to cyberattacks, considering them an act of terrorism. Days later, at a press conference, he stated that the country was in a state of war and that there was evidence that people inside Costa Rica were helping Conti, calling them traitors and filibusters (Delfino 2022). On May 31, 2022, at dawn, the Hive Ransomware Group carried out an attack against the Costa Rican Social Security Fund, forcing the institution to turn off all its critical systems, including the Unique Digital Health File and the Centralized Collection System (Delfino 2022). The former stores sensitive medical information of patients using Social Security, while the latter is used to collect the population's insurance fees.

Conti has been responsible for hundreds of ransomware incidents since 2020. The FBI estimates that, as of January 2022, there were more than 1000 victims of attacks associated with Conti ransomware, with victim payouts exceeding $150 million, making Conti's the most damaging ransomware strain ever documented (Delfino 2022). There have been other related cybersecurity extortion attacks. For example, in May 2022, the Hive hacker group (who also attacked Costa Rica when Conti shut down) attacked the Community of Navarra, Spain, forcing 100 institutions to use pen and paper while systems were recovered (Delfino 2022). That same month, Hive also attacked the Central Bank of Zambia; however, the entity refused to pay the ransom, stating that it had the means to recover its systems (Delfino 2022). Finally, and ironically, although China has been suspected for some of the cyberattacks, it does appear that most have been linked to Russia. In fact, China was the target of a data breach in 2022. The Shanghai National Police Database (SHGA Database) experienced a cyber data breach by Chinese hackers. The stolen data included personal information of Chinese residents and police cases. It was publicly sold by an unknown hacker on the Internet at the price of 10 bitcoins (Zheng 2022). The data allegedly amounted to 23 terabytes of information of more than 1 billion mainland Chinese residents, including names, addresses, places of birth, resident ID card numbers, phone numbers, photos, mobile phone numbers, and information on criminal cases (Zheng 2022). Screenshots circulated on the Internet revealed that the data provide a huge amount of detailed police information, including the time of reporting criminals, the phone number of the reporting person, and the reasons for reporting (Zheng 2022). Preliminary analysis of the data samples showed that the personal information in the database came from residents across mainland China, not just the city of Shanghai (Zheng 2022).

Although China controls most of the media in its country, some social media outlets suggested it would be the largest, most unprecedented data leak incident since 1949 if the amount of data is accurate (Zheng 2022). Some information reported that Weibo, a social platform in mainland China, has applied censorship on some keywords to stop the news from spreading (Zheng 2022). Bloomberg faxed inquiries to the Central Cyberspace Administration of China and the Shanghai Police Bureau, and no responses have been received yet (Zheng 2022). Bloomberg asserted that data breaches within the People's Republic of China are rarely disclosed, mentioning that several data leakage incidents occurred in mainland China over the past few years, such as the leakage of personal information of Communist Party members in 2016, the leakage of Weibo account information in 2020, and the information leakage of Xinjiang re-education camps (Zheng 2022). China is the largest country in the world and one of the few remaining communist societies, so it is interesting that cyber hackers internal to the country are attacking their government and extorting it.

CYBERATTACK SYNOPSIS AND MITIGATION RECOMMENDATIONS

Table 1.2 represents our analysis of the major global cyberattacks by hacker central motive during 2020–2022 (to the time of writing), based on our data review. We also visually summarized our cyberattack data from Table 1.2 as a chart, as shown in Figure 1.1. It can be seen from Table 1.2 that extortion is the most common central motive, at 44% of global cyberattacks, but service disruption (32%) and data theft (24%) are not that far behind.

The cyber hacker central motive patterns become much clearer when examining the extortion by central motive, where we see 36% were for bitcoin ransom, with 20% being directed to end users or customers and 16% of the attacks being targeted at company executives or owner/stockholders. Only 8% of cyberattacks where a ransom was demanded were extorted from governments, and in many cases, the government refused to pay. This suggests we could expect to see more cyberattacks targeted at customers of large companies, particularly in the healthcare/medical field, where patients are extorted for ransom in bitcoin. It also indicates that pretty much all cyber extortions demanded payment in bitcoin. If the government were to regulate the bitcoin industry, policies and safeguards could be developed to impede cyber extortion.

Although data theft at 24% was the lowest of the cyberattack types we reviewed, we consider foreign intelligence spying a considerable risk beyond its representation in Table 1.2 at 12%. We

TABLE 1.2
Major Global Cyberattacks by Type and Central Motive

Central Motive	Data Theft	Disruption	Extortion	Grand Total
Company bitcoin ransom			16%	16%
Customer bitcoin ransom			20%	20%
Disrupt government service		12%		12%
Disrupt nonprofit service		8%		8%
Expose government corruption	4%	8%		12%
Foreign intelligence spying	12%	4%		16%
Government bitcoin ransom			8%	8%
Stealing trade secrets	8%			8%
Grand Total	**24%**	**32%**	**44%**	**100%**

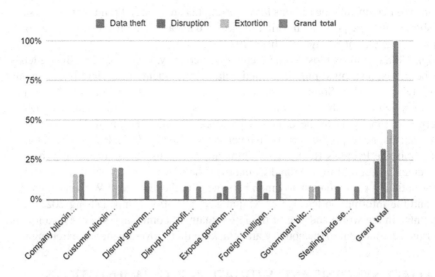

FIGURE 1.1 Synopsis of global cyberattacks.

consider national intelligence data theft the costliest in terms of strategic potential as compared to the actual impact of cyber extortion. The reason data theft could be the costliest in the future is due to the nature of what was stolen; in many cases the data breaches were pharmaceutical drug trade secrets (8%) and government defense industry classified material (12%). A cyber data breach of government secrets could allow communist groups to develop powerful weapons to kill numerous innocent people.

Finally, cyberattacks for service disruption, at 32%, were largely attributed to the Russian invasion of Ukraine, which we estimate was 20%, with the remaining 8% being to expose government corruption of another country and foreign intelligence spying (4%). Thus, if NATO, the European Union, and NATO's largest member, the United States, were to amplify efforts to help Ukraine mitigate and prevent future cyberattacks, this could easily reduce that 20% to almost zero for the remainder of 2022 and future years.

Another subtle yet strategic observation we make regarding the Russian invasion of Ukraine is that the data indicate longitudinal cyberattack and espionage by Russia on the United States and allies of the United States. Strategically, US passive help to Ukraine by way of economic sanctions on Russia will be exactly what the United States has hoped for by forcing Russia to drain its financial reserves, thus making it less of a threat in future years. Note that the United States made similar strategic maneuvers with China during the pandemic: once the United States recognized its dependence on the global supply factory of China, it introduced trade sanctions using trivial excuses to reduce its dependency on Chinese imports and to reduce China's financial reserves – it seems to have worked.

The most strategic cyberattack mitigation is for NATO, European Union, and United States to continue to depress the advancing economic power of Russia and keep vigilance on China's production. More so, NATO and US allies ought to attract the support of other international economic consortiums, such as the African Union and various other international trade groups, including those in Asia and South America, to join in solidarity against cyberattacks and illegal warfare. Involving international trade unions in the fight against cyber terrorism will have a significant effect on reducing the economic ability of hacker groups in communist countries to continue to operate. Additionally, if international trade unions along with NATO alliance countries were to cooperate in the war more fully against cyber terrorism and extortion, their combined vigilance would provide faster global early warning systems and a shared global collection of subject matter experts to combat new cyberattack methods.

INDUSTRY 4.0 INFRASTRUCTURE AND INTERDEPENDENCY WITH CYBERSECURITY

In this section, we will explain Industry 4.0 is legitimately used by businesses for cryptosecurity strategies, and how terrorists use contemporary technology for cyber warfare. The Boston Consulting Group identified nine major building blocks for Industry 4.0 as enabling technologies. Big data and analytics, autonomous robots and vehicles, additive manufacturing, simulation, augment and virtual reality, horizontal/vertical system integration, Internet of Things, cloud/fog/edge technologies, and blockchain-cybersecurity are the nine technologies mentioned (Rosa et al. 2020). These are discussed in the following in terms of how they were or could be used for cybersecurity attacks and as cyber defenses. A decision maker such as the chief information officer or chief technology officer could discuss these issues with their staff and ensure these defenses are in place.

INTERNET OF THINGS (IoT)

The Internet of Things (IoT) paradigm refers to the vast interconnection of the "things" that surround us, allowing them to provide and consume services (Rubio, Roman, and Lopez 2018). When the Internet of Things (IoT) is used in an industrial setting, it is known as the Industrial IoT, or IIoT (Rubio, Roman, and Lopez 2018). The IIoT vertically integrates all the architecture's components, including control systems and machines. IoT encompasses many products, including home appliances, automation systems, watches, and automobiles (Thames and Schaefer 2017). Sensors, assembly-line components, healthcare gadgets, and autos are all examples of IIoT devices (Thames and Schaefer 2017). Another term frequently used in this context is cyber-physical systems (CPS), which differs from IIoT in that CPS focuses on feedback between systems in a local setting, whereas IIoT has a global connectivity dimension. The Internet of Things (IoT) and cyber-physical systems are key developments in the fourth industrial revolution which and are explained in this chapter. One of Industry 4.0's technology cornerstones is the utilization of big data and artificial intelligence (AI) analytics powered by machine learning (ML) and deep learning (DL) algorithms applied to data in real -time. AI has the potential to transform a variety of industries and fields. Methods for learning relationships from data without accepting assumptions about the underlying mechanisms are included in machine learning (ML), a subset of AI.

PROBLEMS AND ISSUES

Industry 4.0 environments with a broad mix of technologies have their own set of security and privacy challenges and typical cybersecurity challenges (Sawik 2022). Social engineering, malware infection, and insider attacks are some of the cybersecurity issues influencing Industry 4.0 0– enabling technologies (Rubio, Roman, and Lopez 2018). Privacy protection, authentication, information management, and access control to heterogeneous resources are the primary cybersecurity concerns for the IIoTs (Rubio, Roman, and Lopez 2018). One of the most prevalent cybersecurity attacks on IIoT devices is overloading the devices' resources, particularly the node resources such as processor, memory, and battery, with traffic and repetitive requests (Rubio, Roman, and Lopez 2018).

Cloud computing and fog computing are both vulnerable to cybersecurity assaults, with denial of service (DoS) attacks against cloud services being the most common type of attack (Rubio, Roman, and Lopez 2018). The service theft attack, in which the attacker exploits cloud resources at the expense of other clients, is an example of such an assault. Because of the prevalence of malware and the faith placed in the service provider, which has complete access to the stored data, cloud and fog computing are equally vulnerable to data integrity and confidentiality issues (Rubio, Roman, and Lopez 2018).

RECOMMENDED SOLUTIONS

Cybersecurity investments are critical by organizations using Industry 4.0 0–enabling technologies and environments. Gordon and Loeb (2002) suggest that the optimal budget for investment to reduce the risk related to a related vulnerability is considerably lower than the loss caused by an incident. This amount usually never exceeds 37% of the expected loss. Cybersecurity investment aims to prevent assets from being compromised by utilizing the Parkerian hexad's six elements of information security. Confidentiality, control, integrity, authenticity, availability, and utility are the six aspects of the Parkerian hexad (Sawik 2022).

Intrusion detection systems (IDSs) that meet the main requirements, such as coverage, holism, intelligence, and symbiosis, are one of the techniques for dealing with cybersecurity threats on Industry 4.0 0–enabling technologies and infrastructure (Rubio, Roman, and Lopez 2018). Due to the increased attack surface presented by Industry 4.0, the IDS must be able to cover all possible interactions and aspects of the deployment and could be easily upgraded with new detection algorithms (Rubio, Roman, and Lopez 2018). The IDS system should be able to consider the interconnections of the various sections of the ecosystem, given the ecosystem's overall and cooperative nature. The IDS should work as a protection system and interface with other Industry 4.0 services' prevention systems and forensics.

CONCLUSION AND FUTURE RESEARCH RECOMMENDATIONS

The advantages of Industry 4.0 technologies are apparent, and the increasing number of IoT devices is likely to push more countries towards the adoption of Industry 4.0 technologies. However, security and privacy issues need to be addressed because of the large number of users and interconnected devices. Unless these issues are addressed, there will be a lack of trust among users and the potential for exploitation of these security issues by hackers and misuse by companies. This chapter presented some of these cybersecurity challenges and recommended some of the solutions. Also, detailed analysis is required to be conducted in various developing countries, and the results need to be compared with the security challenges faced by developed countries. However, future research can focus on each of these challenges separately. A detailed analysis of the issues is needed to understand the pros and cons of issues and potential solutions. Decision makers in organizations using Industry 4.0 applications and environments need to assess their cybersecurity vulnerabilities and ensure that properly designed policies following benchmarks are put in place to handle cybersecurity challenges.

REFERENCES

Bamunuarachchi, Dinithi, Abhik Banerjee, Prem Prakash Jayaraman, and Dimitrios Georgakopoulos. 2020. "Cyber twins supporting industry 4.0 application development." Proceedings of the 18th International Conference on Advances in Mobile Computing & Multimedia, Chiang Mai, Thailand. https://doi.org/10.1145/3428690.3429177.

Blinken, Anthony. J. 2022. Attribution of Russia's Malicious Cyber Activity against Ukraine [Press Release, May 10]. Washington, DC: US Secretary of State. Retrieved June 30, 2022 from www.state.gov/attribution-of-russias-malicious-cyber-activity-against-ukraine/

Burnson, Robert. 2020. "Steve Wozniak sues YouTube over Twitter-like Bitcoin scam." Bloomberg News. Retrieved July 19, 2022 from www.bloomberg.com/news/articles/2020-07-23/steve-wozniak-sues-youtube-over-twitter-like-bitcoin-scam#xj4y7vzkg

Calder, Simon. 2020. "EasyJet hack: what does it mean for me and my personal data? Cyberattack leads to nine million passengers having their data 'accessed'." Independent [Newspaper]. [May 19]. Retrieved June 16, 2022 from www.independent.co.uk/travel/news-and-advice/easyjet-data-hack-news-cyberattack-passengers-personal-information-a9522241.html

Delfino. 2022. "Sala IV declara 'con lugar' más de 200 amparos contra el MEP por atraso en pago de salarios." Delfino Newspaper. [May 31]. Retrieved July 11, 2022 from https://delfino.cr/2022/05/sala-iv-declara-con-lugar-mas-de-200-recursos-de-amparo-contra-el-mep-por-atraso-en-pago-de-salarios

DHS. 2021. *Apache Log4j Vulnerability Guidance*. Washington, DC: US Department of Homeland Security, Cybersecurity & Infrastructure Security Agency (DHS). Retrieved April 20, 2022 from www.cisa.gov/uscert/apache-log4j-vulnerability-guidance

Diphoko, Wesley. 2021. "Transnet website still down and chaos gets worse." *Independent Online – Fast Company SouthAfrica(IOL).* [July 27]. Retrieved July 9, 2022 from www.iol.co.za/technology/software-and-internet/transnet-website-still-down-and-chaos-gets-worse-7a3fe743–5994–4c5e-aa96–900c7733e8f0

Dobberstein, Laura. 2022. "Red Cross forced to shutter family reunion service following cyberattack and data leak." *The Register*. [January 20]. Retrieved July 7, 2022 from www.theregister.com/2022/01/20/red_cross_hit_by_cyberattack/

DOJ. 2021. "Ukrainian arrested and charged with ransomware attack on Kaseya." *US Department of Justice (DOJ)*. [November 8]. Retrieved July 31, 2022 from www.justice.gov/opa/pr/ukrainian-arrested-and-charged-ransomware-attack-kaseya

FBI. 2021. *Internet Crime Complaint Center 2020 Internet Crime Report, Including COVID-19 Scam Statistics* [Report, March 17]. Washington, DC: US Federal Bureau of Investigations (FBI). Retrieved May 16, 2022 from www.fbi.gov/news/press-releases/press-releases/fbi-releases-the-internet-crime-complaint-center-2020-internet-crime-report-including-covid-19-scam-statistics

Fung, Brian, Zachary Cohen and Geneva Sands. 2021. "Ransomware gang that hit meat supplier mysteriously vanishes from the internet." *CNN Business*. [July 14]. Retrieved July 17, 2022 from www.cnn.com/2021/07/13/tech/revil-ransomware-disappears/index.html

Gordon, Lawrence A., and Martin P. Loeb. 2002. "The economics of information security investment." *ACM Transactions on Information and System Security* 5 (4): 438–457. https://doi.org/10.1145/581271.581274.

Ingram, David and Kevin Collier. 2020. "Biden, Gates, Musk: Bitcoin scam breaches some of world's most prominent Twitter accounts: Twitter believes suspected Bitcoin scammers grabbed control of high-profile accounts by targeting its employees." *NBC News*. [July 15]. Retrieved July 20, 2022 from www.nbcnews.com/tech/security/suspected-bitcoin-scammers-take-over-twitter-accounts-bill-gates-elon-n1233948

Kantchev, Georgi and Warren P. Strobel. 2021. "How Russia's 'info warrior' hackers let Kremlin play geopolitics on the cheap." *Wallstreet Journal*. [January 2]. Retrieved July 10, 2022 from www.wsj.com/articles/how-russias-info-warrior-hackers-let-kremlin-play-geopolitics-on-the-cheap-11609592401

Lee, Micah. 2020. "Hack of 251 law enforcement websites exposes personal data of 700,000 cops." *The Intercept*. [July 15]. Retrieved July 15, 2022 from https://theintercept.com/2020/07/15/blueleaks-anonymous-ddos-law-enforcement-hack/

Mallin, Alexander and Luke Barr. 2021. "DOJ seizes millions in ransom paid by colonial pipeline." *ABC News*. [June 7]. Retrieved May 15, 2022 from https://abcnews.go.com/Politics/doj-seizes-millions-ransom-paid-colonial-pipeline/story?id=78135821

Modderkolk, Huib. 2021. "Russian and Chinese hackers gained access to EMA." *de Volkskrant [Dutch News]*. Retrieved March 15, 2022 from www.volkskrant.nl/nieuws-achtergrond/russian-and-chinese-hackers-gained-access-to-ema~bdc61ba59/

O'Loughlin, Ann. 2021. "HSE seeks order to help find who uploaded or downloaded files stolen in cyberattack." *Irish Examiner*. [June 25]. Retrieved June 10, 2022 from www.irishexaminer.com/news/courtandcrime/arid-40322462.html

Pannett, Rachel. 2021. "FBI email system compromised by hackers who sent fake cyberattack alert." *Washington Post*. [November 14]. Retrieved May 30, 2022 from www.washingtonpost.com/nation/2021/11/14/fbi-hack-email-cyberattack/

Perez, Dan, Sarah Jones, Greg Wood, and Stephen Eckels. 2021. "Check your pulse: suspected APT actors leverage authentication bypass techniques and pulse secure zero-day" [Threat Research Report]. *Mandiant*. [April 20]. Retrieved July 29, 2022 from www.mandiant.com/resources/suspected-apt-actors-leverage-bypass-techniques-pulse-secure-zero-day

Psaki, Jen, and Anne Neuberger. 2021. *Jen Psaki and Deputy National Security Advisor for Cyber and Emerging Technology* [Press Briefing]. Washington, DC: US Government Executive Branch. Retrieved March 14, 2022 from www.whitehouse.gov/briefing-room/press-briefings/2021/02/17/press-briefing-by-press-secretary-jen-psaki-and-deputy-national-security-advisor-for-cyber-and-emerging-technology-anne-neuberger-february-17–2021/

Ralston, William. 2020. "A dying man, a therapist and the ransom raid that shook the world." *Wired Magazine*. [December 12]. Retrieved June 11, 2022 from www.wired.co.uk/article/finland-mental-health-data-breach-vastaamo

Robinson, Andy. 2021. "Nintendo says it increased security following a prolific leak of game prototypes: the Gigaleak saw an unprecedented amount of game data leaked online." *Video Game News.* Retrieved July 23, 2022 from www.videogameschronicle.com/news/nintendo-says-it-increased-security-following-a-prolific-leak-of-game-prototypes/

Ropek, Lucas. 2021. "The NRA has reportedly been hacked." *Gizmodo.* [October 27]. Retrieved July 11, 2022 from https://gizmodo.com/the-nra-has-reportedly-been-hacked-1847948727

Rosa, Paolo, Claudio Sassanelli, Andrea Urbinati, Davide Chiaroni and Sergio Terzi. 2020. "Assessing relations between circular economy and Industry 4.0: A systematic literature review." *International Journal of Production Research* 58 (6): 1662–1687. https://doi.org/10.1080/00207543.2019.1680896

Rubio, Juan E., Rodrigo Roman and Javier Lopez. 2018. "Analysis of cybersecurity threats in Industry 4.0: the case of intrusion detection." Proceedings of the 12th International Conference on Critical Information Infrastructures Security, Lucca, Italy. https://doi.org/10.1007/978-3-319-99843-5_11

Russell, Emma. 2021. "Waikato DHB cyberattack: privacy commissioner warns all DHBs to fix its IT vulnerabilities." *New Zealand Herald.* [May 25]. Retrieved July 17, 2022 from www.nzherald.co.nz/nz/waikato-dhb-cyberattack-privacy-commissioner-warns-all-dhbs-to-fix-its-it-vulnerabilities/7IUV5PHBRJZJEE44YZ55DTWAEM/

Sawik, Tadeusz. 2022. "A linear model for optimal cybersecurity investment in Industry 4.0 supply chains." *International Journal of Production Research* 60 (4): 1368–1385. https://doi.org/10.1080/00207543.2020.1856442

Thalen, Mikael. 2021. "Epik hack reveals prominent, Trump-supporting websites under subpoena investigation." *Daily Dot Magazine.* [September 27]. Retrieved July 27, 2022 from www.dailydot.com/debug/epik-hack-subpoenas-data-preservation-leak/

Thames, Lane and Dirk Schaefer. 2017. "Industry 4.0: an overview of key benefits, technologies, and challenges." In *Cybersecurity for Industry 4.0: Analysis for Design and Manufacturing*, edited by Lane Thames and Dirk Schaefer, 1–33. Cham: Springer International Publishing.

Zheng, Sarah. 2022. "Hackers claim theft of police info in China's largest data leak." *Bloomberg News.* [July 4]. Retrieved July 30, 2022 from www.bloomberg.com/news/articles/2022-07-04/hackers-claim-theft-of-police-info-in-china-s-largest-data-leak

2 Nature, Forms, and Remedies of Cyberbullying on Social Media Platforms
A Brief Philosophical Perspective

Sooraj Kumar Maurya

CONTENTS

DOI: 10.1201/9781003319887-2

INTRODUCTION

Cyberbullying is described as the online publishing of hurtful words about another individual. To understand the severity of cyberbullying at length, quantitative analysis is at the forefront. Study regarding cyberbullying is primarily done on the specific age group of children from 9 to 18. Moreover, the prominent theme of research or surveys is the incidence and severity of cyberbullying faced by different age groups. Study materials regarding cyberbullying and its possible causes and remedy are not abundant, even in academia. The term "cyberbullying" is a contemporary word coined about excess use of the internet and the ease of availability of internet connectivity for the vulnerable age group. Nevertheless, only seven such documents refer to the influence of cyberbullying on certain sections of internet users, which represents a gap in the literature in this regard. Cyberbullying is faced today by everyone who uses the internet in any way due to the ease of connection and availability of technology (Al-Othman & Ali, 2014). This research explains the possible causes and types of internet media in cyberbullying and its influence on young people's intelligence, social, and psychological growth.

PROBLEM RATIONALE AND RESEARCH QUESTIONS

The tangibility and severity of the theme undertaken in this research are interesting, as today's young generation, including older members, is more prone to and exposed to cyberbullying. This entrenched distribution in the lives of individuals demands additional advanced research to reflect upon the essential and accidental characteristics of cyberbullying. Today's youth often suffer from varied sorts of bullying; the victim tends not to share it with others, including family and friends, due to possible unwanted sociocultural consequences.

Therefore, this chapter has the following aims to examine the following open research questions related to cyberbullying:

RQ1: How does a philosopher reflect upon the very practicality of cyberbullying among young minds?

RQ2: What are the roots, routes, and nature of cyberbullying in general?

RQ3: What are the possible remedies to deal with the mindsets of the cyberbully and cyberbullied?

LITERATURE REVIEW AND SYNTHESIS

PHILOSOPHICAL REFLECTION

In modern times, the use of social network sites (SNSs) has become a necessary component of today's generation regardless of gender and age. For instance, Facebook, Twitter, YouTube, and LinkedIn not only attract today's generation's attention, but these social media platforms have been an extension of their selves or lives. However, this chapter is an attempt to direct discussion on the roots of cyberbullying. This will be done using a reflection method devoid of merely quantitative analysis manipulation embedded in SNSs. However, reflection on personal characteristics such as issues related to willingness to discuss and cope with cyberbullying is needed. Another reflection uses a philosophical lens. Philosophy has the vision to analyze critically and reflect upon the issues of human life and understanding. Following this, the theme of this chapter is a unique reflection based on a clear ethical and philosophical understanding. This is more likely to be the answer to RQ1. A philosophical account of cyberbullying can be initiated from two different concrete perspectives:

A. Quantitative or Descriptive Reasons (Perspective)
B. Qualitative or Philosophical Reasons (Perspective)

A. **Quantitative or Descriptive Reasons (Perspective):** The mentioned age groups use the internet for many unavoidable reasons, including enjoyable activities such as participating in online communities or playing computer games. The abundant use of the internet is one factor that easily increases the possibility of being cyberbullied. These reasons are not directly related to the personality or individuality of users as they are probably faced by every modern human regardless of their personal characteristics.

B. **Qualitative or Philosophical Reasons (Perspective):** Furthermore, there can also be different human characteristics of a person that are crucial reasons they are cyberbullied. For example, due to the COVID-19 pandemic, it has become more obvious and observable that individuals are very vulnerable due to their lifestyle and less-desired attitudes toward sociability. Therefore, modern individuals suffer from undesirable deviations in the normal course of consciousness and intentionality, reflected in their social and behavioral psychology. For instance, individuals are more prone to alienation, isolation, despair, poor self-esteem, social anxiety, inferiority complex, and educational anxieties. These kinds of people are more vulnerable to cyberbullying.

Furthermore, the aftermath of cyberbullying can take several severe forms, such as having physiological and emotional harm for these individuals and creating psychosocial issues like behavioral issues, alcohol consumption, smoking, despair, and a lack of academic focus. With increased levels of emotional anguish, victims of cyberbullying are hesitant to concentrate on their education, and their school performance suffers consequently. Cyberbullying has a depressing effect on victims, since they are often psychologically hurt. This prevents them from excelling in their education. Anxiety, depression, drug abuse, low self-esteem, social troubles, family disputes, and educational underperformance have been linked to cyberbullying victimization among university pupils.

In the contemporary world, technology has become necessary to ensure the livelihood of one's family. Technological facilities have become an essential evil for today's generation. This has led to excessive use of certain social media platforms like Facebook, WhatsApp, and Instagram. Moreover, using these social media platforms has become an essential and integral part of life today. These social media platforms are creating an altogether different virtual world of sociability, forming a new mode of social interaction, doing activities, and organizational functioning together. Hence, the new world order of virtual sociability is positively replacing the traditional media. Still, this has brought up some crucial consequences of the virtual world. However, despite all positives of the virtual world, it has led to many undesired actions, such as cyberbullying, which are disrespectful or hazardous to people.

Given the previous discussion, it can be concluded that "cyberbullying" is the use of ICT, including such email, messages on cell phones and pagers, instant messaging, defamatory web sites, blog posts, videogames, as well as false and misleading personal online voting web sites, to assist intentional, repeated, as well as hostile behavior by such a person or group that is meant to hurt someone else (Dredge et al., 2014). Cyberbullying may harm many people because of features including anonymity, ease of technological interaction, and quick public dissemination. Students use the Internet more often and widely than just about any other population group in educational institutions. "According to a Pew Research Center poll of 1006 young people in the United States performed in 2014 (Dredge et al., 2014), 97% of young adults aged 18 to 29" are using email and the Internet or access the Internet through a smartphone. Ninety-one percent of them were college students. After understanding the etymological meaning of cyberbullying, the following sections discuss the paper's main theme: the nature and causes of cyberbullying and possible remedies or preventive measures to cope with it.

METHODS

It is interesting to note that cyberbullying is comparatively new in origin and form. This is why there are few comprehensive and substantial pieces of literature on it. However, recent research and studies have been conducted to tackle cyberbullying and its related aftermath. The very issue of cyberbullying is that it changes forms and media frequently; this compels academicians to do research based on its relativity. However, by following philosophical tradition, the current chapter primarily focuses on a qualitative understanding of cyberbullying. Hence, the chapter uses qualitative methodologies, such as reflective, analytic, critical, and synthetic-analytic methods, to discuss the nature, forms, and remedies of cyberbullying.

DISCUSSION AND RESULTS

Means to Execute Cyberbullying

The following are the most prevalent shared mediums in which cyberbullying may happen:

- Electronic mail (email) is a way for an author to send digital communications to one or more receivers.
- Instant messaging is a sort of internet conversation that allows two people to exchange text in real time.
- Chat rooms are a kind of real-time online conversation among strangers who have the same interest or another comparable bond.
- The process of authoring and transmitting a short electronic message between two or more smartphones is known as text messaging.
- Social networking services provide a platform for individuals with similar interests, hobbies, histories, or real-life ties to develop social networks or relationships.
- Web sites are service platforms that may be used for individual, business, or government needs.

Per surveys, college students are the most likely to be bullied online through email as well as least likely to be bullied online through chat rooms. Based on another study, online communication is the most common technical channel used to commit cyberbullying.

KINDS OF CYBERBULLYING

Seven kinds of cyberbullying are observed frequently and on social media platforms: online nuisance, flaming, cyberstalking, masquerading, trickery, outing, and exclusion.

Flaming is delivering angry, harsh, or profane comments by text or email, either individually or to an electronic community (Peled, 2019). Cyberstalking involves the culprit delivering frightening messages to their target via the online network, while harassing frequently uses offensive messages. Denigration occurs whenever a cyberbully spreads false or harsh information about another person to others. Masquerading is a kind of cyberbullying in which a cyberbully impersonates someone else and sends or uploads potentially harmful or damaging information about the individual to others. Trickery and outing are observed whenever a cyberbully persuades someone to provide embarrassing, private, or secret information; the cyberbully then exposes or distributes the information for everyone to see (Hidayatullah et al., 2021).

Cyberbullying may also take the form of fraping when one accesses a victim's social media page and manipulates it to be amusing or damage the user's image and dignity. Dissing is sharing or posting hurtful material on the internet to harm one's image or relationship with others. Trolling is the act of disparaging someone online to elicit a reaction (Peled, 2019). Catfishing is the theft of an individual's online identity to build false social networking identities. One example is registering for a subscription in the victims' names such that the target gets electronic mail or other possibly humiliating items like gay-rights periodicals or incontinence therapy. Phishing is a technique that involves duping (Bashir Shaikh et al., 2020), convincing, or influencing the mark into disclosing individual or monetary data about themselves and their family members. Exclusion is defined as repeatedly avoiding, ignoring, or rejecting somebody, especially in social networks. Sending sexually explicit images or texts through smartphones is known as sexting.

Occurrence of Cyberbullying

According to previous research, cyberbullying among university students may vary from 9% to 3%. Beebe conducted a study with 200 college students across the United States (Peled, 2019). Per the data, 51% of undergraduates in the study said they had been the victim of online bullying either once or twice during their college days. Furthermore, 37% of college students indicated they were victims of cybercrime at least once a month. Based on Dlmaç's study, 23% of 650 pupils at Selcuk University in Turkey acknowledged cyberbullying at least once in their lifetime, while 55.35% claimed to be victims of cyberbullying. In a survey of 131 pupils from seven undergraduate courses in the United States, 11% said they had been victims of cyberbullying at the institution. The most often utilized technologies were Facebook (64%), mobile phones (43%), and instant messaging (43%) (Peled, 2019). According to students, half of the online bullying was done by coworkers, 60% came from outside the school, and 40% had no clue who was attacking them.

Nature of Cyberbullying

Exclusion

A. The purposeful action of keeping somebody out is known as exclusion.
B. Exclusion may take a variety of forms:
   • Your child may be barred from attending parties or events with their peers.
   • Your child's friends are conversing on the internet and tagging various friends, but they are not tagging them.
   • If your child does not utilize social networking websites or have a cellphone, he or she is intentionally excluded from talks by others.

Harassment

Harassment is a kind of bullying involving sending unpleasant or frightening texts to your child or a group of children regularly. This is a particularly hazardous kind of cyberbullying. It may have major consequences on your child's health (Hinduja & Patchin, 2008). The messages are often cruel or vicious, and they may adversely affect a child's self-esteem and trust and scare them. There is no relief from the cyberbully due to the ongoing messaging. The cyberbully goes to great lengths to instill fear and anguish in others.

Outing

Outing is a purposeful act to publicly shame your child or a group by revealing sensitive, private, or humiliating material online without their permission. Outing may take many forms, and the information exposed might be important or insignificant. Personally identifiable data should not be published, and when someone intentionally discloses personal details, make sure your child understands how to identify it as cyberbullying.

Cyberstalking

This kind of cyberbullying may develop into a cyberbully posing a physical danger to your child's health (Chan et al., 2017). Adults using the Web and seeking to connect with young people for sexual interaction are "cyberstalking." It is a particularly deadly sort of cyberbullying, with catastrophic implications if nothing is done to combat it right away.

Fraping

Fraping happens when somebody enters a social media profile illicitly and updates it with offensive content. Fraping is a severe offense that many individuals mistakenly assume is amusing and enjoyable, but it is not. Trying to impersonate somebody online and tarnishing their image may have significant consequences. Note that Google never forgets, so anything offensive and otherwise objectionable placed on the internet will never be completely erased even if it is removed.

Fake Profiles

Fake accounts might be made for someone to mask their true identity to bully your child online. The cyberbully may even cyberbully somebody else via their email or cell phone. That would also make it look like the attacks were sent by somebody else. Because the cyberbully is terrified of their name being disclosed, they create fake identities. Since the culprit would not have to disguise their name if your child did not know them, this typically suggests the cyberbully is somebody your child knows well.

Dissing

Dissing is when someone transmits or publishes hurtful material about someone else online to harm their image or connections. It may also include uploading content on the internet, such as images, screenshots, or movies. The cyberbully wishes to make other individuals believe your child is not cool. Generally, the cyberbully is somebody your child recognizes. This can be really distressing.

Trickery

Trickery is when a cyberbully gains your child's confidence to get them to divulge secrets or humiliating data, which the cyberbully subsequently posts openly online. The cyberbully will "befriend" your child and fool them into thinking they are safe before betraying their confidence and disclosing their personal information to third parties.

Trolling

Tolling is the purposeful act of inciting a reaction on internet forums, including social media sites, by using insults or foul language. The troll will directly attack your child. Their major goal is to enrage them to the point that they will behave similarly (Kowalski & Limber, 2007). Trolls spend most of their time hunting for those who are weak and can be exploited. They are generally seeking ways to make themselves feel better by making other people feel awful.

Catfishing

Catfishing occurs when someone takes your child's identity online, generally images, and uses it to construct false social networking profiles. A catfish would be somebody who wants to remain anonymous. They will look at your child's social media profiles and collect any data they need to establish a false identity. Although it may be difficult to comprehend why a catfish would do such a thing, it is critical to recognize that they may harm your child's internet reputation.

Risk of Cyberbullying

The research on cyberbullying has identified several risk factors. Characteristics divided into demographic and psychological components enhance the chance of youngsters being cyberbullied. Teenagers who experience higher societal pressure and a desire for fame are more inclined to make and spread damaging recordings and photographs of their instructors and classmates.

Gender and Age

There is a discussion about gender regarding cyberbullying. According to studies, it has been observed that girls may be both cyberbullies and cyber victims, and this is the same with boys. Girls are less aggressive than boys, and boys openly bully people, but girls are more discreet and frequently bully in packs. Moreover, the discussion can differ when it comes to age. It is because the chance of being a cyber victim is directly proportional to age.

Education

Cyberbullying may be influenced by the victim's or cyberbully's academic performance. Kids with poor academic accomplishments, as opposed to average students or those with excellent academic accomplishments, are much more prone to be cyberbullied. Some studies discovered that being in a transition year at high school was among the risk variables for cyber victimization. On the other hand, elevated concentrations of anti-social behavior were risk variables for cyberbullies. Teachers need to be equipped with certain tools to handle victims of cyberbullying and provide them with desirable assistance.

Socio-Economic Factors

Based on education, employment, and income, socio-economic status is a complete assessment of an individual's social and economic standing. Monitoring a partner's social media profile and bothering connections are examples of cyber dating abuse. According to studies, a vast number of adults using social media are bullied in some way.

Ethnicity

There are mixed outcomes when it comes to the association between cyberbullying and ethnicity, just as there are with gender. In a survey, it was discovered that Black girls and boys were more likely than Hispanic males to engage in sexting behavior. Female Hispanic students were the least likely to engage in sexting behavior. Non-dominant and mixed-ethnicity English and Austrian students reported cyberbullying more frequently than dominant-ethnicity students. (Schneider et al., 2012). Non-white British culture was a non-dominant ethnicity in England, while non-Austrian ethnicity was a non-dominant ethnicity in Austria. Schneider et al. (2012) investigated the relationship between cyberbullying and conventional bullying occurrences and psychological discomfort.

Psychological Factors

One of the key motivations for cyberbullying is psychological problems. Several mental conditions may increase the risk of cyberbullying or becoming a victim of cyberbullying.

Self-Esteem

Low self-esteem has been identified as a frequent indicator of adolescent cyberbullying in studies. Self-esteem is defined as one's assessment of their feelings and value. Low self-esteem is accompanied by a lack of belief in one's skills. A cyberbully's implantation of a negative notion might lead to difficulties in gaining self-esteem as well as trust.

Depression and Suicide

Being cyberbullied often results in depressive symptoms. Scholarly work has addressed the impact of depression on cyber victims. In a study of 925 United States youths, Kowalski and Limber (2007) discovered a high link between cyber victims and sadness. In a study of 1500 Mexican teens who experienced cyberbullying (Swearer et al., 2012), This supports the notion that cyberbullies lack compassion and therefore do not consider the consequences of their acts.

Empathy

One facet of cyberbullying is the cyberbully's lack of compassion. Empathy is defined as the capacity to connect to other people or the ability to put oneself in another's shoes (Dredge et al., 2014). According to the University of California Berkeley (2014), empathy may be divided into two categories:

A. Affective: the emotional state and feelings we have in reaction to other people's emotions. Compassionate care, like empathic concern, is an extreme response, that is, expressing sympathy and kindness to another person's emotional reaction.
B. Cognitive: involves our capacity to recognize and comprehend others' feelings and emotions.

According to research, cyberbullies have low degrees of empathy and compassion. Longitudinal research by Schultze-Krumbholz et al. (2016) looked at whether poor intellectual and attentive compassion contribute to cyberbullying. Sixty-seven seventh- and eighth-grade students took part in the study.

Internet Addiction

Internet addiction is a key variable in forecasting cyberbullying. The findings revealed that users who were classified as having no addiction problems in the first evaluation but were using the internet to a great extent had higher sadness and anger levels. Moreover, users who had online addiction in the first evaluation but did not have an internet obsession in the evaluation stage exhibited higher anxiety issues but lower despair and hostility (Rachoene & Oyedemi, 2015). Young persons with depressive disorders were more prone to internet addiction, according to Cho et al. (2013). Individuals who are socially nervous are more prone to forming connections online. When contrasted with face-to-face dialogue, online engagement reduces anxiety issues. In research by Kuss et al. (2014), 3105 Dutch teens completed a survey that included the Obsessive Online Use Measure and the Quick Big Five Scale. According to the findings, 3.7% of the participants were classed as possibly dependent on the Internet. The availability of internet games and social media programs (such as Facebook and Twitter) raised the danger of being addicted to the Internet.

The usage of the Web for data had a beneficial relationship with bullies, victims, and onlookers. The moral and social rule that governs the online world is known as netiquette. Cyberbullying was less common among pupils with better netiquette, perhaps as a bully, sufferer, or witness. On the other hand, investing more time online does not always imply better netiquette.

Self-Image

A teenager's self-image is very important in their life, and they will do anything and everything to maintain it. The impact of a teenager's obesity on cyberbullying has been studied. Obese teens are 2.5 times more likely than their normal-weight peers to be cyberbullied. Obese teens who were tormented via the internet and conventional bullying tactics had poor mental health. Suicidal ideation was more common among obese children who had been cyberbullied. On the other hand, Anderson et al. (2014) looked at the impact of weight-based cyberbullying on bystander conduct. Two hundred subjects were subjected to Facebook message tampering. Bystander remarks were determined to be supportive or favorable to the victim in the research.

EFFECTS OF CYBERBULLYING

Cyberbullying is difficult to prevent, whereas direct mistreatment may be prevented by remaining inside. Cyberbullying may emerge anytime and in any location since children consistently access their smartphones or tablets. They may assume that they have no control over the situation. The tormenter can sometimes threaten the child's life or the lives of their family and friends if the youngster exposes the bully, which even the child accepts. This can lead to psychological issues, such as depression, humiliation, isolation, anger, and illness.

Cyberbullying is a serious issue that impacts not just the children who are bullied but also their families, the aggressor, and anybody who witnesses it. Online harassment, on either side, may have the most detrimental effect on the victim, as they may experience a range of behavioral problems that affect their academic and social abilities, as well as their overall psychological health (Naaz, 2020). Moreover, a parent might have never been a victim of cyberbullying. It may be difficult to comprehend how a few words on a computer monitor can cause such distress. Bullying has always been an issue in school and on the playground (Wang et al., 2009). Maybe one was a victim of bullying in school. That is why it is being said that bullying is an unavoidable aspect of school life. In contrast, a victim of cyberbullying can simply switch off the computer or ban a bully on social networks.

Regrettably, it is not as easy to cope with the cyberbullying mindset. While the consequences of real-world bullying should not be overlooked, the consequences of cyberbullying may be even more severe. It is the responsibility of one as a parent to grasp the actual effect of cyberbullying, detect changes in children's behavior because of cyberbullying, and discover a helpful approach to assist the affected child.

Low Self-Worth

Cyberbullying has a detrimental influence on the self-esteem of its victims (Cornu et al., 2022). Individuals who have been abused online may acquire low self-esteem and self-consciousness. This is especially true when the assault is focused on their physical attractiveness. Teenagers and young individuals who have been "trolled" for their appearance may acquire an aversion to their physique. Consequently, these individuals will consider themselves less appealing to everyone else. They may become self-conscious about going out in society or socializing with others. Cyberbullying sufferers and offenders have significantly lower self-esteem than the average person. This indicates that there are bad outcomes for both victims and perpetrators of cyberbullying. Cyberbullying benefits no one else in the long term, since the feel-good factor is transitory.

Reduced Status

The effects of cyberbullying may be observed in several aspects of the human body. This may be observed in students' scores. Bullies and sufferers of cyberbullying both have difficulties in school. This is linked to a loss of interest in previously pleasurable undertakings (Cassidy et al., 2013). Individuals who have been the victims of cyberbullying may decide to discontinue studying. Some may put less effort into school, placing themselves in danger of failing.

Despair

Cyberbullying victims are at risk for several stress-related disorders. Stress and despondency are only two examples. When victims lose trust in themselves, their mental health suffers. Understandably, some cyberbullying sufferers would experience isolation and be miserable if they did not speak out for fear of more ridicule. People are also unsatisfied because of being exposed to online harassment. Whenever an individual is dissatisfied, they may become depressed over time.

Chance of Falling Ill

A person might become ill due to the stress associated with being cyberbullied. Enduring online abuse may cause migraines, insomnia, chest discomfort, and many other health anxieties. This worry may lead to skin issues and rashes, further eroding a person's self-esteem. Survivors may develop eating disorders as a protective mechanism. They may drop more fat or overfeed if they have been informed they are excessively skinny. Such activities are harmful to one's health.

Suicidal Inclinations

When somebody is abused online, the most prevalent motive for online bullying is when the offender wants retribution. Unfortunately, vengeance is futile. This just serves to foster increased cyberbullying (Barlińska et al., 2012). Online harassment, per a study, may enhance suicidal behavior in some victims. It creates a feeling of powerlessness. When individuals are repeatedly mistreated online, they may think that suicide is their only alternative.

The Emotional Impact of Cyberbullying

Cyberbullying may adversely influence sufferers since it can be a considerable source of pressure in their lives. Per research, three out of every ten child victims of cyberbullying show symptoms of trouble.

Embarrassment

Sharing obnoxious postings, messages, or texts that have been made public may be considered harassment. Since so many individuals are now aware of them, it may cause your child embarrassment and humiliation.

Shame and Guilt

Abusers may post sensitive data about your child on the Internet, which may cause a great deal of emotional harm to the youngster (McFarland & Ployhart, 2015). They may feel guilty for getting online and humiliating themselves and their families. It's critical to maintain your composure with your child and make them understand that although the situation is terrible, they have your support.

Anxiety

The child may get worried as well as lack attention in their education, sports, and everyday routines for apparent reasons. This might lead to a recurrence of concerns in the future, which could lead to a breakdown or despair. It's critical to sit down with the child and have a heart-to-heart conversation about their concern.

Isolation

When children are subjected to cyberbullying, they may avoid seeing their friends or attending school or group events. They may lose out on essential friendships because of this. Parents may demand that their children hand in their devices to make things worse. This may lead the children to become even more isolated, since cellphones are a primary means of communicating with family and friends. Cyberbullying victims often struggle to feel secure (Jaradat, 2017). They may feel helpless and defenseless. If you see several of the following indications, your child may be a target of bullying:

- When the child sees or uses their phone, they become unhappy or terrified.
- When the child's phone sounds, they feel anxious.
- The child's online existence has become a well-guarded secret.

- The child has lost their desire to go out.
- Your child begins to withdraw from you, other family, and even their friends.
- The child is unable to get a good night's sleep.
- The child is not eating as much as they used to.

Ways to Stop Cyberbullying

Bullying has evolved beyond the days of after-school brawls and lunch money theft. To keep up with the technology, harassment has moved online, shifting to text, emails, and internet media. Because digital media encourages rapid dissemination but also lacks "take-back" or "delete" keys, the shift to digital has exacerbated bullying's bad effects. What may begin as a little playground altercation may suddenly grow into a catastrophe. Here are the top ten tactics to halt bullies in their paths, as well as a glimpse at cyberbullying by the statistics.

The following are some ways to keep oneself safe in the aftermath of cyberbullying.

Tell Someone

The great majority of teenagers, 90%, feel cyberbullying is an issue, and 63% think it is a significant one. Regrettably, most youths believe that institutions, authorities, and social media companies have failed to address the problem. The good news is that most teens feel their relatives are also helpful friends. Even so, parents must be watchful and approach their children if they suspect an issue. When teenagers are cyberbullied, they sometimes fear notifying their parents or even other adults (Camacho et al., 2018). This barrier is often caused by shame or anxiety. Survivors fear that parents and teachers will be unable to prevent bullying and that if the bully learns that they have informed an adult, the abuse will only become harsher (Bauman, 2013).

Keep Everything

Bullying may sometimes cross the line from annoyance to felony assault or threatening. According to a 2018 study, children and young individuals bullied online are more than twice as likely to self-harm or commit suicide. Channing Smith, Gabbie Green, and Dolly Everett are all victims of misfortune. Homicide is only one of many potential negative effects. But, beginning today, you can alter that. These are some simple but powerful ways to assist your family in preventing and overcoming cyberbullying.

Don't Engage

Per a poll in the year 2021 on kids' online behavior, over 60% of children who use social networks have observed some type of bullying (Salawu et al., 2022). Most youngsters ignore the behavior for different reasons. A combination of acknowledgment and aversion is suggested to overcome this. Witnesses must be ready to alert relatives and acquaintances, as well as teachers, about the attacks. Bullied people are often better off ignoring attacks than responding to them (Salawu et al., 2022). The goal of every bully is to arouse rage in the victim, so "reaching to" the targeted and pushing them to confess to making absurd claims or making derogatory remarks.

Learn More

Per enough.org, over half of all young people have been victims of cybercrime as of February 2018. Instructors now regard cyberbullying as the number-one class security concern, per a 2018 Google poll. Parents must understand all they can about their children's online and smartphone activities. Examine cybersecurity strategies aimed at ensuring the safety of children online.

Understand the Possibility

Many people assume that social media platforms are the most probable venues for bullying, and they are partially correct in this regard. However, with 95% of teenagers now owning a smartphone, the risk of injury is significantly larger. Bullying may take place on "social media sites such as Twitter, Facebook, and Instagram, as well as through Snapchat, emails, and texts sent directly from bullies" (Bozzola et al., 2022). In contrast to almost universal smartphone use, 45% of children report near-constant online engagement, which may lead to bullying. To keep ahead of any possible hazards, it is critical to monitor one's children's mobile phones as well as online conduct on a regular basis, given the fast developments in innovation.

Recognize the Signs

A cyberbullied teenager seems to be like any other adolescent, hesitant to chat about his or her day or provide personal details. Other indicators that one's child has been the victim of cyberbullying include a lack of interest in favored hobbies, an inexplicable drop in grades, missed classes, and depressive symptoms, including changes in sleep and eating or dietary habits. Although any of those might indicate a variety of issues, be particularly cautious if you observe a dramatic loss of desire to use the computer or a propensity to grow irritated after being online or on their smartphones, or, in the case of an aggressive child, intense rage if you take away their computer or smartphone access.

Keep Data Secure

Bullies were able to create bogus Facebook pages for the victims in the instances of Izzy Dix and Gabbie Green, allowing a whole different level of torture. It is necessary to pay extra attention and take care regarding the use of social media platforms. Therefore, the best way to cope with cyberbullying is to limit the amount of personal information, photographs, and data on social media platforms. Make sure you and your children are aware of how to generate safe passwords. Bullies have been reported to "hijack" or hack into victims' social media accounts to publish unpleasant and abusive remarks (Lowry et al., 2017). Teens should also keep their social media accounts in "private" mode and delete communications from people they cannot identify. Password administration techniques and other cybersecurity elements are included in today's comprehensive online security systems, which may help keep your kids' financial records and digital identity safe (Messina & Iwasaki, 2011).

Don't Lose Strength

Many victims fight back against abusers and eventually become bullies themselves, according to dosomething.org. While this may appear to be one solution, what typically occurs is a "kind of back-and-forth between victim and aggressor," which tends to keep the behavior going and aggravate it (Rakovec-Felser, 2014). Make sure your child understands the importance of online respect for others' emotions and privacy. Hence, it is necessary to train young minds that revenge is not a desirable practice to cope with it. It is better to stay out of these kinds of online bad practices in the long term. This is the only practice that can be considered morally desirable for the co-existence of society.

Be United

It's critical to unite and search for long-term answers to cyberbullying and its aftermath. In 2015, Canada approved a law to counter-attack cyberbullying: it is unlawful to share photos of persons without their agreement, and the police can get permits for data about internet operators if they have "reasonable grounds to suspect" that an infraction has been committed. The measure wasn't perfect, but it acted like a template for subsequent legislation meant to keep children safe online. However, since laws in the United States differ by state, it's critical to know your rights and report incidents to the appropriate powers if they get out of control.

CONCLUSIONS AND RECOMMENDATIONS

The globally rising use of social networks, particularly social networking sites by the young generation, has increased cyberbullying worldwide. The very philosophy of development in relation to progress in the world is that development can lead to progress but also other results. The same applies to the use of SNSs. For instance, it is undoubtedly up to the user as to how SNSs should be used, to construct or to destroy. Hence, this very use of advanced media is due to the individual; this leads to ethical and philosophical consideration of the issues and remedies of cyberbullying. Kant proposed that one cannot use anybody merely as a means, whatever the case is. In the course of cyberbullying, a cyberbully is using someone else's existence to fulfil their own prospects. This raises many questions on the very essence of cyberbully as a human. It can be said that a cyberbully is very active and current in terms of using advanced digital media platforms; however, every human action must be performed with due diligence, respecting human existence. Otherwise, human existence can be said to have degraded to animal instincts only; that is what no one wants (Zhang & Leidner, 2018). Moreover, cyberbullying involves many players, including victims, classmates, instructors, parents, social media sites, and Internet providers. Cyberbullying is exacerbated by risk variables such as Internet usage, age, gender, psychological problems, and education (Iacus & Porro, 2021). This proves that this very complex technological problem demands multi-layered, multi-dimensional remedies.

Consequently, remedies have been discussed; however, these remedies can be viewed in two different but supplementary ways. The first is psychological and the second through a philosophical lens. For instance, suppose your child is being bullied on the internet; the best thing you can do is tell them not to reply to the bully. Advise them to save the texts, emails, images, and other means of communication to record each episode of cyberbullying. If required, screenshots may be used. Make sure that your child provides you with these details so that you can keep track of everything. Furthermore, report incidences of cyberbullying to your school's instructor, administrator, or administrative personnel if the bullying is coming from a school connection (Beale & Hall, 2007). One must also report bullying conduct to the police if it involves serious bullying or threatening. Above all, encouraging your young ones that they really are not at fault for online bullying is critical. Sometimes victims may believe that their actions caused the crisis or that they are to blame somehow. As a result, your child must understand that what occurred was not their doing. Hence, they need to be treated with due empathy, compassion, and care by their caretakers. This involves simultaneously looking at the victim's psychology with due care and ethical reflection on the behaviors of cyberbullied and cyberbully.

Moreover, dealing with bullies and trying to find answers is not sufficient for victims of cyberbullying. Such victims are quite often emotionally upset and, therefore, unable to seek assistance. It is our collective responsibility as a society to strive toward establishing a cluster of psycho-philosophical mental practices and prohibitory technical mechanisms to detect the negative practices on social media platforms. It is now high time for public agencies to formulate a normative framework that can detect such practices just after they take place on any social media platform; it should also be compulsory for developers and service providers without a detection policy for cyberbullying. Moreover, it can also be made necessary to create a separate grievance redressal system for cyberbullying specifically. It can minimize the rising cases of cyberbullying. However, cyberbullied children and teenagers are still learning how to manage their feelings and emotional circumstances (Landstedt & Persson, 2014). Cyberbullying at this stage may have protracted consequences. To assist victims of cyberbullying in managing their mental health, mental health services should be made available (Giumetti & Kowalski, 2022). These unwanted senses of fear and emotions will not be considered only a part of today's technological generation. If one reports similar cases, it should be welcomed, and they should be taken seriously to address them. This can also be an inhibiting psychological factor for a cyberbully: if he or she no longer has anything to gain, the behavior will cease. This implies that any instances of online bullying should be disregarded. Furthermore, public awareness efforts should emphasize that online bullying is unacceptable and a sign of low social standing (Almakanin et al., 2018). Above all, parents and teachers should be aware of the adverse effects of cyberbullying, and they should care for and help their children with empathy by understanding their psychological state of mind concerning these effects of technological advancement as part and parcel of today's life.

REFERENCES

Al-Othman, K., and Ali, A. 2014. "Cyber Bullying among Students in General Education." *Psychological Study* 24 (2): 185–212.

Almakanin, Hisham A., Najati A. Younis, and Ghaleb M. Alhiary. 2018. "Electronic Bullying among a Sample of Students with Emotional and Behavioral Disorders in Zarqa City." *Journal of Educational and Psychological Studies [JEPS]* 12 (1): 179. https://doi.org/10.24200/jeps.vol12iss1pp179-197.

Anderson, J., M. Bresnahan, and C. Musatics. 2014. "Combating Weight-Based Cyberbullying on Facebook with the Dissenter Effect." *Cyberpsychology, Behavior, and Social Networking* 17 (5): 281–86.

Barlińska, Julia, Anna Szuster, and Mikołaj Winiewski. 2012. "Cyberbullying among Adolescent Bystanders: Role of the Communication Medium, Form of Violence, and Empathy." *Journal of Community & Applied Social Psychology* 23 (1): 37–51. https://doi.org/10.1002/casp.2137.

Bashir Shaikh, Farhan, Mobashar Rehman, and Aamir Amin. 2020. "Cyberbullying: A Systematic Literature Review to Identify the Factors Impelling University Students Towards Cyberbullying." *IEEE Access* 8: 148031–51. https://doi.org/10.1109/access.2020.3015669.

Bauman, Sheri. 2013. "Cyberbullying: What Does Research Tell Us?" *Theory into Practice* 52 (4): 249–56. https://doi.org/10.1080/00405841.2013.829727.

Beale, Andrew V., and Kimberly R. Hall. 2007. "Cyberbullying: What School Administrators (And Parents) Can Do." *The Clearing House: A Journal of Educational Strategies, Issues and Ideas* 81 (1): 8–12. https://doi.org/10.3200/tchs.81.1.8-12.

Bozzola, E., G. Spina, R. Agostiniani, S. Barni, R. Russo, E. Scarpato, A. Di Mauro, A.V. Di Stefano, C. Caruso, G. Corsello, and A. Staiano. 2022. "The Use of Social Media in Children and Adolescents: Scoping Review on the Potential Risks." *International Journal of Environmental Research and Public Health* 19 (16): 9960. doi: 10.3390/ijerph19169960.

Camacho, Sonia, Khaled Hassanein, and Milena Head. 2018. "Cyberbullying Impacts on Victims' Satisfaction with Information and Communication Technologies: The Role of Perceived Cyberbullying Severity." *Information & Management* 55 (4): 494–507. https://doi.org/10.1016/j.im.2017.11.004.

Cassidy, Wanda, Chantal Faucher, and Margaret Jackson. 2013. "Cyberbullying among Youth: A Comprehensive Review of Current International Research and Its Implications and Application to Policy and Practice." *School Psychology International* 34 (6): 575–612. https://doi.org/10.1177/0143034313479697.

Chan, Tommy K.H., Christy M.K. Cheung, and Zach W.Y. Lee. 2017. "The State of Online Impulse-Buying Research: A Literature Analysis." *Information & Management* 54 (2): 204–17. https://doi.org/10.1016/j.im.2016.06.001.

Cho, S.M., M.J. Sung, K.M. Shin, K.Y. Lim, and Y.M. Shin. 2013. "Does Psychopathology in Childhood Predict Internet Addiction in Male Adolescents?" *Child Psychiatry & Human Development* 44 (4): 549–555. doi: 10.1007/s10578-012-0348-4.

Cornu, Christophe, Parviz Abduvahobov, Rym Laoufi, Yongfeng Liu, and Sylvain Séguy. 2022. "An Introduction to a Whole-Education Approach to School Bullying: Recommendations from UNESCO Scientific Committee on School Violence and Bullying Including Cyberbullying." *International Journal of Bullying Prevention* 4 (1): 47–54. https://doi.org/10.1007/s42380-021-00093-8.

Dredge, Rebecca, John F. Gleeson, and Xochitl de la Piedad Garcia. 2014. "Risk Factors Associated with Impact Severity of Cyberbullying Victimization: A Qualitative Study of Adolescent Online Social Networking." *Cyberpsychology, Behavior, and Social Networking* 17 (5): 287–91. https://doi.org/10.1089/cyber.2013.0541.

Febro-Naga, January, and Mia-Amor Tinam-Isan. 2022. "Exploring Cyber Violence against Women and Girls in the Philippines through Mining Online News." *Comunicar* 30 (70): 125–38. https://doi.org/10.3916/c70-2022-10.

Giumetti, Gary W., and Robin M. Kowalski. 2022. "Cyberbullying via Social Media and Well-Being." *Current Opinion in Psychology* 45: 101–314. https://doi.org/10.1016/j.copsyc.2022.101314.

Hidayatullah, Moch. Syarif, Rizqi Handayani, Abdullah Zubair, and Mohammad Syairozi Dimyathi. 2021. "Cyber Bullying against Indonesian Muslim Leaders Through Social Media." *Psychology and Education Journal* 58 (1): 5348–55. https://doi.org/10.17762/pae.v58i1.1792.

Hinduja, Sameer, and Justin W. Patchin. 2008. "Cyberbullying: An Exploratory Analysis of Factors Related to Offending and Victimization." *Deviant Behavior* 29 (2): 129–56. https://doi.org/10.1080/01639620701457816.

Hossain, Aftab, Juliana Abdul Wahab, Md. Rashedul Islam, Md. Saidur Khan, and Arif Mahmud. 2022. "Cyberbullying Perception and Experience among the University Students in Bangladesh." *Handbook of Research on Digital Violence and Discrimination Studies*, 248–69. https://doi.org/10.4018/978-1-7998-9187-1.ch012.

Iacus, S.M., and G. Porro. 2021. "Subjective and Social Well-Being." *Subjective Well-Being and Social Media*, 1–46. https://doi.org/10.1201/9780429401435-1.

Jaradat, Abdul-Kareem M. 2017. "Gender Differences in Bullying and Victimization among Early Adolescents in Jordan." *People: International Journal of Social Sciences* 3 (3): 440–51. https://doi.org/10.20319/pijss.2017.33.440451.

Kowalski, Robin M., and Susan P. Limber. 2007. "Electronic Bullying among Middle School Students." *Journal of Adolescent Health* 41 (6). https://doi.org/10.1016/j.jadohealth.2007.08.017.

Kuss, D.J., M.D. Griffiths, L. Karila, and J. Billieux. 2014. "Internet Addiction: A Systematic Review of Epidemiological Research for the Last Decade." *Current Pharmaceutical Design* 20: 4026–52.

Landstedt, Evelina, and Susanne Persson. 2014. "Bullying, Cyberbullying, and Mental Health in Young People." *Scandinavian Journal of Public Health* 42 (4): 393–99. https://doi.org/10.1177/1403494814525004.

Lowry, Paul Benjamin, Gregory D. Moody, and Sutirtha Chatterjee. 2017. "Using It Design to Prevent Cyberbullying." *Journal of Management Information Systems* 34 (3): 863–901. https://doi.org/10.1080/07421222.2017.1373012.

McFarland, Lynn A., and Robert E. Ployhart. 2015. "Social Media: A Contextual Framework to Guide Research and Practice." *Journal of Applied Psychology* 100 (6): 1653–77. https://doi.org/10.1037/a0039244.

Messina, Emily S., and Yoshitaka Iwasaki. 2011. "Internet Use and Self-Injurious Behaviors among Adolescents and Young Adults: An Interdisciplinary Literature Review and Implications for Health Professionals." *Cyberpsychology, Behavior, and Social Networking* 14 (3): 161–68. https://doi.org/10.1089/cyber.2010.0025.

Naaz, Kashfi. 2020. "Suicidal Ideation among Cyber Bullying Victim College Students." *Paripex Indian Journal of Research*, 1–3. https://doi.org/10.36106/paripex/9104021.

Peled, Yehuda. 2019. "Cyberbullying and Its Influence on Academic, Social, and Emotional Development of Undergraduate Students." *Heliyon* 5 (3). https://doi.org/10.1016/j.heliyon.2019.e01393.

Rachoene, Matjorie, and Toks Oyedemi. 2015. "From Self-Expression to Social Aggression: Cyberbullying Culture among South African Youth on Facebook." *Communicatio* 41 (3): 302–19. https://doi.org/10.1080/02500167.2015.1093325.

Rakovec-Felser, Z. 2014. "Domestic Violence and Abuse in Intimate Relationship from Public Health Perspective." *Health Psychology Research* 2 (3): 62–67. doi: 10.4081/hpr.2014.1821.

Salawu, Semiu, Jo Lumsden, and Yulan He. 2022. "A Mobile-Based System for Preventing Online Abuse and Cyberbullying." *International Journal of Bullying Prevention* 4 (1): 66–88. https://doi.org/10.1007/s42380-021-00115-5.

Schneider, Shari Kessel, Lydia O'Donnell, Ann Stueve, and Robert W. Coulter. 2012. "Cyberbullying, School Bullying, and Psychological Distress: A Regional Census of High School Students." *American Journal of Public Health* 102 (1): 171–77. https://doi.org/10.2105/ajph.2011.300308.

Schultze-Krumbholz, A., M. Schultze, P. Zagorscak, R. Wölfer, and H. Scheithauer. 2016. "Feeling Cybervictims' Pain – The Effect of Empathy Training on Cyberbullying." *Aggress. Behav.* 42: 147–56.

Smith, Peter K., and Georges Steffgen. 2013. Essay. In *Cyberbullying through the New Media: Findings from an International Network*. London: Psychology Press.

Swearer, Susan M., Cixin Wang, John W. Maag, Amanda B. Siebecker, and Lynae J. Frerichs. 2012. "Understanding the Bullying Dynamic among Students in Special and General Education." *Journal of School Psychology* 50 (4): 503–20. https://doi.org/10.1016/j.jsp.2012.04.001.

Wang, Jing, Ronald J. Iannotti, and Tonja R. Nansel. 2009. "School Bullying among Adolescents in the United States: Physical, Verbal, Relational, and Cyber." *Journal of Adolescent Health* 45 (4): 368–75. https://doi.org/10.1016/j.jadohealth.2009.03.021.

Zhang, Sixuan, and Dorothy Leidner. 2018. "From Improper to Acceptable: How Perpetrators Neutralize Workplace Bullying Behaviors in the Cyber World." *Information & Management* 55 (7): 850–65. https://doi.org/10.1016/j.im.2018.03.012.

3 Cybersecurity and Human Factors

A Literature Review

Natasha Cecilia Edeh

CONTENTS

INTRODUCTION

Information security is a multidisciplinary field of study and professional activity that focuses on safeguarding and protecting information technology from a wide range of threats and dangers. Initially, information security was distinguished by a highly technical approach that was best left to technical experts. Even at this early stage, those in charge of implementing information security recognized the importance of top management involvement (Georgiadou et al. 2020). Cybersecurity is a major concern for every nation's and industry's security. Overall, cyberattacks have primarily targeted commercial organizations to gain access to money. These days, any person or organization with valuable digital data can fall prey to some form of cyberattack (Lau et al. 2018; Gutzwiller et al. 2019). In today's world of great technological advancements, cybersecurity risks are becoming increasingly hard to control. Humans are regarded as the primary risk because technology is inherently neutral and used by humans. However, it can be used detrimentally or beneficially (Corradini and Nardelli 2019). To effectively detect and address cybersecurity issues – threats, vulnerabilities, and risks – many organizations have spent huge amounts of money on IT systems and software (Triplett 2022). The recent global pandemic saw a surge in cybercrime across many industries, especially because many business processes had to be conducted individually from home. Cyberattackers discovered and exploited blind spots and weaknesses in organizational security structures (Groenendaal and Helsloot 2021). Usually, cybersecurity has been handled by the IT department. IT professionals, on the other hand, along with research in the cybersecurity domain, have long argued that an organization's cybersecurity should be the responsibility of everyone. When attempting to mitigate cybersecurity risks, Jeong et al. (2019) suggested taking human factors into account.

DOI: 10.1201/9781003319887-3

Humans must play an important role in any effective cybersecurity strategy (Evans et al. 2016; Oltramari et al. 2015). It is critical to establish a resilient cybersecurity philosophy in all organizations so that staff are constantly aware of the potential consequences of their actions and perform accordingly (Corradini and Nardelli 2019).

PROBLEM RATIONALE AND RESEARCH QUESTION

The domain of cybersecurity has generally been looked at from a technical perspective. But the concept and range of cybersecurity are broader, including information, technology, and, most significantly, human beings (Rahman et al. 2021; Grobler, Gaire, and Nepal 2021). Human-centric cybersecurity is an intangible concept that is difficult to define due to the inherent link between humans and technology, as well as humans and security systems Grobler, Gaire, and Nepal (2021). The role of humans and their link to cybersecurity have largely not been researched in depth in cybersecurity literature (Pollini et al. 2022). While there has recently been an increase in the literature addressing human factors in cybersecurity, the theory is still less than sufficient. One sector that has seen an increase in the literature about human factors/human links in cybersecurity is the health sector, and rightly so, since cybersecurity is becoming a major concern among healthcare workers as they adopt digital technologies to improve the quality of care provided to patients (Nifakos et al. 2021). But most of these studies focus less on using human factors as a means to curb cybersecurity issues or from the perspective of insider threat (Hadlington 2018). It is worth noting that almost all of this research into the role of humans in cybersecurity sees human as the weakest security link (the problem) rather than the solution (Triplett 2022). Only a handful of cybersecurity research addresses the fact that the human link in cybersecurity can be a positive aspect. By considering humans as a solution to cybersecurity issues faced by organizations, this chapter will contribute to the literature on cybersecurity and human factors by posing the question: How can human factors be considered a cybersecurity solution?

LITERATURE REVIEW

Cybersecurity is the act of safeguarding computer networks and computer systems against theft of software or digital information and against damage to hardware components of these computer systems (Chang et al. 2019). Cybersecurity threats are acts that attempt to cause harm that disrupt the normal flow of digital information (Humayun et al. 2020). A vulnerability is a security weakness or a susceptible part that allows cybercriminals to gain unauthorized access to an organization's data, equipment, or other resources (Ulven and Wangen 2021). The likelihood of an organization being exposed to harm or losing money because of a cyberattack or data breach is referred to as cybersecurity risk or cyber risk. A far more comprehensive explanation is the potential loss or injury to an organization's technological infrastructure, use of technology, or reputation. Human activities (human factors), as well as system and technology failures, are major cyber risks (Sardi et al. 2020).

Cyberattacks include social engineering, phishing, malware attacks, denial of service attacks, and password attacks, among others (Kure, Islam, and Razzaque 2018). Human mistakes in cybersecurity continue to be a problem for organizations, resulting in data breaches, cyberattacks, and lasting damage. These attacks are explained in the following.

Malware attacks are the most common type of cyberattack. Malware is harmful software that is installed on a computer when a user clicks on a malicious link or email, such as spyware, ransomware, viruses, and worms. Once inside the system, malware can, among other things, block access to critical network components, harm the system, and collect confidential information (Khan, Brohi, and Zaman 2020; Ghate and Agrawal 2017). **Phishing** is an email-based attack in which the recipient is tricked into providing personal information or downloading malware by clicking on a link in the message. Phishing emails are sent by cybercriminals and appear to be from reputable sources (Pranggono and Arabo 2021; Monteith et al. 2021). **Service denial** is an attack that occurs when a cyberattacker seizes control of a large number of devices and uses them to invoke the operations of a target system, such as a website, causing it to crash due to a demand overload (Dissanayake 2020; Lezzi, Lazoi, and Corallo 2018). **A password attack** occurs when a cyberattacker uses the correct password to gain access to a large amount of data. Social engineering is a type of password attack used by cybercriminals that relies heavily on human interaction and frequently involves duping people into violating standard security procedures (Khan, Brohi, and Zaman 2020). Password attacks can also be carried out by breaking into a password database or guessing openly. **Social engineering** is the practice of exploiting human flaws through manipulation to achieve a harmful goal. Individuals and organizations are more vulnerable than ever to social engineering attacks (Andrade, Ortiz-Garces, and Cazares 2020). Cyberattackers' favorite targets are large telecommunications corporations and other comparable organizations with large client bases and a large collection of sensitive data (Van der Kleij and Leukfeldt 2020). Despite technological safeguards such as antivirus software, firewalls, or intrusion detection systems, social engineering attacks remain common and pose a significant threat (Aldawood and Skinner 2018). One other reason security tools are frequently ineffective in averting social engineering attacks is that some social engineering attacks occur solely in the physical domain, like the theft of security credentials, devices, and delicate files. As a result, Daniel Ani, He, and Tiwari (2016) conclude that, despite the widespread disposition of technological solutions to protect industrial control systems, human factors continue to play an important role in the implementation of a necessary cybersecure setting. Alternatively, organizational security can be completely undermined if employees fail to understand and uphold their roles in an organization's security solution (Daniel Ani, He, and Tiwari 2016).

By applying best practices and cybersecurity technologies, most organizations try hard to mitigate the constant barrage of cyber threats and vulnerabilities (Nobles 2018). Most organizations operate in sociotechnical environments, and because technology will continue to advance, cyberattacks and threats will continue to occur. Research has further shown that nearly all of the identified cybersecurity issues in organizations are related to humans in their various roles in some way (Zimmermann and Renaud 2019). Cybercrimes/attacks have seen an increase in many sectors, including the education sector (Ulven and Wangen 2021), the health sector (Sardi et al. 2020; Nifakos et al. 2021), the maritime industry (Chang et al. 2019), and more. Despite this, solutions that include leveraging the human factor have not been explored much or given enough attention (Aldawood and Skinner 2018; Bada, Sasse, and Nurse 2014).

CYBERSECURITY AND HUMAN FACTORS

According to the 2015 IBM Cybersecurity Intelligence Index, human error was responsible for nine out of every ten information security incidents that year. Most human-centered cybersecurity vulnerabilities stem from inadequate protection against potential attacks. There are many instances of how organizations fail to secure and protect their information. Some of these include failure to revoke technical authorization from previous workers and the lack of official processes for granting access to IT systems (Glaspie and Karwowski 2018). Recent research has identified the human factor as the weakest link in cybersecurity. Even the most advanced cyberattacks are habitually backed by human susceptibilities (Van der Kleij and Leukfeldt 2020). The consensus of many cybersecurity experts is that human behavior, which oftentimes compromises existing technical safeguards, is the greatest challenge to effective technical security solutions (Patterson 2016, 2019). There are many employee behaviors that make organizations susceptible to cybersecurity risks. Employees who are not happy with their organizations are most likely to orchestrate spiteful attacks that threaten their security (Hadlington 2018). Employees can also compromise the security of their organizations unintentionally when they engage in seemingly innocent everyday work routines like storing delicate documents on personal devices or in unsafe places, leaving workspaces unwatched, unknowingly sharing their organization's information on social media sites, writing information like login details on post-it notes, and using unsafe public networks to access work materials (Nobles 2018).

Nobles (2018) also stated that links from email application vulnerability and downloads from the web are among the top three threat vectors for compromising security authorizations. Comparing the cybersecurity risks caused by human factors in organizations to how humans use seat belts in cars, Hadlington (2018), quoting Wilde (1998), states that a false sense of security is then felt because of the use of the seat belts, and people will tend to engage in riskier behavior. Likewise, putting this in the context of information security conduct, he argues that humans will assume they are more protected in their workplaces and carry out security behavior of poorer quality because of the available security measures set in place at their organization. Agreeing with the seat belt example, most research has concluded that almost all the data breaches that occur are caused by human inattention and inaccuracy. A counter-argument was made by Kam et al. (2020) in their research; they argued that the majority of people are quite concerned about security issues to a large extent. Extending this argument, Shappie et al. (2019) stated that in general, people tend to comply with cybersecurity guidelines, so it's perplexing how people can engage in actions that disrupt guidelines while also setting their own sensitive data and that of others in danger.

According to research, most organizations are aware of security concerns and use available technological tools to eliminate security threats, but they continue to ignore the human factor. According to Nobles (2018, 74), "despite the influx of technological capabilities coupled with operational, administrative and technical corrective measures; there is a continued failure to address human factors concerns in information security." The problem of human factors in cybersecurity is heightened by the fact that employees recurrently put their organizations at risk and effectively negate any technological preventive methods put in place by acting carelessly and failing to follow security procedures. Based on a report by the Health Information Trust Alliance in 2014, cybersecurity is not aimed at ignorant human threat actors like well-intentioned but erroneous employees. In comparison to investments in cybersecurity tools and structures, organizational investments in cybersecurity human factors appear immaterial (Glaspie and Karwowski 2018; Evans et al. 2016). The question is why. To answer this, several notions are proposed in the literature. Wisniewska et al. (2020) postulate that one reason human factors have consistently been ignored is that in cybersecurity, human factor knowledge is inadequate, and organizations tend to have a lapse in risk warnings and ways to prevent these risks. Many organizations also make the mistake of focusing on attacks that are external, with very little room for internal attacks, which by a large margin pose a more serious threat, because many big organizations continue to consistently hold the notion that outside threats are the most dangerous to them. Therefore, they focus more attention on these threats and spend money and energy on high-end technological solutions to curb them. Nobles (2018) states that there is a continual need for advancing technology, assimilating the new technology, and leveraging that integration to ease and improve the quality of work without giving much thought to the cultural, social, and organizational implications of such incorporation. Focusing on the context of cybersecurity, he further claims that an unbalanced emphasis on automated technology has had the unintended consequence of diminishing the role of cybersecurity professionals (Nobles 2018). According to Cobb (2016), a dearth of trained cybersecurity professionals forces organizations to invest even more in computerized cybersecurity technologies, resulting in a perplexing puzzle in which organizational over-budget in technology causes a lack of cybersecurity specialists, and the scarcity causes even more over-investment in technology.

There lies a huge gap in the conclusion drawn by research and the security culture/security structures that most organizations employ; this is because human factors have consistently been ignored (National Institute of Standards and Technology 2018). It is an established fact that despite the use and application of cybersecurity tools, the harmful effects of human factors in cybersecurity have still not been curbed until now because disregarding human factors in the buildout and distribution of cybersecurity guidelines sets up these activities for failure (ENISA 2017). While organizations can change these approaches and safeguard their information from human-assisted errors, another plausible solution would be a change of mindset from viewing humans as a problem to seeing them as a solution.

CYBERSECURITY MANAGEMENT METHODS

Organizations employ many methods to alleviate cybersecurity threats. Most of these methods always take on a technical approach, while the field of cybersecurity becomes progressively multifaceted (Oltramari et al. 2015). When it comes to the management and mitigation of cyber threats and risks, organizations are quick to find solutions by taking the technological route, as evident by the numerous methods/frameworks for mitigating these risks. The approach created by Aksu et al. (2017) is a quantitative cybersecurity threat assessment approach for IT systems that identifies low- and high-risk levels in an organization's assets. This framework has been made freely available by the authors for organizations that want to implement the suggested procedure in their IT systems. Another method for managing cyber risk, still from a technology perspective, is that introduced by Algarni, Thayananthan, and Malaiya (2021). The goal of this approach is to prevent information breaches in the business networks of an organization. Similarly, another approach for managing cybersecurity risk examines cybersecurity threats from the perspective of a cyberattacker and what they would do to achieve their goals and recommends ways of responding to the attack by the protector equally in the early and later stages of the attack to break the link. The approach focuses primarily on technical aspects of cybersecurity, such as attackers and defenders. One of its disadvantages, as with most approaches to managing cybersecurity issues, is that it does not address the human and organizational aspects of cyber risk.

Social engineering is one of the ways humans are used as pawns by cyberattackers to obtain information. While the fact that human factors in cybersecurity have been largely ignored has gained traction in research, the commonly proposed methods of curbing cybersecurity threats when human factors are seen as an element in the cybersecurity equation are awareness and training programs (Aldawood and Skinner 2018; Uchendu et al. 2021). Following a thorough examination of the most widely used security frameworks, fundamental human-associated security elements were recognized and categorized by developing a domain-agnostic security model. The authors then presented each component of their proposed model in detail and attempted to compute them to accomplish a practicable assessment method. Following that, it was suggested that this methodology be applied to the design and development of a security culture evaluation tool that organizations can use to provide recommendations and alternative tactics to workers' preparation programs and techniques. This model was created with the goal of being easily adaptable to a variety of application areas while concentrating on their distinct characteristics (Georgiadou et al. 2020). It should be noted that this framework is meant for assessing the readiness level of an organization in terms of cybersecurity. Other research suggests that cybersecurity frameworks should be socio-technical in nature (Malatji, Von Solms, and Marnewick 2019). Sadok, Alter, and Bednar (2020) have argued that, in some cases, corporate policies emphasizing information security are frequently detached from real work practices and habits and are not given high importance in daily work practices. Most workers do not partake in risk assessment or security practice development. In their real-world settings, security practices stay illusory. It has been proposed that organizations conduct cybersecurity response-readiness drills in the same way that they do fire or emergency drills in their buildings. If any flaws in the security network are discovered during these drills, they are fixed for future use and retested and repeated as needed. This method is still ineffective in eliminating cyber threats (Aljohani 2021). All levels of management, from the highest level of decision makers to the board of directors and unit heads, must adhere to best practices in cybersecurity. This will be used to train the rest of the workforce. When it comes to the board of directors' role in cybersecurity management, Lipton et al. (2020) agree that cybersecurity management is more than just a business and operational responsibility for a company's management team; it's also a governance issue that the board has control over, and this method, according to them, is one of the most effective methods of handling cybersecurity risks. Research has also shown that there is a gap between knowing security procedures and actually following through with those policies and procedures in times of a threat or attack, mostly because human errors can undermine the security, privacy, and trustworthiness of an organization's data, as well as the current technological security barriers (Gundu 2019). In earlier work, Bada, Sasse, and Nurse (2014), on why awareness programs still fail to change the security behavior of individuals, suggested that simple knowledge transfer about good security practices is insufficient. Knowledge and awareness are necessary but not sufficient for changing behavior, which is why they must be used in conjunction with other influencing stratagems.

Considering the advantages of humans in any socio-technical environment, and the fact that humans cannot be completely removed from the security network, the lack of literature on how to use these advantages for security solutions in the field of cybersecurity is appalling.

RELATED WORKS

This section shows related works in literature on human factors and their role in cybersecurity. In their research, Suryotrisongko and Musashi (2019) sought to create taxonomies related to various application areas of cybersecurity in their paper. They identified eight different research areas: applied cybersecurity, applications of data science in cybersecurity, cybersecurity education, incidents, policy management, foundational technologies, and theoretical and human factors. Amazingly, they identified human factors among the eight topics in cybersecurity research, but out of the 99 articles that were included for the purpose of their final literature review, only 4 were considered under the category of human factors in cybersecurity. This highlights the rarity of research currently available in the context of the role played by human factors in cybersecurity. Hamm, Harborth, and Pape (2019) conducted a study on the reproducibility of user research in human-centric cybersecurity research. They concluded that user research was the most used method for cybersecurity studies in humans, although such data have never been published. In addition to reporting the results, the authors recommended that future studies should publish the data to ensure the reproducibility of the study.

In a study, Tahaei and Vaniea (2019) examined how software developers write security-compliant code. They perceive various functional and non-functional challenges as downsides to the developer community, such as a lack of a dedicated security team, a lack of communication among members of the team, and a lack of security knowledge. The issue with this study is that it focuses on a specific user group, such as software developers. Sánchez-Gordón and Colomo-Palacios (2020), in their paper, focused on development and operations issues that require close collaboration between development and operations teams. In particular, the focus was on the security aspects that the human factor introduces into various DevOps routines. They proposed a DevOps culture taxonomy scheme containing 13 different attributes, including collaboration, knowledge sharing, feedback, trust, accountability, and leadership. The conclusions drawn by them are novel, but the focus of the paper was on the specialized area of DevOps. However, end users of cybersecurity systems were ignored, therefore, not shedding enough light on human-centric cybersecurity aspects.

METHODS

The goal of this research is to examine papers about human factors in cybersecurity in order to provide an accurate description and evaluation of current practices in the field. A scoping review was chosen to fit the purpose of this chapter. A scoping review was preferred over a systematic literature review because, unlike a systematic review, a scoping review is conducted with the goal of identifying knowledge gaps, scoping a body of literature, clarifying concepts, or investigating research conduct. Scoping reviews can also be used as a precursor to systematic reviews, confirming the relevance of inclusion criteria and potential questions (Gray 2018). Given the exploratory nature of the proposed aim for this chapter, as well as the fact that few studies investigate human factors as a solution in the cybersecurity domain, the decision to adopt a scoping review will lay the groundwork for conducting more detailed research in the future.

To begin the search, some keywords were generated based on an initial analysis of the subject literature. They include terms like "cybersecurity" and "human factors." These keywords,

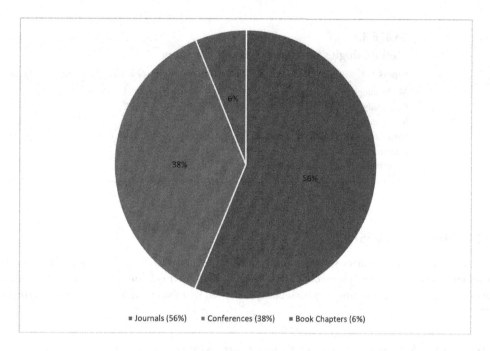

FIGURE 3.1   Article type distribution from 16 publications.

combined with "human factors in cybersecurity" and "the role of humans in cybersecurity," were then used to search for articles in Google Scholar, Research Gate, and Science Direct. A total of 43 articles were discovered. An inclusion and exclusion criterion were used to extract the relevant articles from the total list and eliminate the irrelevant ones. The system used was to include only articles that had a study that focused on human factors in cybersecurity, either as a problem or a solution. Also included were articles that focused on human factors as a means for organizations to develop new solutions. The irrelevant articles were removed in two stages using the inclusion and exclusion criteria.

The article's topics and keywords were examined in the first stage, and the abstract was examined in the second. Following this, there were 16 articles left, which were used to conduct the initial review. The references of the 16 articles were examined further to find additional papers relevant to the study. In the end, none of the articles from the 16 articles' references fit the subject matter. All the included articles were thoroughly reviewed to identify recurring themes based on the objectives, methodologies used, theories applied, and conclusions drawn in each article. To go about answering the aim and question proposed in this chapter, the information from the 16 articles was synthesized to find common themes and relevant insights. Figure 3.1 shows the percentage of publications in book chapters/journals/conferences.

Analyzing the 16 papers on human factors in cybersecurity showed that 9 of the papers were journal articles (56%), 6 were conference papers (38%), and 1 (6%) was a book chapter. All the studies from the 16 articles were geared toward the needs of practitioners; none was written for the academic community, with 1 paper having a section dedicated to steps practitioners can take. To address the human factor issues, 14 (87.5%) of these papers were qualitative studies, with 9 (64.2%) of them having no defined methodology. One (6%) paper out of the 16 used both qualitative and quantitative methods (mixed methods). The two papers that used a case study did not specifically indicate that they used a case study methodology. Table 3.1 shows the method/approach used by the included 16 articles.

TABLE 3.1

Methodologies Used in the Selected Papers

Papers	$N = 16$
Methodology:	
Case study	2
Mixed method	1
Qualitative with no precise approach	9
Literature review	2
Quantitative (survey, questionnaire)	2

DISCUSSION AND RESULTS

This section will discuss various themes derived from the analysis of the 16 included articles that talk about human factors in cybersecurity. An argument will be made in this section so that human factors can be seen as a solution to cybersecurity issues so that the phenomenon can be investigated further.

HUMAN FACTOR STRATEGIES TO REDUCE CYBERSECURITY MISTAKES

From the analyzed papers, human factors in cybersecurity were addressed from an angle of a lack of set-in-place awareness programs for addressing human-related errors that cause incidents leading to losses. Nobles (2018) stressed the fact that many organizations need to have a human factors program that can lay the groundwork for addressing and mitigating human-centric problems and that properly training the workforce of an organization by incorporating psychology-centered experts as decision makers to address human factors-related issues can aid in the reduction of cybersecurity oversights. Agreeing with the conclusion drawn by Nobles (2018), Proctor and Chen (2015) suggest that experts in human factors/ergonomics should use their knowledge to show that positive changes and contributions can be made by employing a scientifically backed human factors method in the field of cybersecurity.

CYBERSECURITY AND LEADERSHIP

Triplett (2022) described human factors in terms of the leadership of an organization. This is the only study among the analyzed articles that explicitly viewed organization leaders and not simply workers as human factors. The author argues that some human errors that lead to cybersecurity threats are unintentional because of incorrect strategic implementation or accurate but inadequate cybersecurity plan implementation. Therefore, cyber leaders can inspire the augmentation of positive mindfulness and toughen human behaviors concerning cybersecurity by educating workers through awareness programs.

ORGANIZATIONAL CYBERSECURITY CULTURE AND HUMAN FACTORS

Pollini et al. (2022) argued that one of the main reasons workers fail to follow proper cybersecurity measures stems from the organizations' implicit culture of security rather than a lack of understanding of the right security behavior, exposing the organization to human weaknesses. Corradini and Nardelli (2019) stressed the need for analyzing employees' risk perception before creating training/awareness programs. The authors also highlight the need for organizations to have a resilient risk philosophy to help mitigate cybersecurity issues.

HUMAN FACTORS AS A POSITIVE LINK IN CYBERSECURITY

Evans et al. (2016) argue in their paper that the effectiveness of cybersecurity awareness programs to curb human errors that lead to data breaches should be checked if, despite these programs, cyber threats and risks continue to increase. For organizations to achieve true cybersecurity assurance, they further argued for the use of operational practices such as "human reliability assessment," as well as improved authentication techniques such as statistical quality control. In their papers, Zimmermann and Renaud (2019) and Rahman et al. (2021) argued for humans to be considered a solution rather than a problem in the cybersecurity chain. It should be noted, however, that the work by the latter focused on the current research trends of the computer science community.

It can be noted that most of these papers consider human factors the "weakest link" in cybersecurity. There has been a shift in dealing with cybersecurity issues from a solely technical point of view to a sociotechnical point of view (Rahman et al. 2021; Jeong et al. 2019). An argument can be made that humans, who are a vital part of the cybersecurity network, can be considered a solution rather than a problem. Because some of the errors by humans that lead to security breaches are unintentional, Hadlington (2018) outlined how awareness programs can be amped up for effectiveness. He also provided evidence from the literature on different methods that organizations can apply to help reduce human errors. Awareness programs and organization security culture play a huge role in how security issues are handled. Along with technical solutions and awareness programs, behaviors programs and psychological programs included in security training will lead to effective handling of cyber threats and risks in organizations. Finally, most of the reviewed articles called for more research exploring human factors in cybersecurity.

CONCLUSION AND RECOMMENDATIONS

Human factors in cybersecurity have generally not been explored in depth. Many of the available studies see humans as the weakest link in the cybersecurity chain. While there have been a few papers calling for an interdisciplinary approach to tackling cybersecurity issues, not many studies have tried to view humans as a form of solution to persisting cybersecurity issues. This chapter has explored existing literature on the role of human factors in cybersecurity. It started by giving an overview of cybersecurity, including the common types of cybersecurity threats faced by organizations. It went further to explain the current state of the literature on human factors in the cybersecurity domain, how humans are considered the weakest link in the cybersecurity chain due to intentional and unintentional errors, and the various methods that have been suggested and used to alleviate cybersecurity threats in organizations. This chapter made the case for how most methods for managing cybersecurity threats are technical and do not include a multidisciplinary perspective (including human factors) and has shown themes that lead to the conclusion that with the right connection of the available methods used by organizations to tackle cybersecurity issues, the human link in the cybersecurity chain can be exploited as a type of solution to security issues in organizations. This review contributes to the literature by drawing attention to an aspect of cybersecurity that is commonly overlooked. Decision makers in organizations can benefit from this chapter and build upon the findings presented to curb security issues in their organizations.

As previously stated in this chapter, more research on human factors and their role in cybersecurity is required because of the lack of focus on human factors as a solution rather than as vulnerabilities in the cybersecurity link. Another reason is that professional human security experts have the awareness and knowledge to predict human behavior and use that knowledge to predict cyber threats, cyber-criminal behavior, and the reasons attackers target specific organizations. Human factors may be considered by some a broad term; researchers can pick a specific human factor like trust, as presented in the paper by Oltramari et al. (2015), and research its role and effects on the security of organizations, more specifically how these factors can be leveraged as security solutions instead of problems. Additional search engines other than the ones used for this research can be used in future work to acquire more articles on human factors in cybersecurity and answer the question of how human factors can be considered a solution in cybersecurity to ensure generalization.

REFERENCES

Aksu, M. Ugur, M. Hadi Dilek, E. Islam Tatli, Kemal Bicakci, H. Ibrahim Dirik, M. Umut Demirezen, and Tayfun Aykir. 2017. "A Quantitative CVSS-Based Cybersecurity Risk Assessment Methodology for IT Systems." In Proceedings – International Carnahan Conference on Security Technology, 1–8. https://doi.org/10.1109/CCST.2017.8167819.

Aldawood, Hussain, and Geoffrey Skinner. 2018. "Educating and Raising Awareness on Cybersecurity Social Engineering: A Literature Review." In Proceedings of 2018 IEEE International Conference on Teaching, Assessment, and Learning for Engineering, TALE, 62–68. IEEE. https://doi.org/10.1109/TALE.2018.8615162.

Algarni, Abdullah M., Vijey Thayananthan, and Yashwant K. Malaiya. 2021. "Quantitative Assessment of Cybersecurity Risks for Mitigating Data Breaches in Business Systems." *Applied Sciences (Switzerland)* 11 (8). https://doi.org/10.3390/app11083678.

Aljohani, Hassan. 2021. "Cybersecurity Threats during the Pandemic." *Journal of Contemporary Scientific Research* 5 (1): 1–14.

Andrade, Roberto O., Ivan Ortiz-Garces, and Maria Cazares. 2020. "Cybersecurity Attacks on Smart Home during Covid-19 Pandemic." In Proceedings of the World Conference on Smart Trends in Systems, Security and Sustainability, WS4, 398–404. https://doi.org/10.1109/WorldS450073.2020.9210363.

Bada, Maria, Angela M. Sasse, and Jason R. C. Nurse. 2014. "Cybersecurity Awareness Campaigns: Why They Fail to Change Behavior." In International Conference on Cybersecurity for Sustainable Society, 38. www.cs.ox.ac.uk/publications/publication9343-abstract.html%0Ahttp://discovery.ucl.ac.uk/1468954/1/Awareness CampaignsDraftWorkingPaper.pdf.

Chang, C.-H., S. Wenming, Z. Wei, P. Changki, and C. A. Kontovas. 2019. "Evaluating Cybersecurity Risks in the Maritime Industry: A Literature Review." In Proceedings of the International Association of Maritime Universities (IAMU) Conference, 1–9.

Cobb, Stephen. 2016. "Mind This Gap: Criminal Hacking and the Global Cybersecurity Skills Shortage, a Critical Analysis." In Virus Bulletin Conference, 1–8. www.virusbulletin.com/uploads/pdf/magazine/2016/VB2016-Cobb.pdf.

Corradini, Isabella, and Enrico Nardelli. 2019. "Building Organizational Risk Culture in Cybersecurity: The Role of Human Factors." *Advances in Intelligent Systems and Computing* 782: 193–202. https://doi.org/10.1007/978-3-319-94782-2_19.

Daniel Ani, Uchenna P., Hongmei Mary He, and Ashutosh Tiwari. 2016. "Human Capability Evaluation Approach for Cybersecurity in Critical Industrial Infrastructure." *Advances in Intelligent Systems and Computing* 501: 169–82. https://doi.org/10.1007/978-3-319-41932-9_14.

Dissanayake, Viraj. 2020. "A Review of Cybersecurity Risks in an Augmented Reality World." https://Virajdissanayake.Blogspot.Com/2019/02/a-Review-of-Cyber-Security-Risks-in.Html?M=1.2020; www.researchgate.net/publication/339941469_A_review_of_Cyber_security_risks_in_an_Augmented_reality_world.

Evans, Mark, Leandros A. Maglaras, Ying He, and Helge Janicke. 2016. "Human Behaviour as an Aspect of Cybersecurity Assurance." *Security and Communication Networks* 9 (17): 4667–79. https://doi.org/10.1002/sec.1657.

Georgiadou, Anna, Spiros Mouzakitis, Kanaris Bounas, and Dimitrios Askounis. 2020. "A Cyber-Security Culture Framework for Assessing Organization Readiness." *Journal of Computer Information Systems* 62 (3): 1–11. https://doi.org/10.1080/08874417.2020.1845583.

Ghate, Shweta, and Pragyesh Kumar Agrawal. 2017. "A Literature Review on Cybersecurity in Indian Context." *Journal of Computer & Information Technology* 8 (5): 30–36. https://doi.org/10.22147/jucit/080501.

Glaspie, Henry W., and Waldemar Karwowski. 2018. "Human Factors in Information Security Culture: A Literature Review." *Advances in Intelligent Systems and Computing* 593: 267–80. https://doi.org/10.1007/978-3-319-60585-2_25.

Gray, Amber. 2018. "Systematic Review or Scoping Review? Guidance for Authors When Choosing between a Systematic or Scoping Review Approach." *BMC Medical Research Methodology* 18 (143): 1–7. https://doi.org/10.4324/9781315159416.

Grobler, Marthie, Raj Gaire, and Surya Nepal. 2021. "User, Usage and Usability: Redefining Human Centric Cybersecurity." *Frontiers in Big Data* 4 (March): 1–18. https://doi.org/10.3389/fdata.2021.583723.

Groenendaal, Jelle, and Ira Helsloot. 2021. "Cyber Resilience during the COVID-19 Pandemic Crisis: A Case Study." *Journal of Contingencies and Crisis Management* 29 (4): 439–44. https://doi.org/10.1111/1468-5973.12360.

Gundu, Tapiwa. 2019. "Acknowledging and Reducing the Knowing and Doing Gap in Employee Cybersecurity Compliance." In 14th International Conference on Cyber Warfare and Security, ICCWS 2019, 94–102.

Gutzwiller, Robert S., Dan Cosley, Kimberly Ferguson-Walter, Dustin Fraze, and Robert Rahmer. 2019. "Panel: Research Sponsors for Cybersecurity Research and the Human Factor." *Proceedings of the Human Factors and Ergonomics Society Annual Meeting* 63: 422–26. https://doi.org/10.1177/1071181319631383.

Hadlington, Lee. 2018. "Human Factors in Cybersecurity; Examining the Link between Internet Addiction, Impulsivity, Attitudes Towards Cybersecurity, and Risky Cybersecurity Behaviours." *Heliyon* 3 (7): 1–18. https://doi.org/10.1016/j.heliyon.2017.e00346.

Hamm, Peter, David Harborth, and Sebastian Pape. 2019. "A Systematic Analysis of User Evaluations in Security Research." In Proceedings of the 14th International Conference on Availability, Reliability and Security – ARES '19, Canterbury, United Kingdom. doi:10.1145/3339252.3340339. https://doi.org/10.1145/3339252.3340339.

Humayun, Mamoona, Mahmood Niazi, Nz Jhanjhi, Mohammad Alshayeb, and Sajjad Mahmood. 2020. "Cybersecurity Threats and Vulnerabilities: A Systematic Mapping Study." *Arabian Journal for Science and Engineering* 45 (4): 3171–89. https://doi.org/10.1007/s13369-019-04319-2.

Jeong, Jongkil, Joanne Mihelcic, Gillian Oliver, and Carsten Rudolph. 2019. "Towards an Improved Understanding of Human Factors in Cybersecurity." In Proceedings – 2019 IEEE 5th International Conference on Collaboration and Internet Computing, CIC 2019, 338–45. https://doi.org/10.1109/CIC48465.2019.00047.

Kam, Hwee Joo, Philip Menard, Dustin Ormond, and Robert E. Crossler. 2020. "Cultivating Cybersecurity Learning: An Integration of Self-Determination and Flow." *Computers and Security* 96: 101875. https://doi.org/10.1016/j.cose.2020.101875.

Khan, Navid Ali, Sarfraz Nawaz Brohi, and Noor Zaman. 2020. "Ten Deadly Cybersecurity Threats Amid COVID-19 Pandemic." *TechRxiv Powered by IEEE*, 1–6. www.techrxiv.org/articles/Ten_Deadly_Cyber_Security_Threats_Amid_COVID-19_Pandemic/12278792.

Kure, Halima Ibrahim, Shareeful Islam, and Mohammad Abdur Razzaque. 2018. "An Integrated Cybersecurity Risk Management Approach for a Cyber-Physical System." *Applied Sciences (Switzerland)* 8 (6). https://doi.org/10.3390/app8060898.

Lau, Nathan, Robert Pastel, Melissa R. Chapman, Jennifer Minarik, Jonathan Petit, and Dave Hale. 2018. "Human Factors in Cybersecurity – Perspectives from Industries." *Proceedings of the Human Factors and Ergonomics Society* 1: 139–43. https://doi.org/10.1177/1541931218621032.

Lezzi, Marianna, Mariangela Lazoi, and Angelo Corallo. 2018. "Cybersecurity for Industry 4.0 in the Current Literature: A Reference Framework." *Computers in Industry* 103: 97–110. https://doi.org/10.1016/j.compind.2018.09.004.

Lipton, Martin, Daniel A. Neff, Andrew R. Brownstein, Steven A. Rosenblum, John F. Savarese, Adam O. Emmerich, and David M. Silk 2020. "Risk Management and the Board of Directors." *Computer Law Reporter* 45 (6): 793–99.

Malatji, Masike, Sune Von Solms, and Annlizé Marnewick. 2019. "Socio-Technical Systems Cybersecurity Framework." *Information and Computer Security* 27 (2): 233–72. https://doi.org/10.1108/ICS-03-2018-0031.

Monteith, Scott, Michael Bauer, Martin Alda, John Geddes, Peter C. Whybrow, and Tasha Glenn. 2021. "Increasing Cybercrime Since the Pandemic: Concerns for Psychiatry." *Current Psychiatry Reports* 23 (4). https://doi.org/10.1007/s11920-021-01228-w.

National Institute of Standards and Technology (2018). "Framework for Improving Critical Infrastructure Cybersecurity" [PDF]. https://nvlpubs.nist.gov/nistpubs/CSWP/NIST.CSWP.04162018.pdf.

Nifakos, Sokratis, Krishna Chandramouli, Charoula Konstantina Nikolaou, Panagiotis Papachristou, Sabine Koch, Emmanouil Panaousis, and Stefano Bonacina. 2021. "Influence of Human Factors on Cybersecurity within Healthcare Organisations: A Systematic Review." *Sensors* 21 (15): 1–25. https://doi.org/10.3390/s21155119.

Nobles, Calvin. 2018. "Botching Human Factors in Cybersecurity in Business Organizations." *HOLISTICA – Journal of Business and Public Administration* 9 (3): 71–88. https://doi.org/10.2478/hjbpa-2018-0024.

Oltramari, Alessandro, Diane Henshel, Mariana Cains, and Blaine Hoffman. 2015. "Towards a Human Factors Ontology for Cybersecurity." *CEUR Workshop Proceedings* 1523: 26–33.

Patterson, W., C. Winston, and L. Fleming. 2016. "Behavioral Cybersecurity: Human Factors in the Cybersecurity Curriculum." *Advances in Intelligent Systems and Computing Advances in Human Factors in Cybersecurity*, 253–266. https://doi.org/10.1007/978-3-319-41932-9_21.

Patterson, W., and C. E. Winston-Proctor. 2019. *Behavioral Cybersecurity: Applications of Personality Psychology and Computer Science*. Boca Raton, FL: CRC Press Taylor & Francis Group. https://doi.org/10.1201/9780429461484.

Pollini, Alessandro, Tiziana C. Callari, Alessandra Tedeschi, Daniele Ruscio, Luca Save, Franco Chiarugi, and Davide Guerri. 2022. "Leveraging Human Factors in Cybersecurity: An Integrated Methodological Approach." *Cognition, Technology and Work* 24 (2): 371–90. https://doi.org/10.1007/s10111-021-00683-y.

Pranggono, Bernardi, and Abdullahi Arabo. 2021. "COVID-19 Pandemic Cybersecurity Issues." *Internet Technology Letters* 4 (2): 4–9. https://doi.org/10.1002/itl2.247.

Proctor, Robert W., and Jing Chen. 2015. "The Role of Human Factors/Ergonomics in the Science of Security: Decision Making and Action Selection in Cyberspace." *Human Factors* 57 (5): 721–27. https://doi.org/10.1177/0018720815585906.

Rahman, Tashfiq, Rohani Rohan, Debajyoti Pal, and Prasert Kanthamanon. 2021. "Human Factors in Cybersecurity: A Scoping Review." In ACM International Conference Proceeding Series, 1–11. https://doi.org/10.1145/3468784.3468789.

Sadok, Moufida, Steven Alter, and Peter Bednar. 2020. "It Is Not My Job: Exploring the Disconnect between Corporate Security Policies and Actual Security Practices in SMEs." *Information and Computer Security* 28 (3): 467–83. https://doi.org/10.1108/ICS-01-2019-0010.

Sánchez-Gordón, Mary, and Ricardo Colomo-Palacios. 2020. "Security as Culture: A Systematic Literature Review of DevSecOps." In Proceedings – 2020 IEEE/ACM 42nd International Conference on Software Engineering Workshops, ICSEW 2020, 266–69. https://doi.org/10.1145/3387940.3392233.

Sardi, Alberto, Alessandro Rizzi, Enrico Sorano, and Anna Guerrieri. 2020. "Cyber Risk in Health Facilities: A Systematic Literature Review." *Sustainability* 12: 1–16.

Shappie, Alexander, Dawson, Charlotte, and Debb, Scott. 2019. "Personality as a Predictor of Cybersecurity Behavior." *Psychology of Popular Media Culture* 9 (4): 475–80.

Suryotrisongko, Hatma, and Yasuo Musashi. 2019. "Review of Cybersecurity Research Topics, Taxonomy and Challenges: Interdisciplinary Perspective." In Proceedings – 2019 IEEE 12th Conference on Service-Oriented Computing and Applications, SOCA 2019, 162–67. IEEE. https://doi.org/10.1109/SOCA.2019.00031.

Tahaei, Mohammad, and Kami Vaniea. 2019. "A Survey on Developer-Centred Security." In Proceedings – 4th IEEE European Symposium on Security and Privacy Workshops, EUROS and PW 2019, 129–38. IEEE. https://doi.org/10.1109/EuroSPW.2019.00021.

The European Network and Information Security Agency (ENISA). 2017. https://techtarget.com.

Triplett, William J. 2022. "Addressing Human Factors in Cybersecurity Leadership." *Journal of Cybersecurity and Privacy* 2 (July): 573–86. https://doi.org/10.3390/jcp2030029.

Uchendu, Betsy, Jason R. C. Nurse, Maria Bada, and Steven Furnell. 2021. "Developing a Cybersecurity Culture: Current Practices and Future Needs." *Computers and Security* 109. https://doi.org/10.1016/j.cose.2021.102387.

Ulven, Joachim Bjørge, and Gaute Wangen. 2021. "A Systematic Review of Cybersecurity Risks in Higher Education." *Future Internet* 13 (2): 1–40. https://doi.org/10.3390/fi13020039.

Van der Kleij, R., and R. Leukfeldt. 2020. "Cyber Resilient Behavior: Integrating Human Behavioral Models and Resilience Engineering Capabilities into Cybersecurity." *Advances in Human Factors in Cybersecurity* 960: 16–27. https://doi.org/10.1007/978-3-030-20488-4_2.

Wilde, G. J. 1998. "Rish Homestasis Theory: An Overview." *Injury Prevention* 4 (2): 89–91.

Wisniewska, M., Z. Wisniewski, K. Szaniawska, and M. Lehmann. 2020. "The Human Factor in Managing the Security of Information." *Advances in Human Factors in Cybersecurity* 960: 38–47. https://doi.org/10.1007/978-3-030-20488-4_4.

Zimmermann, Verena, and Karen Renaud. 2019. "Moving from a' h Uman-as-Problem' to a' Human-as-Solution' Cybersecurity Mindset." *International Journal of Huma-Computer Studies* 131: 169–87.

4 An Introduction to Cybercrime and Cybersecurity
The Whys and Whos of Cybersecurity

Riddhita Parikh

CONTENTS

DOI: 10.1201/9781003319887-4

INTRODUCTION

In the past decade, information technology (IT) has seen a dramatic rise in its usage. Internet users range from academic and government sectors to the industrial sector. There has been a surge in usage of devices pertaining to IT. These devices, namely mobile phones and other digital applications, have transformed people's lifestyle. This upgraded lifestyle has led to an increasing demand for online connectivity. The digitalization has expanded to the educational sector, social platforms, businesses, and even banking. Hence, surfing various websites and utilizing various web engines have inevitably become an integral parts of human life.

Contrariwise, when the need for digitalization bolsters the use of internet services, the netizens that is, the people who use the internet, lack the needed awareness of various threats use of the internet may pose. Many of internet users fail to protect their computer devices and become victims of hacking. In some cases, netizens may be subjected to online obscenity and stalking as well. Thus, this chapter focuses on basic, essential aspects of cybersecurity like the origin of the notion of "cyber," familiarizing the reader with the types of cybercrimes prevailing on the internet. What is cybersecurity? And who needs it?

LITERATURE REVIEW

THE ORIGIN

The word "cyber" is taken from the Greek word *kybernetes*, which means "steersman" or "governor." The word "cyber" is used as a prefix to describe a person, thing, or idea related to computer or information technology. For instance, the word "cybernetics" is used for people using the internet, and "cybercrime" is a word denoting online crimes. "Cyber-criminal" is a word used for people engaging in online crimes. "Cyber-punk" refers to a lawless subculture wherein computer technology dominates an oppressive society. "Cyber-culture" is a social condition that has come into existence due to the wide spread of computer networks for communication, business, and entertainment.

The word "cybernetics" was first coined by Norbert Wiener, an American mathematician and philosopher, in the year 1948. He used this term in his book *Cybernetics: Or Control and Communication in the Animal and the Machine*. Warren S. McCulloch, along with M. Pitts, published an article on logic and the nervous system in 1943. The article mentioned "cyber," but from a different perspective. Norbert Wiener considered Leibniz his historical patron. This is because of Leibniz's interest in the construction of machines that could perform calculations and his attempt to build a calculus ratiocinator. On the other hand, McCulloch believed that Descartes had believed in holistic conception, wherein he recommended the decomposition of difficulties related to logic into parts.

J. Von Neumann was one of the most renowned mathematicians of his time. He is widely known as a Hungarian American mathematician, physicist, computer scientist, engineer, and polymath. Neumann contributed immensely in the fields of mathematics, physics, economics, computing, and statistics. It is noteworthy that Neumann contacted Wiener and McCulloch to join the Telelogical Society, which was informally known as the "Cybernetic Club." The other associations for cybernetics included Cyber-netiques in France and the Ratio Club in Great Britain.

Another names to be mentioned in the history of cybernetics is Claude E. Shannon – who made his contribution in communication theory. William Ross Ashby contributed immensely from the perspective of "control" from the viewpoint of "requisite variety." The early theory of autonomy was conceived by P. Vendryes. The general role of retroaction was given by S. Odobleja and P. Postelnien. The general science of regulation loops was given by H. Schmidt, and the notion of "reflex machines" was given by J. Cafittee. The word *cybernetics* is also mentioned by historical contributors; Plato used it as a metaphor in *The Republic* and *Gorgias* to present the art of government. A. M. Ampere, in his essay on the philosophy of science, used the word *cybernetique*. *Kiberneitki* was a word used by S. Trentowski in his book on management.

Thus, going through the history of cybernetics, cybernetics can be defined as: "The science of control and data processing in animals, machines, and society."

CYBERSPACE AND NETIZENS

CYBERSPACE

It was William Gibson who first coined the term "cyberspace" in his book *Neuromancer*, written in 1984. He later descried his book as an "evocation and essentially meaningless" – a buzzword that could serve as an encryption for all of his cybernetic ideas. However, currently the word "cyberspace" is used to define anything associated with computers, the internet, information technology, and the diverse internet culture. Cyberspace is an electronic application which is equivalent a human psyche – cyberspace is the domain where objects are entirely made up of information and data manipulation. There is no existence of physical objects or even a representation of the physical world.

Chip Morningstar and F. Randall Farmer are of the opinion that cyberspace should be more defined by the social interactions that it involves than the technical implementations. The core characteristic of cyberspace must be that it consists of an environment that has many participants who possess the ability to affect and influence each and every person associated with it. In cyberspace, the computer system acts as a medium to increase and expand communication channels between real people. Thus, it can be concluded that cyberspace is the electrical medium of computer networking, in which virtual communication is undertaken and individuals can interact, exchange ideas, share information, provide social support, conduct business, direct actions, create artistic media, play games, engage in political discussions, and so on.

Virtual reality integrates scores of capabilities (sensors, signals, connections, transmissions, processors, and controllers) and leads to an online communicative experience accessible regardless of geographic location (Beran and Li 2005). Cyberspace permits the inter-reliant network of information technology and telecommunication systems such as the internet, computer systems, integrated sensors, system control networks, and implanted processors and controllers, to create global control and communications. The term has become conventional to designate anything and everything associated with computers, information technology, the internet, and the diverse internet culture. Consequently, cyberspace is a computer-generated space where the internet works and human beings connect through computer and telecommunication, with no regard given to physical geography.

The Features of Cyber-World

a. The physical/real world is analogous to the earth, and cyberspace is analogous to the virtual world, that it, the world wherein individuals are connected through computers and networks, where it is computer programming that works and data are processed (Beran and Li 2005).
b. There has been an ever-increasing expansion in the boundaries of ICT, computers, and internet technology in cyberspace.

    c. Cyberspace provides an easy and convenient way to roam about in the virtual world and find all the necessary and important information.

    d. With tremendous speed and unlimited reach, it is also easy to enter and exit the virtual world.

    e. The resources needed to enter the virtual world are few, less expensive (affordable by all), and very easily available.

    f. Cybernetics provides the benefit to disguise one's real identity in cyberspace.

    g. The influence of cyberspace and the real world on each other is mutual.

    h. To maintain law and order in the cyber world, cyber laws have been created.

CYBERSPACE AND THE 21ST CENTURY

Statistics from 2022 show that 4.9 billion people actively use the internet. This trend indicates that there is around a 4% rise in internet users annually. This means that roughly 196 million new people enter the world of netizens on an annual basis. In 2000, it was only 361 million people worldwide; this statistic itself shows the flashing speed at which internet users are increasing day by day and year by year. Data from 2020 show that an average internet user spends 145 minutes per day online, amounting to 17 hours per week (Goni 2022).

Netizens

Students need to adhere to the rules and regulations of the institute that they are in. They also need to follow the norms and ethics of the educational institute that they are associated with. Likewise, any person in cyberspace is referred to as a netizen and must follow the norms, ethics, rules, and regulations of cyberspace. In the progressive society of the 21st century, it is difficult to escape becoming a netizen. However, at the same time, it is essential to see that law and order prevail in cyberspace, which is why cyber laws were created (Goni 2022).

According to the Collins English Dictionary, a netizen is "a person who regularly uses the internet." However, according to another definition, "a netizen is a person who becomes part of and participates in the larger internet society, which recognizes few boundaries save language." The word "netizen" comes from the combination the two words "internet" and "citizen." Per a 2020 report, India ranked second of the top 20 countries with highest number of internet users. China ranked first, and the United States ranked third, followed by countries like Germany, Switzerland, Norway, Austria, Denmark, Sweden, Netherlands, Canada, and Ireland (Goni 2022).

It is essential to note that cyberspace has eliminated physical boundaries and provides netizens with the opportunity to interact with any other netizen around the globe. It is perceived that netizens are smarter than other citizens; enjoy more privileges, freedom, and expression of thought; and have better communication with their peers as well as with nodal authorities (Maurseth 2018).

Despite the privileges given to netizens, they are governed by the cyber laws of the country in which they reside. These laws are specifically created to maintain law, order, and peace in cyberspace. Beyond this, netizens are also expected to abide by the rules and regulations of telecom services for their internet connection. Attempts have also been made to supervise and restrict the undue freedom enjoyed by netizens for their own benefit and security. This has been done on regular basis by organizing a biennial World Conference on Information Technology (WCIT). The main goal of this conference is to review the international telecommunications regulations which serve as the rules of digital connections and the interoperability of telecommunications and satellite networks. It is also a platform that provides various IT experts, government officials, and policy and decision makers from around the globe to meet and discuss various challenges and solutions related to cyberspace (Patchin and Hinduja 2006).

Two major concerns identified during these conferences pertaining to netizens and civil society were (Maurseth 2018):

- Countries deploying authoritarian censorship and surveillance on their netizens will be given the opportunity to draft the global rules for the internet. This in turn would generate greater worldwide censorship and scrutiny.
- The coordination functions of the Internet Corporation for Assigned Names and Number (ICANN) will be undertaken by the United Nations.

CYBERCRIME

This section of the chapter focuses on cybercrime, its definition, and the types of cybercrimes prevailing in society. The term "cyber" is used to refer to anything and everything related to cyberspace, that is, virtual space – the place where computers become the source for providing information. Crime is social or economic in nature, and its existence in society is as old as society itself. Siegel defines crime as a "violation of societal rules of behavior as interpreted and expressed by a criminal legal code created by people holding social and political power. Individuals who violate these rules are subject to sanctions by state authority, social stigma, and loss of status." In its simplest form, cybercrime can be defined as "Any unlawful act where computer is either a tool or target or both" (Hinduja and Patchin 2008).

Consequently, cybercrimes are offenses committed when a computer, networking, or any other medium of information and communication technology has been used to commit a crime. Such crimes may include an array of offenses, like economic crimes, misusing a person's identity, and downloading illegal files or pornography. Such crimes can be committed very easily, in fractions of seconds, but the damage caused may leave a person mentally, physically, and financially drained.

The United Nations (UN) foresaw the probable negative impact of the digital era in the early 20th century. It cautioned countries against the excessive use of internet and to be vigilant about netizens' behavior. Nevertheless, problems pertaining to excessive use of the internet and anti-social behaviors continued to rise. Today, there has been an intense surge in crimes associated with cyberspace, widely ranging from financial to women and child trafficking and sexual crimes (Mohsin 2021).

According to the Section 65 of Indian IT Act, a person is said to have committed a cybercrime when "a person intentionally conceals, destroys, alters, intentionally, knowingly causes some other person to conceal, destroy or alter any computer source code used for a computer, computer program, computer system or network when a computer source code is required" (Hinduja and Patchin 2008).

CLASSIFICATION OF CYBERCRIME

The following is a classification of cybercrimes.

a. **Crimes committed with the use of computers:** Based on this category, cybercrime can be divided as follows:
   i. **Crimes "on" the internet**
      Factors like global access and internet speed have made it easier for criminals to commit crimes on internet. Moreover, such crimes seem to be cheaper and risk free, can be carried out efficiently, and allow high profit (Mohsin 2021). A few examples of such misdemeanors are threats, fraud, defamation, deceitfulness, and so on.
   ii. **Crimes "of" the internet**
      Offences like hacking, planting viruses, and theft relating to intellectual property fall under this category.

Let us go through some of the very common crimes that could be committed with the use of computers around the globe.

Forgery and Counterfeiting

Here the computer is used as a medium to either forge or counterfeit a document. The latest upgraded hardware and software allows the criminal to produce a counterfeit that would exactly match the original document. The copy generated is so similar that it is difficult to judge its authenticity without the help of a forgery expert.

Software Piracy and Crime Related to Intellectual Property Rights

Software piracy refers to an illegal distribution and reproduction of software either for personal use or for business (Kumar and Priyanka 2019). This crime falls under the category of intellectual property rights infringement. Crimes pertaining to downloading movies or songs illegally may fall under this category.

Cyber Terrorism

Here the internet is used to conduct a violent act that may result in either a loss of life or may cause significant harm to the body. The main goal behind the attack could be to obtain some political or ideological gain (Laqueur et al. 2002). Some experienced cyber terrorists may engage in hacking and cause massive damage to government systems or data, leaving the country in a state of fear and anxiety about future attacks.

Phishing

In this type of cybercrime, an offender may obtain an individual's personal information through email by disguising himself or herself as a reliable, trustworthy, and dependable entity. The main purpose here is to steal the identity and personal information like the individual's username, password, and card numbers to steal money from their account. When the same information is obtained via the use of a telephone, it is called vishing, *voice phishing*. However, when the customer is lured through SMS, it is referred to as *smishing*.

Cyber Vandalism

Vandalism means purposefully destroying another person's or a company's property due to malicious intentions. Cyber vandalism may include things like hacking, defacing the website, posting fake news or reviews, purposefully providing wrong reviews, cheating, posting a virus or malware so that others may download it unintentionally, and so on (Kumar and Priyanka 2019).

Computer Hacking

Computer hacking involves the modification of either the computer hardware or software or both to attain a target that could be quite different than the creator's original purpose. A person may hack a computer for various reasons ranging from simply demonstrating his/her technical abilities to malevolent intentions like destroying, stealing, or modifying the information due to monetary, political, social, or personal reasons (Laqueur et al. 2002). Nowadays, the corporate world hires hackers to intentionally hack the computers of an organization and then fix the security vulnerabilities. Hackers can be classified into the following on the basis of the kind of hacking they undertake (Bhadury 2022):

  i. **White Hat:** These hackers are also known as ethical hackers. White hat hackers hack to identify the security vulnerabilities of a system. Furthermore, they notify companies, which in turn take adequate actions to prevent and protect the system from alien hackers. White hat hackers are employees working in an organization. They are mainly appointed to safeguard the internet security system and overcome loopholes. They may also work as freelancers.

ii. **Black Hat:** As the name suggests; these are hackers who work and engage in hacking due to bad intentions. These people hack the system to feed their economic, personal, social, or political goals (Richard et al. 2000). They try to find the pitfalls in a security system, keep the limitations to themselves, and exploit the person or the organization. The exploitation ends only when the opposite party comes to know about the illegal hacking and fixes the problem. Such hackers are known as crackers.

iii. **Grey Hat:** These hackers work on a consultation basis. The grey hat hacker's role is to identify security lapses, report to administrators, and fix security bugs.

iv. **Blue Hat:** A blue hat hacker is one who tests software for a probable bug even before its launch in the market (Richard et al. 2000). Their focus is to look for vulnerabilities so that the software can be improved prior to its release to the common population.

b. **Creating and distributing viruses over the internet**

Distribution of viruses can cause an organization business and financial loss. The loss may be in connection with the repair of the system, loss in business due to downtime, or cost incurred due to loss of opportunity. If a hacker is found responsible for such malfunctioning, the organization can sue him/her for an amount greater than or equivalent to the loss endured by the organization.

Spamming

Spamming is the process of sending unsolicited bulk messages or mails to a particular mail address. A person who performs this act is called a spammer. Spam messages may cause irritation to the recipient, overload their network, waste the recipient's time, and unnecessarily occupy space in the mailbox (Bhadury 2022).

The criteria for a spam email are as follows:

i. **Mass Mailing:** This email is not targeted to a particular person but sent to many groups.

ii. **Anonymity:** The real identify of the sender is not known.

iii. **Unsolicited:** It is a totally unwelcome email for the recipient.

Cross-Site Scripting

Here malicious scripts are injected into trusted websites. As soon as these scripts are added, the browser executes the malicious script, gaining access to cookies and other private information. This information is then sent to remote servers where it can be utilized to gain either financial information or access to the system benefits (Aloul 2012).

Online Auction Fraud

Online auctions are offered by many genuine websites. Using the goodwill of these reputed websites, criminal minds lure customers to various online auction fraud schemes where the end user either lands up overpaying for a product, or the payment is sent but delivery of the product never happens (Wilson 2021).

Cyber Squatting

Cyber thieves usually steal the domain name of a listed trademark so that advantage can be taken of the trademark owner's goodwill and reputation (Pittaro 2007). In other words, it refers to the act of obtaining a registered domain name illegally and then selling it off to the lawful owner, who is totally unaware of the trick.

Logic Bombs

Malevolent code is injected into legal software. Unethical actions are triggered due to specific conditions. When these conditions arise, vindictive actions begin, and based on the code, information is either destroyed or the computer becomes unusable in the future.

Internet Time Theft

There are some criminals who may illicitly use usernames and passwords and surf internet at their cost.

Denial of Service Attacks

This is a kind of cyberattack in which a legitimate network is obstructed by choking the network with unwanted traffic (Zwilling 2020).

Salami Attack

Under a salami attack, the attacker proceeds with minor increments which when summed up lead to a major hack of bank accounts. The person may illegally access online banking accounts and withdraw small amounts, which might go unnoticed by the owner. These small withdrawals may gradually lead to larger amounts (Aloul 2012).

Data Diddling

This refers to changing data prior to or during the time when entry is done into a computer system and then immediately changing it back as soon as the process is done (Pittaro 2007). It is difficult to track the changes made, and it may affect the data output as well. It may be done either while the data is being entered or by a virus that may be programmed to change the data. A programmer may also be involved, or it could be done by someone involved in creating, recording, encoding, examining, checking, converting, or transmitting data (Algburi and Igaab 2021).

Email Spoofing

Spoofing refers to a malicious action wherein the original details are transformed in such a way that the source of origin appears different. Fake emails are usually sent so that the receiver remains unaware of the original source.

c. **Crimes based on victimization**

This type of crime is divided into three broad categories:

   i. **Crimes against Individuals:** These crimes target individuals. They may include harassment of a person via mail, obscenity, online stalking, morphing, and many more (Vinnakota et al. 2021).
   ii. **Crimes against Organizations:** Under this category, an individual may have unauthorized information, control, or access over an organization's network and thus have direct control over the company's data (Zwilling 2020). It could be either a private or government organization. The best example of this is cyber terrorism.
   iii. **Crime against Society:** Such crimes may include offenses like trafficking (child or female), pornography, crimes related to finances, unethical selling of articles or materials, and so on.

Let's look in detail at some of the most prevalent crimes in this category.

Cyber Stalking

When internet, email, or any other digital communication instrument is used to stalk another person, it is referred to as cyber stalking. Cyber stalking may also include cyber bullying. Cyber stalking and bullying are synonymous. When electronic communication devices like mobile phones, emails, various social media platforms, messages, or websites are repeatedly or intentionally used by a person or a group to mistreat others, it is referred to as cyber bullying. The main purpose here could be defaming the other person (Algburi and Igaab 2021). The person may engage in false accusations, threats, exploitation, and so on with the sole purpose of harassing or troubling the other person.

E-stalking is on the rise, with more female victims being targeted. The stalker may not physically be around the person but may harass the victim through online abuse, following her online activities, gathering information about her, and engaging in verbal abuse or intimidation.

Child Pornography

This is a branch of pornography wherein pictures of children and videos are made. These videos have sexual sounds which aim at arousing the sexual desires of the people watching it. Child pornography is a very heinous crime; however, owing to advancements in technology, the market for child pornography has surged, and it has become even more vicious and dangerous than it was (Vinnakota et al. 2021).

Adult Pornography

There exists a relationship between pornography and the surge in sexual crime against women. E-pornography is a threat to women who use internet services. These crimes incorporate websites or magazines that produce pornographic materials using computers and the internet.

Harassment Through E-Mail

Prior to the internet era, harassment happened via writing unknown letters to the victim. However, with digitalization, now e-harassment includes blackmailing, bullying, threatening, or conning via email (Rattan and Rattan 2019). The case of digital harassment intensifies, especially when mail has been sent using fake mail IDs.

Defamation

Defamation is when a person verbally abuses another to gain publicity. The defamer may go to the extent of issuing defamatory information about a targeted victim on a website or circulating it among their friends and social media circle. This would directly target the reputation of the victim, leading to psychological trauma.

Morphing

Morphing refers to editing an original picture so that it appears to be completely different from the original one. Criminals usually target women as victims of this crime by downloading their pictures from websites and morphing them so that the women seem to be in compromising situations, to present that the women were involved in such acts. After creating these images, criminals tend to blackmail the women either by threatening to release their images on the social media or send them to their relatives or friends, thereby diminishing the status of these women in society.

Trolling

Trolling is slang that is very frequently used on the internet to describe someone, especially those who spread negativity on online platforms (Verma et al. 2022). Trolls usually use harsh comments and gestures to bully, intimidate, or harass people virtually (Borg 2000). Teenagers are deeply affected when their peers, someone known, or a stranger trolls them. Trolling directly or indirectly creates an atmosphere of a cold war in cyberspace, and trolls are not easily traced.

CYBERSECURITY AND ITS IMPORTANCE

At the time of communication, there may be chances that e-records may be misused or hacked by people with malicious intentions. Hence there comes the question of protecting the secrecy, privacy, and authenticity of e-records. This question leads us to develop network securities to safeguard networks against unauthorized users like hackers. The added advantage of security is that it provides authorized users with sense of security, and users feel safe and secure about their data (Rattan and Rattan 2019).

THREATS TO CYBERSECURITY

The National Bureau of Standards identified the following threats insofar as cybersecurity concerned (Borg 2000):

a. An individual might misuse online information to obtain important information pertaining to finances or the market from a competitive private or government organization.
b. To obtain unauthorized information about individuals.
c. Intentional fraud could be committed by illegally accessing a person's digital data accounts.
d. Government accounts could be hacked to disrupt the rights of individuals
e. It could be easier to infringe an individual's rights via an artificial intelligence system.

TYPES OF THREATS

Threats that may pose a danger to cybersecurity are of two types (Singh 2021):

- Active threats
- Passive threats

Active Threats

Probable active threats can be classified into three types:

a. **Message Stream Modification:** In this kind of active threat, unauthorized access is involved. It could also be that parts of legitimate messages may be modified or altered, and the message may be either delayed or replayed or recorded to produce an unlawful effect. The simplest example of such a message could be that "Mr. X can read these confidential files" can be altered to "Mr. Y can read these confidential files" (Vallée 2012).
b. **Denial of Service:** Here the person may be prevented from using or managing communication facilities normally. This kind of threat could even target a specific group or person so that the messages do not reach the desired destination. At times, an entire network could be destroyed either by disabling the network or overloading the servers so that efficiency is degraded (Singh 2021).
c. **Masquerade:** This means misrepresentation. A person may misinterpret the hacker to be someone else, and security access would be granted (Teresia 2011). Such incidents usually take place due to capturing or replaying authentic sequences.

Passive Threats

Unlike active threats, it is difficult to detect passive threats. Nevertheless, it is possible to stop them from succeeding in their goals. The attacker would want to know that information has been transmitted. There are two main types of passive threats:

a. **Threat of Release of Message Content:** Every person is under fear or stress that their personal or confidential data will get into the hands of anti-social actors. Hence, users want their telephone conversations, messages, emails, and files to be safe and secure.
b. **Traffic Analysis:** This threat involves monitoring the patterns of communication or messages sent. The hacker can find the location as well as the identity of the person who is communicating. They are also in a position to understand the length and the frequency of the messages. Such things help the hacker know the nature of the conversation taking place. Often, this kind of threat encompasses decryption, which means converting encrypted data into readable text.

Meaning of Cybersecurity

Cybersecurity is protecting information systems and services against any possible manipulation, errors, or tragedies (Pande 2017). The main goal of a security system is to minimize, reduce, or eliminate the significant effect of threats and minimize their negative impact. Cybersecurity may also be the protection of online resources against illegal leaks, alterations, restrictions, operation, or devastation (Stevens et al. 2021). Internet security at an individual level has always been a subject of concern and research for both data processors as well as communication services. However, in the field of computers, concerns for both are a combined factor.

Key Elements of Cybersecurity

The key elements of cybersecurity are as follows:

a. **Assurance:** This means the system performs as expected.
b. **Identity Authentication:** When communication happens between a user and the program, both parties must recognize each other and be aware of with whom they are interacting.
c. **Accountability:** This is the ability of security to identify who performed a particular operation, when, and where. Users should be held responsible and accountable for their actions. The program should be able to find an automatic audit trail to monitor, analyze, and detect breaches in security – an essential element of network security.
d. **Access Control:** This feature of network security ensures that only registered users have the right to access the system (Srinath 2006). Furthermore, only registered candidates and programs can make alterations in the available data as and when needed.
e. **Accuracy:** The main goal of accuracy revolves around observing that objects are comprehensive and precise or correct.
f. **Secure Data Exchange:** It fundamentally includes the following aspects:
    i. **Confidentiality:** It asserts that data should remain private and confidential while being transmitted to the other party.
    ii. **Integrity:** While data are being transmitted, they should remain complete and accurate. Authentication should be required while the data are being mailed or various programs are communicating with each other (Singh and Rathi 2021). This is vital because, in some situations, it is essential to know the source of information, commonly known as nonrepudiation of origin, and the sender requires proof that the message has been received by the intended receiver – nonrepudiation of receipt (Pande 2017).
    iii. **Secure Data Communication:** Secure data communication is essential so that the data exchanged are secured. Some methods, like digital signatures and public key encryption, are specifically used for this purpose.
    iv. **Reliability of Service:** Reliability refers to the probability that the system or its components will perform the specific functions for the stipulated time under the specified conditions. The aspect of reliability is dependent on the individual components of the system as well as on the system organization.
    v. **Legal Compliance:** The information that is obtained, used, processed, transmitted, or destroyed – all these things must be handled per the legislation of the country one is residing in.

Measures – Cybersecurity

General Security Measures

a. **Privileges and Rights:** The privileges and rights assigned to users, system operators, and administrators should be in line with their roles and responsibilities (Singh and Rathi 2021). Also, the categories of users and the access granted should be documented and kept safe.

b. **Data Encryption Technologies:** This should be developed when it is crucial to protect the privacy of sensitive information.
c. **Password:** The most widely used and authentic security measure is to have a password which is hard to guess. It is also imperative to change passwords on regular basis.
d. The installation of software to varied systems must be undertaken through the source media user only.
e. The right to modify and write access permissions must be disabled for all executive and binary files. Only few authorized individuals should be given the right to access the files, configured files, and directories.
f. The auditing and scanning of servers should happen at regular intervals, preferably daily, to remain alert and vigilant in case of any attacks or intrusions. A logbook must be kept, keeping note of all administrative activities.
g. The anti-virus system should be updated on regular basis. A full system scan should be encouraged on an everyday basis.

Access to Server

a. The system should be safeguarded against any illegal use, damage, or loss.
b. Accessing the server is something that is crucial; hence it should be limited to only the administration and few of the server operators.
c. Logging out of and shutting down the server are vital before leaving the office. Also, the server room must be kept locked, with access granted only to a limited population.
d. Installation of an uninterruptable power supply along with adequate battery backup is recommended to avoid any data loss or corruption due to power failure.

Physical Security

a. Biometric authentication must be a key to access the system via administrator login.
b. Additional human security forces should be ensured to protect the system from fire, theft, or power failures (Singh 2021). This is especially true if the system is operational 24/7.

Backup and Media Management

a. **Server Data Backup:** Backup plans should be defined per policies and procedures and must happen at the scheduled time.
b. **Storage of Backup Media:** Media backup should be saved (onsite/offsite) depending on the backup policy. It should be labeled properly for quick identification and retrieval.
c. **Backup Retention:** Backups should be retained/stored per the policy.
d. **Verification of Backup Integrity:** Backups taken should be verified to confirm the integrity and precision of the data.
e. **Media Identification and Traceability:** The backup of media must be marked by tags such as date, sever name, application name, and so on for speedy identification.
f. **Recovery from Backup Media:** Situations may arise where the server might crash due to a fault/defect in the hardware/software (Singh 2021). At such times, it is essential to have the methods of reloading the operating system and software and reinstallation of applications documented. This speeds the recovery process. The servers should also have hard disk recovery software and anti-virus software installed.
g. **Firewall Security:** This is a system that blocks unauthorized users from entering the intranet. The firewall is responsible for monitoring the activities of the internet and the other networks, looks for suspicious files/data, and prevents unsanctioned access. It is basically placed as the gateway server of the entire network. It inspects network packets

to decide whether they should be forwarded to the appropriate destination. The firewall is connected to the public through the router. These routers have several network interface units (NIUs), and each of these requires an internet protocol (IP) address. In short, the firewall is installed to perform the following functions:

i. Prevent an unlawful person from accessing the data.
ii. Prohibit access to unethical sites such as games, pornography, and many more.
iii. Filter email that may have suspicious intentions, like that pertaining to advertisements or from suspect sources.
iv. Forbid remote login into the computer.

Intrusion Detection Systems

This system complements other technologies related to security. It alerts the site administrator. The intrusion detection system allows identification of attacks handled by other components of security. It also makes efforts to signal the probability of new attacks that other components would have foreseen. It provides forensic information to detect the origin of cyberattacks. Thus, it makes hackers accountable for their actions and acts as a preventive measure to imminent attacks.

CONCLUSION: WHY DO WE NEED CYBERSECURITY?

In the year 2021, the world lost $6 trillion to cybercrimes. It is estimated that by the year 2025, cybercrime costs will amount to $10.5 trillion. With the increase in digitalization, problems pertaining to cybercrimes are also increasing. To address it strongly, a robust cybersecurity system is critically important. Cybersecurity systems are needed by all: individuals, companies, government organizations, non-government organizations, and educational institutes. Our future is dependent on digital technology and its evolution: devices will be upgraded, the number of users will increase, global supplies will increase, and data storage is bound to happen digitally. Thus, to minimize the risk of invasion, well-secured cybersecurity is vital.

REFERENCES

Algburi, B. Y. J., & Igaab, Z. K. (2021). "Defamation in English and Arabic: a pragmatic contrastive study." *International Linguistics Research* 4 (2): 31.

Aloul, F. A. (2012). "The need for effective information security awareness." *Journal of Advances in Information Technology* 3 (3): 176–83. doi:10.4304/jait.3.3.176-183.

Beran, T., & Li, Q. (2005). "Cyber-harassment: a study of a new method for an old behaviour." *Journal of Educational Computing Research* 32: 265–77.

Bhadury, S. (2022). "Child pornography in India: issues and challenges." *Journal of Positive School Psychology* 6(6): 6524–29. http://journalppw.com.

Borg, M. (2000). *UNDP Consultant. "The IT Global Revolution," Ministry of Information, Fiji.* Cambridge, MA: MIT Press.

Goni, O. (2022). "Cyber crime and its classification." *Journal of Multidisciplinary Engineering Technologies* 10 (1): 34–41.

Hinduja, S., & Patchin, J. W. (2008). "Cyberbullying: an exploratory analysis of factors related to offending and victimization." *Deviant Behavior* 29: 129–56.

Kumar, S., & Priyanka. (2019). "Cyber crime against women: right to privacy and other issues." *Journal of Legal Studies and Research* 5 (5): 154–166.

Laqueur, W., Smith, C., & Spector, M. (2002). "Cyberterrorism." In *Facts on File* (pp. 52–53). Oxford, UK: Oxford University Press.

Maurseth, P. B. (2018). "The effect of the Internet on economic growth: counter-evidence from cross-country panel data." *Economics Letters* 172: 74–77. doi:10.1016/j.econlet.2018.08.034.

Mohsin, K. (2021). "The internet and its opportunities for cybercrime – interpersonal cybercrime." Available at SSRN 3815973.

Pande, J. (2017). *Introduction to Cybersecurity.* Uttarakhand: Open University.

Patchin, J. W., & Hinduja, S. (2006). "Bullies move beyond the schoolyard: a preliminary look at cyberbully-ing." *Youth Violence and Juvenile Justice* 4: 148–69.

Pittaro, M. L. (2007). "Cyber stalking: an analysis of online harassment and intimidation." *International Journal of Cyber Criminology* 1: 180–97.

Rattan, J., & Rattan, V. (2019). *Cyber Laws and Information Technology*. New Delhi: Bharat Law House Private Limited.

Richard L. Doernberg, & Luc Hinnekens (2000). *Electronic Commerce and International Taxation*. New Delhi: Taxmann Allied Services Pvt. Ltd.

Singh, A. K. (2021). *E-mail Spoofer*. School of Computing Science and Engineering, New Delhi: Galgotias University. 4 (1): 739–748.

Singh, A. K., & Rathi, A. (2021). "Current scenario of cyber crime in India." *International Journal of Law Management & Humanities* 4: 739.

Srinath, B. J. (2006). *Cybersecurity Awareness for Protection of National Information Infrastructure*. New Delhi, India: Department of Information Technology. Ministry of Communication & Information Technology, Government of India.

Stevens, F., Nurse, J., & Arief, B. (2021). "Cyber stalking, cyber harassment, and adult mental health: a systematic review." *Cyberpsychology, Behaviour, and Social Networking* 24 (6): 367–76. http://doi.org/10.1089/cyber.2020.0253

Teresia, N. W. (2011). "Crime causes and victimization in Nairobi City slums." *International Journal of Current Research* 3 (12): 275–85.

Vallée, R. (2012). *Systems Science and Cybernetics – History of Cybernetics*, Vol. III. New York, NY, USA: Encyclopedia of Life Support Systems (EOLSS).

Verma, D. K., Verma, V., Pal, A., & Verma, D. (2022). "Identification and mitigation of cyber crimes against women in India." *International Journal of Advanced Research in Computer and Communication Engineering* 11 (4): 220–227. doi:10.17148/IJARCCE.2022.11440 2022

Vinnakota, D., Arafat, Y. S. M., & Kar, S. (2021). "Pornography and sexual violence against women in India: a scoping review." *Journal of Psychosexual Health* 3 (3): 216–221. doi:10.1177/26318318211023935–2021

Wilson, C. (2021). "Botnets, cybercrime, and cyberterrorism: vulnerabilities and policy issues for congress." www.everycrsreport.com. Retrieved 5 September 2021.

Zwilling, M. (2020). "Cybersecurity awareness, knowledge and behaviour: a comparative study." *Journal of Computer Information Systems* 62 (1): 82–97. doi:10.1080/08874417.2020.1712269

5 Cybersecurity Attack Case Studies
Lessons Learned

D. V. Manjula, Aisshwarya Nallamilli, and Dulkarnine Raseeda

CONTENTS

INTRODUCTION

An effort to manipulate computers, steal data, or use a computer system that has been infiltrated to launch more attacks is known as a cyberattack. Cybercriminals launch cyberattacks using phishing, man-in-the-middle attacks, ransomware, malware, and other methods (Rosch 2022). We classified the different types of attacks according to their features and elements that contributed to them, as shown through the analysis of related case studies. All organizations, including people, small enterprises, and huge corporations, are facing more cyber threats, which can result in losses of various severity. In addition to quickly spreading around the world, major cyberthreats that can cause enormous financial loss and damage to one's reputation have shockingly become common at many well-known businesses. This chapter focuses on understanding the features of various types of cyberattacks via a detailed investigation of case studies of real cyberattacks. Different forms of cyberattacks in industry are explained in Table 5.1.

TABLE 5.1

Examples of Cyberattacks

Phishing	Phishing is a method of disseminating fake emails that look to have come from a reliable source. The goal is to either infect the victim's computer with malware or to steal or get sensitive data, such as login and credit card information (Lee 2017). Phishing is a cyberthreat that is happening more often.
Malware	Malware is the term used to describe malicious software, which includes viruses, worms, ransomware, spyware, and other threats (Rosch 2022). Malware infiltrates a network by exploiting a weakness, frequently when a user opens a harmful link or email attachment that subsequently prompts the installation of risky software (Lessing 2020).
Denial-of-service attack	Denial-of-service attacks cause systems, servers, or networks to become overloaded with traffic, consuming bandwidth and other resources. Because of this, the system cannot satisfy valid requests (Lee 2017). This exploit is also carried out by attackers using several hacked devices.

(Continued)

DOI: 10.1201/9781003319887-5

TABLE 5.1 (*Continued*)

Phishing	Phishing is a method of disseminating fake emails that look to have come from a reliable source. The goal is to either infect the victim's computer with malware or to steal or get sensitive data, such as login and credit card information (Lee 2017). Phishing is a cyberthreat that is happening more often.
DNS tunneling	DNS tunneling sends non-DNS communication via the DNS protocol on port 53. Traffic using HTTP and other protocols is sent through DNS. There are several legitimate justifications to use DNS tunneling. However, DNS tunneling may be used for illegal activities as well. By masking outgoing traffic as DNS, it may be used to hide data that are typically shared through an internet connection.
MITM attacks	Man-in-the-middle (MITM) attacks are a type of cybersecurity vulnerability that let an attacker eavesdrop on data being sent back and forth between two users, networks, or computers (Lessing 2020). This kind of assault is referred to as a "man in the middle" attack because the assailant places himself in the middle of the two persons who are attempting to communicate. The attacker is really observing how the two persons interact.
SQL injection attack	Several things can happen if a SQL injection is accomplished, including the disclosure of sensitive information or the alteration or deletion of essential information. Additionally, an attacker can run administrator actions like a shutdown command, which can stop the database from working.

COUNTRY-WISE CYBERATTACKS

Some attackers target certain nations to harm those nations' public image or for other reasons. Figure 5.1 shows a list of the top 20 nations where cyberattacks have occurred (Lessing 2020). Since the United States is a well-developed nation with numerous significant companies that deal with the data of individuals all over the world, it is the most-targeted country for cyberattacks, accounting for roughly 25% of all cyberattack incidences (Columbus 2021). China is the second most vulnerable nation (9%) to cyberattacks. Every year, there are around 3% more cyberattacks in India (Columbus 2021).

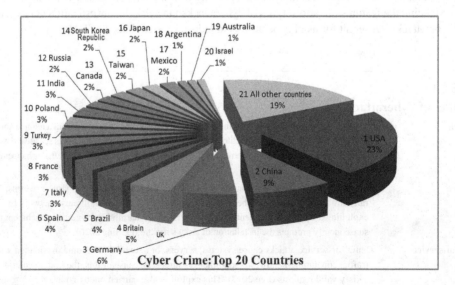

Cyber Crime: Top 20 Countries

FIGURE 5.1 Country-wise cyberattacks.

DISTRIBUTION OF TARGETS

Hackers can attack any department or even individual so that they can benefit by getting money or extract confidential data of a particular country organization. Figure 5.2 is a pie chart of the distribution of targets.

Figure 5.2 makes it clear that cyberattacks on people occur more frequently than on other types of targets. Attacker prey on people, stealing their personal information and extorting money from them. Industries, government administrations, and social security offices are the next most impacted sectors. Hackers can obtain all the data of a nation or the data of individuals worldwide from these types of companies.

COST OF CYBERCRIME

The expense of preventing cybercrimes is rising significantly each year, as shown in Table 5.2.

Here we explain seven case studies of domestic and foreign firms that have experienced cyberattacks. Anyone can learn how to avoid cyberattacks on businesses and organizations to some extent from these case studies. A summary of the cases and lessons learned is presented in Table 5.3.

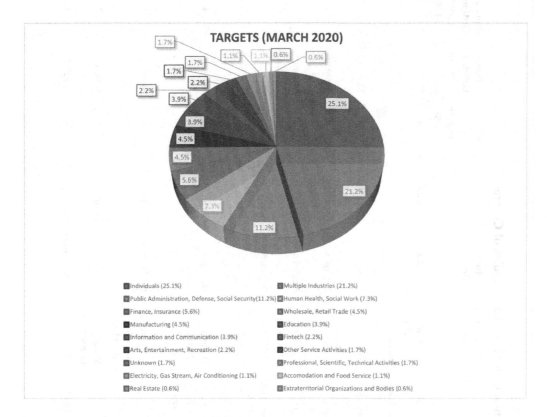

FIGURE 5.2   Distribution of targets in 2020.

TABLE 5.2
Evaluation Criteria for Case Studies of Cyberattacks

Cases	Cyberattack Types	Human Elements	Industry	Intensity of Finance (3–5)	Finance-Unrelated Intensity	Number of Customers Impacted (1–5)	End User Trust and Loyalty	Policy Issues	Training and Acknowledgment	Technology Adoption	Investment
Living Social Hack and Password Hack 2013	Password Attacks/SQL Injection	Negligence	Communication	4	PII	5	No	Yes	No	No	No
Stuxnet Attack through USB	APT	Negligence	Communication	3	Maturity	3	No	Yes	No	No	No
Hacktivism – Estonia Reputation	DOS	Negligence	Financial/Education	4	Reputation	4	No	Yes	No	Yes	No
Reputation	Password Attacks	Negligence	Retail	3	Maturity	3	No	Yes	No	No	No
TJX Cyberattack: WEP (Wired Equivalent Privacy) Attack	Malware	Negligence	Retail	5	PII	5	No	Yes	No	No	No
SQL Injection Attack at the Federal Reserve Bank	Database Attack.	Negligence	Financial	5	PII	4	No	Yes	Yes	No	Yes
Man in the Middle	Software/Browser-Based Attack	Negligence	Retail	4	Maturity	4	No	Yes	No	No	No
Tailgating	Social Engineering	Negligence	Retail	3	Maturity	3	No	Yes	Yes	No	No
Evernote DDOS Attack	DOS	Configuration	Retail	4	Credibility	3	No	Yes	Yes	No	No

Cases	Cyberattack Types	Human Elements	Industry	Intensity of Finance (3–5)	Finance-Unrelated Intensity	Number of Customers Impacted (1–5)	End User Trust and Loyalty	Policy Issues	Training and Acknowledgment	Technology Adoption	Investment
Adobe Password Breach 2013	Password Attacks	Configuration	Technology	4	Reputation	4	No	Yes	Yes	Yes	No
Dairy Queen International Data Breach	Malware	Configuration	Food & Agriculture	4	PII	4	No	Yes	No	No	No
Microsoft DOS Attack	DOS	Configuration	Technology	3	Reputation	5	Yes	No	Yes	Yes	Yes
Cyber espionage – Titan Rain Attack	APT	Configuration	Entertainment	4	Reputation	4	No	Yes	Yes	No	No
Flame Malware Attack	Malware	Configuration	Energy	4	Privacy	3	Yes	Yes	No	No	No
Smurf Attack	DOS	Configuration	Education	3	Credibility	3	Yes	Yes	Yes	Yes	No
Logic Bomb Attack in South Korea Banks and Broadcasting Organizations	Database Attack	Configuration	Financial/ Entertainment	3	Reputation	3	No	Yes	No	No	No
Bating	Social Engineering	Deceit	Transportation	3	Privacy	2	No	Yes	-	No	No
Stuxnet Cyber Warfare	Malware (Worm)	Ignorance	Nuclear	5	Reputation	4	No	Yes	No	No	Yes
RSA APT Attack	APT	Ignorance	Technology	3	Credibility	5	Yes	Yes	No	No	Yes
eBay Account Hack	Password Attacks	Ignorance	Technology	3	Reputation	4	No	Yes	No	No	No

(Continued)

TABLE 5.2 (*Continued*)

Cases	Cyberattack Types	Human Elements	Industry	Intensity of Finance (3–5)	Finance-Unrelated Intensity	Number of Customers Impacted (1–5)	End User Trust and Loyalty	Policy Issues	Training and Acknowledgment	Technology Adoption	Investment
German Steel Plant Attack	Social Engineering	Ignorance	Manufacturing	3	Maturity	3	No	Yes	No	No	No
Heartland Payment System Data Breach 2008	SQL Injection Attack	Ignorance	Financial	5	Credibility	5	Yes	No	No	Yes	Yes
Home Depot Data Access Attack	Malware (worm)	Ignorance	Retail	5	Reputation	5	No	Yes	No	No	No
UAV (Unmanned Aerial/Air Vehicles) Feed Interception	Cyber-Physical Attack	Ignorance	Communication	5	Maturity	5	No	Yes	No	No	No
Trojan Attack	Malware (Worm)	Ignorance	Financial	4	Maturity	4	No	Yes	No	No	No
South Korea Financial and TV Station Cyber-Attack – Summer of 2013	SocialEngineering/Malware	Ignorance	Entertainment/ Financial	3	Reputation	4	No	Yes	No		
Francophoned	DOS	Social Engineering	Financial	3	Maturity	3	No	Yes	No	No	No
Interactive Voice Response (IVR) or Phone Phishing	Social Engineering	Ignorance	Financial	3	Maturity	4	No	Yes	No	No	No

Cases	Cyberattack Types	Human Elements	Industry	Intensity of Finance (3–5)	Finance-Unrelated Intensity	Number of Customers Impacted (1–5)	End User Trust and Loyalty	Policy Issues	Training and Acknowledgment	Technology Adoption	Investment
Sony – The Wiper Malware Attack in 2014	Malware (Worm)	Negligence	Entertainment	5	Reputation	5	No	No	Yes	No	Yes
P.F. Chang's Sales Machine Hacked	Malware	Negligence	Food	4	Maturity	4	No	Yes	No	No	No
Epsilon Data Breach Attack	Malware	Negligence	Financial	5	Reputation	5	No	Yes	No	No	No

Note: Evaluating cyberattack case studies on a set of factors and their scales

Case Studies: All case studies on cyberattacks

Cyberattack Types: Categorization of cyberattacks

Human Elements: Ignorance, negligence, configuration, deceit

Industry: Technology, health, entertainment, advertisement, transportation, energy, food and agriculture, communication, nuclear, financial, manufacturing, retail, education

Intensity of Finance: Moderate (3) = less than $500k, High (4) =less than $1 million, Huge (5) = greater than $1 million

Finance-Unrelated Intensity: Biometric, health, reputation, credebility, maturity, privacy, PII (personally identifiable information)

# of Customers (Victims) Impacted: Low (1) = less than 50k, Moderate (2) = less than 100k, Moderate (3) = less than 250k, High (4) = less than 500k, Huge (5) = greater than 500k

End User Trust and Loyalty: Commitment to protecting the company's digital assets by adhering to cyber policies and buying into them inside the business

Policy Issues: Poor or nonexistent cybersecurity policy (Yes = policy problems or no policy, No = sound cybersecurity policy)

Training and Acknowledgement: Providing the staff with sufficient cyber threat education

Technology Adoption (for Cybersecurity Prevention): Efficient technology applied to protect from cyber threats

Investment: Enough funding (investment) on cybersecurity implementation/precautions

TABLE 5.3
Cases and Lessons Learned

Cases Considered	Lesson Learned (Good to Know)
1. Costa Rican Ransomware Attack	Organizations must regularly test their systems, strengthen or upgrade the security, and educate their staff on the many risks they face and their responsibilities.
2. Cyberattack on Air India Company	Organizations must secure the infected systems, hire outside data security experts, alert credit card companies, and change passwords for frequently used programs.
3. Phishing Attacks on CISOs and CIOs	Increase enterprise budgets for cybersecurity and the hiring of full-time cybersecurity personnel for the enterprises. Beware of malicious QR codes that may be used to access websites, make purchases, and more without the user's consent. Managed services providers (MSPs) are targeted by cyberattacks since all of the clients are exposed as soon as a hacker gains access to the internal system of the MSP. MSPs that have been compromised are being used by threat actors to execute cyberattacks against corporate systems.
4. Crypto Currency Mining Malware Attack on Operational Technology	All the systems in the firm should have high processor availability so that attacks may reduce to some extent. Organizations must test their security systems often.
5. WannaCry Ransomware Attack	All businesses, regardless of size, are significantly disrupted by ransomware. The threat environment has been dramatically changed by the quick evolution of ransomware. Only the greatest security can stop cyberattacks and keep companies safe, since deadly attacks often happen without warning.
6. DDoS Attack on Dyn	High levels of network security are ensured. Pay attention to the warning signs. Monitor network traffic continuously. Using several spread-out servers makes it challenging for hackers to target every server at once.
7. Google and Facebook	DMARC and trust graph are two automated strategies that are now being utilized to safeguard employees from spear phishing. Organizations are protected by DMARC from a certain kind of spear phishing assault. It is preferable to nothing.

CASE STUDY 1: COSTA RICAN RANSOMWARE ATTACK

Location	Costa Rica
Date	April 17, 2022
Attack Type	Cyberattack (Ransomware)

ABOUT THE COMPANY

Costa Rica Government Institutions affected by attack: On April 17, 2022 (UTC-6:00), a cyberattack began against approximately 30 government bodies, including the National Meteorological Institute, Ministry of Science, Innovation, Technology and Telecommunications (MICITT), State Internet Service Provider RACSA, Costa Rican Social Security Fund, Ministry of Labor and Social Security, Fund for Societies, and Ministry of Finance. The Costa Rican government ministry in charge of regulating the fiscal policy on public resources in accordance with the concepts of economy, efficiency, and effectiveness is the Ministry of

Finance. The majority of the country's public health system is under the control of the Costa Rican Social Security Fund. In Costa Rica, it plays a crucial role in the development of the country's national health policies as the administrator of healthcare facilities.

HOW THE ATTACK HAPPENED

The first wave of assaults was attributed to the pro-Russian organization Conti Group, which also requested a $10 million ransom for material taken from the Ministry of Finance that would contain private data on Costa Rican people's tax forms and businesses that do business there. The Hive Ransomware Group attacked the Costa Rican Social Security Fund on May 31, 2022, at daybreak, causing the organization to shut down all of its vital systems, including the Centralized Collection System and the Unique Digital Health File. The former is used to keep private medical data for patients who utilize Social Security, while the latter is used to collect insurance premiums from the public.

CONSEQUENCE

The productive sector suffered losses of almost $30 million per day because of the government being forced to turn off the computers used for tax declaration, import and export administration, and control. In the same way, the Ministry of Science, Innovation, Technology, and Telecommunications' websites were taken down from the internet (Young 2022).

CASE STUDY 2: CYBERATTACK ON AIR INDIA COMPANY

Location	India
Year	2021
Attack Type	Cyberattack (Data Breach)

ABOUT THE COMPANY

The national airline of India, Air India, has its main office in New Delhi. After the transaction was finalized by Air India Limited's previous owner, the Government of India, Talace Private Limited, a Special-Purpose Vehicle (SPV) of Tata Sons, acquired it. The fleet of Air India's Airbus and Boeing aircraft covers 102 domestic and international destinations. The Indira Gandhi International Airport in New Delhi serves as the airline's hub and other focal cities across India. With a share of the market of 18.6%, Air India is the biggest airline operating from India. More than 60 foreign sites on four continents are served by Air India. The airline became the 27th member of Star Alliance on July 11, 2014.

HOW THE ATTACK HAPPENED

In March, Air India said that SITA had alerted it to a cyberattack that occurred during the last week of February, alleging that it resulted in the exposure of some passengers' personal information. The airline informed the affected passengers that personal information recorded between August 26, 2011, and February 20, 2021, was subject to the cyberattack that compromised the data of millions of travelers from around the world. Name, date of birth, contact information, passport information, ticket information, frequent flyer data, and credit card information were among the data that had been compromised, according to the report (Threat Intelligence Team 2022).

CONSEQUENCE

On May 21, 2021, it was announced that Air India had been the target of a hack in which 4.5 million customers' personal information, including passport, credit card, birth date, name, and ticket information, had been compromised.

CASE STUDY 3: PHISHING ATTACKS ON CISOS AND CIOS

Location	Worldwide
Year	2021
Attack Type	Cyberattack (Supply Chain)

ABOUT THE COMPANY

CISOs and CIOs: The chief information security officer, or CISO, is a senior-level executive who oversees creating and implementing an information security program that includes guidelines and policies for safeguarding assets, systems, and communications within an organization from both internal and external threats. CIOs play a crucial role in an organization's digital transformation. For this job, new difficulties include big data analytics, cloud computing, mobile computing, and technical collaboration platforms.

HOW THE ATTACK HAPPENED

In 2020, chief information security officers, chief information officers, and their cybersecurity teams were under attack from a digital pandemic of breaches, ubiquitous supply chain assaults, and inventive uses of human engineering to enter company networks. Bad actors acted quickly to breach as many important corporate systems as they could by taking advantage of the instability the COVID-19 epidemic produced. Attackers began focusing on the millions of remote employees who had basic security measures and inadequate training to recognize hacking and phishing efforts, which led to an increase in data breaches. These types of attacks can be occurred by scanning malicious QR codes. The fastest-growing danger vector today is touchless commerce, or QR codes. To get access to victims' bank accounts, steal money, and infect devices with malware, fraudsters used social engineering with quickly made QR codes.

CONSEQUENCE

Supply chains in the real world are susceptible to cyberattacks. Cybercriminals and advanced persistent threat (APT) groups are impersonating trusted entities (pharmaceutical companies and healthcare providers, for example) to obtain privileged access credentials in attacks against the COVID-19 vaccine supply chain, according to the threat analysis from the US Department of Homeland Security's Cybersecurity & Infrastructure Security Agency (CISA) (Threat Intelligence Team 2022). Attackers use methods including phishing, spreading malware, posing as respectable websites by employing COVID-19-related phrases, and exploiting remote access and teleworking infrastructure. A global phishing campaign targeted the COVID-19 vaccine cold chain in 2020, according to IBM Security X-threat Force's intelligence task force monitoring COVID-19 vaccine cyber threats.

CASE STUDY 4: CRYPTOCURRENCY MINING MALWARE ATTACK ON OPERATIONAL TECHNOLOGY

Year	2018
Location	Europe
Attack Type	Cyberattack (Cryptocurrency Mining Malware)

ABOUT THE COMPANY

Manufacturing and industrial equipment are monitored and managed by operational technology (OT). Since we began using machinery and equipment driven by electricity in industries, buildings, transportation systems, the utility business, and so on, OT has existed – considerably longer than IT or information technology.

HOW THE ATTACK HAPPENED

The operational technology network of a water utility in Europe was affected by cryptocurrency mining malware attack. It was detected by the critical infrastructure security firm, Radiflow. They announced this was the first known instance of mining malware being used against an industrial control system. Connecting iSID to the network was the first step in the process of identifying and removing malware from the utility's SCADA network (Turner 2021). Radiflow's multi-engine platform for keeping an eye on SCADA networks is called iSID. Six engines are included for asset management, topological abnormalities, and identifying known vulnerabilities. On January 21, 2018, a Radiflow Smart-Probe was used to link the network to the iSID Intrusion Detection System. The Smart-Probe enables the deployment of iSID at a central location and the transmission of mirrored network traffic to iSID through a secure IP tunnel via diodes (Threat Intelligence Team 2022).

CONSEQUENCE

The researchers point out that the virus was created to operate covertly in the background while mining the cryptocurrency Monero with the least possible impact on the system. The miner was also made to avoid being flagged by security scanners and other protection measures and even to deactivate them. An industrial control program may stop, pause, or even crash because of such a malware assault, possibly impairing the capacity of an operator to run a plant (Turner 2021).

CASE STUDY 5: WANNACRY RANSOMWARE ATTACK

Date	12 May, 2017
Location	Worldwide
Attack Type	Cyberattack (Ransomware)

ABOUT THE COMPANY

In May 2017, the WannaCry ransomware crypto worm launched a global attack against machines running the Microsoft Windows operating system, encrypting data and demanding ransom payments in the Bitcoin cryptocurrency. The National Security Agency (NSA) of the United States used EternalBlue, a Windows-specific vulnerability, to disseminate it.

HOW THE ATTACK HAPPENED

EternalBlue was secured and made available by the Shadow Brokers a month before to the attack. Even while Microsoft had previously released remedies to close the vulnerability, a significant percentage of WannaCry's spread came from businesses that either hadn't implemented the fixes or were using obsolete Windows systems (Quader and Janeja 2021). Although many of these patches were not applied because their significance was not understood, they were crucial for enterprises' cybersecurity. Some have cited the requirement for round-the-clock operation, resistance to the possibility of previously functioning apps malfunctioning due to patch updates, and a lack of staff or time to install them, among other justifications.

CONSEQUENCE

On May 12, 2017, the attack started at 07:44 UTC and was stopped at 15:03 UTC by the registration of a kill switch that Marcus Hutchins had identified. The kill switch stopped WannaCry from encrypting or propagating to previously affected systems. According to estimates, the assault infected more than 200,000 machines in 150 different countries, causing hundreds of millions to billions of dollars in losses. In August 2018, a new WannaCry variant compelled Taiwan Semiconductor Manufacturing Company (TSMC) to temporarily shut down several its chip-fabrication operations (Quader and Janeja 2021). In the most cutting-edge facilities of TSMC, the virus spread to 10,000 machines.

CASE STUDY 6: DDOS ATTACK ON DYN COMPANY

Date   October 21, 2016
Location   North America and Europe, mainly the Eastern United States
Attack Type   Cyberattack (Distributed Denial of Services)

ABOUT THE COMPANY

Dyn was a provider of solutions for monitoring, controlling, and optimizing online infrastructure as well as domain registration services and email products. It also provided web application security services.

HOW THE ATTACK HAPPENED

The domain name system (DNS) provider Dyn was the target of three separate distributed denial-of-service attacks on October 21, 2016. Large portions of users in Europe and North America were unable to access important Internet platforms and services as a result of the assault. Although no proof was offered, the hacker collectives Anonymous and New World Hackers claimed responsibility for the attack (Mukul 2022).

CONSEQUENCE

Customers of various web properties were unable to access the internet on Friday, October 21, due to a distributed denial of service attack on internet performance management company Dyn. As a DNS service, Dyn assisted several significant businesses in resolving domain names to specific IP addresses. Brands including Twitter, Amazon, Reddit, Netflix, and others experienced service outages several times during the day as a result of the attack (Mukul 2022).

CASE STUDY 7: GOOGLE AND FACEBOOK

Date	2013–2015
Location	Worldwide
Attack Type	Cyberattack (Phishing)

ABOUT THE COMPANY

Google is an American multinational technology firm with an emphasis on consumer electronics, cloud computing, computer software, quantum computing, e-commerce, and search engine technology. Because of its competitiveness, data collection, and technological advantages in artificial intelligence, it has been referred to as the "most powerful corporation in the world." The American corporation Meta Platforms is the owner of the social media and networking website Facebook. Devices with Internet connectivity, such as laptops, tablets, and smartphones, can access Facebook. After registration, users may create a profile that contains information about them. They may exchange text, pictures, and other types of material with other users who have accepted to be their "friends" or, depending on the privacy settings, with the whole public.

HOW THE ATTACK HAPPENED

Evaldas Rimasauskas followed the steps to create a fictitious company and send phishing emails to Google and Facebook workers. According to the US Attorney's Office for the Southern District of New York, the scam ultimately defrauded those multibillion-dollar businesses out of more than $100 million in total between 2013 and 2015, and in 2016, prosecutors accused Rimasauskas of setting up a firm under the name of Taiwan-based Quanta Computer, which really transacts business with Facebook and Google. The only member of the board of directors of the fictitious company was Rimasauskas, who also "opened, managed, and controlled multiple accounts at banks" in Cyprus and Latvia, according to the authorities (Newma 2018).

CONSEQUENCE

In the scam, Rimasauskas and his cohorts created forgeries that seemed to have been sent by employees of the actual Quanta in Taiwan by using fake email accounts. Phishing emails with fake invoices were sent to employees at Facebook and Google, who "often conducted multimillion-dollar transactions" with Quanta; as a result, these individuals deposited more than $100 million to the bank accounts of the fictional company. It is evident from the accompanying line graph that there has been a fast rise in the expense of combating cybercrime. This cost covers the money lost by the businesses, the money spent on loss recovery, and the money used to implement safety measures for avoiding future cyberattacks (Macej 2016).

CONCLUSION

The frequency and severity of cyberattacks are increasing. Some findings from the case studies are: 1) ignorance and carelessness, two factors involving people, appear to be connected to most of the cyber risks out of the four primary human variables. 2) Along with technology, health, and energy, the entertainment, retail, and financial institutions are the major targets of hackers. 3) Cyberattacks typically have significant effects on customers. The organization's reputation is at risk, and there might be significant financial damage. 4) For protection against cyber threats, having a solid cybersecurity policy is essential. To put it another way, to keep digital assets secure, we must make sufficient security investments, train our staff, establish and enforce a robust cybersecurity strategy, and, most importantly, adopt and maintain cutting-edge technology to combat both new and old security threats. Strong security policies may be created and adopted to assist raise awareness, offer chances for education, and develop mechanisms to thwart cyberattacks.

REFERENCES

Louis Columbus, "Top 10 cybersecurity lessons learned one year into the pandemic", March 11, 2021. Available online: https://venturebeat.com/2021/03/11/top-10-cybersecurity-lessons-learned-one-year-into-the-

Timothy B. Lee, "The WannaCry ransomware attack was temporarily halted. But it's not over yet", May 15, 2017. Available online: www.vox.com/new-money/2017/5/15/15641196/wannacry-ransomware-windows-xp

Marlese Lessing, "Case study: WannaCry ransomware", July 9, 2020. Available online: www.sdxcentral.com/security/definitions/what-is-ransomware/case-study-wannacry-ransomware/

Grace Macej, "DDoS attack on Dyn took down the bulk of the internet on Friday", October 24, 2016. Available online: https://blog.avast.com/ddos-attack-on-dyn-took-down-the-bulk-of-the-internet-on-friday

Pranav Mukul, "Explained: What is the Air India data breach that has hit its customers?", August 10, 2022. Available online: https://indianexpress.com/article/explained/explained/air-india-sita-data-breach-explained-7325501/"

Lily Hay Newma, "Now cryptojacking threatens critical infrastructure, too", February 12, 2018. Available online: www.wired.com/story/cryptojacking-critical-infrastructure/

Faisal Quader and Vandana P. Janeja, "Insights into organizational security readiness: Lessons learned from cyberattack case studies", *Journal of Cybersecurity and Privacy* 1 (4): 638–659. November 11, 2021.

Carla Rosch, "A massive cyberattack in Costa Rica leaves citizens hurting". Available online: https://restof-world.org/2022/cyberattack-costa-rica-citizens-hurting/

Threat Intelligence Team, "The Conti ransomware leaks", March 1, 2022. Available online: https://blog.malwarebytes.com/threat-intelligence/2022/03/the-conti-ransomware-leaks/

Dwan M. Turner, "Air India's massive data breach – following best practices for data security is more important than ever", Cryptomathic.com June 21, 2021. https://www.cryptomathic.com/news-events/blog/air-indias-massive-data-breach-compliance-to-major-rules-of-data-security-of-more-important-than-ever

Kelli Young, "Cyber case study: The Mirai DDoS attack on Dyn", January 10, 2022. Available online: https://coverlink.com/case-study/mirai-ddos-attack-on-dyn/

6 Towards a Cybersecurity Awareness Program for Non-Technical Audiences in Malaysia

Shafiq Ul Rehman and Selvakumar Manickam

CONTENTS

INTRODUCTION

In today's world, online scams have been recorded as one of the main problems faced by many Internet users. According to Bernama (2019), statistics from Malaysia Computer Emergency Response Team (MyCERT) and Cybersecurity Malaysia (CSM) indicate that cyber fraud is the most reported cybercrime since 2008, indicating that Internet users in the country are less aware of the issue. We can conclude that, before these advanced technologies, there was cheating and fraud, but the number of cases was less compared to online scams, and online scams will be on the top list every year in Malaysia.

A report by Bernama (2019) indicated that 5123 cyber fraud cases were reported in 2018, and 3127 cases were reported in 2019 in Malaysia. It shows that many people are being cheated online even though some of them are educated and know well on how to do business online or perform online transactions. The increasing daily use of online social network (OSN) platforms around the world leads to more threats to information privacy in this attractive environment (Jain et al., 2021; Al-Charchafchi et al., 2019). While users can get many benefits by using OSN services, users have many concerns regarding their information privacy at the same time (Mosca & Such, 2022). Lately, several online scams in Malaysia are spreading uncontrolled and becoming widespread, especially

DOI: 10.1201/9781003319887-6

on social media platforms like Facebook, Twitter, and WhatsApp. Online scam texts were delivered through WhatsApp. Our expert interviews have demonstrated that platforms such as Facebook and Instagram have rapidly become the primary channels for online scams.

Malaysia is one of the countries, cities, or regions with a high risk of online fraud (Mokhsin et al., 2018). This shows that Malaysians have high chances to be cheated by scammers or be the victims for online fraud. This is due to more technologies and advancement being introduced and applied in developing countries, including Malaysia. Therefore, there are high chances for people to fall prey to online scams.

Usually, online buyers have to make a payment before they can receive their products. However, there is no guarantee that products that have been purchased will be sent in good condition or even be sent to the customer in the first place. A study done by Mokhsin et al. (2018) said that most victims in Malaysia filed police complaints of not obtaining goods they had paid for, receiving products late, receiving products that were not original and not as promoted, and failure to include product and sales terms and conditions. They also stated the number of online shopping scams in Selangor, where the information was given by Selangor Commercial Crimes Investigation Department Deputy Chief Supt Ng Keok Chai. In 2012 there were about 445 cases reported compared to 2010 with 247 cases. He further added that most internet fraud occurs when money paid into the seller's account is transferred to another person's bank account. From January to May 2016, Selangor recorded 302 cases, with total losses of RM1.5 million.

According to federal police Commercial Crime Investigation Department (CCID) director Datuk Mazlan Mansor, the number of online victims of cybercrime, especially online scams, has risen since 2017. He also mentioned that in 2017, losses incurred through these crimes totaled RM266 million, and the figure went up to RM398 million in 2018. In addition, he stated that the number increased in 2019, where RM64 million losses were recorded in the first three months (Tan et al., 2021). This clearly shows that the number of online victims in Malaysia has increased.

Besides that, many Malaysians have bee victims of online dating scams, where scammers obtain money by creating fake profiles on an online dating site. The victims in this kind of cases are both male and female. Deputy Home Minister Datuk Azis Jamman mentioned that, out of the 1303 parcel scam or love scam cases reported in 2019, there were 1070 female victims and 230 male victims, with a total loss of RM67,737,419.38. Obviously good and convincing persuading skills or messages would have caused many Malaysians to fall into the trap. Cyber criminals also take empathy and sincere feelings into consideration, which helps to distract victims from making sound decisions about the content of emails or online messages (Hai-Jew, 2020).

The motivation for the awareness program is to educate all Malaysians using the Internet to strengthen the awareness level of non-technical users. If there are local communities that are not adequately educated, their technological devices may remain unprotected. In this study, we set out to understand the current level of security awareness among common Internet users in Malaysia and develop a program that will help raise their awareness. Therefore, this research seeks to address the following questions:

RQ1: What is the level of security awareness that is influenced by the knowledge, behavior, and attitude of Malaysia non-technical users?

RQ2: How can an online scam awareness toolkit raise cybersecurity awareness among Malaysian non-technical users?

The main objectives of this research are:

1. To observe the pattern of security awareness of non-technical audience before completing the program.
2. To assess the effectiveness of the program in raising awareness among non-technical audiences.

This research work has several contributions. We designed an online survey that includes pre- and post-tests to fulfill our study goals and administered it to (a non-technical) audience on a website.

Using an online scam awareness toolkit will help people to understand and respond better to online scams. This can aid in the resolution of concerns as well as the reduction of cybercrime. Moreover, this research will benefit researchers who want to improve people's understanding and awareness of online scams. Also, this is the first toolkit or web application developed to raise awareness of internet scams. As a result, it is intended that this toolkit will help not only the participants in this study but everyone in the world. Finally, this toolkit aims to aid in the mitigation of the country's negative effects from online scams. In the following sections, we provide a literature review, applied research methods, and implementation process. Then in later sections, we present the results and analysis, recommendations, research limitations, and future research directions.

LITERATURE REVIEW

This section discusses the background information of issues related to online scams, including understanding, awareness, and the spread of online scams. This section also discusses the findings of various studies that have attempted to raise public awareness and provide possible solutions to decrease the spread of online scams. A scam is defined as fraud or a dishonest scheme where people are cheated, and the aim of scammers will typically be financial gain. The same meaning applies to online scams where scammers use the Internet as the main tool to gain benefits by defrauding Internet users. Previously, scammers used Short Message Service (SMS) messages and phone calls to defraud people, but as technology has advanced, scammers are being smarter and making use of Internet services or software to earn money. Scammers are also called cybercriminals, and they can find victims through dating apps; email accounts; social networking sites like Facebook, Instagram, and WeChat; or other social media sites where they are able to fool victims without revealing their actual details.

An article written by Bliss (2021) mentions that many effective Internet scams have the same outcome: scam victims lose money or do not receive the funds promised by the scammer. There are a few different kinds of online scams, such as phishing, fake shopping websites, quick-money promises, overpayment scams, Facebook impersonation scams, and romance scams. According to Button et al. (2014), there are syntactic (technical), semantic (social), or blended (both) scams. Syntactic scams involve the scammer exploiting a technical weakness to gather personal information by using malware such as viruses, keyloggers, worms, spyware, and trojan horses. Blended uses invariably involve a problem created on a computer where the scammers then create situations and get money or personal information from the victims. Atkins and Huang (2013) stated that social engineering can be further divided into two different categories: computer-based and human-interaction–based deception. Usually, background research would be done before an attack; the scammer would gather all the information and plan well. In computer-based deception, scammers depend on technology to cheat the victim, while the human-interaction approach is based on human interaction.

Online shopping is a trend nowadays. Many people, including teenagers, working parents, and even students, prefer to shop online because they can save time and energy. Usually, these groups of people are the victims, as scammers can create fake accounts and easily cheat them. Consumers may be at risk from online shopping scams. There are third parties who take advantage of the convenience. They set up a false account with a fake name and fake business that seem authentic to get customers to buy from them (Dabrowski & Janikowski, 2018). People make a payment and wait for the arrival of the product; unfortunately, they do not receive the right product, or they may receive a lower-quality product or something that is totally different. It is quite difficult to trace the seller, as the purchasing was done online.

Dabrowski and Janikowski (2018) comment that it's important to remember the highly skilled nature of offenders who will use social engineering techniques to manipulate and exploit individual vulnerabilities. Good persuasion skills can be another factor that help online scammers fool people. While persuading someone, it is very important to use the proper words, as this can make people have trust and confidence in you. Therefore, a very good potential scammer will make sure he or she has good persuading skills. Their politeness is usually intended to gain the victims' trust and make them feel comfortable talking to them. This has been proven in research by Naksawat et al. (2016). They stated that there are multiple kinds of persuasive statements provided by scammers to persuade victims, such as, "The Internet led me to your e-mail address in search of a reliable person who could help me. . . . He advised me, however, to provide a trustee who would act on my behalf." Hence, the scammer will use all the possible tricks that he or she can to achieve their goals.

According to a study by Atkins and Huang (2013), using social engineering, scammers skillfully manipulate human weakness to carry out emotional attacks on innocent victims. Additionally, they found that social engineers used both positive and negative statements to entice readers to fall for their scams. Thus, scammers use e-mail to exploit users' emotions, such as enthusiasm, pity, and terror. The employment of authoritative and, in some cases, emotive persuasions prompts readers to let their guard down when it comes to potential dangers. Everyone could be a victim of fraud, according to Button and Cross (2017), if approached in the right way at the right time by a highly competent offender. There are various factors that contribute to the success of online scams. Usually, for every problem that arises, there are reasons the problem continues or becomes worse. There are factors that could contribute to the success of online scams, such as the attitude of the consumer or public. Consumers are so naive that they believe all the online information and buy things without verifying them. In other words, these groups of people can be easily cheated because of their carelessness and blind trust. Some even spend thousands buying things online and at the end complain of not receiving the products or items that they have bought or receiving the wrong products.

As evidence, Mokhsin et al. (2018) cited statements made by *Malaysian Digest* in an article that stated that many of the reports were about not receiving products consumers had paid for, receiving products late, receiving products that were unoriginal and not as advertised, and failing to provide terms and conditions about products and sales. There are also people who are so innocent and helpful that they are willing to help people, even a stranger. Most of the conversation will be on the Internet or via phone calls where the fraudsters will seek financial help. Atkins and Huang (2013) discovered that most people are usually helpful in attitude and tend to believe in this type of attack, and they are often fooled into being the victims of online fraud. Also, scammers being smart enough to create a fake profile where no one can trace them easily, such as on Facebook or Instagram, has made more people their victims.

In a statement in a national newspaper, police said victims of the scam are being misled by fake Facebook accounts which appear to belong to their friends or family members (Lawrence, 2021). Scammers can use the environment of social media to trap their victims by creating a fake profile that cannot be traced. Mokhsin et al. (2018) commented that it's important to remember the highly skilled nature of offenders, who will use their social engineering techniques to manipulate and exploit individual vulnerabilities. This shows that people can fall easily to scammers who have planned well and chosen the potential victims.

In order not to be caught by the police, thieves use different methods and locations to steal. It was proved by Potter (2019) that robbery is a risky business, and robbers are usually nervous. They do not transport money at the same time every day and do not use the same route every time. Hence, the same thing will be done by scammers. They will change their methods to get money. Usually, they will think of any possible methods that could benefit them and make sure they are not trapped. For example, Cross (2016) stated that scammers asked some victims to buy prepaid debit cards and forward these on rather than sending cash through a remittance agency or bank transfer. Offenders still receive something of monetary value.

METHODS

Research designs such as "before and after" or "pre-experimental" methods are also known as pretest and post-test designs. This design involves selecting participants, pre-testing them, and finally exposing them to a learning intervention. It is evident that improvements have been made in terms of results and actions. In most evaluations, some type of measurement is required before and after the intervention (Marsden & Torgerson, 2012).

A pre-test design extends the post-test model without equivalents, and it is one of the simplest approaches to assessing the efficacy of a procedure. Two groups are addressed in this model, and the results are presented at the end. It is worthwhile to note that the control group is not treated but undergoes the same test at the same time as the treatment group (Shuttleworth, 2009). The term survey research refers to the process of collecting data through an inquiry on a person, a document, a mobile device, or the Internet. Surveys are one of the most common types of investigations that collect data directly from the source. Other parties can access the data produced because of secondary research. Survey research is used to learn about the opinions, abilities, and sentiments of certain groups of people, which are generally chosen for demographic sample objectives. According to Johnson and Christensen (2019), a "pre-post-test" design is 61% more effective than a control group in psychological, educational, and behavioral treatment research.

This research is based on a survey titled "Cybersecurity Awareness Program for Non-Technical Malaysian Users" to investigate and determine the level of online cybercrime awareness among Malaysians. All the information gathered is kept strictly confidential. During the collecting, storage, and dissemination of research materials, the responses were kept anonymous. For cybersecurity awareness to be implemented effectively, it must include all people with access to the internet, including those using smartphones. An effective cybersecurity awareness campaign must ensure that it is reaching women and girls. It is not sufficient to argue that the technology is gender neutral and women and girls are targeted no differently from men in technical campaign materials. Inclusion in the benefits of the enhanced protection that comes from adopting cybersecurity messages contributes to their economic empowerment and lessens cyber bullying, as well as making the campaign more effective. Cybersecurity is maximized when everyone adopts cybersecurity practices. Therefore, we took these things into consideration while designing our cybersecurity awareness program, and we made sure it reached the non-technical audience regardless of gender, disabilities, language, and cultural diversity.

A pre-evaluation of selected responses was conducted prior to using the toolkit. As a follow-up to the toolkit's implementation, the same respondents were evaluated according to the same criteria by which they were pre-assessed. The toolkit's effectiveness in raising online scam awareness was determined by the outcomes of the post-evaluation. Surveys were conducted to learn more about people's perspectives on cybersecurity awareness. The data for the study were collected via a questionnaire. The study was entitled "Survey on Cybersecurity Awareness." A quantitative survey was used to collect the information. Changes in cybersecurity awareness were measured using a pre-test-post-test methodology. A quantitative research approach was chosen for this study. Users were able to search for information from digital sources, such as the Internet or other services, which necessitates using quantitative research methods. As a result, discrete quantitative analysis allows scientists to use data and information concepts within data and information theory quickly and effectively (Adhiarso et al., 2018).

In an online form, 18 questions about people's understanding and use of social media associated with online scams were produced. The responses to this questionnaire were utilized in the study's data gathering. The questions' overall approach was based on previous measurements and techniques. The survey was distributed throughout Malaysia using an online form with the goal of collecting 381 responses. After receiving 381 responses, the data were analyzed. Two hundred respondents participated in the pre- and post-tests. In a pre-test, respondents were tested on their awareness of online scams without having accessed information about them, while in the post-test, they were tested on their awareness of online scams after gaining information.

RESEARCH DESIGN

This study uses multiple-choice surveys, a Likert scale, and dichotomous questions. One of the most popular sorts of closed-ended questions is multiple-choice questions, which present respondents with a set of specific response alternatives as possible answers. Multiple-choice questions are used by researchers in surveys to collect data on respondents' activities, beliefs, and demographic attributes. When using multiple-choice questions, response options can be arranged or unordered, and researchers can give respondents the option of selecting only one answer or multiple answers. The Likert scale is a special sort of summary scale composed of a number of ranking elements in an ordered category. Respondents in this study were particularly instructed to choose a scale of agreement or disapproval. Also, researchers use dichotomous questions to obtain a clear understanding of the respondents' experiences, qualities, and opinions about a particular subject. These question types play a pivotal role in uncovering their choices.

There are two sections of questions in the questionnaire, listed in the following. The focus was assessing respondents' experiences with and awareness about online scams. The study examined how individuals respond to online scams, as well as their beliefs about news sources. Furthermore, these questions examine respondents' ability to differentiate between genuine and fake offers as well as their awareness of current events. Individuals and society might suffer negative consequences if they are unaware of how to recognize online scams and how to prevent contributing to their growth. These questions are intended to gauge respondents' views on the prevalence of online scams and how to spot them on social media.

Scam Awareness

The aim of this section was to measure respondents' knowledge and experience with online scams. The purpose of the scam's knowledge questionnaire is to see if the respondents are aware of the veracity of the news on the existing fact-checking website. Its purpose is to assess users' knowledge and awareness of online scams, as well as their ability to recognize them.

Scenarios

In this section, the focus was assessing respondents' experiences with and awareness about online scams. The focus was on what individuals do when they come across an online scam, as well as their confidence and trust in the news they read. These questions are also intended to assess respondents' ability to discriminate between genuine and fake offers, as well as their awareness of current events. Individuals and society might suffer negative consequences if they are unaware of how to recognize online scams and how to prevent contributing to their growth. These questions are intended to gauge respondents' views on the prevalence of online scams and how to spot them on social media.

Survey

Surveys are one of the most common types of investigations that collect data directly from the source. Other parties can access the data produced because of secondary research. Survey research is used to learn about the opinions, abilities, and sentiments of certain groups of people, which are generally chosen for demographic sample objectives. It was vital to determine the users' comprehension and perspective of online scams before using the toolkit, so a survey was created. This research is based on survey questions to investigate and determine the level of online scam awareness among non-technical Malaysian students and employees. All the information gathered was kept strictly confidential. During the collecting, storage, and dissemination of research materials, the responses were kept anonymous. Prior to using the toolkit, the suggested web application conducted a pre-evaluation on the level of understanding for selected responses. The cybersecurity awareness questionnaire is presented in Table 6.1.

Following the toolkit's implementation, the same respondents were evaluated using the same criteria as the pre-assessment. The toolkit's effectiveness in raising online scam awareness was

TABLE 6.1
Cybersecurity Awareness Questionnaire

Number	Questions	Questions Type
1.	Do you share your personal information when requested by the authority or any business entity?	Scam Awareness
2.	Do you perform a background check on the company or individual seeking your personal information?	Scam Awareness
3.	In your opinion, is online scam a major issue in Malaysia?	Scam Awareness
4.	What is your opinion on Malaysians' online scam awareness?	Scam Awareness
5.	How concerned are you about being scammed over the Internet?	Scam Awareness
6.	Have you ever been contacted by a scammer? If yes, which platform did they use to approach you? (Choose all that apply)	Scam Awareness
7.	If you have ever been involved in a financial-related scam, was it:	Scam Awareness
8.	Have you ever been a victim of an online scam? If yes, what type of scam were you a victim of? (Choose all that apply)	Scam Awareness
9.	You purchase a drill for a friend from a small online hardware store. The seller sends you a message that says your purchase did not go through due to issues with the site. However, he requests that you send your billing details to him via email, and he will ensure quicker, one-day shipping in return for the hassle. Should you email him your billing details?	Scenarios
10.	You receive a Facebook message from a friend you have not been in touch with for ages. The message says, "Hey, this is very funny. Check it out: http://bit.ly.bV7l22cb." Do you click the link?	Scenarios
11.	You receive a call from the court. The officer tells you that you have a pending case, and you need to make a payment to avoid the case from being brought to court. The officer provides the bank details for the payment to be done. Should you make the payment?	Scenarios
12.	You receive an SMS from a number you don't recognize. The message says, "Please login into your EPF account and update your information if necessary." Do you think this is a legitimate SMS from EPF?	Scenarios
13.	There is no way to disprove the notion that Malaysians are particularly susceptible to Internet scams. Finding out the underlying reasons is necessary to protect our fellow citizens. Please answer "yes" to this question for us to ascertain that you are reading and responding as a responsible citizen.	Scenarios
14.	You signed up online to get email updates and vouchers from a local business you shop at frequently. You later receive an email from them asking you to click the provided link to verify your email, even though you have already permitted them. Do you click the link?	Scenarios
15.	You received an email from your bank. The email states that your account has been compromised, and you must change your password immediately. The bank provides a link to allow you to change your password. Do you proceed to change your password?	Scenarios
16.	You receive an email from the Inland Revenue Board (IRB) saying you have unpaid taxes. The notice says RM20,000 for the most recent tax year. The email instructs payment to be made via the IRB's portal, JomPay, or by visiting the relevant branch. Do you think this is legitimate?	Scenarios
17.	Someone got in touch with you on the dating network, and soon, you two started communicating frequently. Eventually, soon enough, this person shares a story with you and asks you for money due to medical bills, expenses for transport, the death of a family member, or some other crisis. Will you help this person and transfer money?	Scenarios
18.	You receive a winning letter, email, or text message informing you of a sure thing, such as a lottery prize. This message seems to be from persons or organizations with established reputations. However, this prize requires you to purchase a voucher, incur a deposit, or provide your banking information to claim it. Will you go ahead and make a payment as asked?	Scenarios

determined by the outcomes of the post-evaluation. Surveys were conducted to learn more about people's perspectives on internet scams. The data for the study were collected via a questionnaire. A quantitative survey was used to collect the information. Changes in online scam awareness were measured using a pretest-posttest methodology. The quantitative research approach was chosen for this thesis because of the study's scope. The Internet information storage system allows users to search for information using digital sources such as the Internet or other services, which necessitates the use of quantitative research methodologies. Therefore, the use of discrete quantitative analyses enables scientists to use digital data/information concepts as rapidly or effectively as appropriate in the type of data and information theory and is academically responsible (Adhiarso et al., 2018). The survey's results and data were analyzed, and people responded to the survey. After receiving the findings, users discovered misconceptions, unknown facts, and basic knowledge that they were unaware of. The data were then gathered to better comprehend the misconceptions and perceptions of online scams, as well as to raise awareness.

TOOLKIT USED

Two tools were used in this research, an online form and Wix.com (a web site builder). The questionnaire and test were designed, verified, and distributed to respondents via an online form. The survey was conducted by using an online form since it is both cost and time effective. Furthermore, the online form spreadsheet was pre-populated with survey and test replies, making data collection and analysis easy. The online form was easy to use, the survey could be made and analyzed instantly on mobile phones easily and effectively. When the survey form is completed, it can be emailed; embedded on a website; or shared on social media sites like Facebook, WhatsApp, or Twitter by giving the URL in a conversation or email. In this research, the online form was used to distribute the survey. Individual responses can be seen via the "Responses" tab, and the survey results can be obtained instantly and presented with charts and graphs. This study was designed to gather responses from many states in Malaysia, making it easy to use internet resources.

Wix.com was used as a podium to develop the toolkit model in this study. Wix.com is very helpful, as it builds a website quickly and easily. Wix.com is a one-stop shop for creating websites. It assists in the development of websites using its software and tools, and the websites are hosted on its servers. It's also an online platform that allows us to create our own websites without having to know how to code. Wix.com offers two types of website builders: traditional template-based platforms and more advanced artificial intelligence (AI) platforms (Carmichael, 2019).

In this study, all information, such as the home page, introduction page, and pre-test and post-test pages, were created using this platform. SPSS is software used by researchers to analyze complex statistical data. Hence, SPSS was used for data analysis. The SPSS Visualization Development Program allows researchers to easily construct a range of visualizations, such as density charts and radial boxplots, using their data. SPSS also offers data management tools that enable researchers to categorize cases, create derived data, and reshape files.

RESULTS AND ANALYSIS

There are two sections in the online scams awareness questionnaire to identify whether respondents were fully aware of online scams. The sections are scam awareness and scenarios.

SCAM AWARENESS

About 154 out of 381 respondents always share their personal information when requested by an authority or any business entity. Figure 6.1 shows that 40.4% share their personal information with untrusted organizations.

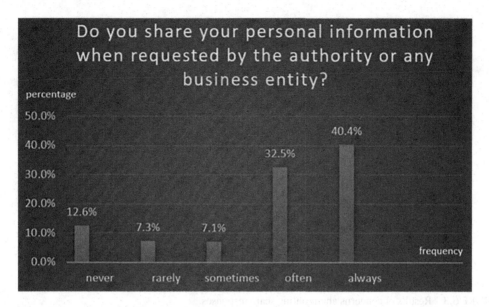

FIGURE 6.1   Results of sharing personal information responses.

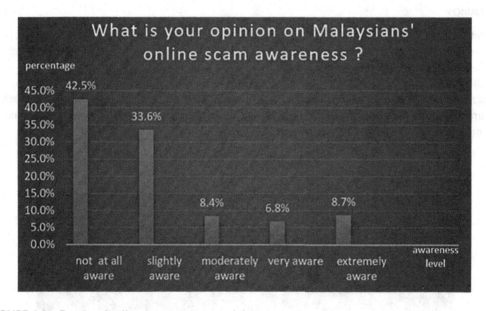

FIGURE 6.2   Results of online scam awareness opinion responses.

About 162 out of 381 respondents were not aware of online scams. Apparently, 128 respondents are only slightly aware of online scams. Figure 6.2 shows that 42.5% and 33.6% are extremely aware and slightly aware of Malaysian online scams, respectively.

About 129 out of 381 respondents were not at all concerned about being scammed over the internet. Moreover, 116 respondents were only slightly concerned about being scammed over the Internet. Figure 6.3 shows that 33.9% were not at all concerned and 30.4% were slightly concerned about being scammed over the Internet, respectively.

FIGURE 6.3   Results of concerns about online scam responses.

SCENARIOS

About 222 out of 381 respondents chose yes as their answer for clicking links. However, 159 respondents chose no as their answer. Figure 6.4 shows 58.3% opted to click on the link, whereas 41.7% opted not to click on the given link.

About 226 out of 381 respondents chose yes as their answer for making a payment to the bank. However, 155 respondents choose no as their answer for making a payment to the bank. Figure 6.5 shows that 59.3% said yes to making the payment, whereas 40.7% said no to making the payment.

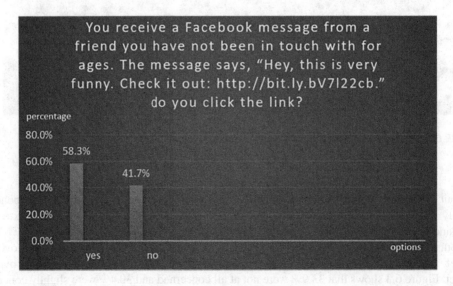

FIGURE 6.4   Results of people's responses to clicking unknown links.

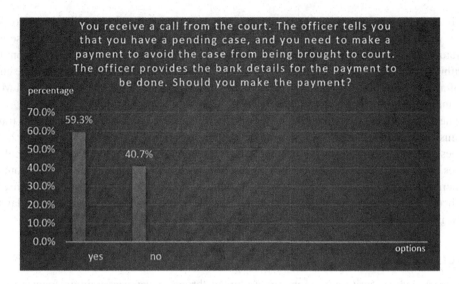

FIGURE 6.5 Results of responses to scams/fraud calls.

According to the results, most respondents are not aware of online scams. Scammers still con many people. However, data analysis shows that respondents were more aware of scams after the post-test. It is evident from the post-test results that most respondents are now more knowledgeable about online scams.

RECOMMENDATIONS

Ongoing relevance is central to the sustainability of the any cybersecurity awareness campaign. The objective of any cyber awareness program should be to make as many people as possible aware of risks, precautions, and remedies related to malicious internet-based activity. The sustainability of a cybersecurity awareness campaign comes from the awareness itself. At this point, awareness of the importance of cybersecurity leads to new legislation and inclusion in school curricula. For instance, this topic should be included in school syllabi, which could create better awareness among future generations.

RESEARCH LIMITATIONS

In this research, 381 respondents participated in answering questionnaires, but not all of them were able to sit for the pre-test and post-test. This shows that the use of a small sample size is one of the limitations for this research, as there were only 200 people who did the test. Another limitation to this study was that the sample had more respondents from the age group of 18–45 years. This study should be repeated over time, with a wider population from varied age groups, especially the age group of 46 and above. Also, most of the samples were from the north of Malaysia, which includes Perak and Penang, so it needs to have more balanced respondents taken from all over Malaysia.

FUTURE RESEARCH DIRECTIONS

In future work, we will conduct the survey in a larger population to obtain detailed outcomes from the respondents. Moreover, the toolkit will be expanded into a more structured training or seminar format, with content covering subjects such as the introduction to and awareness of online scams and possible preventive measures. Moreover, in this specific project, cybersecurity will be promoted through awareness training focusing on the newly released broadband capability and knowledge transfer within local communities. To evaluate the current level of cyber-awareness, a series of exploratory surveys will be distributed to less technologically resourced entities in local communities within Malaysia. By analyzing the results of the surveys, it is possible to benchmark the current level of awareness. These observations can then be extrapolated to the larger group of local Malaysian communities.

The next stage of the awareness evaluation project is to develop cybersecurity awareness training programs for local communities in their native languages, aiming to improve the current level of awareness. The processes required are preparation, evaluation, and training of Malaysian local communities about cybersecurity awareness. This research work will continue with funding from local and international donors. This recognizes that cybersecurity awareness raising is an ongoing task, partly because the message needs to be continuously reinforced and partly because every day there are new internet users who need awareness training.

CONCLUSION

In this work, cybersecurity education was promoted through awareness training focusing on the newly released broadband capability and knowledge transfer within local communities. To evaluate the current level of cyber-awareness, a series of exploratory surveys were distributed to less technologically resourced entities in local communities within Malaysia. In this study, we designed the online Scam Awareness toolkit that can be used to develop and affect the awareness of cybercrimes. To achieve the research objectives, the aspects that influence the level of online scam awareness were examined. Pre- and post-surveys were conducted throughout Malaysia. These surveys were used to answer research questions and achieve the research objective. The data for each different category and answer scales were also analyzed. After analyzing the results of the surveys, we conclude that it is possible to benchmark the current level of cybersecurity awareness among non-technical people. These observations can then not only be extrapolated to the larger group of local Malaysian communities but also to international communities, especially developing countries around the world.

REFERENCES

Adhiarso, Dendy Suseno, Prahastiwi Utari, and Sri Hastjarjo. "The influence of news construction and netizen response to the hoax news in online media." *Jurnal The Messenger 10*, no. 2 (2018): 162–173.

Al-Charchafchi, Ahmed, Selvakumar Manickam, and Zakaria N. M. Alqattan. "Threats against information privacy and security in social networks: A review." In *International Conference on Advances in Cybersecurity*, pp. 358–372. Singapore: Springer, 2019.

Atkins, Brandon, and Wilson Huang. "A study of social engineering in online frauds." *Open Journal of Social Sciences 1*, no. 3 (2013): 23.

Bernama. "Cyber scams top the list every year." *New Straits Times*, August 13, 2019. www.nst.com.my/news/nation/2019/08/512452/cyber-scams-top-list-every-year

Bliss, Erika. "Analyzing temporal patterns in phishing email topics." PhD diss., Rochester Institute of Technology, 2021.

Button, Mark, and Cassandra Cross. *Cyber Frauds, Scams and Their Victims*. Oxfordshire, UK: Routledge, 2017.

Button, Mark, Carol McNaughton Nicholls, Jane Kerr, and Rachael Owen. "Online frauds: Learning from victims why they fall for these scams." *Australian & New Zealand Journal of Criminology 47*, no. 3 (2014): 391–408.

Carmichael, Charlie. "Wix review | 7 crucial things to know before you use Wix." *Website Builder Expert*. October 6, 2019. www.websitebuilderexpert.com/websitebuilders/wix/wix-review/

Cross, Cassandra. "Fraudsters change tactics as a crackdown cuts some losses due to online scams." *The Conversation* (2016). https://theconversation.com/fraudsters-change-tactics-as-a-crackdown-cuts-some-losses-due-to-online-scams-54905

Dabrowski, Marek, and Lukasz Janikowski. "Virtual currencies and central banks monetary policy: challenges ahead." *Depth Analysis. Policy Department for Economic, Scientific and Quality of Life Policies 7*, no. 1 (2018): 1–4.

Hai-Jew, S. "The remote woo: Exploring faux transnational interpersonal romance in social imagery." *Social World Sensing Via Social Image Analysis from Social Media* (2020).

Jain, Ankit Kumar, Somya Ranjan Sahoo, and Jyoti Kaubiyal. "Online social networks security and privacy: Comprehensive review and analysis." *Complex & Intelligent Systems 7*, no. 5 (2021): 2157–2177.

Johnson, R. B., and L. Christensen. *Educational Research: Quantitative, Qualitative, and Mixed Approaches.* Thousand Oaks, CA: SAGE Publications, 2019.

Lawrence, S. "Police warn of fake Facebook profile scam that's cost one victim $55,000." *National*, 2021. www.stuff.co.nz/national/125622858/police-warn-of-fake-facebook-profile-scam-thats-cost-one-victim-55000

Marsden, E., and C. J. Torgerson. "Single group, pre-and post-test research designs: Some methodological concerns." *Oxford Review of Education 38*, no. 5 (2012): 583–616.

Mokhsin, M., A. A. Aziz, A. S. Zainol, N. Humaidi, and N. A. A. Zaini. "Probability model: Malaysian consumer online shopping behavior towards online shopping scam." *International Journal of Academic Research in Business and Social Sciences 8*, no. 11 (2018): 1529–1538.

Mosca, Francesca, and Jose Such. "An explainable assistant for multiuser privacy." *Autonomous Agents and Multi-Agent Systems 36*, no. 1 (2022): 1–45.

Naksawat, Chitchanok, Songyut Akkakoson, and Chek Kim Loi. "Persuasion strategies: Use of negative forces in scam e-mails." *GEMA Online® Journal of Language Studies 16*, no. 1 (2016): 1–17.

Potter, T. *A Guide to Robbery Prevention and Response to Robbery* (pp. 1–14, R. M. Sizer, Ed.). Portland, OR, 2019. www.portlandoregon.gov/police/article/31555.

Shuttleworth, Martyn. 2009. "Pretest-posttest designs – experimental research." *Explorable.com.* https://explorable.com/pretest-posttest-designs (accessed September 22, 2019).

Tan, H. S., H. Abas, and N. Shafie. "A systematic literature review of crime prevention through environmental design principles against banks ATM physical security effectiveness." *Open International Journal of Informatics 9*, no. 1 (2021): 30–44.

7 Raising Awareness of Social Engineering among Adolescents

Psychological and Cybersecurity Perspective

Ruchi Joshi and Shafiq Ul Rehman

CONTENTS

INTRODUCTION

Technology is related to almost all walks of human life. There is practically no field that is not touched and affected by technology, advancements, or lapses. While the importance of technology is never questioned, it was the pandemic (Covid-19) that further stressed the fact that we are dependent on technology as the entire world shifted to online mode, be it business, financial transactions, or education. However, as we scale new heights in the field of information and technology and develop new ideas to improve existing facilities to enhance the quality of life, we are simultaneously leaving behind a trail that leads to exploitation of the gullible and naïve rather easily. One of the ways to achieve this goal is through social engineering. The concept of social engineering refers to the manipulation of individuals to obtain private information, access, or valuables by exploiting human error. Cybercriminals use these "human hacking" scams to force unsuspecting users to expose their data, spread malware infections, or open restricted systems to them.

There are variety of approaches employed when it comes to definition of social engineering that are related to the situations and contexts in which social engineering attacks are made. The definitions are diverse and usually refer to one aspect of an approach relevant to a particular work. There is a lack of unanimity regarding a universally accepted definition; however, one of the most popular definitions of social engineering is provided by Mitnick and Simon (2002), who defines it as "using influence and persuasion to deceive people and take advantage of their misplaced trust in order to obtain insider information." Mouton et al. (2014) divide social engineering attack into two main categories: indirect attacks and direct attacks. An indirect attack occurs when, in any incident, a third-party medium is used as a way of communicating and when a medium is retrieved by a target without direct interaction with the social engineer, for instance, flash drives or web pages.

DOI: 10.1201/9781003319887-7

In case of a direct attack, there are incidents where two or more than two individuals are engaged in direct conversation. This communication can be both one sided and two sided. Attacks falling under category of direct attacks can be further classified into two ways of communication, bidirectional or unidirectional. Bidirectional communication takes place when two or more individuals or organizations participate in communication. One of the popular examples of this type of attack is an impersonation attack where social engineers impersonate the target for financial gain or to gain access to personal and sensitive information. Unidirectional communication is a conversation that is one sided in nature where the social engineer communicates with the target, but the target cannot communicate back. An example of this kind of attack would be bulk e-mails or short message services (SMSs).

Social engineering is inseparably related to the discipline of psychology. In fact, both psychology and technology go hand in hand; psychology seeps in right from the moment a decision about a password is made. According to a report, every 39 seconds, there is a possibility of occurrence of a cybersecurity attack, and the worldwide cost of such attacks will be around $10.5 trillion by 2025 (Morgan 2020). There are three main types of cybercrime: crimes in the device, crimes using the device, and crimes against the device. Crimes in the device are related to content on the device which is otherwise prohibited, for example, content that incites violence against specific communities, hate crimes, and the sale and purchase of illegal content and commodities. The next category involves crimes using the device in such a manner where digital systems are employed to deceive victims, for example, a criminal pretending to be an accounts official tricking students into divulging details of their bank accounts or credit or debit cards. In the third category are crimes against the device, which relates to incidents that compromise the device or system in some manner or another. Crimes of this nature directly target fundamental principles of cybersecurity, such as confidentiality and integrity of systems and data.

Social engineering is very closely associated with the application of principles and theories of social psychology. Social engineers attack not technical loopholes but elements of basic human tendencies like greed and the urge to conform, comply, and obey; they tap into the vulnerabilities of humans involved. It has been observed that these attacks usually attempt to exploit many human psychological traits such as a willingness to trust others and to be kind, the impact of anxiety and stress on decision making, personal needs and desires, and in some cases the naivete and gullibility in decision making.

According to a report (Security Magazine 2017), over the last two years, the major mediums for conducting social engineering attacks were social media sites. They can also take place through simple phone calls, where scammers can impersonate an acquaintance. Americans lost $29.8 billion to phone scams alone over the past year (Leonhardt 2021). Scammers' attacks are difficult to prevent, as access to confidential information is not a result of lapses of psychology but the involvement of the human element that tends to conform, comply, and trust easily. Often firewalls and security systems are outdated or not updated regularly, and organizations still prefer to use the outdated programs or security systems if they meet their identified needs and resolve the most visible and obvious threats. Some frequently used techniques of social engineering are phishing, quid-pro-quo, baiting, pretexting, and tailgating (Stern 2016).

SOCIAL ENGINEERING TECHNIQUES

A detailed description of some of the popular social engineering techniques follows.

1. Phishing: A widely used and successful technique of social engineering attacks falls under the category of phishing. Phishing scams usually start with a scam email that tricks the victim, for instance, a email that appears to have been sent through an authentic source or an invitation to click on a link to win a prize. While most of them are detected and blocked by various technical solutions, some of them manage to evade security measures.

A single lapse can result in grave security consequences that lead to financial losses or loss of confidential information. The techniques of luring victims depend on the objective of the scammer as well as the personal and behavioral attributes of the target. Some types of phishing attacks are

a. Spear – targeting a specific person or organization.

b. Whaling – targeting a high-profile individual. This type of attack requires considerable research and time to find an opportunity to target the credentials of such individuals.

c. Vishing – voice phishing, which is making fraudulent calls to acquire the information or credentials of an individual.

d. Social media phishing: This technique involves observation of the target individual's social media and sites they visit regularly with a purpose of collecting information that can be used to trap the intended victim in numerous ways.

2. Scareware: This is a type of social engineering attack that is based on human emotions like anxiety and shock. The attacker exploits and manipulates such emotions to install malicious software. Usually, hackers make use of pop-up-based alerts on different sites to attract targets. Once the intended target clicks on the pop-up, it leads to misinformation. This misinformation leads the target to act due to panic. The intended act might encourage the victim to purchase products to solve a technical issue. In this manner human emotions are manipulated and exploited for the purpose of harm to victims.

3. Reverse social engineering: Reverse social engineering attacks are very simple to carry out. They operate in twofold processes. A malicious problem is created for the intended target with an intention of initiating interaction, followed by proposing a solution. Over time, the social engineer wins the trust of the victim, who ends up sharing important and sensitive information.

4. Deepfake: This technique involves cybercriminals using deepfakes to forge images, audios, and videos to deceive victims into divulging sensitive information.

5. Dumpster diving: This technique does not involve any sophisticated technical know-how and involves the relatively simple act of going through trash and discarded documents containing information related to the target. Papers containing information about passwords, bills, and credit card information can be used to deceive the target through identity theft.

6. Watering hole: A watering hole attack in social engineering resembles a method of hunting employed by predators in jungle. Like predators wait for their prey near watering holes, the online attacker identifies the target individual or organization and uses surveys and other means to observe and note their browsing habits in terms of websites frequently visited by them. Later they compromise a legitimate website by directing the target to the malicious website from the original one. This malicious website then attempts to identify the vulnerabilities of the victim through various methods such as operating fingerprints and analyzing the user agent string.

7. Pretexting is a form of social engineering that involves creating a pretext or doctored scenario. These attacks usually involve impersonating people, winning the trust of the target, and misleading them into sharing important and sensitive information. Unlike phishing, instead of using feelings of fear or panic, pretexting focuses on winning the trust of the victim.

8. Baiting is like phishing in many ways, with the difference that baiting involves luring victims with promises of goods and items or arousing and piquing the curiosity of an individual. Offers of free downloads of music or movies are an example of social engineering that involves baiting.

9. Quid pro quo is a technique of social engineering similar to baiting, with the difference that quid pro quo promises something in exchange for information. These benefits mostly involve providing a service, whereas baiting usually involves certain goods.

10. The tailgating technique of social engineering involves social engineers accessing password-protected or off-limit locations, for instance, a social engineer holding a heavy door for a regular employee or as a delivery person and walking into unauthorized access space when the door is about to close.

Apart from these techniques, many novel and innovative means are devised by social engineers. As we make progress in intelligence and technology, loopholes are spotted by scammers and hackers to dupe vulnerable sections of society into passing on confidential information that can be misused to the advantage of social engineers. While psychology can be used with technology to improve mental health, treat disorders, and assist in preventive mental health care, scammers exploit basic human nature as chink in the armor that would lead to victims offering their sensitive information on a platter. Conformity, compliance, and obedience are some of the most influential aspects of social psychology that are employed for the purpose of social influence.

Conformity, in very simple words, can be defined as a desire or effort to "fit in." The desire to confirm stems from the fact that every culture has certain spoken and unspoken rules or norms indicating how people belonging to that culture should be behave or act in certain situations. While in some cases norms are explicit and detailed, some situations call for adherence to unspoken norms or rules. For example, following traffic rules while driving is very direct and written and has consequences for non-adherence. There are still some unwritten, indirect rules like not standing too close to people who are not within your immediate circle, not looking at someone's emails or pictures on your cell phone unless asked to do so, or saying "please" or "thank you."

Whether rules are implicit or explicit, one fact is very clear: most people obey them most of the time. It happens because people like to go along with the expectations of society or the group they belong to and to become a part of a particular group, society, or culture. In the first instance, it may look like people only confirm because they would like to be a part of the group they belong to. However, conforming behavior also prevents social chaos. For instance, if we did not conform to the norms of politely waiting for our turn at supermarkets or cafes and tried to jump the line, it may lead to an argument, which may or may not escalate into a full-blown fight.

A ground-breaking experiment in the field of social psychology conducted by Solomon Asch (1951, 1955) demonstrates important insights into our behavior as to how we conform in social situations. In his research, Asch asked the participants of the study to reply to a series of simple perceptual problems. The participant's task was to indicate which of the comparison lines matched with the standard line. However, apart from the participant, there were several other persons present who, unknown to the respondent, were assistants of the experimenter. On several occasions, the accomplices purposely offered the wrong answer by unanimously choosing the wrong line as the match. It was observed that in such situations, the participant would doubt their own judgment, and about 76% went along with the wrong answer at least once. The overall rate of agreeing with the wrong answer was 37%.

This experiment clearly reflected how we change our behavior against our best judgment with the wrong opinions and decisions of others around us. This also holds true in the case of unsafe cyber practices. For instance, if we see many people around us not being very vigilant about sensitive information like passwords or one time passwords (OTPs), we may tend to lower our own guards as well.

If conformity is a desire to fit in, then compliance is a form of social influence involving direct requests from one person to another in very simple words, Compliance is getting others to say yes to your demands or requests. We can make people comply with our requests through six basic principles: friendship, commitment, scarcity, reciprocity, social validation, and authority. Some of the popular techniques are:

1. Foot in the door technique: A procedure for gaining compliance where a small request is made, which when granted leads to the actual larger one. For example, an employee asks for half a day's leave, and when that is granted, she asks for a full day's leave, which was the original intent.

2. Door in the face technique: While the foot in door the technique of compliance begins with a smaller demand and leads to an actual bigger one, the door in the face technique is a procedure to gain compliance in which the requester begins with a large request, and when refused, a retreat is made to original smaller one, for instance, an adolescent asking his parents' permission to travel abroad, knowing well that the request will be turned down. When it is refused, the sulking adolescent asks for permission for a weekend trip to a nearby city, which was the original request.

3. That's not all technique: In this technique of compliance, requesters offer the target person added benefits before they arrive at a decision to accept or reject the request.

4. Playing hard to get technique: This type of compliance technique is based on the suggestion that an object or a person is scarce and difficult to obtain or achieve. This technique is often employed in case of romantic and intimate relationships and includes communicating with people other than intended mates, offering limited communication and affection.

5. Deadline technique of compliance: This technique is used to enhance compliance in which the target audience is convinced that there is a very limited time offer attached with an advantageous opportunity and to have the maximum benefit, they must cooperate within the limited time.

6. Pique technique of compliance: This compliance technique involves employing very unusual demands or requests, as such strange requests tend to pique or attract attention, which leads people to comply to understand the detailed nuances of the original demands.

Apart from these, there are other techniques of compliance which are used by persuaders to get their requests accepted depending upon the situation and intent in our day-to-day lives. Sometimes we are aware of these, and at times we act out unconsciously to fit in and cause others to obey. Often social engineers employ one of the mentioned tactics to carry out malicious designs intended to harm an individual or an organization for personal gains.

Obedience is a form of social influence in which one person simply orders one or more than one person to follow instructions or perform a action. Experiments conducted in the field of social psychology demonstrate that many people readily obey orders even if these orders tend to harm other individuals. The reasons for unquestioned obedience range from persistent and blind belief in the person issuing orders, for instance, the belief of Germans in the ideology of Adolf Hitler, or fear for the safety of one's own self or close ones. However, unquestioned obedience often leads to the infringement of rights of some section of society.

Many social engineering strategies, such as authority, scarcity, and social proof, are used to influence judgment. Bullée et al. (2015) explored how interventions minimize the risk of social engineering attacks. In their study, they sent 31 investigators acting as offenders to visit 118 employees and, based on a script, they asked them to hand over office keys and established that authority, one of the principles of persuasion, plays a significant role in facilitating social engineering attacks.

PROBLEM RATIONALE AND RESEARCH QUESTION

In the present chapter, with help of case studies, it will be explained how conformity. compliance, and obedience play an instrumental role in providing access to extremely sensitive and personal information and how decision makers and authorities should be aware of psychological tactics and techniques that social engineers employ to exploit the vulnerabilities of unsuspecting victims, especially when they are of an impressionable age and share the same explicitly with the target audience. The chapter also addresses the role of counsellors in association with cyber and legal experts to raise awareness about unsafe practices on the net and their rights as defended by the law. The chapter further attempts to highlight the role of the effectiveness of combined psychological, cybersecurity, and legal approaches for prevention, redressal, and rehabilitation of those affected by social engineering. Victims of social engineering experience psychological trauma, low self-esteem, anxiety, stress, and in some cases even self-harming and suicidal tendencies. Cybersecurity measures in terms of training and information dissemination from different approaches will be beneficial for all stakeholders concerned: school administration, teachers, students, parents, and society at large.

LITERATURE REVIEW

Safeguards against cyberattacks are improving day by day, and so are the techniques of cyberattackers. As mentioned earlier, social engineers exploit the psychological vulnerabilities of victims. The most popular techniques of social engineering are phishing, dumpster diving, scareware, watering hole attacks, and reverse social engineering. Siddiqi et al. (2022) identified social influence, persuasion, and attitude and behavior as some of the key components of influence methodologies employed in social engineering attacks. Six principles of persuasion: authority, social proof, liking/similarity, commitment/consistency, scarcity, and reciprocation Cialdini (1984), are associated with phishing attacks on emails.

Coluccia et al. (2020), through their review study on relational dynamics and psychological characteristics, provided qualitative and quantitative evidence that some psychological characteristics seems to be highly associated with risk of being victimized in a scam such as female gender, middle age, neuroticism, sensation seeking, impulsiveness, and susceptibility to addiction. A romance scam, popularly known as a sweetheart scam, is a matter of grave concern, given the number of people who are affected by it all over the world. These scams are initiated by criminals through online dating sites who offer affection to victims who are looking for romantic relationships. The intent, however, is to deceive the victims into financial fraud. Scammers set up fake profiles on various dating and popular social media sites and use pictures of attractive models or popular artists or celebrities and supply inaccurate but very appealing personal information. They tempt the victims into establishing an online relationship off the site, which can be termed "grooming" the victim or, in other words, developing a hyperpersonal relation until they feel the victim can spend a small or large amount of money. Scams of this nature tend to have an extremely adverse impact on the victims, as these scams are not just about financial losses but also lead to feelings of low self-worth, stress, anxiety, and at times even depression and self-harming tendencies.

Khooshabeh and Lucas (2018) recognized normative social influence or yearning to be liked and known by others as one of the important factors of social engineering. If a predator can identify a person with a proclivity for gaining approval from others, possibly communicating the message that an employee from an organization will be helping the requester immensely by providing information, the victim is more likely to share sensitive information (Del Pozo et al. 2018). By complying with the request for information, the employee's wish to be liked and accepted by others tends to outweigh the concerns for security and the safety and well-being of an organization.

Tetri and Vuorinen (2013) emphasized the importance of not just the context of social engineering situations but also how people tend to interpret these situations when they find themselves in them, since the perception of two people of a single situation can be different and varied, based on upbringing, personality, and organizational culture. This idea of perception poses a challenge to researchers or professionals in practice who are trying to better understand the factors that lead to social engineering attacks (Del Pozo et al. 2018).

Another study conducted by Happ et al. (2016) used reciprocity to analyze how compelled people felt to do something in return for a gesture that was done for them by someone. Guadagno et al. (2013) studied the principle of likeability exclusively in the context of an online setting and concluded that it was not an important influencer in that type of environment. Observing the principles of persuasion, apart from understanding how likely an individual is to fall for one of them, helps a social engineer to plan and execute successful attacks on unsuspecting victims. How susceptible an individual is to being a victim of social engineering also depends upon their emotional state and traits (Guadagno et al. 2013). Emotions are powerful means of influencing an individual's moods and attitudes. Depending upon emotional states, people might respond to one of the persuasion techniques easily. The mentioned literature clearly indicates how the emotional and psychological weakness of unsuspecting victims is exploited by social engineers for their advantage.

CASE STUDIES

The present chapter explores case studies across the world to assess how social engineers exploit psychological traits, weakness, and vulnerabilities of unsuspecting victims. One of the case studies is of an adolescent girl from a city of Rajasthan, India. The girl was student at a senior higher secondary and was quite active on social media platforms but was introverted in her personal life, with few or no friends. She received a connection request on social media from a famous local radio jockey in her city. She was elated upon receiving a request from a local celebrity and accepted it instantly. She soon started receiving messages from him and befriended him. The chats led to more intimate conversation, and after a few days, he asked her for pictures of her in compromising situations. When she refused, he stopped talking to her, saying he knew of many women who would do so readily (principle of scarcity), and blocked her.

The adolescent was restless and very upset after he blocked her. A few days later, he unblocked her and repeated the request. The experience left the girl very disturbed; she therefore gave in to his demands. He also made her make a few purchases for him and ended up getting access to her parents' credit card. No sooner than a week into providing her pictures and credit card credentials, the RJ's ID was deleted, leaving the girl devastated. Soon after, her classmates informed her about her pictures on a popular porn site. Huge financial transactions were made on the credit card as well. This led the girl to experience immense anxiety and stress, and she attempted suicide, but timely medical intervention saved her life. When asked about her suicide attempt, she confessed to sharing pictures of a private nature and credit card credentials with the RJ. Her parents immediately informed the cyber police to take down her pictures from the porn site and void the financial transactions made on their card.

When police questioned the local radio jockey, he denied having ever connected with the victim. The inquiry by cyber police led to the conclusion that an imposter had committed identity theft, using pictures of the radio jockey and creating a fake profile to befriend the girl and exploit her. The pictures were removed from the site; however, the trauma left a lasting impact on the girl, and she quit school and left the city along with her family. This case study is a classic example of social engineering where the social engineer methodically researched the profile of the girl, found she liked posts related to introversion, and realized she had few friends. Thus, attacking her vulnerabilities, he connected with her and persuaded her to comply with his requests.

Identity theft by criminals involves accumulating information about individuals and using this information to steal their identities. Usually there are two major techniques of gathering information by social engineers. Individuals are monitored on social media based on their interactions and posts on social networking sites, thereby gathering and exploiting personal information from earlier security breaches. The first method resembles phishing or, in other words, the tendency to overshare, but with poor security and privacy management. A major study done by fraud prevention organization Cifas discovered that Twitter, Facebook, and LinkedIn are the preferred options for identity theft, as these sites contain information related to personal details such as such as birthdates, details of family members, school and university attended, and the organization one works for. Romance scams are very widespread on the Internet through online websites offering dating. Social engineers tend to offer the victims romantic relationships. However, the ulterior aims are financial gains. The technique usually involves seeking vulnerable people looking for romance, love, and companionship.

In the last five years, people have reported losing an astounding $1.3 billion to romance scams. The numbers have skyrocketed in recent years, and 2021 was no exception: $547 million were lost. It has been found, however, that it is the loss of the romantic relationship more than financial losses that traumatizes victims most. Another form of popular social engineering scam is catfishing, where social groupings with fake identities are created to lure unsuspecting individuals looking for romantic relationships. Sextortion is another consequence of unsafe cyber behavior that involves threats to expose sexual images of victims unless additional pictures, sex, or money are given. Children and adolescents are most likely to end up as victims in incidents related to sextortion.

However, unlike conventional scams, the main motive is not just financial gain but notoriety as well. For instance, American football player Manti Te'o was misled into believing that he was in a relationship with Stanford University student Lennay Kekua, who did not exist: Te'o ended up as victim of a year-long girlfriend hoax. This also highlights the lack of awareness among users of social networking platforms about safety and security aspects. Just as availability of opportunities of networking are not a sufficient situation, suitable knowledge about the good, bad, and ugly sides of this usage is essentially important. The internet is a two-edged sword: while it offers opportunities for gaining and sharing information, creating, and maintaining contacts, it can also lead to disastrous consequences that may adversely affect the mental, physical, and emotional wellbeing of those affected.

DISCUSSION AND RESULTS

The case studies are just the tip of the iceberg on how social engineers can manipulate people into providing access to sensitive and valuable information that leads to calamitous effects on victims/survivors, especially in cases of vulnerable populations. Numerous reports across the globe speak volumes about how security experts and predators are in a neck-and-neck competition (Bullée et al. 2015). While technology can prevent financial or data theft, it cannot control whom an individual will share information and of what nature.

The available literature also indicates psychological and emotional states often act as a chink in armor, exposing unsuspecting parties to attacks by social engineers. Apart from the purely technological aspect of social engineering, psychological underpinnings in the behavior of oversharing play an extremely important role. Psychological research shows that there are six basic factors that account for this behavior and end up creating what is termed the "online disinhibition effect": dissociative anonymity (separation of online actions from offline identities), invisibility (opportunity to be physically invisible and unseen), asynchronicity (lack of immediate and real-time reactions), solipsistic introjection (merging of minds with other online individuals), dissociative imagination (impression of the online world as make believe and not connected to reality), and minimization of status and authority (based on the perspective that everyone online is equal) (Mouton et al. 2014).

In addition to these six factors mentioned, romantic imagery is also found to have played an important role in facilitating the plots of social engineers. Romantic imagery can be defined as the mental imagery of an object or romantic love. It has been found that strong romantic imagery is required to maintain online romantic relationships compared to conventional relationships, as more actual contact is experienced in the latter (Bullée et al. 2015). School counsellors play an extremely important role in the academic, personal, social, and overall well-being of students. School counsellors inspire confidence among students to share their personal and academic problems owing to qualities like empathy, unconditional positive regard for the client, active listening, and benevolence that are partly inherent to counsellors and partly instilled through education and training in psychology.

Most counsellors act pro-actively by holding workshops, career talks, seminars, and group counselling sessions. If similar talks can be held about cybersecurity dos and don'ts by school counsellors in association with IT and legal experts, it could lead to a better understanding of tactics used by predators and how such attacks can be prevented, as school counsellors act as both moderators and mediators who can facilitate knowledge dissemination by experts.

As the world moved towards virtual meetings, digital currency, and exchange, it is essential that rules and regulations to address both proper function and malfunctioning, along with prevention and punitive and retributive aspects, be systematically stated and regulated. In India, for instance, there are four predominant cyber laws to cover preventative and punitive aspects related to cyberspace and cyber behavior: the Information Technology Act 2000 for reliable legal inclusiveness for e-commerce, the Indian Penal Code (1980), the Companies Act of 2013, and NIST Compliance (Akbar 2014).

The United Kingdom has the Computer Misuse Act 1990, Data Protection Act (1998), and Data Protection Act (2018). The State and Local Government Cybersecurity Act of 2021 in United States was designed to improve coordination between the Cybersecurity and Infrastructure Security Agency (CISA) and state, local, tribal, and territorial governments. Under the new law, these bodies will be able to share security tools, procedures, and information more easily. Under the proposed cybersecurity regulation, which was published March 22, 2022, all European Union (EU) institutions, bodies, offices, and agencies will be required to have cybersecurity frameworks in place for governance, risk management, and control. They will also be required to conduct regular maturity assessments, implement plans for improvement, and share any incident-related information with Computer Emergency Response Team (CERT-EU) (Van Kleef et al. 2015).

Likewise, almost all countries have specific cyber laws for domestic and international cyber usage. Legal experts addressing laws will not only empower adolescents and young adults against cyber criminals but also act as a deterrent for many, as the consequences will be laid down clearly (Akbar 2014). However, owing to the scarcity of resources and technology that is changing with the blink of an eye, governments, especially in developing countries, are finding it difficult to protect the naïve and at times the well-informed from falling prey to social engineering attacks. In the case studies discussed, most of the victims experienced acute stress, anxiety, guilt, and low self-esteem. The role of mental health professionals such as psychologists and counselors in educational settings can help alleviate the adverse effect on mental health that is experienced by victims of social engineering.

The use of advanced technologies backed by the latest research and development is one of the most influential and effective ways to prevent social engineering attacks. Siddiqi et al. (2022) emphasized the use of machine learning, reinforcement learning, natural language processing, and deep learning in countering cyber-based social engineering attacks. A combined effort from all stakeholders, such as technocrats, administrators, mental health professionals, and legal experts, can help not only manage and control damage created by social engineers but also prove useful in preventing such attacks by online hackers and cyber criminals.

CONCLUSION

The present chapter takes a psycho-cyber approach in tackling the menace of social engineering, specifically for vulnerable and impressionable populations, adolescents, and young adults. A case study from city of Rajasthan was used to explain how, despite knowing that certain actions would lead to disastrous consequences, an adolescent willingly fell into the trap of a social engineer, which led to adverse effects on her overall well-being. The case study also highlights the importance of knowledge dissemination in schools and educational institutes for the safety and well-being of all stakeholders involved. Social engineering is a psychological attack. It can be countered by understanding the psychology of both victims and predators. Dawson and Thomson (2018) acknowledged the interdisciplinary nature of the field. They discovered that while IT and cybersecurity professionals may have expertise related to the nitty-gritty of their field, they lack the understanding of broader social aspects that significantly affect data protection. Comprehension and understanding of personal and social characteristics were mostly overlooked in the past, but many industries understand and acknowledge the importance of this knowledge while building their information technology departments (Vogel 2016).

No discipline can work and thrive in isolation; an interdisciplinary approach is a requirement in and around the cybersecurity filed, especially social engineering, where principles of social psychology can help in preventing and mitigating such attacks.

The present chapter identifies and assesses the role of social influence that facilitates the work of social engineers, thereby making vulnerable and unsuspecting sections of society easy targets for exploitation. We correlated theories of social psychology with unsafe cyber behavior and through a review of the literature established how compliance, conformity, and obedience influence internet usage, especially on social media platforms. However, the study had the following limitations to bear in mind for future research:

1. The study is exclusively focused on influence, behavior, and cyber behavior of adolescents and does not include larger sections of society who are equally vulnerable, like the elderly; people with physical, mental, and emotional disabilities; and the LGBTQ community, for safe cyber conduct.
2. The study only includes two case studies. More case studies can be included to make the review more comprehensive.
3. The study relies heavily on secondary data in terms of research articles, book chapters, books, and newspaper reports. Interviews with real-life victims of social engineers would have made the study more comprehensive.

REFERENCES

Akbar, Nurul. 2014. "Analyzing persuasion principles in phishing emails." Master's thesis, University of Twente.

Asch, Solomon E. 1951. "Effects of group pressure upon the modification and distortion of judgments." *Organizational Influence Processes* 58: 295–303.

Asch, Solomon E. 1955. "Opinions and social pressure." *Scientific American* 193, no. 5: 31–35.

Bullée, Jan-Willem, Montoya, L., Pieters, Wolter, Junger, Marianne, and Hartel, Pieter H. 2015. "The persuasion and security awareness experiment: Reducing the success of social engineering attacks." *Journal of Experimental Criminology* 11: 97–115. https://doi.org/10.1007/s11292-014-9222-7

Cialdini, R. 1984. *Influence: The Psychology of Persuasion*. New York: Quill.

Coluccia, Anna, Pozza, Andrea, Ferretti, Fabio, Carabellese, Fulvio, Masti, Alessandra, and Gualtieri, Giacomo. 2020. "Online romance scams: Relational dynamics and psychological characteristics of the victims and scammers. A scoping review." *Clinical Practice and Epidemiology in Mental Health* 16, no. 1: 24–35. https://doi.org/10.2174/1745017902016010024

Dawson, Jessica, and Thomson, Robert. 2018. "The future cybersecurity workforce: going beyond technical skills for successful cyber performance." *Frontiers in Psychology* 9: 744.

Del Pozo, Ivan, Iturralde, Mauricio, and Restrepo, Felipe. 2018. "Social engineering: application of psychology to information security." In 2018 6th IEEE International Conference on Future Internet of Things and Cloud Workshops (FiCloudW), Barcelona, Spain, 12(1), pp. 108–114.

Guadagno, R., Nicole, L., Lindsay, M., Rice, M., and Roberts, N. 2013. "Social influence online: the impact of social validation and likability on compliance." *Psychology of Popular Media Culture* 2, no. 1: 51.

Happ, C., Melzer, A., and Steffgen, G. 2016. "Trick with treat – reciprocity increases the willingness to communicate personal data." *Computers in Human Behavior*: 372–377.

Khooshabeh, Peter, and Lucas, Gale. 2018. "Virtual human role players for studying social factors in organizational decision making." *Frontiers in Psychology* 9: 194.

Leonhardt, M. 2021. "Americans lost billions of dollars to phone scams over the past year." Retrieved from https://www.cnbc.com/2021/06/29/americans-lost-billions-of-dollars-to-phone-scams-over-the-past-year.html

Mitnick, K. D., and Simon, W. L. 2002. *The Art of Deception: Controlling the Human Element of Security*. Indianapolis, IN: Wiley Publishing.

Morgan, S. 2020. "Cybersecurity magazine online." 2020. Retrieved from https://cybersecurityventures.com/hackerpocalypse-cybercrime-report-2016/

Mouton, F., Leenen, L., Malan, M. M., and Venter, H. S. 2014. "Towards an ontological model defining the social engineering domain." In: Kimppa, K., Whitehouse, D., Kuusela, T., and Phahlamohlaka, J. (eds) *ICT and Society. HCC 2014. IFIP Advances in Information and Communication Technology*, vol. 431. Berlin; Heidelberg: Springer. https://doi.org/10.1007/978-3-662-44208-1_22

Security Magazine. 2017. "Hackers attack every 39 seconds". Retrieved from www.securitymagazine.com/articles/87787-hackers-attack-every-39-seconds

Siddiqi, Murtaza Ahmed, Pak, Wooguil, and Siddiqi, Moquddam A. 2022. "A study on the psychology of social engineering-based cyberattacks and existing countermeasures." *Applied Sciences* 12, no. 12: 6042.

Stern, A. 2016. "SOCs require more than a band-aid approach." Retrieved from Information-management.com.

Tetri, Pekka, and Vuorinen, Jukka. 2013. "Dissecting social engineering." *Behaviour & Information Technology* 32, no. 10: 1014–1023.

Van Kleef, Gerben A., Van den Berg, Helma, and Heerdink, Marc W. 2015. "The persuasive power of emotions: Effects of emotional expressions on attitude formation and change." *Journal of Applied Psychology* 100, no. 4: 1124.

Vogel, R. 2016. "Closing the cybersecurity skills gap." *Salus Journal* 4, no. 2: 32–46.

Wolak, J., Finkelhor, D., Walsh, W., and Treitman, L. 2018. "Sextortion of minors: characteristics and dynamics." *Journal of Adolescent Health* 62: 72–79. https://doi.org/10.1016/j.jadohealth.2017.08.014.

8 Intelligent Named Entity-Based Cybercrime Recognition System for Social Media Network Platforms

Kathiravan Pannerselvam, Saranya Rajiakodi,
and Shanmugavadivu Pichai

CONTENTS

INTRODUCTION

Social media is a fascinating world where people express their emotions anonymously with or without intention. People of all ages share text, audio, photos, and video on social media to get public attention, likes, and positive comments. But social media has a dark side (Baccarella et al. 2018). Analysis of the interactions between different people/groups on social media platforms such as Twitter, Facebook, Instagram, and Reddit is known as social media post analysis (SMPA). In the past, rumors spread slowly through word of mouth (Antonakaki, Fragopoulou, and Ioannidis 2021; Baccarella et al. 2018; Gupta 2021). With the increased usage of social media platforms, rumors spread faster, making it much harder to maintain the authenticity of information (Hagar 2013). Nowadays, social media has become a new target for cybercriminals. They are trying to exploit people's trust in their social media platforms by spreading malicious software and sending spam messages. SMPA is gathering and analyzing social media posts to draw actionable knowledge that assists in identifying internet communities, viral marketing, and investigation of revolutionaries and terrorists by examining social media posts that they frequently exchange within their communities. SMPA includes tasks such as named entity recognition (NER), classification, clustering, and prediction. This experimental research work is about NER systems for cybersecurity content.

Information extraction (IE) includes NER, which is an important field of study and application that looks into how to extract knowledge (information) from massive amounts of unstructured text data

DOI: 10.1201/9781003319887-8

(Behera, Kumaravelan, and Kumar 2019; Avidhya and Aghila n.d.; Kathiravan and Haridoss 2018). In 1996, the first NER system was introduced at the Sixth Message Understanding Conference (MUC-6), which identifies entities such as people, organizations, locations, time, and quantity using Standard Generalized Markup Language (SGML) from the given textual data (Khanam et al. 2016; Lin et al. 2016). Because of semantic ambiguity, accurate identification, and classification of named entities remain challenging for computers. For example, a proper noun has different senses according to the context. For illustration, in the first sentence, "An apple a day keeps the doctor away," an apple is a fruit. However, in the second sentence,˙ "Apple is previewing a groundbreaking security capability that offers additional specialized protection to users who may be at risk of highly targeted cyberattacks from private companies developing state-sponsored mercenary spyware," Apple is an organization. Cybersecurity-related social media posts contain terms like apple, apple employee, and Apple products, which humans easily distinguish by inferring the respective context using their natural intelligence. However, computers can't easily handle such ambiguity and may not be able to differentiate between the fruit and organization unless the associated semantics is grasped. NER involves the following tasks (Khanam et al. 2016; Rajendran and Subalalitha 2019):

- Identify proper names in the text.
- Classify these names into a set of predefined categories of interest, such as person names, organizations (companies, government organizations, committees), locations (cities, countries, rivers), date, time, and quantity (number) expressions.

This task consists of three subtasks identifying entity names, temporal expressions, and number expressions. The expressions to be annotated are unique identifiers of entities (organizations, persons, locations) ENAMEX, times (dates, times) TIMEX, and quantities (monetary values, percentage) NUMEX (Khanam et al. 2016; Ma et al. 2021; Sari, Hassan, and Zamin 2010; Singh et al. 2019; Jing Li et al. 2022). Computers may not be able to differentiate between those entities. To overcome this challenge, we propose an enhanced NER system using machine learning (ML) and deep learning (DL) architectures such as random forest (RF), long short term memory (LSTM), and improved bidirectional LSTM (BiLSTM). Nowadays, researchers use different methods such as rule-based NER, machine learning-based NER, and hybrid NER to identify names from text.

This experimental research work addresses the following research questions (RQs).

RQ 1. How does SMPA enhance cybersecurity through NER systems?
RQ 2. Why are DL architectures such as LSTM and enhanced LSTM, such as BiLSTM, preferred by researchers to develop NER systems?

The objective of this work is derived from these two research questions.

- To review recent research articles on using SMPA to govern the significance of NER systems on cybersecurity issues.
- To address the role of DL architectures in sequential data like textual data collected from social media platforms.

The next section describes the related works such as datasets, domains, and techniques (ML and DL) used in NER systems. Then the methodology section briefly describes the experimental setup of our empirical study. It also includes various theoretical perspectives of ML and DL algorithms. Finally, in the results and conclusion section, the NER system's accuracy is evaluated by suitable metrics, and the section also addresses the issues and future scope of NER systems for cybersecurity using social media posts.

RELATED WORKS

This section illustrates the existing research on developing NER systems with reference to the reported methodologies. Jiakang Li et al. (2022) developed a Chinese clinical named entity recognition (CNER) using RoBerta Glyce-flat lattice transformer-CRF (RG-FLAT-CRF) model. They used pre-trained models to produce vectors containing medical features, and a convolutional neural network was used in the model to extract the morphological information concealed in Chinese characters. They used various datasets, such as CCKS 2017, 2019, and 2020. The RG-FLAT-CRF model produced scores of 95.61%, 85.17%, and 91.2% for F1. Using the mimic learning technique, Bannour et al. (2022) proposed shareable, privacy-preserving models for French clinical named entity recognition to facilitate knowledge transfer from a teacher model trained on a private corpus to a student model. Without gaining access to the original sensitive data, this student model might be available to the public. The novel dictionary-based models produced better performance and data privacy preservation.

Li et al. (2022) developed a multi-model NER system for military intelligence information using BERT-BiLSTM-CRF. They developed a novel military entity corpus with three types (classes), an abbreviation type, scientific or English name type, and novel and casual type. Zhang et al. (2022) proposed a medical NER system using deep convolutional neural networks (DCNN) with multiple word features. They used three different datasets, CCKS-2017, CCKS-2018, and Hospital-BJ. CCKS-2017 and CCKS-2018 contain 600 electronic health records, and Hospital-BJ contains 1200 electronic health records. Further, they replaced traditional CNN with DCNN to enhance the processing speed and used BiLSTM for hierarchical encoding to work on multiple feature words. Song et al. (2015) developed a NER tool by integrating dictionary-based entity extraction and rule-based relation extraction called PKDE4J. Starting with the Stanford CoreNLP, the performance of this tool was evaluated on different corpora. The result shows that this tool significantly outperforms existing systems, with average F-measures of 85% for entity extraction and 81% for relation extraction. Furthermore, the execution time of PKDE4J is arguably a critical issue to be addressed because it does not work well on large-scale datasets. Eftimov, Seljak, and Korošec (2017) proposed a novel rule-based NER called DrNER for evidence-based dietary recommendations. It consists of two phases. The first phase involves detection and determination of entities, and the second phase consists of selection and extraction of entities. The method was evaluated using various dietary recommendations from heterogeneous sources like scientific blogs and journals. The result shows that it is well suited to extracting knowledge for evidence-based nutritional recommendations.

Ek et al. (2011) reported on background NER from Short Message Service (SMS), such as abbreviations and emoticons (pictorial icons with special characters, numbers, and letters, which express emotions or sentiments). They proposed a novel NER application for Android mobiles to extract named entities from Swedish-language SMS. Regular expressions and corpus-driven classifiers were used with an F-score of 86% in this work. The corpus for parts of speech (POS) tagger training was retrospectively collected from newspaper text, whose format and language usage are different from SMS texts, so it degraded the tagger accuracy significantly.

Yanrui (2020) proposed a Chinese NER using a word vector consisting of word position (start word, middle word, and end word). The Chinese Wikipedia corpus with 16,691 entries and Word-2Vec were used in this work. Various classifiers models were built, such as BiLSTM + CRF and IDCNN + CRF, to evaluate the performance of the NER. Finally, the BiLSTM with CRF produced a markedly better F-score of 92.1% than other classifiers. To extract named things from the 1028 Tamil documents that were acquired from the Forum for Information Retrieval Evaluation (FIRE), Rajendran and Subalalitha (2019) employed supervised learning methods. The morphological and context features were extracted using a POS tagger and REGEX. They then used the naive Bayes approach to create a classifier with an F-measure of 83.54%. Theivendiram et al. (2018) proposed a novel NER system called the margin-infused relaxed algorithm (MIRA) and compared it to conditional random fields (CRFs) on Tamil BBC news text data. MIRA produced an F1-measure of 81.38%, while CRF produced a figure of 79.13%. Hariharan, Anand Kumar, and Soman (2019) combined LSTM with the fastText word embedding technique to create a NER system. The data were retrieved from FIRE-18 and Tamil Wikipedia. The outcomes contradict several word embedding methods, including GloVe. Results from the LSTM with fastText were more notable than those

TABLE 8.1

Comprehensive Details of Related Research Work on NER

Reference	Year	Application/Dataset	Language	Technique
Jiakang Li et al. (2022)	2022	Clinical named entity	Chinese	RG-FLAT-CRF
Bannour et al. (2022)	2022	Clinical named entity	French	Dictionary-based models
H. Li et al. (2022)	2022	Military intelligence information	English	Multimodel (BERT-BiLSTM-CRF)
R. Zhang et al. (2022)	2022	Medical	Chinese	DCNN
Song et al. (2015)	2015	Biomedical	English	Dictionary-based models and rule-based relation extraction
Eftimov, Seljak, and Korošec (2017)	2017	Evidence-based dietary recommendations	English	Rule-based NER
Ek et al. (2011)	2011	SMS	Swedish	Regular expressions and corpus-driven classifiers
Yanrui (2020)	2020	General	Chinese	BiLSTM with CRF
Rajendran and Subalalitha (2019)	2019	News articles	Tamil	Naïve Bayes algorithm
Theivendiram et al. (2018)	2018	Tamil BBC News data	Tamil	Margin-infused relaxed algorithm (MIRA)
Hariharan, Anand Kumar, and Soman (2019)	2019	FIRE-2018	Tamil	LSTM
Abinaya et al. (2015)	2015	FIRE	Tamil	Random kitchen sink algorithm

from the LSTM with GloVe. For Tamil NER, Abinaya et al. (n.d.) suggested a statistics-based supervised learning approach called random kitchen sink (RKS). The results were compared to those of support vector machines (SVM) and CRF algorithms. Compared to SVM and CRF, the RKS had a higher accuracy rating of 87.88%. Table 8.1 illustrates the related works, ordered by year, including application/dataset, language, and techniques used in the NER system.

METHODOLOGY

Figure 8.1 illustrates the various phases of this experimental research study. It begins with data collection and ends with data visualization. There are two more phases between these two: data preparation and model development using deep learning (Naseem, Razzak, and Eklund 2021; Alawad et al. 2020; H. Li et al. 2022). The DL model needs testing data to evaluate its performance. So the dataset is separated into two parts, training data and testing data, once the data preparation phase is completed (Kanimozhi, Shanmugavadivu, and Rani 2020; Ameri et al. 2021; Alsharef et al. 2022). The following subsections describe this process clearly.

EXPERIMENTAL DATASET

The NER corpus dataset used for this analytical research study and shown in Table 8.2 was obtained from the GitHub repository (" GitHub – Aiforsec/CyNER: Cybersecurity Concepts Extracted from Unstructured Threat Intelligence Reports Using Named Entity Recognition" n.d.). The CyNER dataset consists of a cybersecurity corpus with appropriate tags. There are 11 tags used in this corpus: I-Malware, O, B-Malware, B-System, I-System, B-Organization, B-Indicator, I-Organization, I-Indicator, B-Vulnerability, and I-Vulnerability. Table 8.2 illustrates an example dataset with two

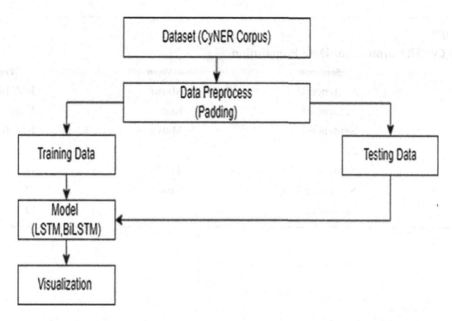

FIGURE 8.1 Phases of CyNER.

TABLE 8.2
Illustration of a Dataset (CyNER)

Word	Tag
Mario	I-Malware
DroidJack	B-Malware
12.2	I-System
Pokemon	B-System
Micro	I-Organization
Trend	B-Organization
//apple-icloud	I-Indicator
video.3gp	B-Indicator
memory	I-Vulnerability
CVE-2015–5119	B-Vulnerability
instance	Other

attributes, Word and Tag. The CyNER dataset is segregated into training (71,001), testing (20,017), and validation (20,342), with separate instances mentioned in parentheses.

DATA PREPARATION

The CyNER dataset has two attributes. For the experiment, the dataset of 8263 words was randomly chosen from CyNER, and an attribute called Sentence was added manually to create sequential data because a social media post is sequential. It consists of a collection of words that express people's intentions. In the CyNER dataset, wherever the token (.) appeared, it was

TABLE 8.3

A New CyNER Corpus after Data Preparation

	Sentence	Word	Tag
0	Sentence:1	Mario	I-Malware
1	Sentence:1	Run	I-Malware
2	Sentence:1	Malware	I-Malware
. . .	. . .	. . .	. . .
8260	Sentence: 340	The	O
8261	Sentence: 340	name	O
8262	Sentence: 340	.	O

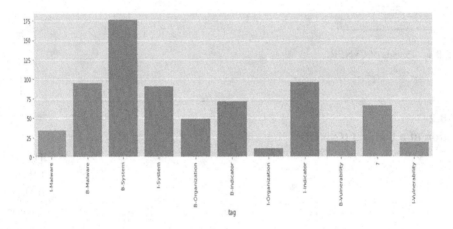

FIGURE 8.2   Visualization of entity counts in CyNER.

considered the end of the sentence, and we manually assigned a sentence number. This way, 340 sentences were generated and used in this experimental research study ("GitHub – Aiforsec/ CyNER: Cybersecurity Concepts Extracted from Unstructured Threat Intelligence Reports Using Named Entity Recognition" n.d.). Table 8.3 shows the CyNER dataset with three categorical attributes: sentence, word, and tag.

Figure 8.2 shows the number of entities with their respective counts in the CyNER dataset. This phase is followed by data preprocessing.

DATA PREPROCESSING

The preprocessing step consists of a padding activity, which makes the sentences equal in length, because deep learning models, such as long short term memory, work with fixed-length input. Figure 8.3 depicts the distribution of the sentence lengths of our experimental dataset.

After this phase, the dataset was partitioned into two parts: training and testing data. The training data is used to develop a DL model, and testing data is used to evaluate its accuracy. The next phase is CyNER model development.

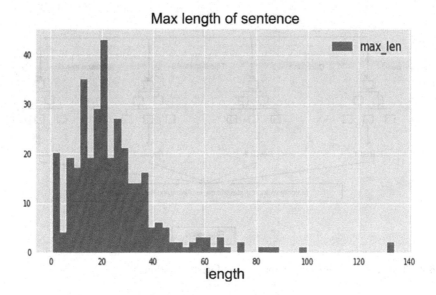

FIGURE 8.3 Distribution of word length of each sentence in a dataset.

NER MODEL DEVELOPMENT

This section describes the state-of-the-art ML and DL models, which play a vital role in information extraction (IE) (Kathiravan and Haridoss 2018; Rajendran and Subalalitha 2019). The NER is a subset of IE and an application of NLP (Khanam et al. 2016).The CyNER model was built using various ML and DL techniques, such as random forest, LSTM, and BiLSTM. Those are significantly used in existing works discussed in the related work section in detail. The RF is one of the most popular ML ensemble algorithms for solving classification and regression problems (Storcheus, Rostamizadeh, and Kumar 2015; Alawad et al. 2020).

RANDOM FOREST ALGORITHM

Figure 8.4 depicts the generic structure of RF, where the dataset is divided among different decision trees, and the result of each decision tree is processed using majority voting/averaging to get the result. The following pseudocode illustrates the overall working procedure of RF (Alawad et al. 2020; Hossain et al. 2021; Ankit and Saleena 2018). It begins with a random selection of *n* records from a given dataset to build the decision tree (DT) for each sample record. Once the DTs are created, the output of each DT is analyzed. The outcome of the random forest is decided based on majority voting or averaging, and thus, a classifier or regression model is created (Ameri et al. 2021; Ahuja et al. 2019; Dong and Qian 2022).

Pseudocode for random forest (RF) algorithm

Step 1: n = random(k)   // *k instances on dataset*
Step 2: For i in k
   DT = create()
      For j in DT
         Output = Generate()

Step 3: RF=majority_voting()   // *to build a classifier, the final output is considered based on majority voting.*

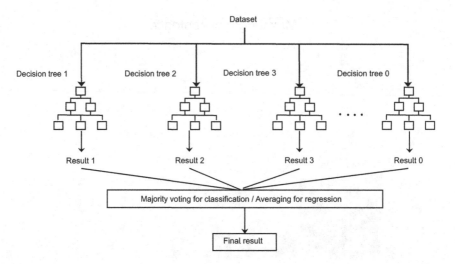

FIGURE 8.4   The general architecture of the random forest algorithm.

LSTM

In real-time streaming data such as social media posts, Internet of Things (IoT) sensor data, signal and video content, and time series analysis, recurrent neural networks (RNNs) are typically used (Subramani et al. 2019; Ameri et al. 2021; L. Zhang, Hall, and Bastola 2018; Feizollah et al. 2019; Singh et al. 2019). Although they do not handle large sequences, they effectively take sequential data. So the improved versions of RNN, that is, LSTM, were used in this experimental research study. The LSTM works well in sequential data. The BiLSTM is a sequence processing model comprising two LSTMs, one receiving input in a forward manner and the other in a backward way (Lashkarashvili and Tsintsadze 2022; H. Li et al. 2022).

Figure 8.5 illustrates an LSTM model. It is an improved version of the RNN. Since it is the first algorithm to have internal memory that remembers its input, it is ideal for machine learning problems dealing with sequential data. The LSTM takes the padded (same length of data) sentences as

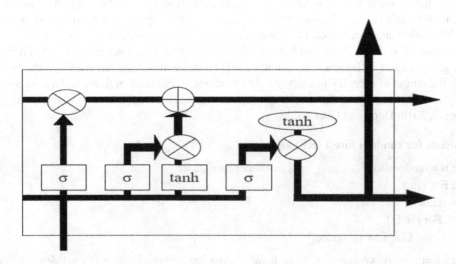

FIGURE 8.5   Architecture of LSTM model.

input and processes. A recurrent neural network that can learn order dependency is a long short-term memory network. During the current RNN phase, the output from the previous step is used as the input. It addressed the problem of RNN long-term reliance, where the RNN can predict words based on recent data but cannot predict words kept in long-term memory. With increasing gap lengths, an RNN does not function efficiently (Behera, Kumaravelan, and Kumar 2019; Behera and Kumaravelan 2021). Information stored by default in the LSTM may be retained for an extended period. It is done by processing, predicting, and classifying time-series data. The LSTM consists of three gates (forget gate, input gate, and output gate), one intermediate cell state, and one cell state (Adhikari et al. 2019; "Bidirectional LSTM Model Showing the Input and Output Layers. The Red . . . l Download Scientific Diagram" n.d.). The forget gate is the first sigmoid activation function in the network. It is represented by ft. It decides which information must be taken and which must be dropped. The information from the previous hidden state and the current input gets through the sigmoid function, and the output arrives. The output of this sigmoid activation function is in the range of 0 to 1. The information must be forgotten if the value is near 0 and is retained near the value of 1. The following formula is the computation procedure for f_t using the sigmoid activation function.

$$f_t = \sigma\left(W_f \times S_{t-1} + W_f \times X_t\right) \tag{1}$$

Eq. 8.1 denotes the computation of f_t using the weight of forget gate as W_f, the old state information as S_{t-1}, and the input value as X_t.

$$i_t = \sigma\left(W_i \times S_{t-1} + W_i \times X_t\right) \tag{2}$$

Eq. 8.2 consists of input value i_t, which is a second sigmoid activation function and the first tanh activation function of the network. W_i is the weight of the input gate, S_{t-1} is the information of the old state, and X_t is an input value.

$$O_t = \sigma\left(W_o * S_{t-1} + W_o * X_t\right) \tag{3}$$

Eq. 8.3 illustrates the sigmoid function of the output gate, where W_o is a weight of output value, S_{t-1} is old state information, and X_t is an input value. This sigmoid function highlights the information which should be passed to the next hidden state. An intermediate cell state uses Eq. 8.4, where the tanh function works with a weight of the intermediate cell state (W_c), old state information (S_{t-1}), and (X_t) as shown in Eq. 8.4.

$$C_{t'} = tanh\left(W_c \times S_{t-1} + W_c \times X_t\right) \tag{4}$$

The cell states use Eq. 8.5, where an intermediate cell value is multiplied by the input gate, and the previous cell state value is multiplied by the forget gate. Finally, both are summed and stored in the cell state (C_t).

$$C_t = \left(i_t \times C_{t'}\right) + \left(F_t \times C_{t-1}\right) \tag{5}$$

Eq. 8.6 is used for the new state, where the tanh function is multiplied by the output gate.

$$new\ state = O_t \times tanh\left(C_t\right) \tag{6}$$

Figure 8.6 depicts the working process of these gates (L. Zhang, Hall, and Bastola 2018; Ameri et al. 2021; Singh et al. 2019; Feizollah et al. 2019; Ma et al. 2021; Hariharan, Anand Kumar, and Soman 2019).

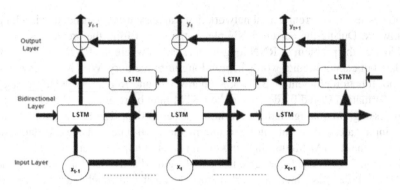

FIGURE 8.6 The architecture of the BiLSTM model.

BiLSTM

Two LSTMs are combined to create a BiLSTM that unifies an extensive sequence of data in both forward and backward directions over a given period, which makes it possible for the concealed state to retain information from the past and future (Subramani et al. 2019; Ameri et al. 2021). Figure 8.6 depicts the working architecture of BiLSTM. The bidirectional layer consists of both forward and backward directional LSTM to improve the model's accuracy.

RESULTS AND DISCUSSION

This section describes the inferences of this research work, addressing the formulated research questions with a discussion. The objective of this research is derived from the following RQs, and this work aims to address the RQs as follows.

RQ 1. How does SMPA enhance cybersecurity through NER systems?
RQ 2. Why are DL architectures such as LSTM and enhanced LSTM, such as BiLSTM, preferred by researchers to develop NER systems?
RQ 1 aims to highlight the importance and significance of SMPA and NER on cybersecurity issues.

Due to the viral impact on society, social media platforms are used by almost everyone in this information era. They have become an easy and new platform for cyber criminals and others performing criminal activities. The increasing volume of criminal activity information available on the internet or blogs helps to explore this insight. State-of-the-art NLP tasks, like NER, help to extract entities such as name, organization, and other essential entities. Those details are used to identify earlier crimes and help highlight crime on social media platforms.

RQ 2 addresses the significance of DL sequential architecture and its advantages. Related studies have revealed that cutting-edge DL architectures (LSTM and BiLSTM) were built and employed extensively in several NER systems. It has shown that sequential data are efficiently managed using LSTM and improved LSTM (BiLSTM). In this experimental research study, three different classifiers, RF, LSTM, and BiLSTM, are examined on the CyNER open access dataset. Table 8.4 depicts various parameter settings of LSTM and BiLSTM with their accuracy, which consists of the optimizer, batch size, activation function, and number of recurrent units. These parameters are known as hyperparameters (Singh et al. 2019; Ma et al. 2021; Ameri et al. 2021; L. Zhang, Hall, and Bastola 2018).

The deep learning model was built with different hyperparameters. Those helped enhance the CyNER system's accuracy by tuning the different parameters. The hyper-parameters used in our experimental research work are described in Table 8.4. We got 100% accuracy for LSTM with the following parameters: Nadam optimizer, batch size = 32, activation function = ReLU, and the

TABLE 8.4

Accuracy of LSTMs and BiLSTMs with Hyperparameter Tuning

Hyper-Parameters	Variants	LSTM Accuracy	BiLSTM Accuracy
Optimizer	Nadam	**100**	**96.13**
	Adam	99.01	88.00
Batch_Size	32	**100**	**96.13**
	64	99.98	88.00
Activation Function	Softmax	99.98	88.00
	ReLU	**100**	**96.13**
No. of Rec Units	64	**100**	**96.13**
	128	99.98	88.00

number of rec units = 64 (Ameri et al. 2021; R. Li 2016; Subramani et al. 2019; L. Zhang, Hall, and Bastola 2018; Lashkarashvili and Tsintsadze 2022; Alawad et al. 2020)

Table 8.5 and Figure 8.7 illustrate various performance metrics used in the CyNER system.

The various machine learning and deep learning techniques and related works are discussed in the section. We selected three predominant techniques from our literature review to empirically evaluate an intelligent NER containing cybersecurity-related content. Table 8.5 and Figure 8.7 depict the performance of CyNER using the evaluation metrics accuracy, precision, recall, and F1-score for

TABLE 8.5

Various Performance Metrics Used in the CyNER System

Classifier	Evaluation Metrics			
	Accuracy %	Precision %	Recall %	F1-Score %
LSTM	100	100	100	100
BiLSTM	96.13	97	96	96
RF	91	87	91	89

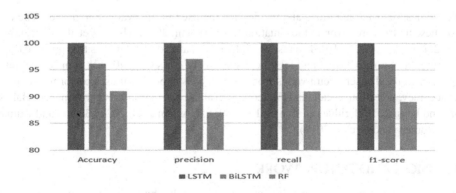

FIGURE 8.7 Comparative performance analysis of CyNER system.

TABLE 8.6
Description of Notations Used in the Evaluation Metrics

Symbol	Description
tp_i	True positive
tn_i	True negative
fp_i	False positive
fn_i	False negative
C_i	Class
M	Total number of classes in the dataset
i	Value is 1 to m

LSTM, BiLSTM, and RF. The accuracy of the CyNER system model is calculated using the following evaluation metrics (Aggarwal and Tiwari n.d.; Goel, Gautam, and Kumar 2017; Chormunge and Jena 2018; Ameri et al. 2021; Bridges et al. n.d.):

$$Accuracy = \frac{\sum_{i=1}^{m} \frac{tp_i + tn_i}{tp_i + fp_i + fn_i + tn_i}}{m} \tag{7}$$

$$Precision = \frac{\sum_{i=1}^{m} |y_i| \frac{tp_i}{tp_i + fp_i}}{\sum_{i}^{m} |y_i|} \tag{8}$$

$$Recall = \frac{\sum_{i=1}^{m} |y_i| \frac{tp_i}{tp_i + fn_i}}{\sum_{i}^{m} |y_i|} \tag{9}$$

$$F1\text{-}Score = \frac{\sum_{1}^{m} |y_i| \frac{2tp_i}{2tp_i + fp_i + fn_i}}{\sum_{i}^{m} |y_i|} \tag{10}$$

Table 8.6 describes the notations and the description used in the evaluation metrics. The computation of these metrics are given in the equations (Ameri et al. 2021; Alsharef et al. 2022; Jiakang Li et al. 2022; Hammar et al. 2019). The results of the model are consolidated as true positive (tp_i), true negative (tn_i), false positive (fp_i), and false negative (fn_i) of class C_i [2,40–43]. If m is the total number of classes in the dataset, then i varies from 1 to m. This experiment uses performance measures such as accuracy, precision, recall, and F1-score to evaluate the classifier's performance (Bahassine, Madani, and Kissi 2016; Bridges et al. n.d.; Kaul 2015; Hossain et al. 2021; Behera and Kumaravelan 2021; Romero and Becker 2019).

CONCLUSION AND FUTURE WORK

This chapter summarizes cybersecurity's significance by analyzing social media posts. Social media is an essential forum in today's technologically advanced and digital-enabled society, where people can freely express their emotions. Furthermore, hackers and crooks primarily come through these platforms. They spread malware and steal user data by sharing malicious website URLs on social media. An intelligent NER system is proposed to detect named cybersecurity-related entities from social media posts. It can be used on textual data such as blogs, websites, and short messages (SMS, emails). This system is developed by an annotated CyNER dataset with the deep learning sequential architecture known as LSTM. The accuracy was compared with another familiar deep learning architecture called BiLSTM and a machine learning classifier – random forest. The foremost model (LSTM) produced 100% accuracy, the second (BiLSTM) produced 96.13%, and the machine learning ensemble technique called random forest classifier gave 91%. Comparatively, LSTM produced better accuracy on CyNER. This same research work will be improved in the future with a more annotated NER corpus for other fields like legal, scientific, and medical writings. Additionally, this endeavor will test Indian regional languages like Tamil and Hindi.

REFERENCES

Abinaya, N., M.A. Kumar, and K.P. Soman. 2015. "Randomized Kernel Approach for Named Entity Recognition in Tamil." *Indian Journal of Science and Technology* 8: 1–7. Accessed July 15, 2022. www.academia.edu/download/56119359/21_Randomized_kernel_approach_for_Named_Entity_Recognition_in_Tamil.pdf.

Adhikari, Ashutosh, Achyudh Ram, Raphael Tang, and Jimmy Lin. 2019. "DocBERT: BERT for Document Classification." http://arxiv.org/abs/1904.08398.

Aggarwal, Abhishek, and Atul Tiwari. n.d. "Multi Label Toxic Comment Classification Using Machine Learning Algorithms." Accessed August 2, 2022. https://doi.org/10.35940/ijrte.A5814.0510121.

Ahuja, Ravinder, Aakarsha Chug, Shruti Kohli, Shaurya Gupta, and Pratyush Ahuja. 2019. "The Impact of Features Extraction on the Sentiment Analysis." *Procedia Computer Science* 152: 341–48. https://doi.org/10.1016/j.procs.2019.05.008.

Alawad, Mohammed, Shang Gao, John X. Qiu, Hong Jun Yoon, J. Blair Christian, Lynne Penberthy, Brent Mumphrey, Xiao Cheng Wu, Linda Coyle, and Georgia Tourassi. 2020. "Automatic Extraction of Cancer Registry Reportable Information from Free-Text Pathology Reports Using Multitask Convolutional Neural Networks." *Journal of the American Medical Informatics Association* 27 (1): 89–98. https://doi.org/10.1093/jamia/ocz153.

Alsharef, Ahmad, Sonia Karan Aggarwal, Deepika Koundal, Hashem Alyami, and Darine Ameyed. 2022. "An Automated Toxicity Classification on Social Media Using LSTM and Word Embedding." *Computational Intelligence and Neuroscience* 2022 (1): 1–10. https://doi.org/10.1155/2022/8467349.

Ameri, Kimia, Michael Hempel, Hamid Sharif, Juan Lopez Jr., and Kalyan Perumalla. 2021. "CyBERT: Cybersecurity Claim Classification by Fine-Tuning the BERT Language Model." *Journal of Cybersecurity and Privacy* 1 (4): 615–37. https://doi.org/10.3390/jcp1040031.

Ankit, Rhode, and Nabizath Saleena. 2018. "An Ensemble Classification System for Twitter Sentiment Analysis." *Procedia Computer Science* 132: 937–46. https://doi.org/10.1016/j.procs.2018.05.109.

Antonakaki, Despoina, Paraskevi Fragopoulou, and Sotiris Ioannidis. 2021. "A Survey of Twitter Research: Data Model, Graph Structure, Sentiment Analysis and Attacks." *Expert Systems with Applications* 164: 114006. https://doi.org/10.1016/j.eswa.2020.114006.

Avidhya, Karunakaran, and Aghila, Gnanasekaran n.d. "Text Mining Process, Techniques and Tools: An Overview." *International Journal of Information Technology and Knowledge Management* 2 (2): 613–22.

Baccarella, Christian V., Timm F. Wagner, Jan H. Kietzmann, and Ian P. McCarthy. 2018. "Social Media? It's Serious! Understanding the Dark Side of Social Media." *European Management Journal* 36 (4): 431–38. https://doi.org/10.1016/J.EMJ.2018.07.002.

Bahassine, Said, Abdellah Madani, and Mohamed Kissi. 2016. "An Improved Chi-Square Feature Selection for Arabic Text Classification Using Decision Tree." In SITA 2016–11th International Conference on Intelligent Systems: Theories and Applications, December. https://doi.org/10.1109/SITA.2016.7772289.

Bannour, Nesrine, Perceval Wajsbürt, Bastien Rance, Xavier Tannier, and Aurélie Névéol. 2022. "Privacy-Preserving Mimic Models for Clinical Named Entity Recognition in French." *Journal of Biomedical Informatics* 130: 104073. https://doi.org/10.1016/J.JBI.2022.104073.

Behera, Bichitrananda, and G. Kumaravelan. 2021. "Text Document Classification Using Fuzzy Rough Set Based on Robust Nearest Neighbor (FRS-RNN)." *Soft Computing* 25 (15): 9915–23. https://doi.org/10.1007/S00500-020-05410-9/TABLES/2.

Behera, Bichitrananda, G. Kumaravelan, and Prem Kumar. 2019. "Performance Evaluation of Deep Learning Algorithms in Biomedical Document Classification." *Proceedings of the 11th International Conference on Advanced Computing* 29 (5): 220–24. https://doi.org/10.1109/ICoAC48765.2019.246843.

"Bidirectional LSTM Model Showing the Input and Output Layers. The Red . . . | Download Scientific Diagram." n.d. Accessed July 15, 2022. www.researchgate.net/figure/Bidirectional-LSTM-model-showing-the-input-and-output-layers-The-red-arrows-represent_fig3_344554659.

Bridges, Robert A., Corinne L. Jones, Michael D. Iannacone, Kelly M. Testa, and John R. Goodall. n.d. "Automatic Labeling for Entity Extraction in Cybersecurity." Accessed July 15, 2022. www.osvdb.org/.

Chormunge, Smita, and Sudarson Jena. 2018. "Correlation Based Feature Selection with Clustering for High Dimensional Data." *Journal of Electrical Systems and Information Technology* 5 (3): 542–49. https://doi.org/10.1016/J.JESIT.2017.06.004.

Dong, Jia, and Quan Qian. 2022. "A Density-Based Random Forest for Imbalanced Data Classification." *Future Internet* 14 (3): 90. https://doi.org/10.3390/FI14030090.

Eftimov, Tome, Barbara Koroušić Seljak, and Peter Korošec. 2017. "A Rule-Based Named-Entity Recognition Method for Knowledge Extraction of Evidence-Based Dietary Recommendations." *PLoS One* 12 (6). https://doi.org/10.1371/JOURNAL.PONE.0179488.

Ek, Tobias, Camilla Kirkegaard, Håkan Jonsson, and Pierre Nugues. 2011. "Named Entity Recognition for Short Text Messages." *Pacific Association for Computational Linguistics (PACLING 2011)* 27: 178–87. https://doi.org/10.1016/j.sbspro.2011.10.596.

Feizollah, Ali, Sulaiman Ainin, Nor Badrul Anuar, Nor Aniza Binti Abdullah, and Mohamad Hazim. 2019. "Halal Products on Twitter: Data Extraction and Sentiment Analysis Using Stack of Deep Learning Algorithms." *IEEE Access* 7: 83354–62. https://doi.org/10.1109/ACCESS.2019.2923275.

"GitHub – Aiforsec/CyNER: Cybersecurity Concepts Extracted from Unstructured Threat Intelligence Reports Using Named Entity Recognition." n.d. Accessed July 15, 2022. https://github.com/aiforsec/CyNER.

Goel, Ankur, Jyoti Gautam, and Sitesh Kumar. 2017. "Real Time Sentiment Analysis of Tweets Using Naive Bayes." In Proceedings on 2016 2nd International Conference on Next Generation Computing Technologies, NGCT 2016, October, 257–61. https://doi.org/10.1109/NGCT.2016.7877424.

Gupta, Kriti. 2021. "SJSU ScholarWorks Fake News Analysis and Graph Classification on a COVID-19 Twitter Dataset." Master's Projects, 1013. https://doi.org/10.31979/etd.sf7y-8v3d.

Hagar, Christine. 2013. "Crisis Informatics: Perspectives of Trust – Is Social Media a Mixed Blessing?" *School of Information Student Research Journal* 2 (2): 2. https://doi.org/10.31979/2575-2499.020202.

Hammar, Kim, Shatha Jaradat, Nima Dokoohaki, and Mihhail Matskin. 2019. "Deep Text Mining of Instagram Data without Strong Supervision." In Proceedings – 2018 IEEE/WIC/ACM International Conference on Web Intelligence, WI 2018, 158–65. https://doi.org/10.1109/WI.2018.00-94.

Hariharan, V., M. Anand Kumar, and K. P. Soman. 2019. "Named Entity Recognition in Tamil Language Using Recurrent Based Sequence Model." *Lecture Notes in Networks and Systems* 74: 91–99. https://doi.org/10.1007/978-981-13-7082-3_12.

Hossain, Md Murad, Md Asadullah, Abidur Rahaman, Md Sipon Miah, M. Zahid Hasan, Tonmay Paul, and Mohammad Amzad Hossain. 2021. "Prediction on Domestic Violence in Bangladesh during the COVID-19 Outbreak Using Machine Learning Methods." *Applied System Innovation* 4 (4): 77. https://doi.org/10.3390/ASI4040077.

Kanimozhi, G., P. Shanmugavadivu, and M. Mary Shanthi Rani. 2020. "Machine Learning-Based Recommender System for Breast Cancer Prognosis." *Recommender System with Machine Learning and Artificial Intelligence*, 121–40. https://doi.org/10.1002/9781119711582.ch7.

Kathiravan, P., and N. Haridoss. 2018. "Preprocessing for Mining the Textual Data-A Review." *International Journal of Scientific Research in Computer Science Applications and Management Studies IJSRCSAMS* 7 (5). www.ijsrcsams.com.

Kaul, Sheetal. 2015. "Agenda Detector: Labeling Tweets with Political Policy Agenda." Graduate Theses and Dissertations. https://lib.dr.iastate.edu/cgi/viewcontent.cgi?article=5560&context=etd.

Khanam, Humera, A. Khudhus, and M. S. P. Babu. 2016. "Named Entity Recognition Using Machine Learning Techniques for Telugu Language." *2016 7th IEEE International Conference on Software Engineering and Service Science* (ICSESS), Beijing, China, pp. 940–44, doi: 10.1109/ICSESS.2016.7883220.

Lashkarashvili, Nineli, and Magda Tsintsadze. 2022. "Toxicity Detection in Online Georgian Discussions." *International Journal of Information Management Data Insights* 2 (1): 100062. https://doi.org/10.1016/J. JJIMEI.2022.100062.

Li, Hui, Lin Yu, Jie Zhang, and Ming Lyu. 2022. "Fusion Deep Learning and Machine Learning for Heterogeneous Military Entity Recognition." *Wireless Communications and Mobile Computing* 2022 (1): 1–11. https://doi.org/10.1155/2022/1103022.

Li, Jiakang, Ruixia Liu, Changfang Chen, Shuwang Zhou, Xiaoyi Shang, and Yinglong Wang. 2022. "An RG-FLAT-CRF Model for Named Entity Recognition of Chinese Electronic Clinical Records." *Electronics* 11 (8): 1282. https://doi.org/10.3390/ELECTRONICS11081282.

Li, Jing, Aixin Sun, Jianglei Han, and Chenliang Li. 2022. "A Survey on Deep Learning for Named Entity Recognition." *IEEE Transactions on Knowledge and Data Engineering* 34 (1): 50–70. https://doi. org/10.1109/TKDE.2020.2981314.

Li, Rihui. 2016. "Classification of Tweets into Policy Agenda Topics." ProQuest Dissertations and Theses, 73. https://login.pallas2.tcl.sc.edu/login?url=https://search.proquest.com/docview/1845053991?accountid= 13965%0Ahttp://resolver.ebscohost.com/openurl?ctx_ver=Z39.88-2004&ctx_enc=info:ofi/ enc:UTF-8&rfr_id=info:sid/ProQuest+Dissertations+%26+Theses+Global&rft_v.

Lin, Wei San, Hong Jie Dai, Jitendra Jonnagaddala, Nai Wun Chang, Toni Rose Jue, Usman Iqbal, Joni Yu Hsuan Shao, I. Jen Chiang, and Yu Chuan Li. 2016. "Utilizing Different Word Representation Methods for Twitter Data in Adverse Drug Reactions Extraction." In TAAI 2015–2015 Conference on Technologies and Applications of Artificial Intelligence, 260–65. https://doi.org/10.1109/TAAI.2015.7407070.

Ma, Pingchuan, Bo Jiang, Zhigang Lu, Ning Li, and Zhengwei Jiang. 2021. "Cybersecurity Named Entity Recognition Using Bidirectional Long Short-Term Memory with Conditional Random Fields." *Tsinghua Science and Technology* 26 (3): 259–65. https://doi.org/10.26599/TST.2019.9010033.

Naseem, Usman, Imran Razzak, and Peter W. Eklund. 2021. "A Survey of Pre-Processing Techniques to Improve Short-Text Quality: A Case Study on Hate Speech Detection on Twitter." *Multimedia Tools and Applications* 80 (28–29): 35239–66. https://doi.org/10.1007/s11042-020-10082-6.

Rajendran, Srinivasan, and Subalalitha Chinnaudayar Navaneetha. 2019. "Automated Named Entity Recognition from Tamil Documents." *2019 IEEE 1st International Conference on Energy, Systems and Information Processing (ICESIP)*, Chennai, India, pp. 1–5, doi: 10.1109/ICESIP46348.2019.8938383.

Romero, Simone, and Karin Becker. 2019. "A Framework for Event Classification in Tweets Based on Hybrid Semantic Enrichment." *Expert Systems with Applications* 118 (March): 522–38. https://doi.org/10.1016/j. eswa.2018.10.028.

Sari, Yunita, Mohd Fadzil Hassan, and Norshuhani Zamin. 2010. "Rule-Based Pattern Extractor and Named Entity Recognition: A Hybrid Approach." *Proceedings 2010 International Symposium on Information Technology – Engineering Technology, ITSim' 10* (2): 563–68. https://doi.org/10.1109/ ITSIM.2010.5561392.

Singh, Vinay, Deepanshu Vijay, Syed Sarfaraz Akhtar, and Manish Shrivastava. 2019. "Named Entity Recognition for Hindi-English Code-Mixed Social Media Text." *Proceedings of the Seventh Named Entities Workshop*, 4 (1): 27–35. Association for Computational Linguistics, Melbourne, Australia. https://doi.org/10.18653/v1/w18-2405.

Song, Min, Won Chul Kim, Dahee Lee, Go Eun Heo, and Keun Young Kang. 2015. "PKDE4J : Entity and Relation Extraction for Public Knowledge Discovery." *Journal of Biomedical Informatics* 57: 320–32. https://doi.org/10.1016/j.Jbi.2015.08.008.

Storcheus, Dmitry, Afshin Rostamizadeh, and Sanjiv Kumar. 2015. "A Survey of Modern Questions and Challenges in Feature Extraction." *The 1st International Workshop Feature Extraction: Modern Questions and Challenges* 44: 1–18.

Subramani, Sudha, Sandra Michalska, Hua Wang, Jiahua Du, Yanchun Zhang, and Haroon Shakeel. 2019. "Deep Learning for Multi-Class Identification from Domestic Violence Online Posts." *IEEE Access* 7: 46210–24. https://doi.org/10.1109/ACCESS.2019.2908827.

Theivendiram, Pranavan, Mokanarangan Thayaparan, Sanath Jayasena, and Gihan Dias. 2018. "Named-Entity-Recognition (Ner) for Tamil Language Using Margin-Infused Relaxed Algorithm (Mira)." In *Computational Linguistics and Intelligent Text Processing*. LNCS 9623. Cham: Springer: 465–76. https://doi.org/10.1007/978-3-319-75477-2_33.

Yanrui, Du. 2020. "Named Entity Recognition Method with Word Position." *2020 International Workshop on Electronic Communication and Artificial Intelligence (IWECAI)*, Shanghai, China: IEEE, pp. 154–59. doi: 10.1109/IWECAI50956.2020.00038.

Zhang, Ling, Magie Hall, and Dhundy Bastola. 2018. "Utilizing Twitter Data for Analysis of Chemotherapy." *International Journal of Medical Informatics* 120: 92–100. https://doi.org/10.1016/j.ijmedinf.2018.10.002.

Zhang, Ruoyu, Pengyu Zhao, Weiyu Guo, Rongyao Wang, and Wenpeng Lu. 2022. "Medical Named Entity Recognition Based on Dilated Convolutional Neural Network." *Cognitive Robotics* 2 (January): 13–20. https://doi.org/10.1016/J.COGR.2021.11.002.

9 A Case Study on Zonal Analysis of Cybercrimes Over a Decade in India

Diya C. R., Umme Salma M., and Chaitra R. Beerannavar

CONTENTS

DOI: 10.1201/9781003319887-9

INTRODUCTION

People are exposed to sophisticated digital transactions in the present technologically progressive world with e-business, e-commerce, e-governance, and e-procurement. Forsaking aspects of the internet for the new "digital native" generation means missing innumerable social connections. All legal issues related to internet crime are dealt with through cyber laws and cybersecurity. India does not have a staunch cybersecurity law. The Information Technology Act 2000, when read with the rules and regulations drawn under it, deals mainly with cybersecurity measures and the cybercrimes associated therewith. Information security practices mainly focus on protecting confidentiality, integrity, and availability of information, while cybersecurity is the ability to protect or defend the use of cyberspace from cyberattacks. Cyberspace is nothing but an interconnected network of information systems or infrastructures such as the Internet, telecommunications networks, computer systems, embedded processors and controllers, and many other systems. Information security has limited coverage of risks emanating from cyberspace such as cyber warfare, negative social impacts of people's interaction (trolling, defamatory viral messages, online fraud etc.), software and services on the Internet, and threats from the Internet of Things (IoT). These and various other threats in online mode are not classic information security issues and thus need to be covered under a separate strict cybersecurity framework. The emerging latest technologies and online tools in cyberspace are rapidly increasing organizations' exposure to new vulnerabilities, thereby causing risk. The inability of legislators to keep cybercrime legislation ahead of fast-moving technological advances leads to frustration among law enforcement officials. Using the technological tools available and benefits of cyberspace, organizations manage their risk effectively through a robust cybersecurity framework.

BACKGROUND

The growth of communication systems and information technology has made immense changes in the digital modern world. The internet came to India in 1985 with the Educational and Research Network (ERNET) project of the Department of Electronics (Arora & Banwet, 2006). In August 1995, Videsh Sanchar Nigam Ltd. (VSNL), a public-sector undertaking, started offering internet service to individuals. This opened a hitherto unexplored market (Arora & Banwet, 2006). The resolution of the General Assembly of the United Nations dated January 30, 1997, gave birth to the Information Technology Act, which led to the adoption of Model Law on Electronic Commerce on International Trade Law. The Indian bill was drafted by the Department of Electronics (DoE) in July 1998. It could only be introduced in the House on December 16, 1999, when the new IT Ministry was formed and alterations were made related to e-commerce and matters about the World Trade Organization (WTO) obligations. The bill was introduced in Parliament and was referred to the 42-member Parliamentary Standing Committee following demands and suggestions from the members. One of the suggestions that were greatly argued about was that a cyber café owner must maintain a register to record the names and addresses of all people visiting the café and a list of the websites that they browsed. This suggestion was made as a precautionary measure to curb cybercrime and to facilitate speedy locating of cyber-criminals. This was criticized to a large extent, as it would invade a net surfer's privacy and would not be economically viable. This suggestion, after a lot of expert opinions, was dropped by the IT Ministry in its final draft. The development of electronic commerce has pushed the requirement for dynamic and compelling administrative components which would additionally fortify and secure the legitimate foundation so urgent to the achievement of electronic commerce. To make suitable amendments to the existing laws to facilitate e-commerce and give legal recognition to electronic records and digital signatures, the government of India introduced the Information Technology Bill 1999, and later it had the assent of the president and came to be known as the Information Technology Act 2000. The IT Act is based on the UNCITRAL model law on e-commerce. The preamble of the IT Act specifies that the act is aligned with affording legal recognition to transactions carried out electronically. The scope of the IT Act goes much beyond its preamble but centers on legal recognition of electronic records. It covers multiple areas, including data protection and security, privacy, cybercrimes, adjudication of cyber disputes, government-mandated surveillance of digital communication, and intermediary liability.

PROBLEM RATIONALE AND RESEARCH QUESTIONS

The case study will answer the following research questions

Q1. What is the distribution of cybercrime data across various zones in India?
Q2. What variations are observed related to incidences of crime in states and union territories?
Q3. Which cybercrimes have a high incidence rate?
Q4. What are the top ten places where high cybercrimes are witnessed?
Q5. What is the trend observed?
Q6. What safety measures are ensured by the government of India?

LITERATURE REVIEW

Cyber Victimization of Women and Cyber Laws in India

This chapter provides a situational analysis of cybercrimes against women in India and laws that prevent cyber victimization. This chapter deals with the current legal protections that are available to women victims in India for cybercrimes such as offensive communication, offences against cyber privacy, hacking, stalking, and related crimes.

CYBERCRIME SCENARIOS IN INDIA AND JUDICIAL RESPONSE

This chapter explains how cybercrime is emerging as a serious threat and examines worldwide initiatives by governments, police departments, and intelligence units to curb cross-border cyber threats. It also gives us an awareness of special cyber cells across the country for educating personnel. *Cyber Law and Cybercrimes* by Barowalia and Aarushi Jain explains the various kinds of cybercrime, loopholes in Indian information technology laws, and the various preventive measures to tackle it from the government as well as private entities.

MEANING AND DEFINITION OF CYBERCRIME

Cybercrimes are criminal activities which are carried out with the help of computers or the internet. Due to the wide use of the internet, nameless and faceless crimes involving computers are emerging rapidly. A computer may be used as a tool or as a target in commission of a cybercrime. Cybercrime ranges across a spectrum of activities which includes breaches of individual and corporate privacy, identity theft, malware attacks, hacking, cyber pornography, grooming, denial of service attacks, and so on. The first recorded cybercrime took place in the year 1820 when Joseph-Marie Jacquard, a textile manufacturer in France, produced a loom. The loom allowed the repetition of a series of steps in the weaving of fabrics. This generated fear among his employees that machine power would replace manpower, and their traditional employment and livelihood were being threatened. An act of sabotage was committed to discourage Jacquard from using the new technology.

DEFINITION OF CYBERCRIME

However, in general, the term cybercrime means any illegal activity which is carried out with the help of the internet by using computers as a tool or target (Chopra and School, n.d.). The Oxford

Dictionary defined the term cybercrime as "Criminal activities carried out by means of computers or the Internet." Professor S.T. Viswanathan gave three definitions in his book *The Indian Cyber Laws with Cyber Glossary* as follows:

a) Any illegal action in which a computer is the tool or object of the crime.
b) Any incident associated with computer technology in which a victim suffered or could have suffered loss and a perpetrator, by intention, made or could have made a gain.
c) Computer abuse is considered as any illegal, unethical, or unauthorized behavior relating to the automatic processing and transmission of data.

(Vishwanathan, 2001)

TYPES OF CYBERCRIME

a) Harassment via e-mail: It is a very common type of harassment through sending letters or attachments of files and folders.
b) Cyber-stalking: A specific victim is targeted by following the person virtually, creating fear using computer technology such as the internet, e-mail, phones, text messages, webcam, websites, or videos.
c) Dissemination of obscene material: This includes indecent exposure/pornography (or child pornography) or hosting of web sites containing these prohibited materials. These obscene materials may cause harm to the mind of the adolescent and tend to deprave or corrupt their mind (Halder & Jaishankar n.d.)
d) Hacking: This is taking unauthorized control/access over a computer system, and the act of hacking destroys data as well as computer programs. Hackers usually hack telecommunication and mobile networks (Halder & Jaishankar, n.d.).
e) Cracking: This is one of the gravest cybercrimes known to date. It is a dreadful feeling to know that a stranger has broken into your computer systems without your knowledge and consent and has tampered with precious confidential data and information.
f) E-mail spoofing: A spoofed e-mail misrepresents its origin. It shows its origin to be different from where it actually originates.
g) SMS spoofing: Spoofing is a blocking through spam, which is unwanted, uninvited messages. Here an offender steals the identity of another in the form of a mobile phone number, sends an SMS via the internet, and the receiver gets the SMS from the mobile phone number of the victim. It is a very serious cybercrime against any individual.
h) Phishing: A cyber-criminal posing as a real service provider sends an email requesting credit card details and passwords to update their records. Debit and credit cards are then used by criminals for their financial benefit through withdrawing money from the victim's bank account fraudulently ("Cybercrime during Coronavirus Pandemic – Coronavirus (COVID-19) – India" n.d.).
i) Child pornography: This involves the use of computer networks to create, distribute, or access materials that sexually exploit minor children.
j) Intellectual property crimes: Intellectual property is a bundle of rights given to a person for a creative work. When the owner is deprived completely or partially of their rights by an unlawful act, then it is an offence. The usual form of violation is software piracy; infringement of copyright, trademark, patents, or designs; service mark violation; theft of computer source code; and so on.
k) Cyber squatting: This is where two persons claim the same domain name, either by claiming that they registered the name first on by right of using it before the other or using something like it previously.

l) Cyber vandalism: Cyber vandalism means destroying or damaging data when a network service is stopped or interrupted. It may include within its purview any kind of physical harm done to the computer of any person. These acts may take the form of theft of a computer, some part of a computer, or a peripheral attached to the computer.

m) Malware: Viruses are programs that attach themselves to a computer or a file and then circulate themselves to other files and to other computers on a network. They usually affect the data on a computer either by altering or deleting it. Worm attacks transmit copies from a user's computer to other computers.

n) Cyber terrorism: The main aim of this attack is to cause physical or virtual violence to national interests or damage a public utility service managed by computer systems. Cyber terrorism activities endanger the sovereignty and integrity of the nation.

o) Cyber warfare: This refers to politically motivated hacking to conduct sabotage and espionage. It is a form of information warfare sometimes seen as analogous to conventional warfare.

ZONAL ANALYSIS OF CYBERCRIMES OVER A DECADE IN INDIA: A CASE STUDY

Case Analysis and Discussion

Sample Size

The data chosen for the study are related to cybercrime (CC). The sample size of the data is restricted to the top-layer administrative units, that is, states and union territories of the country India. Ten years of data related to cybercrime are collected from 28 states and 8 union territories from the years 2011 to 2020. The main aim of restricting the sample size to states and union territories (UTs) over ten years is to conduct a case study on zonal analysis of cybercrimes over a decade in India.

Data Collection

Online websites are used as the means to collect the cybercrime data required for analysis. The main reason for choosing this digital platform is that the websites used to collect the data are authentic and authorized by the government of India, thus providing genuine information. Three different websites, NCRB (https://ncrb.gov.in/), Indiastat (www.indiastat.com), and CERT (www.cert-in.org. in), are used to collect data related to cybercrime.

The NCRB data are used for zone-wise analysis of cybercrime in India over a decade ranging from 2011 to 2020. Crime-wise analysis is done using Indiastat data, and an analysis with respect to handling of cybercrime incidents over the past 10 years is done using CERT data.

A three-phase analysis is done to conduct the case study. Phase 1 deals with zone-wise analysis, Phase 2 deals with crime-wise analysis, and Phase 3 deals with analyzing the measures taken to handle the cybercrime.

Zone-Wise Analysis

The first phase of the analysis begins with grouping the data into seven zones: central, east, west, north, south, north-east, and union territories. The grouped data are then examined to identify which zone has the highest cybercrime incidences. The main outcome of this phase is to identify which zone(s) require immediate measures to be taken to provide cybersecurity.

Questions answered in this phase are as follows:

Q1. What is the distribution of cybercrime data across various zones in India?

Q2. What variations are observed related to incidences of crime in states and union territories?

TABLE 9.1

Zonification of Geographical Regions of India

Zone	Region Covered	Count
Central zone	Chhattisgarh and Madhya Pradesh	2
East zone	Bihar, Jharkhand, Odisha, West Bengal	4
West zone	Goa, Gujarat, Maharashtra, Rajasthan	4
North zone	Haryana, Himachal, Punjab, Uttarakhand, and Uttar Pradesh,	5
South zone	Andhra Pradesh, Karnataka, Kerala, Tamil Nadu, Telangana	5
North-east zone	Arunachal Pradesh, Assam, Manipur, Meghalaya, Mizoram, Nagaland, Sikkim, and Tripura	8
UT	Andaman & Nicobar Island, Chandigarh, D&N Haveli and Daman & Diu, Delhi, Jammu & Kashmir, Ladakh, Lakshadweep and Puducherry	8

TABLE 9.2

Zone-Wise Analysis of Cybercrimes Reported in India from 2011 to 2020

Zone	2011	2012	2013	2014	2015	2016	2017	2018	2019	2020	10-year Sum
Central zone	181	256	443	412	334	348	661	879	777	996	5287
East zone	140	401	611	686	1206	1363	2545	2482	4154	5359	18947
West zone	594	825	1339	2865	3403	3714	5379	5346	7528	8173	39166
North zone	256	533	1216	2194	2679	3235	5831	7177	12399	12472	47992
South zone	822	1244	1657	2627	3102	2737	5957	8886	17289	18872	63193
North-east zone	58	87	196	501	573	762	1252	2161	2364	3836	11790
UT	118	158	231	337	295	158	166	317	224	327	2331

Table 9.1 clearly provides the answer to Q1. From Table 9.2, the highest number of crimes are recorded in the south zone, followed by north and west. The union territories show the lowest ratio.

The answer to Q2 is provided in Table 9.3. From Table 9.3, the highest cybercrime rate was observed in the year 2020 and the least in 2011. That is, the crime rate follows an upward trend irrespective of the zone. A major observation to be considered is the distribution of crime rate across states and union territories. Around 98.76% of cybercrimes are witnessed in states where the administration is federal in nature; on the other hand, only 1.24% of crimes are observed in union territories where there is unitary administration. However, the sizes of states cannot be ignored. Generally, states are larger in size compared to union territories: the larger the size, the bigger the population, which may result in higher percentage of crime. However, the answer for Q2 is that the gap in the crime rate is significant between states and UTs.

Crime-Wise Analysis of Cybercrime in India

In Phase 2, we mainly focus on crime-wise analysis of cybercrime in India. Data collected from the Indiastat website are used. The data collected cover the ten cybercrimes as attributes: computer-related offences, cybercrimes against women, identity theft, cheating using computer resources, publishing, or transmitting obscenity in electronic form, ransomware, cybercrimes against children,

TABLE 9.3
Zone-Wise Analysis of Cybercrime Data

Zone	Minimum CC in 10 Years	Corresponding Year Minimum CC	Maximum CC in 10 Years	Corresponding Year Maximum CC	Average Rate CC in 10 Years	CC Percentage in 10 Years
Central zone	181	2011	996	2020	528.7	2.801713
East zone	140	2011	5359	2020	1894.7	10.04049
West zone	594	2011	8173	2020	3916.6	20.75504
North zone	256	2011	12472	2020	47992	25.43215
South zone	822	2011	18872	2020	63193	33.48754
North-east zone	58	2011	3836	2020	11790	6.247814
States only total	2051	2011	49708	2020	186375	98.76475
UT total	118	2011	337	2014	2331	1.235255
India total	2169	2011	50045	2020	188706	100

TABLE 9.4
Crime-Wise Analysis of Data

Number	Cybercrime Type	10yrs_Total	Percentage	Maximum	Place	Year	Zone
1.	Computer-related offences	84723	41.3834	11700	Karnataka	2019	South
2.	Cybercrimes against women	29579	14.44802	2859	Jharkand	2020	East
3.	Identity theft	28549	13.94491	10482	Kerala	2019	South
4.	Cheating using computer resources	25603	12.50592	6486	Jharkand	2019	East
5.	Publishing or transmitting obscenity in electronic form	22641	11.05912	2120	Uttar Pradesh	2020	North
6.	Ransomware	4259	2.080331	1136	Uttar Pradesh	2018	North
7.	Cybercrimes against children	4049	1.977756	234	Andhra Pradesh	2013	South
8.	Violation of privacy	3620	1.768208	628	Uttar Pradesh	2019	North
9.	Tampering with computer source documents	1573	0.76834	192	Uttar Pradesh	2018	North
10.	Cyber terrorism	131	0.063988	11	Tamil Nadu	2018	South

violation of privacy, tampering with computer source documents, and cyber terrorism. The questions mainly addressed in Phase 2 are:

Q3. Which cybercrimes have a high incidence rate?
Q4. Which are the top ten places where high cybercrimes are witnessed?
Q5. What is the trend observed?

The crime-wise analysis of data is provided in Table 9.4.

The answer to Q4 is provided in Table 9.4 and Figure 9.1. Computer-related offences top the chart with 84,723, while cyberterrorism is at 131.

It is also important to find which year witnessed the most cybercrimes. Table 9.5 helps us to identify it. From Table 9.5, the year 2020 witnessed the most cybercrimes, so a zone-wise analysis for 2020 was conducted. The result of the analysis reveals in which zones which cybercrime was dominant and its corresponding place of incidence. The details of the analysis are given in Table 9.6.

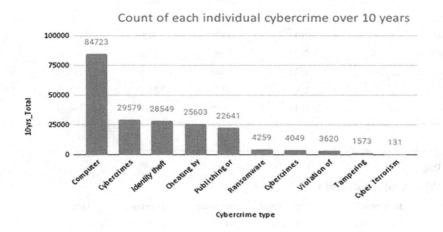

FIGURE 9.1   Count of each individual cybercrime over ten years.

TABLE 9.5
Total of All Cybercrime Incidence Reported Year-Wise

Year	Total_of_10 Crimes
2011	1812
2012	4119
2013	4496
2014	11952
2015	9875
2016	490
2017	22992
2018	34800
2019	56278
2020	57913
Total	204727

TABLE 9.6

Highest Cybercrimes Reported in 2020

Zone	Crime Type	Total	Location of Maximum Incidence
Central zone	Cybercrimes against women	391	Madhya Pradesh
East zone	Computer-related offences	10289	Jharkhand
West zone	Cybercrimes against women	2369	Maharashtra
North zone	Computer-related offences	6912	Chhattisgarh
South zone	Cybercrimes against women	1639	Assam
North-East zone	Computer-related offences	1576	Telangana
UT	Computer-related offences	1014	Kashmir

TABLE 9.7

Top Ten Locations Witnessing Highest Crime Rate

Rank	Location	Sum of All Crimes over 10 Years
1.	Uttar Pradesh	81782
2.	Karnataka	71990
3.	Maharashtra	50171
4.	Telangana	24414
5.	Assam	21137
6.	Rajasthan	16874
7.	Andhra Pradesh	16362
8.	Odisha	11975
9.	Jharkhand	9056
10.	Gujrat	8275

Table 9.6 reveals that computer-related offences were reported more in 2020, the highest being in Jharkhand, followed by Chhattisgarh, Telangana, and Kashmir. Cybercrimes against women also predominated in the regions of Maharashtra, Assam, and Madhya Pradesh.

To answer Q4, that is, to find the top ten locations witnessing the highest cybercrime rate, we calculated the sum of all the years' data across all 28 states and 8 union territories. The results are given in Table 9.7.

Table 9.7 reveals that Uttar Pradesh, Karnataka, and Maharashtra had the highest incidence of cyber-crimes reported across ten years. Even though cyber terrorism incidences are reported the least in India, it is highly important to analyze the data with respect to cyber terrorism because of national security reasons. Figure 9.2 provides a zone-wise distribution of cyber terrorism incidences in India. From Figure 9.2, we see the south zone contributes around 28% in cyber terrorism, followed by the west and north-east zones.

Further analysis revealed that Tamil Nadu, Assam, and Gujarat, respectively, are the top three locations where cyber terrorism was reported. 2011 witnessed 27 incidents, 2020 witnessed 26, and 2018 witnessed 21. From the analysis, cyber terrorism is more prevalent in metropolitan cities and is increasing yearly. The government needs to take efficient security measures to handle cybercrimes.

Zone-wise analysis of cyber terrorism incidence from 2011 to 2020

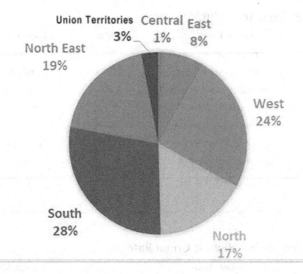

FIGURE 9.2   Zone-wise analysis of cyber terrorism from 2011 to 2020.

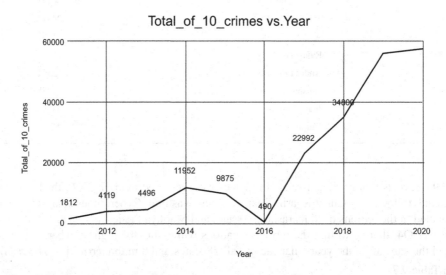

FIGURE 9.3   Total of all ten crimes recorded every year.

When it comes to analyzing the trend of cybercrime, Figure 9.3 provides the answer to Q5. Figure 9.3 clearly reveals that crime incidence follows an uptrend over time. However, a sudden fall in the year 2016 is also observed, where the crime incidents reported were at the lowest value, 490.

Cybersecurity Measures in the Indian Legal Framework

Cybersecurity law is a rather new field for many countries and is still developing worldwide. The issues pertaining to cybersecurity and the increasing threats it imposes in the cyberspace are a huge cause of concern to many countries, as cybersecurity impacts the economy of nations as well as their sovereignty by threatening the power and authority of governments. As there is no effective international framework on cybersecurity, countries are taking individual initiatives to come up with their own national legislations to deal with cybersecurity attacks. These many attempts to regulate cybersecurity issues, both nationally and internationally, have given birth to a new body of cyber jurisprudence focusing on the logical structure, the implications and uses of its concepts, and the formal terms and ways of operation of cyber law. Legal issues relating to electronic communication, computer systems, and networks in cyberspace are a new kind of jurisprudence, that is, cyber jurisprudence with a cybernetic approach. Cyber jurisprudence defines the principles of legal concerns of cyber law, which absolutely regulates cyberspace and internet and deals with the complex idea of cyber jurisdiction.

The Information Technology Act 2000 not only contains provisions that are aimed at safeguarding electronic data, information, or records and preventing unauthorized or unlawful use of a computer system but also provides legal recognition and protection for transactions carried out through electronic data interchange and other means of electronic communication. Further, in accordance with the Information Technology (The Indian Computer Emergency Response Team and Manner of Performing Functions and Duties) Rules 2013 (the CERT Rules), the Computer Emergency Response Team (CERT-In) is the nodal agency under the Ministry of Electronics and Information Technology responsible for the collection, analysis, and dissemination of information on cyber incidents, reporting on vulnerabilities, and promoting effective IT security practices throughout the country by taking emergency measures to contain such incidents.

CYBERSECURITY MEASURES IN THE FORM OF LEGISLATION, RULES, AND REGULATIONS

INFORMATION TECHNOLOGY ACT 2000

The Information Technology Act, 2000 deals with issues of cybercrimes in two broad groups. One is Chapter IX, which deals with penalties and adjudications under sections 43 to 47, and another is Chapter XI, which deals with offences under sections 65 to 75. The act defines cybersecurity under Section 2 (nb) as shielding information, equipment, devices, computers, computer resources, communication devices and the information stored therein from unauthorized access, use, disclosure, disruption, modification, or destruction. In case of any damage to computers, computer systems, and so on, there is a penalty up to Rs. 1 Crore under Section 43. Tampering with computer source documents and hacking computer systems is an offense bringing a penalty of imprisonment up to three years, a fine, or both under Sections 65 and 66. Section 67 deals with publishing or transmitting obscene material in electronic form and provides for imprisonment up to a term of ten years and also a fine up to Rs. 2 lakhs. Section 66B deals with dishonestly receiving stolen computer resources or communication devices, with punishment up to three years, 1 lakh rupees, as fine or both. Section 66C deals with electronic signatures or other identity theft causing financial fraud by using another's password or electronic signature. Section 66D deals with cheating by impersonation using an electronic device or a computer and is punishable with imprisonment for a term which may extend to three years and shall also be liable for a fine up to 1 lakh rupee. Section 66E deals with privacy violations – publishing or transmitting private information from any person without his or her consent is punishable with three years' imprisonment, a 2-lakh fine, or both. Section 66F deals with cyber terrorism with an objective to threaten the unity, integrity, security, or sovereignty of the nation and denying access to any person authorized to access a computer resource or attempting to access a computer resource without authorization. It is an attack on military installations, power plants, air traffic control, banks, traffic controls, telecommunication networks, which are the most likely targets. Other targets of attacks are police, medical, fire, and rescue systems. Cyber terrorism is a striking option for modern terrorists for several reasons. It is cheaper and more anonymous than traditional terrorist methods. Cyber terrorism can be conducted remotely, and the variety and number of targets are enormous. Section 70B in the Information Technology Act 2000 mentions the Indian Computer Emergency Response Team, which shall serve as the national agency for cybersecurity.

Its function in cybersecurity includes gathering, analysis, and dissemination of information on cyber incidents; to forecast and warn about cybersecurity attacks; to take emergent measures on cybersecurity instances; and to manage cyber incident response activities and issue guidelines, advisories, susceptibility notes, and whitepapers relating to information security practices, procedures, prevention, response, and reporting of cyber incidents. Section 72 prescribes the punishment for breaching privacy and confidentiality to third person punishable by imprisonment up to two years, a fine of up to 1 lakh rupees, or both. This was first judicially upheld in the case of State of Tamil Nadu v. Suhas Katti (2004), where the accused, Katti, posted obscene, defamatory messages about a divorced woman in a Yahoo message group and advertised her as a soliciting sex. This was considered one of the first cases to be booked under section 67 of the Information Technology Act 2000.

The Information Technology (Reasonable Security Practices and Procedures and Sensitive Personal Data or Information) Rules 2011 (The SPDI Rules)

The SPDI Rules protect personal data collected by an individual who is involved in commercial or professional undertakings. This is because all obligations under the 2011 Rules are incident applicable to corporate bodies. A "corporate body" is defined under Section 43A of the IT Act as "any company and comprises a firm, sole proprietorship or other association of individuals engaged in commercial or professional undertakings." Therefore, an individual or a person who is not engaged in commercial or professional activities would fall outside the ambit of the 2011 Rules. Rule 3 explains sensitive personal data or information such as passwords; financial information; physical, physiological, and mental health conditions; sexual orientation; medical records; history; and biometric information. These details provided to the corporate body for providing services come under a lawful contract or otherwise provided that, any information that is freely available or available in public domain or provided under the Right to Information Act, 2005. Hence, a body corporate must provide a policy for privacy and disclosure of information. There is an onus placed upon body corporates under Rule 5 as to the procedure for collection of information. This requires the body corporate to inform users about the purpose of data collection, security of data collected, and how long it is retained, and the body corporate shall appoint a grievance officer and publish his or her name and contact details on its website. The grievance officer shall redress grievances at their earliest convenience or within one month of receipt of the grievance. Further, by virtue of Rule 6, a body corporate has an obligation to comply with the procedure for disclosure of information in which the information is to be collected with consent and sensitive personal data shall not be disclosed to any other person. A body corporate or a person on its behalf shall be considered to have complied with reasonable security practices and processes if they have executed these security practices and standards and have a comprehensive documented information security program and information security policies that contain managerial, technical, operational, and physical security control measures that correspond to the information assets being protected with the nature of business under Rule 8.This is considered a reasonable security practice. In the event of an information security attack, the body corporate or a person on its behalf shall be required to prove, as and when called upon to do so by the agency mandated under the law, that they have executed security control measures per their documented information security program and information security policies. An audit of reasonable security practices and measures shall be carried cut by an auditor at least once a year or as and when the company or a person on its behalf undertakes significant upgrades to its procedure and computer resources.

Information Technology (Intermediaries Guidelines) Rules 2018 and Exemptions

The Information Technology Act was amended in 2008 to provide exemption to intermediaries from liability for any third-party information, among others. Per this, the IT (Intermediary Guidelines) Rules 2011 were outlined under Section 79(2) of the act to specify the due diligence requirements for intermediaries to claim such exemption. The Supreme Court has clarified that threat to public safety cannot be a ground to restrict freedom of speech. The court stated that any restriction placed on freedom of speech must relate to the grounds specified under Article 19(2) (Secy., Ministry of Information & Broadcasting, Govt. of India v. Cricket Assn. of Bengal 1995 AIR 1236).

In 2015, when the Supreme Court examined Section 79(3)(b) of the Information Technology Act 2000, it was observed that intermediaries are required to remove or disable access to certain types of content based on user requests. The Supreme Court stated that it would be difficult for intermediaries to judge the legitimacy of each item with high volumes of content. The provision reads that content needs to be removed or incapacitated only if: (i) it is done based on the order of a court or government, and (ii) the order relates to one of the restrictions under Article 19(2) of the Constitution such as national security and public order (Shreya Singhal vs. Union of India AIR 2015 SC 1523).

Indian Penal Code 1860

Identity thefts and associated cyber fraud are embodied in the Indian Penal Code (IPC), 1860 – invoked along with the Information Technology Act of 2000.The primary relevant sections of the IPC that cover cyber frauds are forgery (Section 464), forgery pre-planned for cheating (Section 4), false documentation (Section 465), a forged document as genuine (Section 471), and reputation damage (Section 469).

Companies (Management and Administration) Rules 2014

Under the Companies Act 2013, there now exist several mechanisms under which affected parties may seek to hold management liable for cybersecurity-linked failures in a post-incident scenario. These include fiduciary duties of directors and through class actions. These forms of liability are co-existent with remedies which may be available under other frameworks including sectoral regulations (if any) and the Information Technology Act (Gifty, Bharathi, & Krishnakumar, 2018).

ROLE OF GOVERNMENT AND ITS ORGANIZATIONS IN ENSURING CYBERSECURITY IN INDIA

THE MINISTRY OF ELECTRONICS AND INFORMATION TECHNOLOGY

The functions of the Ministry of Electronics and Information Technology (MeitY) include policy matters relating to information technology; electronics; internet (all matters other than licensing of internet service providers); promotion of internet, IT, and IT-enabled services, promotion of digital transactions including digital payments; assistance to other departments in the promotion of e-governance, e-commerce, e-medicine, and e-infrastructure; promotion of information technology education and information technology–based education; matters relating to cyber laws; and administration of the Information Technology Act 2000 and other laws related to information technology. It deals with areas relating to promotion and manufacturing of semiconductor devices in the country, excluding all matters relating to Semiconductor Complex Limited (SCL) interactions in IT-related materials with international agencies and bodies, such as Internet for Business Limited (IFB), Institute for Education in Information Society (IBI), and International Code Council – online (ICC). Initiative is taken on bridging the digital divide and matters relating to Digital India Corporation.

CERT-In

This is the nodal agency to deal with cybersecurity threats and is an office within the Ministry of Electronics and Information Technology. A computer emergency response team (CERT) is a group of information security experts responsible for protection against, detection of, and response to an organization's cybersecurity incidents. CERT-In was an initiative by the Indian Department of Information Technology in 2004 and operates under the auspices of that department. Per the provisions of the Information Technology Amendment Act 2008, CERT-In is responsible for managing the administration of the act. The purpose of CERT-In is to react to computer security incidents immediately, report on vulnerabilities, and stimulate effective IT security practices throughout the country. Throughout the world, CERT organizations are independent entities, although there may be coordinated activities among groups. The first CERT group was formed in the United States at Carnegie Mellon University. CERT-In is a government body established to gather, analyze, and publish information on cyber incidents, as well as provide forecasts and alerts about cybersecurity incidents, provide emergency measures to deal with cybersecurity incidents, and coordinate cyber incident response actions. Such notifications are required to be made within a reasonable time to leave scope for appropriate action by the authorities. The importance of following "breach notice obligations" depends upon the "place of incidence of such breaches" and whether Indian customers have been targeted. CERT issues guiding principles, advisories, vulnerability notes, and whitepapers involving information security practices, procedures, prevention, response, and reporting of cyber incidents.

Reserve Bank of India

The Reserve Bank of India (RBI) guidelines associated with the cybersecurity framework will enable banks to formalize and adopt cybersecurity policies and cyber crisis management plans. The necessity of sharing information on cybersecurity incidents with RBI will also help to structure practical threat identification and modification. Reserve Bank Information Technology Private Limited (ReBIT) is an arrangement by the Reserve Bank of India to serve its information technology and cybersecurity needs and to improve the cyber resilience of the Indian banking industry. Banks need to assess their cybersecurity vigilance under the active guidance and oversight of the IT Sub Committee of the board or the bank's board directly. Banks are required to report to the Cybersecurity and Information Technology Examination (CSITE) Cell of the Department of Banking Supervision, Reserve Bank of India, which has the following functions to identify the gaps with reference to cybersecurity/resilience framework, propose measures/controls and their expected efficacy, ensure milestones with timelines for executing the proposed controls/measures, and measure standards for assessing their effectiveness, including the risk evaluation and risk management procedure followed/proposed by the bank.

The National Association of Service & Software Companies

Rather than the government, the private sector has taken the initiative and made efforts to comply with the demands of privacy principles and self-regulation. In this line, the National Association of Service & Software Companies (NASSCOM) is India's national information technology business group and has taken various steps to drive private sector efforts to improve data security (Barowalia & Jain, 2022).

National Institute of Standards and Technology

This agency is responsible for improving the cybersecurity of critical infrastructure under Executive Order (EO) 13636. The National Institute of Standards and Technology (NIST) published a report on 13/10/2020 NISTIR 8286, *Integrating Cybersecurity and Enterprise Risk Management (ERM).* This report highlights understanding of the connection between cybersecurity risk management and ERM and the benefits of including those approaches. The growing frequency, inventiveness, and severity of cybersecurity attacks means that all enterprises should guarantee that cybersecurity risk is receiving proper attention within their enterprise risk management agendas. The intention of this document is to facilitate individual organizations within an enterprise to expand their cybersecurity risk information, which they provide as inputs to their enterprise's ERM processes through communications and risk information sharing. Through this, enterprises and their constituent organizations can better recognize, assess, and manage their cybersecurity risks in the context of their wider mission and business objectives. This document explains the value of bottom-level measures of risk usually addressed at lower system and higher organization levels to the broader enterprise level.

The National Security Council

The National Security Council (NSC) was introduced by the National Security Act of 1947. It is the highest body of the three-tiered structure of the national security management system in India. These structures are the Strategic Policy Group, the National Security Advisory Board, and a secretariat from the Joint Intelligence Committee. It is the president's main medium for considering national security and foreign policy matters with his national security advisors and cabinet.

The National Technical Research Organization

The National Technical Research Organization (NTRO) is an intelligence agency which is technically set up under the national security advisor in the prime minister's office. This includes the National Institute of Cryptology Research and Development (NICRD), which is first of its kind in Asia. The NTRO functions as the primary advisor on security-related problems to the prime minister and the Union Council of Ministers of India. It also offers technical intelligence to other Indian agencies. NTRO's activities include satellite and terrestrial monitoring. While the agency does not disturb the working of the technical wings of various intelligence agencies or those of the Indian Armed Forces, it acts as an excellent feeder agency for facilitating technical intelligence on internal and external security to other agencies.

The Ministry of Home Affairs

The Ministry of Home Affairs (MHA) continuously monitors the internal security situation; issues appropriate advisories; shares intelligence inputs; interacts with the PM; provides international event/conference clearances online; and extends human resources and financial support, guidance, and expertise to the state governments for maintenance of security, peace, and harmony. It discharges multifarious responsibilities such as details about the Indian Cyber Crime Coordination Centre (I4C) Scheme, National Cyber Crime Research, and Innovation Centre, Cyber and Information Security (C&Is) Division. Besides these bodies, there is a Cyber and Information Security (C&Is) Division dealing with cybersecurity, cyber crime, national information security policy, and guidelines. The Cybercrime Prevention against Women and Children (CCPWC) Scheme provides a central repository for all such crimes, which will be used for publishing an annual analytical report regarding cyber-crimes, their trends, and remedial measures. The research and development unit needs to take up research and development activities in partnership with research and academic institutions of national importance. Further, the Indian Cybercrime Coordination Centre Scheme adopts measures to prevent the misuse of cyberspace for furthering the cause of extremist and terrorist groups and suggest amendments, if required, in cyber laws to keep stride with fast-changing technologies and international cooperation. This scheme organizes all activities related to execution of mutual legal assistance treaties (MLATs) with other countries related to cybercrimes in consultation with the relevant nodal authority in Ministry of Home Affairs. The Ministry of Defense also deals with cybersecurity policy, the e-mail policy of the government of India, guidelines on approved social media frameworks, guidelines for the use of IT devices on government networks, and information security best practices.

National Cybersecurity Policy

Cyber-crime has been increasing at a massive rate in India. To tackle this menace, the Indian government released its first national cybersecurity policy with the aim to monitor and protect information and strengthen defenses from cyberattacks (Barowalia & Jain, 2022). The national cybersecurity policy is a framework of rules dealing with security in cyberspace by the Department of Electronic and Information Technology (DEIT) that aims at protecting public and private infrastructure from cyberattacks. Cybersecurity policy is a developing task, and it focuses on needs of the whole spectrum of ICT users and providers, including home users; small, medium, and large enterprises; and government and non-government entities. It serves as a secure framework for defining and administering actions related to security of cyberspace. Per the needs of individual sectors and organizations, appropriate cybersecurity policies are designed. The policy delivers an overview of what it takes to protect information, information systems, and networks effectively and gives insight into the government's approach and strategy for protection of cyberspace in the country. It also gives directions to enable the collaborative working of all key players in public and private to safeguard the country's information systems. The aim of this policy is to create a cybersecurity framework that points out specific actions and programs to improve the security of the country's cyberspace. National policies/strategies provide an important framework and roadmap for the security and growth of a country.

A comprehensive cybersecurity policy is a must for the comprehensive regulation of cyberspace. It provides a roadmap and focused approach to regulate and control the negative effects of cyberspace. Cyberspace is a phenomenon which cannot be regulated through a single institution or agency. It requires a holistic and comprehensive approach and state-sponsored mechanism to build a solid foundation for the establishment of cyber power and constructing more cyber-secure societies. It is true that cyberspace is a global challenge and difficult to control through domestic legislation, but national policies provide an important framework to promote international agreements and standards to support the intergovernmental collaboration that put in place the educational and industrial policies. The purpose of the policy is to protect information and information infrastructure in cyberspace; build abilities to prevent and respond to cyber threats; reduce vulnerabilities; and minimize damage from cyber incidents through a combination of institutional structures, people, processes, technology, and cooperation. Despite this robust legal and regulatory framework in India, the rate of cybercrimes continues to grow alarmingly.

ANALYZING THE MEASURES TAKEN TO HANDLE CYBERCRIMES

From the Phase 1 and Phase 2, study it is clear that cybercrimes, irrespective of their type, are increasing. Majorly computer related offences are the highest form of cybercrimes creating the menace. As a matter of local and national security, it is very important to handle cybercrime issues seriously.

This section focuses on Q6: What safety measures are ensured by the government of India?

The government of India (GoI) is addressing this issue related to computer related offences. Under computer-related offences, phishing, probing, virus attacks, website defacement, spam, and website intrusion are to be handled effectively. The data used in Phase 3 are collected from the CERT website, which is an official website of the GoI. Table 9.8 provides the answer to Q6. Information related to what percentage of cybercrimes related to cybersecurity incidents handled from 2011 to 2020 is presented in Table 9.8.

From Table 9.8, one can see that probing is the cybersecurity incident handled most effectively, followed by virus code attack and website defacement. Probing is an initial step for any cyberattack and allows the hacker to access network information and attack. The GoI is trying its best to curb these issues. However, many other factors like breaches, open proxy server issues, and security drills need to be worked on more.

The three-phase analysis clearly provides valuable insights related to zone-wise, crime-wise, and measure-wise analysis of cybercrime data collected from the NCRB, Indiastat, and CERT websites. The analysis was helpful to answer all six questions and provided valuable insights.

TABLE 9.8
Cybersecurity Incidents Handled from 2011 to 2020

Cybersecurity Incidents Handled	Percentage Handled
Phishing	0.33
Probing	68.76
Virus code	12.64
Website defacement	8.30
Spam	6.99
Website intrusion	1.49
Others	1.47

ISSUES AND CHALLENGES IN THE INDIAN CYBERSECURITY REGIME

This reflects issues and challenges that are present in the system and need to be addressed immediately. The research has identified the following issues and challenges in the existing legal framework. The Information Technology Act 2000 does not define cyber-terrorism, and the IT Amendment Act of 2008, by adding Section 66F, only provides for punishments. Given this ambiguity, the global fight against cyber terrorism is necessary, as incidents of cyber terrorist attacks are increasing alarmingly. The IT Act doesn't provide a definition of personal data. The definition of "data" has more relevance in the field of cyber-crime.

Data protection consists of a framework of security measures which is technical and is designed to guarantee that data are handled in such a manner as to ensure that they are safe from unexpected, unintended, unwanted, or malicious use. The absence of geographical borders may give rise to a condition where an act legal in the country where it is done may infringe the laws of another country, resulting in jurisdictional conflicts. In India, the Information Technology Act, by virtue of Section 75, convenes extraterritorial jurisdiction. This section makes it clear that whether an offence is committed outside or in India, the offender shall be governed by the provisions of Information Technology Act whether he or she is Indian or not provided such an offence relates to computer systems or networks that are situated in India. Thus, the solution provided by Indian laws to the problem of enforcement is limited (Arya, 2019). The absence of a uniform and harmonized law governing the jurisdictional aspects of disputes arising using the Internet makes this process more complicated. Jurisdiction in cyberspace requires clear principles rooted in international law. Jurisdiction is the authority by which a court of law or an official must enforce laws. It may be implemented through legislative, executive, or judicial actions. The usual approach to jurisdiction requires a court whether it has the territorial, pecuniary, or subject matter jurisdiction to entertain the case brought before it. With the advent of the internet, the question of "territorial" jurisdiction has become complex, largely because the internet is borderless. Hence, in the cyber world, there are no borders between one region and the other within a country and no borders even between countries. There are no standard documented procedures for searching, seizing, or collecting digital evidence, and there is a lack of standard operating procedures for forensic examination of digital evidence. In India the conviction rate is very low due to the lack of standard procedures for seizure and analysis of digital evidence.

The Budapest Convention is the first international treaty on crimes committed via the Internet and other computer networks, dealing particularly with infringements of copyright, computer-related fraud, child pornography, and violations of network security. It also contains a series of powers and procedures such as the search of computer networks and interception. Without international cooperation, national cyber laws are useless. This highlights the importance of an international cyber law treaty or convention that can provide a "harmonized framework" for cyber law across the globe (Arya, 2019).

CONCLUSION

The challenges discussed here suggest that there is an urgent need to establish a strong national cybersecurity regime which would deal with various concerns and issues in cybercrime. A collective approach to cybersecurity can be developed, executed, and encouraged by applying the principles of governance, management, and completeness. This would encourage a system of cybersecurity which would ultimately lead to the development of an instinct for what is safe and what is risky. There is a need for the development of an international, multi-stakeholder regime that would include industry, governmental, international, and non-governmental organizations focused on cybersecurity in cyberspace. Apart from this, the emergence of cyber jurisprudence around the world has promoted the growth of new dimensions in law and cyberspace. The most fatal threat today for various countries is cyber terrorism. The Information Technology Act 2000 was amended in 2008 and Section 66 F was inserted via the Amendment Act of 2008, which attempted to define and penalize cyber terrorism. However, it does not cater to the required efforts to control and mitigate this growing menace. A single provision is not enough to deal with this huge security threat, so there is an urgent need to have a detailed legislative and regulatory framework with political, legal, and technical infrastructure. The present policy completely overlooks this issue of immense importance to national security (Bamrara, Singh & Bhatt, 2013). The issue of cyber jurisdiction has a global character which cannot be genuinely addressed by passing only national legislation. Therefore, cyber jurisdictional issues require a global solution. Hence, an international treaty relating to uniform rules applicable to cyber-crimes in all jurisdictions badly needs to be addressed. The government of India is trying its best to confront the issues. The Convention on Cybercrime, also known as the Budapest Convention on Cybercrime, is the first international treaty seeking to address Internet and computer crime by harmonizing national laws, improving investigative techniques, and increasing cooperation among nations. However, India is not a signatory to this convention, which is of concern ("Cyber-Threats and International Law" n.d.).

The three-phase analysis clearly provided valuable insights related to zone-wise, crime-wise, and measure-wise analysis of cybercrime data collected from NCRB, Indiastat and CERT websites. The analysis was helpful to answer all six questions and provided valuable insights. However, many other factors like breaches, open proxy server issues, and security drills need to be worked on more. Proactive measures are needed to eradicate cybercrimes. Measures to enhance cross-border collection of evidence need to be taken. Domestic legislation needs to be enhanced and re-worked to facilitate traceability of cyber criminals. A separate dispute resolution body that specially deals with cybercrime should be established. International cooperation is needed in direct trans-border access, mutual legal assistance, and public–private partnership. Traditional methods used by legal systems have miserably failed in dealing with technology. Criminals are intelligent enough to use innovative methods in cyberspace for committing crimes. To tackle this, a developing and digitally advancing country like India should establish an efficient legal framework with the help and co-operation of other countries. Every stakeholder should be diligent and actively involved in preventing and solving the negative aspect of ICTs – cybercrimes – with an appropriate balance between regulations and self-regulation subject to the different types of crimes in cyberspace to optimize the more creative side or benefits of ICTs. High-tech resources and procedural tools are required to investigate cybercrime, and India lacks both. India also needs to be part of international conventions on cybercrime and assign more resources to fighting cybercrime in terms of updating cybersecurity cells, making use of state-of-the-art technology, and regularly training officials to give them highly specialized skills and make them competent to fight cybercrime.

REFERENCES

Arora, Rajiv, and D.K. Banwet. 2006. "E-Commerce Implementation in India: A Study of Selected Organizations." *Asia-Pacific Development Journal* 1 0(1): 69–95. https://doi.org/10.18356/64e662cb-en.

Arya, Nidhi. 2019. "Cyber Crime Scenario in India and Judicial Response." *International Journal of Trend in Scientific Research and Development* 3 (4): 1108–12. https://doi.org/10.31142/ijtsrd24025.

Bamrara, Atul, Gajendra Singh, and Mamta Bhatt. 2013. "Cyberattacks and Defense Strategies in India: An Empirical Assessment of Banking Sector." *SSRN Electronic Journal* 7 (1): 49–61. https://doi.org/10.2139/ssrn.2488413.

Barowalia, J.N., and A. Jain. 2022. "Cyber Law & Cyber Crimes." *Bharatlawhouse.in.* www.bharatlawhouse.in/shop/cyber-law-information-technology-computer-internet-e-commerce-mobile-law/cyber-law-cyber-crimes-by-jn-barowalia-aarushi-jain/.

Chopra, Aarushi, and Amity School. n.d. "Cybercrime Is the Bane of the Internet: Is India Ready?" Accessed September 30, 2022. https://supremoamicus.org/wp-content/uploads/2020/07/A1-2.pdf.

Cyber Crime during Coronavirus Pandemic – Coronavirus (COVID-19) – India. n.d. *www.mondaq.com.* Accessed February 27, 2022. www.mondaq.com/india/operational-impacts-and-strategy/921026/cyber-crime-during-coronavirus-pandemic.

Cyber-Threats and International Law. n.d. "Security and International Law." Accessed September 30, 2022. https://doi.org/10.5040/9781474201612.ch-014.

Gifty, R., R. Bharathi, and P. Krishnakumar. 2018. "Data Management and Security of Big Data in Internet of Things (IOT) Enabled Cyber Physical Systems." *Journal of Computational and Theoretical Nanoscience* 15 (11): 3218–22. https://doi.org/10.1166/jctn.2018.7602.

Halder, Debarati, and K. Jaishankar. n.d. "Cyber Victimization of Women and Cyber Laws in India." *Cyber Crime*, 742–56. Accessed September 30, 2022. https://doi.org/10.4018/978-1-61350-323-2.ch403.

Viswanathan, Suresh, T. 2001. *The Indian Cyber Law Glossary*. 2nd edition. New Delhi: Bharat Law House.

10 Taming the Confluence of Space Systems and Cybersecurity

Syed Shahzad, Keith Joiner, Felicity Deane, and Li Qiao

CONTENTS

INTRODUCTION

Human spaceflight has allowed humanity the chance to observe our universe from a new perspective. From Yuri Gagarin's first orbital flight to the early exploration of the Moon, the International Space Station (ISS) orbiting the Earth, landing on Mars, and the latest James Webb telescope, these human marvels accumulate over six decades of experience in space exploration. Consequently, over the years, space infrastructure has started to play a crucial role in our daily lives and has become part of critical national infrastructure. The European Commission states:

> Space infrastructure is critical infrastructure on which services that are essential to the smooth running of our societies and economies and our citizens' security depend. It must be protected, and that protection is a major issue for the EU, which goes far beyond the individual interests of the satellite owners.
>
> *(E Commission 2021)*

DOI: 10.1201/9781003319887-10

Space-based technology supports vital societal functions such as modern navigation, communication, weather, finance, timing, defense, and science. Therefore, the security of space infrastructure is critical for society, particularly as these service offerings are challenging to restore if attacked.

Like today's mostly digitized critical infrastructure such as communication, water, chemical, and emergency response, space infrastructure is vulnerable to cyberattacks in a cyberwar. According to the Oxford Dictionary, cyberwar is defined as "the use of computer technology to disrupt the activities of a state or organization, especially the deliberate attacking of information systems for strategic or military purposes," and "cyberwar is asymmetric, which means it benefits lesser military powers as much as military goliaths." Hence, the rapid advancements in new technologies and war-fighting domains have evolved from the old "attack-response" paradigm. As a result, cyberwar is fought in a contemporary, digital realm, with almost no rules of engagement, hard-to-identify enemies (threat actors), and even sometimes obscure motives. Therefore, a cyberwar in space would be devastating and pose critical threats to humanity. Ample evidence suggests that significant dependency on space infrastructure poses a new but critical and under-recognized cybersecurity predicament for space technology providers, international policymakers, and governments. This chapter specifically looks at how space infrastructure is vulnerable to cyberattacks and furthermore how space "weaponization" and "militarization" are major regulatory concerns. The chapter covers the concepts across space architecture, cyber vulnerabilities, cyber weapons, and legal aspects of cyber war in outer space.

LITERATURE REVIEW

The research for this chapter is multidisciplinary in nature, crossing space, cyber, and legal domains. Figures 10.1 and 10.2 highlight eight potential inquiry questions in those domains for this interdisciplinary research. In relation to space-related legal frameworks, the study found limited research published. Furthermore, given the multidisciplinary nature of the topic, the study identified only a few authoritative research sources for space and cybersecurity. The literature review is based on a protocol for discovery and eligibility adapted from the Preferred Reporting Items for Systematic Reviews and Meta-Analyses (PRISMA) framework.

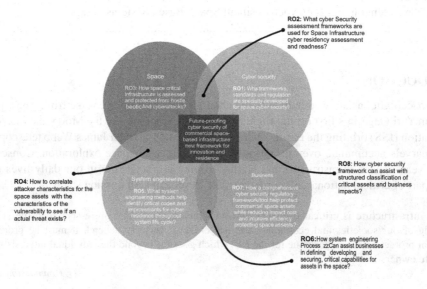

FIGURE 10.1   Research questions Venn diagram.

Search	Keyword 1	Condition	Keyword 2	Google Results	UNSW Results
Any field	space assets	or	cybersecurity	27,000	3,705
Any field	critical space infrastructure	or	standards	6,050	67,000
Any field	space systems cybersecurity	and	framework	2,000	302
Any field	space assets frameworks	and	cybersecurity	6,810	1271
Any field	space assets policy	and	cybersecurity	9,340	1,948
Any field	space assets policy	or	cybersecurity	33	62
Any field	critical space infrastructure	or	cyber resiliency	.	5
Any field	Space infrastructure	and	cyber resiliency	186	21
Any field	Space infrastructure	and	cyber	420	36
Any field	space cyber frameworks	or	assessment	2	.
Any field	cybersecurity assessment frameworks	and	Space	4	.
Any field	critical space infrastructure	and	cyber attacks	42	63
Any field	Space infrastructure	and	governance	857	685
Any field	Space infrastructure	and	cyber attacks	308	63
Any field	Space infrastructure	and	kinetic attacks	1,100	34
Any field	Space infrastructure	and	attacks	1,940	268
Any field	Space infrastructure	and	current threats	3,420	378
Any field	cyber vulnerability assessment	or	space	115	5
Any field	attack vectors	or	critical assets	12,800	400
Any field	cyber security threats	and	SCADA or ICS or IoT	649	268
Any field	cyber security space	and	security models	318	4
Any field	critical infrastructure	and	attacker behaviour	17,800	368
Any field	cyber attack	and	motivation	20,900	630
Any field	system engineering	and	cybersecurity (cyber security)	3,940	767
Any field	system engineering	and	cyberresiliency (cyber resiliency)	3,520	210
Any field	system engineering	and	space	133,000	9,040
Any field	Space system engineering	and	security	336	7
Any field	system engineering frameworks	and	space	33	29
Any field	systems engineering	and	business	21,700	2,297
Any field	systems engineering	and	business process / management	20,300	2,064
Any field	systems engineering	and	business framework	13,800	1,463
Any field	systems engineering	and	business management	16,600	1,978
Any field	systems engineering	and	business process modeling	16,600	1,978
Any field	system engineering	and	risk management	366,000	129,000
Any field	regulatory framework	and	cybersecurity (cyber security)	9050/3990*	787/140*
Any field	regulatory framework	and	cyber resiliency/resilience	3,370	72
Any field	regulatory framework	and	space	20,000	4,349
Any field	business efficiency	and	space	3,310	146
Any field	business	and	regulatory framework	22,700	7,024
Any field	cybersecurity	and	risk assessment frameworks	334	21
Any field	cybersecurity	and	asset classification	509	591
Any field	cybersecurity	and	risk categorisation	70	248
Any field	cybersecurity	and	business impact	3,430	2,233
Any field	cybersecurity	and	risk assessment	31,500	1,775

FIGURE 10.2 Selected search terms.

Space Systems

Like early nuclear technology, space systems were originally analogue and isolated assets that were designed with safety features and minimum external interfaces. Although security was not considered at design, admittedly, this approach had one benefit of the attack surface being insignificant and, to a degree, limited to threats only from sophisticated and state-based entities with resources. Even government organizations that developed and managed space systems did not take cybersecurity seriously. One good example is the Iridium satellite constellation, which offered the Pentagon satellite-based services. There were no special cybersecurity measures implemented when the constellation was first built because engineers believed the technology was too sophisticated to be compromised (Porup, 2015). Contrary to the engineers' beliefs, the introduction of new digital technologies and cyber physical systems (CPS) created more opportunities for space-based systems but brought cyber-threat risks to these once-isolated platforms. These new risks had never been seen before, and no counter measures were planned to tackle the new digital cyberspace challenges, both technical and legal (Yaacoub et al., 2020).

Space infrastructure is a textbook complex system of systems (SoS), caused by multigenerational system and software reuse, subject to cascading and escalating failures, increasing the impact of the damage (Georgescu et al., 2019). A typical space system provides capability or service by combining space-based elements such as satellites and terrestrial ground stations to communicate and control. How it delivers these capabilities is determined by its architecture and constituent components, and those components dictate both space systems' susceptibility to threats and the methods available for incorporating resilience features that mitigate those threats. Figure 10.3 provides a summary of these definitions.

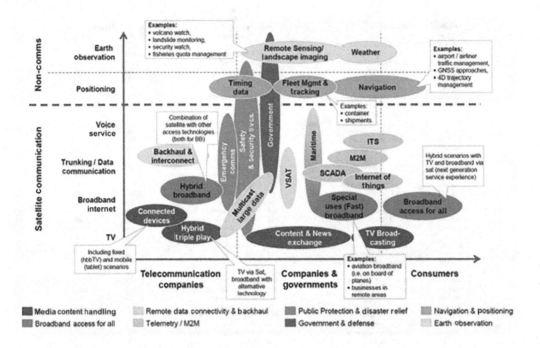

FIGURE 10.3   The increasing satellite use cases.

SPACE SYSTEM COMPONENTS

> The world architecture means "arrangement of the functional elements into physical blocks" (Ulrich and Eppinger, 2012) and in an engineering context it is known as "an abstract description of the entities of a system and the relationships between those entities."
>
> (Ulrich and Eppinger, 2012)

Space systems are intended to perform functions that are usually mission-critical, as their end users implement them in mission-critical systems. Therefore, the quality of service, security, reliability, and resilience of such platforms are of the utmost importance (Georgescu et al., Critical Space Infrastructures). Space systems are typically broken into three physical parts: space, ground, and launch segments.

1. Space segment: can be placed in space such as a satellite, launch vehicle, rover, or flying object like Ingenuity.
2. Ground segment: directly supports space activities.
3. Launch segment: responsible for delivering space equipment into orbit.

A conventional space mission consists of various pieces of equipment; in the case of a mission to launch a satellite, a routine task would be to orbit the Earth and carry one or more payloads. These payloads are highly sophisticated and include communication and computing components such as processors, antennas, cameras, and transmitters. Typically, these payloads are lodged on the spacecraft assembly known as the "bus," which provides the power, data exchange, and other command and control features.

> Some of the famous space systems that some commercial organizations and governments provide include:
>
> - Global positioning systems (GPS),
> - Remote sensing systems,
> - Geostationary Operational Environmental Satellite (GOES) for the weather, and
> - Space-based infrared system (SBIRS) for early missile warning.

The ground segment is also known as the control segment or earth station. There are two possible distinguishing locations for these stations: the surface of the planet or the atmosphere surrounding it. Usually ground stations are constructed to communicate radio signals in the super high frequency (SHF) and extremely high frequency (EHF) bands, tracking and determining a space asset's location and sharing the data received from the space with various users and applications. The satellite ground stations typically consist of a reception antenna (may be protected by a Radome), feed horn, waveguide, and receiver. Sophisticated satellite networks warrant satellite operations centers (SOCs) that are part of the ground segment, and this is where satellite operations are designed, developed, managed, and implemented. One good example of a SOC is the US Air Force Satellite Control Network (AFSCN), which supports multiple space systems and ground applications. Another example is the global positioning system (see Figure 10.4), a global network of satellites and ground facilities, including a master control station in Colorado, an alternate master control station, 11 command and control antennas, and 16 monitoring sites.

The launch providers are responsible for launching and successfully deploying the space systems in the correct orbits. It is a highly contested area within the global space economy, where private corporates like SpaceX, Blue Ocean, OneSpace and state-owned agencies such as NASA, DARPA, and JAXA compete in innovation and commercial success. Typically, the design of a space system consists of a mix of operational and information technology. In addition, they contain essential components such as field programmable gate arrays (FPGA) and other commercial off-the-shelf (COTS) processing and computational systems. These components, in turn, drive architectural and design

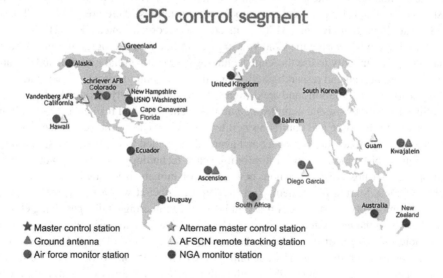

FIGURE 10.4 GPS: The global positioning system.

specifications. All space systems have communication and computing components with architectural and operational design elements mainly specific to a space system's unique and sole intended use. Typically, the most common architectural design approaches for safety and contingency are parallel, series, and hybrid.

In parallel architecture, several space components work together to provide an aggregated capability or service. Therefore, the loss of one segment results in a "proportional loss of capability," whereas, in series architecture, components depend on each other with a single chain of links (data/information). The hybrid model incorporates parallel and series designs for better redundancy and resilience (Mckelvin et al., 2015). However, all three architectures have similar cyber threats, which we will cover in detail in the coming sections.

Regardless of the architecture and design approach, space systems face mission challenges, computing limitations, communication necessities, and hardening requirements, all of which mandate employing multidisciplinary engineering frameworks for operational safety, security, and governance (Georgescu et al., 2019). In addition, the combination of the space segments adds complexity to a range of cyberattack surfaces.

Definition of attack surface:

The total number of potential points of entry for unauthorized access into any system is known as the attack surface. According to the Australian Cybersecurity Centre, attack surface is "The amount of ICT equipment and software used in a system. The greater the attack surface the greater the chances of an adversary finding an exploitable security vulnerability."

(ACSC, 2022)

RISE OF SMALL COMMERCIAL SATELLITES

The Artificial Earth satellite is the most widely used, has the greatest number of launches, and is the most efficient space system compared to other human space assets. However, there is no definitive count of the number of satellites, operational or otherwise. According to the Union of Concerned Scientists (UCS), which keeps a record of operational satellites, there are 6542 satellites, out of which 3372 satellites are active, and 3170 are inactive, as recorded January 1, 2021.

What started in the 60s during the Cold War to place military technologies in orbit for reconnaissance has changed humanity to use the same technology for commercial, science, and research purposes. Today, commercial and research satellites are the most common asset in outer space. They are small; they work in constellations and are designed to be commercially affordable. In contrast, military satellites have high cost and complexity, and their reliability and resilience are mostly mission critical. The most affordable and common satellite type is low earth orbit (LEO) (see Figure 10.5); orbiting at a lower altitude, they are faster and generally intended to work in a constellation.

The evolving proliferation in low earth orbiting space technology and entrepreneurship for new, low-cost space start-ups created a whole new sector of miniaturized satellites, the most famous called the CubeSat. Started by academics in the 1980s, CubeSat was a small satellite project for the scientific community to assess feasibility and design engineering challenges (Pang et al., 2016). CubeSats belong to the nanosatellite category, which consists of satellites weighing between 1 and 10 kg (without the weight of the chipset). According to the CubeSat Design Specification (CDS) guide, their dimensions range from 1U (one unit) (10 × 10 × 11.35 cm) to 12U (12 × 20 × 34.05 cm) ("CDS Announcement"; Sweeting, 1982). Although no official authority or agency regulates CDS, most countries of manufacture adhere to best practices and comply with flight safety regulations

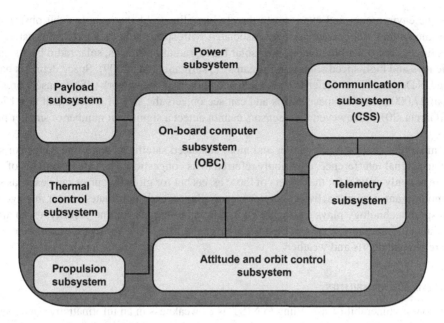

FIGURE 10.5 Components and subsystems of a LEO satellite.

(Berk et al., 2013). According to the CDS guide, four main roles exist in the development and launch of a CubeSat (Heiney, 2018):

1. **Developer**: Organization or an individual who designs and develops the CubeSat.
2. **Dispenser Integrator**: Organization or individual who safely stows the CubeSat in the launch vehicle.
3. **Dispenser Manufacturer**: Organization or individual who constructs the CubeSat dispenser.
4. **Launch Provider**: Organization or individual responsible for the launch infrastructure (including the vehicle) and/or successfully delivering the CubeSat into orbit.

These four roles contribute to space systems' overall cybersecurity posture, attack surface, and weaknesses.

CYBERSECURITY VULNERABILITIES, THREATS, AND WEAPONS FOR SPACE SYSTEMS

The Soviet Union launched Sputnik 1, the first man-made satellite, in 1957 "equipped with two radio transmitters and four antennas that broadcasted a constant beep while circling the Earth for 21 days" (Ker Than, 2007). Numerous satellite launches have taken place since then, placing thousands of space systems in orbit around the planet. As of 2022, more than 50 nations have produced artificial satellites, which have launched from 12 different countries. The first space system with an integrated circuit, or cyber-enabled, was Explorer 18 in 1963 ('Developing the First Ics to Orbit Earth', n.d.). Currently, a comparatively small number of satellites are in use, with hundreds being abandoned spacecraft and satellite components in orbit around the Earth as space junk.

SPACE'S UNIQUE CHALLENGES

Space systems combine several mission-critical systems, including sensitive and highly vulnerable components. The outer space infrastructure has several unique challenges, most of which are related to the unique environment and exposure to threats like climate phenomena to orbit obstructions. The most known and recognized risks are associated with space junk or debris from natural and artificial sources. The other phenomena are "solar flares, radiation storms, solar radio bursts, galactic cosmic rays and high-speed solar wind streams" (Tsurutani et al., 2009). Space debris is hard to track. The US Department of Defense's global Space Surveillance Network (SSN) sensors presently track about 27,000 pieces of space debris and can see objects the size of a basketball at a 15-mile distance (Garcia, 2015). However, their sensors cannot detect a significant number of smaller pieces of debris.

Furthermore, the new wave of smaller and more advanced satellites creates the danger of space crowding and signal interference, commonly referred to as congestion. The safe operations of space systems are not only critical for the owners of those assets but for global security and peace, as space systems monitor anti-terrorist activities, perform surveillance, and coordinate disaster management. Although space technology plays a critical role in relation to commerce and security, it can also be seen as a threat to international peace (Bhattacherjee et al., 2018). The vulnerabilities to outer space systems are beyond debris and weather.

Space Systems Vulnerabilities

The definition of vulnerability, according to NIST, is a "weakness in an information system, system security procedures, internal controls, or implementation that could be exploited or triggered by a threat source" (NVD – Vulnerabilities). Besides the space debris challenge, the weakness of space infrastructure is unique, as space infrastructure combines several mission-critical systems, including sensitive and highly vulnerable components. Space assets incorporate an ICT environment where ground stations, launch pads, and spacecraft are linked in a more complex interconnected network. There are multiple entry points such as corporate networks, communication stations between facilities and satellites, and any system that connects to the space network to use its services. Therefore, understanding attackers' characteristics and attack vectors to protect the space systems correctly is essential. The security improvement of space systems starts by measuring the impact of vulnerabilities and system weaknesses that are potentially exposed to threats. However, measuring security and calculating the return on risk mitigation investments is challenging (Hubbard and Seiersen, 2016). For example, empirical data can help to identify attacker behavior and characteristics. However, exploits by a "single team" are likely to go undetected or not fall under the behavior of a typical attacker.

Another entry point, and sometimes easy access for attackers, is through the space capability's supply chain. Today's commercial space operators work for operational and commercial success, with competitive budgets that often favor price points. Yet the ability to rapidly design, deploy, adjust, recover, and sustain space-based assets, even during conflict and pandemics, is the key to a dynamic, responsive, and viable service-focused business. The supply chain can be argued to be the weakest link (Simon and Omar, 2020).

Vulnerability is "the inability to resist a hazard or to respond when a disaster has occurred." A vulnerability in cybersecurity is a flaw that could be used by cybercriminals to break into a computer system without authorization. A cyberattack can run malicious code, install malware, and even steal sensitive data after exploiting a vulnerability. At the same time, risk is an unavoidable aspect of life. Every time you do something with an uncertain outcome, whether it's as simple as crossing the street or as complex as undergoing surgery, you take a risk. Risk is a function of uncertainty; there is no risk if there is no uncertainty. Risk is approached differently in different business fields, but the general principles remain the same: the likelihood of an adverse event is mapped against the effect that event would have if it occurred.

There are several threat actors in the space segment, from governments to individuals supported by adversaries.

THREAT ACTORS IN SPACE

Space infrastructure is under new anti-satellite attacks, and adversaries are increasingly developing new cyber threats, perhaps even to achieve coordinated cyber-storming (Austin, 2018) within what the Australian defense minister termed "grey zone" tactics short of actual war (Walker, n.d.). Russia, China (Chari, 2007), India, and the United States have shown their capabilities for kinetic weapons to destroy satellites in low Earth orbit, including a nuclear-powered missile by Russia tested on its own obsolete satellite (Egeli, 2021). These weapons have been shown to cause a large debris field that threatens other satellites and pollutes the space domain beyond recovery, whereas cyberattacks are stealthy and would likely limit significant damage to the targeted space asset. The resources required to disrupt space infrastructure are still considered complex, expensive, and relatively difficult to build or acquire. Therefore, the threat actors for the space domain are not as familiar as for any other critical infrastructure where cyber-threat propagation is extensive (Heinl, 2016). Some of those actors are mentioned in the following.

NATION-STATE

Threat actors from nation-states operate on a national scale and typically seek out information about the nuclear, financial, or technological industries. This kind of threat typically refers to military or government intelligence services, which are well-trained and resourced.

STATE-SPONSORED

Attacks that are sponsored by states are typically the most sophisticated and well targeted, and criminals with state support have almost the same capabilities. State-sponsored criminals can carry out the most valuable attacks because they have more resources, time, and expertise than regular cyber criminals.

CYBER TERRORISTS

Cyber terrorists have a political agenda, and they are motivated to spread their message or disrupt to draw attention to their cause. Attacks of this nature are becoming more frequent due to crowdfunding, and they typically disrupt business operations.

Each of these threat actors deploys different types of cyberattacks. Some of those attacks are discussed in the next section.

TYPES OF CYBERATTACKS

The space industry is projected to reach $1 trillion in revenue by 2040, and it is expected to grow exponentially because of new, cheaper launch platforms (Sheetz, n.d.). The growth comes with its own challenges, and cybersecurity is one of the major concerns for the fast-paced industry with a lot of new private players. The private sector is playing a key role in outer space activities where the public sector was once driving innovation and technology. In 2022, more than 50 countries operated satellites in space. The growth in outer space activities is mainly driven by the commercial demand that comes from new satellites for space transportation. This is called "Space 2.0", where from new space thinking has come new or adapted technologies, new market entrants, new launcher systems, new ways of financing space ventures, new satellite architectures, efficient new small satellite designs, new types of ground antenna systems with electronic tracking, and market shifts toward networked services (Pelton and Madry, 2020). As noted earlier, this new wave of smaller and more advanced satellites creates a danger of space crowding and signal interference. The safe operations of space systems are not only critical for the owners of those assets but for global security and peace, as space systems monitor anti-terrorist activities, perform surveillance, and coordinate disaster management.

The easiest way to take over a space system is ultimately to compromise the ground station because it offers the tools and software needed to appropriately operate and track it. Some mainstream threats to space systems that arise are physical attacks, intentional malware injection at the design stage, denial-of-service, distributed denial-of-service (DDOS), jamming and spoofing, network exploitation, unauthorized access to the cloud, and man-in-the-middle attacks. Here are some examples from the recent past to understand how these attacks were executed. For example, a string of satellite-related issues began in April 2007 when an Intelsat satellite, which is located over the Indian Ocean, was allegedly compromised by Tamil rebels in Sri Lanka for the purpose of spreading propaganda (Vacca, 2017). NASA's Landsat-7 was also hacked around the same time, and a similar attack was recorded in 2008 when the Terra AM-1 satellite operated by NASA went out of service for a few minutes (Falco, 2018). An embarrassing example of an incident was the alleged use of a $29 program called SkyGrabber by insurgents in Iraq installed on a mediocre laptop to eavesdrop on the satellite and small drone communications of US special forces (Arthur, 2009). Cyber-physical attacks may totally disable a ground operation and supply chain by introducing time-related malware or a backdoor to activate at a certain duration or from a signal by the attacker. Network and cloud attacks are classic cases of unauthorized access where an attacker may compromise the whole network. One great example of gaining unauthorized access is phishing or spear-phishing. Cloud providers are not always very reliable, and a failure of the cloud infrastructure could have devastating effects. Similarly, a DDOS attack can cause major disruption to availability.

Another type of attack is signal jamming, which is the act of overpowering a weak RF signal on a specific frequency with a stronger one on the same frequency to interfere with satellite or ground station communications. Similarly, spoofing is a clever form of interference that tricks the receiver into thinking it is somewhere else. Although jamming and spoofing come under communications and signal intelligence, with today's software-defined radios, these computers, processors, and hardware interfaces allow jamming and spoofing through cyberattacks. Some of those cyberattacks combined with other kinetic weapons are famously known as anti-satellite weapons, which we discuss in detail in the following section.

ANTI-SATELLITE WEAPONS

Besides the specific space phenomena, orbital debris, and harshness of the outer space temperatures and radiation, deliberate threats to critical space systems come from the state, rogue states, and non-state actors. The threat levels vary from highly capable and costly to less probable but affordable weaponry. These threats come from four distinct attacks and weapons known as anti-satellite weapons (ASATs), described as kinetic physical, non-kinetic physical, electronic, and cyber (Shahzad and Qiao, 2022). These methods are deployed by adversaries in three main segments of the space infrastructure: space segment, ground segment, and launch segment.

> The existing CDS guide contains a brief section on testing but does not mention any security-related testing. In 2014, for instance, LibreCube, an open-source CubeSat design initiative, was launched to provide a valuable framework for CubeSats and prevent the duplication of similar design steps across organizations and academic institutions (Scholz and Juang, 2015). In addition, LibreCube provides no design-level security guidance.

> *There are over 3000 nanosatellites and CubeSats as of April 2021.*

Kinetic physical attacks target both space systems and on-ground infrastructure. They are normally grouped under three categories: direct-ascent ASAT, which uses a ground-to-space missile to destroy the target; co-orbit ASAT, in which a space-to-space attack is achieved; and ground station ASAT, usually physical or cyber strike. Non-kinetic physical attacks are non-physical in nature, but their impact could be complete damage to the physical asset. Such attacks are most likely to be achieved using high-powered laser and microwaves and electromagnetic pulses. Electronic attacks involve spoofing and jamming, which are covered in detail in the later sections in this chapter. Cyberattacks target data integrity and the platform that generates and consumes that data. Typical cyberattacks are around data interception, corruption, and control (Pavur and Martinovic, 2019).

As a result of new assault weapons, space systems and the services they deliver have been subjected to cyberattack by what are known generally as advanced persistent threats (APTs) (Sarkunavathi and Srinivasan, 2018). Assault by APTs is divided into three different areas: ground-based threats, space-based threats, and interference-oriented threat. However, the nature of cyber-security for space systems and vehicles is shifting as the new space infrastructure is equipped with onboard computers and networked hardware with connectivity for remote analytics, configuration, and upgrades. This creates new opportunities for both cyberattacks and cyber-defense. Also, the new ground station operator's risk profile has been altered by the increasing use of cloud solutions such as Microsoft Azure Orbital and Amazon Web Services Ground Station (AWS Ground Station). One example of ground-based threats are natural disasters. For space-based threats, it could be solar activity, temperature, and, as previously mentioned, debris. Interference-oriented threats are related to information technology that focuses on interference, including those brought on by unintentional or malicious human interference with terrestrial and space-based wireless systems or computer systems (AWS, 2022).

> "An Advanced Persistent Threat (APT) is a broad term to describe highly sophisticated, continuous, and clandestine attack campaign that has long term goals to stay on the target network to collect sensitive data."
>
> (Cole, 2013)

Current space cybersecurity is a combination of several critical challenges from lack of standards and regulatory frameworks; complex supply chains; off-the-shelf commercial and open-source technology; and a small, highly specialized workforce. Despite the apparent cybersecurity risks and potential impact across multiple jurisdictions, space cybersecurity is not well defined, regulated, or governed by any independent body. As the most representative global organization today, the United Nations (UN) plays a pivotal role in international policymaking and security affairs.

JURISDICTIONAL CHALLENGES FOR CYBERSECURITY IN SPACE

Abandoned rocket "hits the Moon" – scientists.

(BBC News, 2022)

After mistaken identity and confusion, a piece of space junk slams into the Moon.

(Grush, 2022)

Whose rocket was it? The short answer is that no one knows for sure. The questions of ownership, attribution, and governance in space remain without answers. For example, who owns space? Who is responsible for space's safety, security, and governance? Whose assets are flying in space? Despite there being thousands of space systems, it remains difficult to answer those questions. These issues are aligned with the concerns of jurisdictional boundaries as explored by military and commercial space companies, with national borders and the ownership of space fundamentally uncertain. According to a Australian Department of Defense report on the ideas of sovereignty ('It's All about Sovereignty – Australian Defense Magazine' n.d.), cyberspace and outer space are two new frontiers for national security. Neither area adheres to traditional notions of "borders, sovereignty, and defense strategy," and they therefore have changed the conventional understandings of war and peace, creating severe challenges for defense organizations and lawmakers (Heinl, 2016). This problem is also quite prominent in international trade and negotiations.

WHAT IS CYBERSPACE AND ITS EFFECTS ON OUTER SPACE?

The definition of cyberspace, as described by NIST, is "global domain within the information environment consisting of the interdependent network of information systems infrastructures including the Internet, telecommunications networks, computer systems, and embedded processors and controllers" (Editor, 2022).

Another way to describe cyberspace is a non-physical environment that does not have boundaries and does not necessarily exist within perceived geographical borders. Therefore, due to the de-regionalized nature of cyberspace, fundamental issues around the implementation and jurisdictions of domestic laws and international agreements have become significantly challenging. A prominent example of these territorial jurisdiction challenges is a transnational cyber threat. These threats go across several international boundaries, exploiting the global interconnected network (Heinl, 2016). They violate several legal and technical boundaries, affect multiple organizations in their path, and can be carried out by anyone from individuals to state-owned actors. It is always hard to find who the real perpetrators are (Maglaras et al., 2018). This creates a real challenge for regulators to understand and develop solutions to address increasingly common and disruptive attacks, mainly when they try to address them through laws with uncertain jurisdiction.

The Internet was initially developed for military purposes and later extended to the scientific community to communicate. It could only be accessed with a limited capacity through fixed and known desktop computers. However, today's Internet is entirely different compared to its original design. With fiber optic cables spread across the continents, transmitting large amounts of data at a speed never envisaged before, with billions of devices connected to thousands of networks providing connectivity to globally interconnected systems, cloud computing, and almost unlimited data storage, these combine to create an unimaginable challenge and tension between national sovereignty and the borderless nature of the digital activity (Lipschultz, 2000). Moreover, the same Internet is shared between many different technologies, interests, social values, and political systems. According to the Internet & Jurisdiction Global Status Report 2019, "almost 80% of stakeholders think that there is not sufficient international coordination and coherence to address cross-border legal challenges on the Internet." The report highlights three main challenges that, without the right legal framework, become acute ('Internet and Jurisdiction Global Status Report 2019', n.d.).

1. The dependency on the interconnected global network, the Internet
2. The dependency on social and financial aspects of societies
3. The fight over who owns the Internet

> "Internet is a network of networks, what that means is that it is a global network that is creating by linking smaller networks of computers and servers. Cyberspace is nothing more than a symbolic and figurative space that exists within the scope of Internet."
>
> (CybersecurityIntelligence, n.d.)

The challenges of the internet or cyberspace is now part of the new wave of rapid and more advanced digitally connected space systems. The latest array of space infrastructure is built on the new digital technology based on the industrial Internet and the Internet of Things (IoT). "The origin of the threat posed by cyberspace is found in the architecture of the Internet itself" (Stahl, 2011), and it is no different to today's "Space 2.0" (Rao et al., 2017).

Technological challenges are not the only threat today's space systems face. It is also how they are protected and governed by laws, treaties, and international agreements in the uncontrolled environment of outer space. In this way, cyberspace infrastructure faces challenges to areas outside the exclusive economic zones of the oceans. That is, no state or states have sovereignty. In the past, during the age of exploration, this matter was unimportant (Craig, 2020), and the high seas were considered common property. But in 1967, the United Nations first suggested the idea of binding treaties to define the ownership, rights, and responsibilities to the oceans. Laws like the Law of the Sea clarified that the international waters remained international, and they were "the common heritage of all mankind." The "territorial sea" idea was established, and nations agreed on methods to calculate its boundaries (Beckman, 2013). Unfortunately, for outer space, the progress in international legal controls is slow.

CURRENT LEGAL FRAMEWORKS AND UN CONTRIBUTION ON SPACE

Space and nuclear technologies were once the frontiers of exorbitant research and development for industrialized governments. However, international space law does not cover the space activities of the private sector. As international agreements are made between nation or state governments, they do not proport to regulate the actions of private entities. However, these international agreements can guide, limit, or harmonize domestic regulations, which in turn can impact private entities. However, there has been very little impact on the actions of private entities to date. This is problematic, as the private sector is responsible for most of the activity in space. By law, private-sector entities are to be under the supervision of the state of their jurisdiction, and their activities are to be assumed to be within the framework of relevant national laws and policies. However, "There is no national legislation in many states on space-related matters, and many key issues relating to liability, technical safeguards, security and innovation are not addressed adequately" (Oltrogge and Christensen, 2020).

Despite the increasing advancement in space technology with rapid growth, international space lawmakers have not progressed beyond the initial five treaties and non-binding resolutions in the last 50 years (Recent Developments in Space Law, 2017). There is no governing body that oversees cybersecurity standards for space systems. Further, UN treaties on outer space activities do not adequately facilitate commercial space activities. The current corpus of space law comprises treaties and agreements that are only accepted and adopted by the full signatories. Although this is common to the nature of international agreements, such non-universal recognition and buy-in have seriously undermined the applicability of space law despite its adoption by unanimous approval in the UN General Assembly (Sachdeva, 2017). As described by Yevgeniya Oralova, the "*Jus Cogens* of Space Law, is the fundamental principle that carry unanimous acceptance among the comity of nations as peremptory norms and command invariable adherence from states." Oralova further clarifies that

Potential derogation from the principles of non-appropriation of outer space and of freedom of exploration and use of outer space, which is essential for the whole system of international space law is inconsistent with the natural state of outer space and can threaten international space and security.

(Oralova, 2015)

These laws provide:

1. Outer space as province of mankind
2. Freedom of access to all states for exploration and use
3. State responsibility to humanity
4. Prohibition on placement of weapons in earth orbit
5. Rescue and return of astronauts and space objects

The threat of space weaponization was acknowledged in the UNGA Resolution on Legal Principles. However, it didn't factor potential digital or, as we now know, cyber threats, and the resolution hasn't been changed to deal with these new difficulties ('Legal Principles', n.d.). The UNGA authors only factored in scenarios involving kinetic attacks, such as military operations. Article IV gained international consensus:

State-Parties to undertake not to place in orbit around the earth any objects carrying nuclear weapons or any other kinds of weapons of mass destruction, install such weapons on celestial bodies, or station weapons in Outer Space in any other manner

The increasing use of space systems for military reasons and several other conflicting issues make space systems vulnerable to attack. A study by the secretary-general of the United Nations Group of Governmental Experts on transparency and confidence-building measures (TCBMs) in outer space activities concluded that "the World's growing dependence on space-based systems and technologies and the information they provide requires collaborative efforts to address threats to the sustainability and security of outer space activities." However, our structured literature review has found there is generally a lack of peer-reviewed research in cybersecurity for space infrastructure, and not much work has been done in space reference architecture, governance frameworks, and tools.

Despite the gap in the literature, governments and industry have started to address cybersecurity for space infrastructure. For instance, the White House recently unveiled a space policy directive (SPD5) titled "Cybersecurity Principals for Space Systems" (Federal Register, 2020), which lays out a comprehensive set of principles for space companies to follow when creating their cyber protection strategies. These recommendations include:

- Protecting vital space vehicle functions from unauthorized access.
- Structural safeguards intended to lessen the susceptibility of a spacecraft's command, control, and telemetry receiver systems.
- Defense against communication spoofing and jamming.
- Protection of information processing systems, operational technology, and ground systems through the deliberate adoption of cybersecurity best practices. The National Institute of Standards and Technology's cybersecurity framework should be adopted in order to reduce the risk of malware infection and unauthorized access to systems, including from insider threats.
- Adoption of appropriate physical security measures for automated information systems, cybersecurity hygiene practices, and intrusion detection techniques for system components.
- Managing risks in the supply chain that have an impact on the cybersecurity of space systems by racking manufactured goods; requiring the use of reputable suppliers; spotting fake, fraudulent, and malicious equipment; and evaluating other risk mitigation options.

There is an urgent need for like-minded nations to develop legislation and standardize them with international law, and there has been a drive from the international community to develop "risk-based" frameworks for both public and private sectors (Johnson and Yepez, 2011).

NEED FOR CYBERSECURITY FRAMEWORKS FOR CYBER-WORTHY SPACE SYSTEMS

Modern space infrastructure is made up of vital ground and space systems whose loss or disruption can catastrophically influence other critical infrastructure. Space assets are fundamental elements of today's digital economies. Some countries consider them critical national infrastructure, as they are an integral and crucial part of modern navigation, financial services, research, and the military. Space-based services are difficult to replace, as they provide technological solutions otherwise either too expensive or not possible to replicate, such as across-globe satellite communication and reconnaissance. The physical, cyber, and borderless-geographical aspects of space infrastructure, as noted earlier for satellites themselves, make space infrastructure a complex system-of-systems, caused by multigenerational system and software reuse, subject to cascading and escalating failures, and increasing the impact of the damage (Hossain et al., 2020). Space infrastructure is a new frontier for adversaries to disable, degrade, and destroy; hence its security is critical for national security and vital commercial operations. Research into the regulation and legal frameworks for secure and sustainable space operations is essential and urgent for nations to develop and preserve their critical space infrastructure.

CURRENT STATE OF CYBER-WORTHINESS AND RESILIENCE FRAMEWORKS

There are few studies and commercial attempts that specifically investigate how vulnerable the space infrastructure is to cyberattack scenarios and how to make it resilient. However, despite its importance, applying any new cybersecurity frameworks to space infrastructure has its challenges and complexity spanning from the policy to the resources needed to secure these systems (Shahzad and Qiao, 2022).

Few academics have conducted systematic research into cyber resilience engineering frameworks for critical space infrastructure; with the exceptions being, none could be found, especially with any balance between legal, business, and engineering disciplines in such frameworks. Commercially, however, there have been some attempts, such as MITRE Corporation's recent paper, "Cyber Best Practices for Small Satellites," to address some of the issues raised by Space Policy Directive 5 (SPD 5).

In addition, ISAC has created a framework for describing threats in the operations, business systems, provider, and communication sectors. Aside from that, a few private organizations, such as the Aerospace Industries Association, have published some work, such as the first National Aerospace Standard NAS9924, citing it as a "Cybersecurity Baseline." The Aerospace Industries Association developed baseline controls focusing on cybersecurity for the aerospace and defense supply chain.

Although the public and private sectors have made significant efforts to address the cybersecurity and cyber-worthiness issues facing space infrastructure (Fowler and Sitnikova, 2019), little has been done to create standard cybersecurity and cyber resilience frameworks for assessing space infrastructure's cyber worthiness and stability. A comprehensive regulatory framework can provide efficient management and operations and create a lasting positive effect on the regulated areas. It assists in raising public confidence, reduces compliance costs and, in some cases where a legal basis is required, better ensures the universality and compulsoriness of applicable systems (Deane, 2012). One such example was after the global financial crisis of 2008, when the banking industry went through significant reforms to mitigate risks. The Basel Committee, a consortium of central banks from 28 countries, introduced Basel III, an international regulatory accord, to enhance international banking by requiring them to better manage risk by maintaining leverage ratios and certain reserve capital levels (Vousinas, 2015). Some of the potential disadvantages of regulation, especially cybersecurity in health care (Glennon, 2012) and aviation (De Gramatica et al., 2015), have been researched by scholars.

Space infrastructure threats come from four distinct anti-satellite weapons. Their main target is the core segments of space equipment, ground stations, and launch providers. The new space infrastructure is equipped with onboard computers and networked hardware with connectivity for remote analytics, configuration, and upgrades. This creates new opportunities for both cyberattacks and cyber-defense. In recent years, researchers have become increasingly interested in anti-satellite cyber threats, as their strategic, legal, and technical implications are not well understood. Scholars have argued the limitations of a "non-binding doctrine" of jus ad bellum to cyber conflicts known as the "Tallinn Manual" (Heinl, 2016). They claimed that it has limited scope and insufficiencies in the definition and contextualization of cyberattacks only confined to the military context, whereas space systems are widely used in civilian functions as well (Wallace and Jacobs, 2018).

WHY THE TALLINN MANUAL FAILED

The Tallinn Manual claims to be the most comprehensive work on the topic of cyber warfare. However, it addresses only the most disruptive cyberattacks whose severity would allow states to respond in self-defense either through cyber or kinetic warfare without a rubric to match the type of attack with the response. The manual supports peaceful conflict resolution by providing a threshold for when it is legal to wage war within the jus ad bellum framework. As the manual is not a legally binding document and only provides guidance on how existing laws of armed conflict apply to cyber war, the threshold of breach and proportion of self-defense is ambiguous and only serves as a guide. Second, the manual authors ignored international consent; they developed rules based on military manuals from just four countries: Canada, Germany, the United Kingdom, and the United States. Countries like China and Russia did not participate. Therefore, the lack of inclusion and consensus is one of the significant flaws of the Tallinn Manual (Schmitt and NATO Cooperative Cyber Defense Centre of Excellence, 2017).

Another complexity legal and technical experts face in the Tallinn Manual is in attempting to translate complex terms, such as the "use of force," into the cyber domain. The term has significant importance and is already defined by the UN Charter. The manual does not provide conclusive advice on "if the attack is a use of force or not" and suggests referring to Schmitt Analysis for further explanation without specific definitions. For example, the Stuxnet cyberattack and the scale of its damage to the Natanz nuclear facility could be considered an armed attack against Iran, "triggering Iran's right for self-defense" (Foltz, 2012). Experts have recognized the attribution problem, which is another challenge in the cyber domain that makes the use of force difficult without knowing the enemy. The final and most substantial issue with the Tallinn Manual is the lack of legal consensus on the implementation of the laws in the cyber domain. The international group of experts failed to reach a conclusive answer on when a cyberattack constitutes a "use of force" or when the "right to self-defense" should be exercised (Norris, 2013).

Despite the failure of the Tallinn Manual, there are examples of successful negotiations between countries on matters that are traditionally outside state sovereignty. For instance, the Antarctic Treaty System (ATS) is a unique set of legally binding agreements between all countries interested in Antarctica. The treaty is made up of four major international treaties:

1. 1959 Antarctic Treaty
2. 1972 Convention for the Conservation of Antarctic Seals
3. 1980 Convention on the Conservation of Antarctic Marine Living Resources
4. 1991 Protocol on Environmental Protection to the Antarctic Treaty

The treaty binds signatory nations to keep Antarctica weapons free (including nuclear free) and ready for inspection. It has successfully managed Antarctica and the surrounding areas since 1961 despite conflicting sovereignty claims. Despite the legal and technical issues around claims, minerals, and mining, the treaty is valid only until 2048.

WHAT SHOULD BE THE NEW RESILIENCE FRAMEWORK FOR SPACE SYSTEMS?

"New Space" is driven by private corporations, and their infrastructure combines several mission-critical systems, including sensitive and highly vulnerable components. Outer space infrastructure has challenges of its own, from climate phenomena to orbit obstructions. Just like any digital infrastructure, today's space technology incorporates an ICT environment where ground stations, launch pads, and spacecraft are linked with each other in a more complex interconnected network. Because in the past, attacks have not been of immediate concern, the scope and functionality of space platforms related to cybersecurity controls were limited. The tightening of security measures has changed as threats and verified exploitations started to increase. Several scholars have argued in favor of not just technical but also regulatory frameworks from operational and legal standpoints for the space domain. Rocket Lab entrepreneur Peter Beck observed that space, which has hitherto been a government domain, is now more democratized and acceding towards commercial control. There have been voices of concern that "democratization involves the disappearance of the state and the rise of capital."

Any proposed resilience framework must recognize that space businesses should assess their cybersecurity risk management on a cost-benefit basis but appropriately balanced by new regulators against public risk. The challenge is how to measure cyber risk. Although we know that, for example, more established fields of banking and insurance better measure risk against specified risk units, for cyber risk, the challenge is how to compare and measure different risk reduction approaches, monitory implications, and rate of return or return on investment. Academics have suggested that despite

> several cyber risk management frameworks, risk assessment methodologies, quantitative risk models, industry surveys and security analytics tools in the market, little has been done to standardize the measurement unit for cyber risk.
>
> *(Ruan, 2017)*

Another great theory of integrating cyber risk management and economics into what is called "cybernomics" has taken root in the studies of economics (Suh and Han, 2003). Although there is a range of qualitative and quantitative cyber risk management frameworks and methodologies used in the corporate sector, they lack a cost-benefit analysis. One example is the National Institute of Standards and Technology cybersecurity framework v1.1. The framework is voluntary guidance based on existing standards that recognize that businesses must assess their cyber posture and risk management based on a cost-benefit basis. However, it does not provide guidance on how to execute such an analysis. There is evidence of integrating cost-benefit assessment into the NIST framework by proposing a new Gordon-Loeb mode (Gordon et al., 2020). They argue that "the NIST cybersecurity framework has been instrumental in providing a common language and approach for organizations to use as they strive to improve the way they manage cybersecurity risks." However, it does not provide any guidance on financial returns.

To date, no study has explicitly looked at forming a comprehensive regulatory or engineering framework for the cybersecurity of space infrastructure that would adopt a risk and systems-based approach to securing commercial space systems. The suggested framework would additionally look at security costs, loss probability, new cyber-resilience technology, and the effectiveness of security controls and investment optimization.

NEED FOR NEW TECHNOLOGIES FOR CYBER-RESILIENT SPACE-BASED SYSTEMS

Threats to space systems come from multiple entry points such as corporate networks, communication stations between facilities and satellites, and any system that connects to the space network to use its services. Therefore, understanding the attackers' characteristics and attack vectors is essential to correctly protect the space systems. The security improvement of space systems starts by measuring the impact of vulnerabilities, risks, and system weaknesses that are potentially exposed to threats. However, measuring security and calculating the return on risk mitigation investments is challenging.

Therefore, most scholars and commercial operators are stressing the "security by design" aspect of design and development of space infrastructure. Today's space infrastructure is software intensive and inevitably introduces defects and vulnerabilities which adversaries can exploit. A system must be developed with agile security in mind from the beginning to remain reliable and secure to evolving threats, such as remote reprogramming. The concept of agile and secure development is not new. In the late 1990s, as computers and the Internet quickly proliferated, numerous security holes and problems in the era's operating systems, software, and hardware were made public. As viruses and worms increased in number, customers cried out for action. When most developments used the "waterfall" model, this was a challenge; in the era of Agile and other, more iterative methodologies, the challenge has never been greater.

Another excellent way to test the reliability, security, and resilience of space infrastructure is by developing and testing designs on small satellites, the CubeSats. The CubeSats are a brilliant, affordable, and rapid development platform for testing and evaluation of a wide range of space missions at a lower cost and timeframe. An example of how to systematically evaluate the resilience of complex infrastructure operations is given by Hossain et al. (2020), albeit for a maritime port, not space infrastructure. Similar approaches are needed for space infrastructure. Some scholars have suggested the use of a digital twin testbed to test and verify the security and resilience behavior and context of space systems (Jones et al., 2020).

There are examples of successfully generic digital twin cybersecurity testbeds for LEO space systems (Ormrod et al., 2021).

CONCLUSION

Space infrastructure supports vital functions of society to operate sensitive and crucial services for health, mobility, security, and peace, and it is increasingly commercially derived. Although the importance of space infrastructure is significant and there is a possibility of increased cybersecurity risks, threats, and attacks; the global community is yet to define, negotiate and mandate a treaty or instrument for the confluence of these domains. Researchers have become increasingly interested in anti-satellite cyber threats in recent years as their strategic, legal, and technical implications are not well understood. Currently, no agencies or governing bodies monitor and restrict the use of satellites to provide assurance of their resilience in the face of numerous and growing threats and vulnerabilities. The lack of overarching governance is creating a vacuum in security design and operational cyber resiliency for the private sector that is playing a vital role in the outer space activities where the public sector once was driving innovation and technology. The literature survey research outlined in this chapter has spawned case studies and further research into the requirements for balanced legal, business, and engineering frameworks to urgently address the cyber-resilience of space infrastructure. Until these frameworks are fully developed and validated with the associated communities, cybersecurity decision makers for space systems are recommended to take the following proposed precautions outlined earlier in this chapter:

1. Cyber-ASATs are not theoretical threats, as they have been successfully demonstrated by several nation-states. These weapons are based on widely available technologies available to almost every threat actor. Therefore, undertaking a cyber threat assessment across all segments of space infrastructure is critical.

2. Space assets are critical infrastructure; therefore, a cyberattack on them may be classified as a "use of force." Although the law of international space is inconsistent and weak, nation-states must agree to their own local laws and jurisdiction for self-restraint and self-regulation.

REFERENCES

ACSC. 2022. 'Attack Surface'. www.cyber.gov.au/acsc/view-all-content/glossary/attack-surface.

Amazon Web Services. 'AWS Ground Station'. Accessed 5 August 2022. https://aws.amazon.com/ground-station/.

Arthur, Charles, and Technology Editor. 2009. 'SkyGrabber: The $26 Software Used by Insurgents to Hack into US Drones'. Accessed 17 December 2009. sec. Technology. www.theguardian.com/technology/2009/dec/17/skygrabber-software-drones-hacked.

Austin, Greg. 2018. *Cybersecurity in China. SpringerBriefs in Cybersecurity*. Cham: Springer International Publishing. https://doi.org/10.1007/978-3-319-68436-9.

BBC News. 2022. 'Abandoned Rocket "Hits the Moon" – Scientists'. Accessed 4 March 2022. sec. Science & Environment. www.bbc.com/news/science-environment-60596449.

Beckman, Robert. 2013. 'The UN Convention on the Law of the Sea and the Maritime Disputes in the South China Sea.' *American Journal of International Law* 107 (1): 142–63.

Berk, Josh, Jeremy Straub, and David Whalen. 2013. 'The Open Prototype for Educational NanoSats: Fixing the Other Side of the Small Satellite Cost Equation'. In 2013 IEEE Aerospace Conference, 1–16. Big Sky, MT: IEEE. https://doi.org/10.1109/AERO.2013.6497393.

Bhattacherjee, Debopam, Waqar Aqeel, Ilker Nadi Bozkurt, Anthony Aguirre, Balakrishnan Chandrasekaran, P. Brighten Godfrey, Gregory Laughlin, Bruce Maggs, and Ankit Singla. 2018. 'Gearing Up for the 21st Century Space Race'. In Proceedings of the 17th ACM Workshop on Hot Topics in Networks, 113–19. Redmond, WA: ACM. https://doi.org/10.1145/3286062.3286079.

Chari, P.R. 2007. 'China's Asat Test: Seeking the Strategic High Ground'. *Institute of Peace and Conflict Studies*. www.jstor.org/stable/resrep09262.

Cole, Eric. 2013. *Advanced Persistent Threat: Understanding the Danger and How to Protect Your Organization*. Amsterdam; Boston, MA: Syngress, an Imprint of Elsevier.

Craig, Robin Kundis. 2020. 'The New United Nations High Seas Treaty: A Primer'. *Natural Resources and Environment* 34 (4): 1–3.

CybersecurityIntelligence. n.d. Accessed 5 August 2022. www.cybersecurityintelligence.com/.

Deane, F. 2012. 'The WTO, the National Security Exception and Climate Change'. *Carbon & Climate Law Review* 6 (2): 149–58. https://doi.org/10.21552/CCLR/2012/2/213.

De Gramatica, Martina, Fabio Massacci, Woohyun Shim, Alessandra Tedeschi, and Julian Williams. 2015. 'IT Interdependence and the Economic Fairness of Cybersecurity Regulations for Civil Aviation'. *IEEE Security & Privacy* 13 (5): 52–61. https://doi.org/10.1109/MSP.2015.98.

'Developing the First iCs to Orbit Earth'. n.d. Accessed 6 August 2022. https://bit.ly/3jcHKDY.

Editor, CSRC Content. n.d. 'Cyberspace – Glossary | CSRC'. Accessed 5 August 2022. https://csrc.nist.gov/glossary/term/cyberspace.

Egeli, Sitki. 'Space-to-Space Warfare and Proximity Operations: The Impact on Nuclear Command, Control, and Communications and Strategic Stability'. *Journal for Peace and Nuclear Disarmament* 4 (1): 116–40. https://doi.org/10.1080/25751654.2021.1942681.

Falco, Gregory. 2018. 'The Vacuum of Space Cybersecurity'. In 2018 AIAA SPACE and Astronautics Forum and Exposition. Orlando, FL: American Institute of Aeronautics and Astronautics. https://doi.org/10.2514/6.2018-5275.

Federal Register. 2020. 'Cybersecurity Principles for Space Systems'. www.federalregister.gov/documents/2020/09/10/2020-20150/cybersecurity-principles-for-space-systems.

Foltz, Andrew C. 2012. 'Stuxnet, Schmitt Analysis, and the Cyber Use of Force Debate. Air War College Maxwell Air Force Base United States'. *Joint Force Quarterly* 67 (1): 40–48.

Fowler, Stuart, and Elena Sitnikova. 2019. 'Toward a Framework for Assessing the Cyber-Worthiness of Complex Mission Critical Systems'. In 2019 Military Communications and Information Systems Conference (MilCIS), 1–6. Canberra: IEEE. https://doi.org/10.1109/MilCIS.2019.8930800.

Garcia, Mark. 2015. 'Space Debris and Human Spacecraft'. *NASA*. Accessed 13 April 2015. www.nasa.gov/mission_pages/station/news/orbital_debris.html.

Georgescu, Alexandru, Adrian V. Gheorghe, Marius-Ioan Piso, and Polinpapilinho F. Katina. 2019. 'Critical Space Infrastructures: Risk, Resilience and Complexity'. In *Topics in Safety, Risk, Reliability and Quality*, Vol. 36. Cham: Springer International Publishing. https://doi.org/10.1007/978-3-030-12604-9.

Glennon, Michael J. 2012. "The Dark Future of International Cybersecurity Regulation." *Journal of National Security Law & Policy* 6: 563.

Gordon, Lawrence A., Martin P. Loeb, and Lei Zhou. 2020. 'Integrating Cost – Benefit Analysis into the NIST Cybersecurity Framework Via the Gordon – Loeb Model'. *Journal of Cybersecurity* 6 (1): tyaa005. https://doi.org/10.1093/cybsec/tyaa005.

Grush, Loren. 2022. 'After Mistaken Identity and Confusion, a Piece of Space Junk Slams into the Moon'. *The Verge*. Accessed 4 March 2022. www.theverge.com/2022/3/4/22958705/chinese-rocket-space-debris-moon-collision-change-5-t1.

Heiney, Anna. 2018. 'CubeSat Launch Initiative Resources'. *NASA*. 17 January. www.nasa.gov/content/cubesat-launch-initiative-resources.

Heinl, Caitríona H. 2016. 'The Potential Military Impact of Emerging Technologies in the Asia-Pacific Region: A Focus on Cyber Capabilities'. In *Emerging Critical Technologies and Security in the Asia-Pacific*, edited by Richard A. Bitzinger, 123–37. London: Palgrave Macmillan. https://doi.org/10.1057/9781137461285_10.

Hossain, Niamat Ullah Ibne, Raed M. Jaradat, Michael A. Hamilton, Charles B. Keating, and Simon R. Goerger. 2020. 'A Historical Perspective on Development of Systems Engineering Discipline: A Review and Analysis'. *Journal of Systems Science and Systems Engineering* 29 (1): 1–35. https://doi.org/10.1007/s11518-019-5440-x.

Hubbard, Douglas W., and Richard Seiersen. 2016. *How to Measure Anything in Cybersecurity Risk*. Hoboken, NJ: Wiley.

'Internet and Jurisdiction Global Status Report 2019 | Shaping Europe's Digital Future'. n.d. Accessed 5 August 2022. https://digital-strategy.ec.europa.eu/en/library/internet-and-jurisdiction-global-status-report-2019.

'It's All about Sovereignty – Australian Defence Magazine'. n.d. Accessed 5 August 2022. www.australiandefence.com.au/adm/editorials/it-s-all-about-sovereignty.

Johnson, Chris, and Atencia Yepez. "Cyber security threats to safety-critical space-based infrastructures." *In Proceedings of the Fifth Conference of the International Association for the Advancement of Space Safety*, no. 1. 2011.

Jones, David, Chris Snider, Aydin Nassehi, Jason Yon, and Ben Hicks. 2020. 'Characterising the Digital Twin: A Systematic Literature Review'. *CIRP Journal of Manufacturing Science and Technology* 29 (May): 36–52. https://doi.org/10.1016/j.cirpj.2020.02.002.

Ker Than. 2007. 'The Scientific Legacy of Sputnik'. *Space.com*. www.space.com/4421-scientific-legacy-sputnik.html.

'Legal Principles'. n.d. Accessed 5 August 2022. www.unoosa.org/oosa/en/ourwork/spacelaw/principles/legal-principles.html.

Lipschultz, Jeremy Harris. 2000. *Free Expression in the Age of the Internet: Social and Legal Boundaries*. Boulder, CO: Westview Press.

Maglaras, Leandros, Mohamed Ferrag, Abdelouahid Derhab, Mithun Mukherjee, Helge Janicke, and Stylianos Rallis. 2018. 'Threats, Countermeasures and Attribution of Cyberattacks on Critical Infrastructures'. *ICST Transactions on Security and Safety* 5 (16): 155856. https://doi.org/10.4108/eai.15-10-2018.155856.

Mckelvin, Jr., Mark L., Robert Castillo, Kevin Bonanne, Michael Bonnici, Brian Cox, Corrina Gibson, Juan P. Leon, Jose Gomez-Mustafa, Alejandro Jimenez, and Azad M. Madni. 2015. 'A Principled Approach to the Specification of System Architectures for Space Missions'. In AIAA SPACE 2015 Conference and Exposition. Pasadena, CA: American Institute of Aeronautics and Astronautics. https://doi.org/10.2514/6.2015-4462.

Norris, Michael J. 2013. 'The Law of Attack in Cyberspace: Considering the Tallinn Manual's Definition of "Attack" in the Digital Battlespace.' *Inquiries Journal* 5 (10).

Oltrogge, Daniel L., and Ian A. Christensen. 2020. 'Space Governance in the New Space Era'. *Journal of Space Safety Engineering* 7 (3): 432–38. https://doi.org/10.1016/j.jsse.2020.06.003.

Oralova, Yevgeniya. 2015. 'Jus Cogens Norms in International Space Law'. *Mediterranean Journal of Social Sciences* 6 (6): 421–27. https://doi.org/10.5901/mjss.2015.v6n6p421.

Ormrod, David, Jill Slay, and Amy Ormrod. 2021. 'Cyber-Worthiness and Cyber-Resilience to Secure Low Earth Orbit Satellites.' In ICCWS 2021 16th International Conference on Cyber Warfare and Security, 257. Academic Conferences Limited.

Pang, W. J., B. Bo, X. Meng, X. Z. Yu, J. Guo, and J. Zhou. 2016. "Boom of the CubeSat: A Statistic Survey of CubeSats Launch in 2003–2015." In Proceedings of the 67th International Astronautical Congress (IAC), Guadalajara, Mexico, 26–30.

Pavur, James, and Ivan Martinovic. 2019. 'The Cyber-ASAT: On the Impact of Cyber Weapons in Outer Space'. In 2019 11th International Conference on Cyber Conflict (CyCon), 1–18. New York: IEEE. https://doi.org/10.23919/CYCON.2019.8756904.

Pelton, Joseph N., and Scott Madry. 2020. *Handbook of Small Satellites Technology, Design, Manufacture, Applications, Economics and Regulation*. Cham: Springer International Publishing. https://link.springer.com/10.1007/978-3-030-20707-6.

Porup, J. M. 2015. 'It's Surprisingly Simple to Hack a Satellite'. *Vice* (blog). 21 August. www.vice.com/en/article/bmjq5a/its-surprisingly-simple-to-hack-a-satellite.

Rao, R. Venkata, V. Gopalakrishnan, and Kumar Abhijeet 2017. *Recent Developments in Space Law: Opportunities & Challenges*. Singapore: Springer. https://doi.org/10.1007/978-981-10-4926-2.

Recent Developments in Space Law. 2017. New York, NY; Berlin; Heidelberg: Springer.

Ruan, Keyun. 2017. 'Introducing Cybernomics: A Unifying Economic Framework for Measuring Cyber Risk'. *Computers & Security* 65 (March): 77–89. https://doi.org/10.1016/j.cose.2016.10.009.

Sachdeva, G. S. 2017. "Select Tenets of Space Law as Jus Cogen." In *Recent Developments in Space Law*, 7–26. Singapore: Springer.

Sarkunavathi, A., and V. Srinivasan. 2018. 'A Detailed Study on Advanced Persistent Threats: A Sophisticated Threat'. *Asian Journal of Computer Science and Technology* 7 (S1): 90–95. https://doi.org/10.51983/ajcst-2018.7.S1.1797.

Schmitt, Michael N., and NATO Cooperative Cyber Defence Centre of Excellence, eds. 2017. *Tallinn Manual 2.0 on the International Law Applicable to Cyber Operations*. 2nd edition. Cambridge; New York, NY: Cambridge University Press.

Scholz, Artur, and Jer-Nan Juang. 2015. 'Toward Open Source CubeSat Design'. *Acta Astronautica* 115 (October): 384–92. https://doi.org/10.1016/j.actaastro.2015.06.005.

Shahzad, Syed, and Lily Qiao. 2022. 'Need for a Cyber Resilience Framework for Critical Space Infrastructure'. *International Conference on Cyber Warfare and Security* 17 (1): 404–12. https://doi.org/10.34190/iccws.17.1.52.

Sheetz, Michael. n.d. 'The Space Industry Is on Its Way to Reach $1 Trillion in Revenue by 2040, Citi Says'. *CNBC*. Accessed 5 August 2022. www.cnbc.com/2022/05/21/space-industry-is-on-its-way-to-1-trillion-in-revenue-by-2040-citi.html.

Simon, Jay, and Ayman Omar. 2020. 'Cybersecurity Investments in the Supply Chain: Coordination and a Strategic Attacker'. *European Journal of Operational Research* 282 (1): 161–71. https://doi.org/10.1016/j.ejor.2019.09.017.

Space ISAC. n.d. 'Space ISAC – Space Information Sharing and Analysis Center'. Accessed 5 August 2022. https://s-isac.org/.

Stahl, William M. 2011. 'The Uncharted Waters of Cyberspace: Applying the Principles of International Maritime Law to the Problem of Cybersecurity'. *Georgia Journal of International and Comparative Law* 40: 247.

Suh, Bomil, and Ingoo Han. 2003. 'The IS Risk Analysis Based on a Business Model'. *Information & Management* 41 (2): 149–58. https://doi.org/10.1016/S0378-7206(03)00044-2.

Tsurutani, B. T., O. P. Verkhoglyadova, A. J. Mannucci, G. S. Lakhina, G. Li, and G. P. Zank. 2009. 'A Brief Review of "Solar Flare Effects" on the Ionosphere: SFES ON IONOSPHERE'. *Radio Science* 44 (1). https://doi.org/10.1029/2008RS004029.

Ulrich, Karl T., and Steven D. Eppinger. 2012. *Product Design and Development*. 5th edition. New York, NY: McGraw-Hill/Irwin.

Vacca, John R., ed. 2017. *Computer and Information Security Handbook*. 3rd edition. Cambridge, MA: Morgan Kaufmann Publishers, an Imprint of Elsevier.

Vousinas, Georgios L. 2015. 'Supervision of Financial Institutions: The Transition from Basel I to Basel III. A Critical Appraisal of the Newly Established Regulatory Framework'. *Journal of Financial Regulation and Compliance* 23 (4): 383–402. https://doi.org/10.1108/JFRC-02-2015-0011.

Walker, J. n.d. 'Call for UK to Flex Muscles in Pacific'. www.theaustralian.com.au/nation/defence/call-for-uk-to-flex-muscles-in-pacific/.

Wallace, David A., and Christopher W. Jacobs. 2018. 'Conflict Classification and Cyber Operations: Gaps, Ambiguities and Fault Lines'. *University of Pennsylvania Journal of International Law* 40: 643.

Yaacoub, Jean-Paul A., Ola Salman, Hassan N. Noura, Nesrine Kaaniche, Ali Chehab, and Mohamad Malli. 2020. 'Cyber-Physical Systems Security: Limitations, Issues and Future Trends'. *Microprocessors and Microsystems* 77 (September): 103201. https://doi.org/10.1016/j.micpro.2020.103201.

11 Regulating Cyber-Physical Systems for Safety Consequences

Mark van Zomeren, Keith Joiner,
Elena Sitnikova, and Li Qiao

CONTENTS

DOI: 10.1201/9781003319887-11

INTRODUCTION

The cyber-physical systems (CPS) discussed in this chapter operate with dynamic and critical phys-ical outputs that have the potential to create significant hazardous outcomes for people because of their actions or inaction. Inherent in CPS is an increased risk of unintended and erroneous operation due to a greater number of interactions occurring within the system and an increase in the size of the cyber-vulnerable attack surface presented to external cyber threats. As the ability of more CPS to be networked improves, an ever-increasing number of individuals and seemingly innocuous systems can interact with each other long after each initially went into operational use. These systems and their products (e.g., data and physical action) are exposed to unintended, undesirable interactions and malicious agents alike (NIST, 2017b). Furthermore, when internal flaws or external threats alike compromise the nominal operation of a CPS, there is also an increased risk to the health and safety of humans that interact with, or are in proximity to, that CPS.

The National Institute of Standards and Technology (NIST) of the United States defines cyber-physical systems as:

> Cyber-Physical Systems integrate computation, communication, sensing, and actuation with physical systems to fulfil time-sensitive functions with varying degrees of interaction with the environment, including human interaction.
>
> *(NIST, 2017b)*

The term cyber-worthiness, as it is utilized in this chapter, is best defined as:

> Cyber-worthiness can be viewed as the possession of an acceptable level of cyber resiliency, which is defined as "the ability of a nation, organization, or mission or business process to anticipate, withstand, recover from, and evolve to improve capabilities in the face of, adverse conditions, stresses, or attacks on the supporting cyber resources it needs to function."
>
> *(Fowler and Sitnikova, 2019)*

Figure 11.1 depicts how cyber-worthiness is mapped from cybersecurity settings and the capability systems and processes within a modern defense force. Within any modern defense force, CPS are

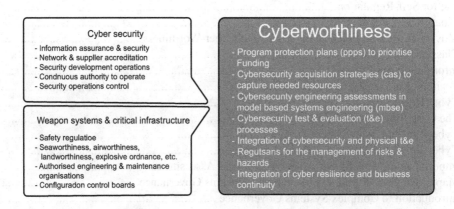

FIGURE 11.1   Mapping of defense cybersecurity and systems processes to cyber-worthiness.

utilized extensively as capability assets in warfighting. They are also pervasive within infrastructure and facilities used for basing capability assets and the training of forces.

RESEARCH FOCUS

The research predicated on this literature aims to systematically investigate the most viable and effective ways to determine the cyber-worthiness of any given CPS. This research is interested in how CPS deal with cyberspace risks and any interactions with physical hazards, such that the overall cyber-physical system remains safe for people and overall mission effectiveness in the physical domain while remaining fit for purpose in the cyber domain.

Figure 11.2 provides a graphical depiction of complex systems of complex cyber-physical systems, where the dotted lines identify cyber interfaces between the physical capability and critical infrastructure systems of a generic modern defense force. It should be noted that these cyber interfaces, and the cyber-threats they present, were not necessarily present or anticipated when each individual system was initially designed and deployed. As more cyber-physical systems are brought into service that can interact with an increasing number of new and legacy systems, systematically ensuring that these interactions do not result in undesirable outcomes becomes increasingly difficult. It follows that any knowledge that assists in the achievement of through-life technical assurance of cyber-capable systems will be valuable to organizations that seek to minimize the effect of malicious actors in the cyber domain.

RESEARCH PROBLEM

This research aims to provide systematic and comprehensive consideration of how to avoid the combined harm that could be caused by operating fully integrated CPS within the expansive cyberspace as defined by the US DoD (2021) and the physical domain. The research considers systematic and comprehensive test and evaluation (T&E) activities, which are utilized within the classical systems engineering process, required to provide an assurance of system security engineering (Nejib et al., 2017) or cyber-worthiness. These assurances are needed to confidently operate multiple cyber-physical systems as a larger complex system of complex cyber-physical systems that display complex interdependencies and interactions in highly contested cyberspace.

Figure 11.3 provides a graphical consideration of the complex interactions between the cyber and physical domains of cyber-physical systems and the manner with which extant systems engineering, and in particular T&E, is applied differently to each and shows the gaps.

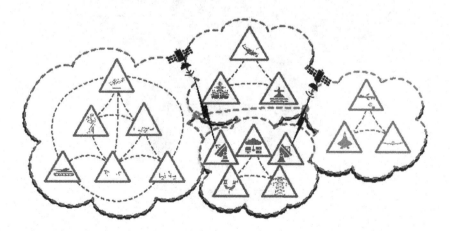

FIGURE 11.2 Depiction of a complex system of complex cyber-physical systems interfacing across a complex organization.

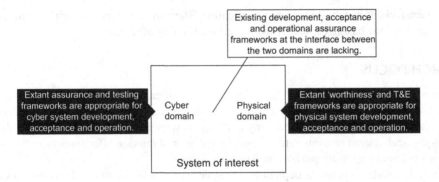

FIGURE 11.3   Test and evaluation gaps within the interactions between the cyber domain and the physical domain.

In addition to the systematic and comprehensive T&E required to ensure the cyber-worthiness of CPS, this research also seeks to explore the way complex organizations that utilize CPS should govern these CPS, particularly where they form part of larger systems of CPS. The application of complex systems governance (CSG) is explored in detail to determine how this broad theory may be applied to CPS that are integral to the operations of large and complex organizations such as modern defense forces, advanced manufacturing organizations, or operators of critical infrastructure. Figure 11.4 provides a graphical representation of the nine interrelated meta functions associated with CSG as described by Keating and Katina (2016).

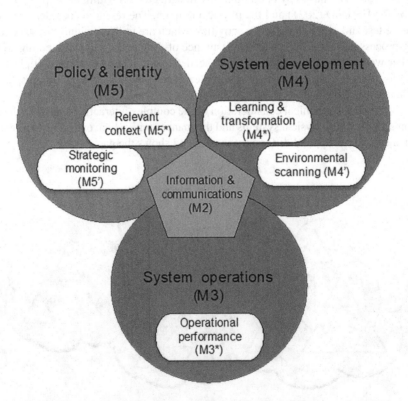

FIGURE 11.4   Nine interrelated functions and communication channels for the metasystem.

Source: (Adapted from Figure 3, Keating and Katina, 2016)

CYBER-WORTHINESS RESEARCH QUESTIONS AND SUB-QUESTIONS

The following research questions are posed to address the issue of cyber-worthiness in cyber-physical systems:

- How can complex systems theory and complex system governance be applied to complex cyber-physical systems to:
  - achieve adequate governance of a complex system of complex cyber-physical systems to ensure ongoing mission-critical and safe operations?
  - develop an appropriate regulatory framework for cyber-physical governance of a complex system of complex cyber-physical systems?
  - develop an appropriate management framework in through-life cyber-worthiness of a complex system of complex cyber-physical systems?
- In achieving assurances of cyber-worthiness, what is the optimal sequencing and timing of T&E techniques and activities for cyber-physical systems from the perspectives of:
  - complex system theory?
  - cybernetics and the law of requisite variety?
  - complex system governance?

While the cyber-worthiness research questions stated here are about cyber-worthiness, they share considerable similarities with the overarching research questions of this book. At the end of this chapter, a summary of cyber-worthiness recommendations and takeaways are provided within the context of the research questions of the book.

SYSTEMATIC LITERATURE REVIEW

The purpose of reviewing the literature is to identify the literature gaps to focus on for this research project. As systems engineering by its nature is focused on the broad concept of a system, it stands to reason that any research on the governance of complex systems of complex systems will need to begin from a broad perspective before narrowing in on appropriately bounded literature gaps.

As detailed in O'Brien and Mc Guckin (2016, pp. 6–13), the systematic literature review consists of two primary activities, the development of a search strategy and the implementation of the systematic literature review. The advantages of the systematic literature review are that it reduces the impact of bias and provides a credible and repeatable process (O'Brien and Mc Guckin, 2016, p. 4) to provide confidence in the veracity of the literature review that is better able to withstand scrutiny.

METHODOLOGY DEVELOPMENT OF SEARCH STRATEGY

Initially, a review of the literature was undertaken to develop a general sense of the breadth and content of relevant literature. Due to the broad scope of the literature associated with the research topic, a comprehensive and detailed literature review was then undertaken to determine the broader literature gaps in the context of the research questions identified earlier. Based on the initial literature review, several literature topics were determined to be relevant, giving an initial broad view of the research. These terms are listed in the following:

- Cyber-worthiness
- Complex system theory
- Cyber test and evaluation
- Cybernetics
- Cyber-physical
- Cyber governance

- Cyber regulation
- Cyber resilience
- General system theory
- Operations technology and information technology
- Requisite variety
- Requisite complexity

There were some terms that, although highly relevant to the literature, were so dominant in test search results that using them in the search resulted in a greatly inflated number of results. Accordingly, while carefully ensuring that more constrained terms are included in the search that could represent the excluded terms in a better context, some terms were not included directly in the search terms, as follows:

Cybersecurity – This search term is too broad and resulted in an overwhelming number of results that were purely about the security of IT systems, which did not add to the relevance of the search results to the research problem.

Cyber testing – This search term led to many results relating to red teaming or pen testing, and, although valid cyber tests, they skewed the search results to these very narrow examples of testing.

A Logical Combination of Search Terms

(Cyberworth* OR Cyber-worth*)
OR
("Cyber Test" OR "Cyber Evaluation")
OR
(Cyber AND ("General System Theory" OR "Complex System Theory"))
OR
(Cybernetics AND ("Requisite Variety" OR "Requisite Complexity"))
OR
("Information Technology" AND "Operation* Technology")
OR
("Cyber Governance")
OR
("Cyber Resilien*")
OR
("Complex Cyber Physical System")

The logical combination of search terms was then run through relevant literature databases, with each database requiring some adjustments to properly execute in its advanced search engine. The databases queried are provided in Table 11.1, along with the number of returns for each search term through each database query.

The raw results were sorted for duplication, and then the titles were screened to determine documents that were relevant and irrelevant to the research questions. Irrelevant documents were manually excluded from the search results that were downloaded for further analysis. Some examples of these were journal articles with the following terms in their titles: social media, information overload in researchers, cyber-bullying, and so on. In general, a more conservative approach leaned towards keeping articles in for further analysis with MAXQDA, which is a software tool for qualitative data analysis, so articles that seemingly related only to cyber-security (based on the abstract)

TABLE 11.1
Literature Review Search Databases

Database	Raw Results
ACM Digital Library	202
IEEE Xplore	3122
Scopus	2917
Web of Science	263

were typically retained. In addition to the search databases identified previously, several sources of literature are of direct relevance to the research topic:

- National Institute of Standards and Technology (USA) – 24 documents
- European Union Agency for Network and Information Security – ENISA – 3 documents
- US Department of Defense – US DoD – 6 documents

LITERATURE REVIEW CODING STRUCTURE

Using MAXQDA, it is possible to bulk–auto code many relevant documents using categories related to the literature review search terms. The advantage of using these automated coding techniques is that the production of rapid literature analysis is possible using the Category Matrix browser function to quickly assess the overall relevance of a new document based on occurrences of coded categories in the document.

The Code Map viewer can readily depict gaps in the literature when considering all the documents together and their linkages to multiple coded categories by identifying where one or more coded terms appear within any given document in the literature review. The resulting Code Map, shown in Figure 11.5, provides a number in brackets with each coded term that represents the number of times that the term (or specified derivation of the term) appears overall in all the documents included in the analysis.

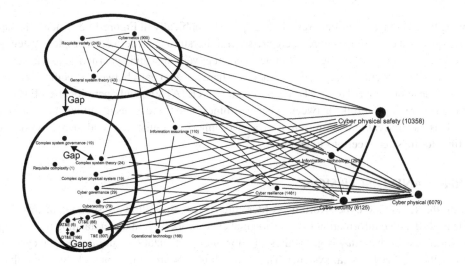

FIGURE 11.5   MAXQDA code map of search terms applied to 2091 documents from the literature review.

The MAXQDA Code Map then identifies where two terms are present within the same document via a connection line between two terms. The thickness of each line between two coded terms gives a visual indication of how many separate documents the two terms co-existed; the thicker the line, the more documents the two coded terms were both included within. However, this function of the MAXQDA Code Map does not identify whether the two terms were linked within the document or if their co-inclusion was a mere coincidence. Conversely, any coded term with no connecting lines had no other coded terms present in any of the documents in which it was found.

LITERATURE GAPS

An initial and less formal manual literature review was undertaken in advance of the systematic literature review, which was based on heuristics and the use of the better-known literature as they were applied to a range of cyber-physical systems. The initial issues found with the coverage of the literature that this informal literature review uncovered were able to guide the more comprehensive and formal systematic literature review. These initial issues identified that the possible broader literature gaps were:

- Misapplication of the information technology cybersecurity triad: confidentiality, integrity, availability to operational technology. From a systems engineering perspective, this triad does not allow for a holistic system engineering approach to the cyber-worthiness of a cyber-physical system.
- The lack of a workable through-life designed assessment framework of deployed cyber-capable systems in an evolving cyber-environment, including the ability to test multiple interactions.
- The lack of a detailed methodology for applying new and developing test designs to the best phase(s) of a generic cyber-capable system lifecycle.
- A lack in designing for degraded cyber operational states in cyber-reliant physical systems.
- A lack of regulation of artificial intelligence/machine behavior (the intersection of the laws of people, nature, and algorithms).
- A lack of principles-based regulation of human behavior to ensure cyber-worthiness of enterprise-level complex systems of cyber-physical systems.

Following the systematic literature review, as depicted graphically in Figure 11.5, when considering the cyber-physical domain literature, there are several literature gaps between complex system governance and complex systems theory, complex system governance and cybernetics, and a weak link between complex systems theory and cybernetics. There are also gaps between specific T&E activities such as developmental T&E (DT&E), acceptance T&E (AT&E) and operational T&E (OT&E). There is a general lack of links between cyber-worthiness and these areas identified, but this is to be expected, as the concept and definition of cyber-worthiness are quite new, and there has not been a lot of time for these connections to be made.

FINDINGS AND DISCUSSION

Based on the systematic cyber-worthiness literature review, the following sections of this chapter provide more detailed information for decision makers to work with in understanding the concept of cyber-worthiness as they may begin addressing how their organization can improve the cyber-worthiness of their cyber-physical systems. The overarching research questions of this book that are most relevant to each section are highlighted at the beginning of each section.

CYBER-PHYSICAL SYSTEMS

This section provides a high-level guide to the broad constituent parts of a generic cyber-physical system, from the more mundane internet-of-things to advanced capability assets utilized by modern defense forces and complex systems of cyber-physical systems that support modern civilization.

By providing clear descriptions of the components of cyber-physical systems that are vulnerable to cyberattacks, this section primarily addresses Research Question #1: Why should decision makers be aware of cybersecurity, what should this awareness include, and who should be informed? This section provides compelling reasons decision makers who are responsible for cyber-physical systems should be aware of the cybersecurity requirements of these systems.

CYBER-PHYSICAL SYSTEM COMPONENTS

At their most basic, cyber-physical systems incorporate several simple networked electronic input devices, sensing devices, and actuating components that are connected within the system boundary through information technology (IT), working in unison with the physical parts of the system to undertake a physical process or provide a physical or electrical power output. While traditional IT, or cyber systems, are primarily concerned with the creation, processing, exchange, storage, and retrieval of data, CPS extend this to physical processes and outputs. Several key terms need explaining with basic CPS to enable a later discussion on the research on regulatory needs for CPS.

Informatioznology and Operational Technology (IT/OT) and Industrial Control Systems (ICS): The physical, or electromechanical, components of a CPS are traditionally known as industrial control systems (ICS). However, more contemporary CPS build on this by offering greater data processing, data sharing and greater overall network connectivity between I and O components. The use of I components within physical systems is fast becoming ubiquitous. This trend is primarily due to the efficiency and productivity advantages that the IT/OT combination brings to remote sensing, monitoring and operation, as well as a more holistic integration with broader enterprise systems. However, these benefits do bring additional risks to the successful operation of CPS, and indeed to wider enterprises where they are deployed.

Input Devices and Sensors: Input devices allow a cyber-physical system to receive data directly from a range of input sources, which the system will then process along with data from other input devices or sensors. These input devices can range from a single button that a human or animal can purposefully activate to the direct input of volumes of data from another cyber or cyber-physical system. Within cyber-physical systems, sensors are used to continually sense and measure a discrete physical phenomenon. These measurements are converted into data that the system can process along with other data to determine set physical actions to perform. The cyber-physical system may be designed to perform a given activity based on the data provided by sensors alone or via a combination of sensors and inputs from input devices.

Programmable Logic Controllers (PLCs): Programmable logic controllers (PLCs) are a cornerstone of operational technology due to their ability to gather discrete data from a range of inputs or sensors, compute the data received using discrete and tailored logic programming suited to an operational requirement, and initiate a desired electromechanical activity. PLCs are used extensively in hazardous industrial environments to automate activities, thereby removing humans from the hazardous activity or environment.

Supervisory Control and Data Acquisition (SCADA): The supervisory control and data acquisition (SCADA) component of a cyber-physical system enables centralized monitoring and control of several disbursed PLCs, input devices, and sensors. The SCADA is typically set up to provide a human controller with a useful dashboard on the overall status and critical operations of the broader system. The SCADA component may also allow for a human controller to remotely override the operation of a PLC, remotely request sensors to provide data at different rates, and remotely troubleshoot the erroneous operation of the cyber-physical system. SCADA is typically an instance of software residing within a more substantial operating system on a desktop computer or similar, and this computer may be internet-facing to allow for further remote operation. The broader CPS may be able to continue operation for a period without SCADA monitoring and control; however, this may force the CPS into a degraded state of operation, and the continued stable and safe operation would likely diminish over time.

Human–Machine Interface (HMI): The human machine interface (HMI) is typically the graphical representation of the SCADA component of the CPS. The HMI provides the options available to the human controller in manipulating the system and includes the input device such as a keyboard or mouse. Instances of a HMI may also be provided more locally to a PLC or bank of PLCs to allow for direct operation of the PLCs, allowing further opportunities for override, testing, and troubleshooting.

Internet of Things (and Industrial Internet of Things): The Internet of Things (IoT) is a broad term which generally encompasses discrete electronic devices that are capable of independently connecting to an established network, or the internet, directly through a router or direct connection (typically wireless), bypassing the need to connect to a fully functional operating system to in order establish and control its network connection. These discrete electronic devices may be capable of generating their own ad-hoc network by linking with many similar devices. They may also form part of a distributed cyber-physical system by functioning as input devices or as sensors and/or actuators connected via a local area network or the internet.

In much the same vein as IoT, the Industrial Internet of Things (IIoT) refers to a generalized network of electronic devices utilized in industrial settings. IIoT devices are more likely to be connected to a local area network as part of a cyber-physical system. This local area network may be connected to a broader network (possibly internet facing) extending far beyond the physical location of the IIoT devices. This type of configuration would allow the operation and outputs of the industrial cyber-physical system to be remotely monitored and controlled.

Putting It All Together

Advanced capability assets in present-day high-speed air, land, and sea transport are all examples of CCPS. The sensors, actuators, and IT/OT integrated into these systems are required to undertake ongoing and precise measurements and computations to initiate physical responses at very high refresh rates to keep these systems stable in operation. Advanced fifth-generation fighters incorporate networked mission and weapons systems, which collectively present the potential for extreme hazards to humans.

Space systems hold a comparatively precarious position as an example of CCPS. This is because they are not only costly and resource intensive to get into operational service, but they typically utilize sensors, actuators, and computational units that are required to operate reliably in a hostile environment for many years without the possibility of maintenance or repair. As a result, all on-board space system components, including IT, need to undergo extensive space testing, and as a result, they tend to be many generations older than their terrestrial counterparts. This adds to the complexity of systems of CCPS, as space systems tend to have components that are considered obsolete to the terrestrial systems they interact with remotely.

Challenges of Cyber-Physical Systems

As NIST describe in their framework for CPS, there are several aspects that make CPS different to conventional systems that lack interconnectedness (NIST, 2017b) and these differences typically

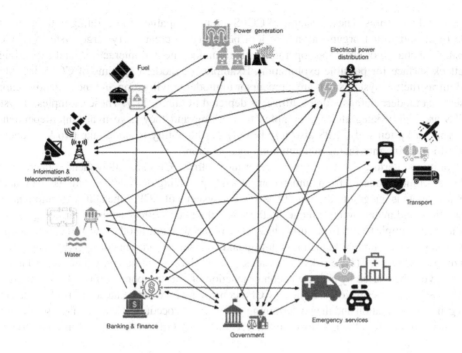

FIGURE 11.6   Concept of the interdependencies of each critical infrastructure.

Source: (Adapted from Figure 5, European Union Agency for Network and Information Security [ENISA], 2017)

present significant challenges. These challenges range from the potential for the development of emergent behaviors to interoperability issues. There is no clear threshold to identify when a cyber-physical system has enough complexity to be considered a truly complex cyber-physical system. As with any system, the greater the number of components, the greater the complexity tends to become. Certainly, the general definitions of complex systems apply, and if the number of interconnections is large, and there are multigenerational elements, then CPS become part of systems of systems (SoS) and emergent and unpredictable results can emerge (Keating& Katina). The systems of systems phenomenon also can extend to software-intensive systems where there is multigenerational code reuse (Ferreira et al). More on systems of systems involving CPS will be covered in the next section.

The interconnected system of critical infrastructure comprising energy and utility supply and storage relies on geographically dispersed, physically interconnected, and networked systems comprising countless ICS and IT/OT. Large populations rely on these CCPS to not only supply hazardous materials and power safely but also rely on these CCPS to ensure a largely uninterrupted supply to preserve life. Figure 11.6 depicts a concept for the interdependencies across many of the sectors of critical infrastructure in modern society.

SYSTEMS OF COMPLEX CYBER-PHYSICAL SYSTEMS

Many organizations have been managing systems of complex systems through human management and organizational structure over extended periods of time to great effect. These organizations range from national governments and their defense forces to manufacturers of complex systems, multinational logistics companies, and space agencies. Over time, as an increasing number of ICS and IT/OT have been integrated into the systems comprising these systems of complex systems, many CCPS have been networked to create systems of CCPS. This has driven efficiency in the overall management of systems of systems by automating much of the human management and simplifying organizational structures. These systems of CCPS are now capable of integrating with other CCPS outside of an individual organization's system boundary to create very large systems of CCPS, increasing the chance of erroneous operation due to undocumented interactions and expanding the cyberattack surface for possible exploitation. Examples of modern systems of CCPS include the critical infrastructure systems that are a precursor to modern civilization and the collective capability assets that modern defense forces utilize, as depicted in Figure 11.7. These examples of systems of CCPS are highly integrated via complex networking and they have many interdependencies. These types of systems of CCPS also rely heavily on the ability to undertake two key functions: machine-to-machine interfacing and autonomous operations.

The ability to interface one CCPS with one or more other CCPS and allow them to operate with a high degree of independence from human control while providing one another with the data that they require to operate is integral to driving efficiency. For systems of CCPS, the ability to automate physical operations and interactions with one another takes the machine-to-machine interfacing a step further. Allowing multiple CCPS to perform physical activities with one another, as well as transfer power or materials with very limited human monitoring and control, can present considerable safety risks to large numbers of people. These risks to human safety can have extreme consequences for large populations and can be caused by a single action or inaction of one component of one CCPS in a system of CCPS. Defense forces have a significant CCPS construct where the greatest risk is of cybersecurity threats gaining information and then determining and storing procedures for a denial-of-service attack. The following quote from the US Government Accountability Office (GAO, 2018) is appropriate:

> Cybersecurity issues can vary widely across different types of systems, so weapon systems cybersecurity challenges may be very different than those of some IT systems. . . . Although some weapon systems are purely IT systems, most – such as aircraft, missiles, and ships – are what the National Institute of

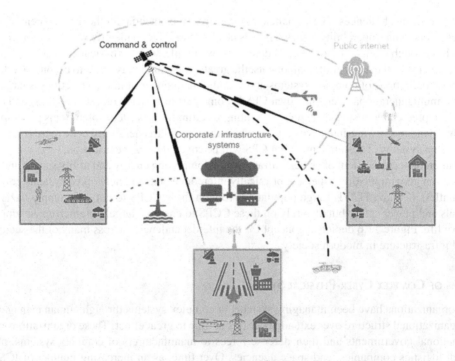

FIGURE 11.7 Weapon systems are connected across the armed services and to networks that may connect them to many other cyber-physical and information technology systems.

Source: (Adapted from Figure 4, United States of America Government Accountability Office [GAO], 2018).

Standards and Technology (NIST) and sometimes DOD refer to as "Cyber-Physical Systems." NIST defines these systems as "co-engineered interacting networks of physical and computational components." These cyber systems can affect the physical world so the consequences of a cyberattack may be greater than those of attacks on other types of systems. For example, an attack on a weapon system could have physical consequences that may even result in loss of life.

(GAO, 2018)

SAFETY CONSEQUENCES OF CYBER-PHYSICAL SYSTEM OPERATION

While cyber-physical systems present immense benefits to modern quality of life, they also present great challenges to humans and their environment when compared to traditional physical systems and traditional cyber systems. This section is a broad guide to many of the various standards and frameworks that can be applied to CPS to help address their vulnerability to cyber threats. This section then goes on to consider the risks specific to CPS, CCPS, and systems of CCPS that lead to unique hazard sets that require careful management to ensure system safety.

By identifying standards and frameworks that organizations can use to assess the cybersecurity vulnerabilities of their CPS, this section has a strong association with Research Question #2 – How can organizations assess their cybersecurity vulnerabilities and what benchmarks, indicators or maturity levels would be relevant? These standards and frameworks provide organizations with methods of assessing their own maturity levels as well as techniques that can be employed to improve on them.

CYBERSECURITY STANDARDS AND FRAMEWORKS CYBER-PHYSICAL SYSTEMS

Due to the very diverse nature of CPS, there is no single publication that can deal with all CPS risks and hazards. Each CPS will hold a unique set of risks and hazards associated with its bespoke operation. Typically, the more complexity that exists within any given CPS, the greater the risks and hazards associated with it. There are many standard-setting organizations and many more standards that can be used to guide risk assessments relating to CPS.

While most of the standards and specifications produced by these organizations are not produced specifically for risk assessments or CPS, they all include risk assessment guidance or useful tools to aid in cybersecurity or the safety of typical CPS components. The following information provides an overview of some of the more prominent and established standard-setting organizations that produce standards that apply to CPS.

The European Network and Information Security Agency (ENISA): ENISA provides standards on cybersecurity as well as reporting on specific areas of cybersecurity such as protecting industrial control systems. While ENISA provides these artifacts specifically for the European context, they are generally applicable worldwide.

The International Atomic Energy Agency (IAEA): IAEA develops nuclear safety standards, nuclear security standards, and reports specifically relating to the management of nuclear power. These standards also relate to the management of nuclear material. Due to the hazards that nuclear material presents to people and the environment, CPS are used extensively in the handling and processing of nuclear material.

The International Electrotechnical Commission (IEC): IEC establishes standards and specifications in relation to electrical power generation and distribution systems including the information security of the ICS related to these systems. The IEC also provides reports on electrical power and distribution systems including cybersecurity. The IEC co-publishes several standards with the ISO.

The International Organization for Standardization (ISO): ISO produces standards for the management of risk, including those specific to CPS. The ISO produces a family of standards on the Information Security Management System Standard, which includes information security risk management. Also relevant to the safety aspects of CPS is the ISO family of standards that provide guidance on occupational health and safety risks.

The Institute of Electrical and Electronics Engineers Standards Association (IEEE): IEEE produces standards for electrical and electronics safety, including software safety. The IEEE also publish peer-reviewed journal articles, including CPS.

The MITRE Corporation: MITRE undertakes reporting on the status of cybersecurity across a range of sectors and produce a range of tools that can assist in the identification, analysis, and mitigation of cybersecurity risk.

The National Institute of Standards and Technology: NIST provides a comprehensive framework for establishing and maintaining cybersecurity. NIST supports this framework through the publication of standards on cybersecurity, including ICS and CPS.

CYBER-PHYSICAL SYSTEM RISK

Fundamentally, a risk is the potential for an event to occur with an outcome that is negative from the perspective of a person or organization perceiving the potential event (Pojasek, 2019). The person or organization will therefore be most interested in the likelihood of the risk occurring and the likely overall consequence if it does. In the context of CPS, the overarching negative outcome that is to be mitigated against is the loss of the controlled use of a CPS. The consequences of losing control of a CPS will vary and depend on circumstances. There exists a wide variety of causes of a loss of control event, and there is a broad range of outcomes that can follow a loss of control event, each CPS having its unique set. Losing control of a CPS is likely to not only lead to the risk of further negative outcomes such as loss of productivity and loss of sensitive data or information, but a loss of control event can pose significant hazards to human health and safety.

The broad cyber safety standards, frameworks, and tools for CPS described earlier provide a strong foundation for the identification and treatment of risks associated with CPS. The key to understanding the appropriate context of CPS when undertaking a CPS risk assessment is three-fold: first, the way in which data is used by the CPS in all its functions and operations needs to be understood such that all manifestations of CPS operations, both intended and unintended, are known. Second, all possible outcomes and limitations of the physical operation of the CPS must be determined in all states of operation. Third, the consequences of the CPS not providing a specific output need to be determined.

Multiplier Effect: There is a potential for a significant number of components to reside within a CCPS that all need to interact with each other to varying degrees and in varying ways for the overall CPS to operate as intended. When many components are coupled with data inputs and outputs reliant on logical processes and software, which may have many internal interactions and potential for logic failure, there is a significant potential for undocumented interactions to occur, leading to undesirable outcomes.

Adding multiple CCPS together to form a system of CCPS multiplies the potential for unintended interactions to occur and, therefore, a greater risk of unwanted outcomes. For CCPS, there also exists the significant risk that the IT systems could be compromised by an external actor intent on forcing deleterious outcomes (Gendron, 2013). With systems of CCPS, there is a greater risk still of flow-through from one CCPS to another through their networked connections. This could make the consequences of a realized risk considerably more significant. Where the CCPS within a system of CCPS have critical interdependencies through physical inputs and outputs, the consequences of a realized risk may be worse still.

HAZARDS ASSOCIATED WITH CYBER-PHYSICAL SYSTEMS

Fundamentally, hazards are tangible things that could cause harm. When considered in the context of risk, the aim is to determine how likely it is that a hazard will end up causing harm and how serious that harm is likely to be. For the purposes of this chapter, the focus is the hazards the CPS may cause to human health and safety. Although CPS are likely to be hazardous to other CPS and property and even livelihoods, the realization of such hazards is considered part of the multiplier effect or interdependencies. Where these multiplier effects and interdependencies lead to hazards for human health and safety, there is relevance to this section, even where the lack of physical output of a CPS leads to human harm. This complexity is the nature of highly networked CCPS and systems of CCPS.

Considering the vast range of CPS in existence, the hazards associated with CPS vary greatly depending on the operational context and their interaction with other CPS and people. While many of the potentially hazardous outcomes are limited to humans in the proximity of malfunctioning CPS, hazards can have a global reach when considering the potential reach of systems of CCPS and their interdependencies. While many interactions are also likely to initiate CPS downtime, there may also be a greater risk that a failure of a physical output could result in harm (Castiglione and Lupu, 2020). For example, a loss of national electricity distribution, leading to harm to thousands of people on life support systems reliant on a reliable power supply.

It is critical to include cybersecurity considerations when assessing hazards associated with highly networked systems of CPS, as they may be particularly vulnerable to a breach of cybersecurity. When considering breaches, or attempted breaches, of cybersecurity, it may be necessary to consider the motivations of actors. This necessity is due to the idea that the success of a cybersecurity breach may often be dependent on the resources available to the actor carrying out the attack. While it may seem impractical, or even impossible, to protect against a determined superpower nation-state actor, the hazards associated with a breach may necessitate the expenditure of significant resources. This is likely to significantly affect the trade space of the broader CPS.

Risk of Hazardous Cyber-Physical System Operation: When considering the risk associated with a hazard, there are two important factors that must be considered: the application of appetite for risk and tolerance for risk. These concepts give an indication of how an individual or organization might perceive the negative outcome of a risk that is realized (Leech and Gupta, 2015). When dealing with hazards to human safety and health, the idea that individuals or organizations can apply an appetite or tolerance to the realization of an outcome that negatively affects humans is typically not palatable to the broader community.

So, even if an individual or organization has a large appetite and high tolerance for dealing with the human impacts of their deleterious actions, legislation passed by governments typically dictates minimum standards for addressing hazards. In the context of CPS, it may be difficult to readily apply all legislation, and the application of the legislation may be ambiguous for some CPS. In such cases, the concept of appetite should be replaced with the concept of as low as reasonably practicable, and systems engineering approaches must be taken to the development and operation of CPS to demonstrate due diligence.

Identification and Assessment of Hazards: Hazard and operability studies (HAZOP) (Crawley and Tyler, 2015) are a useful methodology for the identification of hazards associated with the operation of CCPS, as well as identifying issues with their ongoing operation. While HOZOPs are generally resource intensive and require the involvement of expert domain leads, employing them early in the design of the CCPS can offset high rework costs during future stages of design and operation. Scenario-based assessments used for determining hazards that may be present during various stages of the CCPS lifecycle may also be utilized in conjunction with HAZOPS to maximize the utility of the assessment.

MITIGATION AND MANAGEMENT OF CYBER-PHYSICAL SYSTEM HAZARDS

A key outcome of undertaking risk identification and assessment and hazard identification and assessment is to determine the most effective ways to avoid, eliminate or treat risks and hazards to minimize the amount of risk acceptance and hazard exposure practicable.

As with all systems involving risks and hazards, it is important to ensure that risk and hazard identification and assessments are undertaken on CPS on a regular and ongoing basis. Due to the nature of the cyber domain, risk and hazard assessments must include ongoing assessments of the CPS attack surface against newly discovered vulnerabilities of the IT components. For systems of CCPS, it is also important to consider reviewing all intra-system interfaces when modifying or incorporating a new CCPS into the broader system of CCPS.

> **Cyber-Physical System Hazard Mitigation:** Early and detailed planning is the first step in hazard mitigation of a CCPS. Following the systems engineering process, the early establishment of needs, goals, and objectives of the CCPS is useful in early planning (Faulconbridge and Ryan, 2014). More advanced planning should involve developing detailed requirements and identifying system boundaries and interfaces, particularly if the CCPS operated within a system of CCPS.

As a result of the different design methodologies typically employed during software design compared to physical system design, there is likely to be a degree of conflict between the IT aspects and the physical aspects of a CPS during all stages of system design. There is likely to be more conflict between the two the longer it takes to design and produce the CCPS, due to the rapid pace of IT technological change compared to the physical components. These conflicts require close and ongoing management during CCPS development, with regular design space trade studies that consider changing technologies and cybersecurity trends.

Considering the ongoing need to keep up with potential cyberattacks, it is also important to ensure that the configuration of the systems is well documented from design to allow for ongoing table-topping cyber vulnerability assessments. The design should also consider incorporating multiple redundant and independent methods for verifying the operation of critical system functions (Singh and Rajput, 2016).

> **Through-Life Hazard Management of Cyber-Physical Systems:** There are many mitigation strategies available to help manage the hazards associated with CPS, CCPS and systems of CCPS. The development of safety management systems (SMS) (Inayat et al., 2021; Bieder, 2021) for the various modes of operation on of the CCPS is a key consideration of ongoing hazard management. For systems of CCPS, safety management systems should be standardized to as great a degree as possible.

Considering the ongoing need to keep ahead of potential cyber-threats, it is important to conduct regular penetration testing of the CCPS, and if part of a system of CCPS, then consideration should be given to incorporating the penetration testing with the broader system of systems. While penetration testing should consider the multiple and redundant methods for verifying the operational performance of critical system functions, any recommendations should be cognizant of the likelihood of all methods being compromised by an external actor at the same time.

REGULATION FOR PUBLIC RISK POSED BY CYBER-PHYSICAL SYSTEMS

Through identifying how cybersecurity attacks on cyber-physical systems can impact the safety of people across different industries, organizations, and different countries, this section primarily addresses Research Question #3 – How have cybersecurity attacks impacted different industries, organizations, and countries; what are the case studies and lessons learned? This section also utilizes some case studies to demonstrate how self-regulation of cybersecurity practices can be employed to minimize the risk of organizations experiencing hazardous outcomes from errant cyber-physical system operations caused by cyber threats.

As identified in the preceding section of this chapter, CCPS and systems of CCPS have the potential to cause significant harm to large numbers of people if they deviate from their expected operational boundaries. There are also many standards and frameworks that are available for managing risks and hazards relating to CCPS. While it may be considered prudent for owners and operators of CCPS to be aware of and follow the standards and frameworks relevant to their system, some owners and operators may not be inclined to do so. There are also likely to be pressures on owners and operators of CCPS to discard discretionary standards due to budgetary constraints or the pursuit of efficiency and profits.

To counter these individual and organizational drivers and behaviors, governments may regulate the people and their activities relating to the operation of CCPS. It is important to note that laws apply to people and entities that make up groups of people. No matter how autonomous a CCPS is, government laws and regulations can only seek to regulate a CCPS through the actions or omissions of people and the entities that own or operate the CCPS.

Any criminal and/or civil liability associated with any harm caused by the action or inaction of a CCPS or system of CCPS rests with the people and/or organizations that develop, produce, operate, and maintain a CCPS over their full lifecycle. Given the sheer complexity involved with CCPS over their full lifecycle, it is extremely challenging to regulate all aspects of CCPS and their operation. For this reason, regulations associated with CCPS can be quite broad and tend to specify that activities are to be undertaken by the developers, owners, and operators of CCPS at various stages of the CCPS lifecycle. These activities may include the development of a safety management system, or a safety case for a particular CCPS, which result in artefacts that help to manage the safe operation of the CCPS throughout its operational.

Any legislation or regulations may require certain records to be kept, such as maintenance records or the competencies of personnel operating CCPS. The aim of regulating these types of activities and demanding artifacts be produced is for individuals and organizations to be able to demonstrate that due diligence has been carried out to ensure CCPS safety. If due diligence can be demonstrated prior to initial operations of a CCPS, and regularly throughout the operation of the CCPS, then there is an expectation that negative outcomes will largely be avoided.

Many modern industrial processes involve a high degree of complexity coupled with requirements for precision timing that humans simply cannot perform without the assistance of CPS. Creating a positive feedback loop, increasingly capable ICS and IT/OT allow for the creation of materials and physical conditions that are far too hazardous for direct human interaction. When then considering that work health and safety requirements trend towards becoming more onerous, there exists a need for continuous improvement in the management and assurance of IDC.

Legislation may be produced for specific types or categories of CCPS, such as air transport or nuclear power reactors, and target specific known hazards. Regulators that are given powers by legislation may disallow the commissioning of a particular CCPS based on the absence of required information in a mandated artefact. Through the operational life of CCPS, regulators may then query that certain activities have taken place by auditing records such as operational logs and maintenance records. Regulators may also undertake inspections of the CCPS, which may provide direct evidence of issues with the CCPS or demonstrate inconsistencies between the state of the CCPS and the artefacts provided. These activities are all undertaken to help reduce the likelihood of losing operational control of a CCPS and realizing specific harms that CCPS may cause.

THE CASE FOR SELF-REGULATION

While legislation set by governments plays a significant role in maintaining public safety around CCPS and through the actions or inactions of CCPS, legislation cannot be seen as the only way to ensure public safety. Regulations, codes of practice, and standards alike do not and cannot provide a comprehensive and complete set of rules for CCPS to follow to ensure public safety. There are simply too many variables in the operating environments (in both the cyber domain and the physical domain) for generalized legislative frameworks to capture all risks and eliminate all hazards for each bespoke CCPS that may be operating in a wider CCPS.

While some may argue that there is a case to do away with government regulation and entirely self-regulate the operation of CCPS, this is not the case for self-regulation being made here, as community expectations must be reflected through government regulations. The argument here for self-regulation is for organizations utilizing CCPS to regulate themselves to a higher standard than the community expectation. History is rich with examples of self-regulation that lead to disaster, with the Boeing 737 Max 8 aircraft crashes of 2017 and 2018 (Palmer, 2020) serving as a contemporary example of the harms of handing regulation back to the entities designing high-hazard CCPS. Instead, there is a strong case to argue that individuals and organizations alike, who develop, operate, and maintain CCPS should consider legislation, regulations, codes of practice and standards a minimum and aspire to excellence in self-regulation more than the legal minimum.

A pertinent example of excellence in self-regulation is the example of the United States Naval Reactor Regulator, which is responsible for US Naval Reactors. The US Naval Nuclear Propulsion Program self-regulated lifetime radiation exposure limits to a higher level than that of the federal regulations, leading the federal regulator to adopt the same limits for all nuclear reactors in the United States (US DoE & DoN, 2020). One of the primary drivers for self-regulation more than statutory requirements is the clear signal that it sends to anyone dealing with the CCPS, including the public, that system safety is a priority. Self-regulation also helps to ensure that appropriate resourcing is being applied to ensuring CCPS safety.

WHAT TO SELF-REGULATE

When considering what to self-regulate, consideration should be given to the CCPS that is being developed, operated, or maintained by the organization or organizations responsible for the CCPS. The hazards and extant regulations that apply to the CCPS should be known, and the organization dealing with the CCPS should already have a high level of maturity with respect to their understanding of the CCPS in both the cyber context and the physical context. Careful consideration also needs to be given to how a CCPS may operate within a system of CCPS, particularly where the organization does not have ownership or control of all CCPS working within the system of CCPS. Key areas to self-regulate are described in the following.

> **Roles and Qualifications** – Key roles and qualifications may already be specified within the legislative framework that applies to the CCPS. If this is the case, then these key roles should be identified early, and the organization may consider imposing self-regulation to ensure that succession planning is properly considered and appropriately funded. Where possible, there should be regular overlap in role responsibilities and duties to ensure that the right people are available whenever they are needed. Consideration should also be given to regulating career path development for key personnel, coupled with a program for maintaining up-to-date qualifications and upskilling. The latter aspects are particularly critical for personnel responsible for the IT, or cyber, aspects of the CCPS, as IT jobs are typically in high demand.
>
> **Interfaces and Interactions** – Particularly when dealing with systems of CCPS that incorporate CCPS across multiple owners and operators, it may be necessary to impose self-regulation on the interfaces that each CCPS has with the other CCPS. Limitations may also need to be placed on the number and types of interactions that each CCPS has with other CCPS in the broader system. Given the disbursed nature of systems of

CCPS, these types of self-imposed regulations help to standardize across industries and sectors, which may eventually coalesce into industry standards or codes of practice and may eventually be subsumed into legislation. Interfaces and interactions also require regular testing to ensure that the integrity of the overall system of CCPS remains intact to emerging cyber threats.

Technology – As the IT components within a CCPS are likely to become obsolete well before many of the physical and electromechanical components, consideration should be given to regulating maximum system design review periods. This process may include scope for planning upgrades and retrofits in line with new CCPS that may be entering service into a broader system of CCPS. If the operational life of the CCPS is measured in decades, then consideration may be given to self-regulating processes for actively identifying new technology that is available for sensing, computation, and networking of the CCPS.

MOVING FROM TRADITIONAL CYBERSECURITY TO CYBER-WORTHINESS

This section provides a high-level overview of the key principles of cybersecurity and plots course via information assurance and cyber-resilience to make a case for the use of cyber-worthiness tools by organizations that utilize cyber-physical systems. Accordingly, this section addresses aspects of Research Question #1 – Why should decision makers be aware of cybersecurity, what should this awareness include, and who should be informed? This section then continues to address parts of Research Question #2 – How can organizations assess their cybersecurity vulnerabilities and what benchmarks, indicators, or maturity levels would be relevant? These aspects are addressed by identifying the awareness that decision makers should have in relation to the cybersecurity of cyber-physical systems, as well as the benchmarks to utilize in the context of cyber-worthiness.

CLASSIC CYBERSECURITY

The classic model for cybersecurity is focused on the needs that individuals and organizations have in relation to the creation, transmission, storage, and retrieval of data and information. While the relative importance and significance of the specific data and information that require cybersecurity have some bearing on the overall needs, the primary aim of cybersecurity is to achieve information assurance while providing a degree of resilience to the individual or organization. Classic cybersecurity does not consider the operation or physical outputs of CPS and so is only concerned with physical systems in so much as the specific having concern for the physical systems that the information is created, transmitted, stored, or retrieved on remains operational.

INFORMATION ASSURANCE

Information assurance is fundamentally based on three key principles as they relate to data and information (Wilson, 2013):

- Confidentiality – keeping data and information available only to authorized individuals; ensuring that no data or information is disclosed to unauthorized individuals, processes, or systems.
- Integrity – ensuring that the data and information remain intact and readable through the designated means of viewing the information. Integrity applies to the entire data set, such that the unauthorized modification or destruction of data and information is not permitted.
- Availability – having the data and information available to authorized individuals in a timely manner through the designated means of viewing the data and information.

RESILIENCE

Broadly, resilience is the ability to maintain a specific purpose, with integrity, through uncertain and variable conditions. This can be applied to the smallest microorganisms and to the largest civilizations of people alike. There are many variations on the definition, including psychological definitions relating to an individual's ability to recover from adversity (Langeland et al., 2016).

CYBER RESILIENCE

When applied to cyber systems and CPS, these definitions continue to apply, and given that these systems rely on the input of individuals and organizations, it is valid to consider multiple perspectives when considering resilience in the context of cyber systems. Cyber resilience is closely related to business continuity for organizations, which is primarily about the ability of an organization to carry on its business in adverse conditions or under stress. Cyber resilience can be described as the ability for an information system to continue operation under adverse conditions and stress and the ability to rapidly recover from an adverse event (Carayannis et al., 2021).

The US NIST (NIST, 2017a) articulates the organizational objectives and functions to have trustworthiness and assure cybersecurity. Organizations need to have cybersecurity expertise at functional, operational, and technical levels of "preventing, protecting and restoring." In addition, they need to have organizational processes for trustworthiness and assurance, which are evidenced through "assessment and test." Key definitions are as follows (NIST, 2017b):

- Cybersecurity. Prevention of damage to, protection of, and restoration of computers, electronic communications systems, electronic communications services, wire communication, and electronic communication, including information contained therein, to ensure its availability, integrity, authentication, confidentiality, and nonrepudiation
- Trustworthiness, in this context, means worthy of being trusted to fulfil whatever requirements may be needed for a component, subsystem, system, network, application, mission, business function, enterprise, or other entity. Trustworthiness requirements can include attributes of reliability, dependability, performance, resilience, safety, security, privacy, and survivability under a range of potential adversity in the form of disruptions, hazards, threats, and privacy risks.
- Assurance is the measure of confidence that the system functionality is implemented correctly, operating as intended, and producing the desired outcome with respect to meeting the security and privacy requirements for the system – thus possessing the capability to accurately mediate and enforce established security and privacy policies.

The NIST CPS framework is depicted in Figure 11.8, where it can be seen that assurance is one part of the CPS framework and that the CPS needs to be conceptualized in the context of the aspects and concerns specific to the CPS.

THE CASE FOR CYBER-WORTHINESS

One of the earlier uses of the term cyber-worthiness utilizes seaworthiness as an analogy to express the need for cyber-worthy software to be able to withstand cybersecurity risks the way a ship is required to withstand the risks associated with the high seas (Trope, 2004). Applied to warranties for software only, Trope (2004) argued that "A warranty of Cyber-worthiness" would consist of specific assurance and rectification activities that would be undertaken before and after the release of the software. These activities would serve to assure users of the software that the software is safe from cyberattacks and that in turn their information would remain confidential.

While this early work is useful in gaining an understanding of the concept of cyber-worthiness, it is extremely limited in that it only applies to software and adheres to the traditional cybersecurity paradigm of confidentiality of the information and touching lightly on control of a computing device. In a military context (US DoD, 2021), the terms cyber-resilience and cyber-survivability are used as a means for military systems to be tested or put through trials. These trials would prove their ability to operate effectively in the physical world while also operating IT components critical to the physical operations of the CCPS within a contested cyber domain. These concepts convey a similar meaning to the idea of the cyber-worthiness of a system operating in the cyber domain where it will be subjected to ongoing cyber-risks. The more modern cyberspace, or cyber domain, has evolved into something far more complex that is generally considered "co-equal with air, land, and sea" domains (US DoD, 2021), while the US DoD defines cyberspace as:

> A global domain within the information environment consisting of the interdependent network of information technology infrastructures and resident data, including the internet, telecommunications networks, computer systems, and embedded processors and controllers.
>
> *(US DoD, 2021)*

A more contemporary definition of cyber-worthiness would need to consider the risks associated with cyberspace as defined by the US DoD. Further to this, the definition would also need to include not only the cyber-worthiness of software and the confidentiality, integrity, and availability of associated information, but it would need to consider fully integrated cyber-physical systems and the combined harm that could be caused across these domains. Figure 11.1 provides a generic mapping of cybersecurity and cyber-physical system governance processes to achieving cyber-worthiness in the context of the modern defense force.

CYBER-WORTHINESS IN SYSTEM DESIGN

When designing a CPS to incorporate cyber-worthiness, requirements for cyber-worthiness should be considered early in the requirements setting phase. To achieve this, the concept of cyber-worthiness needs to be defined for the specific CPS of interest, given the context of its specific cyber and physical operating environments. This definition of cyber-worthiness should consider the operating organization's settings on resilience, business continuity, and information assurance.

Once the requirements are set for the cyber-worthiness of the CPS under development, the methods for validating that the cyber-worthiness construct is appropriate for the operational concepts of the CPS need to be established. This will allow ongoing checks as the system develops to validate that the system continues to adhere to the established cyber-worthiness needs. Verification that the cyber-worthiness requirements that were originally set have been addressed in the final CPS configuration can be achieved through developmental and acceptance T&E. To undertake T&E measures of performance, measures of effectiveness will need to be set. Developing the measures of performance and measures of effectiveness can be difficult for any system under development. CPS have the additional challenge of creating measures in both the physical and the cyber domains.

CYBER-WORTHINESS IN THE SYSTEM LIFECYCLE

Particularly when dealing with large systems of CCPS, the cyber-worthiness of each CCPS must be considered an aspect of the system that requires ongoing management. To be considered carefully is the need to plan for obsolescence and the need to prepare for the retirement of individual CCPS that are part of the broader system of systems, as well as anticipating the integration of new CCPS into the broader system. Key aspects to consider in this regard are maintaining configuration management and undertaking extensive operational T&E for existing CCPS. The generic process of system assurance shown over a generic capability life cycle, such as approval-to-solicit (market/tender) and approval-to-contract, is depicted in Figure 11.8.

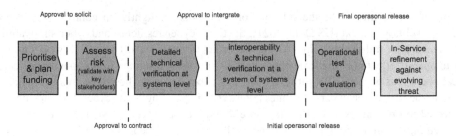

FIGURE 11.8   Generic assurance process for defense capabilities.

IMPORTANCE OF MODEL-BASED CYBER-WORTHINESS ASSESSMENTS

This section provides useful information to decision makers on the types of model-based systems engineering (MBSE) tools that can be utilized by their organizations to undertake rapid and dynamic assessments of cyber-worthiness through threat and risk assessments, which pertains to Research Question #4 – Which cybersecurity applications or defenses ought to be selected for prevention or mitigation, and how/when/where should they be implemented? This question is addressed by describing the use of Systems Modeling Language applications to develop MBSE models that is also an effective communication tool for conveying technical information on cybersecurity and cyber-worthiness to non-technical personnel. Cybersecurity threats are continually evolving (Klemas and Chan, 2018), and as the pace of evolution increases, iterations of cumbersome and time-consuming static assessments of cyberattack surfaces, kill-chains (i.e., threat paths), and key controls become inadequate. To deal with this pace of evolution, dynamic and highly adaptable model-based assessments are needed. Model-based systems engineering techniques in universal languages like Systems Modeling Language (SysML) are increasingly used by organizations to model complex system requirements, obsolescence, and supply-chain management with improved efficiency (Rogers and Mitchell, 2021).

Fowler et al. (2021) and Barzeele et al. (2021) are undertaking research into MBSE frameworks to have cyber-worthiness assessments of CCPS based on modeling cyberattack surfaces and possible kill chains using activity diagrams, misuse cases, and safety-focused bow-tie diagrams. These efforts are utilizing improved SysML-based packages like Cameo and Munich Agile MBSE Concept (MAGIC) (Salehi and Wang, 2019; Rogers and Mitchell, 2021). One distinct advantage in the enterprise use of MBSE in cybersecurity activities and requirements setting is the ability to link the supply-chain management of IT and OT suppliers to risk manage the confluence of key controls to contractors or countries of concern, that is, to assist cyber-provenance (Carnovale and Yeniyurt, 2021; Sigler et al., 2017). Other advantages preferred by Fowler et al. (2021) and Barzeele et al. (2021) for MBSE use in modeling cyber-worthiness assessments are:

- Greater consistency between programs and projects.
- Greater reuse of common modules.
- More detailed, informed, and nuanced cyber table-topping or risk assessments.
- More informed and thus fairer investment decisions at development iterations, technical refreshes, or upgrade opportunities.
- The more robust basis for determining the most important cases to verify with pen test (i.e., representative sampling and combinatorial test design like high throughput testing (Hagar et al., 2015; Kuhn et al., 2016; NIST, 2010).
- Greater efficiency and flexibility to aggregate cyber-worthiness assessments on systems-of-systems that are formed to meet operational demands.
- Ease in updating cyber-worthiness assessments to new threats, subsystems, suppliers, or software refreshes to keep pace with advanced persistent threats.

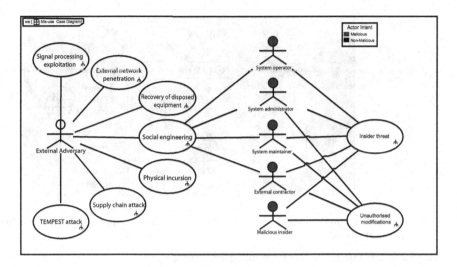

FIGURE 11.9 A generic mis-use case schematic that may be applied to cyber-physical systems.

Source: (Adapted from Figure 1, Fowler and Sitnikova, 2021).

Using MBSE to undertake assessments of cyberattack surfaces and kill chains also requires verification and validation (V&V) (Thrasher and Pippard, 2018; Christensen, 2017). However, due to their time-consuming and resource-intensive nature, focusing only on V&V techniques is often risk focused and does not cover all interactions of CPS As a result, organizations may make the decision to change key controls without considering all interactions and likely outputs of a CPS. Focusing on MBSE approaches inherently links the safety consequences of engineered physical systems in methods like failure modes effects and criticality analysis (FMECA) with new cyber-threats to facilitate risk management decisions. They may also form a systematic basis to move systems design from a focus on designing them for functions or use cases to balancing this with vulnerabilities to misuse cases. Finally, they help merge systems engineering management with information assurance management, such as system security engineering (Nejib et al., 2017) or cyber-worthiness. Figure 11.9 provides an example output of MBSE using a SysML application Cameo.

When verifying and validating such cyber-worthiness assessments, the process for CCPS often involves cyber-range infrastructure and challenges to get consistency (repeatability) with independence in penetration testing (Joiner and Tutty, 2018; Christensen, 2017). New scripting environments like APT2 (Compton, 2016) provide the wherewithal for large organizations to build consistent pen-testing with traceability and test design and analysis tools.

The development of digital twinning within complex systems appears to be the next evolution from selective or even universal MBSE (Madni and Purohit, 2021) and extends cyber-resilience assessment into CPS (Flammini, 2021). Figure 11.10 depicts the process cycle between the virtual and physical world through the construct of digital twinning.

MAPPING CYBER-WORTHINESS TO COMPLEX SYSTEMS GOVERNANCE

This section explores the application of complex systems governance to the pursuit of cyber-worthiness of cyber-physical systems utilized by large and complex organizations. This investigation of the application of complex systems governance to cyber-worthiness for cyber-physical systems addresses Research Question #7 – What are the literature gaps and what future research is needed to advance the state-of-the-art in the cybersecurity field for stakeholders? This section describes current research being undertaken for the advancement of cybersecurity in cyber-physical systems.

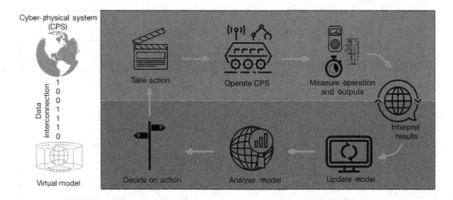

FIGURE 11.10 A representation of digital twin components and high-level processes applicable to cyber-physical systems.

Source: (Adapted from Figure 1, Van Der Horn and Mahadevan, 2021).

As identified throughout this chapter, cyber-physical systems can be very complex systems, particularly when utilizing them within a broader system of systems. Coupling this complexity with the potential for CCPS to cause significant harm to large numbers of people when not operating as intended, the overall governance requirements of these CCPS can be as complex as the systems themselves. Although CCPS do have a large amount of complexity, when considering them in isolation, they do not fit any definition that could identify them as a truly complex system. Even when considering systems of CCPS, the threshold is not crossed to judge them as complex systems. However, when considering CCPS as parts of systems of CCPS that operate within complex and organically derived human organizations, there is reason to view their operation as part of a truly complex system.

INTRODUCTION TO COMPLEX SYSTEMS GOVERNANCE

One methodology for managing complex systems is the emerging field of complex systems governance, which considers system design, execution, and evolution of a group of metasystem functions that assert control over and coordination within the complex system. CSG is ultimately focused on the overall complex systems performance and ongoing viability. CSG is grounded at the intersection of the associated fields of systems theory, management cybernetics, and governance. The benefit that CSG can provide to CCPS is that it considers the CCPS within its organizational and regulatory constructs, as well as its operational environment. As a result, when applying CSG to CCPS, or systems of CCPS, there is an inherent need to query the organizational construct, as well as the legislation and regulations that the CCPS work within. Where deficiencies are found in the organization that owns or operates the CCPS, changes can be made to rectify these deficiencies. Where deficiencies are found in the overarching legislation and regulations, changes can be proposed to legislators, or the organization can impose self-regulation.

META FUNCTIONS

CSG considers nine meta-functions of a system of interest. By identifying how a given CCPS fits within its operating environment, greater organizational construct, and regulatory framework considering these nine meta-functions, the operation of the CCPS can be better understood. With this renewed understanding of the CCPS, a functional assessment can be conducted to determine how it is performing within its broader organization and regulatory framework. If the CCPS is not functioning as well as expected, then a pathological assessment can be undertaken to see which meta functions are most responsible for impacting performance (Katina, 2015; Keating and Katina, 2019). These nine meta functions, depicted in Figure 11.4, are:

- Policy and identity
- System context
- Strategic monitoring
- System development
- Learning and transformation
- Environmental scanning
- Operational performance
- Information and communication
- System operations

COMPLEX SYSTEMS GOVERNANCE IN CYBER-WORTHINESS

As cyber-worthiness is concerned with how well CPS, CCPS, or systems of CCPS operate in both the contested cyber domain and the contested physical domain, CSG provides a sound framework for bringing domain specialists together to consider overall system performance and initiate positive feedback mechanisms for ongoing system development. Currently, research is being undertaken considering critical CSG meta functions within very large organizations that utilize advanced capability and critical infrastructure cyber-physical systems incorporating high-hazard physical outputs. The aim of this research is to determine the CSG meta functions that contribute most to the ongoing cyber-worthiness of systems of CCPS in order to develop strategies for rapid and real-time assessments of whole-of-organization cyber-worthiness.

RECOMMENDATIONS AND FUTURE WORK

As complex cyber-physical systems become more complex and begin to incorporate advanced machine learning and artificial intelligence, there will be a greater need to govern potential emergent features of the systems. While some emergent features of complex systems can be beneficial, many may not be, and all are likely to operate outside the expected parameters of the CCPS. Therefore, a robust framework for rapidly assessing the cyber-worthiness of CCPS is likely to be even more significant as CCPS trend toward becoming truly complex systems. The ongoing investigation on the use of complex systems governance may shed some light on how owners and operators might confidently prepare for the advent of emergent features in their cyber-physical systems.

IMPORTANCE OF CYBER-WORTHINESS TO THE DECISION MAKER

While the central cyber-worthiness research questions and sub-questions stated in the introductory section of this chapter are about cyber-worthiness, they share considerable similarities with the overarching research questions of this book. This section provides a summary of recommendations and takeaways that the cyber-worthiness literature review can provide a decision maker who is interested in both the cybersecurity and the quality of the physical outputs of cyber-physical systems.

> RQ1. Why should decision makers be aware of cybersecurity, what should this awareness include, and who should be informed?

Through the cyber-worthiness literature review conducted, it is evident that decision makers should be aware of the degree to which their organization relies on the cyber domain and the way their business or undertaking is dependent on the cyber domain in delivering its outputs. Decision makers should make themselves aware of the contemporary cyber-threats that are likely to impact their operations, how they are best mitigated, and the resources required to adequately mitigate them.

Where a decision maker's business or undertaking is reliant on the safe and ongoing operation of cyber-physical systems, they are obliged to understand how these threats may impact the health and safety of their workers and the impact that the physical outputs (or lack of them) may have on the users of their CPS. Accordingly, decision makers, workers, and customers alike should be informed of potential impacts on the cyber-worthiness of the CPS that they rely upon.

RQ2. How can organizations assess their cybersecurity vulnerabilities, and what benchmarks, indicators, or maturity levels would be relevant?

Organizations that utilize CPS should strongly consider integrating cybersecurity into system design, upgrades, modifications, and operational procedures of their CPS. As an initial step in reducing cybersecurity vulnerabilities, careful consideration should be given to ensuring that their CPS are separated from their general enterprise networks and to limit any internet-facing networking capabilities. While cybersecurity alone does not provide robust cyber-worthiness for CPS, it is likely that organizations utilizing CPS that have a higher cybersecurity maturity will also demonstrate greater cyber-worthiness.

Depending on their specific sector and business or undertaking, organizations that utilize CPS will be subjected to varying cybersecurity vulnerabilities and threats. Therefore, each individual organization will be required to tailor its cybersecurity maturity based on the needs of its organizational structure and the types of CPS it utilizes. To assess and uplift cybersecurity maturity levels, organizations should consider utilizing robust frameworks such as the NIST Framework for Improving Critical Infrastructure Cybersecurity (NIST, 2018) or the Cybersecurity Capability Maturity Model (C2M2) developed by the Department of Energy in the United States (US DoE, 2022).

RQ3. How have cybersecurity attacks impacted different industries, organizations, and countries; what are the case studies and lessons learned?

While the degree of risk associated with CPS utilized by defense forces will demand more robust risk analysis and treatment to ensure their ongoing safety, CPS utilized by critical infrastructure operators are under renewed pressure to assure cybersecurity. The 2011 Stuxnet cyberattack that was conducted on an Iranian nuclear enrichment facility heralded a paradigm shift for the cybersecurity requirements of industrial control systems used worldwide (Siwar et al., 2012). The 2020/21 cyber hacking of the chemical dosing system of a United States united water utility provides a stark warning about the physical harm that cybersecurity weaknesses in critical infrastructure can have on large communities (Grubbs et al., 2021).

The lessons learned from these cyberattacks are twofold: (1) even when industrial control systems are purposely kept separate from broader networks and the internet, they contain inherent cybersecurity vulnerabilities which must be actively addressed, and (2) as more an industrial control systems are allowed to be connected to broader networks for the convenience of remote monitoring and control, the attack surface they provide to nefarious actors increases. Therefore, cybersecurity protections commensurate with the overall risks and hazards associated with critical infrastructure CPS must be applied.

RQ4. Which cybersecurity applications or defenses ought to be selected for prevention or mitigation, and how/when/where should they be implemented?

There are myriad cybersecurity applications that could be recommended, each with unique advantages and disadvantages for organizations. When considering what can be used to assist in the assessment of the cyber-worthiness of CPS, the use of MBSE techniques and their associated Systems Modeling Language applications are recommended. The use of MBSE and SysML applications can be used at any stage of a CPS lifecycle to assess and enhance the cyber-worthiness of CPS, and they have the additional advantage of being both relatively user friendly and very effective as a communication tool for non-technical audiences. One example of a practical application of MBSE to the cyber-worthiness assessment of CPS is the Cyber-worthiness Evaluation and Management Toolkit (CEMT)[1]. This toolkit provides a customized SysML profile that can be imported into commercial MBSE tools to streamline the development of model-based cyber-worthiness assessments.

> RQ7. What are the literature gaps and what future research is needed to advance the state of the art in the cybersecurity field for stakeholders?

As identified in the literature review undertaken as part of the cyber-worthiness research underpinning this chapter, there are clear indications that while there are stronger ties between general T&E and both cybersecurity and cyber-physical literature, there is a distinct literature gap between the traditional subsets of T&E (i.e., DT&E, AT&E and OT&E) in the cybersecurity and cyber-physical contexts. This indicates difficulty in the adjustment of traditional T&E to cyber T&E, and this requires research to confirm, quantify, address, and measure.

When considering the cyber-physical domain literature, there are several literature gaps between complex system governance and complex systems theory, complex system governance and cybernetics, and a weak link between complex systems theory and cybernetics. These gaps are significant for large organizations that utilize complex systems of cyber-physical systems with a broad range of high-hazard physical outputs, such as modern defense forces. This significance is derived from the fact that in combination with the organization itself, the complex system of cyber-physical systems is part of a complex system that is subject to the theories of cybernetics, complex system theory, and complex system governance.

CONCLUSIONS AND FUTURE WORK

Through the information gathered during the conduct of a systematic literature review contributing to greater research on the cyber-worthiness of cyber-physical systems, this chapter provides a solid foundation for decision makers to identify the key terminology and the foundation components of their cyber-physical systems. With this information, decision makers are in a better position to begin to effectively address the cybersecurity of their cyber-physical systems through the range of cybersecurity standards and cyber-physical frameworks identified. The safety-critical aspects and challenges associated with the complexity of complex systems of cyber-physical systems are further explored, and decision makers are provided with useful concepts to utilize in further consideration if a path of self-regulation for improved safety outcomes is appropriate for their organization.

The key concepts of cyber-worthiness of cyber-physical systems are explored in the context of classic cybersecurity, information assurance, and cyber-resilience such that the decision maker can consider the cybersecurity and safety of their cyber-physical systems form a broader organizational perspective. This perspective also extends to complex systems of cyber-physical systems, considering the interdependencies that cyber-physical systems can have with each other and broader networking infrastructure. Model bases systems engineering tools such as Systems Modeling Language and digital twinning are presented to the decision maker to demonstrate some of the advanced and cutting-edge tools available to them in the pursuit of cyber-worthiness. By introducing the use of complex systems governance in the assessment of organizational cyber-worthiness, the decision maker can consider the near future work that is being undertaken in the field of cyber-worthiness. With the rapid development of artificial intelligence and machine learning paving the way for true complexity in cyber-physical systems, ongoing research into addressing cyber-worthiness through complex system governance is vital.

NOTE

1. https://github.com/stuartfowler/CEMT/

REFERENCES

Barzeele, J., Siu, K., Robinson, M., Suantak, L., Merems, J., Durling, M., Moitra, A., Meng, B., Williams, P., and Prince, D. 2021. Experience in Designing for Cyber Resiliency in Embedded DoD Systems. *INCOSE International Symposium*, vol. 31, no. 1, pp. 80–94.

Bieder, C. 2021. *Safety Science: A Situated Science an Exploration Through the Lens of Safety Management Systems*. Amsterdam, NL: Elsevier.

Carayannis, E. G., Grigoroudis, E., Scheherazade, S., Rehman, S. S., and Samarakoon, N. 2021. Ambidextrous Cybersecurity: The Seven Pillars (7Ps) of Cyber Resilience. *IEEE Transactions on Engineering Management*, vol. 68, no. 1.

Carnovale, Steven, and Yeniyurt, Sengun. 2021. *Cybersecurity and Supply Chain Management: Risks, Challenges and Solutions*. Hackensack, NJ: World Scientific.

Castiglione, L. M., and Lupu, E. C. 2020. Hazard Driven Threat Modelling for Cyber Physical Systems. Session 1: CPS & IoT Security. CPSIOTSEC'20, November 9. Virtual Event. New York, United States, 4(1), pp. 13–24. https://doi/10.1145/3411498.3419967

Christensen, P. 2017. Cybersecurity Test and Evaluation: A Look Back, Some Lessons Learned, and a Look Forward! *ITEA Journal*, vol. 38, no. 3, pp. 221–228.

Compton, A. 2016. Scripting Myself Out of a Job – Automating the Penetration Test with APT2, ed. Rapid 7 conference: YouTube. www.youtube.com/watch?v=psBtbekLntg

Crawley, F., and Tyler, B. 2015. HAZOP: Guide to Best Practice, 3rd Edition Describes and Illustrates the HAZOP Study Method, Highlighting a Variety of Proven Uses and Approaches. Elsevier, Amsterdam, Netherlands.

Norfolk Virginia, B. K. Payne and H. Wu, Eds., 12–13 March. Academic Conferences and Publishing International Ltd, pp. 127–134. doi: 10.34190/ICCWS.20.006.

European Union Agency for Network and Information Security (ENISA). 2017. Communication Network Dependencies for ICS/SCADA Systems. doi: 10.2824/397676. https://www.enisa.europa.eu/publications/ics-scada-dependencies

Faulconbridge, I., and Ryan, M. J. 2014. *Systems Engineering Practice*. Canberra: Argos Press.

Flammini, F. 2021. Digital Twins as Run-time Predictive Models for the Resilience of Cyber-Physical Systems: A Conceptual Framework. *Philosophical Transactions of The Royal Society A Mathematical Physical and Engineering Sciences*, vol. 379, p. 20200369. https://doi.org/10.1098/rsta.2020.0369

Fowler, S., Joiner, K., and Sitnikova, E. 2021. Assessing Cyber-Worthiness of Complex System Capabilities using MBSE: A New Rigorous Engineering Methodology. www.techrxiv.org/articles/preprint/

Fowler, S., and Sitnikova, E. 2019. Toward a Framework for Assessing the Cyber-worthiness of Complex Mission Critical Systems. Presented at the Military Communications and Information Systems Conference, Canberra, Australia, 12–14 November. https://doi.org/10.1109/milcis.2019.8930800

GAO. 2018. Weapon Systems Cybersecurity: DoD Just Beginning to Grapple with Scale of Vulnerabilities. Report to the Committee on Armed Services, US Senate, GAO-19-128.

Gendron, A. 2013. Cyber Threats and Multiplier Effects: Canada at Risk. *Canadian Foreign Policy Journal*, vol. 19, no. 2, pp. 178–198. doi: 10.1080/11926422.2013.808578

Grubbs, Robert L., Stoddard, Jeremiah Trent, Freeman, Sarah G., and Fisher, Ronald Earl. 2021. Evolution and Trends of Industrial Control System Cyber Incidents Since 2017. *Journal of Critical Infrastructure Policy*, vol. 2, no. INL/JOU-21–65119-Rev000.

Hagar, J. D., Wissink, T. L., Kuhn, D. R., and Kacker, R. 2015. Introducing Combinatorial Testing in a Large Organization. *Computer*, vol. 48, no. 4, pp. 64–72.

Inayat, I., Farooq, M., and Inayat, Z. 2021. *Safety and Security Risks Management Process for Cyber-Physical Systems: A Case Study. Software: Evolution and Process.* New York: Wiley.

Joiner, K. F., and Tutty, M. G. 2018. A Tale of Two Allied Defence Departments: New Assurance Initiatives for Managing Increasing System Complexity, Interconnectedness, and Vulnerability. *Australian Journal of Multidisciplinary Engineering*, vol. 14, pp. 4–25. http://dx.doi.org/10.1080/14488388.2018.1426407

Katina, P. 2015. *Systems Theory-Based Construct for Identifying Metasystem Pathologies for Complex System Governance.* Norfolk, VA: Old Dominion University.

Keating, C. B., and Katina, P. F. 2016. Complex System Governance Development: A First Generation Methodology. *International Journal of System of Systems Engineering*, vol. 7, nos. 1–3, pp. 43–74.

Keating, C. B., and Katina, P. F. 2019. Complex System Governance: Concept, Utility, and Challenges. *Systems Research Behavioural Sciences*, vol. 36, pp. 687–705.

Klemas, T. J., and Chan, S. 2018. Harnessing Machine Learning, Data Analytics, and Computer-Aided Testing for Cybersecurity Applications. In CYBER 2018: The Third International Conference on Cyber-Technologies and Cyber-Systems, Athens, IARIA.

Kuhn, D. R., Kacker, R. N., Feldman, L., and White, G. 2016. Combinatorial Testing for Cybersecurity and Reliability. *Information Technology Bulletin*. www.nist.gov/publications/combinatorial-testing-cybersecurity-and-reliability

Langeland, K. S., Manheim, D., McLeod, G., and Nacouzi, G. 2016. *How Civil Institutions Build Resilience: Organisational Practices Derived from Academic Literature and Case Studies.* Santa Monica, CA: Rand Corporation.

Leech, T., and Gupta, P. 2015. Board Oversight of Management's Risk Appetite and Tolerance: Regulators Claim They Expect It But Change Will Not Come Easy. *EDPACS*, vol. 51, no. 4, pp. 9–14. doi: 10.1080/07366981.2015.1038159

Madni, A. M., and Purohit, S. 2021. Augmenting MBSE with Digital Twin Technology: Implementation, Analysis, Preliminary Results, and Findings. In 2021 IEEE International Conference on Systems, Man, and Cybernetics (SMC), pp. 2340–2346. doi: 10.1109/SMC52423.2021.9658769.

National Institute of Standards and Technology (NIST). 2010. Practical Combinatorial Testing, Special Publication (NIST SP), Gaithersburg, MD, [online], Special Publication (NIST SP) – 800-142. https://doi.org/10.6028/NIST.SP.800-142

National Institute of Standards and Technology (NIST). 2017a. National Initiative for Cybersecurity Education (NICE) Cybersecurity Workforce Framework. NIST Special Publication 800–181.

National Institute of Standards and Technology (NIST). 2017b. NIST Special Publication 1500–2001 Framework for Cyber-Physical Systems: Volume 1, Overview. Version 1.0. https://doi.org/10.6028/NIST.SP.1500-201

National Institute of Standards and Technology (NIST). 2018. Framework for Improving Critical Infrastructure Cybersecurity. https://nvlpubs.nist.gov/nistpubs/CSWP/NIST.CSWP.04162018.pdf

Nejib, P., Beyer, D., and Yakabovicz, E. 2017. Systems Security Engineering: What Every System Engineer Needs to Know. In 27th Annual INCOSE Int. Symposium, Adelaide, July. https://onlinelibrary.wiley.com/doi/abs/10.1002/j.2334-5837.2017.00370.x

O'Brien, A. M., and Mc Guckin, C. 2016. *The Systematic Literature Review Method: Trials and Tribulations of Electronic Database Searching at Doctoral Level. Sage Research Methods Cases.* London: Sage Publications.

Palmer, C. 2020. *The Boeing 737 Max Saga: Automating Failure Engineering.* Amsterdam, NL: Elsevier.

Pojasek, R. B. 2019. *How New Risk Management Helps Leaders Master Uncertainty.* New York, NY: Business Expert Press.

Rogers, Edward B., and Mitchell, Steven W. 2021. MBSE Delivers Significant Return on Investment in Evolutionary Development of Complex SoS. *Systems Engineering*, vol. 24, no. 6, pp. 385–408. https://doi.org/10.1002/sys.21592.

Salehi, Vahid, and Wang, Shirui. 2019. Munich Agile MBSE Concept (MAGIC). *Proceedings of the Design Society*, vol. 1, no. 1, pp. 3701–3710. https://doi.org/10.1017/dsi.2019.377

Sigler, Kenneth, Kohnke, Anne, and Shoemaker, Dan. 2017. *Supply Chain Risk Management: Applying Secure Acquisition Principles to Ensure a Trusted Technology Product* (1st edition). Boca Raton, FL: CRC Press.

Singh, L. H., and Rajput, H. 2016. Ensuring Safety in Design of Safety Critical Computer Based Systems. *Annals of Nuclear Energy*, vol. 92, no. 1, pp. 289–294.

Siwar, K., Bouissou, M., and Piètre-Cambacédès, L. 2012. Modeling the Stuxnet Attack with BDMP: Towards More Formal Risk Assessments. In 2012 7th International Conference on Risks and Security of Internet and Systems (CRiSIS), pp. 1–8. New York: IEEE.

Thrasher, D., and Pippard, J. 2018. Independent Verification and Validation Tools. *ITEA Journal*, vol. 39, pp. 180–182.

Trope, R. 2004. A Warranty of Cyber-worthiness. *IEEE Security and Privacy*, vol. 2, no. 2, pp. 73–76.

United States of America, Department of Defence (US DoD). 2021. Cybersecurity Maturity Model Certification (CMMC). www.acq.osd.mil/cmmc/

United States of America, Department of Energy (US DoE). 2022. *Cybersecurity Capability Maturity Model (C2M2)*. Pittsburgh, PA: Carnegie Mellon University.

United States of America, Department of Energy (US DoE) and United States of America, Department of the Navy (US DoE & DoN). 2020. The United States Naval Nuclear Propulsion Program. https://navalnuclearlab.energy.gov/nuclear-propulsion-program/.

Van Der Horn, E., and Mahadevan, S. 2021. Digital Twin: Generalisation, Characterisation and Implementation. *Decision Support Systems*, vol. 145, p. 113524.

Wilson, K. S. 2013. *Conflicts among the Pillars of Information Assurance Security*. New York: IEEE.

12 Mapping the State of the Art
Artificial Intelligence for Decision Making in Financial Crime

Borja Álvarez Martínez, Richard Allmendinger,
Hadi Akbarzadeh Khorshidi, Theodore Papamarkou,
Andre Feitas, Johanne Trippas, Markos Zachariadis,
Nicholas Lord, and Katie Benson

CONTENTS

INTRODUCTION

"Financial crime" is a broad term that includes a wide range of different offences, including money laundering, terrorism financing, cyber financial crime, corruption, and different types of fraud and bribery (Ünvan, 2020). Such breadth is problematic as the term incorporates diverse offences and actors that are qualitatively distinct; thus, while it is an accepted label with some shared meaning, as an analytical construct, it lacks precision. Offences pertaining financial crime are generally grouped into four categories: corruption, fraud, theft, or manipulation (Gottschalk, 2010). Given the enormous impact of these crimes on individuals, companies, organizations, and governments alike, there is currently a race between financial criminals, enforcement, and financial institutions to increase the scope and complexity of criminal activities and their respective countermeasures (Ünvan, 2020). In the context of this growing complexity, financial crimes are becoming increasingly transnational and electronic (Yeoh, 2019), so that development of both technologies and human expertise is needed to respond to this challenge (Kurum, 2020). Further, this development means that an interdisciplinary approach to such a truly global problem is required (Garcia-Bedoya et al., 2020) and it is precisely this interdisciplinary scope that frames the chapter as we explore the role of artificial intelligence (AI) and machine learning (ML) applications in the context of financial crime.

AI is increasingly being deployed in various countermeasures against financial crimes (Yeoh, 2019). Prevalent application areas include fraud detection, anti-money laundering, compliance, tax evasion, and risk management, among others. Considering this, the goal of this review is to provide the relevant stakeholders and decision makers in industry, academia, and enforcement agencies with

DOI: 10.1201/9781003319887-12

a broad overview of the most current innovations, relevant tools, and developments within the field of AI applications to detect, combat, or prevent different types of financial crimes. This will be done by contextualizing such tools within their contemporary research, synthesizing what they offer, and, equally importantly, discussing their limitations and implementation issues. We aim for our work to contribute in a robust and considered way to the effort of incorporating AI research into actual real-world, industry applications that can produce tangible benefits while recognizing the challenges and hurdles that may be met. In doing so, this work aims to reduce the implementational gap between research and practice that has already been problematized by, among others, Ryman-Tubb et al. (2018). To achieve this, we will map the cutting-edge techniques that are being applied to financial crime issues, allowing decision makers, academics, and practitioners a quick overview of how AI/ML applications are being developed. Some issues pertaining to regulatory frameworks, datasets, and implementational issues will be discussed succinctly to raise awareness of both potentialities and limitations of AI/ML techniques. Furthermore, we will analyze the trends in the relationships between diverse actors in the field of AI/ML and financial crime, namely industry, academia, and governmental authorities, and assess how this is impacting developments on the field.

The structure of the chapter is as follows: in the next section, we discuss the methodological considerations that underpin this systematic literature review, focusing on the databases searched and the strings and criteria employed. The AI and ML in financial crime section then provides a brief overview of the evolution of different AI techniques in the field of financial crimes, followed by a discussion of initial research activities in this field covering the years of 2018–2020. The discussion section provides more details about the most recent developments starting in 2021 with the goal of providing decision makers and stakeholders with a critical framework including capabilities, potential drawbacks, and information pertaining to datasets used for AI development in the context of diverse financial crimes. The trends and the key issues section examines trends and key issues of AI in financial crime considering existing research efforts. Finally, the conclusion and recommendation section concludes the chapter and discusses directions for future research.

METHODOLOGY OF THE SYSTEMATIC REVIEW

A systematic literature review was undertaken to identify, assess, and analyze the AI-based techniques applied to combatting financial crime generally and from this the implications for the relevant stakeholders of the current state of the art. Doing so allowed a synthesis and critique of the associated body of literature while permitting us to address contradictions, gaps, or inconsistencies (Siddaway et al., 2019). To do so, two combinations of keywords directly related to the project at hand were selected. The keyword combinations were "financial crimes" and "artificial intelligence." Once the baseline keywords had been decided, they were combined with the Boolean indicator "AND" into the query that was then used to systematically search for the existing literature on the topic. While it is usually recommended that at least two different datasets be employed (Siddaway et al., 2019), duplicating the number would naturally increase the reliability of the review, and so in total four databases were queried for this chapter. The databases employed for this systematic review were Scopus, ACM Digital Library, ProQuest, and Web of Science. The strings of terms were searched for within the abstract, title and keywords fields. As it was intended to gain an understanding of the long-term trends in this field, no temporal criteria were used to artificially limit the search. Table 12.1 shows the frequency of hits for the strings of search terms across the four employed databases.

The combined results from across all four databases produced an initial dataset of 53 papers that were analyzed for this review. These were in turn manually cross-referenced to avoid duplications between each of the databases. The remaining papers were then manually reviewed to ensure that they remained topical, to establish that the included papers were at the forefront of current research, that they covered the range of available tools, and that they addressed their advantages and short-comings when applied by relevant stakeholders. After following this two-step process, 34 papers remained that were directly relevant to the application of AI within different fields associated with

TABLE 12.1

A Detailed Overview of the Systematic Review That Is the Basis of This Chapter, Including the Databases Employed, Dates in Which They Were Searched, Terms Used, and Hits Obtained

Date of Search	Database	Strings of Terms	# Hits
26–06–2022	Scopus	"Financial Crime" AND "Artificial Intelligence"	26
26–06–2022	ACM Digital Library	"Financial Crime" AND "Artificial Intelligence"	12
27–06–2022	ProQuest	"Financial Crime" AND "Artificial Intelligence"	10
27–06–2022	Web of Science	"Financial Crime" AND "Artificial Intelligence"	7

financial crimes broadly. These papers make up the basis for the following discussion. A narrative and historical approach is taken to discuss the selected body of literature. This allowed for coherence in the structure of the paper, which also incorporated interdisciplinary insights while ensuring clarity for decision makers reading the chapter who are working in this field.

AI AND ML IN FINANCIAL CRIME: TRACING THE DEVELOPMENT

In this section an overview of the different applications of AI and ML techniques that are developed and employed to combat, identify, or prevent financial crime is provided. The goal is not to explain them in detail but rather to provide the reader with the basic information and adequate references to obtain technical details on each specific approach in its original literature as needed. As such, it is important to understand that AI and ML-based techniques have a long history of application in financial crime-related issues. In this chapter, proposals as old as 2005 were identified. In Figure 12.1, it is possible to see an increasing interest within academia in AI/ML applications for the field of financial crime since 2019, a still-growing trend. The first identified work already sought and

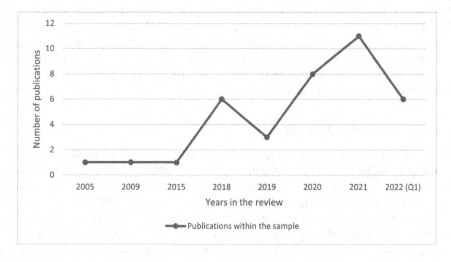

FIGURE 12.1 The yearly evolution of the publications considered for this survey.

successfully managed to apply automated data mining for anomaly detection in the context of insurance fraud detection (Rejesus et al., 2005). At such an early stage, it was acknowledged that these comparatively simple methods proved a significantly more efficient identification of anomalies and, ultimately, fraud detection when compared with the contemporary widespread practice of randomized manual selection of cases for analyst investigation, which ultimately led to better overall fraud identification (Rejesus et al., 2005). The model proposed by Rejesus et al. (2005) used a combination of both publicly available and proprietary datasets (belonging to government agencies) to create its own dataset for anomaly detection. While the combination of proprietary datasets with publicly available data remains the ideal approach, it was rare in the reviewed papers for authors to use both proprietary and public datasets, with researchers often choosing either public or proprietary datasets for reasons of economy or data availability.

Graph-based techniques were also evident in the early papers, techniques that were both promising and which were employed many later studies as we discuss in Section 3.1. Jedrzejek et al. (2009) showed how graph mining could be used to identify various types of fraudulent transactions, which nonetheless still required significant human oversight in the decision-making stages to evaluate whether a suspicious pattern was fraudulent. In their view they saw this as a first step, one that needed fuller development. As Edwards et al. (2015) would later demonstrate, this then became a decade-long trend of increasingly automated data-mining systems, including applications for financial crime, though many of these ultimately relied on implementing social network analysis (SNA) and derivatives once the data had been automatically mined. The literature in this review then clearly showed observable growth of stakeholder interest in applying AI solutions to different financial crime-related issues around 2020.

The growth had to be contextualized within a wider increased interest in the field of AI and financial crime, as Figure 12.1 shows, with 2021 being an inflection point (that year yielding more results than all preceding years), and simultaneously an increase in the degree of complexity of AI applications, such as the development of fuzzy methods for blockchain-related financial crimes research also increases (Kadena and Holicza, 2018). To help decision makers and stakeholders quickly grasp the different applications of specific AI-based techniques, a representative sample of publications which discussed specific implementations along with brief information pertaining to the datasets they employed (if available) is summarized in Table 12.2.

Having quickly mapped some of the key implementations of AI solutions for specific financial crimes, we can see how there are two emerging markers, the complexity of the methods employed and the types of datasets used, that distinguish the 2018–2020 period from the 2021–2022 period. In the first period, the AI/ML techniques discussed are relatively simpler, and the publications generally focus on outlining theoretically possible AI/ML applications to diverse financial crime issues. The 2021–2022 period generally includes more complex AI/ML techniques paired with a more widespread use of bigger (often multi-million–entry), partner-provided, real-world datasets. In the two following sections, we will discuss in more depth this temporal evolution of the state of the art in this field, and then discuss and synthesize some of the key overarching issues and concerns that decision makers must be aware of in this context.

THE FIRST RESEARCH BOOM: 2018–2020

The first key set of research outputs that relate to more advanced artificial intelligence applications to the realm of financial crime appeared at the end of the 2010s. As such, in this section we will discuss in more depth the papers published between 2018 and 2020. At this stage, as Esther Omolara et al. (2018) pointed out, anomaly detection and neural networks (NNs) were already clearly taking leading roles in the detection, analysis, and prevention of financial crime, particularly in financial fraud. The authors already emphasized the variety of methods "proposed for data collection, storage, transport, processing, and analysis in the selected studies" (Esther Omolara et al., 2018). This characteristic methodological diversity remained more than a decade later. Within this

TABLE 12.2

A Comparison of Some Methods and Datasets for AI in Financial Crime Across the Review

Author	Technique	Dataset	Purpose
Dorofeev et al., 2018	Support vector, random forest, boosting	n.a.	Map potential AML AI methods
Turner and Irwin, 2018	Graph analysis	Live, Apache-based data scrapping, not publicly available	Cryptocurrency ownership tracking in relation to financial crimes
Suzumura et al., 2019	Federated graph learning	Financial Crimes Authority dataset (synthetic), not publicly available	Detection of financial crime-associated transactions
Garcia-Bedoya et al., 2020	Graph analysis	Panama Papers subset (real-world), publicly available[1]	Detection of money-laundering networks
Rouhollahi et al., 2021	Expert-supervised and unsupervised anomaly detection (neural-network and random-forest mainly	Undisclosed banking transaction dataset, not publicly available	Detection of suspect money laundering transactions
Olber and Warczak, 2021	K-nearest neighbor	Ecommerce fraud data (synthetic, Kaggle available), publicly available[2]	Financial fraud detection by law enforcement
Desrousseaux et al., 2021a and 2021b	Neural networks (adaptive resonance theory + self-organizing maps)	Proprietary (HSBC-owned) and semi-open datasets (world-check) (real world), not publicly available	Risk analysis in AML environmental crime detection
Giacomo et al., 2021	Graph analysis + SNA	State provided tax and fiscal data (real world)	Tax evasion risk assessment
Lebichot et al., 2021	Neural network (batch trained vs incremental learning)	Partner-provided e-commerce fraud dataset (real world), not publicly available	Credit card fraud detection
Day, 2021	AI-meta learning to complete a knowledge graph	Cryptocurrency research (2014–2021) on Web of Science, publicly available	Generation of a cryptocurrency AML knowledge graph
Granados et al., 2022	Convolutional neural networks + long short-term memory network	Unspecified open dataset (real world)	Facial recognition for financial services security

first research wave, it emerged clearly in this review that a focal point for the AI applications in the financial crime environment was that of automated fraud detection/prevention. Ryman-Tubb et al. (2018) already produced a comparative benchmark in which they assessed contemporary AI and ML based methods for payment card fraud detection. In their research, they illustrated clearly that neural network-based approaches offered the best opportunities for industry application based on comparatively high discriminatory capabilities and quick analytical turnover, given that they flagged fewer false positives reducing the overall need for human analyst to follow up cases. Still, nevertheless, they already identified problems relating to researchers employing datasets which widely varied in size, from the low thousands to multi-million entries, different characteristics (real-world or synthetic, different granularity of transactional data, among others), and generally a high degree of data imbalance (the fraudulent transactions representing a marginal part of the overall sample) (Ryman-Tubb et al., 2018, Suzumura et al., 2019).

Other ML techniques, such as support vector machine models (combined with graph paths that can be used to represent, for example, transaction patterns relevant for anti-money laundering (AML) were also developed at that point to be deployed in fraud detection applications (Dorofeev et al., 2018, Esther Omolara et al., 2018). Their decision tree proved to be more accurate and with better discriminatory power when measured with a Mathews correlation coefficient than its neural-network counterparts. Nevertheless, there was a tendency at that point to view AI and ML applications as possible future solutions rather than present-day industry tools to predict, pre-empt, or combat financial crimes generally and fraud particularly (Hasham et al., 2019). Within fraud detection in the financial crime environment, it was also fundamental to discuss the role of graph computing techniques, specifically, graph anomaly detection, which provided effective to differentiate fraudulent characteristics within the large-scale size of real-world transactional data (Kurshan and Shen, 2020). Given these capabilities, graph computing techniques unsurprisingly gained traction quickly in academic and practitioner circles alike (Kurshan et al., 2020). Besides anomaly detection, graph-based techniques also offered the possibility of sub-graph analysis and mining. Sub-graphs proved useful with either semi or unsupervised learning to analyze local graph patterns related to fraud, which allowed to identify abnormal patterns related to small-scale fraud rings (Kurshan et al., 2020). Although sub-graph-based techniques may be limited on account of their need for adjustment to detect multi-stage cases, they remained a valuable tool for investigation and alert resolution in large scale graphs (Kurshan and Shen, 2020). Another technique that had potential applications for financial crime, and within it, fraud specifically, was the use of directed acyclic graphs (DAGs) combined with ML algorithms (supervised and unsupervised). The combination was explored by Turner and Irwin (2018), who posited that DAG could then be combined with ML algorithms, such as the open-source LINGO employed in their experiment. The combination of DAG with LINGO allowed Turner and Irwin (2018) to scrutinize the actual ownership of otherwise opaque cryptocurrencies by using social media and blockchain data, which has direct implications for both money laundering and fraud.

Graph methods were also combined with federated ML, and as Suzumura et al. (2019) demonstrated, such an approach can make local models trained on transaction models and graph features based on privacy-compliant, inter-institutional data sharing identify potentially criminal scenarios comparatively more accurately than centralized models trained on transaction features only. This was, however, mostly an experimental venture that needed to be piloted with more extensive and broader datasets. It is however worthy of note that this technique was developed with synthetic data facilitated by the Financial Conduct Authority, representing a very early example of academia-practitioner collaboration. Yet, despite the potential capabilities of graph and NN-based methods overviewed in this heading they also have drawbacks. Some of the drawbacks identified by Kurshan et al. (2020) included algorithmic complexity, which was presented as a major problem for large-scale and real-time data interpretation, and the need for constant data updates for machine learning, which required data from millions of daily transactions. Moreover, the graph and NN-based methods had to scrutinize a significant number of fast-occurring transactions (Kurshan and Shen, 2020) in a shifting adversarial environment in which financial criminals proactively seek to avoid pattern and anomaly detection (Kurshan et al., 2020). These difficulties in deploying and implementing the techniques within real-life crime detection applications make it so that despite their potential capabilities, graph-based methods require application-specific development (Kurshan and Shen, 2020).

Beyond fraud detection and prevention, AI/ML has also been discussed as leverageable in anti-money laundering scenarios. The possibilities within AML environments differ from personal screening to diminish false positives during customer checks for AML investigators by analyzing data from pre-existing transactions, automated know-your-customer (KYC) onboarding, to AI-driven politically exposed persons (PEP) assessments (Kurum, 2020). However, Kurum (2020) acknowledged that these applications needed case-specific AI development, and it ought not to be assumed that neither regulators nor human resources in the AML sector are necessarily ready for AI implementation. There was, nonetheless, research aimed at covering the theory-practice gap identified by both Kurum (2020) and Ryman-Tubb et al. (2018). Garcia-Bedoya et al. (2020) posited a graph-based framework directly designed around pre-identified Colombian compliance AML needs. The model proposed by Garcia-Bedoya et al. (2020) was attractive because it used an entirely real-world dataset directly linked to AML issues, the Panama Papers (although not a problem-free dataset either), therefore catering to the potential needs of practitioners, in a demonstration of their industry-led approach. While the framework posited by Garcia-Bedoya et al. (2020) provides a good basis for further development, it meets limitations regarding the need for AI training and the complexity of AML data.

Further peripheral uses of AI in the financial crime environment appeared within the literature reviewed. One such example is the potential use of deep learning and supervised learning to create models for form jacking detection (Dharmavaram, 2020). But while Dharmavaram (2020) provided technically compelling arguments, it did not elaborate on how end-users in retail would be capacitated to overcome the technical and implementational difficulties already stated elsewhere in our review and acknowledged that large amounts of data with very different characteristics were needed to train the models (Dharmavaram, 2020). Further applications were also proposed by Mundada et al. (2020), who proposed the application of AI-based methods within the financial crimes context to facilitate court case work by automating several stages along the processes of case filtering and assignment. The authors expected that in the context of quickly increasing financial crimes, AI-assisted case processing could help to reduce the number of cases pending litigation. But even in their current stage of development, the application of AIs in the financial crime environment could be considered potentially problematic. While high-tech applications of sophisticated AML applications are being increasingly deployed to combat an array of financial crimes, the development of these processes and practices happens in a context of what Truby (2020) describes as regulatory inertia, in which few standardized evaluation or auditing techniques exist. The regulatory context is important because AI/ML techniques and researchers (Yeoh, 2019) in financial crime must tackle a broad array of ethical concerns, particularly around privacy, the limits of surveillance (Edwards et al., 2015) and issues pertaining the need for explainability (Suzumura et al., 2019; Harris, 2022). Explainability is the legal requirement imposed on certain AI applications which requires that the internal logic and decision-making process of the AI is clarifiable and justifiable to the individuals or entities impacted by the AI decision (Truby, 2020). Explainability and its importance in the financial crime context will be discussed more in depth in section 4.

In this regard, Truby (2020) emphasized the importance of not overregulating, which was seen as essential in a quickly developing sector but highlighted simultaneously the fact that AI applications can lack transparency and trustworthiness, while pointing out the existing lack of oversight, scrutiny, or even common developmental principles. The balancing act between maximalist and minimalist regulatory frameworks distinctly brings into focus the need for shared legal structures and common frameworks that can be applied to dynamic, interconnected, and often, cross-border scenarios, such as financial crime and associated AI applications. Given the variety of regulations that can potentially impact AI/ML processes applied to financial crime, it is important to engage candidly on how to further develop the appropriate legal frameworks. Thus, how the regulatory framework is shaped in the future will be fundamental in ensuring that AI systems are developed in such a way that allows them to become more of an antidote to financial crimes than an accelerator (Yeoh, 2019). Problematizing regulatory frameworks is also relevant given that the general approach in key economies such as the United States and United Kingdom is that of a liberal *laissez-faire* attitude when it comes to both policies and regulations, with a view to ensure that a competitive edge is maintained in the research and development of AI/ML (Yeoh, 2019). Because of this, Yeoh (2019) argued that the current legal frameworks meant that it was still up for policymakers and regulators to ensure that AI was leveraged as a crime deterrent, being wary that it could just as easily as be employed to increase the complexity of financial cybercriminal endeavors.

REFINING THE APPLICATIONS: 2021–2022

In this section, the focus is on how financial crime AI applications evolved in the second 2021–2022 period, which was illustrated in Figure 13.1. Despite the twofold problem that characterized research pertaining AI/ML and its application to financial crimes at the turn of the decade, that is, the growing gap between academic research output and industry implementation and appetite (Kurum, 2020), and the equally increasing distance between the capabilities and potentialities of AI in the realm of financial crimes and their actual regulation both at national and supranational levels (Yeoh, 2019, among others), developments continued at a quick pace. An example of how ML applications were evolving to become increasingly targeted, not necessarily by the techniques employed, but also by their intended context of application, can be found in Olber and Warczak (2021), who purported to identify payment fraud within datasets available to law enforcement, both banking and non-banking. As a proof of concept, they employ several supervised ML methods, including K-nearest neighbor and support vector clustering with a synthetic dataset available through Kaggle (Olber and Warczak, 2021), which, given that it is proposed by members of the law enforcement community, showcases an increasing readiness and capability to implement AI/ML approaches into real-world practices.

Further evidence of the growing spread of increasingly complex approaches appeared in models that combined expert-supervised and unsupervised learning for the purpose of anomaly detection in the context of AML. Among others, NN, random forest, naïve Bayes, and nearest neighbor appear interlinked in different ways for AML applications (Rouhollahi et al., 2021). But the potential of AI/ML in the context of financial crimes is not only becoming increasingly broad in terms of the community that applies them and the techniques it employs: the goals it pursues are also becoming much more specific. Case in point is the application of an adaptive resonance theory (ART) based-neural network technique combined with a self-organizing map (SOM) by Desrousseaux et al. (2021a), creating a technique that both allowed incremental learning with real-world datasets and allowed for the discovery of previously undetected financial risk clusters, demonstrating both direct real-world applicability and an improvement on the current industry model employed by their collaboration partner (HSBC). Their model was further developed into a procedure that used fuzzy ART with SOM-trained weights, creating a NN ML model that, using their HSBC-provided real-life dataset, was able to overcome high data imbalance and identify suspicious activity with fewer false positives. The reduced number of false positives meant that fewer transactions were incorrectly flagged as potential AML concerns than HSBC's current approach (Desrousseaux et al., 2021b), which in turn diminished both the number of cases human analysts needed to deploy human intervention and the number of false positive alerts (Desrousseaux et al., 2021b).

As the applications of AI to combat, prevent, and monitor financial crime kept becoming more diverse across the industry, increasing in their technical complexity and involving more stakeholders (i.e., industry, academia, law enforcement) while pursuing more context-specific outcomes, several efforts have been made to keep up-to-date maps of such developments. Tiwari and Saxena (2021) showed that within the financial industry AI could be directly applied to financial crime and financial compliance through, among others, real-time fraud detection, AML detection, transaction blocking, KYC processes, automatic pattern recognition, estimation of risk parameters, and asset quality monitoring. Decision trees, naïve Bayes, K-nearest neighbor, neural networks, and support vector machines were the most employed AI/ML techniques in the field of financial crime generally (Tiwari and Saxena, 2021), all of which have already been discussed here and the previous section (see Table 12.2). Further surveys had identified approaches to tackle financial crime within specific axes: stocks and securities investment fraud, fraud detection and AML, customs frauds, tax evasion, SIM-swapping/social engineering/phishing and romance fraud-based financial crimes (Nicholls et al., 2021). For the more specific field of fraud and tax evasion, the prevalent methods appeared to be neural networks (specifically graphic convolutional networks [GCNs] and recurrent neural networks [RNNs] and SNA (Nicholls et al., 2021). The review by Cao (2021) also underlined that the preferred deep learning models applied in the financial crime environment were convolutional neural networks (CNN), with GCN and RNN specifically being particularly useful methods for detecting financial crime. Neural networks, particularly deep neural networks, were also among the preferred methods specifically targeted towards fraud detection within AI research (Cao, 2021).

Furthermore, CNN techniques including GCN and RNN are being developed into procedural pipelines that can combine several of the methods to offer practitioners and decision makers enhanced analysis and increased validity. An example of this multi-methodological approach could be found in the MALDIVE system, in which automatedly mined data is employed for SNA and graph pattern matching, both used to create and train an automated forecasting and risk diffusion model to identify the risk of tax evasion (Giacomo et al., 2021). The increasingly broad avenues for implementation have prompted data scientists to consider the best learning strategies to accomplish the highest degree of detection accuracy in different learning algorithms (Lebichot et al., 2021). Using a real-world e-commerce credit card fraud dataset (not publicly available) to compare batch, retrained, and incremental (supervised and unsupervised) learning algorithms with partner-provided online neural networks, Lebichot et al. (2021) concluded that incremental learning can not only compete with batch learning in terms of accuracy, but it also has nonanalytical advantages by avoiding the storage of GDPR-sensitive data. Furthermore, Lebichot et al. (2021) explored which specific variants of incremental learning could improve fraud detection accuracy, concluding that ensemble learning offered more prospects of accuracy increase. Within financial services, in risk mitigation, compliance and crime prevention, AI can also prove useful in enhancing online facial recognition. By using an edge-computed CNN combined with long short-term memory (LSTM), the authors proposed a financial-services oriented facial recognition tool (Granados and Garcia-Bedoya, 2022). While the authors acknowledged that such a resource-intensive, state-of-the-art algorithm would require significant graphic processing unit or tensor processing unit GPU/TPU capabilities and bandwidth, they sought to overcome these constraints by proposing a hybrid architecture employing both cloud and edge computing (Granados and Garcia-Bedoya, 2022).

Yet not all the applications of AI in the financial crime context were necessarily deployed in a prevention/detection/enforcement role. AI has also been used to generate knowledge graphs, particularly domain-specific, in the field of cryptocurrency AML (Day, 2021). By employing a meta-learning AI that uses a few-shot learning model, it was possible to textually analyze leading research automatically, creating knowledge graphs around high-frequency keywords (Day, 2021). The resulting knowledge graphs allowed for an intuitive mapping of a field that is developing quickly while ascertaining its conceptual interrelations. But regardless of the clearly expanding application potential showcased by AI/ML research in the 2021/2022 period, the regulatory quagmire that had been already documented and problematized in Yeoh (2019), among other issues discussed in the current and previous section, remained unresolved. While there was agreement around the fact that AI offers opportunities for financial crimes risk management, compliance and enforcement, the legal frameworks and responses remained lacking. Particularly in financial markets, which could often find themselves trailing behind regulators, the current state of both domestic and international legal frameworks was troublesome (Harris, 2022). In principle, the data volume, transaction speed and complexity inherent to the financial industry should make the use of AI as a regulatory compliance support tool interesting by default. Harris (2022) already posited that it was becoming clear that the lack of adequate normative frameworks oriented around AI deployment and application were hindering its actual use in an industry which was increasingly concerned with regulatory compliance.

DISCUSSION: TRENDS AND KEY ISSUES IN AI AND FINANCIAL CRIME

Having briefly outlined the most relevant aspects of the works analyzed in our review, in this section, some of the key issues that need to be considered by decision makers will be addressed. To do so, commonalities across the different reviewed papers will be discussed, and the recurring themes, opportunities, and drawbacks that appeared through the literature sampled for the chapter will be addressed succinctly. That is, the changes in the relationship between academia, industry, and

TABLE 12.3

An Overview of the Key Aspects Highlighted through This Chapter

Key trends	Increase of working partnerships between different stakeholders, including academia, industry, and governmental bodies
	Datasets used across research are increasingly real-world datasets and are improving in terms of quality and quantity
Favored techniques	Fraud (payment and credit card): NN, DT/random forest, federated graph learning
	AML/tax evasion: CNN (GCN/RNN) + SNA, fuzzy ART+SOM, random forest+NN
Key issues	Regulatory maturity: legal frameworks must contend with complex ethical and privacy issues while allowing compliance and development
	Explainability remains an issue for some techniques given that stakeholders must remain accountable

governmental bodies will be discussed. Second, key implementational issues, focusing on explainability, will be tackled. This section will finish with a brief note on datasets and data availability. For quick reference, the key findings of our survey that will be discussed in the present section, plus an overview of the most common techniques discussed in Section 3, are summarized in Table 12.3.

The first fundamental take-away point for any decision maker or stakeholder is that the literature review shows a gradual but important change in the relationship between academic researchers and industry, broadly understood as the wide range of practitioners interested in applying AI-related solutions to financial crime problems. As the comprehensive survey by Ryman-Tubb et al. (2018) critically noted, research was struggling to translate into actual practical application through industry solutions. In their opinion, this was related to the little incentives they had to adopt newer methods that required balancing improvements against IT system changes, which in turn needed additional support, time, and funding. However, our review shows evidence that the pattern of industry reticence is starting to change, with diverse stakeholders taking a hands-on research approach. While this can potentially lead in the future to issues such as conflicts of interests and disclosure among others, for the time being, it has provided useful to overcome challenges associated with key data access, which is fundamental to AI/ML development. For instance, Rouhollahi et al. (2021) were already employing real-world datasets facilitated by an undisclosed bank. Further evidence of the banking industry increasing its stakes within AI research for financial crime applications can be seen in Desrousseaux et al. (2021a, 2021b). The authors directly collaborated with HSBC to improve the application and design of online learning neural networks with direct industry implementation in mind through a joint industry-academia project.

However, it is not only banks that are becoming interested in furthering AI research in financial crime and its direct application by engaging in different types of partnerships. KPMG, a financial audit, tax, and advisory firm, is also interested in furthering the applications of AI for AML compliance (Kurum, 2020). Leading payment service Worldline provided confidential data to Lebichot et al. (2021) by sharing a dataset containing more than 50 million real-world transactions. While partnering with industry that provides confidential data or confidential code creates obvious issues of both code and data availability for other researchers, it also allows development of specific applications of AI, such as in the example of Lebichot et al. (2021), to detect credit card fraud, that directly tackle by design industry concerns such as data management and incremental learning. Moreover, besides bank and other financial services providers, it is worth noting that our review also highlights how governmental bodies are becoming interested in developing AI solutions to diverse financial crime issues. In Giacomo et al. (2021), several research projects are outlined, including collaborations with the Italian Revenue Agency and the Financial Intelligence Agency of the San Marino Republic. The ad-hoc partnership between academia and financial authorities demonstrates a growing interest in generating processes and resources that have a real-world application from a multiplicity of financial crime stakeholders. The interests of industry and governmental agencies are not directly overlapping, however: while private actors were more concerned with suspicious activity reports and card fraud (for obvious compliance-related reasons), governmental agencies such as in the work of Giacomo et al. (2021) were interested in the application of AI-based techniques for tax evasion risk determination. Law enforcement agencies are also showcasing an increased interest in the application of AI to combat financial crime, as investigated by Olber and Warczak (2021), both researchers of the Polish National Police Academy. Their research has a clear view to being applied to support enforcement and investigation activities by law enforcement agencies, particularly to detect financial fraud and money laundering cases (Olber and Warczak, 2021).

Nevertheless, the closer relationship between academic researchers, industry, and practitioners should not give decision makers the idea that AI can be a panacea for financial crime (Yeoh, 2019). Awareness must be raised about the fact that the literature problematizes several aspects of implementing AI solutions in the field of financial crime (see, among others, Kurshan et al., 2020, Kurum, 2020, Tiwari and Saxena, 2021, Nicholls et al., 2021). The implementation problems of AI techniques for financial crime detection generally arise from the size, speed, complexity, and adversarial nature inherent to financial operations and their datasets. (Kurshan et al., 2020). Moreover, financial operations require real-time data processing with very fast response times. The enormous datasets involved need constant updating, data quality assurance, data labeling, system scaling, ample infrastructure support, high levels of energy consumption. Furthermore, other issues that must considered by practitioners and decision makers are the deployment of adversarial tactics by financial criminals, the requirements by different regulatory bodies for the AI/ML applications to be interpretable and explainable, concerns about their role within governance and regulatory compliance, and the need for ultimately human-in-the loop investigations by crime/fraud/compliance analysts (Kurshan et al. 2020, Nicholls et al., 2021). Other research further highlighted how some issues were weighing heavily against technology adoption: experts were consulted in a Delphi panel (a double-round questionnaire with feedback to ascertain consensus among participants) in Kurum (2020), where it was highlighted that besides the aforementioned need for human supervision and constant system updates adoption industry broadly perceived that stakeholders still required more time to adapt and integrate AI/ML solutions across their processes.

Decision makers must also be aware that both compliance with general data protection frameworks and explainability remain key challenges for AI implementation (Tiwari and Saxena, 2021). Explainability is the requirement for the logic and criteria behind certain AI/ML decisions, such as flagging a transaction or denying a purchase, to be describable and possible to clarify to the individual (or organization) impacted by the decision (Truby, 2020). Several regulations (FINRA rules in the United States and GDPR in the EU) require that AI/ML applications be explainable by design (Nicholls et al., 2021). The explainability mandate is very important because two of the most used methods in financial crime applications, those based around NN, on account of its "black box" decision making, and those based around graph techniques, have inherent explainability problems (Suzumura et al., 2019, Kurshan and Shen, 2020). By contrast to NN and graph-based methods, decision tree (DT)–based applications have a better level of explainability (Ryman-Tubb et al., 2018), but nevertheless DT remains a far less widespread method in financial applications.

Given the explainability requirements imposed by various regulators, there is ongoing effort to further ML knowledge to achieve NN explainability (Suzumura et al., 2019), and similar research is happing within the field of graph computing to optimize model explainability (Kurshan and Shen, 2020). Examples of this drive towards better explainability and can be found in the mix of SOM and fuzzy ART proposed by Desrousseaux et al. (2021a), discussed before in the chapter, which was designed with a view of achieving necessary thresholds of explainability for industry, achieving this in their NN outputs. Besides explainability and data protection, a less clear-cut issue is cost.

AI implementation costs are associated with complex data and computational resources as well as manpower requirements, and it appears as a critical concern in Tiwari and Saxena (2021), but only just below a third of the experts in the Delphi study by Kurum (2020) considered this factor relevant in actual implementation.

Last, it is essential to raise awareness of the very different datasets used in the past and that continue to be used for AI/ML research in the context of financial crime. When assessing the potential that certain techniques have in relation to a specific industry or other stakeholders' needs, the output of researchers within academia needs to be contextualized within the differences in the available data. Some researchers employ synthetic data, while others have access to real-world data. And while most datasets in the review were secondary, some researchers are beginning to use primary data collected specifically for their research. Dataset sizes also vary from the low thousands to datasets involving dozens of millions of data entries. Decision makers need to also understand that the nature, size, and availability of the data can contribute to shape the research design decisions made by academics or industry stakeholders, which can then ultimately impact the performance of certain AI/ML solutions, and the researchers' choices of AI/ML techniques to design a tool to tackle a specific financial crime problem. Also, worth noting when discussing the relevance of datasets for AI/ML research in financial crime is the link between the increasing relationship of academia and practitioners and data availability. As stated elsewhere in the chapter, partnerships usually include access to proprietary data which are mostly confidential in nature. The confidentiality of the data is troublesome, since it does not allow transparent replication and verification by other academics or practitioners, who not only will not have access to the datasets but may also not have synthetic equivalents.

The overall challenges discussed in this section highlight how, in the end, AI must be applied in what essentially is an ever-evolving defensive landscape (Nicholls et al., 2021). Furthermore, given their present applications (AML, card fraud detection, and tax evasion risk, among others), involved stakeholders and decision makers must be aware that AI will need to make decisions based on data that will be either uncertain or incomplete, even when the ML systems are entirely updated with real-time incident data, thus ultimately requiring human operators to be involved at different stages of the different processes (Nicholls et al., 2021). In the end, AI/ML solutions are only as good as the data that is fed to them.

CONCLUSIONS AND RECOMMENDATIONS

To bring the chapter to an end, several fundamental takeaways will be highlighted. First and foremost, it is fundamental to understand that AI applications for financial crime are evolving quickly. The evolution in terms of techniques, datasets, and types of financial crimes tackled was illustrated in Tables 12.2 and 12.3 and Sections 3.1 and 3.2. Nevertheless, there is already enough maturity within the research to identify some best practices. For example, neural networks and graph-based techniques are more broadly employed across the field. They are generally used to tackle suspicious transactions, money laundering networks, and tax evasion risks. As such, they will be important within key financial stakeholders such as banks, payment processing companies, or auditors' compliance and risk management departments but also increasingly in governmental bodies such as law enforcement and tax and revenue agencies. AI/ML applications in the field of financial crime will consequently need to adapt to the specific set of priorities, interests, and agenda of each financial actor. We have showcased how techniques such as neural networks are being developed for specific AML applications and credit card fraud detection, which are also criminal offences of extreme interest for a variety of the financial institutions and agencies mentioned. Other applications combining several different techniques such as deep learning and graphs (Nicholls et al., 2021) or graphs and social networks analysis (Giacomo et al., 2021) are being developed to cover other areas of interest for financial stakeholders such as suspicious activity reports or tax evasion. While the evolution in both the techniques and their applications is significant and should guide prospective decisions around which are the best tools for a given financial crime-related issue, it must be noted that no one-stop shop exists for any criminal typology.

The lack of predetermined AI/ML solutions should not be considered a deterrent to the application of diverse AI techniques to tackle financial crimes. On the contrary, as it has been highlighted through the chapter, there are many ways in which they can be successfully and efficiently deployed. As such, this lack of a clear matchup between a specific financial crime issue and a particular AI/ML technique should rather be considered an encouragement to seek ad-hoc solutions. These solutions can then cater to industry-specific needs and requirements in terms of resourcing, capability, and implementation, thus ensuring that any given AI/ML application is fit for purpose. Evidence that purpose-built solutions are increasingly becoming the golden standard can be seen from the growing number of academia-stakeholder partnerships discussed in the previous heading. Academia-stakeholder partnerships allow either tailoring existing solutions to the specific needs of industry in terms of scale, speed, levels of automation, and target accuracy or designing them from the ground up with specific toolkits using one or more of the techniques discussed in this chapter. It is also important to conclude that even cutting-edge systems will require human oversight at different points of their application within the context of the financial crime. Whether these are compliance officers, law enforcement officers, AML analysts, or fraud investigators, they will play a vital role in successfully deploying AI systems. Moreover, given that some of the issues inherent to the applications if AI/ML for financial crime, such as size, speed, and complexity, are common to other applications such as automated trading in stock markets, self-driving applications both for consumer and logistics, and many others, sharing expertise across these fields should be a key priority.

Last, AI solutions are in themselves not entirely trouble free: decision makers must be aware of the need to adopt systems with adequate scalability and processing times; the benefits and drawbacks of cloud and edge computing; and the high likelihood that complex graph-based solutions will require GPU-intensive computing systems making use of platforms such as Tensor/CUDA, OpenCL, or ROCm. Increasing computing requirements and the need for a crime prevention or mitigation system to be dynamic and fast-changing will require quick decision processes to implement versatile AI solutions in the financial crime environment that can prove both cost efficient and long lasting, in accordance with the resource commitments they require. AI should be harnessed to deal with data issues such as imbalance data and minimize the performance deterioration due to changes such as concept drift. But even when considering the complex environment that AI/ML applications must navigate, the final note must be that AI/ML solutions offer huge promise to improve the responses to a broad range of crime issues to a variety of stakeholders and that the environment for cooperation between industry and academia has been markedly evolving since the turn of the decade. It is therefore up to the involved stakeholders to commit to further work across boundaries.

ACKNOWLEDGMENTS

This study is supported by Manchester–Melbourne Joint Research Seed Fund for the project FinTech and Financial Crimes: Methods, Applications, and Regulations. We thank Fiona Haines from the University of Melbourne for her insightful feedback and commentary on the early drafts of this chapter.

NOTE

1. Available at https://offshoreleaks.icij.org/pages/database
2. Available at www.kaggle.com/datasets/aryanrastogi7767/ecommerce-fraud-data

REFERENCES

Cao, Longbing. 2021. "AI in Finance: Challenges, Techniques and Opportunities." *SSRN Electronic Journal* 55 (3). https://doi.org/10.2139/ssrn.3869625.

Day, Min Yuh. 2021. "Artificial Intelligence for Knowledge Graphs of Cryptocurrency Anti-Money Laundering in Fintech." *Proceedings of the 2021 IEEE/ACM International Conference on Advances in Social Networks Analysis and Mining, ASONAM 2021*, 439–46. https://doi.org/10.1145/3487351.3488415.

Desrousseaux, Roxane, Gilles Bernard, and Jean Jacques Mariage. 2021a. "Predicting Financial Suspicious Activity Reports with Online Learning Methods*." *Proceedings – 2021 IEEE International Conference on Big Data, Big Data 2021*, 1595–603. https://doi.org/10.1109/BigData52589.2021.9671716.

Desrousseaux, Roxane, Gilles Bernard, and Jean Jacques Mariage. 2021b. "Profiling Money Laundering with Neural Networks: A Case Study on Environmental Crime Detection." *Proceedings – International Conference on Tools with Artificial Intelligence, ICTAI 2021-Novem*, 364–69. https://doi.org/10.1109/ICTAI52525.2021.00059.

Dharmavaram, Vijaya Geeta. 2020. "Formjacking Attack: Are We Safe?" *Journal of Financial Crime* 28 (2): 607–12. https://doi.org/10.1108/JFC-07-2020-0138.

Edwards, Matthew, Awais Rashid, and Paul Rayson. 2015. "A Systematic Survey of Online Data Mining Technology Intended for Law Enforcement." *ACM Computing Surveys* 48 (1). https://doi.org/10.1145/2811403.

Esther Omolara, Abiodun, Aman Jantan, Oludare Isaac Abiodun, Manmeet Mahinderjit Singh, Mohammed Anbar, and Kemi Victoria Dada. 2018. "State-of-The-Art in Big Data Application Techniques to Financial Crime: A Survey." *International Journal of Computer Science and Network Security* 18 (7): 6–16.

Garcia-Bedoya, Olmer, OscarGranados, and JoséCardozo Burgos. 2020. "AI against Money Laundering Networks: The Colombian Case." *Journal of Money Laundering Control* 24 (1): 49–62. https://doi.org/10.1108/JMLC-04-2020-0033.

Giacomo, Emilio Di, Walter Didimo, Luca Grilli, Giuseppe Liotta, and Fabrizio Montecchiani. 2021. "Visual Analytics for Financial Crime Detection at the University of Perugia BT." In *Advanced Visual Interfaces. Supporting Artificial Intelligence and Big Data Applications*, edited by Thoralf Reis, Marco X. Bornschlegl, Marco Angelini, and Matthias L. Hemmje, 195–200. Cham: Springer International Publishing.

Gottschalk, Petter. 2010. "Categories of Financial Crime." *Journal of Financial Crime* 17 (4): 441–58. https://doi.org/10.1108/13590791011082797

Granados, Oscar, and OlmerGarcia-Bedoya. 2022. *Deep Learning-Based Facial Recognition on Hybrid Architecture for Financial Services. Internet of Things.* https://doi.org/10.1007/978-3-030-80821-1_3.

Harris, Hannah. 2022. "Artificial Intelligence and Policing of Financial Crime: A Legal Analysis of the State of the Field." *Financial Technology and the Law, Law, Governance and Technology Series* 47.

Hasham, Salim, Shoan Joshi, and Daniel Mikkelsen. 2019. "Financial Crime and Fraud in the Age of Cybersecurity." *McKinsey & Company* 1–11.

Jedrzejek, Czeslaw, Maciej Falkowski, and Jaroslaw Bak. 2009. "Graph Mining for Detection of a Large Class of Financial Crimes." *CEUR Workshop Proceedings* 483.

Kadena, Esmeralda, and Peter Holicza. 2018. "Security Issues in the Blockchain(Ed) World." In *18th IEEE International Symposium on Computational Intelligence and Informatics, CINTI 2018 – Proceedings*, 211–15. https://doi.org/10.1109/CINTI.2018.8928212.

Kurshan, Eren, and Hongda Shen. 2020. "Graph Computing for Financial Crime and Fraud Detection: Trends, Challenges and Outlook." *International Journal of Semantic Computing* 14 (4): 565–89. https://doi.org/10.1142/S1793351X20300022.

Kurshan, Eren, Hongda Shen, and Haojie Yu. 2020. "Financial Crime Fraud Detection Using Graph Computing: Application Considerations Outlook." *Proceedings – 2020 2nd International Conference on Transdisciplinary AI, TransAI 2020* 125–30. https://doi.org/10.1109/TransAI49837.2020.00029.

Lebichot, Bertrand, Gian Marco Paldino, Wissan Siblini, Liyun He-Guelton, Frédéric Oblé, and Gianluca Bontempi. 2021. "Incremental Learning Strategies for Credit Cards Fraud Detection." *International Journal of Data Science and Analytics* 12 (2): 165–74. https://doi.org/10.1007/s41060-021-00258-0.

Mundada, Kapil, Mihir Kulkarni, Samruddhi Mandakhalikar, and Atharva Kulkarni. 2020. "Computer Aided Commercial Case Classifier Using Artificial Intelligence Algorithm." In *Proceedings of the 2nd International Conference on Inventive Research in Computing Applications, ICIRCA 2020*, 468–72. https://doi.org/10.1109/ICIRCA48905.2020.9183292.

Nicholls, Jack, Aditya Kuppa, and Nhien An Le-Khac. 2021. "Financial Cybercrime: A Comprehensive Survey of Deep Learning Approaches to Tackle the Evolving Financial Crime Landscape." *IEEE Access* 9: 163965–86. https://doi.org/10.1109/ACCESS.2021.3134076.

Olber, Pawel, and Wojciech Warczak. 2021. "Application of Artificial Intelligence to Support Law Enforcement Agencies in Combating Financial Crime." *Archibald Reiss Days* 11.

Rejesus, Roderick M., Bertis B. Little, and Ashley C. Lovell. 2005. "Using Data Mining to Detect Crop Insurance Fraud: Is There a Role for Social Scientists?" *Journal of Financial Crime* 12 (1): 24–32. https://doi.org/10.1108/13590790510625052.

Rouhollahi, Zeinab, Amin Beheshti, Salman Mousaeirad, and Srinivasa Reddy Goluguri. 2021. "Towards Proactive Financial Crime and Fraud Detection through Artificial Intelligence and RegTech Technologies." In *ACM International Conference Proceeding Series*, 538–46. https://doi.org/10.1145/3487664.3487740.

Ryman-Tubb, Nick F., Paul Krause, and Wolfgang Garn. 2018. "How Artificial Intelligence and Machine Learning Research Impacts Payment Card Fraud Detection: A Survey and Industry Benchmark." *Engineering Applications of Artificial Intelligence* 76: 130–57. https://doi.org/10.1016/j.engappai.2018.07.008

Siddaway, Andy P., Alex M. Wood, and Larry V. Hedges. 2019. "How to Do a Systematic Review: A Best Practice Guide for Conducting and Reporting Narrative Reviews, Meta-Analyses, and Meta-Syntheses". *Annual Review of Psychology* 70. https://doi.org/10.1146/annurev-psych-010418-102803.

Tiwari, Aviral Kumar, and Deepak Saxena. 2021. "Application of Artificial Intelligence in Indian Banks." In *2021 International Conference on Computational Performance Evaluation, ComPE 2021*, 545–48. https://doi.org/10.1109/ComPE53109.2021.9751981.

Truby, Jon. 2020. "Governing Artificial Intelligence to Benefit the UN Sustainable Development Goals." *Sustainable Development* 28 (4): 946–59. https://doi.org/10.1002/sd.2048.

Turner, Adam, and Angela Samantha Maitland Irwin. 2018. "Bitcoin Transactions: A Digital Discovery of Illicit Activity on the Blockchain." *Journal of Financial Crime* 25 (1): 109–30. https://doi.org/10.1108/JFC-12-2016-0078.

Ünvan, Yüksel Akay. 2020. "Financial Crime: A Review of Literature." In *Contemporary Issues in Audit Management and Forensic Accounting (Contemporary Studies in Economic and Financial Analysis, Vol. 102)*, edited by S. Grima, E. Boztepe, and P. J. Baldacchino, 265–72. Bingley: Emerald Publishing Limited. https://doi.org/10.1108/S1569-375920200000102019

Yeoh, Peter. 2019. "Artificial Intelligence: Accelerator or Panacea for Financial Crime?" *Journal of Financial Crime* 26 (2): 634–46. https://doi.org/10.1108/JFC-08-2018-0077.

13 Understanding and Measuring the Impact of Cyberattacks on Businesses
A Systematic Literature Review

Xiuqin Li, Richard Allmendinger,
Elvira Uyarra, and James Mercer

CONTENTS

INTRODUCTION

The coronavirus pandemic has accelerated existing future of an operating model in which working from home has become the "new normal." Businesses are speeding up their digital transformation by adopting frontier digital technologies, such as the Internet of Things (IoT), artificial intelligence (AI), quantum computing, and robotics. This has given increased prominence to ensuring trust and security in the cyberspace, thereby achieving the objectives of contemporary societies: innovation, productivity, competitiveness, and collaboration. However, the increased reliance on digital solutions

DOI: 10.1201/9781003319887-13

has raised major concerns around cybersecurity, as it has opened new opportunities for people to undertake cyberattacks (OECD 2020). According to the UK Cybersecurity Breaches Survey (CSBS) 2021, nearly half of businesses report having cyberattacks in the last year. With the onset of the COVID-19 pandemic, cyberattacks grew in frequency and severity. The Beaming Report (2021) shows that commercial cybersecurity attacks on UK businesses were up 11% year-on-year in Q1 2021 and that UK businesses lost almost £13 billion due to cyberattacks in 2019. One of the reasons for the spike in cyberattacks may be related to the fact that remote working does not guarantee the same level of cybersecurity as an office environment (Deloitte 2021). Apart from financial losses, cyberattacks could also cause a wide range of critical damages to businesses, such as productivity, business reputation, customer trust, and penalties (Smith 2004; Makridis and Dean 2018; Lee 2021).

Cyberattacks are becoming more sophisticated. The negative use of AI, for example, could create problems for businesses (Guembe et al. 2022). As such, cybersecurity has become a key business priority (Sonnenreich et al. 2006) and a critical component in risk management (Lee 2021). A recent study shows that "cybersecurity and privacy issues" were ranked as the first IT management issues and concerns by European IT executives (Kappelman et al. 2019; Guembe et al. 2022). There is strong demand from upper management for economic justification of cybersecurity expenditures (Gordon et al. 2018; Leszczyna 2013). However, it is difficult to justify investment benefits due to a lack of suitable analytical models (Lee 2021). There is no consensus on how to measure the impact on businesses (Paoli et al. 2018). Most of the studies and policies often cover only some of the costs, that is, direct, or tangible financial cost, and tend to neglect other indirect or intangible costs, such as losses in reputation, productivity, customer loyalty, and social utility (Böhme et al. 2019). This could be explained partly by a lack of accessible and quantifiable data (Lagazio et al. 2014, Armin et al. 2016) and obscure methodology.

Our study aims to contribute to the still-developing area of cyberattacks from the perspective of impact measurement. We undertook a systematic literature review to provide a comprehensive analysis of previous studies on assessing the business impacts of cyberattacks between 2000 and 2021. The findings can provide practical insights for a broad range of researchers and practitioners not only to identify contemporary research trends, key authors, methods, and barriers but also to recognize future research directions and encourage the consideration of appropriate solutions in the field. This is important because a lack of understanding could hinder the adoption of adequate measures and technologies to curb cyberattacks in the future. Businesses may overlook opportunities to achieve significant benefits from investing in cybersecurity (Lee 2021). This is all the more pressing considering the increase of online activities because of the COVID-19 pandemic and the economic significance of ecommerce sectors.

The rest of the chapter is structured as follows. The next section describes the methodology we employed to carry out the literature review. The results section analyzes the identified literature, and the discussion section presents the key findings. The future research directions section highlights the research gaps and future research directions as identified via the literature review. The chapter ends with conclusions in the conclusion and implications section.

METHODOLOGY

We undertook a systematic literature review following the guidance provided by Kitchenham et al. (2009) and Brereton et al. (2007). It often follows fixed steps, as outlined in Figure 13.1.

RESEARCH QUESTIONS

As shown in Figure 13.1, the systematic review process starts with clearly defined research questions. This study aims to answer the research questions listed in Table 13.1. These questions were framed with multiple goals in mind, including getting a general idea about what research is ongoing in the field of cyberattacks and their effect on business as well as zooming in to methodologies used to measure different types of impact on business.

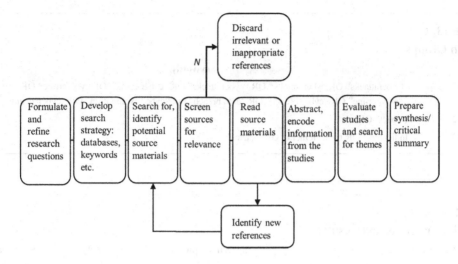

FIGURE 13.1 Systematic literature review flowchart.

TABLE 13.1

Research Questions to Be Addressed in This Chapter

No.	Research Questions	Intentions
RQ 1	How has the focus of scientific publications evolved since 2000?	The intention is to understand the size and trend of the research field.
RQ 2	Who is working on measuring the impact of cyberattacks on businesses?	The intention is to map out the distribution of the research community. This includes individual researchers, the organization to which researchers were affiliated, and the country in which the organization is located.
RQ 3	What impacts of cyberattacks have been addressed in the literature?	The intention is to identify how cyberattacks affect business and what indicators have been used.
RQ 4	What methods have been used to measure the impact of cyberattacks?	The intention is to understand whether there are well-accepted impact measurements regarding cyberattacks and which approaches and indicators have been used for impact assessment.
RQ 5	What are the major barriers for businesses to measure the impact of cyberattacks?	The intention is to find out current barriers or challenges faced by practitioners when evaluating cyberattacks impacts.

SEARCH PROCESS

We selected four databases to identify relevant literature: Web of Science, Scopus, Science Direct, and ProQuest. The four databases were selected because they were known to index a wide range of computer science and management literature in terms of journals, conferences, and book chapters (Grover et al. 2018). Furthermore, a multiple-database search strategy allows us to cover a wide range of literature.

Following a review of key papers in the field, a search on Google Scholar, and multiple discussions with cybersecurity experts from academia and industry, an iterative approach allowed us to agree on several search terms, including cyberattacks, impact, measurement, indicators, cyber exploitation, cybersecurity, cybercrime, cyberbreach, data breach, cost, and metrics.

TABLE 13.2

Search Groups

Group	Keywords
Group 1	"Cyberattacks" OR cyberattacks* OR "cyberattacks" OR "cyber-crime" OR cybercrime* OR "cybercrime" OR "cyber breach" OR "data breach" OR "cyber exploitation" OR "cybersecurity"
Group 2	Impact* OR cost*
Group 3	Indicators* OR measurement* OR metrics*

TABLE 13.3

Search Constructs and Results

Search Constructs*	Source	Search Scope	#Hits	Date of Search
("cyberattacks" OR "cyberattacks" OR cyberattacks* OR "cybercrime" OR "cyber-crime" OR cybercrimes* OR "cyber breach" OR "data breach" OR "cybersecurity" OR "cyber-security" OR "cyber exploitation") AND (impact* OR cost*) AND (Indicators*OR measurement*OR metrics*)	Web of Science	Search scope was set to "Topic," which includes title, abstract, author keywords, and keywords plus	244	2021–04–16
	Scopus	Search scope was set to "Article title, Abstract, Keywords"	360	2021–04–16
	Science Direct	Search scope was set to "Title, abstract or author-specified keywords"	483	2021–04–16
	ProQuest	Search scope for Group 1 was set to "Document title"; search scope for Group 2 and 3 was set to "Abstract"	180	2021–04–16

Notes: *Search constructs are slightly different across different databases.

The keywords were thematically grouped (see Table 13.2), and each group was linked using Boolean logic. A wildcard (asterisk) was used to shorten search terms.

The search process was a manual search of publications written in English and published between January 2000 and April 2021. The search construct was tailored to the specific search requirements of four databases, as shown in Table 13.3. The initial search returned 1267 publications in total.

INCLUSION AND EXCLUSION CRITERIA

The initial search results were further screened based on the inclusion and exclusion criteria, as shown in Table 13.4.

QUALITY ASSESSMENT

All papers were evaluated separately by three different researchers based on four quality assessment (QA) questions, as shown in Table 13.5. The questions were scored as Y (included) or N

TABLE 13.4

Inclusion and Exclusion Criteria

Selection Criteria	Scientific Database
Inclusion	• Peer-reviewed research articles, book chapters, and reports • Published between 2000 and 2021 • Written in English • Investigated cyberattacks and their impacts/cost on business • Presented empirical data related to measuring the cyberattacks impact, vulnerabilities, and risk
Exclusion	• Published out of timeframe restrictions • Written in non-English • Studies related to the impact of cyberattacks on governments, regions, and individuals (e.g., victims, consumers, employees, researchers, teenagers etc.) • Technical papers that only discuss cybersecurity technologies, architectures • Studies only related to cybersecurity education, legislation, policy, culture • Studies only related to behavior analysis of attackers

TABLE 13.5

Quality Assessment Questions Considered to Filter out Relevant Literature

QAs	Quality Assessment Questions
QA 1	Did the paper discuss cyberattacks/breach/crime?
QA 2	Did the paper provide enough context?
QA 3	Were the data adequately described?
QA 4	Did the paper discuss the impact/cost of cyberattacks/breach/crime?

(excluded). When there was a disagreement, we discussed the issues until we reached a group consensus. Only studies that met all four criteria were selected and proceeded to data extraction and analysis.

DATA COLLECTION

Following the guidance of Kitchenham et al. (2009), one researcher extracted details about each identified paper (see Table 13.6), and the other two checked the extraction. Disagreements were discussed and resolved by group discussion.

DATA ANALYSIS

The data were analyzed to show the following (with reference to Table 13.1):

- The number of papers published per year and their source (addressing RQ1)
- The affiliations of the authors, their institutions, and the country where the institutions locate (addressing RQ2)
- The results of the paper (addressing RQ3)
- Whether the paper proposed methods/indicators to measure the impact (addressing RQ4)
- Whether the paper highlighted major issues (addressing RQ5)

TABLE 13.6
Attributes Extracted for Each Identified Relevant Paper

No.	Attributes	Details
1.	Reference	Provides the citation of the paper
2.	Document types	Journal articles, book chapter, or reports
3.	Institutions	Provides author(s)' institutions
4.	Country	Provides the country where the institutions are located
5.	Research objectives	Provides a short description of research aims
6.	Research methods	Lists the methods used by the study
7.	Impacts	Lists the key impacts and/or cost examined by the study
8.	Indicators	Lists the key indicators used to measure the impacts/costs
9.	Barriers	Lists the key barriers for impact measurement
10.	Future research streams	Lists future research areas reported in the primary study

RESULTS

Following the methodology outlined in the previous section, this section presents and analyzes the search results and data extraction results. We also perform a keyword co-occurrence analysis to understand if we can make up clusters of similar research activities within the literature of cyber-attacks. Such a cluster analysis can help inform us, for instance, about the number and focus of different research strands within a field and their connectivity.

SEARCH RESULTS

Figure 13.2 shows the flow of search process adopted and the number of papers (records) identified/removed/added at each stage. We identified 1267 publications from the search (Table 13.3). In the phase of title and abstract screening, we removed 469 duplicates and excluded 725 publications according to the inclusion and exclusion criteria (Table 13.4). The paper count reduced to 73. Three industrial reports and one book chapter, which focus on measuring the costs of cyberattacks, were

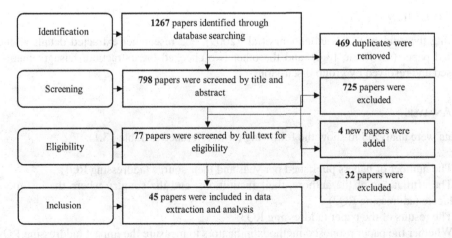

FIGURE 13.2   Flowchart of the search process adopted, and the number of papers handled at each stage.

TABLE 13.7

Extracted Data for Papers Meeting Our Search Criteria

	Ref.	Loc.	Research Objectives	Methods	Impacts	Barriers and Challenges	Future Research Streams
1.	Derbyshire et al. (2021)	UK	To understand how cyber risk assessment is conducted in practice	Semi-structured interviews	• Financial losses • Reputation	• Middle management: lack of understanding. • Board member: see cybersecurity as a disabler but not enabler	• Develop supplement data about costs and effects of controls; develop practical impact framework
2.	Böhme et al. (2019)	Austria	To develop a conceptual framework for quantitative modeling of cyber risk	Economic modeling	• Financial losses (assets' value) • Reputational damage • Data loss, breach, or abuse	• Incoherent cybersecurity standards and certificates. • Very hard to measure indirect cost (e.g., reputational damage) • Absence of empirical data	• More systematic collection and evaluation of data
3.	Layton and Watters (2014)	Australia, New Zealand	To estimate the cyber costs to Australian businesses	Case studies, cost modeling	• Tangible cost (investigating vulnerabilities; hiring staff, restoring data, communication, legal, insurance) • Intangible cost (reputation, identity theft, missed opportunity cost, staff and customer turnover etc.)	• Difficult to measure damage to company reputation	• Quantify the likelihood of data breach
4.	Lagazio et al. (2014)	UK	To understand the impact of cybercrime on the financial sector	Surveys, interviews, system dynamics	• Direct losses (e.g., financial losses) • Indirect losses (e.g., opportunity cost) • Defense losses (cost of security measures, security services, law enforcement etc.)	• Lack of consensus on the definition, classification, and impact of cyber-attacks. • Under-reporting;	• Understand the systematicity and complexity of cybercrime activities and their consequences

(Continued)

TABLE 13.7 *(Continued)*

	Ref.	Loc.	Research Objectives	Methods	Impacts	Barriers and Challenges	Future Research Streams
5.	Kappelman et al. (2019)	USA	To report the findings of a study of information technology management issues and practices	Survey, Delphi	• Revenue losses • Customer satisfaction	• Lack of formal cybersecurity leadership. • Lack of alignment between cybersecurity and business strategy	• In-depth comparative research is needed to under cultural, economic and legal areas
6.	Kjaerland (2006)	Norway	To understand cyber incidents towards the commercial and government sectors	Multidimensional scaling	• Disruption • Distort • Destruct • Disclosure • Unknown	• The lack of reporting • Problematic threat assessment for firms • Unreliable data	• Collect additional data on a large-scale basis; undertake comparative studies across sectors
7.	Srinidhi et al. (2015)	USA	To develop an analytical model for optimally allocate investment to productive and cybersecurity assets	A decision support model	• Aggregate cost: the direct and financial distress costs (e.g., direct legal and administrative costs, indirect cost due to loss of market share and employees)	• Misalignment of interests between managers and investors	• Can be broadened to address resource allocation
8.	Leszczyna (2013)	Poland	To provide practical method for measuring the cost of security to plan effective security strategies	Economic modeling	• The total cost of activities associated with the establishment and operation of cybersecurity • The total cost of activities related to cybersecurity professionals	• Very difficult to assess the costs on the users' side • The calculation formulas and methodologies are mostly implicit	• Propose a systematic approach to the determination of physical assets involved in the cybersecurity management process.

	Ref.	Loc.	Research Objectives	Methods	Impacts	Barriers and Challenges	Future Research Streams
9.	CSBS (2021)	UK	To understand the nature and significance of the cybersecurity threats they face, and support the government to shape policy	Survey, interview	• Financial costs: • Short-term direct costs (payments to external IT consultants, attackers) • Long-term direct costs (training, system upgrade, recruitment, legal) • Other indirect costs (staff could not do their jobs, loss of intellectual property, replacing devices)	• Senior management attitudes had not hugely shifted. • Under reporting (external reporting)	• Improve approach to cybersecurity management • Help management boards to understand that cybersecurity is an integral component of business resilience
10.	Armin et al. (2016)	Poland	To gain an understanding of the impact of cybercrime on stakeholders	Delphi survey,	• Impacts on stakeholders (most significant impact: loss of staff time, distraction from business purpose, reputational damage to the brand)	• Low reporting rate • Lack of quantifiable data • The absence of standards and benchmarks • Confused definition of cybercrime	• Reliable data • Build clear taxonomy • Build reliable model for quantifying the cost
11.	Smith (2004)	USA	To develop model that allowing companies to study the effects of cybercrime on online consumer confidence	Literature review	• Hinder the growth of e-commerce • Retailer's reputation • Trust	• Lack of legislative actions • Lack of understanding on cybercrimes and their impact on customer trust	• The strategic impacts of retailers' disclosures of online privacy and security policies on consumer confidence
12.	Lee (2021)	USA	To discuss the trends of cyberattacks and present cyber risk management framework	Economic modeling	• Financial loss • Reputation damage • Government penalties and sanctions • Costs of recovering data	• Lack of proper analysis models and techniques • Lack of quantitative historical data	• Expand to the qualitative risk assessment (Delphi) • Combine financial methods in cyber investment decision

(Continued)

TABLE 13.7 (*Continued*)

	Ref.	Loc.	Research Objectives	Methods	Impacts	Barriers and Challenges	Future Research Streams
13.	Rees et al. (2011)	USA	To help planners in reducing security risk by forming a cost-effective portfolio of countermeasures	Risk analysis modeling – genetic algorithm	• Financial losses (dollar loss caused by security event)	• Uncertainty	• Point estimate scenarios adapted from the categorical data
14.	Gupta and Sharman (2012)	USA	To analyze data security breaches and categorize the incident and loss trends, so as to help security decision in practice	Survey – PRC database	• Cost for hardware, software • Time on replacing/ restoring the laptop • Reputation and confidence loss • Potential loss of customers • Liabilities from laws	• There was no intention to make data available on the Internet • Internal attacks are often underreported to public	• Include more record sets • Expand time period
15.	Gordon et al. (2018)	USA	To report the results of a survey to better understand the driver of cybersecurity investment in private sector firms	Survey	• Private costs (e.g., financial loss) • Externalities (e.g., costs to customers)	• Cybersecurity is often viewed as cost saving rather than revenue generating project • Uncertainty of benefits	• Conduct laboratory experiment
16.	Bürger et al. (2019)	Germany	To support decision makers in their attempts to protect digitized production environments by estimating the impact of incidents	Bayesian networks (BNs) and attack graphs	• Impact the value creation process • Reduce functionality of the attacked network nodes itself • Spread of damage within both information and production networks	• Difficult to collect empirical data due to strict confidentiality agreements and concerns about reputation loss	• The model should be justified and applied to multiple products in large-scale networks

	Ref.	Loc.	Research Objectives	Methods	Impacts	Barriers and Challenges	Future Research Streams
17.	Smith et al. (2019)	USA	To examine the impact of cybercrime on stock prices of a sample of publicly traded companies.	Event study, case studies	• Stock prices • Customers • Damages economic growth, trade, and competitiveness	• Companies are not fully aware of their losses • Many cases are unreported	• More publicly traded firms • Specific types of industries • Larger samples
18.	Tariq (2018)	Pakistan	To explore impact of cyberattacks on financial institutions	Case study	• Direct loss (money theft, data breach) • Indirect loss (customer frustration, destruction of PR)	• Lack of awareness of cybersecurity	• Invest in cybersecurity measures and assessment
19.	Alali et al. (2018)	Saudi Arabia, USA	To describe the impacts of criminal activities	Fuzzy inference model	• Economically, socially, physically • Hinder the success of business • Loss of intellectual property	• Subjective to the loss • Vague information	• N/A
20.	Gordon et al. (2015)	USA	To develop an economics-based analytical framework for assessing the impact of government regulations to offset the underinvestment in cybersecurity	Survey	• Private costs • Externalities • The costs of detecting and correcting breaches • Actual loss of physical assets • Stock market returns	• Underinvestment in cybersecurity • Lack of reliable empirical data	• Develop national database to track cybersecurity investments • Better understand the determinants to cybersecurity investment
21.	Morse et al. (2011)	USA	To examine the impact of a disclosure of data breaches on the behavior of stock markets	Event study	• Economic consequence of a breach depends on the nature and value of the assets compromised by the breach • Loss of market value	• Lack of alignment in top management team to manage cybersecurity	• Consider absolute size of stock market reaction • Include more variables that may affect the market price

(Continued)

TABLE 13.7 *(Continued)*

	Ref.	Loc.	Research Objectives	Methods	Impacts	Barriers and Challenges	Future Research Streams
22.	Makridis and Dean (2018)	USA	To introduce a new dataset containing data breach and financial outcome at the firm level	Survey – PRC database	• Undermine consumer trust • Reduce cash flow • Stock prices • Decline in productivity	• No ready-to-use database • Firm heterogeneity • Less likely to report incidents	• Compare with analysis based on other datasets • Build data sources to remedy data deficiencies
23.	Winder and Trump (2015)	UK	To discuss mitigating cybercrime through meaningful measurement methodologies	Review	• Financial losses • Reputational damage	• Fear, uncertainty, doubt • Lack of consistent measurement method and clarity concerning the definition of cybercrime	• Clarify the definition of cybercrime
24.	Jana and Ghosh (2018)	India	To propose a type-2 fuzzy logic controller for improving risk assessment model for cybersecurity	Fuzzy assessment model	• Consequence: the impact given that the attack occurs and succeeds	• Difficult to improve risk assessment of cybersecurity in imprecise environment	• The model based on real time data can be investigated
25.	Almutairi and Thomas (2020)	UK	To present two performance models of a web-based sales system, one without an attack and the other with a denial-of-service attack	Performance Evaluation Process Algebra modeling	• Delay the processing of orders • Failed customer orders • Delay on selling products • Products being discarded • Revenue loss	• There are few existing models in this domain	• Obtain more realistic parameter values from a real system to validate the model
26.	Weintraub (2017)	Israel	To define, formulate, illustrate a quantitative integrity impact measure	Security assessment models	• Steal data, change software • Degradation of confidentiality • Damage the database • Downgrade networks' availability to users	• Lack of complete data • Lack of methods for providing a complete impact solution	• Mathematical formalization of algorithm, usefulness using real cases • Data mining models for risk prediction

	Ref.	Loc.	Research Objectives	Methods	Impacts	Barriers and Challenges	Future Research Streams
27.	Aissa et al. (2010)	USA	To illustrate the proposed quantitative model using an e-commerce application	Cybersecurity econometrics model; cost-benefit analysis	• Customer (loss of confidential information) • Merchant (the loss of business and the loss of customer loyalty) • Technical intermediary (the loss of business and reputation) • Financial intermediary (the loss of business, and reputation)	• Require real-time data	• Call for more economics-based analysis to quantify security attributes and provide resource for decision making
28.	Russell (2017)	UK	To raise businesses' awareness around cyberattacks	Review	• Financial losses • Reputational damage	• Lack of public awareness around cybersecurity	• To develop proactive approach and place focus on the technology, governance and processes
29.	Kamiya et al. (2021)	SGP, HK, Cyprus, USA	To investigate the impact on corporations of successful cyberattacks	Event study; risk assessment model	• Reputation and trust loss • Decrease sales growth and stock price • Recovery costs and litigation costs • Decreases the risk-taking incentives of management	• Limited information available in public sources and the difficulty to judge the timing of each event	• N/A
30.	Kotenko and Doynikova (2018)	Russia	To discuss the issues of countermeasure selection for ongoing computer network attack	Attack graphs; review	• Damage system operation • High financial losses	• Short sequences of attacks • Low numbers of events	• Consider characteristics and motivations of different types of attackers to increase the accuracy of the model

(Continued)

TABLE 13.7 *(Continued)*

	Ref.	Loc.	Research Objectives	Methods	Impacts	Barriers and Challenges	Future Research Streams
31.	Hiller and Russell (2013)	USA	To review the nature of cyber threats and compare the US and EU approach to promoting cybersecurity	Review	• Negative implications for customers' privacy, investors' lost profits, business IP theft and industry competitiveness, and loss of jobs in the economy	• Lack of new law • Difficulty of agreeing on the best approach	• Require sustained attention from both the public and private sectors
32.	Furnell et al. (2015)	UK	To discuss the challenge of measuring cyber-dependent crimes	Review	• Direct and indirect financial loss • Loss of reputation • Loss of shareholder value • Real or potential loss of stolen data and clean-up costs	• Various terminology • Various data sources and data collection methods • Vender reports do not treat things in the same way, issue of consistency • Difficult to obtain data	• Consistent terminology • Clear data collection methodology • Need to find ways to improve visibility of incidents
33.	Cabinet Office & Detica (2011)	UK	To estimate the cost of cybercrime in the UK	A causal model (scenario-based approach)	• Direct and indirect costs • Impact on business value chain • Effects of IT theft on UK business (reduced turnover, reduced profitability, reputational damage, reduction in share price, loss of competitive advantage, additional costs, opportunity costs etc.)	• Lack of available data • Lack of a clear reporting mechanism • Under-reporting of cybercrime • Lack understood topic	• Business needs to invest in cybersecurity • Government and businesses need to build awareness, share insights and measure cybercrime

Ref.	Loc.	Research Objectives	Methods	Impacts	Barriers and Challenges	Future Research Streams
34.	Buil-Gil et al. (2021)	UK	To analyze the impact of companies' online activities and cybersecurity measures on victimization	Survey	• New measures needed, additional staff time, stopped staff from daily work, repair or recovery costs, software damaged, loss of revenue or share value, reputational damage, lost assets, fines from regulators, etc.	• Lack of available and reliable sources of data • Under-reporting	• Need new research in other geographic contexts and using alternative sources of data
35.	Juma'h and Alnsour (2020)	USA	To analyze the effect of data breaches on companies' overall performance	Event studies (ROA, ROE)	• Losing data control • Affect company stock value • Affect a company's overall performance (e.g., sales, revenue, liquidity, profitability, and sustainability)	• Subjective to the loss • Vague information	• Need more data to validate the findings • Integrate qualitative factors • Investigate the relationship between IT investment and occurrence of data breach
36.	Paoli et al. (2018)	Belgium	To develop a conceptual framework to examine how cybercrime affects businesses	Survey	• Direct cost • Opportunity cost: revenue lost	• No consensus on how to measure cybercrime • High sensitivity of the topic	• Develop standardized methodology • Regular assessment
37.	Gordon et al. (2011)	USA	To help solve conflicting evidence from previous studies on the effect of security breaches on market returns of firms	Event study (basic one-factor CAPM market model)	• Explicit costs (costs of detecting and correcting breaches) • Implicit costs (lost current and future revenues resulting from affecting the relationships with customers and business partners; legal liabilities)	• The market is not efficient, so the event study formulation could not be expected to capture the economic impacts of breaches	• Researchers, practitioners, and policy makers need to devote resources to address the concern on growing tolerance by investors for security breaches

(Continued)

TABLE 13.7 *(Continued)*

	Ref.	Loc.	Research Objectives	Methods	Impacts	Barriers and Challenges	Future Research Streams
38.	Schatz and Bashroush (2016)	UK	To examine the influence of information security breach on an organization's stock market value	Event study	• Direct and indirect cost • The market reaction to such an incident	• Lack of information security-specific public data	• More available public information • Law and regulations become more explicit on reporting such event
39.	Caldwell (2014)	UK	To discuss the financial impact of a data breach on the organization	Review	• Direct cost (cost of engaging law firms, security experts, PR consultants) • Indirect cost (the cost of fines and compensation to the victims of the breach)	• Difficult to calculate a true total cost • Each incident is unique • Very difficult to measure the reputation damage, the loss of customer confidence and royalty	• Grow awareness of the potential impact of a data breach
40.	Donalds and Osei-Bryson (2019)	Jamaica and USA	To present and illustrate a new cybercrime ontology	Design science (DS)	• Financial losses • Loss of access • Reputational damage	• Varying terminologies • Insufficient and fragmented classification	• Conduct more robust evaluation • Involve other researchers • Use text mining and AI technologies
41.	Furnell et al. (2020)	UK	To explore the issue of cybersecurity breaches and understand the full costs	Review	• Direct loss (short-, medium-, long-term) • Indirect loss (short-, medium-, long-term)	• Difficult to estimate time-related costs • Ambiguous to measure the longer-term costs	• Understand the longer-term costs of cyber breach • Standardize methods of collecting information
42.	Dumitraş (2015)	USA	To report on empirical studies to understand the vulnerability lifecycle for risk assessment against cyberattacks	Security metrics	• Financial costs	• Existing security metrics and models do not provide an adequate assessment of security • Not available data	• Require empirical studies conducted at scale, using comprehensive field data

	Ref.	Loc.	Research Objectives	Methods	Impacts	Barriers and Challenges	Future Research Streams
43.	Home Office (2018)	UK	To take the research community closer towards achieving better estimates of the costs of cybercrime as part of future studies	Review	• Costs in anticipation of cybercrime (technology costs, training, security practices, government activities) • Costs because of cybercrime (costs of fixing an attack, financial losses, other) • Costs in response to cybercrime (Law enforcement, prisons, and probation)	• Challenges in developing robust estimates • Inconsistent definitions of both costs and cybercrime • Most studies did not measure the same thing	• Approach research design in a systematic fashion • Focus on notable gaps • Investigate the costs and benefits to offenders • Assessing the impact on business reputation • Explore using survey data
44.	Jaganathan et al. (2015)	India	To propose a mathematical model to predict the impact of an attack based on significant factors that influence cybersecurity	Mathematical model	• Impact on IT asset (metrics: assess vector, access complexity and authentication)	• Underinvestment in cybersecurity • Lack of reliable empirical data	• The technical analyst can analyze the impact and take preventive actions • Need to generalize and customize the model to the needs of individual firms
45.	Corbet and Gurdgiev (2019)	Ireland	To examine the impact of cybercrime on equity market volatility across publicly traded corporations	Exponential GARCH model	• Negative impact on stock volatility • Direct financial costs • Theft of IP • Software and data destruction	• Inconsistent research methods • Lack of tools • Limited data	• Regulatory needs to take urgent action and develop strategy to mitigate the potential cybercrime

later suggested and added by team members. This led to 77 publications that were eligible for full text screening. We then evaluated the eligibility of publications based on four quality assessment questions (Table 13.5). In this phase, we excluded any publications that were not relevant to measuring the impact of cyberattacks on business. Finally, 45 publications were selected for data extraction (Table 13.6).

DATA EXTRACTION RESULTS

Table 13.7 shows the key results of data extraction. This includes reference, location, research objectives, impacts of cyberattacks, impact measuring methods, barriers to measuring impacts, and future research streams. We will draw from information shown in Table 13.7 to answer five research questions.

KEYWORD CO-OCCURRENCE ANALYSIS

Keywords represent important concepts that are addressed in the paper. The co-occurrence analysis of keywords uses visual maps of semantics based on the content analysis technique, thus providing a good glance of research areas related to cyberattacks. VOSviewer was used to develop the co-occurrence bibliometric map, using the authors' keywords abstracted from the four selected databases. A total of 193 keywords was obtained. After merging similar words, 96 keywords remained. Only 21 keywords (or 21.88%) appeared more than once. Fourteen keywords appeared more than three times, eight appeared more than four times, and six appeared more than five times. Many keywords appearing once indicates a lack of continuity and divergence in research.

Table 13.8 shows the six most-used author keywords in terms of occurrence and total link strength. The occurrence means the frequency of a keyword appears; the total link strength indicates the number of papers in which two keywords are used together. The higher this value, the more linkages a keyword has with other keywords. "Cybersecurity" is the most recurring keyword and is used most frequently with another keyword. It is notable that "cost" only appears four times but is more frequently used with other keywords compared to "data breach" and "risk assessment."

Figure 13.2 presents the co-occurrence map for author keywords. These network maps are made up of nodes and links. The nodes are the keywords, and their size represents the number of times that keywords appear. Links indicate a relationship between nodes, and the distance between two nodes indicates the strength of their relationship. Circles in the same color show a similar topic among selected publications.

As shown in Figure 13.3 and Table 13.9, VOSviewer grouped keywords into ten clusters that include at least two nodes. Cluster 5 (cybersecurity) is in the center of the map and has strong connections with the others. This shows that the field is dominated by studies analyzing the risk of cybersecurity by using mathematical models. We can also see that Clusters 5, 2 (data breach), 3

TABLE 13.8
Author Keyword Co-Occurrence

Keyword	Occurrence	Total Link Strength
Cybersecurity	18	85
Cybercrime	11	60
Cyberattack	8	31
Data breach	6	27
Risk assessment	6	25
Cost	4	28

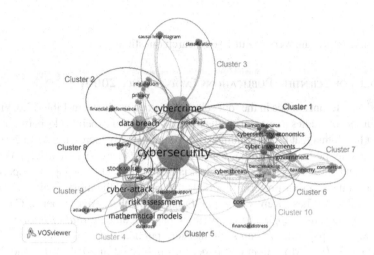

FIGURE 13.3 The co-occurrence network of keywords overlaid with a clustering of the keywords.

TABLE 13.9

Details of Cluster Groups of Keyword Nodes

Topic	Clusters	Top Five Terms	#Terms	Share
1.	Cybersecurity economics	Cyber investment, cyber fraud, metrics, human resource, performance measurement	13	13.53%
2.	Data breach	Financial markets, financial performance, law, non-financial factors, number of breached records	12	12.50%
3.	Cybercrime	Causal loop diagram, classification, economic impact, financial sector, knowledge-based approach	11	11.46%
4,	Cyber risk	Computational infrastructure, cyber investment, cyber risk, cyber threats, information technology	11	11.46%
5.	Cybersecurity	Cybersecurity, data loss, risk assessment, fuzzy, mathematical models	11	11.46%
6.	Benchmarking	Benchmarking, data, DDoS, definition, measurement, methodology	10	10.42%
7.	Government	Cyber incidents, government, commercial, reporting, sectors	8	8.33%
8.	Stock value	Consumer trust, stock value, ethics, security breach announcement, vulnerability	8	8.33%
9.	Cyberattack	Attack graphs, cyberattack, financial institutions, countermeasure selection, security metrics	6	6.25%
10.	Cost	Adversary, cost, financial distress, insurance, resource allocation	6	6.25%

(cybercrime), and 9 (cyberattacks) are closely related to each other. This indicates that cybersecurity is highly analyzed by examining the financial performance after data breach, economic impact of cybercrime, and cost of cyberattacks. In contrast, Clusters 6 (benchmarking), 7 (government), 8 (stock value), and 10 (cost) have less interaction with the other clusters. The distant connectivity between the groups indicates that the research field is in an early stage.

DISCUSSION

In this section, we discuss the answers to our five research questions.

HOW HAS THE FOCUS OF SCIENTIFIC PUBLICATIONS EVOLVED SINCE 2000?

Overall, we selected 45 relevant studies in the four selected sources, as shown in Table 13.6. Figure 13.4 further shows the number of studies in measuring the business impact of cyberattacks between 2000 and 2021. The line chart highlights that the total number has been gradually increasing since 2000, despite some fluctuations. Among the included studies, 41 of them (91.11%) are journal articles. For the rest, three studies (6.67%) and one study (2.23%) are industrial reports and a book chapter, respectively.

Figure 13.5 presents the top four preferred journals that recorded the most significant number of publications on the subject. These were *Computer Fraud & Security* (five papers), *Computers & Security* (four papers), *Decision Support Systems* (three papers), and *Journal of Information Security and Applications* (two papers). We can see consistent publications in the field since 2011 and a gap between 2006 and 2011. More than one paper was published in 2014, 2015, and 2018. The four journals published 14 papers, representing 34.15% of the total. The remaining 27 papers were published by the other 27 journals, such as *European Journal of Information Systems, Journal of Applied Security Research,* and *Journal of Economic and Social Measurement.*

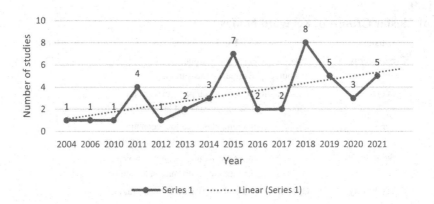

FIGURE 13.4   Time analysis of selected publications.

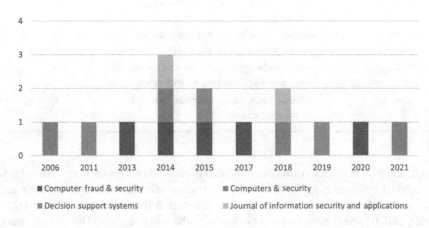

FIGURE 13.5   Top four targeted journals.

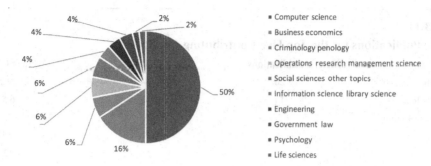

FIGURE 13.6 Journal articles by research area.

The studies covered nine research areas identified by Web of Science. Figure 13.6 presents the journal articles by percentage and research area. We can see that this topic is mainly investigated in the field of computer science (50%). However, researchers also show different interests in other fields, such as business economics (16%), criminology penology (6%), operations research and management science (6%), social sciences (6%), information science (4%), engineering (4%), and government law (4%).

WHO IS WORKING ON MEASURING THE IMPACT OF CYBERATTACKS ON BUSINESSES?

We found that a total of 105 authors participated in producing the 45 publications over the period 2000–2021. Table 13.10 shows the five main authors in the research field. The most prominent author is Gordon, L.A., who co-authored with Zhou, L. and Leob, M.P. on three papers, as well as Lucyshyn, W. in two papers. Meanwhile, Furnell, S. contributed two papers.

Table 13.10 also provides an author's H-index, which uses a score to quantify the results of an individual's research output by comparing documents and citations. It shows that Furnell, S. is the author with the highest index, with 59. The high H-index indicates the high impact of the publications of an author, but it doesn't mean significant impact in the field, since some researchers are interested in several topics.

Contributions to this research were developed by 21 countries. Table 13.11 lists the scientific production of the five leading countries that account for 70.18%. It reveals that the United States leads the group, with 20 publications (35.09%) within the study period, followed by the United Kingdom, Russia, Poland, and India, with 14 (24.56%), 2 (3.51%), 2 (3.51%), and 2 (3.51%), respectively.

TABLE 13.10
Main Authors in Measuring the Business Impact of Cyberattacks

Author	Country	# Papers Selected	Citations	# Total Papers	Total Citations	H-Index
Gordon, L.A.	USA	3	261	162	13,027	45
Leob, M.P.	USA	3	261	90	10,268	34
Zhou, L.	USA	3	261	10	1450	9
Lucyshyn, W.	USA	2	63	141	2661	18
Furnell, S.	UK	2	38	738	14,173	59

TABLE 13.11

Scientific Publications for the Top Five Contributing Countries

Country	# Publications	# Citations	Average Citations
United States	20	584	29.2
United Kingdom	14	91	6.5
Russian Federation	2	29	14.5
Poland	2	7	3.5
India	2	24	12

We noted that the number of citations is consistent with the number of publications, except for Poland, whose citations are low compared to Russia and India. According to the average citations (the number of publications/the number of citations), United States is the most-cited country, while Poland has the lowest number of citations.

A total of 73 organizations participated in this research field, but we cannot see significant scientific links between organizations. The most productive organization is the University of Maryland (USA), which produced three papers with 262 citations. The other institutions produced one paper each.

What Impacts of Cyberattacks Have Been Addressed in the Literature?

The impact of cyberattacks refers to the consequence or effect of a threat or attack leveraging a vulnerability (Derbyshire et al. 2021; Kjaerland 2006). In total, we identified 50 different impacts. Figure 13.7 shows the top ten impacts addressed in the literature.

As illustrated in Figure 13.7, 39 publications (88.9%) discussed direct financial losses or costs. Cyberattacks lead to revenue or sales losses due to investigating vulnerabilities, hiring new staff, training, working with external IT consultants, restoring data, replacing equipment, or updating system. Twenty-three of them (51.1%) were concerned with reputational damage, including brand damage, losing customers, losing future sales, losing positioning within the market, or losing

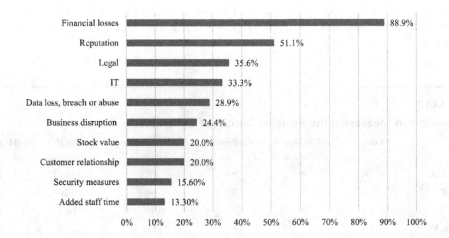

FIGURE 13.7   Top ten business impacts of cyberattacks.

TABLE 13.12

Typology of Business Impacts of Cyberattacks

#	Typology	Citation	Frequency
1.	Direct losses, indirect losses, defense losses	CSBS (2021), Furnell et al. (2020), Paoli et al. (2018), Caldwell (2014), Lagazio et al. (2014)	5
2.	Tangible cost, intangible cost	Layton and Watters (2014)	1
3.	Explicit costs, implicit costs	Gordon et al. (2011)	1
4.	Costs in anticipation, costs consequently, costs in response	Home Office (2018)	1
5.	Private costs, externalities	Gordon et al. (2018)	1
6.	Customer, merchant, intermediary	Aissa et al. (2010)	1

customers' trust. Sixteen of them (35.6%) mentioned legal costs, including legal fees, fines, PR, law enforcement, legislation, government penalties, and sanctions. Fifteen of them (33.3%) discussed IT cost, including changing or upgrading software, databases, or systems and replacing hardware, equipment, or devices. Thirteen of them (28.9%) focused on data loss, breach, or abuse. This is followed by business disruption (11, 24.4%), stock value (9, 20%), customer relationship (9, 20%), new security measures needed for future attacks (7, 15.6%), and added staff time to deal with attacks (6, 13.3%).

There were 14 impacts discussed more than once: recovering cost (e.g., the cost of recovering data and IT systems), opportunity cost (e.g., due to reduced sales, shifts in priorities and strategies, spending defense measures, staff turnover, missing funds, etc.), IP loss, asset loss, economic growth, competitiveness damage, business value chain, training, staff loss, market share loss, hiring staff, payment to attackers or offenders, payment to external IP or security professionals or consultants, and cost of cyber insurance. The remaining 26 impacts were only mentioned once, such as reduced productivity (Makridis and Dean 2018), hindering the growth of e-commerce (Smith 2004), increased cost of borrowing due to reduced credit ratings (Layton and Watters 2014), increased communication cost (Layton and Watters 2014), reduction in R&D investment (Home Office 2018), and decreasing the risk-taking incentives of management cost (Kamiya et al. 2021).

While 35 publications focused on different impacts, 10 (22.22%) proposed or used a typology to estimate the costs of cyberattacks. As shown in Table 13.12, the most frequently used typology is direct losses (i.e., monetary losses, damages experienced by the targeted organizations as a consequence of a cyberattack), indirect losses (i.e., the monetary losses and opportunity costs imposed on organizations when a cyberattack is carried out), and defense losses (i.e., direct defense costs of development, deployment and maintenance of cybersecurity measures, and indirect defense costs from opportunity costs caused by the defense measures) (CSBS 2021; Furnell et al. 2020; Paoli et al. 2018; Caldwell 2014; Lagazio et al. 2014). The remaining five typologies were used once.

WHAT METHODS HAVE BEEN USED TO EVALUATE THE IMPACT OF CYBERATTACKS?

There are debates on which data, methods, and techniques we should use to capture and unpack the complex consequence of cyberattacks (Lagazio et al. 2014). In total, we identified 14 methods. Figure 13.8 presents the top ten methods.

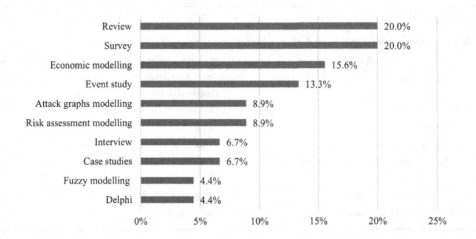

FIGURE 13.8   Top ten methods used to measure the business impact of cyberattacks.

As shown in Figure 13.8, nine publications (20%) are review papers that aim to understand the definition, measurement, methods involved, issues, and challenges. Nine publications (20%) used a survey to capture data and information about organizational spending on cybersecurity, the number of specific incidents faced by companies on a yearly basis, and industry perceptions on the impact of cyberattacks. For example, CSBS (2021) launched an annual cybersecurity survey to map out the current cyber threats and their impact on organizations, thus supporting the government to shape future policy.

Seven publications (15.6%) used economic modeling techniques to capture the behavioral economics of security. The seven used economic modeling techniques such as cost-benefit analysis (CBA) (Aissa et al. 2010), an activity-based costing (ABC) model (Leszczyna 2013), a four-step tangible cost model (Layton and Watters 2014), a cyber cost prediction model (Jaganathan et al. 2015), an economic model of cyber risk transfer (Böhme et al. 2019), an exponential GARCH (EGARCH) model (Corbet and Gurdgiev 2019), and a cyber investment cost analysis model (Lee 2021). In addition, researchers mentioned other well-known economic metrics that are used commonly, such as the rate of return (IRR), return on investment (ROI), and maximum net present value (NPV). These methods could provide quick and rough estimation mainly for illustrative objectives of the financial impact of a security incident on a business (Leszczyna 2013).

Six publications (13.3%) employed an event-study methodology, which is widely used to access the impact of an event on the value of a firm. For instance, Juma'h and Alnsour (2020) used event study to understand the effect of data breaches on company performance, as measured by profitability ratios, return on assets, and return on equity. Morse et al. (2011) used event study to measure the effect of data breach announcements on the behavior of stock markets.

Other frequently used methods include attack graph modeling (4, 8.9%), risk assessment modeling (3, 8.9%), semi-structured interviews (3, 6.7%), case studies (3, 6.7%), fuzzy modeling (2, 4.4%), and Delphi survey (2, 4.4%). The research on cyberattacks in the field of sociology has traditionally relied on interviews with cybersecurity experts and questionnaires to organizations experiencing attacks. This is because experts can provide context to a variety of aspects of impact. Their opinion was considered valuable in the cyber risk and impact evaluation process (Derbyshire et al. 2021). Delphi surveys have increasingly been highlighted as a popularly used expert judgement technique. For example, they have been used to understand the impact of cybercrime on stakeholders, to find out what they see as potential threats both now and in the future (Armin et al. 2016), and to estimate costs for cyber investment analysis (Lee 2021).

The remaining five methods were used once separately. They were performance modeling (Almutairi and Thomas 2020), design science (Donalds and Osei-Bryson 2019), system dynamics (Lagazio et al. 2014), a scenario-based causal model (Cabinet Office and Detica 2011), and multi-dimensional scaling (Kjaerland 2006).

Furthermore, we found that six publications (8.5%) used mixed methods: survey and interview (CSBS 2021); event study and risk assessment modeling (Kamiya et al. 2021); event study and case studies (Smith et al. 2019); survey and Delphi (Kappelman et al. 2019); survey, interview, and system dynamics (Lagazio et al. 2014); and case studies and cost modeling (Layton and Watters 2014).

WHAT ARE THE MAJOR BARRIERS TO MEASURING THE IMPACT OF CYBERATTACKS?

In total, we identified 15 barriers reported by identified publications, which can be clustered into three key issues.

The most frequently reported barrier is a lack of accessible and quantifiable data, which accounts for 48.9% (22 publications). In fact, it is extremely challenging to collect empirical data due to under-reporting issues in the field of cybersecurity (Cabinet Office and Detica 2011; Bürger et al. 2019). On the one hand, there is a lack of a clear reporting mechanism (Cabinet Office and Detica 2011); on the other hand, businesses are often reluctant to report cyber incidents due to the possible negative impact of publicity on business reputation and customer trust (Gordon et al. 2015; Gupta and Sharman 2012; Lagazio et al. 2014; Makridis and Dean 2018). A lack of a ready-to use database also makes it difficult to collect empirical data on the actual level of cyberattacks and their consequences (Gordon et al. 2015; Makridis and Dean 2018). For existing databases, these figures are not all directly comparable, since background, conditions, and methods vary between studies. Some studies are not even transparent about their methodology. The degree to which data are designated as open is questionable. These issues are intertwined with questions of trust in the data, as stakeholders show ambiguity and doubts about information about cyberattacks (Armin et al. 2016). Although academics have flagged these issues, a widely accepted knowledge base is still not within reach.

A lack of proper analysis models and assessment methods is another frequently reported barrier. We notice that many studies use different methods or models to estimate the cost of cyberattacks, but it is difficult to agree on the best approach (Hiller and Russell 2013). While some include implicit costs, others only focus on explicit costs due to the difficulty to measure reputational damage and the loss of customer confidence (Böhme et al. 2019; Leszczyna 2015). This makes it extremely difficult to estimate the true total cost of cyberattacks and justify the benefits of cybersecurity investment (Lee 2021).

Furthermore, many authors highlighted the management issue for cybersecurity. Many studies claim that senior managers and/or board members do not understand the severity of cyberattacks and show limited interest in grasping the technical cyber aspect. Cybersecurity is often viewed as cost savings rather than revenue-generating investment. Compared to the latter, a cost-saving project has a clear disadvantage because of the emphasis on sales growth in businesses (Gordon et al. 2015). This leads to a lack of formal cybersecurity leadership and alignment between cybersecurity and business strategy (Kappelman et al. 2019).

FUTURE RESEARCH DIRECTIONS

Cybersecurity is an emerging research topic that has received growing attention from scholars and practitioners. In parallel, the rise of digitalization in the context of COVID-19 pandemic requires new studies to understand the impact of cyberattacks on business. Moreover, the outlook demands the continuous improvement of existing ways of measuring impacts in support of cybersecurity investment and mitigation activities. Therefore, we have identified six directions in this field that scholars can address in the future.

1) **Measuring indirect costs**: Our results show that most studies only cover parts of the costs and exclude indirect costs, like losses of reputation, losses of customer trust, and negative impact on stock market (Böhme et al. 2019). Future studies could develop supplement data about indirect costs, build a practical impact framework, and involve different methods and researchers. Possible research questions could be: What are the indirect costs? What data are needed and what methods are available to measure indirect costs?

2) **Undertaking large-scale studies**: While many studies propose theoretical models and frameworks for impact assessment, researchers often call for further evaluation against real-world cyber data (Derbyshire et al. 2021). Future research could collect real-time data on a large-scale basis using easy-to-understand format (Kjaerland 2006; Dumitraş 2015; Armin et al. 2016; Weintraub 2017; Jana and Ghosh 2018; Derbyshire et al. 2021) to obtain realistic parameter values from a real system to validate the models (Almutairi and Thomas 2020).

3) **Applying Delphi methods**: To obtain more reliable and efficient estimates, researchers have been calling for using qualitative techniques, such as a Delphi study (Lee 2021). In our review, we found that most studies employed review, survey, economic modeling, and event studies, while only two studies used a Delphi study for impact assessment. A Delphi study is a well-known expert judgement technique, which is effective in developing opinions when quantitative historical data are not available. As such, researchers could explore the possibility of using a Delphi study in identifying the cybersecurity challenges, moderate variables, and evaluation methods. This could be integrated with quantifiable variables and financial methods to better understand the business impact of cyberattacks (Lee 2021; Morse et al. 2011).

4) **Applying artificial intelligence (AI)**: AI has been applied practically across many fields including cybersecurity. There are increasing studies on applying AI in cybersecurity. Apart from detecting various cyberattacks, handling the volume of data, and responding to threats, AI might contribute to developing models to predict the cyber risks and evaluate cyberattacks' impacts (Weintraub 2017; Donalds and Osei-Bryson 2019). Future research could explore how to use AI to generalize and customize the impact assessment model to the needs of individual firms (Jaganathan et al. 2015).

5) **Undertaking comparative case studies:** More cases are needed to compare the impact of cyberattacks on commercial sectors, public sectors, non-profit sectors (Kjaerland 2006), large companies, and SMEs (Lagazio et al. 2014), as well as other geographic contexts (Buil-Gil et al. 2021). In-depth comparative research would help validate the findings and shed some light on understanding the cultural, economic, legal, and other areas involved (Kappelman et al. 2019).

6) **Understanding the roles of senior managers:** For security practitioners, the ability to evaluate the cost of cyberattacks is essential to justify cybersecurity investment. However, it is difficult to convince a firm's senior managers and change their perception that cybersecurity is a cost-saving rather than revenue-generating project (Gordon et al. 2018). Future research could study the issue from a social science perspective to understand why senior managers prioritize cybersecurity or do not. What is the process of cybersecurity management? What are the roles of senior managers? What information or data are required to increase business buy-in? What are the determinants to cybersecurity investment? What are the challenges and how to overcome them?

CONCLUSIONS AND IMPLICATIONS

Cybersecurity has become a major concern for businesses, given the acceleration of digital transformation in the context of COVID-19 pandemic. Amid potential waves of the coronavirus, companies should be proactive in addressing the threats of cyberattacks. Impact measurement could be the first step that allows executive committee to understand the real cost of successful cyberattacks, thus helping to justify cybersecurity investment benefit and mitigate the cyberattack risk in the future (Russell 2017).

The main objective of this chapter was to review and analyze the research progresses around the topic on the business impacts of cyberattacks and how to measure such impacts. The analysis on the number of papers, authors and institutions, and their geographical locations suggests that business impact measurement of cyberattacks as a subject of study is still in its early stage. Scholars have attempted to recognize 50 impacts and use 14 methods to measure those impacts. But the efforts are hindered by various methodologic, organizational, and regulatory barriers. Overcoming these barriers will require a systematic and collaborative multistakeholder approach at the national and global level. The questions for future research could be: How do cyberattacks affect business? What are the methods to measure those impacts? What measures could be taken to reduce the likelihood and impact of a cyberattacks? What are the roles of public- and private-sector stakeholders to mitigate cyber risk and enhance cyber resilience?

PRACTICAL IMPLICATIONS

To help address the absence of empirical data, the government can establish national cyberattack databases that improve visibility of incidents and track cybersecurity investment and incidents (Gordon et al. 2015). Meanwhile, it is important to develop standardized reporting mechanism, unify data collection methods (Furnell 2015), build standards and benchmarks, and provide effective incentives to facilitate the "data-sharing frameworks" between competitors or within intermediaries to calculate compound loss distribution (Cabinet Office and Detica 2011; Böhme et al. 2019).

Also, our results show that all employees – from staffs to senior board members – need to fully understand the importance of cybersecurity in the organization. Security practitioners have a key responsibility in evaluating the impacts of cyberattacks and raising the awareness of cybersecurity across the organization (Russell 2017). Hence, having an effective and engaging training program and collaborating with universities can be instrumental for practitioners in mitigating cyber risk in the future.

LIMITATIONS

It is important to note that every study has limitations, including ours. Due to time and resource constraints, the analysis was based on searching studies from four databases using self-defined inclusion and exclusion criteria. We could have included more databases, expanded keywords, and involved more researchers. Such a search strategy would, however, be extensive and time consuming. The review and search process of this study strictly followed the guidance provided by Kitchenham et al. (2009) and Brereton et al. (2007), which makes us confident that our review has been carried out thoroughly. The three groups of keywords and four databases have enabled us to identify the relevant contributions.

ACKNOWLEDGMENTS

The authors would like to thank for the financial support provided by the Soteria project funded by Innovate UK as part of the UK ISCF Digital Security by Design (DSbD) Programme (Grant number: 75243).

REFERENCES

Aissa, Anis Ben, Robert K. Abercrombie, Frederick T. Sheldon, and Ali Mili. 2010. "Quantifying Security Threats and Their Potential Impacts: A Case Study." *Innovations in Systems and Software Engineering* 6, no.3 (March): 269–81. https://doi.org/10.1007/s11334-010-0123-2.

Alali, Mansour, Ahmad Almogren, Mohammad Mehedi Hassan, Iehab A.L. Rassan, and Md Zakirul Alam
    Bhuiyan. 2018. "Improving Risk Assessment Model of Cybersecurity Using Fuzzy Logic Inference
    System." *Computers & Security* 74, no.5 (September): 323–39. https://doi.org/10.1016/j.cose.2017.09.011.
Almutairi, Ohud, and Nigel Thomas. 2020. "Performance Modelling of the Impact of Cyberattacks on a Web-
    Based Sales System". *Electronic Notes in Theoretical Computer Science* 353 (November): 5–20. https://
    doi.org/10.1016/j.entcs.2020.09.016.
Armin, Jart, Bryn Thompson, and Piotr Kijewski. 2016. "Cybercrime Economic Costs: No Measure No
    Solution". In *Combatting Cybercrime and Cyberterrorism: Challenges, Trends and Priorities. Advanced
    Sciences and Technologies for Security Applications*, edited by Babak Akhgar and Ben Brewster, 135–
    55. Cham: Springer International Publishing. https://doi.org/10.1007/978-3-319-38930-1_8.
Beaming. 2021. "Cyber Reports: Q1 2021 Cyber Threat Report." www.beaming.co.uk/cyber-reports/
    q1-2021-cyber-threat-report/.
Böhme, Rainer, Stefan Laube, and Markus Riek. 2019. "A Fundamental Approach to Cyber Risk Analysis."
    Casualty Actuarial Society 12, no.2 (February): 161–85. https://informationsecurity.uibk.ac.at/pdfs/
    BLR2019_FundamentalApproachCyberRiskInsurance_Variance.pdf.
Brereton, Pearl, Barbara A. Kitchenham, David Budgen, Mark Turner, and Mohamed Khalil. 2007. "Lessons
    from Applying the Systematic Literature Review Process within the Software Engineering Domain."
    Journal of Systems and Software 80, no.4 (April): 571–83. https://doi.org/10.1016/j.jss.2006.07.009.
Buil-Gil, David, Nicholas Lord, and Emma Barrett. 2021. "The Dynamics of Business, Cybersecurity and
    Cyber-Victimization: Foregrounding the Internal Guardian in Prevention." *Victims & Offenders* 16,
    no.3 (February): 286–315. https://doi.org/10.1080/15564886.2020.1814468.
Bürger, Olga, Björn Häckel, Philip Karnebogen, and Jannick Töppel. 2019. "Estimating the Impact of IT
    Security Incidents in Digitized Production Environments." *Decision Support Systems* 127, no.113114
    (December): 1–11. https://doi.org/10.1016/j.dss.2019.113144.
Cabinet Office & Detica. 2011. "The Cost of Cybercrime." https://assets.publishing.service.gov.uk/government/
    uploads/system/uploads/attachment_data/file/60942/THE-COST-OF-CYBER-CRIME-SUMMARY-
    FINAL.pdf.
Caldwell, Tracey. 2014. "The True Cost of Being Hacked." *Computer Fraud & Security* 2014, no.6 (June):
    8–13. https://doi.org/10.1016/S1361–3723(14)70500–7.
Corbet, Shaen, and Constantin Gurdgiev. 2019. "What the Hack: Systematic Risk Contagion from Cyber
    Events." *International Review of Financial Analysis* 65, no. 101386 (October): 1–18. https://doi.
    org/10.1016/j.irfa.2019.101386.
CSBS. 2021. "Cybersecurity Breaches Survey 2021." www.gov.uk/government/statistics/cyber-security-
    breaches-survey-2021/cyber-security-breaches-survey-2021.
Deloitte. 2021. "Impact of COVID-19 on Cybersecurity." https://www2.deloitte.com/ch/en/pages/risk/articles/
    impact-covid-cybersecurity.html.
Derbyshire, Richard, Benjamin Green, and David Hutchison. 2021. "'Talking a Different Language':
    Anticipating Adversary Attack Cost for Cyber Risk Assessment." *Computers & Security* 103, no.3
    (April): 102163. https://doi.org/10.1016/j.cose.2020.102163.
Donalds, Charlette, and Kweku-Muata Osei-Bryson. 2019. "Toward a Cybercrime Classification Ontology:
    A Knowledge-Based Approach." *Computers in Human Behavior* 92 (March): 403–18. https://doi.
    org/10.1016/j.chb.2018.11.039.
Dumitraş, Tudor. 2015. 'Understanding the Vulnerability Lifecycle for Risk Assessment and Defense
    Against Sophisticated Cyberattacks'. In *Cyber Warfare: Building the Scientific Foundation.
    Advances in Information Security*, edited by Sushil Jajodia, Paulo Shakarian, V.S. Subrahmanian,
    Vipin Swarup, and Cliff Wang, 265–85. Cham: Springer International Publishing. https://doi.
    org/10.1007/978-3-319-14039-1_13.
Furnell, Steven, David Emm, and Maria Papadaki. 2015. "The Challenge of Measuring Cyber-Dependent
    Crimes." *Computer Fraud & Security* 2015, no.10 (October): 5–12. https://doi.org/10.1016/
    S1361–3723(15)30093–2.
Furnell, Steven, Harry Heyburn, Andrew Whitehead, and Jayesh Navin Shah. 2020. "Understanding the Full
    Cost of Cybersecurity Breaches." *Computer Fraud & Security* 2020, no.12 (December): 6–12. https://
    doi.org/10.1016/S1361–3723(20)30127–5.
Gordon, Lawrence A., Martin P. Loeb, William Lucyshyn, and Lei Zhou. 2015. "Increasing Cybersecurity
    Investments in Private Sector Firms." *Journal of Cybersecurity* 1, no.1 (November): 3–17. https://doi.
    org/10.1093/cybsec/tyv011.

Gordon, Lawrence A., Martin P. Loeb, William Lucyshyn, and Lei Zhou. 2018. "Empirical Evidence on the Determinants of Cybersecurity Investments in Private Sector Firms." *Journal of Information Security* 9, no. 2 (February): 133–53. https://doi.org/10.4236/jis.2018.92010.

Gordon, Lawrence A., Martin P. Loeb, and Lei Zhou. 2011. "The Impact of Information Security Breaches: Has There Been a Downward Shift in Costs?" *Journal of Computer Security* 19, no.1 (February): 33–56. https://doi.org/10.3233/JCS-2009–0398.

Grover, Varun, Roger H.L. Chiang, Ting-Peng Liang, and Dongsong Zhang. 2018. "Creating Strategic Business Value from Big Data Analytics: A Research Framework." *Journal of Management Information Systems* 35, no.2 (May): 388–423. https://doi.org/10.1080/07421222.2018.1451951.

Guembe, Blessing, Ambrose Azeta, Sanjay Misra, Victor Chukwudi Osamor, Luis Fernandez-Sanz, and Vera Pospelova. "The Emerging Threat of AI-driven Cyberattacks: A Review." *Applied Artificial Intelligence* 1, no.36 (January): 2037254. https://doi.org/10.1080/08839514.2022.2037254

Gupta, Manish, and Raj Sharman. 2012. "Determinants of Data Breaches: A Categorization-Based Empirical Investigation." *Journal of Applied Security Research* 7, no.3 (July): 375–95. https://doi.org/10.1080/19361610.2012.686098.

Hiller, Janine S., and Roberta S. Russell. 2013. "The Challenge and Imperative of Private Sector Cybersecurity: An International Comparison." *Computer Law & Security Review* 29, no.3 (June): 236–45. https://doi.org/10.1016/j.clsr.2013.03.003.

Home office. 2018. "Understanding the Costs of Cyber Crime." https://assets.publishing.service.gov.uk/government/uploads/system/uploads/attachment_data/file/674046/understanding-costs-of-cyber-crime-horr96.pdf.

Jaganathan, Venkatesh, Priyesh Cherurveettil, and Premapriya Muthu Sivashanmugam. 2015. "Using a Prediction Model to Manage Cybersecurity Threats." *The Scientific World Journal* 2015 (May): e703713. https://doi.org/10.1155/2015/703713.

Jana, Dipak Kumar, and Ramkrishna Ghosh. 2018. "Novel Interval Type-2 Fuzzy Logic Controller for Improving Risk Assessment Model of Cybersecurity." *Journal of Information Security and Applications* 40 (June): 173–82. https://doi.org/10.1016/j.jisa.2018.04.002.

Juma'h, Ahmad H., and Yazan Alnsour. 2020. 'The Effect of Data Breaches on Company Performance." *International Journal of Accounting and Information Management* 28, no.2 (April): 275–301. https://doi.org.manchester.idm.oclc.org/10.1108/IJAIM-01-2019-0006.

Kamiya, Shinichi, Jun-Koo Kang, Jungmin Kim, Andreas Milidonis, and René M. Stulz. 2021. "Risk Management, Firm Reputation, and the Impact of Successful Cyberattacks on Target Firms." *Journal of Financial Economics* 139, no.3 (March): 719–49. https://doi.org/10.1016/j.jfineco.2019.05.019.

Kappelman, Leon, Vess Johnson, Russell Torres, Chris Maurer, and Ephraim McLean. 2019. "A Study of Information Systems Issues, Practices, and Leadership in Europe." *European Journal of Information Systems* 28, no.1 (July): 26–42. https://doi.org/10.1080/0960085X.2018.1497929.

Kitchenham, Barbara, O. Pearl Brereton, David Budgen, Mark Turner, John Bailey, and Stephen Linkman. 2009. "Systematic Literature Reviews in Software Engineering – A Systematic Literature Review." *Information and Software Technology* 51, no.1 (January): 7–15. https://doi.org/10.1016/j.infsof.2008.09.009.

Kjaerland, Maria. 2006. "A Taxonomy and Comparison of Computer Security Incidents from the Commercial and Government Sectors." *Computers & Security* 25, no.7 (October): 522–38. https://doi.org/10.1016/j.cose.2006.08.004.

Kotenko, Igor, and Elena Doynikova. 2018. "Selection of Countermeasures against Network Attacks Based on Dynamical Calculation of Security Metrics." *The Journal of Defense Modeling and Simulation* 15, no.2 (March): 181–204. https://doi.org/10.1177/1548512917690278.

Lagazio, Monica, Nazneen Sherif, and Mike Cushman. 2014. "A Multi-Level Approach to Understanding the Impact of Cyber Crime on the Financial Sector." *Computers & Security* 45, no.9 (September): 58–74. https://doi.org/10.1016/j.cose.2014.05.006.

Layton, Robert, and Paul A. Watters. 2014. "A Methodology for Estimating the Tangible Cost of Data Breaches." *Journal of Information Security and Applications* 19, no.6 (December): 321–30. https://doi.org/10.1016/j.jisa.2014.10.012.

Lee, In. 2021. "Cybersecurity: Risk Management Framework and Investment Cost Analysis." *Business Horizons* 64, no.5 (February): 659–671. https://doi.org/10.1016/j.bushor.2021.02.022.

Leszczyna, Rafał. 2013. "Cost Assessment of Computer Security Activities." *Computer Fraud & Security* 2013, no.7 (July): 11–16. https://doi.org/10.1016/S1361–3723(13)70063-0.

Makridis, Christos, and Benjamin Dean. 2018. "Measuring the Economic Effects of Data Breaches on Firm Outcomes: Challenges and Opportunities." *Journal of Economic & Social Measurement* 43, no.1 (October): 59–83. https://doi.org/10.3233/JEM-180450.

Morse, Edward A., Vasant Raval, and John R. Wingender. 2011. "Market Price Effects of Data Security Breaches." *Information Security Journal: A Global Perspective* 20, no.6 (November): 263–73. https://doi.org/10.1080/19393555.2011.611860.

OECD. 2020. "OECD Digital Economy Outlook 2020." www.oecd-ilibrary.org/sites/bb167041-en/index.html?itemId=/content/publication/bb167041-en.

Paoli, Letizia, Jonas Visschers, and Cedric Verstraete. 2018. "The Impact of Cybercrime on Businesses: A Novel Conceptual Framework and Its Application to Belgium." *Crime, Law and Social Change* 70, no.4 (May): 397–420. https://doi.org.manchester.idm.oclc.org/10.1007/s10611-018-9774-y.

Rees, Loren Paul, Jason K. Deane, Terry R. Rakes, and Wade H. Baker. 2011. "Decision Support for Cybersecurity Risk Planning." *Decision Support Systems* 51, no.3 (June): 493–505. https://doi.org/10.1016/j.dss.2011.02.013.

Russell, Gavin. 2017. "Resisting the Persistent Threat of Cyberattacks." *Computer Fraud & Security* 2017, no.12 (December): 7–11. https://doi.org/10.1016/S1361-3723(17)30107-0.

Schatz, Daniel, and Rabih Bashroush. 2016. "The Impact of Repeated Data Breach Events on Organisations' Market Value." *Information and Computer Security* 24, no.1 (March): 73–92. https://dx.doi.org.manchester.idm.oclc.org/10.1108/ICS-03-2014-0020.

Smith, Alan D. 2004. "Cybercriminal Impacts on Online Business and Consumer Confidence." *Online Information Review* 28, no.3 (June): 224–34. https://doi.org/10.1108/14684520410543670.

Smith, Katherine Taken, Amie Jones, Leigh Johnson, and Lawrence Murphy Smith. 2019. "Examination of Cybercrime and Its Effects on Corporate Stock Value." *Journal of Information, Communication & Ethics in Society* 18, no.1 (March): 42–60. https://doi.org.manchester.idm.oclc.org/10.1108/JICES-02-2018-0010.

Sonnenreich, Wes, Jason Albanese, and Bruce Stout. 2006. "Return on Security Investment (ROSI) – A Practical Quantitative Model." *Journal of Research and Practice in IT* 38, no.1 (January): 45–56. https://doi.org/10.3316/ielapa.937199632104879.

Srinidhi, Bin, Jia Yan, and Giri Kumar Tayi. 2015. "Allocation of Resources to Cyber-Security: The Effect of Misalignment of Interest between Managers and Investors." *Decision Support Systems* 75 (July): 49–62. https://doi.org/10.1016/j.dss.2015.04.011.

Tariq, Nida. 2018. "Impact of Cyberattacks on Financial Institutions." *Journal of Internet Banking and Commerce* 23, no.2 (February): 1–11. www.icommercecentral.com/open-access/impact-of-cyberattacks-on-financial-institutions.php?aid=87130

Weintraub, Eli. 2017. "Quantifying Integrity Impacts in Security Risk Scoring Models." *International Journal of Advanced Computer Science and Applications* 8, no.12 (December): 233–39. https://doi.org/10.14569/IJACSA.2017.081229.

Winder, Davey, and Ian Trump. 2015. "Mitigating Cybercrime Through Meaningful Measurement Methodologies." *EDPACS* 52, no.5 (December): 1–8. https://doi.org/10.1080/07366981.2015.1113058.

14 Problems and Ethical Issues in Cybersecurity Today
Some Critical Readings

Maximiliano E. Korstanje

CONTENTS

INTRODUCTION

I'll explain to readers a personal situation I experienced a couple of days back. It describes with some clarity the essence and limitations of cyber-security and its importance for daily life. I was at home when I received an email message delivered from the economics faculty dean asking "revise esto por favor y decime tu opinion [please review this for me and reply your feedback]." When I double-clicked the marked link, a virus infected my personal computer, corrupting all word processing files. A couple of days back, I had sent my two pending books to the publishers, so it was not a complete disaster, but what is more important, all my files were encrypted and simply emptied. This nightmare begs a more than perplexing question: how may we understand cyber-security and its real effects in daily life?

Over recent years, cybersecurity has occupied a central position in journals, PhD dissertations, conferences, books, and journal articles. Anonymous (an unknown global hacker group who reached fame in 2003) has perpetrated several cyberattacks on different networks to date. Without any doubt, the question of cyber-security has become a priority for governments worldwide (Korstanje 2015; Strang, Korstanje & Vajjhala 2018). As Singer and Friedman (2014) put it, the internet is no longer a thing that facilitates email delivery; it is an essential part of our lives. Having said this, cyber-security risk seems to be one of the major priorities and challenges of governments in the 21st century. Countries are devoting considerable efforts and resources to enhancing cybersecurity or – if needed – disconnecting the worldwide internet (Cavelty 2010; O'Connell 2012). Cybersecurity speaks to us of a new stage of costless war mainly marked by the lack and displacement of troops. In this vein, cyberwar and cybersecurity have not only pressed representatives to issue a set of bills to legislate "cyber stuff" but to interrogate democratic culture as never before. Just after the attacks on the World Trade Center, the declaration of war against terrorism (known as the War on Terror) by Bush's administration, Assange's leaks, and Snowden's scandal, not to mention the manipulation of Trump's election, digital technologies are deployed not only to scrutinize lay citizens but spying embassies and other foreign administrations. The culture of fear not only dominates US politics but also affects the functioning of the checks-and-balances institutions which mainly characterized American democracy (Altheide 2014; Skoll 2014; O'Connell 2012). In consonance with this, Bauman and Lyon (2013) coined the term "liquid surveillance" to denote a new state of alarmism and fear ignited by terrorism. Based on the Marxian premise that all solids melt in the air, the authors

DOI: 10.1201/9781003319887-14

acknowledge that in the *liquid society*, security occupies a central position. Per their viewpoint, e-surveillance acts in two main directions. On the one hand, it provides people with an ontological state of security while portraying the external world as dangerous. On the other, it marks a new (privileged) class of citizens who have something important to be protected. The disposition of electronic instruments to monitor the office, home, or any property denotes an adscription to privileged status in a world where a whole portion of citizens certainly lives below the poverty line. What is more important, under some conditions, technology not only affects the agency's autonomy but also affirms what scholars dubbed "Perrow's paradox."

Charles Perrow (1977) postulated that for each accident that occurs, almost seven similar events happened in the past. Disasters are often seen as catastrophic events that can be avoided, but this does not happen. Disasters follow specific dynamics originally determined by the social background. This suggests that rules and security protocols do not provide real efficiency of the organization. He used the term "bureaucratic paradox" to explain that workers' behavior daily deviates from the end of maximizing their gains but paradoxically runs the risk of future accidents. As he eloquently observes, efficient organizations decentralize their forms of production. The urgency to maximize gains leads organizations to deviant behavior, raising the probability of new accidents. Max Weber's works went in a similar direction. As Weber envisaged, bureaucracy cemented a set of rules and regulations to grease the rails of production. These bureaucracies invariably fall short wreaking havoc on the involved organization. This point will be addressed with more clarity in the next sections.

As the previous argument is given, the present book chapter critically discusses the philosophical dilemmas revolving around cybersecurity and digital technology while laying the foundations for a new understanding of the phenomenon. Technology has pros and cons. It generates more efficient forms of communication but is packaged and automated for critical reasoning. Hence, one of the contradictions of technology is that it generates mechanical behavior, which makes the system more vulnerable to unexpected attacks. Doubtless this is one of the topics the classic literature in cyberspace and cybersecurity undermines. To fill the gap, this chapter deals with Weber and Perrow's paradoxes to give readers a clear diagnosis of this deep-seated issue. The first part critically discusses the role of technology and technological society in forming the sensibility of a new audience sensitive to mass information. At the same time, we hold the thesis – echoing Virilio, Baudrillard, and Ellul – that under some conditions, technology enhances the vulnerability of society. The second section is limited to what we named "the paradoxes of bureaucracy," which means a novel emerging situation where the planning process originally oriented to protect society against global risks leads us irreversibly to a state of disaster.

TECHNOLOGY AND CYBERSPACE

One of the critical voices in the fields of technology has been French philosopher Jacques Ellul. In his viewpoint, technology not only had long-lasting but also devastating effects on society. Technology mediates between citizens and social institutions while interacting with politics and religion. It behooves us to consider that the adoption of technology generates new forms of alienated consumption that displace religion to a peripheral position. Nowadays, it invariably works as a regulator of class or status quo. By this token, there is a dialectical relation between what he named "the technique" and social agency. Having said this, he is mainly worried about the triumph of the technique and the possibility of technological tyranny surfacing. Ellul notably questioned what the act of living in a technological society means. TFor Ellul, the problem does not lie in the machine but in the rational reasoning and protocols created to create automated behavior. Through the division of labor, technology enhances efficiency while undermining human autonomy. The set of protocols and regulations deployed to achieve absolute efficiency recreates the conditions of an artificial system which is designed to subordinate – if not eradicate – the natural world.

In consequence, knowledge production and modern education emerged as training processes that facilitate the decoding of and access to information. As Ellul remarks, the original goals of schools were to prepare young people to deal successfully with the world of information while being able to work with computers and understand their reasoning. Modern technology becomes a sacred phenomenon for our civilization but at the same time its main hazard (Ellul 1962, 1992, 2018, 2021). The paradoxes of technology rest on its capacity to clone reality, not only fabricating a pseudo-reality but also imagined landscapes. Of course, Ellul's legacy was a source of inspiration for many thinkers and philosophers over decades (Jerónimo et al. 2013; Mitcham & Mackey 1971). Similar remarks have been introduced by Paul Virilio and Jean Baudrillard – both leading philosophers who debated the role and effects of technology in modern society. For Baudrillard, technology moves in a climate of mistrust and individualism recreated by a pseudo-reality. For the sake of clarity, he mentions Spielberg's film *Minority Report*, where the Chicago police arrest criminals before a crime has been committed. The Precogs are a type of mutants who are supported by high digital technology to envisage the future. As Baudrillard notes, the same applies to modernity, where risks are fabricated and globally consumed, but they never happen as they have been imagined. Technological society is mainly oriented to a future while eradicating history. At the same time, historical events (facts) set the pace for *pseudo-events* culturally rooted in the future.

The paradox of technology rests on the fact that the system expands, but at the same time, it recedes. Centered on the principle of reversibility, Baudrillard understands that technology not only creates pseudo-realities but also erodes the core of society (Baudrillard 2006). To this end, Paul Virilio holds a similar thesis. It is difficult to resist the impression that technology emancipates the autonomy of human agency. Rather, as he asserts, modern technology has initiated a revolution in transport means which created an excess of time for humans. This excess – far from being empty for leisure purposes – is filled by propaganda and media consumption. The question of whether the Enlightenment saw in science a valid pathway towards human emancipation has been diluted. Science is not only a slave of the liberal market; it is subservient to profits and businesses. As a result of this, humanity is being closed to alienated forms of consumption sustained by the media igniting fear as a form of relationship. For Virilio, cyberspace is not an exception. It regulates human relations to a fixed matrix mainly marked by solipsism and radical transformations of geography: to be more exact, a much deeper transformation of the geographical space (Virilio 2006, 2010, 2012). Equally important, Arturo Escobar et al. (1994) argue that cyberculture reflects specifically the surface of new digital technologies in two main domains: biotechnology and artificial intelligence.

Not surprisingly, their prominence nowadays is determined by the expansion of modern capitalism and the urgency to regulate the workforce. In this respect, cyberculture moves in the arenas of specific discourses, sensibilities, and narrative embodying the self in a rigid cultural matrix. Technology, in this way, opens the doors to new social network institutions and a negotiated construction of reality (Escobar et al. 1994). With the benefits of hindsight, De Mul (2010) suggests that technology survives because of inventions, which give products the opportunity to continue no matter their original function. The question of cyberspace engages the self with hybridized spaces of relations while changing its nature. That is to say, part of what is of interest for humans is decentralized and transferred to virtual environments, but once done, the geographical place melts into the virtual logic. Cyberspace today penetrates and modifies the self, as well as its engagement with time and space.

Exceeding our capacities and skills in the real world, cyberspace offers not only a place beyond our daily life but the possibility to construct a new reality (de Mul 2010). Beyond this discrepancy, sociologists of cyberspace have recently developed mix-balanced argumentation (Kollock & Smith 1995; Turkle 1999; Lyon 1997; Deibert & Rohozinski 2010). For example, Monica Whitty and Adrian Carr (2006) analyze cyberspace romance as a limonoid object that conditions human relationships. Based on Winnicot's contributions, they overtly say that cyberspace mitigates the psychological frustrations of life, offering an alternative experience where the self is not only recomforted but renegotiated. Offline relations are inspired in a type of self-disclosed space that allows people to be honest with others. There is a type of benign disinhibition which leads people to reveal much deeper fears, secret emotions, or frustrated dreams. Cyberspace builds the foundation for an actual self, which is ongoingly negotiated with others; some psychologists toy with the belief that this actual self should be pitted against a true self. For Whitty and Carr, cyberspace represents a playful space that often liberates users while placating their anxieties and frustrations. Anyway, the freedom in this space can be problematic when users go too far beyond the realm of fantasy. Cyberspace speaks to us of two important aspects of capitalism.

First is the rational and individual choice to interact with others or move freely in a virtual space. Second and most important, this freedom ushers some persons into deviant or criminal behavior or acts bordering irrationality. Whatever the case may be, psychology should struggle to embrace an all-encompassing theory that explains with some accuracy cyber-relating. Cyberspace molds specifics-based social identities; even multiple identities inscribe in the process of social reproduction. Having said this, the implication of cyberspaces in the negotiation of identity moves on multiple levels. Beyond inter-class inequalities, cyberspace reaffirms already existent imbalances. Digital technology divides society into two: those who can engage with technology and those excluded from the system that lack the necessary basic information and access to online communities (Wilson & Peterson 2002). This led William S. Bainbridge (1999) to argue convincingly that cyberspace offers a fertile ground for implementing new methods in sociological research. It further interrogates the formation of a new (digital) social identity where users move in a climate dominated by mobilities. At the same time, he warns that digital metrics lay the preconditions for consumers to be segmented, tailored (if not commoditized) by their psychological profile, much deeper drives, and needs.

Cyberspace – far from being a unilateral entity – emerged as a complex combination of factors. The end of WWII, associated with the interest of leading universities like MIT or Stanford in creating a net of communication, as well as the rise of computer hardware and software production, resulted in the triumph of cyberspace as a relational place (Whittaker 2003). In consonance with this, Adams and Warf (1997) discuss the nature and evolution of cyberspace as inevitably linked to a state of dependency on information production. The urgency to deal with and administer mass information in a consuming society has invariably led to the adoption of technological determinism that ultimately changed the sense of geographical space. To some extent, the figure of the internet reflects not only the economic asymmetries between the Global North and South but also some long-dormant disparities in the military power of nations. Echoing this, Manuel Castells calls attention to *an information society* which re-organizes the economic production and social relations. Based on the idea of collective action, he holds that modern societies are structured in a bipolar logic between the self and the net. While the net signals specific-centered organizations that change the integrated hierarchies, the latter refers to the practices exerted by a person to get a social identity. As Castells anticipated, in the Age of information, the self can liberate one's skills and intellectual autonomy, but it increases the risks of resource exhaustion. The generated information serves to protect the autonomy of the digital self but paradoxically disperses it into multiple dimensions and stages. Not surprisingly, industrialism has been replaced by *information*, which marks the hegemony of media information (Castells 1997, 1999, 2010).

Finally, John Naisbitt (1994, 1996) speaks to us about a "global paradox" entirely given by the expansion of transport means and the globalization process. Per his stance, technology played a leading role in expanding the borders of capitalism to the four corners of the globe, but in so doing, it lays the foundations for a new fragility conditioned by interaction (and competence) among countless small players. A new global scenario recreates the conditions for new more unstable competitions mainly marked by negotiations of many virtual tribes. In late global capitalism, mega-corporations become more important but paradoxically more vulnerable to the climate of political fragmentation as well as instability. This happens simply because the ever-changing intervention of small players makes the decision-making process more complex (Lloyd & Naisbitt, 1994). This point will be explained in detail in the next section.

PARADOXES OF BUREAUCRACY AND GLOBAL RISKS

In his seminal book *Risk Society*, Ulrich Beck (1992) introduces readers to the logic of reflexive modernization. This process opens the doors to a new dynamic where laypeople interrogate the net of experts. The capitalist system entered a new stage dubbed the "risk society." In this vein, risk society is the natural evolution of industrialism. Its origins can be traced back to the Chernobyl disaster (Ukraine) in 1986. This foundational event marked a new era where nobody felt safe any time or anywhere. One of the lessons and paradoxes given by this event is that nuclear technology, which theoretically was designed to make people's lives safer – given some conditions – becomes a global danger that may very well eradicate humankind. In a global society, where classes are gradually evaporating, humans are put in equal conditions to disasters. As Beck insists, the production of risk is inversely proportional to the wealth distribution.

For the sake of clarity, a combination of global risks creates a collective course of actions which exceed individual reactions. At a first glimpse, the risk society engenders radical shifts of major caliber following the increasing materiality and empowerment of productive forces. As social constructs engulfed in the communication process, risks derive directly from economic development. To put it bluntly, economic growth paved the way for the rise of complex unexpected situations that policymakers fail to deal with – a least successfully – and exceeding the capacity of society to respond. In consequence, one of the paradoxes of late modernity consists in some minor risks being magnified, while major ones are simply overlooked. It is not simplistic to say that the accumulation of ignored minor risks leads society to the doorstep of disaster. At the same time, the liberal market offers multiple products available to mitigate global risks. The quest for security accelerates a deep technological revolution that invariably ends with the multiplication of major risks. Beck's legacy sheds light not only on the risk paradox but also on the pervasive role of technology and its effects in daily life. Another important point of entry in this debate was certainly given by senior sociologist Cass Sunstein, who holds the thesis that the net of experts is subject to human emotionality, which obscures the decision-making process.

Even when educated and trained to deal with risks, experts often fail to implement successful protocols of security simply because some risks are not correctly evaluated. Sunstein reminds us that humans are subject to irrational emotions, which lead them to exaggerate some risks, while others are simply undermined. Here two elements are of vital importance to describe the process: the heuristic of probability neglect and the cascades of risks. The heuristic of probability neglect signals cognitive distortions orchestrated by the human capacity to rely on different events (disasters) as unilaterally caused by the same factor. Rather, the cascade of risks refers to those distortions explained by the over-simplification of some major risks, while others are systematically magnified (Sunstein 2002, 2005; Kuran & Sunstein 1998; Sunstein & Zeckhauser 2011).

Although from different angles, both scholars (Beck and Sunstein) lay their fingers on the paradox of risk perception. At this point, they deserve our attention and academic recognition. However, the contradictions of modern technology in risk management can be very well understood by returning to the classic texts. Max Weber, it is important not to forget, has made a seminal contribution to the understanding of modern bureaucracy and how the received rules determine future accidents. Weber is today considered one of the founding parents of modern sociology, even though he was a lawyer, not a sociologist in the strict sense of the word. Like Pareto or Durkheim, he was originally obsessed with answering the question of how society stays united. He distinguished social cohesion according to three clear-cut categories (he called them logics): a) traditional authority, b) legal authority, and c) charismatic authority. These are not only sources of authority but legitimate types of social cohesions. The legal authority (of the rule) is certainly based on a system of protocols conducted administratively because of legal issues. Those agents who administer legal authority not only are elected by specific processes and protocols, but they often avoid being governed by others. This is the logic of political authority. Traditional authority is given by a legitimate background which is inherited in a patrilineal regime. This is the rule of kings, princes, or queens. Last, charismatic authority emanates from the charisma of a leader who commands the people through outstanding skills, heroism, and prophecies (Weber 1964). As Weber clarifies, these three types are shifted in time, alternating even in the same organization. He gives the example of the death of the charismatic leader whose legacy is continued by his followers while imposing a bureaucratic regime or a new regime centered on tradition. Their authority is based on the power of the law, not charisma.

These followers not only lack the leader's charisma, but sooner or later they are confronted by a new charismatic leader. Charismatic leadership is certainly emerging in the context of crises or disasters. The construction of bureaucracy is carefully designed to manage external and internal problems (dangers), and if it works efficiently, the traditional authority consolidates. Anyway, unexpected events not only affect the system but also put it in jeopardy, opening the doors to the rise of a new charismatic authority. This cycle goes on and never ends. As Weber explains, these unexpected events are unpredictable simply because the system operates in a set of combined (fixed) rules and a much deep impenetrable legitimacy (Weber 1964; Spencer 1970; Rust 2021). Here is where one of the paradoxes of bureaucracy lies. As Perrow (1977) eloquently noted, the system needs bureaucracy to survive, but in so doing, it runs serious risks of being destroyed in the future.

This exactly explains the effects of viruses and cyberattacks on global systems. It is important not to lose sight of the fact that the first factor which underlies cyberattacks seems to be trust and intimacy. Like the anecdote mentioned at the start of this chapter, the virus intruded once I received an email from a familiar person. Having said this, hackers often target different email accounts as part of massive attacks. The account is also kidnapped and controlled by hackers who write to friends, relatives, and colleagues in the name of the account holder. The hacked email delivers a message to a wider net formed by thousands of people. Like a Trojan horse, once the person clicks on the marked link, a virus infects the computer. Some of these viruses locate vital information of credit cards to commit fraud, while others are designed to corrupt some or all files. What is more important, these cyberattacks work because beyond antiviruses or programs for cyber-security, all information is stored in the same place. This is doubtless the paradox of cybersecurity: once the attack is perpetrated, the costs and generated damage are too high. Starting from the premise that cyber-security rests on a digital bureaucracy formed not only by antivirus software as well as firewalls, or security protocols, no less true is it that an unexpected attack threatens the system. This reminds me of Marc Foster's film *World War Z*: the moment when Garry Lane (Brad Pitt) flies to Israel and successfully manages a quarantine by building a large wall. Israel – as a hosting country – welcomes hundreds of refugees coming from all countries in search of hospitality. Garry realizes that the loud celebratory singing from the refugees has attracted the attention of zombies who ultimately breach the walls. The rest is a real nightmare; zombies enter Jerusalem, which is quickly overrun. This example reminds us exactly what happens with planned cyberattacks.

The second element which should be debated is the password. Anthropologically speaking, the password is an arbitrary string of characters which confirms the user's identity or protects specific information. The password is meant to protect the user's secrecy. Here, the figure of a password can be very well equated to a passport. Both are instrumentalized to protect the user's (holder's) identity. The third element is the surprise factor. The affected person never imagines he or she will be a target of a cyberattack. The surprise factor tends to ignite radical shifts in the rules of the system. New cyberattacks start with new anti-virus software or firewalls which, once created, attract the attention of hackers, who will devote considerable efforts to breaching them. One of the paradoxes of digital technologies is given by the fact that all information is put together in the same place. In the medieval age, information was certainly given by books. Authors and books which were considered dangerous for the king or the church were simply killed or burned. Censorship played a leading role in the medieval social imaginary, preventing potential riots. For instance, handwritten books contained in libraries, which were dispersed across Europe, were the source of knowledge in medieval times. With the invention of print, as well as other technological breakthroughs, produced knowledge tended to be centralized in a few hands. Paradoxically, censorship set the pace for the excess of information.

To put things more clearly, if I try to understand Karl Marx's legacy using Google, I will find almost 1,300,000 entries, including books, papers, conferences, and documents. The limitations of our mind lead us to absorb only a small portion of such information. In the digital society, censorship seems not to be necessary; rather the excess of circulated information keeps citizens' minds behind the veil of ignorance. Whatever the case may be, circulated information is all stored on the same platform, centralized in a few circuits and channels. Once the platform is made vulnerable, the king is checkmated.

CONCLUSION

This chapter has interrogated further the paradox of cyber-security, which punctuates the state of fragility that shows current cybersecurity protocols. Although analysts and policymakers have advanced a lot in the creation of anti-virus software, firewalls, and cyber-security protocols, not less true is that the paradoxical situation is far from being resolved. At the time we move to strengthen cyber-security, the risks of suffering a devastating attack are higher. Charles Perrow and Max Weber have theorized the paradox of bureaucracy monopolized by the modern national state. Their contributions are not only clear but also help us understand the limits and challenges revolving around cybersecurity. Last but not least, the dilemmas of cyber-security rest on two main aspects which need to be revised. On the one hand, technology operates in the fields of produced and circulated knowledge while creating nets of exchange. Unlike in medieval times, where the produced information was certainly dispersed (at libraries), in modern times, information is centralized and stored in a few circuits, which, once compromised, put the system on the brink of collapse. On the other hand, the obsession with a zero-risk society leads us to recreate a strong bureaucracy, mainly marked by traditional authority and the multiplication of rules. Paradoxically, this bureaucracy gives us a false sense of security (if not stability), which undermines our critical reasoning. Of course, the success of modern bureaucracy in dealing with minor risks placates what we dubbed "the natural alert," an instrument that helps us to avoid the state of disaster. At the same time, as more protocols are created, the natural alert becomes weaker. As debated, the question of cyberspace has not only confronted the geographical sense but also has created a real revolution in the creation and dissemination of information. To what extent cybersecurity will give answers to the paradoxes of modern bureaucracy and technology remains unclear – at least for us. In this direction, Jacques Ellul, Jean Baudrillard, and classic sociology (in Max Weber's hands) provide us with a clear diagnosis of the problem.

REFERENCES

Adams, P. C., & Warf, B. (1997). Introduction: Cyberspace and geographical space. *Geographical Review*, 87(2), 139–145.

Altheide, D. L. (2014). The triumph of fear: Connecting the dots about whistleblowers and surveillance. *International Journal of Cyber Warfare and Terrorism (IJCWT)*, 4(1), 1–7.

Bainbridge, W. (1999). Cyberspace: Sociology's natural domain. *Contemporary Sociology*, 28(1), 664–672.

Baudrillard, J. (2006). Virtuality and events: The hell of power. *Baudrillard Studies*, 3(2), 1–10.

Bauman, Z., & Lyon, D. (2013). *Liquid surveillance: A conversation*. New York: John Wiley & Sons.

Beck, U. (1992). *Risk society: Towards a new modernity* (Vol. 17). London: SAGE.

Castells, M. (1997). An introduction to the information age. *City*, 2(7), 6–16.

Castells, M. (1999). *Information technology, globalization and social development* (Vol. 114). Geneva: UNRISD.

Castells, M. (2010). The information age. *Media Studies: A Reader*, 2(7), 152–160.

Cavelty, M. D. (2010). Cyber-security. In P. Burgess (Ed.), *The Routledge handbook of new security studies* (pp. 154–162). Abingdon: Routledge.

Deibert, R. J., & Rohozinski, R. (2010). Risking security: Policies and paradoxes of cyberspace security. *International Political Sociology*, 4(1), 15–32.

De Mul, J. (2010). *Cyberspace odyssey: Towards a virtual ontology and anthropology*. Newcastle upon Tyne: Cambridge Scholars Publishing.

Ellul, J. (1962). The technological order. *Technology and Culture*, 3(4), 394–421.

Ellul, J. (1992). Technology and democracy. In *Democracy in a technological society* (pp. 35–50). Dordrecht: Springer.

Ellul, J. (2018). *The technological system*. London: Wipf and Stock Publishers.

Ellul, J. (2021). *The technological society*. London: Vintage.

Escobar, A., Hess, D., Licha, I., Sibley, W., Strathern, M., & Sutz, J. (1994). Welcome to cyberia: Notes on the anthropology of cyberculture [and comments and reply]. *Current Anthropology*, 35(3), 211–231.

Jerónimo, H. M., Garcia, J. L., & Mitcham, C. (Eds.). (2013). *Jacques Ellul and the technological society in the 21st century* (p. 21). Dordrecht: Springer.

Kollock, P., & Smith, M. (1995). *The sociology of cyberspace: Social interaction and order in computer communities*. Thousand Oaks: Pine Forge.

Korstanje, M. E (2015). *A difficult World: examining the roots of capitalism*. Hauppauge: Nova Science Publishers.

Kuran, T., & Sunstein, C. R. (1998). Availability cascades and risk regulation. *Stanford Law Review, 51*, 683.

Lloyd, B., & Naisbitt, J. (1994). Megatrends and global paradoxes. *Management Decision, 32*(7), 28–32.

Lyon, D. (1997). Cyberspace sociality. *The Governance of Cyberspace, Abingdon, Routledge*, 23–37.

Mitcham, C., & Mackey, R. (1971). Jacques Ellul and the technological society. *Philosophy Today, 15*(2), 102–121.

Naisbitt, J. (1994). Global paradox: The bigger the world economy, the more powerful its smallest players. *Journal of Leisure Research, 26*(4), 406–415.

Naisbitt, J. (1996). Global paradox. *Futures-the Journal of Forecasting Planning and Policy, 28*(1), 91–95.

O'Connell, M. E. (2012). Cybersecurity without cyber war. *Journal of Conflict and Security Law, 17*(2), 187–209.

Perrow, C. (1977). The bureaucratic paradox: The efficient organization centralizes in order to decentralize. *Organizational Dynamics, 5*(4), 3–14.

Rust, J. (2021). Max Weber and social ontology. *Philosophy of the Social Sciences, 51*(3), 312–342.

Singer, P. W., & Friedman, A. (2014). *Cybersecurity: What everyone needs to know*. Oxford: Oxford University Press.

Skoll, G. R. (2014). Stealing consciousness: Using cybernetics for controlling populations. *International Journal of Cyber Warfare and Terrorism (IJCWT), 4*(1), 27–35.

Spencer, M. E. (1970). Weber on legitimate norms and authority. *The British Journal of Sociology, 21*(2), 123–134.

Strang, K., Korstanje, M. E., & Vajjhala, N. R. (2018). *Research, Practices and innovations in global risks and contingency management*. Hershey: IGI Global.

Sunstein, C. R. (2002). *Risk and reason: Safety, law, and the environment*. Cambridge: Cambridge University Press.

Sunstein, C. R. (2005). *Laws of fear: Beyond the precautionary principle*. Cambridge: Cambridge University Press.

Sunstein, C. R., & Zeckhauser, R. (2011). Overreaction to fearsome risks. *Environmental and Resource Economics, 48*(3), 435–449.

Turkle, S. (1999). Looking toward cyberspace: Beyond grounded sociology. *Contemporary Sociology, 28*(6), 643–648.

Virilio, P. (2006). *Art and fear*. London: A&C Black.

Virilio, P. (2010). *University of disaster*. Cambridge: Polity Press.

Virilio, P. (2012). *The administration of fear* (Vol. 10). Cambridge: MIT Press.

Weber M (1964). *The theory of social and economic organization*. New York: The Free Press.

Whittaker, J. (2003). Mapping cyberspace. In J. Whittaker (Ed.), *The Cyberspace Handbook* (pp. 2–14). London: Routledge.

Whitty, M. T., & Carr, A. N. (2006). *Cyberspace romance: The psychology of online relationships*. London, UK: Palgrave Macmillan. https://doi.org/10.1007/978-0-230-20856-8

Wilson, S. M., & Peterson, L. C. (2002). The anthropology of online communities. *Annual Review of Anthropology*, 449–467.

15 An Empirical Investigation of Psychological Factors Affecting Compliance with Information Security Organizational Policies

Tatyana Ryutov

CONTENTS

DOI: 10.1201/9781003319887-15

INTRODUCTION

The frequency, scope, and cost of data breaches have been increasing dramatically in recent years. A primary strategy for addressing security threats to an organization's information resources is to develop and enforce a comprehensive information security policy (ISP). Typical security policies designed to mitigate user-based risks include: (1) data protection, (2) limiting installation of software unrelated to work on organizational mobile devices, (3) retrieval or remote wipe of organizational data from personal mobile devices upon employee termination or loss of a device, (4) password complexity and periodic password updates, (5) screen-lock timeouts, (6) requiring up-to-date firmware and application patches for system operation, (7) mandatory user training to recognize phishing attempts, and (8) non-disclosure of organizational information.

Employees can be required to agree to an organization's ISPs, yet such policies are of limited value unless they are sufficiently enforced. Due to current technological and social trends, verification and enforcement of user compliance with ISPs have become increasingly challenging. For example, the proliferation of mobile devices has led to employees subscribing to "bring your own device" trends (Miller et al., 2012). The result is decreased transparency of user activities and less control over the security of these devices (Hashizume et al., 2013). Similarly, there is little to stop users from sharing information about an organization via social media. At the same time, monitoring social media sites to analyze employees' activity may be not only laborious but also not legally permissible (Putchala, 2013). Consequently, policy enforcement increasingly depends on user awareness, responsibility, and compliance.

Although information security managers recognize that security risks often arise from employees' decisions and behavior, their insights on what shapes employees' compliance with ISPs are frequently limited. Therefore, a detailed understanding of factors that motivate employees to comply with organizations' various ISPs is central to helping information security managers diagnose and mitigate user-based security risks. The goal of this chapter is to provide more insight into the motivational factors applicable to ISPs and their influence on end-user behavior and to offer a theoretical explanation and practical recommendations. This chapter begins with the discussion of the current research on user-based risks. Next, it presents a theoretical model for intentions to comply with ISPs and the methodology used to test the model. The chapter continues with presentation and analysis of the results. Finally, it discusses the practical implications of the results.

PROBLEM RATIONALE AND RESEARCH QUESTION

Simply having a well-documented set of policies and procedures is insufficient to deter information security breaches (Safa & Ismail, 2013). Studies showed that most security problems are caused by employees' non-compliance behavior or violation of the ISPs of their organizations (Myyry et al., 2009). Past studies have found that security behavior is influenced by several factors (discussed in the next section). However, the link between intention to comply and actual compliance behavior has not been sufficiently examined. A better understanding of factors that motivate employees to comply with organizations' ISPs is imperative in helping information security managers diagnose and mitigate user-based security risks. Several motivational factors influence the intentions of end-users to comply with their organization's ISP. However, it is unclear which factors are the most relevant for which risk types.

Advancing existing knowledge, the goals of this chapter are to (1) examine stronger measures of compliance behavior; (2) rather than examining ISP compliance as a single homogenous construct, investigate heterogeneity among key types of user-based security risks; and (3) provide practical recommendations. In this chapter, we research the following questions:

1. *What factors relate, in which degree, to intentions to comply with each of the key types of ISPs?*
2. *Based on these insights, what organizational practices are needed to promote end-user compliance with the ISP?*

The intended audience for this work is anyone making security decisions in an organization, such as security managers and practitioners.

LITERATURE REVIEW

USER-BASED RISKS IN ORGANIZATIONAL SETTINGS

Employees' non-compliance with workplace ISPs plays a major role in security breaches in organizations (AlKalbani et al., 2014; Ullah et al., 2013). Employees have varying levels of access to proprietary information to perform their jobs, and while this is not a new risk, it has become pivotal with new technological trends, including cloud computing, social media, and mobile devices. We examined literature on user-related threats and vulnerabilities (Wang et al., 2014; Putchala et al., 2013; Souppaya & Scarfone, 2021) and identified six risk domains (see Table 15.1). Although the following typology is not exhaustive, it includes key risk types that are particularly relevant to security policy compliance within organizations.

Social engineering risk arises from users' inability to distinguish malicious messages from legitimate communication. Malicious actions are accomplished through human interactions and phycological influences. Currently, social engineering attacks are one of the biggest cybersecurity threats

---

TABLE 15.1

Risk Types and Sources

User-Based Risk Type	Citations
Social engineering risk	(La Marra et al., 2018) (Pavkovic & Perkov, 2011) (Washo, 2021)
Password-related risk	(Furnell, 2005) (Notoatmodjo & Thomborson, 2009) (Florencio & Herley, 2007) (Tam et al., 2010)
Social media risk	(SANS, 2012) (Banerjee, 2014)
Security management risk	(Schoenberg, 2013) (Souppaya & Scarfone, 2021)
Bring your own device (BYOD) risk	(Miller et al., 2012) (Morrow, 2012) (Wang et al., 2014)
Cloud computing risk	(Carroll et al., 2011) (Pring et al., 2009) (Marinelli, 2009) (Rochwerger et al., 2009) (Sqalli et al., 2011) (Subashini & Kavitha, 2011) (Zhang, 2010)

(La Marra et al., 2018; Pavković & Perkov, 2011). Recent studies and surveys report that over 80% of social engineering attacks are successful. The attacks cannot be fully prevented using software or hardware solutions if people are not trained to prevent these attacks.

Password-related risk arises from inadequate password composition and management practices. Chief among these are weak (easily guessed) passwords, sharing and/or reusing passwords, and writing or storing passwords in unsecured locations (Furnell, 2005). Many organizations now require a complex password to ensure security; however, employees may find such passwords difficult to remember and resort to using one password for most accounts (Notoatmodjo & Thomborson, 2009; Florencio & Herley, 2007). Tam et al. (2010) found that many users are fully aware of good password practices but choose not to adopt them because compliance would cause inconvenience in their normal work routine.

Social media risk is caused by users sharing their work and personal information that may result in damage to the organizational reputation and data leakage (SANS, 2012; Banerjee, 2014). While individual users may not be revealing secrets at any given time, attackers gain valuable intelligence about an organization by accumulating small bits of information across users over time. Uploading social media related software can result in targeted spam, sensitive data leakage, malware infection, and so on. For instance, notorious malware (Koobface) was specifically designed to propagate across social networks (e.g., Facebook, MySpace, Twitter, etc.) to infect other computers to build a peer-to-peer botnet.

Security management risk springs from poor management of assets under users' control (e.g., delayed patching, downloads that can unwittingly enable malware to access organizational cyber infrastructure). Users may download and install applications with vulnerabilities that go unpatched, as well as malicious software that actively steals data that resides on users' machines. If an organization does not support centralized patching, users are responsible for updating their operating systems and applications. Users who do not update their applications and operating systems in a timely manner increase the likelihood that vulnerabilities on their systems will be exploited (Schoenberg, 2013).

Bring your own device risk. Among the most popular mobile phone applications, designed to boost productivity, email, calendar, and contact management, are applications that can increase the risk of data breaches, intrusions, and malware incidents. Nearly half of organizations that allow employee-owned devices to connect to a company's network have experienced a data breach. In the context of BYOD, employees are using their personal devices for both business and personal purposes. If the organization's security rules cause inconvenience in personal use, employees are less likely to comply with them (Miller et al., 2012; Morrow, 2012; Wang et al., 2014).

Cloud computing risk stems from a general loss of control over data transferred to the cloud. Users can store unencrypted sensitive data on cloud storage services, some of which may be insecure. Furthermore, vulnerabilities of authentication credentials and networks' vulnerabilities also increase the risk of compromising information security. Overcoming the vulnerabilities associated with cloud computing has become an important issue for guarding information security (Carroll et al., 2011; Pring et al., 2009). Although fruitful research has been conducted to mitigate cloud computing risk from a technical perspective (Marinelli, 2009; Rochwerger et al., 2009; Sqalli et al., 2011; Subashini & Kavitha, 2011; Zhang, 2010), few studies have focused on end-users, who are an important piece of the puzzle.

FACTORS INFLUENCING USERS' COMPLIANCE WITH ORGANIZATIONAL ISPS

While creating ISPs is essential, it is insufficient to ensure employees' compliance. ISPs implemented by security managers can evoke strong emotions (Kabay, 2009), whereby users may become frustrated or angry if they are required to comply with security policies they perceive as interfering with their work (see Table 15.2).

TABLE 15.2

Theoretical Perspectives and Sources

Theoretical Perspective	Citations; Specific Aspect, If Applicable
Deterrence theory (DT)	General: (D'Arcy et al., 2009) (Herath et al., 2009) (Straub & Nance, 1990) (Siponen et al., 2010)
	Penalties: (Theoharidou et al., 2005) (Scholtz, 1997)
	Rewards: (Boss & Kirsch, 2007) (Pahnila et al., 2007)
Theory of planned behavior (TPB)	Subjective norms: (Ajzen, 1991)
	Self-efficacy: (Bulgurcu et al., 2010) (Chan et al, 2005) (Herath et al., 2009) (Myyry et al., 2009) (Pahnila et al., 2007)
Protection motivation theory (PMT)	(Herath et al., 2009) (Lee et al., 2004) (Pahnila et al., 2007) (Johnston et al., 2015)
	(Anderson & Agarwal, 2010) (Ifinedo, 2012) (Posey et al., 2013) (Vance et al., 2012)
	Fear: (Maddux & Rogers, 1983) (Rogers, 1975)
	Avoiding threats: (Warkentin et al., 2011)
	Moral judgment: (Myyry et al., 2009)
Integrative models	TPB and PMT: (Ifinedo, 2012)
	PMT and habits: (Vance et al., 2012)
	DT and social bond: (Cheng et al., 2013)
	TPB and social bond: (Safa & Ismail, 2013)

Research based on a variety of theoretical perspectives (D'Arcy et al., 2009; Bulgurcu et al., 2010; Pahnila et al., 2007; Herath et al., 2009; Straub & Nance, 1990; Siponen et al., 2010; Washo, 2021) has identified various factors that influence employees' non-compliance with ISPs. For instance, studies based on general deterrence theory (D'Arcy et al., 2009; Herath et al., 2009; Straub & Nance, 1990; Siponen & Vance, 2010) have found sanctions, such as penalties or punishments (Theoharidou et al., 2005; Scholtz, 1997; Straub & Nance, 1990), to act as an inhibiting factor which reduces violations, thereby improving compliance. Other studies have found rewards (Boss & Kirsch, 2007; Pahnila et al., 2007) to be a motivating factor which increases compliance with rules and regulations.

Another branch of literature is based on the theory of planned behavior (TPB), a well-supported theory which postulates that behavior is determined by individuals' intention to perform a behavior, which is a function of one's attitude, subjective norms, and perceived control related to the behavior (Ajzen, 1991). Studies have found that factors derived from TPB can significantly influence compliance with ISPs: higher self-efficacy and positive beliefs or attitudes toward ISP policy are associated with higher ISP compliance intention (Bulgurcu et al., 2010; Chan et al., 2005; Herath et al., 2009; Myyry et al., 2009; Pahnila et al., 2007), suggesting there is a link between planned intentions and ISP compliance.

Other studies (Herath et al., 2009; Lee et al., 2004; Pahnila et al., 2007; Johnston et al., 2015) have examined user ISP behavior through the lens of protection motivation theory (PMT), a well-established risk-perception theory outlining an individual's threat and response assessment and their motivation to protect themselves. PMT can be used to explain fear appeals, which are generally defined as messages designed to increase awareness of threats and thereby promoting protective actions (Maddux & Rogers, 1983; Rogers, 1975). Past studies have demonstrated that motivation to avoid threats (Warkentin et al., 2011) and moral judgment (Myyry et al., 2009) have been found to enhance compliance, and past researchers have also applied PMT to the security context. Herath and Rao (2009) found that perceived severity of the threat, response efficacy, self-efficacy, and response cost significantly affect employees' attitudes toward ISPs. Johnston et al. (2015) reported that using fear appeals can positively affect end users' compliance intention, and perceived severity of threat, self-efficacy, and response efficacy are significant predictors of the effectiveness of fear appeals. Many other studies also reported similar results (Anderson & Agarwal, 2010; Ifinedo, 2012; Posey et al., 2013; Vance et al., 2012), suggesting PMT is pertinent in evaluating ISP compliance intention.

Researchers have proposed different integrative models for predicting ISP compliance. Ifinedo (2012) proposed a model based on TPB and PMT and found that attitudes toward ISPs, subjective norms, self-efficacy, and perceived vulnerability significantly influence employee's ISP compliance intentions. Vance et al. (2012) combined a PMT model with habits toward ISP compliance and reported that perceived severity of threat, rewards, response efficacy, self-efficacy, and response cost all significantly affected ISP compliance intention. In another related study, Cheng et al. (2013) developed a model with the social bond and general deterrence theories, and results showed that subjective norms, co-worker behaviors and perceived severity of sanctions for noncompliance significantly impacted ISP compliance intention. Last, in a study, Safa & Ismail (2013) drew upon TPB and social bond theories, and their test revealed that personal norms and commitment significantly influence employees' attitude toward ISPs, which has a substantial effect on ISP compliance intention. However, previous studies primarily focused on investigating the relationship between each factor and ISP rather than exploring links among factors.

In summary, although security behavior is influenced by several factors, the applicability of the possibly conflicting theoretical models is not clear. More importantly, many studies have used ISP compliance intention as the dependent measure rather than observed compliance behaviors (Floyd et al., 2000; Johnston et al., 2015; Milne et al., 2000; Vance et al., 2012), and the link between intention to comply and actual compliance behavior has not been sufficiently examined. This chapter builds on this knowledge by examining stronger measures of compliance behavior across ISPs designed to mitigate user-based risks.

METHODS

THEORETICAL MODEL

The theoretical background of this work is based on a unified model that integrates PMT, deterrence theory, organizational commitment, and TPB. Our effort to understand the predictors of user compliance with organizational ISPs is based on the widely cited work by Herath and Rao. We adopted Herath and Rao's model because it not only provides a comprehensive framework for examining the dynamics among factors but also allows evaluation of the relationship between various predictive factors and ISP compliance intention. Under this model, the following factors have been found to impact security policy compliance (Herath & Rao, 2009; Bulgurcu et al., 2010; Blythe et al., 2015):

1. Security threat – Employees' understanding of the severity of the threat significantly predicts their concern regarding security breaches. However, the certainty of security breaches does not predict security concerns.
2. Productivity – Employees who believe that complying with policies is a hindrance to their day-to-day job activity are less likely to favorably view ISPs.
3. Response cost – Perceived response cost is inversely related to one's attitude towards security policies.
4. Organizational commitment – Employees' level of organizational commitment positively predicts policy compliance intentions.
5. Norms – Employees' normative beliefs related to expectations of superiors, peers, and IT personnel have the most impact on employee security compliance intentions.
6. Deterrence – The certainty of detection has a positive impact on employees' security policy compliance intentions. If employees perceive that there is high likelihood of getting caught if they violate security policies, they report stronger intentions to follow the security policies.

7. Self-efficacy and resource availability – Employees' level of cybersecurity self-efficacy significantly predicts compliance intentions with security policies. Resource availability positively predicts self-efficacy.

CONTRIBUTIONS

Most of the research on employee ISP compliance has focused on compliance intentions as an outcome. Research suggests that although people may formulate an intention to adhere to a behavior, in practice they will not always do so (Albrechtsen, 2007). While studies based on Herath and Rao's model confirm that intentions to comply with ISPs are influenced by several factors described previously, the connection between intentions and behavior has not been sufficiently examined. The present study advances this work in the following ways:

1. Instead of examining ISP compliance as a single homogenous construct, we decomposed ISP compliance in terms of policies related to specific security risks and investigated how Herath and Rao's model applied to each one. This enabled us to investigate the heterogeneity among types of security risks.
2. We constructed a set of choice vignettes to create a more realistic and concrete decision context that would elicit more accurate behavioral intentions. We incorporated situations related to each risk type and typical security policies used to address the risks in our vignettes.
3. We tested the generalizability of Herath and Rao's model. Specifically, whereas the original sample comprised employees at organizations in western New York who used computers and internet daily, our study recruited individuals across the globe in more diverse organizational settings.
4. We included an adapted version of the Impression Management Scale to adjust for socially desirable responding patterns in the self-report data.

PROCEDURES

We developed and administered a survey instrument hosted on Qualtrics, a secure, online survey platform commonly used by researchers. The survey consisted of three main parts. The first part captured participants' demographic information. The second part assessed predictors of ISP compliance based on Herath and Rao's model. The third part introduced a "typical workday" scenario in which respondents were asked to imagine they were an employee at a company at which they'd been working for several years. They read a background story about their role in the company and an outline of its ISPs (Appendix). A series of decision vignettes was then presented to investigate potential differences in compliance across types of IS behaviors and how models using these decision outcomes relate to models using self-reported general intentions to comply.

Respondents were recruited from Amazon Mechanical Turk. They were compensated $1.50 each for participating in the survey, which took an average of 20 minutes to complete. We utilized two separate measures to enhance the reliability and validity of responses. First, we embedded four attention check questions throughout the survey (e.g., "what is the opposite of white?" with response options of: Rain, dog, black, house). Respondents who missed any one of these were excluded from the sample. Second, we included an adapted version of the Impression Management Scale from the Balanced Inventory of Desirable Responding (Paulhus, 2001) to assess and account for socially desirable response patterns.

PARTICIPANTS

To be eligible to participate in the survey, respondents self-reported: (1) age of at least 18 years, (2) US residency, and (3) a history of employment at an organization (profit or non-profit). A total of 408 eligible volunteers took the survey. Of these, 40 respondents (<10%) missed at least one of the four attention check questions embedded in the survey and were excluded from analyses. The final sample ($N = 368$) was 57.3% female with a mean age of 34.4 (SD = 10.17). Nearly all (99.7%) owned a personal computer/laptop and spent an average of 5.81 (SD = 3.81) hours using a computer at work each day. Roughly 84.5% were currently employed, with the remainder (15.5%) employed at an organization in the past. See Ryutov et al. (2017) for full demographic characteristics of the sample.

MEASURES

DEPENDENT VARIABLES

We assessed two types of outcomes. First, general intentions to comply with ISPs were assessed using a single item (i.e., "how likely are you to follow company IS policies?"), with responses provided on a 7-point Likert scale ranging from 1 = very unlikely to 7 = very likely. Second, following the "typical workday" scenario, respondents were presented with decision vignettes representing each of the six risk types (i.e., social engineering, BYOD usage, password-related risk, social media, cloud computing, and security management risk). The ISP summary presented prior to the vignettes outlined the precautionary or correct response corresponding to each risk type. For instance, for the social engineering type, we presented a vignette in which participants were responsible for processing shipments from common shipping companies (e.g., FedEx, UPS). We then presented four emails appearing to be sent from such shipping companies, some of which were fraudulent and represented phishing attempts. Participants were asked how they would respond to each of these messages (i.e., check the tracking number, click the tracking number in the email, do nothing, forward message to IT). They received a score of 1 for every precautionary response and 0 for every non-precautionary response (coding of precaution/compliance varied by message; see Table 15.1 for additional details).

Independent Variables

We adapted survey items from (Herath & Rao, 2009) for use as independent variables (IVs) in the model (Table 15.3). In addition, we considered demographic variables and the sum score of 11 items from the Impression Management Scale of the Balanced Inventory of Desirable Responding.

See Appendix for additional details on item vignettes.

DATA ANALYSIS

To test the applicability of Herath and Rao's model to each of the six risk types, we built partial least squares (PLS) regression models using SmartPLS (Hair, 2014). PLS relies on uncorrelated principle components constructed from predictors for estimation and therefore is particularly useful when predictors exhibit multi-collinearity (Wold, 1982; Wold, 1985). Compared to conventional regression analysis, PLS is capable of handling multiple indicators simultaneously, providing multiple outputs, and has a lower risk of producing erroneous non-zero path coefficients by chance (Gerbing & Anderson, 1988). Compared to covariance-based structural equation modeling techniques, PLS is more suitable when the research goal is to evaluate predictive relationships for target constructs (Hair, 2011; Lowry & Gaskin, 2014). PLS also allows testing path coefficients and measurement models simultaneously (Chin & Newsted, 1999; Fornell & Bookstein, 1982). Standard errors for testing statistical significance of path coefficients were obtained through bootstrapping 500 samples.

TABLE 15.3

Latent Variables, Items, Loadings, Response Scales, and Cronbach Alphas

Construct	Survey Items	Item Loading	Response Scale	Cronbach α
Perceived probability of security breach	Security violation will result in loss of productivity.	0.907***	1 (very unlikely)– 7 (very likely)	0.881
	Security violation causes loss of sensitive data.	0.924***		
	Security violation causes financial loss.	0.865***		
Perceived severity of security breach	Information stored on company computers is vulnerable to security threats.	0.906***	1 (strongly disagree)– 7 (strongly agree)	0.803
	Profitability of the company is threatened by security threats.	0.922***		
Security breach concern level	The IS security issue affects my company directly.	0.891***	1 (strongly disagree)– 7 (strongly agree)	0.754
	I think IS is serious and needs attention.	0.900***		
Response efficacy	Every employee can make a difference when it comes to helping secure the company's IS.	0.918***	1 (strongly disagree)– 7 (strongly agree)	0.817
	If I follow the company's IS security policies, I can make a difference in helping to secure my company's IS.	0.921***		
Response cost	Complying with security policies reduces my personal productivity at my company.	0.790***	1 (strongly disagree)– 7 (strongly agree)	0.831
	Adopting security technologies and practices makes things more difficult.	0.879***		
	It would be inconvenient to follow my company's security policies.	0.917***		
Self-efficacy	I am confident that I could deal efficiently with unexpected events.	0.861***	1 (strongly disagree)– 7 (strongly agree)	0.929
	Thanks to my resourcefulness, I know how to handle unforeseen situations.	0.868***		
	I can remain calm when facing difficulties because I can rely on my coping abilities.	0.892***		
	If I am in trouble, I can usually think of a solution.	0.890***		
	I can handle whatever comes my way.	0.900***		
Security policy attitude	Adopting security technologies and practices is important.	0.942***	1 (strongly disagree)– 7 (strongly agree)	0.868
	It is beneficial to adopt security technologies and practices.	0.938***		
Organizational commitment	I am willing to put in a great deal of effort beyond that normally expected in order to help this company be successful.	0.915***	1 (strongly disagree)– 7 (strongly agree)	0.843
	I really care about the fate of this company.	0.869***		
	This is the company I most want to work for.	0.821***		

(Continued)

TABLE 15.3 (*Continued*)

Construct	Survey Items	Item Loading	Response Scale	Cronbach α
Punishment severity	The company disciplines employees who break information security rules.	0.897***	1(stronglydisagree)– 7 (strongly agree)	0.891
	My company terminates employees who repeatedly break security rules.	0.911***		
	If I were caught violating company information security policies, I would be punished.	0.909***		
Detection certainty	Employee computer practices are properly monitored for policy violations.	0.919***	1(stronglydisagree)– 7 (strongly agree)	0.839
	If I violate security policies, I would probably be caught.	0.936***		
Security policy compliance intention	How likely are you to follow company IS policies?	1.000***	1 (very unlikely)– 7 (very likely)	-
Subjective norm	The information security department in my company thinks that I should follow my company's IS security policies.	0.932***	1(stronglydisagree)– 7 (strongly agree)	0.863
	Computer technical specialists in the company think that I should follow my company's security policies.	0.943***		
Descriptive norm	I believe other employees comply with the company's IS security policies.	0.951***	1(stronglydisagree)– 7 (strongly agree)	0.881
	It is likely that the majority of other employees comply with the company IS security policies to help protect the company's IS.	0.939***		
Social engineering risk+	Email 1	0.421*	0 (not taking precautions), 1 (precautionary response)	0.458
	Email 2	0.721*		
	Email 3	0.710**		
	Email 4	0.598*		
Password related risk+	Item 1	0.902*	0 (not compliant), 1 (complying with policy/rules)	0.491
	Item 2	0.454		
	Item 3	0.485*		
Social Media Risk	How likely are you to post/tweet/blog about your concerns on your favorite social media sites?	1.000	1 (very likely)–7 (very unlikely)	-
Security management risk+	Item 1	0.742***	0 (not compliant), 1 (complying with policy/rules)	0.076
	Item 2	0.564*		
	Item 3	0.456		
Cloud computing risk+	Item 1	1.000	0 (not compliant), 1 (complying with policy/rules)	-

Construct	Survey Items	Item Loading	Response Scale	Cronbach α
Bring your own device risk	How likely are you to install game applications on your company phone for free?	0.808***	1 (very likely)– 8 (never)	0.959
	How likely are you to install health applications on your company phone for free?	0.900***		
	How likely are you to install sports applications on your company phone for free?	0.780***		
	How likely are you to install dining applications on your company phone for free?	0.799***		
	How likely are you to install shopping applications on your company phone for free?	0.843***		
	How likely are you to install social networking applications on your company phone for free?	0.884***		
	How likely are you to install music applications on your company phone for free?	0.892***		
	How likely are you to install news applications on your company phone for free?	0.831**		
	How likely are you to install entertainment applications on your company phone for free?	0.841***		

Note: *: Significant at $p < 0.05$; **: significant at $p < 0.01$; ***: significant at $p < 0.001$.

RESULTS AND DISCUSSION

PSYCHOMETRIC VALIDATION

We first examined psychometric properties of the measures, including reliability, convergent validity, and discriminant validity. To test reliability, or the extent to which items within a measure produce consistent results, Cronbach's alpha was computed for all constructs all were above the 0.70 threshold (Gefen et al., 2000), indicating acceptable levels of reliability for all measures. To evaluate convergent validity, or the consistency among constructs that are theoretically related, we examined loadings of items representing the same construct on the hypothesized construct. Overall, the measurement model showed satisfactory reliability, convergent validity, and discriminant validity. See Ryutov et al. (2017) for in-depth discussion of the validation methodology.

PLS MODELS

The standardized PLS model using ISP compliance intention as the outcome is shown in Figure 15.1. From the model summary, 36.9% of the variance in security policy attitude is explained by security breach concern, response cost, and response efficacy; likewise, 39.6% of the variance in ISP compliance intention is explained by security policy attitude, self-efficacy, punishment severity, and descriptive norms.

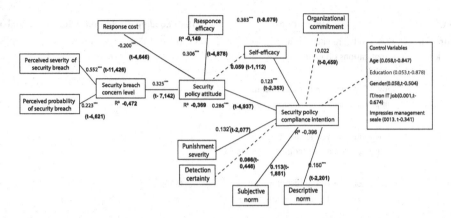

FIGURE 15.1   PLS model summary.

Note: *: significant at $p < 0.05$; **: significant at $p < 0.01$; ***: significant at $p < 0.001$.

Focusing on constructs related to protection motivation theory, employees' perceived severity of security breach ($\beta = 0.552$, $p < 0.001$) and perceived probability of security breach ($\beta = 0.223$, $p < 0.001$) both significantly predict employees' security breach concern level. Security breach concern level had a significant effect on security policy attitude ($\beta = 0.325$, $p < 0.001$). Security policy attitude significantly predicts security policy compliance intention ($\beta = 0.286$, $p < 0.001$). Response efficacy significantly predicts attitudes toward security policy ($\beta = 0.306$, $p < 0.001$), whereas response cost has a significant negative relationship with security policy attitude ($\beta = -0.200$, $p < 0.001$). Self-efficacy does not significantly predict security policy attitude ($\beta = 0.059$), but significantly predicts ISP compliance intention ($\beta = 0.123$, $p < 0.05$).

For constructs related to general deterrence theory, punishment severity significantly predicts intention to comply with security policies ($\beta = 0.132$, $p < 0.05$), but detection certainty did not significantly predict compliance intention ($\beta = 0.086$). For constructs related to theory of planned behavior, subjective norm did not significantly predict intention of complying with security policies ($\beta = 0.117$). However, descriptive norm significantly predicts security policy compliance intention ($\beta = 0.150$, $p < 0.001$). Last, organizational commitment significantly predicts response efficacy ($\beta = 0.383$, $p < 0.001$) but does not significantly predict security policy compliance intention ($\beta = -0.022$). Out of the five control variables (age, education, gender, job in IT, and IM), only impression management significantly predicts intention of complying with security policies ($\beta = 0.127$, $p < 0.001$).

These results show that if employees believe the severity and likelihood of security breach are high, they are likely to be more concerned about potential security breaches. When employees are concerned about security breaches, they will have more positive attitudes toward security policies. Furthermore, if employees believe complying with security protocol interferes with their work, they are more likely to have negative attitudes toward security policies. If employees are confident that compliance behaviors will positively affect their organization, they are more likely to have positive attitudes toward security policies.

We next examined the applicability of the model to each of the six user-based risks. To identify significant predictors associated with each risk type, we created six new models that replaced ISP compliance intention with the behavioral indicators from the vignettes and tested each model. In each model, the dependent variable represents compliance with an ISP corresponding to one of the six user-based risks. The next section summarizes significant findings from each model and implications for management practice. Refer to Ryutov et al. (2017) for detailed discussion of the PLS models and theoretical results.

CONCLUSIONS AND RECOMMENDATIONS

We next discuss the proposed solutions to the two research questions.

1. *What factors relate, in which degree, to intentions to comply with each of the key types of ISPs?*
2. *Based on these insights, what organizational practices are needed to promote end-user compliance with the ISP?*

For each of the six risk types, we summarize our findings that indicate the relevant factors and the degree they correlate with the intentions to comply with corresponding ISPs. We next follow with the recommendations that outline organizational practices needed to promote end-user compliance with the ISPs.

SOCIAL ENGINEERING RISK

FINDINGS

For social engineering risk, age had a significant negative effect on compliance ($\beta = -0.212, p < 0.001$), which indicates that older employees are less likely to distinguish malicious messages from legitimate communication.

These findings are consistent with prior research (Castle et al., 2012; Ruffman et al., 2012; Ebner et al., 2015) that suggested that sensitivity to untrustworthy information declines with age. Older adults display diminished ability to detect lies (Ruffman et al., 2012). These findings support well-documented age-related positivity bias: older adults show a significant information processing bias toward positive versus negative information. More specifically, older adults exhibit reduced attention and memory to negative compared to positive information (Chan et al., 2014).

Recommendations

Many organizations follow a one-size-fits-all approach to security training, which is likely not optimal. Differential susceptibility suggests the need for age-targeted security warnings and training. Phishing awareness training programs should consider motivations and meet the learning requirements of different age groups. For example, the content and design of the training phishing emails can be customized to different age groups. A large-scale study (Li et al., 2020) analyzed the effects of three types of simulated phishing emails on different age groups. The email types included IT/tech support, finance/banking, and e-commerce/package delivery scenarios. The findings of this study revealed that individuals in the youngest age group (less than 27 years old) were significantly more likely to perceive financial emails as genuine than people aged between 27 and 41. The individuals in the oldest age group (greater than 59 years old) were more likely to trust IT help desk email and package delivery emails than other groups.

Age-tailored training can address the following observations:

- The older generation will benefit from learning about Internet technology. Effective training strategy should help older employees to understand how their strengths (e.g., life experiences) and weaknesses (e.g., limited familiarity with new technology) could be used against them in phishing attacks.
- The younger generation, many of whom are highly adept at Internet technology, do not need to be taught how to use the technology. Instead, younger employees should learn the techniques that social engineering attacks typically employ. This knowledge will help them to recognize attacks.

Password-Based Risk

Findings

For password-related risk, subjective norm significantly predicts compliance ($\beta = 0.206$, $p < 0.05$), indicating if employees believe management or IT personnel expect them to comply with information security policy, they are more likely to comply.

Recommendations

It is important for organizations to understand the role of expectations and the impact they have on motivating employees. The end goal is to minimize misunderstandings that employees may have about what is expected of them. For example, employees may falsely assume that, since the company's IT systems are protected by cybersecurity software, and an IT department, their own personal password practices are not important. ISP is a mechanism to hold individuals accountable for compliance with expected behaviors. Therefore, the first step in mitigating password security risks is to develop a strong password policy that clearly sets expectations. It should lay out in plain language its purpose and scope, specific roles and responsibilities, and how the policy is enforced. Some common oversights in terms of password policy management involve sanctions for violations and ongoing policy compliance review and evaluation. The actual policy statement will outline the technical specifics on password requirements (for example, length, complexity, etc.) and which systems, applications, and devices the policy applies to.

If security policies clearly outline employees' responsibilities about the types of information to be safeguarded and the reasons behind them, then people can act accordingly and be held accountable for their actions. Research results (Yıldırım & Mackie, 2019) suggest that password creation methods and persuasive messages provided to users are more likely to convince them to create strong passwords. Therefore, it is essential to communicate organizational expectations and train employees on how to establish and maintain strong passwords on a regular basis.

Typically, employees are required to review these security rules during initial onboarding, but there may insufficient reminders after that. Continuous communication is needed to keep employees aware of the security policies. According to a global study, 56% of IT staff reported that security policies were briefed to new employees at the time of hire, but only 32% of employees reported having been briefed (Cisco, 2008). Moreover, the literature suggests that persuasion attempts are more likely to succeed if the persons are aware of the situation. Thus, informing users about possible attacks if they choose weak passwords and the consequences if their organization falls victim to password cracking and sensitive user information is leaked will likely improve compliance with password guidelines. Proper user education and training will help to raise security awareness and personal responsibility. It is a good practice to keep security reminders visible throughout the workplace (e.g., posters, memos, and e-mail broadcasts) and conduct regular staff survey to test level of awareness and disciplinary measures.

Social Media Risk

Findings

For social media risk, self-efficacy ($\beta = 0.115$, $p < 0.05$), subjective norm ($\beta = 0.195$, $p < 0.001$), whether employees work in IT departments ($\beta = 0.164$, $p < 0.05$), and detection certainty ($\beta = 0.182$, $p < 0.05$) were found to be significant positive predictors of compliance. These findings indicate that employees are less likely to cause security breaches on social media if they strongly believe management or IT personnel expect them to comply with security policies. If employees' violation of information security policies is more likely to be detected, employees are less likely to violate security protocols on social media. Furthermore, if employees work in IT departments, or if they feel more capable of complying with security policy, they are less likely to overshare on social media.

Recommendations

1. Setting Appropriate Expectations

The first step to reduce social media security risks is to develop a formal policy that unambiguously sets expectations about employees' acceptable use of social media. A strong social media policy must outline clear explanations about types of information that employees can and cannot share, legal or regulatory requirements, and consequences of non-compliance. The policy should be a standalone document rather than embedded into a more generic IT security or acceptable usage policy. Another option is to cross-reference social media policies with related standards or policies, such as use and protection of business resources and information and conflicts of interest.

In many organizations, when employees join the company, a code of conduct is used to inform them about regulatory or compliance obligations and expectations in terms of employee conduct. Security managers should remind employees that the code of conduct is also relevant to online activity. Employees who do not work in IT or security roles are not always aware of these security rules or may not think they apply to their jobs. To increase the visibility of the security polices, organizations can make compliance with the policies be part of the job requirements and performance review. To ensure compliance with organizations' security policies and to promote safe secure online behavior, employees must be educated to fully comprehend the social media security risks and the consequences of non-compliance. Organizations need to provide effective security awareness training to employees on a regular basis. Security awareness training should provide detailed explanations of the organization's social media acceptable use and security policy and give examples of various social media attacks. It should outline the proper precautions to mitigate security threats and risks and emphasize the importance of reporting security incidents.

2. Deterring Policy Violations

Deterrence is the combination of the perceived likelihood of a violation being detected and the expected outcome (e.g., sanctions) from that detection. Research on deterrence (Aurigemma & Mattson, 2017) indicates that increasing the likelihood of being caught when breaking the rules and applying sanctions for non-compliance incentivize employees to follow the rules. The practical implications suggest that organizations would benefit from implementing social media monitoring technology and being transparent about its use. Many organizations routinely monitor and log employee internet activity. Social media site monitoring tools such as Google Alerts and Social Mention can generate timely alerts and help quickly detect suspicious activity and threats. Informing employees of the monitoring practices and asking for employees' consent to be monitored will likely increase perceived likelihood of being caught.

Formal sanctions for policy violation provide an important legal foundation, allowing organizations to take clearly defined actions against those who violate policy. However, the results from compliance-related research indicate that formal sanctions may be ineffective in deterring policy violations (Hu et al., 2011; Cheng et al., 2013; Guo & Yuan, 2012; Barlow et al., 2013; D'Arcy & Herath, 2011; Liao et al., 2009) in the social media context; employee monitoring can erode much of the sense of trust between companies and their workers and weaken loyalty. Companies run the risk of being seen as insensitive to employees' privacy if their monitoring is seen as overly aggressive. Thus, in addition to deterrence, organizations should engage in positive means of enforcement. Practical implications suggest that organizations should focus on security awareness activities that address moral beliefs and perceived benefits of compliance. For instance, security training sessions can persuade employees that the violation of ISPs is morally wrong and that compliance with the policies is morally correct.

3. Fostering Self-Efficacy

Organizations should promote employees' beliefs and confidence regarding their ability to protect confidential corporate information and prevent information disclosure using social media.

Self-efficacy, or confidence, as it is commonly known, is an individual's belief in their competence and capacity to successfully accomplish a task. Self-efficacy has been used as the theoretical framework (Bandura, 1999) typically associated with work-related performance in numerous studies. Employee empowerment has been advocated as a useful tool to motivate employees to make decisions on their own without constant referral to their managers, which in turn enhances the employees' self-efficacy beliefs (Greenberg & Baron, 2000).

Employee's self-efficacy expectations for complying with social media policies can be increased through guided experience and mentoring. For example, providing guidance and training employees in how they should conduct themselves online would reduce the amount of time required to reach a certain experience level, thereby enhancing their self-efficacy. Having experienced employees mentor inexperienced individuals about social media etiquette is another option for achieving this same goal. There is strong agreement in the literature that by creating conditions to increase motivation, organizations can enable employees to accomplish their tasks in a confident manner and build a strong sense of self-efficacy (Conger & Kanungo, 1988). Other drivers include effective communication between managers and employees and effective management practices, including the establishment of realistic expectations (Staples, 1997).

Thus, for organizations, it is important to develop a realistic social media policy that enhances employee motivation and self-management without excessive monitoring and controls. To improve effectiveness of communication, in addition to simply disseminating a social media policy, managers could review and discuss the policy and how it applies to the business with employees. Organizations need to consider realistic expectations for the use of social media. For instance, a policy that bans all employee personal use of social media in the workplace may do more harm than good. Employees may still have social media access on their personal devices at work. Morale may suffer if the workplace is seen as being too restrictive, decreasing employees' happiness and motivation.

SECURITY/VULNERABILITY MANAGEMENT RISK

FINDINGS

For security management risk, subjective norm ($\beta = 0.236$, $p < 0.01$) and descriptive norm ($\beta = 0.175$, $p < 0.05$) were significant positive predictors, indicating that employees' security management will improve if they believe most employees comply with security policies and if they believe management or IT personnel expect them to comply.

These results are consistent with the findings of prior research that showed that social influence strongly affects employee intention to follow the ISP guidelines. According to Furth-Matzkin & Sunstein (2018), exposure to information about the majority opinion can significantly influence people's support for specific policies. This is particularly likely in the security policy context, where people often lack fixed and firm convictions.

Recommendations

Conformity is a type of social influence that occurs when a person changes their behavior or beliefs because of perceived social pressure. It is often based on a desire to fulfill others' expectations and gain acceptance (Myers, 2009) and is often driven by a desire to fit in with what the majority considers correct. That usually means copying the actions of others, looking to the group when deciding how to think or behave, or doing what is "expected" based on widely accepted social norms. Organizations should therefore consider leveraging susceptibility to conformity by tailoring security training efforts to emphasize the heightened social desirability of following the vulnerability management policy. Managers should communicate that many or most people in the organization comply with the policy. An effective strategy would be to provide an opportunity to interact with individuals who diligently patch and update servers and end-user devices.

CLOUD COMPUTING AND **BYOD** RISKS

FINDINGS

For cloud computing risk, organizational commitment ($\beta = 0.141$, $p < 0.05$) and whether employees work in IT ($\beta = 0.192$, $p < 0.001$) were found to significantly predict compliance, suggesting that if employees are highly committed to their organizations or work in IT departments, they are less likely to break security policies related to cloud storage services. For bring your own device risk, organizational commitment was found to be a significant predictor ($\beta = 0.122$, $p < 0.05$), indicating that the more committed employees are to their organization, the less likely they are to violate security rules on their own devices. Our results are in line with prior research on policy compliance. Organizational commitment refers to the connection or bond employees have with their employer (the organization). Committed individuals value personal achievement and reputation and would avoid the risk of breaking rules that could jeopardize their career aspirations (Lee et al., 2004). Consequently, employees with more commitment to the organization are less likely to deviate from the security policies.

Recommendations

We have already discussed the recommended actions directed to raising awareness among employees working outside of IT departments. We next discuss the recommendations for increasing organizational commitment to minimize cloud computing and BYOD risks.

1. Increasing Employee Commitment

Organizational support refers to the extent to which the organization acknowledges and values the employees' contribution and cares about their well-being (Shropshire et al., 2015). The research literature indicates that perceived organizational support increases commitment by contributing to the satisfaction of employees' socio-emotional needs such as esteem, approval, and affiliation (Fuller et al., 2003). This satisfaction tends to enhance employees' social identity by being a member of that organization which creates greater commitment. Therefore, organizations would benefit from implementing strategies that enhance perceived organizational support by creating a positive working environment (Beheshtifar et al., 2013). For example, organizations can provide some IT support and safeguards for employees' personal data as well as corporate resources. Managers could periodically conduct surveys to collect feedback from employees on how they believe wellness could be improved at work and gradually implement recurring suggestions where possible.

2. Improving Transparency

Organizational transparency is the practice of sharing information related to the organization's operations with the intent to create clarity, trust, and accountability. Findings of a recent study revealed the strong correlation between employees' perception of managerial transparency and organizational commitment (Bratley et al., 2019). When an organization is transparent with its employees, they will more likely feel valued and develop increased sense of belonging that leads to stronger commitment.

To support transparency, a BYOD policy should clearly communicate the type of devices and data covered by the BYOD policy, the data that IT can access on employee devices, and to what extent devices can be monitored or managed. An organization may want to reserve the right to remote wipe a personal device if it gets lost, stolen, or compromised. Employees need to understand that possibility and acknowledge that they may lose all their personal data if they agree to abide by the BYOD policy. Similarly, the cloud computing use policy should clearly define which organizational data is allowed in the cloud, as well as cloud regulatory compliance and incident response procedures.

Conclusions

As employees' behaviors can impact the security, performance, and reputation of organizations, ISP compliance is an important issue. The study described in this chapter examined predictors of

ISP compliance intentions and behavioral indicators of compliance with ISPs intended to mitigate key user-related risks, including social engineering, passwords, social media, security management, cloud computing, and BYOD. Rather than measuring ISP compliance as a single homogenous construct, we assessed the six user-based risks to explore the heterogeneity of responses across risk types separately. We also used security threat vignettes requiring a specific decision, in addition to assessing general intention to comply.

We partially replicated and extended a previous study (Herath & Rao, 2009), with some important differences. Our model identified several new significant paths, including those from self-efficacy to security policy attitude, and perceived probability of security breach to security breach concern level. These differences may be attributed to a greater sample diversity than Herath and Rao's sample of employees from organizations in western New York. Our results offer several theoretical and practical implications for ISP-related risks.

First, relevant to both theory and practice, we identified differences in predictors of compliance with different ISPs. Theoretically, this suggests that employees perceive different ISPs in distinct ways, and unique factors predict their compliance with them. Hence, composite measures of ISP compliance may obscure important differences among predictors of actual compliance with individual policies. On a practical note, these findings have important actionable implications for organizational IT managers.

First, results suggest that increasing employees' comprehension of the importance and consequences of security breaches may help improve ISP compliance. Second, ensuring that employees are aware that their compliance helps the organization may elevate the level of compliance. Additionally, employee ISP training should define the ISPs in sufficient detail along with the desired compliance behaviors; the training should address different predictors of compliance depending on the specific target ISP. For instance, employees are less likely to comply with password and social media ISPs if they have weak beliefs that they are expected to comply with such policies; however, subjective norms did not predict compliance with the other four risks. Employee communications and outreach that enhance subjective norms surrounding social media and password policy compliance may facilitate compliance.

Social media-related risk may also be lowered if employees: (1) believe they are more capable of complying with a security policy, (2) believe they are expected to comply with a security policy, (3) work in IT, or (4) believe in a high detection probability. Hence, for social media risk in particular, several factors could be targeted by IT managers to enhance compliance with relevant policies. In terms of enhancing compliance to mitigate other risks, the security management risk can be decreased if employees believe the majority complies with security policies or that the IT personnel expect them to comply. Employees working in IT departments are less likely to violate cloud computing policies, whereas those who are more committed to their organization are less likely to violate cloud computing and BYOD policies. Finally, older employees are more susceptible to social engineering risk, which suggests targeted training programs.

STUDY LIMITATIONS AND FUTURE RESEARCH

Our findings should be viewed considering several limitations. First, our sample was recruited from Amazon Mechanical Turk. Prior work has found that studies using MTurk samples replicate results of lab studies (Hauser & Schwarz, 2016), and for the objectives of our study, a sample of online users may generalize well to target populations of computer users. However, our results still may not extend to all other settings, and populations and should be interpreted with caution.

Next, we used decision vignettes for several of our outcome variables, building on prior literature which has assessed only self-reported intentions to comply with ISPs. However, we did not measure actual behavior. Although workplace vignettes have been used in previous ISP studies (Cheng et al.,

2013; D'Arcy et al., 2009; Siponen & Vance, 2010; Ullah et al., 2013), additional work is needed to develop behavioral measures of ISP compliance. On a related point, measurement of some outcomes relied on single-item vignettes. Improved reliability and construct validity could be achieved with multi-item measures. Although other research has found that intentions are among the best predictors of a variety of behaviors, future studies should measure observed behavior. Furthermore, security compliance intention is a single item construct in our model; future studies should consider including more items for this construct to improve reliability and model parameters. Finally, due to the cross-sectional design of our study, the results are correlational only; causality is not addressed and yet to be established. Future studies should use experimental designs to allow stronger conclusions regarding the causal direction of relationships.

ACKNOWLEDGMENTS

This research was supported by National Science Foundation funding under award No. 1314644.

APPENDIX

COMPANY'S POLICIES

1. All forms of sexual harassment are unacceptable in company's work environment and should be reported immediately to HR.
2. Employees are not allowed to possess, or be under the influence of, alcohol or drugs on company premises or while performing work duties.
3. Company-owned computers/devices as well as employee-owned devices used to access company data must have up-to-date operating system and applications security software installed.
4. Employees sign non-competition and proprietary information agreements that restrict what information employees can disclose during their employment and after they leave the company.
5. Social media rules (e.g., Facebook posting, blogging, tweeting, etc.): responding to an offensive or negative post by a customer, sharing negative information about the company, and posting private company information is prohibited.
6. Under no circumstances may company owned computers or other equipment be used on to obtain, view, or reach any non-business-related Internet sites.
7. Employees' access to the company's data is protected by passwords. A password has to be least 10 characters long, include at least one upper case character, at least one number, and one special character (e.g., #), and no dictionary words can be used.
8. Company email can be used to conduct company business only.
9. Employees are allowed to use his/her company smartphone to access the company data at any time; however, only the pre-loaded applications (those that came with the smart phone, such as calendar, email, clock, etc.) and MobileWorkspace (vetted by the company) are permitted to be installed on the smart phones used to access the manufacturing data.
10. Employee is not allowed to store manufacturing data in the cloud, e.g., iCloud, Dropbox, Google Drive, or Microsoft SkyDrive.
11. Employee should be aware about phishing attacks – malicious emails pretending to be legitimate communication. Employees should not provide confidential information, open any attachments or click any links from suspicious e-mails. Phishing emails should be reported immediately to information technology (IT) department.

Items for Compliance Behavior Intentions in Risk Domains:

Social engineering risk	**Your action:** **Check the tracking number** **Track the package by clicking the tracking number** **Do nothing** **Forward email to IT** **Precautionary response: Do nothing or forward email to IT (this is a phishing email). This item tests for compliance with policy 11.**
	Your action: Check the tracking number Do not check Do not check and forward email to IT **Precautionary response: Do nothing or forward email to IT (this is a phishing email). This item tests for compliance with policy 11.**
	Your action: Check the tracking number Do not check Do not check and forward email to IT **Precautionary response: Check the tracking number (this is a legitimate email). This item tests for compliance with policy 11.**
	Your action: Check Do not check Do not check and forward email to IT **Precautionary response: Do nothing or forward email to IT (this is a phishing email). This item tests for compliance with policy 11.**
Password-related risk	Imagine that your typical work day has just started. You had your tea or coffee, and now you need to log in to the company's server. Access to the server is protected by a password. Each time you access company data, you need to input your password. Typically, you will input your password 5–10 times a day. If you are connecting for the first time, you need to create a password. Remember, a password has to be least 10 characters long, include at least one upper-case character, at least one number, and one special character (e.g., #), and no dictionary words can be used. New password: **Compliant response: a compliant password needs to meet all rules stated in the question (at least 10 characters long, at least one upper-case character, at least one number and one special character, and no dictionary words). This item tests for compliance with policy 7.**
	Confirm your password: **Compliant response: confirmed password should match the previously selected password. This item imitates typical password set up environment to check if users are paying attention.**
	A message from your boss asks you to send her the list of company's new vendors. To do that you need to connect to the database: by entering the server name, username, and password. Enter your password. **Compliant response: entered password should match the previously selected password. This item tests if users can retain strong passwords.**
Security management risk	You are in the middle of a time-consuming tedious work task and have several applications opened on your company's computer when you see a pop up: "Security update is available for your operating system. Click 'install' button to install the update and restart your computer." Your action: Do nothing Click install Contact IT Contact HR **Compliant response: Click install or contact IT. This item tests for compliance with policy.**

You receive a memo that announces a security breach experienced by the company. The company's server was hacked, and important data was lost. The cause of the breach was a disabled antivirus software on an employee's machine. Your action:

Ensure my antivirus software is off

Do nothing

Ensure my antivirus software is on

Contact IT

Contact HR

Compliant response: Ensure my antivirus software is on or contact IT. This item tests for compliance with policy.

You download an update to a work-related software. During the download a pop-up appears: "suspicious download, to continue email support." Your action:

Email

Do not email

Compliant response: Email. This item tests for compliance with policy 3.

Cloud computing risk

You have the Dropbox cloud storage application installed at work to share public information with co-workers. An alternative to using Dropbox is to email the files, but the company's email server blocks some types of attachments you want to share. To send these files by email you need to convert them to another format. Select the information below to be shared via Dropbox (check all that apply):

Pictures from the last after work gathering

New HR policies

Customer complaints

Product failure rates report for 2014

Where to have lunch to celebrate a co-worker's birthday: suggested placed with menus

Compliant response: choices that did not include Product failure rates report for 2014 is compliant. This item tests for compliance with policy 10.

REFERENCES

Ajzen, I. (1991), "The theory of planned behavior", *Organizational Behavior and Human Decision Processes*, vol. 50, no. 2, pp. 179–211. https://doi.org/10.1016/0749–5978(91)90020-t

Albrechtsen, E. (2007), "A qualitative study of users' view on information security", *Computers & Security*, vol. 26, no. 4, pp. 276–289. https://doi.org/10.1016/j.cose.2006.11.004

AlKalbani, A., Deng, H., and Kam, B. (2014), "A conceptual framework for information security in public organizations for e-government development", *Proceedings of 25th Australasian Conference on Information Systems*, Auckland, New Zealand, pp. 65–83.

Anderson, C. L., and Agarwal, R. (2010), "Practicing safe computing: a multimedia empirical examination of home computer user security behavioral intentions", *MIS Quarterly*, vol. 34, no. 3, pp. 613–643.

Aurigemma, S., and Mattson, T. (2017), "Deterrence and punishment experience impacts on ISP compliance attitudes", *Information and Computer Security*, vol. 25, no. 4, pp. 421–436. https://doi.org/10.1108/ICS-11–2016–0089

Bandura, A. (1999), *Self-efficacy. The exercise of control*. London: W. H. Freeman & Co. https://doi.org/10.5860/choice.35–1826

Banerjee, A., Banerjee, C., and Poonia, A. S. (2014), "Security threats of social networking sites: an analytical approach", *International Journal of Enhanced Research in Management & Computer Applications*, vol. 3, no. 12.

Barlow, J. B., Warkentin, M., Ormond, D., and Dennis, A. R. (2013), "Don't make excuses! Discouraging neutralization to reduce IT policy violation", *Computers & Security*, vol. 39, pp. 145–159. https://doi.org/10.1016/j.cose.2013.05.006

Beheshtifar, M., and Herat, B. H. (2013), "To promote employees commitment via perceived organizational support," *International Journal of Academic Research in Business and Social Sciences*, vol. 3, no. 1, pp. 306–313.

Blythe, J. M., Coventry, L., and Little, L. (2015), "Unpacking security policy compliance: the motivators and barriers of employees' security behaviors", *Eleventh Symposium on Usable Privacy and Security*, Ottawa, Canada, pp. 103–122. doi: https://dl.acm.org/doi/10.5555/3235866.3235875

Boss, S. R., and Kirsch, L. J. (2007), "The last line of defense: motivating employees to follow corporate security guidelines", in *Proceedings of the 28th International Conference on Information Systems*, Montreal.

Bratley, K. J., and Aloysius, S. M. (2019), "Transparency in managerial practices and affective commitment", *Journal of Business Studies*, vol. 6, no. 2, pp. 61–81. https://doi.org/10.4038/jbs.v6i2.47

Bulgurcu, B., Cavusoglu, H., and Benbasat, I. (2010), "Information security policy compliance: an empirical study of rationality-based beliefs and information security awareness", *MIS Quarterly*, vol. 34, no. 3, pp. 523–548. https://doi.org/10.2307/25750690

Carroll, M., Van Der Merwe, A., and Kotze, P. (2011), "Secure cloud computing: Benefits, risks and controls", *Information Security South Africa (ISSA)*, pp. 1–9. New York: IEEE. https://doi.org/10.1109/issa.2011.6027519

Castle, E., Eisenberger, E. N. I., Seeman, T. E., Moons, W. G., Boggero, I. A., Grinblatt, M. S., and Taylor, S. E. (2012), "Neural and behavioral bases of age differences in perceptions of trust", *Proceedings of the National Academy of Sciences*, vol. 109, pp. 20848–20852. https://doi.org/10.1073/pnas.1218518109

Chan, L., Reed, A. E., and Mikels, J. A. (2014), "Meta-analysis of the age-related positivity effect: age differences in preferences for positive over negative information", *Psychology and Aging*, pp. 1–15. https://doi.org/10.1037/a0035194

Chan, M., Woon, I., and Kankanhalli, A. (2005), "Perceptions of information security in the workplace: linking information security climate to compliant behavior", *Journal of Information Privacy and Security*, vol. 1, no. 3, pp. 18–41. https://doi.org/10.1080/15536548.2005.10855772

Cheng, L., Li, Y., Li, W., Holm, E., and Zhai, Q. (2013), "Understanding the violation of IS security policy in organizations: an integrated model based on social control and deterrence theory", *Computers & Security*, vol. 39, pp. 447–459. https://doi.org/10.1016/j.cose.2013.09.009

Chin, W. W., and Newsted, P.R. (1999), "Structural equation modeling analysis with small samples using partial least squares". In Hoyle, R. (Ed.), *Statistical Strategies for Small Sample Research*. New York: Sage Publications, 1307–1341.

Cisco System, (2008), "Data leakage worldwide: the effectiveness of security policies", available at: www.cisco.com/en/US/solutions/collateral/ns170/ns896/ns895/white_paper_c11–503131.pdf

Conger, J. A., and Kanungo, R. N. (1988), "The empowerment process: Integrating theory and practice", https://doi.org/10.5465/amr.1988.4306983

D'Arcy, J., and Herath, T. (2011), "A review and analysis of deterrence theory in the IS security literature: making sense of the disparate findings", *European Journal of Information Systems*, vol. 20, pp. 643–658. https://doi.org/10.1057/ejis.2011.23

D'Arcy, J., Hovav, A., and Galletta, D. (2009), "User awareness of security countermeasures and its impact on information systems misuse: a deterrence approach", *Information Systems Research*, vol. 20, no. 1, pp. 79–98. https://doi.org/10.1287/isre.1070.0160.

Ebner, N. C., Bailey, P. E., Horta, M., Joiner, J., and Chang, S. W. C. (2015), "Multidisciplinary perspective on prosociality in aging", in *Social Cognition for the Frontiers in Developmental Science Series* (Psychology).

Florencio, D., and Herley, C. (2007), "A large-scale study of web password habits", in *Proceedings of the 16th international conference on World Wide Web*, pp. 657–666. New York: ACM. https://doi.org/10.1145/1242572.1242661

Floyd, D. L., Prentice-Dunn, S., and Rogers, R. W. (2000), "A meta-analysis of research on protection motivation theory", *Journal of Applied Social Psychology*, vol. 30, no. 2, pp. 407–429. https://doi.org/10.1111/j.1559-1816.2000.tb02323.x

Fornell, C., and Bookstein, F. (1982). "Two structural equation models: LISREL and PLS applied to consumer exit-voice theory", *Journal of Marketing Research*, vol. 19, pp. 440–452. https://doi.org/10.2307/3151718.

Fuller, J. B., Barnett, T., Hester, K., and Relyea, C. (2003), "A social identity perspective on the relationship between perceived organizational support and organizational commitment", *The Journal of Social Psychology*, vol. 143, no. 6, pp. 789–791. https://doi.org/10.1080/00224540309600432

Furnell, S. (2005), "Authenticating ourselves: will we ever escape the password?", *Network Security*, 8–13. https://doi.org/10.1016/s1353-4858(05)00212-6

Furth-Matzkin, M., and Sunstein, C. R. (2018), "Social influences on policy preferences: conformity and reactance: conformity and reactance", *Minnesota Law Review*, vol. 102, no. 3, pp. 1339–1379. https://doi.org/10.2139/ssrn.2881494

Gefen, D., Straub, D. W., and Boudreau, M. C. (2000), "Structural equation modelling and regression: guidelines for research practice", *Communications of the Association for Information Systems*, vol. 4, pp. 1–77. https://doi.org/10.17705/1cais.00407

Gerbing, D. W., and Anderson, J. C. (1988), "An updated paradigm for scale development incorporating unidimensionality and its assessment", *Journal of Marketing Research*, 186–192. https://doi.org/10.1177/002224378802500207

Greenberg, J., and Baron, R. A. (2000), *Behavior in Organizations* (7th edition). Hoboken, NJ: Prentice-Hall.

Guo, K. H., and Yuan, Y. (2012), "The effects of multilevel sanctions on information security violations: a mediating model", *Information & Management*, vol. 49, no. 6, pp. 320–326. https://doi.org/10.1016/j.im.2012.08.001

Hair, J. F., Ringle, C. M., and Sarstedt, M. (2011), "PLS-SEM: indeed a silver bullet", *Journal of Marketing Theory and Practice*, vol. 19, no. 2, 139–151. https://doi.org/10.2753/mtp1069–6679190202

Hair, M. (2014), *A Primer on Partial Least Squares Structural Equation Modeling*. Thousand Oaks, CA: SAGE.

Hashizume, K., Rosado, D., Fernández-Medina, E., and Fernandez, E. (2013), "An analysis of security issues for cloud computing", *Journal of Internet Services and Applications*, vol. 4, no. 5, pp. 1–13. https://doi.org/10.1186/1869-0238-4-5

Hauser, D. J., and Schwarz, N. (2016), "Attentive Turkers: MTurk participants perform better on online attention checks than do subject pool participants", *Behavior Research Methods*, vol. 48, no. 1, pp. 400–407. https://doi.org/10.3758/s13428–015–0578-z

Herath, T., and Rao, H. R. (2009), "Protection motivation and deterrence: a framework for security policy compliance in organisations", *European Journal of Information Systems*, vol. 18, no. 2, pp. 106–125. https://doi.org/10.1057/ejis.2009.6

Hu, Q., Xu, Z., Dinev, T., and Ling, H. (2011), "Does deterrence work in reducing information security policy abuse by employees?", *Communications of the ACM*, vol. 54, no. 6, pp. 54–60. https://doi.org/10.1145/1953122.1953142

Ifinedo, P. (2012), "Understanding information systems security policy compliance: an integration of the theory of planned behavior and the protection motivation theory", *Computers & Security*, vol. 31, no. 1, pp. 83–95. https://doi.org/10.1016/j.cose.2011.10.007

Johnston, A. C., Warkentin, M., and Siponen, M. (2015), "An enhanced fear appeal rhetorical framework: Leveraging threats to the human asset through sanctioning rhetoric", *MIS Quarterly*, vol. 39, no. 1, pp. 113–134. https://doi.org/10.25300/misq/2015/39.1.06

Kabay, M. E. (2009), *Computer Security Handbook, Set* (5th Edition). Seymour Bosworth (Editor), Eric Whyne (Editor). Hoboken, NJ: John Wiley & Sons, Inc.

La Marra, C. G. A., Martinelli, F., and Matteucci, I. (2018), "CANDY: A social engineering attack to leak information from infotainment system", in *Proceedings of the IEEE Vehicular Technology Conference*, pp. 1–5. https://doi.org/10.1109/vtcspring.2018.8417879

Lee, T. W., Mitchell, T. R., Sablynski, C. J., Burton, J. P., and Holtom, B. (2004), "The effects of job embeddedness on organizational citizenship, job performance, volitional absences, and voluntary turnover", *Academy of Management Journal*, vol. 47, no. 5, pp. 711–722. https://doi.org/10.5465/20159613

Li, W. D., Lee, J. D., Purl, J., Greitzer, F. L., Yousefi, B., and Laskey, K. B. (2020), "Experimental investigation of demographic factors related to phishing susceptibility", *HICSS*: 1–10. https://doi.org/10.24251/hicss.2020.274

Liao, Q., Gurung, A., Luo, X., and Li, L. (2009), "Workplace management and employee misuse: does punishment matter?", *Journal of Computer Information Systems*, vol. 50, pp. 49–59.

Lowry, P. B., and Gaskin, J. (2014), "Partial least squares (PLS) structural equation modeling (SEM) for building and testing behavioral causal theory: when to choose it and how to use it", *IEEE Transactions on Professional Communication*, vol. 57, no. 2, pp. 123–146. https://doi.org/10.1109/tpc.2014.2312452

Maddux, J. E., and Rogers, R. W. (1983), "Protection motivation and self-efficacy: A revised theory of fear appeals and attitude change", *Journal of Experimental Social Psychology*, vol. 19, no. 5, pp. 469–479. https://doi.org/10.1016/0022–1031(83)90023–9

Marinelli, E. E. (2009), *Hyrax: Cloud Computing on Mobile Devices using MapReduce* (No. CMU-CS-09–164). Carnegie-Mellon Univ Pittsburgh PA School of Computer Science, Pittsburgh, PA.

Miller, K. W., Voas, J., and Hurlburt, G. F. (2012), "BYOD: security and privacy considerations", *IT Professional*, vol. 14, no. 5, pp. 53–55. https://doi.org/10.1109/mitp.2012.93

Milne, S., Sheeran, P., and Orbell, S. (2000), "Prediction and intervention in health-related behavior: A meta-analytic review of protection motivation theory", *Journal of Applied Social Psychology*, vol. 30, no. 1, pp. 106–143. https://doi.org/10.1111/j.1559–1816.2000.tb02308.x

Morrow, B. (2012), "BYOD security challenges: control and protect your most sensitive data", *Network Security*, 5–8. https://doi.org/10.1016/s1353-4858(12)70111-3

Myers, M. D. (2009), *Qualitative Research in Business & Management*. Thousand Oaks, CA: Sage Publications.

Myyry, L., Siponen, M., Pahnila, S., Vartiainen, T., and Vance, A. (2009), "What levels of moral reasoning and values explain adherence to information security rules and quest; an empirical study", *European Journal of Information Systems*, vol. 18, no. 2, pp. 126–139. https://doi.org/10.1057/ejis.2009.10

Notoatmodjo, G., and Thomborson, C. (2009), "Passwords and perceptions", *Proceedings of the Seventh Australasian Conference on Information Security*, vol. 98, pp. 71–78.

Pahnila, S., Siponen, M., and Mahmood, A. (2007), "Employees' behavior towards IS security policy compliance, System Sciences", in *HICSS 2007.40th Annual Hawaii International Conference*, p. 156b. https://doi.org/10.1109/hicss.2007.206

Paulhus, D. L. (2001), "Socially desirable responding: the evolution of a construct". In Braun, H., Jackson, D. N., and Wiley, D. E. (Eds.), *The Role of Constructs in Psychological and Educational Measurement* (pp. 67–88). Hillsdale, NJ: Erlbaum. https://doi.org/10.4324/9781410607454-10

Pavković, P. N., and Perkov, L. (2011), "Social engineering toolkit – A systematic approach to social engineering", *Proceedings of the 34th International Convention MIPRO*, Opatija, Croatia, pp. 1485–1489.

Posey, C., Roberts, T., Lowry, P. B., Bennett, B., and Courtney, J. (2013), "Insiders' protection of organizational information assets: Development of a systematics-based taxonomy and theory of diversity for protection-motivated behaviors", *MIS Quarterly*, vol. 37, no. 4, pp. 1189–1210. https://doi.org/10.25300/misq/2013/37.4.09

Pring, B., Brown, R. H., Frank, A., Hayward, S., and Leong, L. (2009), *Forecast: Sizing the Cloud; Understanding the Opportunities in Cloud Services*. Stamford, CT: Gartner, Inc.

Putchala, S. K., Bhat, K., and Anitha, R. (2013), "Information security challenges in social media interactions: strategies to normalize practices across physical and virtual worlds", *DSCI – Best Practices Meet 2013*, Chennai, India, pp. 1–4, doi: 10.1109/BPM.2013.6615012

Rochwerger, B., Breitgand, D., Levy, E., Galis, A., Nagin, K., Llorente, I. M., and Ben-Yehuda, M. (2009), "The reservoir model and architecture for open federated cloud computing", *IBM Journal of Research and Development*, vol. 53, no. 4, pp. 4–1. https://doi.org/10.1147/jrd.2009.5429058

Rogers, R. W. (1975), "A protection motivation theory of fear appeals and attitude change", *The Journal of Psychology*, vol. 91, no. 1, pp. 93–114. https://doi.org/10.1080/00223980.1975.9915803

Ruffman, T., Murray, J., Halberstadt, J., and Vater, T. (2012), "Age-related differences in deception', *Psychology and Aging*, vol. 27, pp. 543–549. https://doi.org/10.1037/a0023380

Ryutov, Tatyana, Nicole Sintov, Mengtian Zhao, and Richard S. John. (2017), "Predicting information security policy compliance intentions and behavior for six employee-based risks." *Journal of Information Privacy and Security* vol. 13, no. 4, pp. 260–281.

Safa, N. S., and Ismail, M. A. (2013), "A customer loyalty formation model in electronic commerce", *Economic Modelling*, vol. 35, pp. 559–564. https://doi.org/10.1016/j.econmod.2013.08.011

SANS Institute (2012), "Risk assessment of social media", available at: www.sans.org/reading-room/whitepapers/riskmanagement/risk-assessment-social-media-33940.

Schoenberg, C. (2013), "Information security & negligence targeting the C-class", available at: www.infosecwriters.com/text_resources/pdf/InformationSecurityCClass.pdf.

Scholtz, J. T. (1997). "Enforcement policy and corporate misconduct: the changing perspective of deterrence theory", *Law and Contemporary Problems*, vol. 60, no. 3, p. 253. https://doi.org/10.2307/1192014.

Shropshire, J., Warkentin, M., and Sharma, S. (2015), "Personality, attitudes: and intentions: predicting initial adoption of information security behavior", *Computer Security*, vol. 49, pp. 177–191. https://doi.org/10.1016/j.cose.2015.01.002

Siponen, M., and Vance, A. (2010), "Neutralization: new insights into the problem of employee information systems security policy violations", *MIS Quarterly*, 487–502. https://doi.org/10.2307/25750688

Souppaya, M., and Scarfone, K. (2021), "Guide to enterprise patch management planning: preventive maintenance for technology", NIST Special Publication NIST SP 800–40r4. NIST-CSRC Publications, Gaithersburg, MD, pp. 1–28. https://doi.org/10.6028/NIST.SP.800–40r4

Sqalli, M. H., Al-Haidari, F., and Salah, K. (2011), "Edos-shield-a two-steps mitigation technique against EDoS attacks in cloud computing", in *Utility and Cloud Computing (UCC), Fourth IEEE International Conference*, pp. 49–56. New York: IEEE. https://doi.org/10.1109/ucc.2011.17

Staples, D. S. (1997), "An investigation of some key information technology-enabled remote management and remote work issues", in *Conference Proceedings of the Australasian Conference on Information Systems*. https://doi.org/10.3127/ajis.v4i2.362

Straub, D. W., and Nance, W. D. (1990), "Discovering and disciplining computer abuse in organizations: a field study", *MIS Quarterly*, vol. 14, pp. 45–60. https://doi.org/doi.org/10.2307/249307

Subashini, S., and Kavitha, V. (2011), "A survey on security issues in service delivery models of cloud computing", *Journal of Network and Computer Applications*, vol. 34, no. 1, 1–11. https://doi.org/10.1016/j.jnca.2010.07.006

Tam, L., Glassman, M., and Vandenwauver, M. (2010), "The psychology of password management: a tradeoff between security and convenience", *Behaviour & Information Technology*, vol. 29, no. 3, pp. 233–244. https://doi.org/10.1080/01449290903121386

Theoharidou, M., Kokolakis, S., Karyda, M., and Kiountouzis, E. (2005). "The insider threat to information systems and the effectiveness of ISO17799", *Computers & Security*, vol. 24, no. 6, pp. 472–484. https://doi.org/10.1016/j.cose.2005.05.002.

Ullah, K. W., Ahmed, A. S., and Ylitalo, J. (2013), "Towards building an automated security compliance tool for the cloud, trust, security and privacy", in *Computing and Communications (TrustCom), 12th IEEE International Conference, IEEE*, pp. 1587–1593. https://doi.org/10.1109/trustcom.2013.195

Vance, A., Siponen, M., and Pahnila, S. (2012), "Motivating IS security compliance: insights from habit and protection motivation theory", *Information & Management*, vol. 49, no. 3, pp. 190–198. https://doi.org/10.1016/j.im.2012.04.002

Wang, Y., Wei, J., and Vangury, K. (2014), "Bring your own device security issues and challenges", in *Proceedings of the 11th Annual IEEE Consumer Communications & Networking Conference (CCNC)*, pp. 80–85. https://doi.org/10.1109/ccnc.2014.6866552

Warkentin, M., Johnston, A. C., and Shropshire, J. (2011), "The influence of the informal social learning environment on information privacy policy compliance efficacy and intention," *European Journal of Information Systems*, vol. 20, no. 3, pp. 267–284. https://doi.org/10.1057/ejis.2010.72

Washo, A. H. (2021), "An interdisciplinary view of social engineering: a call to action for research", *Computers in Human Behavior Reports*, vol. 4. https://doi.org/10.1016/j.chbr.2021.100126

Wold, H. O. A. (1982), "Soft modeling: The basic design and some extensions". In Joreskog, K. G. and Wold, H. O. A. (Eds.), *Systems under Indirect Observations: Part II* (pp. 1–54). Amsterdam, Netherlands: North-Holland Publishing Company (an Imprint of Elsevier).

Wold, H. (1985), "Partial least squares", *Encyclopedia of Statistical Sciences*, vol. 6, pp. 581–591.

Yıldırım, M., and Mackie, I., (2019), "Encouraging users to improve password security and memorability", *International Journal of Information Security*, vol. 18, pp. 741–759. https://doi.org/10.1007/s10207-019-00429-y

Zhang, X., Wuwong, N., Li, H., and Zhang, X. (2010), "Information security risk management framework for the cloud computing environments", in *Computer and Information Technology (CIT), IEEE 10th International Conference*, pp. 1328–1334. https://doi.org/10.1109/cit.2010.501

16 Nexus between Banking Cybersecurity Breaches, Cyber Vulnerabilities, and Kidnap for Ransom in Nigeria

A Comparative Analysis of Kaduna and Abuja Metropolis, Nigeria

Hassan Abdulazeez and Sule Magaji

CONTENTS

INTRODUCTION

Cybersecurity has been of concern for policymakers for years because of the increasing interconnectivity between computers and telecommunication. The increasing innovation and diffusion of technology which has hitherto been identified with developed nations has over the years taken on a global dimension, which has also led to the emergence/introduction of cyber-based system of banking, that is, connectivity between computers and telecoms. The need to secure them has therefore become paramount because of the vulnerabilities that are inherent in the system.

This chapter aims to examine the platform of the cyberinfrastructure of the E-banking system in Nigeria, established to reduce high cash circulation with an intended concomitant effect of reducing

DOI: 10.1201/9781003319887-16

crime, for example, robbery and corruption. This chapter examines how the system reduced, hindered, or led to the manifestation of other crimes. This chapter uses literature reviews, data from the police and other law enforcement agencies, and surveys from the public to ascertain the typologies of crimes before the E-banking cybersecurity system. In addition, this chapter examines the possible nexus between the cashless system and kidnapping for ransom that is presently ravaging Nigeria.

The threat posed by breaches in the global cybersecurity system is advancing faster than we can keep up with. Billions of naira were diverted from one form of a cyber-security breach or the other; these breaches, known as cybercrime, are recorded in virtually all organizations and are linked to global cyberspace facilitated by the synchronization of the internet and networks of computers. For example, in Nigeria, fraudulent activities were recorded, 60% of which were mainly because of the Internet of Things. In addition, between July and September 2020, about 3.5 billion in the Nigerian currency, naira, was lost, mainly due to cyber-based bank fraud.

PROBLEM RATIONALE AND RESEARCH QUESTIONS

Nigeria is the most populous country in Africa, with an estimated population of 206.1 million (as of 2020), and it has many natural landmarks and wildlife reserves. Nigeria has more than 25 banks, 11 of which have international authorization. It has formidable commercial trade, transportation, insurance, banking, and finance activities. Before the introduction of cyber-based banking systems, the banking system in Nigeria was primarily analogue and had peculiarities in the types of crime recorded within that period. For example, the banking industry in Nigeria experienced a high number of bank robberies, culminating in the loss of a significant volume of depositors' funds and loss of lives. With the use of cash settlements via commercial activities coupled with innovation in global banking and other industries; a shift from analogue to cyber-based system became inevitable, which led the central bank of Nigeria to introduce and enforce what is now known as the cashless policy in 2012.

With the implementation of the policy, new cyber-based products and platforms gave previously unbanked locations platforms for banking services. Meanwhile, banks are supposed to develop cybersecurity infrastructure to ensure depositors' funds are safe. To what extent have banks been able to reduce their vulnerabilities? What are the nature and extent of cybersecurity breaches in the banking industry in Nigeria? What were the nature and extent of crimes that are bank related before the use of the cyber-based system, that is, the electronic banking system? What are the extent and vulnerabilities of the system? What are its impacts on the banking industry? What can be done to turn the tide? These questions interest cyber scholars to offer workable solutions to the problems.

Moreover, manifestations of the system's vulnerabilities and the challenges they pose to the global banking system are enormous. In addition to the vulnerabilities induced by cybersecurity infrastructure, the country is presently witnessing a new form of crime, which this chapter argues is related to the advent of the electronic cyber-based banking system: the menace of kidnap for ransom. We intend to advance the idea that there is a link between widespread implementation of cyber-based electronic banking systems and kidnapping for ransom. Finally, we shall look at how cybersecurity attacks have impacted the banking industry in Nigeria.

LITERATURE REVIEW

TRENDS AND PATTERNS OF CRIME BEFORE E-BANKING

Alemika and Chukwuma (2003) highlighted the patterns of crime before electronic banking systems, which were primarily robbery, murder, assassination, and other violent crimes; the situation led to the launching of "Operation Fire for Fire" aimed at addressing the menace. Disputable as the results might be, researchers measured relative relationships between crime and cash access and found that the overall crime trend was going down after the program implementation – albeit with a few hiccups along the way. All criminal acts fall into four categories: an offence against a person, property, lawful authority, and local crimes. Offences against persons included manslaughter, murder, attempted murder, assault, rape, and child stealing. In contrast, crimes such as armed robbery, house and store breaking, forgery, and theft/stealing are offences against lawful authority. However, the crime data showed crimes such as forgery of currency, gambling, breach of peace, bribery, and corruption. Finally, offences of local acts, including traffic offences and liquor offences, were rampant. Badiora and Afon (2013) employ a systematic sampling technique to study the rate of occurrence of crime measured through an index-tagged crime rate of occurrence index (CROI); the findings were astonishing. Chinwokwu (2014) traced the trend and pattern of violent crimes in Nigeria from the 1980s and believed that the emergence of Boko Haram introduced a pattern of criminal violence that has taken and continues to take on a dangerous dimension and intensity in Nigeria.

CYBERSECURITY VULNERABILITIES AND THE NEW FACE OF CRIME

This section reviews the literature on cybersecurity vulnerabilities that involve the banking sector in Nigeria; the threats posed by breaches of the cybersecurity of financial institutions in Nigeria and elsewhere are overwhelming. Cybersecurity consists of tools, policies, security concepts, security safeguards, best practice assurance, and technologies that can protect cyberspace or organization and user assets (Frank and Odunayo, 2013). Attempts by unscrupulous societal elements to infiltrate and breach safeguards for their selfish ends leads to vulnerabilities in cybersecurity networks. Cybercrime, according to Ibrahim (2020), involves the use of specialized applications in computers and the internet by technically skilled individuals to commit crimes, the consequences of which possibly threaten nations' security architecture and financial wellbeing.

Omodunbi et al. (2016) see cybercrime as a crime committed by criminals using computers as a tool of the internet as a connection to reach various objectives. This concept involves the manifestation of cybercrime, including bank verification number (BVN) scams, phishing, theft of bank cards, and banking fraud. Imran et al. (2018) identify cybersecurity attacks and threats to cyberspace as malware, phishing, eavesdropping, SQL injection attacks, denial of service (DOS), and XSS (crisscross-scripting) attacks, among others. All these crimes have had devastating consequences on the banking sector. In the same vein, Chiappetta (2019) states malware can be transferred from one computer to another in many forms; this is possible because computers are linked, and the internet is widely used in the contemporary business and economic environment.

Kosutic and Pigni (2020) set out to assist companies in addressing the problem of ever-increasing cybersecurity investment that does not produce tangible business value. Vartolomei and Avasilcai (2019) state that, especially given the ever-increasing vulnerabilities of the cyber world/space that come with concomitant cyber threats and data infiltration, this benefits the attacker without the consent of the victim. The studies suggested some strategies to mitigate challenges, including cybersecurity training. Similarly, Ogunwale (2020) argues that commercial banks in Nigeria have experienced numerous cyberattacks, which have, over the years, culminated in substantial financial and valuable losses. The shift from the previous analogue system to the modern, sophisticated internet-based one that ushered in electronic banking. Despite all the measures put in place, the banking sector in Nigeria has continued to remain the most targeted institution in all sectors by cyber hackers and criminals. Eze (2021) asserts that the internet-based banking system has ushered in new forms of crime in Nigeria, such as spamming, credit card fraud, ATM fraud, phishing, identity theft, and other cyber-related crimes. Further arguing that cybercrimes have negatively impacted the online banking system in Nigeria, this often dissuades foreign investors from investing in the country and has led to substantial financial losses.

In addition, Ugwuja et al. (2019) argue that cyber risks in the banking system include unsuccessful transactions through electronic banking platforms such as ATMs and POS, which culminate in accounts being debited without accessing cash. Furthermore, Ugwuja et al. identified vishing, smishing, and others as social engineering threats. In addition, Gupta and Kumar (2020) studied the concept of identity fraud and how it can lead to financial crime. They argued that cybercrime through the medium of identity theft was initially on a small scale. However, with the increasing global digitalization of cyberspace, crime has intensified to the extent that its impacts can hamper the global economy. Also, Wang et al. (2020) believed the transition of the Nigerian banking system catapulted the cybercrime scene from low-tech crimes to much more sophisticated high-tech breaches involving the uses of viruses, worms, or Trojan infections, spam e-mail and hacking being the most-recorded breaches.

Impact of Cybersecurity Attacks on the Nigerian Banking Industry

Dagoumas (2019) examines the challenges of cybersecurity attacks on power systems, which he believes substantially impact the reliability of the whole energy system. Furthermore, the study employed unit commitment (UC) models in tackling renewable uncertainty. It is a view of the dangers cyberattacks posed on the power system. Each transmission system operator needs to examine the combination of cyberattacks and operating conditions to identify crucial cases for system stability and power system cost operation.

Ogunwale (2020) writes on the impact of cybercrime in Nigeria's commercial banking system and asserts that numerous cyberattacks have engendered the loss of a considerable sum of depositors' funds. For example, the central bank of Nigeria confirms that transactions valued at 6.5 trillion were stolen by hackers from commercial banks. Cybercriminals cost $1.5 trillion in 2018 and $2 trillion in 2019 globally through effective hacks and theft from websites and organizations. The paper further argued that cybercrime has been increasing within Nigeria's banking industry, which remains the most vulnerable and targeted by hackers.

Okpa et al. (2020) examined the rising incidence of phishing and maintained that it had a devastating effect on organizations, as it has increased, leading to loss of trade and competitiveness and destroying consumer confidence. Akinbowale et al. (2020) employed a survey of literature and balanced scorecard (BSC) methods in analyzing the effects of cybercrime on the banking sector and believes that an increasing wave of cybercrime has negatively impacted the goodwill of economic growth of financial institutions through the distortion of consumer confidence and trust in the digital banking system. Imran et al. (2018) believe cyberattacks hurt industries, with a resultant increasing percentage of industries victimized by cyberattacks.

Hussain and Ustun (2020) assert that the introduction/penetration of smart inverters has tremendous support for power grid systems. They are, however, vulnerable to cyberattacks; the paper pointed out the impact on the distribution performance of the system. Leevy et al. (2021), in their detection of cyberattacks across different network features, believe the data set covers a wide range of realistic cyberattacks, about 16 million instances. Also, Gogolin et al. (2021) argued that cybercriminals primarily target smaller banks; the phenomenon has had tremendous negative impact on bank branch deposit growth, with concomitant loss of consumer confidence and trust in smaller banks to bigger banks in what they termed "fight to reputation."

The study suggests that cybersecurity investment by banks is crucial for attracting and maintaining customers. Similarly, Khan et al. (2021) believe that banks must enhance their cybersecurity control to minimize the occurrence of cyberattacks. Uba (2021) was more detailed in stating that the impact of a cyberattack on a company is devastating, as it comes with consequences – financial, which often manifests in the following: theft of information like bank details, disruption to online transactions, and loss of business; reputational, which can lead to loss of customers, loss of sales, and reduction in profit; and finally legal due to data leaks. The person could face legal battles, fines, and regulatory sanctions if sensitive data are leaked and an infraction is noted against the culprits.

Literature Synthesis

From the previous literature survey on the trends and patterns of crime before the advent of the cyber-based banking system, otherwise known as the electronic banking system, one thing that comes to mind is the crime realities that dictate the research by various authors. For example, Chinwokwu (2014) centers his work on the then-prevailing crime associated with Boko Haram, an Islamist insurgence movement with attendant devastating consequences on the lives and properties of the Nigerian population, especially in northeast Nigeria. Other studies identified robbery, assault, arson, stealing, burglary, and other nonviolent crimes like corruption. It is pertinent to note that police statistical records confirmed various findings on the true nature and crime trends before the introduction of the cashless banking system. In addition, the records showed there used to be child stealing; however, the present realities of kidnap for ransom and other cybercrimes are, in the opinion of this author, a transition of crimes from what they used to be to what predominates presently.

Furthermore, with the intensification and deepening of the global economy through trade, commerce, finance, insurance, and banking through the internet, the synchronization or interface of wireless telecoms and computers enters new forms of risks associated with it, otherwise known as cyberattacks. Imran et al. (2018) identified cybersecurity attacks such as malware, denial of service, and SQL injection. Chiappetta (2019) notes that malware can be transferred from one remote computer to another.

Eze (2021), believes electronic banking platforms and infrastructures like ATM/credit card fraud and others like spamming and identity theft are the new faces of crime. Wang et al. (2020) earlier held that electronic banking has intensified cybercrime and taken it to a height that is dangerous to the system, especially given the sophistication of cybercrime, for example, the Trojan injections and spam mail. Consequently, Uba (2021) classified the consequences of cyberattacks on internet users into three broad categories: theft of information, loss of business, and reputational damage, all manifesting in different damage, as outlined earlier.

In addition, Akinbowale et al. (2020) argue that cyberattacks hurt industries' banking sector by lowering consumer confidence. Also, Khan et al. (2021) suggest that banks' cybersecurity control enhancement must be paramount to reduce cyberattacks because of their adverse impacts on the industry. Cyberattacks have been on the rise, as alluded to by the literature surveyed; the following are the extent and nature of cyberattacks on Nigerian banks from 2020 to June 2022, as reported by the news media:

1. France-based Nigerian travels to Lagos leads cyberattacks on ten banks – punch.com; 24 June 2022.
2. Cyber fraud rises 534% as Nigerian banks lose ₦3.5billion – businessday.com; 16 February 2022.
3. Alleged cyberattack on the central bank of Nigeria (CBN) causes stir in banks, others – The Guardian; 19 October 2020.
4.
5. Cyberattacks hit 71% of Nigerian businesses from 2021–May 2022. A total of $706,452 was paid ransom to cyber criminals by Nigerian businesses – nairametrics.com.
6. Four banks lost ₦1,77 billion to fraud in 2021, including Access Bank plc, Guaranty trust bank plc, First Monument City Bank, and Wema Bank, as contained in their 2021 financial statements.
7. Momo payment service bank, a new financial services subsidiary of the telecom company MTN Nigeria, suffered a breach in May 2022, days after launch, reportedly losing 22 billion naira, the equivalent of $53 million – qz.com/Africa/2183438.
8. Cybersecurity expert predicts an increase in cyberattacks in 2022 and argues that 2021 will witness unprecedented ransomware attacks with the rise of ransomware-as-a-service (RASS) groups on the dark web – thisdaylive.com/index.php.
9. Fresh cyberattacks hit Nigeria – Adaramola, Z., dailytrust.com (2022).
   Finally, Rufai (2021), in a well-researched work on rural banditry in Zamfara state, traced the origin of robberies and banditry to pre-colonial and colonial Nigeria and argued that the menace continued in the post-colonial era. This study argues that reducing cash in

circulation with the implementation and deepening of the cashless banking system played a vital role in the transition from the crimes of burglary, armed robbery, and others to the kidnap for ransom Nigerians are presently experiencing today. It may not necessarily be the main factor, as other factors may also come into play, as seen in a publication by the center for democracy and development (CDD, 2022). However, according to Abdulazeez et al. (2022), it may explain why robberies are reduced, while the main crime is people being traded for cash as ransom.

METHODS

This section concerns the presentation, analysis, and interpretation of data collected from Kaduna state and Federal Capital Territory (FCT) and from which inferences were drawn. This study uses crime statistical data from the police and interviews with law enforcement agents and attempts a social survey to ascertain the typology of crimes related to cyberbanking security-induced systems concerning the nature and extent of crimes after the introduction of the system. We used a simple percentage method, frequency analysis, and the Likert scale. We administered 650 questionnaires (350 in Kaduna and 300 in Abuja). Out of 650 questionnaires administered, a total of 587 were completed and retrieved; this represented a 90% success rate, as shown in Table 16.1.

Table 16.1 indicates that out of the 350 questionnaires administered in Kaduna state, 317 were retrieved; this represented about a 90.6% success rate. For Abuja, 270 questionnaires were filled and returned out of the 300 questionnaires administered. This represented a 90% return rate.

DESCRIPTIVE ANALYSIS OF THE QUESTIONNAIRE

Table 16.2 presents the respondents' demographic information. The results on the respondent's location according to their gender indicates that most of the respondents, that is, 446, representing about 76%, are male, while 141, representing about 24%, are female. The result showed that the majority of the respondents were between 31–50 years old (228, or 39%), followed by respondents in the age group 29–30 years (175, or 30%). Next was 51 years and above (109, or about 19%), and finally respondents within the age group 18–28 years (75, or about 13%). The frequency and percentage of marital status indicated that 481 respondents, about 82%, are married, and 93 respondents, about 16%, are single. In comparison, 13 respondents, representing 2%, are either divorced, separated, or widowed.

The results on respondents' highest educational qualification showed that most of the respondents had a tertiary education certificate, with a frequency of 398, or about 68%. In comparison, the minority was respondents with no formal education, with 1 (0.1%). The result of the frequency distribution of respondents' religion indicates that most of the respondents, that is, 439, representing about 75%, are Muslims, and 133, representing about 23%, are Christians. In comparison, 15 respondents, representing more than 3%, are traditionalists. The results for respondent occupation

TABLE 16.1
Questionnaire Administered and Retrieved

S/N	Location of Respondents	Questionnaire Administered	Questionnaire Retrieved	Percentage Retrieved
1.	Kaduna State	350	317	90.6%
2.	Abuja, FCT	300	270	90.0%
	Total	650	587	90.3%

TABLE 16.2

Frequency Distribution of Respondents' Demographic Information

Demographic Information	Response	Kaduna	Abuja
Gender	Male	260	186
	Female	57	84
	TOTAL	317	270
Age group	15–29 years	44	31
	30–44 years	101	74
	45–59 years	91	137
	60 years and above	81	28
	TOTAL	317	270
Marital status	Married	267	214
	Single	41	52
	Divorce/separated	6	4
	Widowed	3	0
	TOTAL	317	270
Educational attainment	No formal education	1	0
	Primary school only	32	23
	Secondary school only	78	55
	Tertiary school	206	192
	TOTAL	317	270
Religion	Islam	308	131
	Christianity	9	124
	Tradition	0	15
	TOTAL	317	270
Occupation	Public/civil servant	248	176
	Artisan/unskilled	8	83
	Business/trading	61	11
	TOTAL	317	270
Income level	Less than #30,000	18	5
	#31,000–#60,000	34	76
	#61,000–#90,000	61	93
	#91,000–#150,000	112	55
	#151,000 and above	92	41
	TOTAL	317	270
Ethnic group	Hausa	297	241
	Igbo	1	0
	Yoruba	2	6
	Others	17	23
	TOTAL	317	270

indicate that most respondents, that is, 424, representing about 72%, are either public or civil servants. The results also indicated that 72 respondents, about 12%, are either businesspersons or traders, while 91, representing 16%, are either artisans or unskilled workers.

The frequency distribution of the respondent's income level group shows that 167 respondents, about 29%, earn between N91,000 and N150,000. In contrast, only 13 respondents, about 2%, earn less than N30,000. The frequency distribution of respondents' ethnic groups indicates that the majority (538),

TABLE 16.3
Frequency of Crime before the Introduction of E-Banking

s/n	Statement	Location	Yes (2)	No (1)	Total	Mean Score	Decision
1.	Do you think the introduction of cashless banking has reduced the crime rate?	Kaduna	38	279	317	1.11	No
		Abuja	82	188	270	1.30	No
2.	Was cyber-crime common in Kaduna metropolis and Abuja before the introduction of the cashless banking policy?	Kaduna	248	69	317	1.78	Yes
		Abuja	221	49	270	1.82	Yes
3.	Do you think that cashless banking has reduced cybercrime?	Kaduna	42	275	317	1.13	No
		Abuja	84	186	270	1.12	No
4.	Do you think that the cashless policy has increased financial crime?	Kaduna	285	32	317	1.90	Yes
		Abuja	237	33	270	1.88	Yes

$$Sectional\ mean = \frac{Kaduna}{Abuja} = \frac{1.48}{1.53} = \frac{No}{Yes}$$

representing about 92%, are Hausa by tribe, and 40 respondents, about 7%, are from other ethnic groups. In comparison, nine respondents, representing above 2%, are either Ibos or Yoruba by tribe.

Five questions were answered using frequency distribution, simple percentages, and mean scores. Yes = 2 and No = 1 were used in the research instrument. The scale measurement average is 1.5. The decision rules guiding this analysis are given as follows.

- Yes if the item mean is above 1.5
- No if the item mean is below 1.5

What are the frequencies and patterns of crime before the introduction of e-banking and implementation of the cashless system?

The frequency of crime before the introduction of E-banking is presented in Table 16.3. Table 16.4 presents the item-by-item descriptive analysis of the crimes committed before e-banking in Kaduna state and Abuja. The mean score of items 2 and 4 for the two respondents' locations was more significant than the 2 Likert scale measurement average of 1.5, while the mean score of items 1 and 3 for the two respondents' locations was less than the 2 Likert scale measurement average. The result showed that the sectional mean rating of the respondents located in Kaduna state (mean score =1.48) was less than the 2 Likert scale measurement average of 1.5, while the sectional mean rating of the respondents located in Abuja (mean score =1.53) was more significant than the 2 Likert scale measurement average of 1.5. This result implies that Kaduna-based respondents disagreed that the introduction of cashless banking has reduced the crime rate and cybercrime, while

TABLE 16.4

Response to the Pattern of Crime before the Introduction of E-Banking

Crimes	Kaduna State	Abuja	Total
	Frequency		
Armed robbery	156 (49.2%)	109 (40.4%)	265 (45.1%)
Burglary	77 (24.2%)	82 (30.4%)	159 (27.1%)
Arson	24 (7.6%)	32 (11.9%)	56 (9.5%)
Rape	56 (17.7%)	12 (4.4%)	68 (11.6%)
Others	4 (1.3%)	35 (12.9%)	39 (6.7%)
Total	317 (54.0%)	270 (46.0%)	587 (100%)

Abuja-based respondents agreed that the introduction of cashless banking has reduced the crime rate and cybercrime. It was also discovered from the result presented in Table 16.4 that the two categories of respondents agreed that cybercrime was common in Kaduna metropolis and Abuja before the introduction of the cashless banking policy and that the cashless policy has increased financial crime. Similarly, the results on the pattern of crime before the introduction of e-banking presented in Table 16.4 indicated that armed robbery was the highest crime committed, with a frequency of 265 (45%), followed by burglary, with a frequency of 159 (27%), arson 56 (12%), rape 68 (12%), and other forms of crimes with a frequency of 39 (7%).

What are the challenges and new trends of crime with the introduction of e-banking?

Table 16.5 presents the problems encountered while using e-banking in Kaduna and Abuja. The first problem encountered according to respondents is thieves robbing customers at the POS, with 16.7% (98), followed by robbery at the ATM center at 9% (53); 22.7% (133) hacking the customer's account; and 27.9% (164) ATM debit without dispensing cash. The table also indicates that 139 (23.7%) of the total respondents believed that all four options were seldom encountered while using e-banking in Kaduna and Abuja. The result presented in Table 16.6 indicates that respondents from Kaduna and Abuja agreed that network failure in e-banking, inconveniences in sending and receiving money, debiting by ATM without getting cash from the ATMs, and charging by banks when using e-banking are some of the challenges faced by using cashless banking in Kaduna and Abuja. This result was arrived at because the grand mean response to the statement on the challenges of cashless banking in Kaduna and Abuja, that is, mean scores of 2.64 and 2.59, respectively, were more significant than the 4 Likert scale measurement averages of 2.5.

TABLE 16.5

Response on the Major Problems Encountered in Using E-Banking

Major problems	Kaduna State	Abuja	Total
	Respondents' Locations		
Thieves rob people at POS	61 (19.2%)	37 (13.7%)	98 (16.7%)
Robbery at ATM centers	24 (7.6%)	29 (10.7%)	53 (9.0%)
Hacking of customer's account	45 (14.2%)	88 (32.6%)	133 (22.7%)
ATM debit without dispensing cash	108 (34.1%)	56 (20.8%)	164 (27.9%)
All of the above	79 (24.9%)	60 (22.2%)	139 (23.7%)
Total	317 (56.0%)	270 (44.0%)	587 (100%)

TABLE 16.6

Response to the Challenges and New Trends of Crime with the Introduction of the E-Banking Cashless System in Kaduna and Abuja

s/n	Statement	Location	Yes (2)	No (1)	Total	Mean Score	Decision
1	Do you usually experience network failure in e-banking?	Kaduna	194	123	317	1.61	Yes
		Abuja	176	94	270	1.65	Yes
2	When you want to send or receive money, do you find it very convenient?	Kaduna	57	260	317	1.17	No
		Abuja	211	59	270	1.78	Yes
3	Have you ever been debited by ATM without getting cash from the machine?	Kaduna	194	123	317	1.61	Yes
		Abuja	72	198	270	1.27	No
4	Does the bank rectify the problem quickly?	Kaduna	200	117	317	1.63	Yes
		Abuja	161	109	270	1.60	Yes
5	Do banks charge you when you make use of e-banking?	Kaduna	224	93	317	1.71	Yes
		Abuja	226	44	270	1.84	Yes
6	If you are charged, is it usually much?	Kaduna	220	97	317	1.69	Yes
		Abuja	178	92	270	1.66	Yes
7	Do you think that banks are doing enough to curb financial crime	Kaduna	134	183	317	1.42	No
		Abuja	102	168	270	1.38	No
8	Do you think/ believe those transiting to other types of crime have been all along in other crimes?	Kaduna	182	135	317	1.57	Yes
		Abuja	77	193	270	1.28	No

$$Sectional\ mean = \frac{Kaduna}{Abuja} = \frac{1.55}{1.56} = \frac{Yes}{Yes}$$

DISCUSSION AND RESULTS

TEST OF HYPOTHESIS

Hypothesis one:

H_0: *There is no significant difference between cyberattacks and impacts on the banking industry*

H_1: *There is a significant difference between cyberattacks and impacts on the banking industry*

TABLE 16.7
Two-Tailed T-Test Result of Cyberattacks and Impacts on the Banking Industry

Locations	N	d.f.	Mean	Std. Error	t-Test	t-Critical	P-Value	Decision
Kaduna	317	585	1.48	0.135	1.312	1.96	0.673	Not significant
Abuja	270		1.53	0.168				

RESULT INTERPRETATION

A two independent sample t-test was done to determine if there was a difference between Kaduna state and Abuja (see Table 16.7). The test was statistically insignificant because the mean cyberattacks and impacts on the banking industry (mean = 1.48, SD = 0.135) were not significantly different from Abuja (mean = 1.53, SD = 0.168). The mean difference in cyberattacks in the banking industry was 0.05. This difference was insignificant because the calculated = 1.31 was less than the critical value of 1.96, and the P-value = 0.673 was more significant than the 0.05 level at 585 degrees of freedom. This result implies that there is not enough evidence to reject the null hypothesis; therefore, it is concluded that there is no significant difference between cyberattacks and impacts on the banking industry.

Hypothesis two:

H_0: *There is no significant difference in the mean electronic banking and upsurge of kidnapping between Kaduna and Abuja*

H_1: *There is a significant difference in the mean electronic banking and the upsurge of kidnapping between Kaduna and Abuja.*

A two independent sample t-test was done to determine if there was a difference in electronic banking and an upsurge in kidnapping between Kaduna state and Abuja (see Table 16.8). The test was statistically significant because the mean electronic banking and upsurge of kidnapping in Kaduna state (mean = 1.63, SD = 0.863) were significantly higher than in Abuja (mean = 1.25, SD = 0.434). The mean difference in electronic banking and upsurge in kidnapping between Kaduna state and Abuja was 0.38. This difference was significant because the calculated = 3.77 was greater than the critical of 1.96, and the P-value = 0.00 was smaller than the 0.05 level of significance at 585 degrees of freedom. This result implies that the null hypothesis (H_0) was rejected, and the alternative hypothesis (H_1) was accepted. This study concludes that there is a significant difference in the mean electronic banking and the upsurge of kidnapping between Kaduna and Abuja.

TABLE 16.8
Two-Tailed T-Test Result of Electronic Banking and Upsurge of Kidnapping between Kaduna State and Abuja

Locations	N	d.f.	Mean	Std. Error	t-Test	t-Critical	P-Value	Decision
Kaduna	317	585	1.63	0.863	3.77	1.96	0.00	Significant
Abuja	270		1.25	0.434				

CONCLUSION AND RECOMMENDATIONS

CONCLUSION

The study used descriptive statistics in analyzing data from questionnaires in explaining the frequencies and patterns of crime before the introduction of e-banking and the implementation of the cashless system, where findings show the preponderance of crimes like armed robbery, burglary, rape, and others. The new trends in crime and other related challenges after the introduction of e-banking were examined, and crimes such as robbery, instead of being committed at victims' houses and banks, have now transitioned to ATM platforms, hacking of bank accounts, and bank servers. Challenges like ATM debiting without providing appropriate services were observed.

The following hypotheses are, because of this, rejected and accepted, as the case may be:

1. There is no significant difference between cyberattacks and their impacts on the banking sector.
2. There is a significant difference between Kaduna and Abuja's mean electronic banking and upsurge of kidnapping.

RECOMMENDATIONS

This section is concerned with recommendations the researcher believes may help solve some of the issues identified during this study.

1. The supervising authority of the commercial banking sector should develop more ways to address the challenges experienced by the public from banks.
2. The CBN should enforce extant rules to violators of the rules and regulations guiding the banking system.
3. Commercial and other banks that use electronic banking platforms should ensure their hardware and software are always serviceable and subjected to hackproof/integrity tests often, without which colossal amounts of depositors' funds may continue to be lost.
4. Banks must ensure they continuously vet their staff and subject them to crime checks before and after employment. It is necessary because most bank-related cybercrime is mainly a result of insider connivance.
5. To curtail/reduce the inducement of bank workers by fraudsters, this study recommends that banks investigate their welfare packages and remunerations to make it almost impossible for a fraudster to employ/collude with an insider to perpetrate acts that are detrimental to the banking industry.
6. This study observed that banks employ contract staff to man critical banking system infrastructure, making easy connivance possible. This study, therefore, recommends that banks should be discouraged from employing contract staff for critical electronic banking infrastructure.
7. More technology-based crime prevention systems on platforms should be enhanced, for example, more cyber-related protocols to safeguard the lives and funds of people using the electronic system.
8. The government should enforce the cashless system rules to make it almost impossible for people to collect vast sums of money in cash from banks; this may reduce kidnap for ransom, a crime that manifested with the introduction and wide use of the e-system.
9. The federal Ministry of Education should add crime-related courses or subjects to Nigeria's educational curriculum to highlight their general implications for the nation's economy and general wellbeing, all aimed at discouraging would-be cybercrime offenders. That alone may help in reducing the menace in our society.

10. POS operators, bank agents, and other bank electronic payment platforms should identify their customers through either the "know your customer" (KYC) model or recognized means of identification and keep duplicate records in case of any eventuality.

REFERENCES

Abdulazeez, Hassan, Magaji, Sule, and Ibrahim, Musa. 2022. 'Analysis of Infrastructural Challenges, Cybercrime, & the Cashless Policy in Nigeria.' *Advanced Research on Information Systems Security*, vol. 2, no. 1, pp. 13–27. http://dx.doi.org/10.56394/aris2.v2i1.15

Akinbowale, Oluwatoyin Esther, Klingelhofer, Heinz Eckart, and Zerihom, Mulatu Fekadu. 2020. 'Analysis of Cyber-Crime Effects on the Banking Sector Using the Balanced Scorecard: A Survey of Literature.' *Journal of Financial Crime*, vol. 27, no. 3, pp. 945–958. http://dx.doi.org/10.1108/JFC-03-2020-0037

Alemika, Etannibi and Chukwuma, Innocent. 2003. *Analysis of Police and Policing in Nigeria: A Desk Study of the Role of Policing as Barrier to Change or Driver of Change in Nigeria*. Lagos: Centre for law enforcement education in Nigeria.

Badiora, Adewumi Israel, and Afon, Abel Omoniyi. 2013. 'Spatial Pattern of Crime in Nigerian Traditional City: The Ile-Ife Experience.' *International Journal of Criminology and Sociological Theory*, vol. 6, no. 3, pp. 15–28. https://ijcst.journals.yorku.ca/index.php/ijcst/article/view/36686

Centre for Democracy and Development (CDD). 2022. 'Northwest Nigeria's Bandit Problem.' https://cddwestafrica.org/wpcontent/uploads/2022/04/Conflict-Dynamics-and-Actors-in-Nigerias-Northwest.pdf.

Chiappetta, Andrea. 2019. 'Cybersecurity Benefits and Resilience of Ports.' *European Transport*, no. 75, Paper no. 3. www.researchgate.net/journal/European-TransportTrasporti-Europei-1825-3997

Chinwokwu, C. Eke. 2014. 'Trend and Pattern of Violent Crimes in Nigeria: An Analysis of Boko Haram Terrorist Outrage.' *Journal of Culture, Society, and Development*, vol. 3. https://core.ac.uk/download/pdf/234690917.pdf; www.internationaljournalcorner.com/index.php/ijird_ojs/article/view/132872

Dagoumas, Athanasios. 2019. *Assessing the Impact of Cybersecurity Attacks on Power Systems*. Piraeus, Greece: Energy and Environment Policy Laboratory, School of Economics, Business and International Studies, University of Piraeus, PC 18532. http://dx.doi.org/10.3390/en12040725

Eze Patience AU. 2021. 'Challenges of Cybercrime on Online Banking in Nigeria a Review.' *International Digital Organization for Scientific Research IDOSR Journal of Arts and Management*, vol. 6, no. 1, pp. 63–69. www.idosr.org/wp-content/uploads/2021/07/IDOSR-JAM-61-63-69-2021.pdf

Frank, Ibikunle, and Odunayo, Eweniyi. 2013. "Approach to Cybersecurity Issues in Nigeria: Challenges and Solution." *International Journal of Cognitive Research in Science, Engineering and Education*, vol. 1, pp. 100–110. www.semanticscholar.org/paper/Approach-to-cyber-security-issues-in-nigeria%3A-and-Frank-Odunayo/0d201267556257bb9f7292e05652d7feb4c18f7e

Gupta, Chander Mohan, and Devesh, Kumar. 2020. 'Identity Theft: A Small Step Towards Significant Financial Crimes.' *Journal of Financial Crime*, vol. 27, no. 3. http://dx.doi.org/10.1108/JFC-01-2020-0014

Hussain, Suhail S. M., and Ustun, Taha Selim. 2020. 'Smart Inverter Communication Model and Impact of Cyberattacks.' In *IEEE International Conference on Power Electronics, Drives and Energy Systems (PEDES)*. http://dx.doi.org/10.1109/PEDES49360.2020.9379762

Ibrahim, Umar. 2020. 'The Impact of Cybercrime on the Nigerian Economy and Banking System.' https://ndic.gov.ng/wp-content/uploads/2020/08/NDIC-Quarterly-Vol-34-No-12–2019-Article-The-Impact-Of-Cybercrime-On-The-Nigerian-Economy-And-Banking-System.pdf; www.semanticscholar.org/paper/THE-IMPACT-OF-CYBERCRIME-ON-THE-NIGERIAN-ECONOMY-BY/cce26cbe71054298ee7266344cd245d1bce9fdb2.

Imran, Mohammad, Tasleem, Arif, and Shoab, Mohammad. 2018. 'A Statistical and Theoretical Analysis of Cyberthreats and Its Impacts on Industries.' *International Journal of Scientific Research in Computer Science Application and Management Studies*. www.semanticscholar.org/paper/A-Statistical-and-Theoretical-Analysis-of-and-its-Imran-Arif/2cc23c2b82e423a31900a43c4db60fb0d27a9b8f.

Khan, Anum, Mubarik, Muhammad Shujaal, and Naghavi, Nawaz. 2021. 'What Matters for Financial Inclusions? Evidence From an Emerging Economy.' *International Journal of Finance and Economics* vol. 28, no. 1, 821–838. http://dx.doi.org/10.1002/IJFE.2451

Leevy, L. Joffrey, Hancock, John, Zuech, Richard, and Taghi, M. Khosgoftar. 2021. 'Detecting Cybersecurity Attacks across Different Network Features and Learners.' *Journal of Big Data*, vol. 8, p. 38. https://doi.org/10.1186/s40537-021-00426-w

Ogunwale, Hezekia. 2020. *The Impact of Cybercrime on Nigeria's Commercial Banking System*. Bournemouth: Department of Computing and Informatics, Bournemouth University Dorset. www.researchgate.net/publication/347388290

Okpa, John Thompson, Okorie, Ajah Benjamin, and Egidi, Igbe Joseph. 2020. 'Rising Trend of Phishing Attacks on the Corporate Organization in Cross River State, Nigeria.' *International Journal of Cyber Criminology*, vol. 14, no. 2, pp. 460–478. http://dx.doi.org/10.5281/zenodo.4770111

Omodunbi, Bolaji, Odiase, P. O., Olaniyan, Olatayo, and Esan, Adebimpe. 2016. 'Cybercrime in Nigeria: Analysis. Detection and Prevention.' *Journal of Engineering and Technology*, vol. 1, no. 1. http://dx.doi.org/10.46792/fuoyejet.v1i1.16

Rufai, Murtala Ahmed. 2021. 'I am a Bandit: A Decade of Research in Zamfara State Bandits Den.' Department of History, Usmanu Danfodio University Sokoto – Nigeria. www.academia.edu/51724720/I_AM_BANDIT_a_decate_of_research_in_Zamfara_bandit_den?f_ri=419855.

Uba, J. 2021. 'The Most Serious Cybersecurity Threats Facing Businesses in Nigeria and How to Mitigate Them.' www.mondaq.com/nigeria/security.

Ugwuja, V. C., Ekunwe, P. A., and Henri-Ukoha, A. 2019. 'Cyber Risks in Electronic Banking: Exposures and Cybersecurity Preparedness of Women Agro-Entrepreneurs in the South-South Region of Nigeria." In *6th African Conference of Agricultural Economist*. http://dx.doi.org/10.22004/ag.econ.295693

Vartolomei, V. C., and Avasilcai, S. 2019. 'Challenges of Digitalization in Different Industries Before and After.' In *IOP Conference Series: Materials Science & Engineering*, vol. 568, Annual Session of Scientific Papers IMT ORADEA 2019, 30–31 May, Oradea, Felix S.P.A., Romania. http://dx.doi.org/10.1088/1757-899X/568/1/012086

Wang, Victoria, Harrison, Nnaji, and Jung, Jeyong. 2020. 'Internet Banking in Nigeria: Cybersecurity Breach Practices, and Capability.' *International Journal of Law Crime and Justice* vol. 62, pp. 415–423. http://dx.doi.10.16/j.ijlcj.2020.1000415

17 SME Cybersecurity Misconceptions
A Guide for Decision Makers

Martin Wilson and Sharon McDonald

CONTENTS

DOI: 10.1201/9781003319887-17

INTRODUCTION

Cybersecurity decision makers play a crucial part in protecting businesses against cyberattacks by influencing an organization's approach to implementing protective cybersecurity. Such decision makers in a small business may be internal, such as the owner, manager, or other designated employees. Alternatively, small and medium-sized enterprises (SMEs) have a range of security professionals who engage with client businesses to improve security, such as consultants and specialist governmental departments. Decision makers may hold differing views on risk and what measures are appropriate to protect organizations (Shreeve et al. 2022). This chapter considers the factors influencing small business cybersecurity decision makers by re-examining data collected from a survey of 85 UK-based SMEs (Wilson et al. 2022). We conclude by recommending cybersecurity engagement tactics for small business owners, managers, employees, and those external decision makers who engage with businesses to reduce risk. Before describing our approach and results, we briefly review the issues and existing literature on SME cybersecurity engagement.

PROBLEM RATIONALE AND RESEARCH QUESTIONS

The work presented in this paper was spearheaded by the North-East Business Resilience Centre (NEBRC), a UK-based, not-for-profit partnership between policing, academia, and the private sector which aims to assist SMEs in becoming more resilient to fraud and cybercrime. The NEBRC wanted to understand SMEs' attitudes to cybersecurity adoption and whether SMEs believed they were vulnerable to specific threats (e.g., phishing, network hacks, etc.). This baseline understanding would be used to target the NEBRC's ongoing work with the sector to debunk misconceptions and provide targeted help and support to the SME community.

The original study by Wilson et al. (2022) presented the results of a survey that explored SMEs' perceptions of cyber-security. That study built on previous research by examining SME attitudes regarding the most common cyberattacks SMEs may face and their perceived ability to take preventative steps against such attacks. Understanding SMEs' appraisal of and response efficacy to different cyber threats will enable researchers to identify and target interventions that may help SMEs build better cybersecurity practices.

The reanalysis presented in this chapter goes a step further towards identifying how we might support specific small business cybersecurity decision makers. This is achieved by exploring differences between SME owners', managers', and employees' attitudes to the most common type of cyberattacks that they may face and their perceived ability to take preventative steps against such attacks. This builds on previous work profiling SMEs' attitudes towards cybersecurity threats in general. Therefore, this research is another important step in understanding why SMEs fail to implement proactive and protective cyber-security measures which would reduce their vulnerability to cyberattacks. The understanding generated by our reanalysis may be beneficial in:

1. Influencing small business decision makers to adopt protective cybersecurity.
2. Helping those who engage small business decision makers to improve cybersecurity.

The data analysis presented in this chapter explores the following questions:

RESEARCH QUESTIONS

RQ1 To what extent do small business owners have differing threat appraisals from managers and employees?

RQ2 To what extent do small business owners have differing coping appraisals from managers and employees?

RQ3 Where differences exist, what might be the cause?

RQ4 What recommendations for small business cybersecurity engagement can be made considering these findings?

LITERATURE REVIEW

It is widely accepted that SMEs are critical to the global economy (Rhodes 2016; Department for Business, Energy & Industrial Strategy 2021). However, SMEs have been shown to have poor cybersecurity adoption, as demonstrated by the low uptake of the cyber essentials scheme (DCMS and Ipsos MORI 2022). This is despite the potentially disastrous impacts of attacks (Chen 2016) and considerable encouragement from governments via cybersecurity awareness programs (US Small Business Administration 2020; NCSC 2015).

SMEs rely on information technology (IT) to conduct their day-to-day business. The 2022 cybersecurity breaches survey (DCMS and Ipsos MORI 2022) reported that nine out of ten businesses had some form of digital exposure. SME digitalization has been accelerated by the COVID-19 crisis (OECD 2021). Incentives for IT adoption include increased competitiveness, cost savings, and the creation of new business opportunities such as e-commerce (Khayer et al. 2020). Previous surveys have shown SME respondents reporting cyberattacks (Renaud and Ophoff 2021; Valli et al. 2014), and in a 2021 survey of 1150 American SMEs, 29% reported cyberattacks (CISCO and NSBA 2021). The 2022 UK government cybersecurity breaches survey (DCMS and Ipsos MORI 2022) highlighted that 39% of 1243 businesses reported being attacked; this percentage has remained consistent for the previous five years, and half of all organizations polled experienced at least monthly attacks. (DCMS and Ipsos MORI 2022).

Many internet-born attacks upon organizations seek to leverage and exploit elemental, well-known weaknesses in software. Cybercriminals use automated programs to scan vast IP ranges, simply searching for vulnerabilities in internet-facing devices and web applications. One internet service provider reported seeing over 80 billion malicious scans in one day (Lewis 2018). In this way, attackers indiscriminately target as many devices, services, or users as possible, as some machines or services will always have vulnerabilities (NCSC 2015). The victim could be an SME or a large multi-national corporation; it is the presence of these weaknesses, sometimes referred to as "low-hanging fruit," which increases the risk of these scattergun, untargeted attacks.

Defensive emphasis is placed on removing "low-hanging fruit" via initiatives like the Cyber Essentials Scheme (NCSC 2015) and NCSC small business guide (NCSC 2015). The cyber essentials scheme contains the primary preventative technical measures, which, if adopted, are proven to defend against 99% of automated, untargeted attacks in SMEs (Such et al. 2015). However, the 2022 cybersecurity breaches survey showed that only 6% of businesses polled had achieved Cyber Essential certification, and 1% had Cyber Essentials plus. Given the cyber risk and the potentially disastrous impacts from attacks, and despite the considerable cybersecurity investment by the UK government, SME cybersecurity decision makers are failing to adopt cybersecurity preventative measures. The key questions are why, and, moreover, how might we better influence decision makers to act?

BARRIERS TO SME CYBERSECURITY ADOPTION

Researchers have highlighted the following barriers to SME cybersecurity adoption:

- Lack of resources in time, money, and expertise. Renaud and Weir (2016) highlight that SME decision makers believe the cost of cybersecurity is prohibitive, with SMEs frequently lacking the financial resources to either fund in-house security expertise or to pay for external consultants.
- Failure to understand the impact of an attack. Renaud and Ophoff (2021) believe that risk owners might not appreciate the relevance of cybersecurity to the continuity of their business and therefore fail to act.

- Knowledge vacuum. Osborn and Simpson (2018) interviewed SME IT decision makers, finding that participants lacked knowledge of cyber threats and mitigations.
- De-prioritization of cybersecurity. Other business functions are prioritized at the expense of cybersecurity (Osborn and Simpson 2018). This is unsurprising, given that the failure rate of businesses in the United Kingdom is estimated to be 12% (ONS 2020). SMEs face a myriad of demands with limited resources. When faced with a choice, decision makers will prioritize other business-critical functions such as raising finance ahead of cybersecurity (Osborn 2014).
- Lack of SME provision. The security industry is tailored to large business cybersecurity provision, meaning SMEs are left behind (Kimwele et al. 2005; González et al. 2013; Almeida et al. 2018)
- Discounting vulnerability to attacks. Several studies highlight that SMEs report optimistic risk appraisals concerning the likelihood of a cyberattack (Renaud and Weir 2016; Alahmari and Duncan 2020; Renaud and Ophoff 2021; Wilson et al. 2022). These risk appraisals are a result of various threat landscape misconceptions, such as SMEs believing they are too small to be attacked (Renaud and Ophoff 2021), they have nothing worth stealing (Osborn and Simpson 2018), or their protection is adequate (Saban et al. 2021). They also question why an attacker would choose to target their business (Renaud and Ophoff 2021; Renaud and Weir 2016; Osborn and Simpson 2018).

HUMAN FACTORS AND CYBERSECURITY DECISION MAKING

Issues relating to staff training compliance which influence the adoption of protective cybersecurity are referenced by several researchers (Alahmari and Duncan 2020; Barlette et al. 2017; Gundu 2019; Siponen et al. 2014) and can be divided into three components:

i) Different perceptions and attitudes toward cyber-security based on an individual's role within the business.
ii) General compliance behaviors of employees.
iii) The provision of information and cybersecurity policies and training to support employees.

Taking the issue of an individual's role within the business first, in a survey of 292 French SMEs, Barlette et al. (2017) found differences in the factors affecting reported intention to adopt protective information security measures when they compared business owners to chief executive officers (CEOs) who were not the business owners. The primary driver for non-owner CEOs was coping appraisal: *the ability to cope with and avert the threat*, demonstrating a focus on the practicalities of information security, whereas for business owners, social influence factors, such as comparing their current security practices to those of competitors/partners and their customers' expectations, are their primary drivers to adopt protective information security measures. Other studies have found that cybersecurity decision-making is predicated on security professionals' own experiences and biases. In 2013 a survey and semi-structured interviews were conducted with security managers and found that they mostly used their own judgment and experience when making security decisions (Zinatullin 2013). A study by Shreeve et al. (2022) explored the influence of cyber experience in making security decisions during 208 simulated cyber tabletop exercises by 948 players with differing backgrounds, such as security experts, risk analysts, and board-level decision makers. The findings of this study indicate that no one group of experts made better security game decisions than the other and that hard-to-challenge biases about how systems should be defended were impacting security decisions. The same authors suggest decision makers were at risk of making mistakes when defending unfamiliar systems by applying a one-size-fits-all approach; as how one system is defended may not be suited to defending another (D'Arcy and Hovav 2008; Bernik and Prislan 2016)

Turning to issues of employee compliance, poor information security behaviors demonstrated by employees, either intentionally or unintentionally, can be an open door for hackers (Alahmari and Duncan 2020; Siponen et al. 2014). This issue is of particular concern when clicking on links and visiting suspicious websites (Barlette et al. 2017). Engendering a culture of cyber-secure behaviors is challenging when phishing-based attacks are growing in sophistication. Therefore, it seems reasonable to conclude that implementing training and information security policies within SMEs should be a priority. However, in respect of information security policies, research studies suggest that SMEs may be behind the curve. For example, Berry et al. (2006) surveyed 370 small businesses in the United States about their approach to risk management and cyber threats and found that only 6.5% reported having written policies covering IT security. A written information security policy may establish an organization's expectations vis-à-vis employee behavior, which can be reinforced through appropriate training. However, as Gundu (2019) points out, knowledge and behavior do not always match. In an action research study with 30 employees within a South African SME, Gundu (2019) found that reported behavioral intention following cybersecurity awareness campaigns was high (85%); however, reported behavior scores were low (54%).

METHODS

In this section, we describe the design, piloting, and implementation of our web-based survey.

SURVEY QUESTION DESIGN

In designing our survey, we first needed to identify the constructs that we would measure. To achieve this, we turned to the behavioral models that have been previously used to examine cyber-security adoption within a variety of contexts: home, employee behavior, and SMEs (Barlette et al. 2017; Blythe and Coventry 2018; Anderson and Agarwal 2010). Second, we needed to identify common types of attacks that SMEs might face and the nature of the response measures they might adopt to defend against those attacks. To achieve this, we turned to the National Cybersecurity Centre's guidance for small businesses (NCSC 2015). In the following section, we explain how these sources affected our survey design and present the questions we used.

USE OF BEHAVIORAL MODELS

Behavioral models have been used to help us to understand the relationship between behavior and intended action. Many are examples of expectancy-value theories that hypothesize that our attitudes and/or beliefs will lead to subsequent behaviors. As such, the models are founded upon both cognitive and affective factors, which, when combined, may determine protective behavior.

Two models at the forefront of attention concerning cybersecurity are protection motivation theory (Rogers 1975) and health belief model (Rosenstock et al. 1988). The basis of protection motivation theory (PMT) is that fear, delivered through messages or "fear appeals," triggers threat and coping appraisals which motivate people to change attitudes and behaviors (Shillair 2020). The health belief model (HBM) proposes that people are more likely to take preventative action if they perceive the threat of a risk to be serious and they feel they are personally susceptible and there are fewer costs than benefits to engaging in it (Michie et al. 2014). There is a significant overlap between the models, but both are useful in considering people's attitudes to cybersecurity adoption (Anderson and Agarwal 2010; Dodel and Mesch 2017; Ng et al. 2009; Tsai et al. 2016).

However, it is important to note that while PMT and HBM were used as a source of inspiration for our questions, we did not set out to test or validate these models regarding SME attitudes and behaviors. Doing so would have entailed using multi-item scales for each construct and a measure of behavioral intention. Our purpose was to use some of the constructs from these models to explore

SME attitudes about common attack scenarios and preventative measures. Specifically, we wanted to determine decision makers' perceptions of cyber threats and their perceived ability to address them. We, therefore, adopted the following constructs from protection motivation theory.

> **Threat Appraisal:** the individual assessing the risk of the event or consequence happening to them (*perceived vulnerability*) and the perceived seriousness of the threat if it did occur (*perceived severity*).
>
> **Coping appraisal**: the individual's assessment of their ability to perform the action(s) that may prevent the unwanted outcome (*self-efficacy*); the individual's assessment of the effectiveness of that action in preventing the unwanted outcome (*response efficacy*), and the individual's assessment of the cost of acting (*response cost*). We also wanted to understand what factors might influence a decision maker to adopt cybersecurity measures and the perceived barriers to taking preventative cybersecurity measures.

We adopted the following constructs from the health belief model:

> **Cues to Action**: the internal or external triggers that stimulate an individual to act.
>
> **Perceived Barriers**: perceived impediments to undertaking recommended behaviors.

Cues to action was measured via a 5-point Likert scale, and perceived barriers were addressed through an open, non-compulsory free text question. Each respondent who answered this question was assigned relevant pseudonyms owner, manager, and employee to preserve anonymity.

Finally, we asked our respondents to comment on their engagement with cybersecurity training and their preferences for receiving advice on cybersecurity matters.

NCSC SMALL BUSINESS GUIDE

Cybersecurity for SMEs involves a wide range of processes, technologies, and human factor issues. We wanted to examine whether the type of attack or the nature of preventative measures to defend against an attack would impact participants' appraisal of threat and their ability to cope with that threat. We turned to the five recommendations contained in the NCSC's small business guide as a source of inspiration for our attack-response pairs:

- implementing data backups
- keeping mobile devices safe
- preventing malware damage
- avoiding phishing attacks
- using passwords to protect data

Within the survey, we asked respondents to rate their perceived vulnerability and severity to each type of attack and then to rate the costs and benefits of preventing such attacks and their self-efficacy in doing so. Table 17.1 shows the Likert-scale questions that were used within our survey. These were inspired by Claar (2011) and Ng et al. (2009).

SURVEY PILOTING AND ADMINISTRATION

The survey was prepared using Qualtrics. The survey design and questions were subject to iterative internal review within the research team and through two separate rounds of piloting with 15 people drawn from cybersecurity professionals, SME owners, and cybersecurity researchers. Different respondents were used in each round. The survey was tested for usability across a range of devices (mobile, desktop, and tablet). Care was taken to ensure that the flow through the questionnaire was

TABLE 17.1
Threat and Coping Appraisal Questions

Construct	Question	Attack Scenarios from NCSC Small Business Guide	5-Point Likert Response Options
Threat Appraisal			
Perceived vulnerability	How likely do you feel that the following scenarios will occur in your business?	• Network being hacked • Data being stolen or encrypted • Malware infection • Mobile devices being compromised • Phishing email attack	Highly unlikely (1) to highly likely (5)
Perceived severity	Please indicate the impacts that each of the following scenarios would have on your business if it did occur (in terms of lost time, data, money, and damage to your business reputation).		Very low impact to very high impact
Coping Appraisal			
Response cost	Please indicate the cost of implementing and maintaining the following protective measures for your business (cost refers to expense in time and money).	• Using strong, unique passwords for my business accounts • Taking regular backups of my data • Preventing malware (malicious software, including viruses) infections • Configuring mobile devices so that they can be remotely tracked, wiped, and locked • Avoiding and limiting the impact of phishing email attacks	Very inexpensive (1) to very expensive (5)
Response efficacy	Please indicate the effectiveness of the following protective measures when considering their efficacy in protecting your business from cyberattack.		Very ineffective (1) to very effective (5)
Self-efficacy	Please rate your ability to implement and maintain the following protective measures for your business (ability refers to skills and knowledge).		Very low ability (1) to very high ability (5)
Influencers			
Cues to action	Please indicate how likely it would be that you would seek to adopt protective cybersecurity measures for your business because of the following scenarios.	• Another SME told me that it had suffered a cyberattack • I saw a news report about a cyberattack upon an SME • I received advice from a cybersecurity professional • I recurved advice from government bodies such as NCSC • My business became the victim of cybercrime	Highly unlikely (1) to highly likely (5)

logical and did not present too many of the same type of questions in long sequences, which might overwhelm the participants or induce a response set. The survey duration was estimated to be eight minutes. By keeping the survey short and making it easy to complete, we hoped to improve response rates (Courage et al. 2015). An ethics section was included at the beginning of the survey, and the University of Sunderland's ethics committee approved the study.

Sampling and Dissemination

We considered using random sampling for the survey. However, previous studies within this field have achieved poor response rates. For example, Osborn and Simpson (2018) achieved a response rate of <1% through standard random sampling procedures. Given the difficulty in engaging busy SME owners in research, we decided to leverage the first author's connections within the Cyber Resilience Centre Network, a national network of not-for-profit centers that bring together academia, law enforcement, and private sector businesses together in a trusted nexus to help SMEs adopt cybersecurity ("Northeast Business Resilience Centre" 2022).

The survey was disseminated electronically to SMEs across England, Scotland, Wales, and Northern Ireland via the Cyber Resilience Center Network and existing business support networks, such as chambers of commerce and federation of small businesses, LinkedIn, press releases, and blogs. Business support groups such as the chamber of commerce exist to support, develop, and grow small businesses, providing expert help to thousands of small businesses across various business disciplines, such as tax, accounting, and HR. Groups were contacted personally to negotiate the dissemination of the survey to their members. Some wished to preview the survey prior to agreeing to its distribution. No incentives were offered to complete the survey.

DISCUSSION AND RESULTS

The analysis that follows is based upon 85 completed survey returns. First, we present our analysis of threat appraisal and coping appraisal data; we then present our data on SME advice and training preferences. Finally, we conclude the results by discussing our qualitative data about the barriers to cybersecurity engagement. Before presenting the substantive findings, we first summarize the characteristics of our survey respondents.

Respondent Characteristics

Table 17.2 presents the primary demographic characteristics of our sample. Most respondents reported representing micro businesses in sectors other than IT. Moreover, most of the respondents were business owners or partners and were based within the Northeast and Yorkshire region of the United Kingdom.

SME Threat Appraisal and Coping Appraisal

We present some insights based on SME decision makers from frequency count data for those factors where there is a divergence of opinion between owners, managers, and employees. Data were collected using a 5-point Likert scale for some questions. The midpoint (3) is undecided. For purposes of clarity and ease of presentation, this data has been grouped so that strongly agree (5) and agree (4) form one group, strongly disagree (1) and disagree (2) form another group, and then undecided (3) forms the last group. The charts that follow focus only on the high. The low and undecided groups have been excluded from each figure. Any bars within the charts highlighted in red represent areas of difference between respondent groups. These were determined to be any difference ≥ 20% and can be identified by those bars, which are encompassed by red dashed lines. For clarity, percentages are presented in the figures with whole numbers on the bar charts.

Perceived Vulnerability

Figure 17.1 shows the percentage of respondents from each group who rated their perceived vulnerability to each attack scenario to be high (a rating of 4 or 5).

TABLE 17.2
Sample Characteristics

Demographic Factor	Characteristics
Company size	Micro (Less than 10 employees) 60.0% ($n = 51$)
	Small (11 to 50 employees) 28% ($n = 24$)
	Medium (51 to 250 employees) 12% ($n = 10$)
Respondent	Owner/partner 60% ($n = 51$)
	Management 22% ($n = 19$)
	Employee 18% ($n = 15$)
Region	64.7% North East and Yorkshire ($n = 55$)
	5.9% North West ($n = 5$)
	9.4% Wales ($n = 8$)
	1.2% East Midlands ($n = 1$)
	3.5% London and Southeast ($n = 3$)
	3.5% Scotland ($n = 3$)
	3.5% South West ($n = 3$)
	8.1% Preferred not to say ($n = 7$)
Business sector	20% ($n = 17$) reported their businesses were IT related, with 3 reporting involvement in cybersecurity services.
	80% ($n = 68$) reported being in fields unrelated to IT.

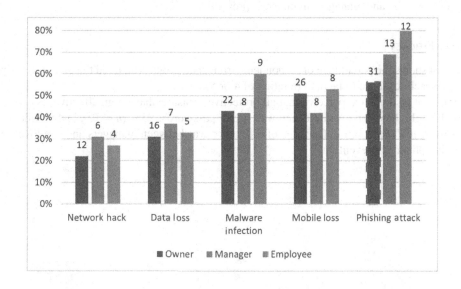

FIGURE 17.1 High perceived vulnerability likelihood ratings (rated as a 4 or 5).

Overall findings are that 66% ($n = 56$) of participants perceived phishing emails were the attack to which they would be most susceptible, with network hacks being at the lower end of their perceived vulnerability spectrum (26%, $n = 22$). Participants commented, "Apart from the spam email, I wonder how much of this is actually real?" (Owner), "I don't know what the likelihood is of my business being attacked" (Owner), and "I don't think I will be the victim of an attack as who really knows about me?" (Owner). Analyzing the findings by the respondent position, owners have a lower perceived vulnerability to a phishing attack when compared to employees.

PERCEIVED SEVERITY

Figure 17.2 shows the percentage of respondents from each group who rated the perceived severity of each attack scenario to be high (a rating of 4 or 5).

Overall findings are that 76% (n = 65) of participants perceived that data loss would have the greatest impact. Owners and employees have differing perceived severity ratings for malware infection and mobile loss. Owners have differing ratings than managers and employees in data loss. Phishing attacks are the only attack scenario with a level of agreement on the severity. Two respondents described the impacts of cyberattacks as being "All hands to the pump" (Manager) and "It's really expensive clearing up after a cyberattack" (Owner).

COPING APPRAISAL

In this section, we present our analysis of SMEs' ratings for response costs, response efficacy, and self-efficacy with respect to implementing measures relating to the NCSC small business guide recommendations.

RESPONSE COST

Figure 17.3 shows the percentage of respondents from each group who rated the perceived cost of each action to be high (a rating of 4 or 5).

Overall, 41% (n = 35) of our respondents felt that preventing malware infections was the costliest preventative action, and only 6% (n = 5) rated strong passwords as costly. Employees had lower ratings than owners and managers in malware prevention.

RESPONSE EFFICACY

Figure 17.4 shows the percentage of respondents from each group who rated the perceived response efficacy of each response to be high (a rating of 4 or 5).

Overall, the respondents perceive that all protective measures have high effectiveness. The category with the highest perceived efficacy was strong passwords, 93% (n = 79), and mobile devices the lowest, with 71% (n = 60). One area of difference was between managers and employees when considering phishing prevention.

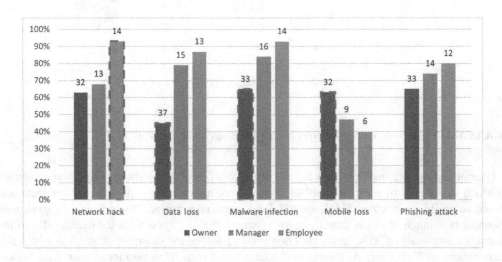

FIGURE 17.2   High perceived severity likelihood ratings (rated as a 4 or 5).

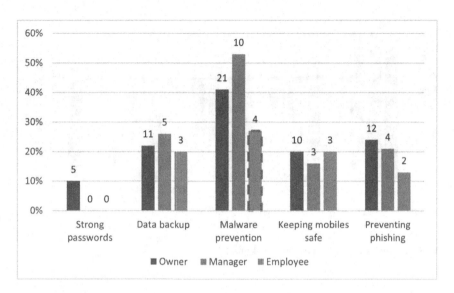

FIGURE 17.3 Response cost ratings (rated as 4 or 5).

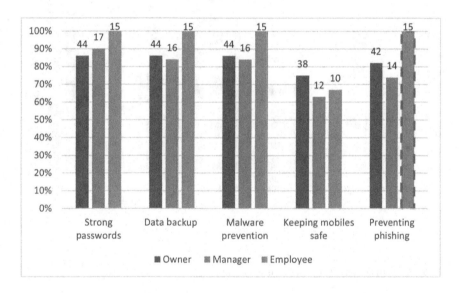

FIGURE 17.4 Response efficacy ratings (rated as a 4 or a 5).

SELF-EFFICACY

Figure 17.5 shows the percentage of respondents from each group who rated the perceived self-efficacy of each response to be high (a rating of 4 or 5)

Respondents reported higher than lower self-efficacy levels for all measures. Configuring mobile devices 71% ($n = 40$) was the measure with the lowest perceived self-efficacy. Some survey respondents gave quotes that demonstrated low self-efficacy, such as, "I don't understand it and don't have the time to learn" (Owner) and "It's all confusing and just another hassle" (Manager). Employees reported lower levels of self-efficacy in data backup, owners in malware prevention, and managers in keeping mobile devices safe.

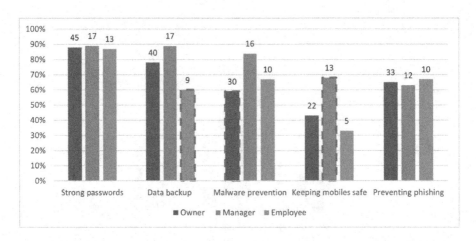

FIGURE 17.5   Self-efficacy ratings (rated as a 4 or a 5).

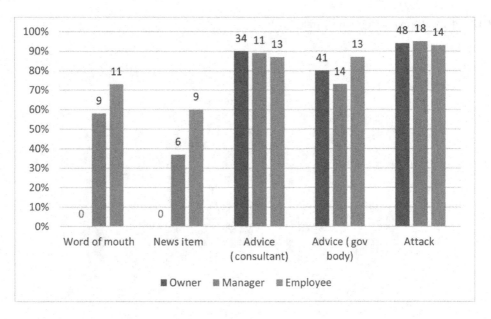

FIGURE 17.6   Cues to action ratings (rated as a 4 or a 5).

CUES TO ACTION

Figure 17.6 shows the percentage of respondents from each group who rated selected cues to action as high (a rating of 4 or 5).

The most effective cue was if the respondent's business was victimized 94% ($n = 80$). One survey respondent was clearly motivated by a previous attack "You don't think about cyberattacks until they happen, we were guilty of thinking it wasn't a huge issue for us at one time" (Owner). Owners seem to be at odds with managers and employees when it comes to word of mouth and news item cues.

Figure 17.7 presents how survey respondents received cybersecurity advice.

Overall, 68% ($n = 58$) of respondents conduct their own research when looking for advice, with 68%% ($n = 39$) of small business owners obtaining advice in this way. Employees reported receiving more training than conducting their own reading. Fewer owners report using consultancy.

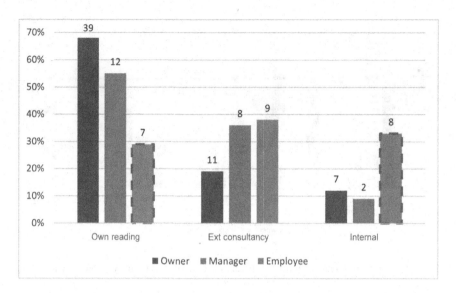

FIGURE 17.7   How survey respondents reported receiving security guidance.

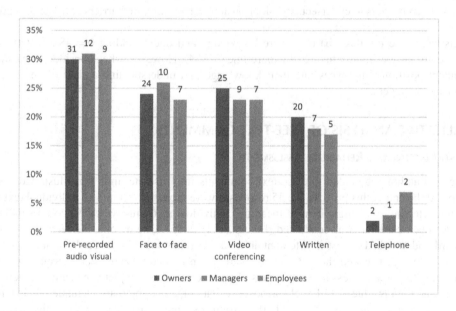

FIGURE 17.8   Survey respondents' high preference formats for receiving cybersecurity guidance.

Preference for Advice

Figure 17.8 shows the percentage of respondents from each decision-making group who ranked their preference for receiving cybersecurity guidance across five different formats as a 1 or a 2 (high preference).

There was broad agreement across all formats, with pre-recorded audio-visual and face-to-face being the preferred options.

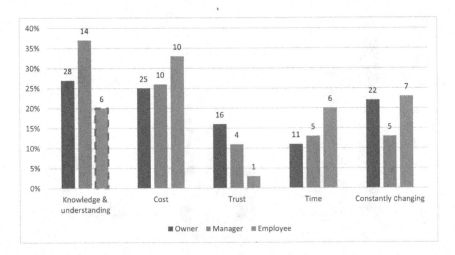

FIGURE 17.9   Survey respondents' ranking of the greatest barriers to their cybersecurity adoption.

BARRIERS TO CYBERSECURITY ADOPTION

Figure 17.9 shows the percentage of respondents from each decision-making group who ranked their perceived barriers to cybersecurity adoption across five different barriers as a 1 or a 2 (greatest challenge).

Holistically, the top three barriers were knowledge and understanding ($n= 48$), cost ($n = 45$), and the constantly changing nature of cybercrime ($n =34$). However, when considering barriers by respondent position, employees rate their knowledge and understanding as less of an issue than owners and managers.

QUALITATIVE ANALYSIS OF FREE-TEXT COMMENTS

CODING PROCESS AND RELIABILITY ASSESSMENT

The second author segmented the free-text comments into discrete units that illustrated a single concept. At the end of this process, the 55 responses were broken down into 73 individual text units: each unit referring to a single item of meaning. Individual text units were printed on small index cards. An open card sort was conducted (Baxter et al., 2015). One by one, the second author read each card and attached a Post-it note containing a short summary label. Cards on the same topic were grouped together, and these groupings were given thematic labels. Large groups were then coded using the same process into subthemes. When the sort was complete, the author reviewed the structure and then produced an Excel spreadsheet that contained the main thematic labels with the individual text units that were allocated to that group. As a measure of coding reliability, the second author recoded the 73 individual text cards after a period of three weeks had elapsed. Cohen's kappa (0.88) was calculated, demonstrating excellent reliability.

DISCOUNTING VULNERABILITY TO ATTACKS

Taken together, our results suggest that all survey respondents underestimate the risk of a cyberat-tack and report phishing as the most likely attack and network hacks as the least likely. While the likelihood of an attack was considered low, our respondents acknowledged that an attack would impact their business operation, and all attack types were rated highly. Regarding the implantation of protective measures, our respondents rated those items more positively that were both simple and under personal control. Using strong passwords was rated as the most cost-effective scenario and the most effective response measure (with maintaining backups).

Using secure passwords was also the measure with the greatest reported self-efficacy. Scenarios that involved other people, such as phishing avoidance, were rated significantly lower for self-efficacy and response efficacy. Regarding cues to action, our respondents rated experiencing an attack the most influential cue, with hearing about an SME or hearing a news report the least. Knowledge and understanding were major barriers to cybersecurity adoption, and, as one respondent said, "I don't know what's appropriate for me and my size of business" (Owner). However, our respondents were very clear about the format in which they prefer to receive cybersecurity advice: pre-recorded audio-visual materials. We now discuss these findings in relation to our qualitative data and the existing literature, starting with threat and coping appraisals, followed by cues to action and training preferences. We close by making conclusions and recommendations and recognizing our study's limitations.

APPRAISAL OF THREAT

Overall, and in line with previous studies such as Renaud and Weir (2016) and Topping (2017), our respondents reported optimistic vulnerability ratings. However, our results highlighted differences in perceived vulnerability to specific types of threats. Respondents reported they believed phishing and mobile insecurity to be the most likely, with network hack and data loss to be the least likely. Revisiting our research questions one and three:

RQ1 To what extent do small business owners have differing threat appraisals from managers and employees?

RQ3 Where differences exist, what might be the cause?

Proportionally, a greater number of employees rated their vulnerability to phishing emails higher when compared to owners and managers, indicating this view was prevalent for that group of respondents (see Table 17.3). It could be anticipated that phishing is rated as most likely due to its prevalence and that it crosses both home and business spheres. Out of all our cyberattack scenarios, it is the most visible and tangible and probably the attack that employees are most likely to encounter directly in the workplace.

Many organizations now attempt to raise phishing awareness via training programs and simulated phishing tests. The aggregation of phishing prevalence, tangibility, and training awareness programs could explain higher phishing perceived vulnerability ratings among our employees. The higher ratings for mobile insecurity may arise simply because devices we carry with us are at an increased risk.

Turning to differing severity ratings in our second and third research questions:

RQ2 To what extent do small business owners have differing coping appraisals from managers and employees?

RQ3 Where differences exist, what might be the cause?

Respondents rated the severity of each of the five scenarios to be high, with a median value of 4. Therefore, while the risk was perceived to be low, our respondents, nonetheless, acknowledge the impact of an attack should it occur. In terms of the five potential attack scenarios, although still rated high with a median value of 4, the severity of mobile insecurity was significantly lower than the highest-rated data loss scenario. A greater proportion of owner respondents rated the severity of this scenario on their business to be higher than managers and employees. This could be attributed to the tangible nature of mobile devices and the cost of replacing lost or stolen hardware. Fewer owners felt that the impacts of data loss and malware infections would be as damaging as managers and employees. Employees rated network hack impacts more highly than managers and owners. Some

TABLE 17.3

Qualitative Themes

Theme	Description	Illustrative Comment	Overall Frequency	Owner Frequency	Manager Frequency	Employee Frequency
Resources	Costs in time and resources that limit respondents' ability to engage with cybersecurity	"Just not able to afford consultancy" (Owner).	5.5% (n = 4)	100% (n = 4)	0% (n = 0)	0% (n = 0)
Limited understanding	Perceived lack of understanding about cybersecurity in general, cybersecurity advice, the threat landscape or specific cybersecurity constructs/practices	"It's all confusing and just another hassle" (Owner).	41.1% (n = 30)	33.3% (n = 10)	33.3% (n = 10)	33.3% (n = 10)
Operational challenges	Specific technological concerns that the respondents report to be challenging	"Setting up hardware firewalls effectively, without causing internal networking issues" (Employee).	19.2% (n = 14)	85.7% (n = 12)	0% (n = 0)	14.2% (n = 2)
Invisibility to hackers	The extent to which respondents feel that they are visible targets to hackers	"I have a website, but no one is going to bother with me" (Owner).	11.0% (n = 8)	100% (n = 8)	0% (n = 0)	0% (n = 0)
Human factors	Issues relating to staff training, compliance	"Ensuring all staff are following the correct procedures" (Manager).	17.8% (n = 13)	53.8% (n = 7)	23.1% (n = 3)	23.1% (n = 3)
Management buy-in	Management attitudes towards cybersecurity	"More awareness and understanding of the importance of cybersecurity with business leaders at the highest level is needed" (Manager).	5.5% (n = 4)	0% (n = 0)	75% (n = 3)	25% (n = 1)

of our managers and employee respondents gave responses that were technical when asked which aspect of cybersecurity they found most difficult, such as, "ensuring all staff apply security patches" (Manager), "data transformation and encryption" (Employee). These responses suggest they are IT professionals/managers, which could account for differing severity ratings, as they will possess more knowledge and understanding of the threat and impact.

Taking perceived vulnerability and perceived severity together, there is a basic incongruence between respondent ratings for network hack and data loss in that both attacks were rated as being unlikely, but their impact if they were to happen was rated as being high. The low vulnerability and high severity ratings suggest a gap between knowledge and action previously observed by Gundu (2019). So, what might account for this discrepancy? Costs would be an obvious mediating factor, and we will return to this in our discussion of coping appraisal. For the moment, however, our qualitative data may be able to provide some insights into the emergent theme of "Invisibility to hackers." Within this theme, there was some indication that despite acknowledging the potential impact, respondents were engaging in dissonance reduction through trivialization, denial, and the addition of additional consonant cognitions: "I have a website, but no one is going to bother with me"(Owner); "My turnover is small, and I do not see myself as a target" (Owner); "As a music teacher I doubt hackers would know what data I keep. I'm more concerned about keeping the pianos in tune" (Owner). Therefore, some respondents reported that their size acted like a cloak of invisibility, making them invulnerable to hackers despite their dependency on IT. As one respondent commented: "We are a small fish in a huge ocean, I think bigger business has more to fear" (Owner), believing that larger organizations with more capital and reputation are more likely to be the victims of targeted cybercrime. Others reported a belief that cybercrime is a problem for financial institutions that must bear the cost of cybercrime activities: "We got caught by a BT survey email, and they took money out of the account, but I got it back from the bank within a day, so there's no hassle really. It's the banks that need to worry about this" (Owner). Our qualitative data exposed a fundamental misconception about how cyber-criminals operate that must be challenged if we are to tackle SME cyber-security behaviors: that cyberattacks are generally targeted, when the reverse is true. For example, the global spread of WannaCry ransomware demonstrates the random and untargeted nature of automated attacks, which take a "scattergun" approach toward victims (NCA and NCSC 2018). Indeed, Osborn and Simpson (2018) suggest that a lack of knowledge about the nature of cyberattacks among SMEs leads them to miscalculate the risk. Indeed, as one respondent commented: "I don't understand how criminals can access my accounts" (Owner). SMEs and public understanding of cyber-crime and the key competencies needed are worthy areas for future study.

COPING APPRAISAL

In this section, we revisit our research questions 2 and 3, which consider if owners have differed coping appraisals and the potential causes of any such differences. To assess coping appraisal, we asked our respondents to rate the costs, benefits, and self-efficacy to implement the five recommendations of the NCSC small business guide. Regarding resource costs, our respondents rated malware prevention as the costliest item in that it was perceived to involve resource outlay in terms of software purchase. Employees rated this area less highly than their respondent counterparts, which could reflect that they are less likely to be involved in cybersecurity funding within their parent organization. The other preventative measures were rated low in terms of cost, demonstrating that they were within the grasp of a small business and, for some, could be achieved via personal vigilance in terms of response effectiveness. Our respondents indicated all actions were effective, with median ratings of 4; the most beneficial was regular backups and using strong passwords, and the least beneficial in terms of effectiveness was protecting mobile devices, although this was still rated highly. Employees rated phishing prevention more highly than managers, and comments contained within our qualitative data suggest managers have experienced issues with employees failing to recognize phishing emails, for example, "Trusting people to act responsibly and not open links in emails" (Manager).

In terms of self-efficacy, ratings were high, but our respondents rated their ability to use strong passwords higher than any other measure. Self-efficacy in the application of mobile security measures was rated lowest with a median of 3, suggesting that at best, participants were unsure of their ability to engage in this activity. These findings echo that of Valli et al. (2014), who reported that

SMEs lacked the necessary knowledge to deal with mobile security in a survey of 50 SMEs in Western Australia. Analysis by respondent position shows that managers were at odds with employees regarding backups, with owners regarding malware prevention and owners and employees regarding the safety of mobile devices. This is unsurprising given that managers are not doers; they are unlikely to have high self-efficacy levels when they don't perform the task. This is likely to be delegated to employees or, in the case of sole traders, the owner.

High coping appraisal suggests that respondents can enact cybersecurity preventive measures. Mobile security and phishing avoidance have low-cost ratings; respondents indicate that these measures may be effective, but their reported efficacy in implementing them is much lower than other measures. While our sample rated the response costs as low across all five scenarios, when we asked respondents to rate five primary barriers to cybersecurity, cost and knowledge came out as the primary limiting factors.

Cost

Our qualitative data suggest that cost becomes a factor when it involves the SME interacting with a third party, such as independent cybersecurity specialists, which was perceived to be expensive. Respondents expressed concerns about how their lack of cybersecurity knowledge could mean they have difficulty determining the level of support needed – "Getting to grips with what we must do rather than may do" (Owner); "Getting the balance of measures to reflect the size of the business" (Employee) – and that their lack of knowledge but a desire for peace of mind could leave them vulnerable to exploitation from unscrupulous consultants: "The number of 'shiny box' sales staff trying to sell their latest version of snake oil" (Owner). Respondents clearly articulated the need for advice to match the business needs, highlighting that they need to know what they should do at a given point in time rather than what they could do.

Knowledge

Small business decision makers will not adopt cybersecurity measures if they do not know or understand the risks. Methodologies behind hacking and data exfiltration can be complex and involve exploiting vulnerabilities in hardware, software, and web applications. Increased knowledge is required to grasp these concepts and to appreciate the inherent vulnerabilities to these types of attacks; for example, as soon as a business connects a computer or server to the internet, they become vulnerable, as attackers use the internet to indiscriminately target as many devices, services, or users as possible. One internet service provider reported seeing over 80 billion malicious scans in one day. Decision makers will self-assess the cyber risk to their business, based on their current knowledge and understanding, before deciding to undertake protective action (Renaud 2016). To make an appropriate risk assessment, they need to understand their vulnerability to cyberattack accurately. Some of our qualitative survey responses suggest a lack of understanding of cyberattacks and speculation about their relevance, for example, "I don't understand it" (Owner); "More awareness and understanding is needed" (Manager); and "Understanding threats" (Employee).

Cues to Action

As might be expected, our respondents indicated that the key event that would cause them to engage with cybersecurity measures would be the experience of an attack. Surprisingly, there was little difference in the reported level of influence between receiving advice from NCSC vs. a consultant or by hearing about a fellow SME being attacked. This finding conflicts somewhat with past research on key SME influencers. Berry et al. (2006) suggest that SMEs tend to be most receptive to advice and guidance from within their own business networks, in other words, internal facing rather than external facing. It was suggested that personal relationships and trust are vital components of SME receptivity and that lower levels of trust were related to external sources such as public bodies and external consultants. In terms of the differences in ratings for the different cues to action by different types of respondents (owners, managers, and employees), small business owners have different factors which affect their intention to adopt cybersecurity compared to non-owners (Barlette et al. 2017). The authors, when surveying 292 SMEs, found what appears to drive owner adoption is when they compare their security position to those of competitors and partners and what their customers expect of them. If there is a variance in that security comparison, then there is an increased likelihood that they will act. News reporting upon business cyberattacks tends to be fear appeals about large multi-national companies who have been attacked, not reports of attacks upon small businesses, and is therefore perceived to be less relevant to small business owners. A literature review by Renaud and Weir (2016) found there was a degree of dissent about whether fear appeals were helpful and concluded further research needs to be conducted in this area.

KNOWLEDGE, TRAINING, AND ADVICE

In line with Renaud and Weir (2016), the majority (68%) of our respondents relied on their own research and learning from the internet (primarily) about cybersecurity, with only 33% paying for the services of expert consultants. Fewer (20%) reported any internal training function, which could be because 60% of this survey's respondents were micro businesses (<10 employees) who are unlikely to possess the funds or skills to conduct their own training. This is also a likely explanation for why employees reported more training than their counterparts. In terms of receiving advice, our respondents reported that they would prefer to receive pre-recorded advice that they can watch and digest at their own pace focusing on practical "how-to" advice that the average lay-person can understand: "easy to understand advice – we are not the technicians here and the specialists find it hard to speak in non-tech terms" (Owner).

SMEs vs. LARGE ENTERPRISES

Professionals who work with small businesses to improve cybersecurity must take a different engagement approach. This research has shown that there are differences in how stakeholders view cyber risk, and using a one-size-fits-all approach to protective cybersecurity is less likely to result in security adoption. Research interviews with 25 SME CEOs and IT executives by Heidt et al. (2019) also found that SMEs differ in their cybersecurity approach from large enterprises, that is, they take a very insular, local geographic approach to cybersecurity. In other words, "it's not what you know, but who you know." This is likely a better lens for organizational IT security investment decisions in SMEs. Future SME research needs to focus on better understanding these differences and recognize that SMEs have differing views of cyber risks compared to their large business cousins.

CONCLUSIONS AND RECOMMENDATIONS

Vulnerability   Overall, respondents perceive *low* risk of hacking and data loss.
    Employees reported *higher* phishing vulnerability than **owners** or **managers**.
Severity   Agreement that all impacts are *high*, with data loss being *the most severe*.
    Owners perceive attacks resulting in data loss, as well as malware infections, as *less severe*.
    Employees rate network hacks being *more severe* than **owners** and **managers**.
    Owners rate mobile loss as *more severe* than managers and employees.
Response-efficacy   Overall, the small business guide recommendations were *effective*.
    Employees rate phishing prevention *more highly* than **managers**.
    Response-cost Overall, respondents felt preventing malware infections was the *costliest*.
    Employees had *lower* cost ratings than **owners** and **managers** in malware prevention.
Self-efficacy   Overall, respondents reported *higher than lower* levels for all measures.

Employees reported *lower* levels of self-efficacy in data backup vs. **managers**.
Owners reported *lower* levels in malware prevention vs. **managers**.
Managers reported *lower* levels in keeping mobile devices safe vs. **employees**.
Cues to action   Overall, the most effective cue was victimization.
Unlike **managers** and **employees**, **owners** *did not rate* word of mouth or news cues.
Advice format   **All groups** prefer *pre-recorded, face-to-face*, and *video conferencing*.
Advice received   Overall, respondents reported conducting their **own reading**
Employees reported receiving more internal training than managers and owners.
Barriers   Top barriers are *knowledge*, *cost*, and *changing nature of cybercrime*.
Employees rate their *knowledge and understanding* as *less of a barrier* than **owners and managers**.
Qualitative themes   Top three: *limited understanding, operational challenges*, and *human factors*.
All groups shared *limited understanding* as their top barrier.
Owners exclusively believed that their businesses *were invisible to hackers*.

RECOMMENDATIONS

Revisiting our fourth research question:

RQ4: What recommendations for small business cybersecurity engagement can be made considering these findings?

Based on our findings, we suggest the following recommendations for engaging with small business decision makers in respect of cybersecurity.

1. **Challenge the misconception about the nature of cyberattacks for managers and owners**. Comments about the protection their small size and turnover provide coupled with the low vulnerability ratings for network hacking suggest that respondents perceived attacks to be more likely to be targeted, when in truth they are more likely to be an untargeted attack. This trend is demonstrated by the Verizon (2021) data breaches report, showing that 61% of data breaches were due to the industrialization of attacks that use stolen username and password pairs in automated credential theft campaigns. Therefore, awareness training and other engagement materials need to emphasize the opportunistic nature of these attacks. Useful tools could include attack demos, showing how the presence of simple vulnerabilities in internet-facing systems is exploited.
2. **Prioritize phishing training with owners.** Phishing is a major risk to all organizations, yet small business owners, when compared to managers and employees, perceive less vulnerability. This perception needs to be countered, as threat actors often target owners when defrauding them via spear-phishing campaigns, and owners are unlikely to act if they do not believe their business to be vulnerable. Useful tools include "real phishing tests/simulations" where recipients receive an email in their inbox and observations are made on how the individual interacts with this email, followed up by appropriate training.
3. **Prioritize data loss training with owners**. Data loss can adversely affect a business in several ways, not limited to regulatory fines, bans on processing data, and reputation damage (Albrecht 2016). Yet only 40% of our owners gave high severity ratings. If owners do not believe the impacts of data loss to be severe, they are unlikely to take protective action. Consider showing data loss case studies from similar-sized companies in the same business context as the owner's business.
4. **Targeted interventions around mobile security for owners and employees**. Our owners and employees reported lower self-efficacy in relation to keeping mobiles secure. Support should be tailored to the recipients; for example, owners are likely to need to understand and realize the benefits of mobile device management such as data encryption, policy

enforcement, and app blocking. Employees, on the other hand, are more likely to need and realize the benefits of device tracking and wiping in the event of theft/loss.

5. **Provide pre-recorded advice and training for employees, managers, and owners**. Our respondents expressed a clear preference for training that is pre-recorded, can be engaged with at the point of need, and can be referred to as needed rather than face to face or web conferencing.

6. **Avoid trying to influence owners via word of mouth and news media**. Owners were clear that cyber information that reached them via word of mouth or news reporting was unlikely to compel them into action. Using case studies of competitors which demonstrate good cybersecurity and emphasizing consumer expectations are more likely to trigger action.

Conclusion

Despite their importance to the UK economy and their dependency on IT, our findings suggest that small business owners, managers, and employees are still discounting their risk of cyberattack. This is despite knowing that the consequences could be significant if an attack were to occur. Perceptions of vulnerability appear to be tied to the notion that most cyberattacks are targeted, fueled by misconceptions about size, turnover, and reputation rather than the indiscriminate, untargeted, industrialized approaches cyber criminals currently use when attacking businesses. However, the news is not all bad. Our survey suggests that our SMEs feel able to action three out of five preventative measures, with their reported self-efficacy waning with respect to phishing avoidance, perhaps because of its prevalence or perhaps because it is difficult to control the behaviors of others and mobile security. The latter suggests an area of focus for training and awareness programs.

Our qualitative data suggest that as businesses grow or their dependency on technology increases, there is a need for further training/knowledge transfer so that SMEs can both garner good advice and understand what actions *should* be taken from the myriad of actions that *may* be taken. Clearly, SME owners and employees are focused on the day-to-day challenges of operating a private concern. Cybersecurity, therefore, while important, may always be one step down on a long list of priorities. So too is engagement with the research community. We are grateful to the 85 respondents who took the time to complete our survey. However, we are mindful that unless researchers can secure the engagement of SMEs to understand how to design better cybersecurity interventions, awareness, and training that will work for them, we will be unable to support SMEs in making accurate assessments of threat and in defining appropriate response measures.

Limitations

A key limitation of this study is the small sample size. However, this is not uncommon; previous studies within this field have achieved poor response rates. For example, Osborn and Simpson (2018) achieved a response rate of <1% through standard random sampling procedures. A key challenge for researchers in this field is securing the engagement of the business community. Moreover, the sample was self-selecting and therefore may have been completed by respondents with more of an interest in cybersecurity. We collected a range of demographic information but did not use some of this within the analysis. Finally, we assessed threat and coping appraisal from one question per construct and triangulated this with qualitative data. We could have used a greater number of items. However, our approach was guided by a desire to increase the response rate by reducing the burden of completion, and therefore this compromise needed to be made. Interviews would, no doubt, have revealed more nuanced insights, and to achieve this, the authors have conducted a follow-up interview study with 30 SMEs from a range of business areas, which is close to publication.

REFERENCES

Alahmari, A., and B. Duncan. 2020. "Cybersecurity Risk Management in Small and Medium-Sized Enterprises: A Systematic Review of Recent Evidence." In *2020 International Conference on Cyber Situational Awareness, Data Analytics and Assessment (CyberSA)*, 1–5. https://doi.org/10.1109/CyberSA49311.2020.9139638.

Albrecht, Jan Philipp. 2016. "How the GDPR Will Change the World." *European Data Protection Law Review* 2: 287–89.

Almeida, Fernando, Inês Carvalho, and Fábio Cruz. 2018. "Structure and Challenges of a Security Policy on Small and Medium Enterprises." *KSII Transactions on Internet and Information Systems (TIIS)* 12 (2): 747–63. https://doi.org/10.3837/tiis.2018.02.012.

Anderson, Catherine L. and Ritu Agarwal. 2010. "Practicing Safe Computing: A Multimethod Empirical Examination of Home Computer User Security Behavioral Intentions." *MIS Quarterly* 34 (3): 613–43. https://doi.org/10.2307/25750694.

Barlette, Yves, Katherine Gundolf, and Annabelle Jaouen. 2017. "CEOs' Information Security Behavior in SMEs: Does Ownership Matter?" *Systèmes d'information & Management* 22 (3): 7. https://doi.org/10.3917/sim.173.0007.

Baxter, Kathy, Catherine Courage, and Kelly Caine. 2015. *Understanding Your Users: A Practical Guide to User Research Methods*. Morgan Kaufmann.

Bernik, Igor, and Kaja Prislan. 2016. "Measuring Information Security Performance with 10 by 10 Model for Holistic State Evaluation." *PLoS One* 11 (9): e0163050. https://doi.org/10.1371/journal.pone.0163050.

Berry, Anthony J., Robert Sweeting, and Jitsu Goto. 2006. "The Effect of Business Advisers on the Performance of SMEs." *Journal of Small Business and Enterprise Development* 13 (1): 33–47.

Blythe, John M., and Lynne Coventry. 2018. "Costly but Effective: Comparing the Factors That Influence Employee Anti-Malware Behaviours." *Computers in Human Behavior* 87 (October): 87–97. https://doi.org/10.1016/j.chb.2018.05.023.

Chen, Jane. 2016. "Cybersecurity: Bull's-Eye on Small Businesses." *Journal of International Business and Law* 16 (1): 97–118. https://scholarlycommons.law.hofstra.edu/jibl/vol16/iss1/10.

CISCO and NSBA. 2021. "US Small Business Recovery and Technology Report." https://nsba.biz/wp-content/uploads/2021/12/Cisco-NSBA-Pandemic-Survey-Final2.rf_.pdf.

Claar, Chester L. 2011. "The Adoption of Computer Security: An Analysis of Home Personal Computer User Behavior Using the Health Belief Model." *All Graduate Theses and Dissertations* 878. https://digitalcommons.usu.edu/etd/878.

D'Arcy, John, and Anat Hovav. 2008. "Does One Size Fit All? Examining the Differential Effects of IS Security Countermeasures." *Journal of Business Ethics* 89 (1): 59. https://doi.org/10.1007/s10551-008-9909-7.

DCMS and Ipsos MORI. 2022. "Cybersecurity Breaches Survey." *GOV.UK*. www.gov.uk/government/statistics/cyber-security-breaches-survey-2022/cyber-security-breaches-survey-2022.

Department for Business, Energy & Industrial Strategy. 2021. "Business Population Estimates for the UK and Regions 2021: Statistical Release (HTML)." *GOV.UK*. www.gov.uk/government/statistics/business-population-estimates-2021/business-population-estimates-for-the-uk-and-regions-2021-statistical-release-html.

Dodel, Matias, and Gustavo Mesch. 2017. "Cyber-Victimization Preventive Behavior: A Health Belief Model Approach." *Computers in Human Behavior* 68: 359–67.

González, Daniel Pérez, Pedro Solana González, and Sara Trigueros Preciado. 2013. "Strategy of Information Security in Small and Medium Enterprises, an Technology-Enterprise Approach: Analysis of Its Relationship with Organizational and Performance Business Variables." *Information (Japan)* 16 (6): 3883–3905.

Gundu, Tapiwa. 2019. "Acknowledging and Reducing the Knowing and Doing Gap in Employee Cybersecurity Compliance." In *Proceedings of International Conference on Cyber Warfare and Security*, Reading, UK, 94 (1), pp. 94–102.

Heidt, Margareta, Jin P. Gerlach, and Peter Buxmann. 2019. "Investigating the Security Divide between SME and Large Companies: How SME Characteristics Influence Organizational IT Security Investments." *Information Systems Frontiers* 21 (6): 1285–305. https://doi.org/10.1007/s10796-019-09959-1.

Khayer, Abul, Md Shamim Talukder, Yukun Bao, and Md Nahin Hossain. 2020. "Cloud Computing Adoption and Its Impact on SMEs Performance for Cloud Supported Operations: A Dual-Stage Analytical Approach." *Technology in Society* 60: 101225. https://doi.org/10.1016/j.techsoc.2019.10.

Kimwele, Michael, Waweru Mwangi, and Stephen Kimani. 2005. "Adoption of Information Technology Security Policies: Case Study of Kenyan Small and Medium Enterprises (SMEs)." *Journal of Theoretical and Applied Information Technology* 18 (2): 11. www.jatit.org/volumes/research-papers/Vol18No2/1Vol18No2.pdf.

Lewis, James. 2018. "Economic Impact of Cybercrime, No Slowing Down." www.csis.org/analysis/economic-impact-cybercrime.

Michie, S. F., Robert West, Rona Campbell, Jamie Brown, and Heather Gainforth. 2014. *ABC of Behaviour Change Theories*. Silverback Publishing.

NCA, and NCSC. 2018. "The Cyber Threat to UK Businesses." www.nationalcrimeagency.gov.uk/who-we-are/publications/178-the-cyber-threat-to-uk-business-2017-18/file.

NCSC. 2015. "How Cyberattacks Work." www.ncsc.gov.uk/information/how-cyberattacks-work.

Ng, Boon-Yuen, Atreyi Kankanhalli, and Yunjie (Calvin) Xu. 2009. "Studying Users' Computer Security Behavior: A Health Belief Perspective." *Decision Support Systems* 46 (4): 815–25. https://doi.org/10.1016/j.dss.2008.11.010.

"North East Business Resilience Centre." 2022. March 28, 2022. https://www.nebrcentre.co.uk/.

OECD. 2021. "The Digital Transformation of SMEs." www.oecd-ilibrary.org/content/publication/bdb9256a-en.

ONS. 2020. "Business Demography, UK – Office for National Statistics." www.ons.gov.uk/businessindustryandtrade/business/activitysizeandlocation/datasets/businessdemographyreferencetable.

Osborn, Emma. 2014. "Business versus Technology: Sources of the Perceived Lack of Cybersecurity in SMEs." *Oxford University Research Archive*. https://ora.ox.ac.uk/objects/uuid:4363144b-5667-4fdd-8cd3-b8e35436107e.

Osborn, Emma, and Simpson, Andrew. 2018. "Risk and the Small-Scale Cybersecurity Decision Making Dialogue – a UK Case Study." *The Computer Journal* 61 (4): 472–95. https://doi.org/10.1093/comjnl/bxx093.

Renaud, Karen, and Jacques Ophoff. 2021. "A Cyber Situational Awareness Model to Predict the Implementation of Cybersecurity Controls and Precautions by SMEs." *Organizational Cybersecurity Journal: Practice, Process and People* 1 (1): 24–46. https://doi.org/10.1108/OCJ-03-2021-0004.

Renaud, Karen, and George R. S. Weir. 2016. "Cybersecurity and the Unbearability of Uncertainty." In *2016 Cybersecurity and Cyberforensics Conference (CCC)*, 137–43. Amman, Jordan: IEEE. https://doi.org/10.1109/CCC.2016.29.

Rhodes, Chris. 2016. "House of Commons Library Briefing Paper Number 06152." November 23. https://researchbriefings.files.parliament.uk/documents/SN06152/SN06152.pdf.

Rogers, Ronald W. 1975. "A Protection Motivation Theory of Fear Appeals and Attitude Change." *The Journal of Psychology* 91 (1): 93–114. https://doi.org/10.1080/00223980.1975.9915803.

Rosenstock, I. M., V. J. Strecher, and M. H. Becker. 1988. "Social Learning Theory and the Health Belief Model." *Health Education Quarterly* 15 (2): 175–83. https://doi.org/10.1177/109019818801500203.

Saban, Kenneth Albert, Stephen Rau, and Charles A. Wood. 2021. "SME Executives' Perceptions and the Information Security Preparedness Model." *Information & Computer Security* 29: 263–82. https://doi.org/10.1108/ICS-01-2020-0014.

Shillair, Ruth. 2020. "Protection Motivation Theory." In Jan Van den Bulck (Ed.), *The International Encyclopedia of Media Psychology*, 1–3. https://doi.org/10.1002/9781119011071.iemp0188. Hoboken, NJ, USA: Wiley.

Shreeve, Benjamin, Joseph Hallett, Matthew Edwards, Kopo M. Ramokapane, Richard Atkins, and Awais Rashid. 2022. "The Best Laid Plans or Lack Thereof: Security Decision-Making of Different Stakeholder Groups." *IEEE Transactions on Software Engineering* 48 (5): 1515–28. https://doi.org/10.1109/TSE.2020.3023735.

Siponen, Mikko, M. Adam Mahmood, and Seppo Pahnila. 2014. "Employees' Adherence to Information Security Policies: An Exploratory Field Study." *Information & Management* 51 (2): 217–24.

Such, J.M., J. Vidler, T. Seabrook, and A. Rashid. 2015. "Cybersecurity Controls Effectiveness: A Qualitative Assessment of Cyber Essentials." www.research.lancs.ac.uk/portal/en/publications/cyber-security-controls-effectiveness(a09a2d28-d121-41dc-86d6-cc24595d8968)/export.html.

Topping, Colin. 2017. "The Role of Awareness in Adoption of Government Cybersecurity Initiatives: A Study of SMEs in the U.K." Student thesis, Luleå University of Technology, DiVA. http://urn.kb.se/resolve?urn=urn:nbn:se:ltu:diva-64870.

Tsai, Hsin-yi Sandy, Mengtian Jiang, Saleem Alhabash, Robert LaRose, Nora J. Rifon, and Shelia R. Cotten. 2016. "Understanding Online Safety Behaviors: A Protection Motivation Theory Perspective." *Computers & Security* 59 (June): 138–50. https://doi.org/10.1016/j.cose.2016.02.009.

US Small Business Administration. 2020. "Stay Safe from Cybersecurity Threats." *Stay Safe from Cybersecurity Threats*. www.sba.gov/business-guide/manage-your-business/stay-safe-cybersecurity-threats.

Valli, Craig, Ian C. Martinus, and Michael N. Johnstone. 2014. "Small to Medium Enterprise Cybersecurity Awareness: An Initial Survey of Western Australian Business." In *CSREA Press* (pp. 71–75). http://worldcomp-proceedings.com/proc/p2014/SAM9779.pdf.

Verizon. 2021. "2021 Data Breach Investigations Report." www.verizon.com/business/resources/reports/dbir/.

Wilson, Martin, Sharon McDonald, Dominic Button, and Kenneth McGarry. 2022. "It Won't Happen to Me: Surveying SME Attitudes to Cyber-Security." *Journal of Computer Information Systems*, 1–13. https://doi.org/10.1080/08874417.2022.2067791.

Zinatullin, Leron. 2013. "Modelling Conflicts between Security Compliance and Human Behaviour." *University College London*. https://zinatullin.com/2013/09/09/comparing-views-on-security-compliance-behaviour-in-an-organisation/.

18 Rethinking the Impact of Informal Organizational Rules on Organizational Cybersecurity

Maharazu Kasim

CONTENTS

INTRODUCTION

The advent of the internet has come along with many unprecedented benefits for various human endeavors: health, education, businesses, and government, among others. Despite these great benefits, the internet has become a haven for criminal activities that could inflict lethal damage on organizations. Like systems that experience a physical breach in organizations, the cyber world is being exposed to threats capable of disrupting the confidentiality, integrity, and availability of critical organizational data (Sallos et al. 2019). Malicious cyberattacks are growing as internet technologies and mobile apps grow in volume and complexity, exposing organizations and society to cyber-security dangers like never before (van Steen et al. 2020). Thus, it has become a critical business for the organization, and it is paramount that they know about the threats that could cause disruption in their systems. A breach of cybersecurity can cause lingering impact that could prove difficult to recover. Information assets can be distorted, accessed without authority, and updated in ways that lead to their losing their value and integrity as a result of cybersecurity flaws (Zwilling et al. 2020).

Organizations are increasingly making efforts to secure their information and communication technologies (ICTs) with the most sophisticated approaches available. Organizations spend a lot of resources to ensure the best cybersecurity mechanisms to protect their critical information. Organizations spend millions to detect the technical, human, and contextual vulnerabilities that expose their ICTs to a series of cyber threats (van Steen et al. 2020). Despite this, organizational cyberse-curity is still a problem. First-class cybersecurity equipment is being purchased. The best human resources are being employed to assess and proffer a better solution to the cybersecurity vulnerabilities that could disrupt operations. However, we could critically say that the threats to cybersecurity

DOI: 10.1201/9781003319887-18

are socio-technical (Ejigu, Siponen, and Arage 2021). They arise not just as a consequence of technological flaws but also, more fundamentally, the result of the deterioration of working methods over time, which pushes an organization to the point where assaults will not only succeed but also have a substantially significant impact on the company (McEvoy and Kowalski 2019).

Additionally, organizations have also identified that the human factor is one of the weakest points associated with organizational cybersecurity (Pollini et al. 2021; Wiafe et al. 2020). Specifically, many studies have raised the alarm on the danger of insider threats in general organizational information security (including cybersecurity). Most studies have agreed that successful information security breaches are most often associated with an insider making advances firsthand to the criminal hacker out there, either intentionally or as a result of human error (Andronache 2021; Hong and Furnell 2022; Lin, Kuo, and Myers 2015; Pollini et al. 2021). It does not seem a surprise given that organizations might spend all their resources on providing technical support for their cybersecurity; the notable impact is on the external forces of hacking. Concentrating on external threats and neglecting internal threats does not lead to a viable information security solution (Ejigu, Siponen, and Arage 2021). Instead, insiders worry less because they have legitimate access to the information within an organization. Thus, developing formal structures to guard against the potential for insider attacks is necessary. Several studies have recognized the possibility of using people to achieve information security and minimize information security risks (McEvoy and Kowalski 2019; Kasim et al. 2022a; Pollini et al. 2021; Andronache 2021; Vance, Siponen, and Straub 2020). Organizations could capitalize on it by identifying those rationale-based factors that determine significant compliance with information security policies (Bulgurcu, Cavusoglu, and Benbasat 2010). The authors argue that human error could become a means of enhancing information security rather than focusing more on its negativity.

This chapter is a review of papers on cybersecurity and information security with the aim of rethinking the impacts of informal rules in promoting or abating cybersecurity-related vulnerabilities. Specifically, the chapter considers human-induced vulnerabilities to have a strong connection with substantive cybersecurity and information security of organizations.

BACKGROUND

Organizations put forth effort to create a secure information security environment. They typically focus on technical aspects of technology and software. As the majority of information system (IS) threats come from outsiders, organizations believe that tackling the problem associated with technology components will fix it (Ejigu, Siponen, and Arage 2021). Internal threats, on the other hand, have been demonstrated in previous studies to constitute a bigger threat. According to some research, desired information systems solutions cannot be realized just via the use of technology tools; equal consideration must be given to the human component, as well as, more importantly, internal threats (Archibald and Renaud 2019). This chapter defines an insider threat as someone who has access to the organization's data and information systems, facilities, and networks. Organizations are commonly subject to cybersecurity vulnerabilities due to human factors. The human component, according to Kasim et al. (2022b), refers to human-induced actions and behaviors that expose a business to cybersecurity vulnerabilities. They act as a weakness that most attackers exploit to do major harm to an organization's information systems and create interruption, distortion, and loss of data and resources. As a result, to reduce the risk of information security breaches and cybersecurity events, businesses create formal structures and processes to protect their information systems. Although informal structures can emerge from formal structures, they typically render organizations more susceptible to cybersecurity threats.

The crucial role of information security policy in ensuring the successful implementation of information security and cybersecurity mechanisms is very strong. In fact, studies have called information security policy the foundation of any information security effort (Tankard 2015; Doherty, Anastasakis, and Fulford 2009). Without it, the potential for information security breaches is high.

As a result, many organizations have developed information security policies to help guide contact with ICT resources. What organizations do is enhance the information security (cybersecurity included) culture among organizational actors. If we take a step backward, we should remember that information security policy is one of the properties of formal structures that stipulate the right direction for adherence to safety rules and cultures. However, sanctioned rules might pose more danger to organizational cybersecurity (Reeves, Delfabbro, and Calic 2021). It might be because the organizational actors, as major stakeholders, have not been involved in developing the information security and cybersecurity strategy. Many frameworks have been developed to enhance information security policy–compliant behavior among organizational actors. However, there seems to be a difference between officially sanctioned behavior and actions and the actual theory-in-use among actors (Patriotta 2003). This is the term "informal structure." It refers to behaviors and actions outside of officially sanctioned rules. However, there are other formal structures, such as intense cybersecurity awareness and education, whose relevance studies have recognized in ensuring compliant behavior.

Not only are formal frameworks insufficient, but there appears to be a dearth of studies examining the function of informal rules in assisting or mitigating cybersecurity threats. Informally sanctioned rules are informally sanctioned activities and behaviors inherent in organizations that may encourage either safe or unsafe actions and behaviors. Organizational actors tend to create informal norms outside of formally sanctioned structures and processes, which can be damaging to operations. For example, an employee may be involved in password sharing with his closest associates both inside and outside of the firm. This may appear normal to the employee, but in a security-conscious firm, this might be a precursor to exploiting the vulnerability, resulting in a cybersecurity breach. Human-caused vulnerabilities are careless practices that could jeopardize the best organizational cybersecurity protocol. However, this chapter is arguing that inasmuch as formal rules have been affirmed as a promoter of cybersecurity-compliant behavior, we cannot dispute the fact that informal rules sometimes promote cybersecurity-compliant behavior among organizational actors.

LITERATURE REVIEW

OVERVIEW

It is true that organizations must deal with vulnerabilities coming from both technical and human angles. However, organizations seem to pay more attention to technical vulnerabilities than they do to human. Given the call by scholars on the danger of human-induced vulnerabilities, many organizations have embarked on developing and adopting measures to minimize the risks associated with human actions and behaviors. As a result, organizations have adopted many formal measures towards enhancing compliant behavior against cybersecurity and information security. Although formal and informal rules have great positive impact on cybersecurity and information security, there exist certain negative impacts that could demonize organizational cybersecurity. So, in this section, the chapter discusses the positive and negative views that emanate from both formal and informal rules. This discussion will enable organizations realize that just as formal rules are a strong promoter of organizational cybersecurity, informal rules can also be harnessed positively to promote organizational cybersecurity.

FORMAL RULES AS A PROMOTER OF CYBERSECURITY-COMPLIANT BEHAVIOR

Deployment of IS makes it pertinent for organizations to look for ways to safeguard their systems against information security breaches and cybersecurity incidents. Formal rules are one of the major approaches organizations use to promote the safety of their critical IS infrastructures from breach. In other to achieve that, many studies have reinstated the crucial role of information security policies (Tankard 2015; Doherty, Anastasakis, and Fulford 2009), organizational culture (Andronache 2021; Orehek and Petrič 2021), awareness and training, and place management (Back and Guerette 2021), among others. All these require the commitment of organizational decision makers.

Formal rules are those strategies and processes designed by an organization's governance and management to guide operations of the organization. These structures and processes are designed to help organizations achieve their strategic goals and objectives. Since IS has become part and parcel of organizational operations (suffice it to say they are at the core center of organizational operations), it is quite necessary to develop strategies to minimize or possibly do away with the growing concern over their security. A number of studies have attributed the success of information security and cybersecurity to compliance with information security policy (Tankard 2015; Doherty, Anastasakis, and Fulford 2009). Information security policy is a formal document that outlines the procedures, rules, and regulations governing the use of IS. Most studies have agreed that organizations that choose to ignore information security policy risk their critical assets being breached and causing disruptions, distortions, and loss of critical information (Ajibesin, Kasim, and Ogundapo 2022). In this regard, there are many studies that have been conducted to look at the employee compliance behavior attributed to information security policy. Most studies believe that the more organizations impose formal sanctions on the misuse of IS, the greater the compliant behavior (Ejigu, Siponen, and Arage 2021). From this, we must understand that formal sanctions/rules are making employees develop compliant behavior with information security policies. And the greater the compliant behavior, the more organizations reduce the chance of being breached because of human error. The emphasis on human error is because it is a threat to organizations given that employees have formal authority on systems. Thus, technical security of systems does not guard against employee social errors. Technical security is more of a protective measure against external invasion.

Restating this, a study conducted by (Back and Guerette 2021) stated that place management can reduce the chances for cybersecurity vulnerabilities caused by human actions and vulnerabilities. The study emphasized the need to borrow the concept of "place management," which originates from criminology, to promote a campaign against insider intrusion. Although it is pertinent, we state here that insider intrusion could be deliberate or otherwise. According to the authors, place management has been found to reduce physical criminal activities, especially as it concerns developing rules and regulations associated with crime actions and behaviors. In fact, absence of place management can cause serious problems to organizations. Adapting this idea, it is quite relevant for organizations to have information security place managers aware and trained on how to tackle behaviors and actions detrimental to their cybersecurity. Place managers can use training and awareness to enhance online users' behaviors and actions. Through this, organizations can minimize losses and mitigate cybersecurity vulnerabilities. Place management is also one of the formal rules that organizations can use to promote information security and cyber secure behavior.

Also, formal rules can help improve the corporate cybersecurity of small and medium-sized enterprises (SMEs). It is believed that cybercrime targeted at SMEs is more lethal and successful. This is a result of weak corporate cybersecurity and poor and inadequate cybersecurity training and awareness, required expertise, and resources (Bada and Nurse 2019). Cybersecurity culture in SMEs can be promoted through intense training and awareness. Training and awareness are a product of formal rules. Organizations have been engaging organizational actors in series of training and awareness associated with cybersecurity and information security. Many studies have established the crucial role of training and awareness in promoting cybersecurity-compliant behavior (Andronache 2021; Drivas et al. 2019). However, when cybersecurity awareness is not taken seriously, there is every possibility to institute cybersecurity culture detrimental to the security of critical information systems assets (Knight and Sadok 2021).

Organizations are deemed to promote safe cybersecurity practice when they continue to keep their employees aware of growing cybersecurity threats through their negligent actions and behaviors. Negligent behavior is an action that organizational actors exhibit and makes their organizations prone to cybersecurity incidents. Negligence evolves through taking for granted actions and behaviors which are a product of non-adherence to the formal rules stated in the information security policy. Thus, organizations can enhance their protective measures by adhering to the stated rules and sanctions governing the use of IS among organizational actors. When organizations become reluctant to use these policies, organizational actors develop actions and behaviors that are taken for granted and institutionalize them. In this regard, adherence to formal rules, structures, and processes enhances information security and cybersecurity-compliant behavior (Ejigu, Siponen, and Arage 2021).

One of the greatest properties of formal rules is the promotion of good information security and cybersecurity culture among employees. Culture is the institutionalized practices within organizations, which could be in their favor or otherwise. Organizations need to be wary of this culture and intensify effort toward formally sanctioning approved information security and cybersecurity culture. A study conducted by Drivas et al. (2019) and one conducted by Pătrașcu (2019) reaffirmed the crucial nature of promoting cybersecurity culture through intense education, training, and awareness about the dangers of cybersecurity threats. The study emphasized that organizations could take proactive and reactive measures through the development of formal rules such as policies in tandem with the organizational goals and IS use. Some of these measures include the development of information security policy and putting contingency plans in place. As Ejigu, Siponen, and Arage (2021) rightly put it, consistent culture can help promote adherence to formal rules and can increase intention to comply with formal rules, processes, and structures (Parsons et al. 2015). The implication is that critical assets of organizations will be less threatened by human-induced vulnerabilities, although if policies and procedures are in contradiction to the moral beliefs of organizational actors, chances are that information security will be breached. Once taken-for-granted actions and behaviors become institutionalized, they are in contradiction to the information security culture sanctioned by the organization.

FORMAL RULES AS A PROMOTER OF CYBERSECURITY NON-COMPLIANT BEHAVIOR

In the quest for enhancing sound cybersecurity and information security culture among employees, organizations mostly cross the line by overexposing organizational actors to cybersecurity information and activities, and the source of these activities is a product of formal rules imposing strict compliance with safety behaviors. Cybersecurity fatigue is one of the negative impacts of overexposure to cybersecurity information and activities on safety behaviors. Some studies refer to this as technostress (D'Arcy, Herath, and Shoss 2014). Technostress has to do with employees showing signs of stress and fatigue because of the accelerating technological demand in the workplace. Usually, organizational actors are expected to develop fear of imposing sanctions by not adhering to formal rules. However, cybersecurity fatigue tends to be a driver of certain behaviors that could easily increase exposure to cybersecurity threats. Employees become disengaged from following the cybersecurity practices sanctioned by formal rules (Reeves, Delfabbro, and Calic 2021). Cybersecurity fatigue leads to cyber-loafing. This is a situation where employees engage in informal activities using an organization's network and information assets (Cheng et al. 2013). So, in instances like this, formal rules expose the organizations to an old and new set of threats, which can cause serious loss and disruptions of organizational critical assets.

Studies have identified the crucial role of organizational culture sanctioned by formal rules. However, if there is misalignment between culture and moral behavior, there is every possibility for actions and behaviors detrimental to organizational information security. Studies have cautioned against promoting a culture in which organizational actors do not share similar views. In other words, organizations develop formal rules without the involvement of employees in the development process. Remember, at the core of any organizational information security and cybersecurity success are policies, structures, and processes. However, this view comes with many irregularities, given fresh evidence. In fact, some studies have established that there is no significant relationship between formal sanctions and intention to exercise compliant behavior (Vance, Siponen, and Straub 2020). According to the authors, compliance with information security safety measures is dependent upon what the employees regard as right or wrong behavior. Because of the eagerness to protect their critical IS assets, organizations impose their approved organizational culture on the employees.

However, it is one of their critical mistakes given that employees will create informal rules to suit their moral beliefs. Most studies have recognized the importance of neutralization in ensuring compliant behavior (Siponen and Vance 2010; Vance, Siponen, and Straub 2020).

One crucial point for the failure of cybersecurity and information security formal rules is lack of compliance from top management. If rules are made, it is necessary that organizations mandate compliance from top to bottom. It is said that top management's compliance will trigger compliant behaviors that will not expose the organizations to threats (Wiafe et al. 2020). Organizational actors will be wary of behaviors contrary to the ones practiced by top management. If sanctions are applied to middle- and lower-level employees because of non-compliance, it will become a stepping stone for the enactment of informal rules that could be detrimental to organizational cybersecurity. The cognitive frames of the middle- and lower-level employees will not be in the favor of the organization. Employees will begin to think that formal rules were set to witch-hunt them rather than supplement their activities. As such, employees could enact behaviors that trigger cybersecurity incidents.

Also, processes are one of the determinants for compliant behavior among employees, especially as it relates to organizational cybersecurity. Thus, processes should not be too complicated nor too simple. Because processes might be invisible, the user is excluded from the solution to the security problem. Processes may be both a hindrance and a helper when it comes to efficient cybersecurity. If processes are overly complex, and the user is unwilling or unable to expand their expertise in order to comply, security is jeopardized (Pham et al. 2019). Furthermore, if processes are overly simplistic, security may be perceived as ineffectual. One technique to ensure a balance between organizational and user demands is to co-create procedures.

INFORMAL RULES AS A PROMOTER OF CYBERSECURITY-COMPLIANT BEHAVIOR

Generally, informal rules are being viewed as having a negative impact on organizational policies, especially as it concerns cybersecurity and information security. However, certain studies have recognized the significant contribution of informal rules in promoting organizational goals, be it cybersecurity, information security, or strategic goals of an organization. Informal rules have the potential to reduce information security policy non-compliance among organizational actors (Ejigu, Siponen, and Arage 2021). So, we could argue that informal rules are very much relevant to enhancing organizational cybersecurity.

While formal rules have a crucial role in deterring cybersecurity human-induced vulnerabilities, some studies argue that informal rules play more vital roles in deterring suspicious cybersecurity behavior. It is believed that perceived informal sanctions prevent cybersecurity incidents more than formal. Individuals who have better ties to traditional family and peers may be less prone to engage in a wide range of cybercrimes because they are afraid of causing shame and humiliation to themselves and their loved ones. This might imply that focusing on informal punishments rather than formal sanctions has a bigger impact on cybercrime and people's desire to perform severe cyber assaults, especially if reintegration shaming concepts are adopted in families, schools, and communities (Bossler 2019; Vance, Siponen, and Straub 2020).

It has been established in the literature that cooperative actions among organizational actors promote more compliant behavior related to cybersecurity. Unlike most studies, which show a strong connection between formal rules and compliant behavior, Daud et al. (2018) show that informal connection, such as cooperative behavior among employees, has high positive influence on the intention to comply with cybersecurity protective behavior. In some instances, formal sanctions do not seem to motivate compliant behavior rather provoke more resistant behavior. The more resistant employees are, the more organizational cybersecurity is at risk. Thus, organizations can mitigate cybersecurity-compliant behavior through promotion of cooperative behavior among employees.

Pham et al. (2019) presented a new model that includes products, price, promotion, place, physical evidence, process, and people. The authors came up with an interesting finding that organizations should consider enhancing employee recognition whenever they are making decisions.

Organizations need to consider aligning their organizational goals with employees' goals. Immersing this into the organizational rules will provide a kind of smooth and successful inception of behavioral change campaign. Typically, this refers to the relevance of informal sanctions. And the study emphasizes that developing innovation of whatever kind provides the best results when there exists alignment between organizational goals and employees. In the context of cybersecurity, there is a need for organizations to understand whether their definition of *product* is in tandem with the employees' definition. If there is conflict in respect to what the employees believe to be right and what the organization does, then the possibility for failure is high. The view is supported by Wiafe et al. (2020). The authors put it in the form of descriptive norms influencing personal norms.

INFORMAL RULES AS A PROMOTER OF CYBERSECURITY–NON-COMPLIANT BEHAVIOR

While informal rules have positive impact, there is a negative side attached to it. Organizational actors develop a neutralized form of behavior to certain organizational rules. So, if the formal rules of an organization match the moral behavior of the employees, it is expected that employees will develop optimism about compliance to organizational cybersecurity. Employees are more likely to break IS security regulations when they believe their workload is heavy, they are busy with other tasks, security policies slow them down, and other work is more essential (Siponen and Vance 2010). Although scholars view neutralization as predisposition for committing a crime, it is still more informal than formal. Thus, we view neutralization as a step for either promoting compliant behavior or enhancing violation of IS security policies. From the bigger picture, a wise organization might use this opportunity to promote change behavior among employees and ensure compliance with IS security policies (cybersecurity inclusive).

Employees develop cybersecurity fatigue as a result of overexposure to cybersecurity details (Reeves, Delfabbro, and Calic 2021). Employees become disengaged with the rules and expose organizational cybersecurity to threats. Although the fatigue is a product of overexposure to cybersecurity formal rules, it may become an informally developed rule among employees. It has been established in the literature that people form communities of practice within an organization, which could be an advantage to the organization or otherwise (Kasim et al. 2022b). When it happens, the community of practice negotiates competence with which members identify themselves. This will generate similar patterns of behavior and actions among the employees.

RECOMMENDATIONS

This chapter established that, inasmuch as formal and informal rules have a positive impact on organizational cybersecurity, organizations must deal with the negative realities that come along with these two concepts. We proffer the following solutions and recommendations:

- Notable among the problems is misalignment between organizational belief and employees' beliefs. Thus, organizations must ensure that they stand on the same side as employees. This can be achieved through engaging employees in the process of establishing any formal rules.
- Formal rules associated with cybersecurity must cover every aspect of the organization. If the rules apply to certain group of people and not another, there is every possibility for the enactment of certain informal settings among the employees. We have established that informal rules do more harm to organizations than good. Formation of informal rules means compromising the approved form of cyber behavior and actions.
- We have established that employees develop cybersecurity fatigue because of too much exposure to cybersecurity requirements. So organizations must deal with the reality that overexposure to cybersecurity awareness, campaigns, and others can make employees feel overwhelmed and begin not to follow the set cybersecurity rules. So it is quite necessary that

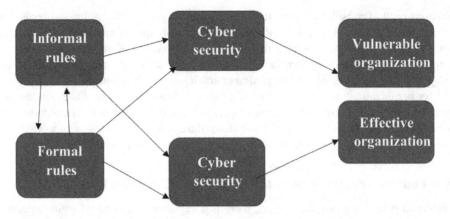

FIGURE 18.1   Organizational cybersecurity and formal and informal rules model.

organizations understand what, when, and how they should embark on activities to avoid cybersecurity fatigue. For example, if an organization mandated that employees should be changing their official email password every two weeks, it may reach a point where the employees will not do it, and it will subject the organization to cybersecurity threats.

- Another crucial point in this section is that empirical studies need to be undertaken from varying perspectives. Most of the studies talking about compliant behavior are coming from a positivist point of view. In IS, philosophy is a crucial factor for the development of new ideas and perspectives to problems. When there is resistant behavior among employees on compliance to rules, it is quite all right to try another angle and see what it offers. Thus, this study suggests that studies rooted in interpretivism and critical realism should be undertaken to develop new understandings. For example, we are more familiar with the interpretivist philosophy, which states that multiple realities exist and are subjective. Thus, we could use interpretivist philosophy to understand how the competence of a community of practice contributes to the enactment of informal rules and resistant behavior associated with compliance with cybersecurity formal rules.

To buttress the problem and the solutions better, a model was developed, depicted in Figure 18.1. This framework provides an explanation of the inter-relationship that exists between formal rules and informal rules, formal rules and cybersecurity-compliant behavior, and informal rules and cybersecurity-compliant behavior

CONCLUSION

Our study was about how formal and informal organizational rules impact the cybersecurity of organizations. We provided background information on the problems. We established that formal and informal rules could have both positive and negative aspects. Organizations should recognize that formal rules not only promote cybersecurity but also pose certain threats. If employees are not on the same page as organizations, the possibility of resistant behavior detrimental to cybersecurity is high. Inasmuch as formal rules promote cybersecurity-compliant behavior, they also promote behaviors detrimental to organizational cybersecurity. Organizations must deal with the reality that informal rules are not always negative to organizational cybersecurity. Organizations can harness informal rules to promote cybersecurity-compliant behavior among employees. For example, fear of causing shame and humiliation to oneself and one's loved ones is believed to guard against any action that leads to cybersecurity vulnerabilities. Organizations could capitalize on this kind of informal structure to understand their employees' weaknesses and take urgent actions to enhance cybersecurity-compliant behavior. Finally, we were able to develop a model that explains the relationship between cybersecurity-compliant or non-compliant behavior and formal and informal organizational rules.

REFERENCES

Ajibesin, Adeyemi Abel, Maharazu Kasim, and Olusegun Ogundapo. 2022. "Information Security Policies in Nigerian Institutions: Evaluation and Readiness." *International Journal of Risk and Contingency Management* 11 (1): 1–22. https://doi.org/10.4018/IJRCM.303103.

Andronache, Alina. 2021. "Increasing Security Awareness through Lenses of Cybersecurity Culture." *Journal of Information Systems & Operations Management* 15 (1). http://jisom.rau.ro/Vol.15%20No.1%20-%20 2021.html.

Archibald, Jacqueline M., and Karen Renaud. 2019. "Refining the PoinTER 'Human Firewall' Pentesting Framework." *Information & Computer Security* 27 (4): 575–600. https://doi.org/10.1108/ICS-01-2019-0019.

Back, Sinchul, and Rob T. Guerette. 2021. "Cyber Place Management and Crime Prevention: The Effectiveness of Cybersecurity Awareness Training against Phishing Attacks." *Journal of Contemporary Criminal Justice* 37 (3): 427–451. https://doi.org/10.1177/10439862211001628.

Bada, Maria, and Jason R.C. Nurse. 2019. "Developing Cybersecurity Education and Awareness Programmes for Small- and Medium-Sized Enterprises (SMEs)." *Information & Computer Security* 27 (3): 393–410. https://doi.org/10.1108/ICS-07-2018-0080.

Bossler, Adam M. 2019. "Perceived Formal and Informal Sanctions on the Willingness to Commit Cyberattacks against Domestic and Foreign Targets." *Journal of Crime and Justice* 42 (5): 599–615. https://doi.org/1 0.1080/0735648X.2019.1692423.

Bulgurcu, Burcu, Hasan Cavusoglu, and Izak Benbasat. 2010. "Information Security Policy Compliance: An Empirical Study of Rationality-Based Beliefs and Information Security Awareness." *MIS Quarterly* 34 (3): 523–548. https://doi.org/10.2307/25750690.

Cheng, Lijiao, Ying Li, Wenli Li, Eric Holm, and Qingguo Zhai. 2013. "Understanding the Violation of IS Security Policy in Organizations: An Integrated Model Based on Social Control and Deterrence Theory." *Computers & Security* 39 (Part B): 447–459. https://doi.org/10.1016/j.cose.2013.09.009.

D'Arcy, John, Tejaswini Herath, and Mindy K. Shoss. 2014. "Understanding Employee Responses to Stressful Information Security Requirements: A Coping Perspective." *Journal of Management Information Systems* 31 (2): 285–318. https://doi.org/10.2753/MIS0742-1222310210.

Daud, Maslina, Rajah Rasiah, Mary George, David Asirvatham, and Govindamal Thangiah. 2018. "Bridging the Gap between Organisational Practices and Cybersecurity Compliance: Can Cooperation Promote Compliance in Organisations?" *International Journal of Business and Society* 19 (1): 20.

Doherty, Neil Francis, Leonidas Anastasakis, and Heather Fulford. 2009. "The Information Security Policy Unpacked: A Critical Study of the Content of University Policies." *International Journal of Information Management* 29 (6): 449–457. https://doi.org/10.1016/j.ijinfomgt.2009.05.003.

Drivas, George, Leandros Maglaras, Helge Janicke, and Sotiris Loannidis. 2019. "Cybersecurity Assessment of the Public Sector in Greece." In *Proceedings of the 18th European Conference on Cyber Warfare and Security ECCWS 2019*, p. 162. University of Coimbra, Portugal: Academic Conferences and Publishing Limited.

Ejigu, Kibrom Tadesse, Mikko Siponen, and Tilahun Muluneh Arage. 2021. "Investigating the Impact of Organizational Culture on Information Security Policy Compliance: The Case of Ethiopia." In *AMCIS 2021: Proceedings of the 27th Americas Conference on Information Systems*. Association for Information Systems. https://aisel.aisnet.org/amcis2021/info_security/info_security/10/.

Hong, Yuxiang, and Steven Furnell. 2022. "Motivating Information Security Policy Compliance: Insights from Perceived Organizational Formalization." *Journal of Computer Information Systems* 62 (1): 19–28. https://doi.org/10.1080/08874417.2019.1683781.

Kasim, Maharazu, Mohammed Bashir Saidu, Abdullahi Isa, and Samuel C. Avemaria Utulu. 2022a. "A Proposal for Social Ethical Hacking Framework for Detecting and Managing Human-Induced Vulnerabilities in Organizational Cybersecurity." In *UK Academy for Information Systems Conference Proceedings 2022*, p. 16. https://aisel.aisnet.org/ukais2022/16.

Kasim, Maharazu, Mohammed Bashir Saidu, Abdullahi Isa, and Samuel C. Avemaria Utulu. 2022b. "Proposal for Social Ethical Hacking Framework for Detecting and Managing Human-Induced Vulnerabilities in Organizational Cybersecurity." In *Proceeding of the UK Academy for Information Systems Conference Proceedings UKAIS 2022*, AIS Press, Oxfordshire, p. 150.

Knight, Victoria, and Moufida Sadok. 2021. "Is Cyber-Security the New Lifeboat? An Exploration of the Employee's Perspective of Cyber-Security within the Cruise Ship Industry." Edited by Peter Bednar, Alexander Nolte, Mikko Rajanen, Anna Sigridur Islind, Helena Vallo Hult, Fatema Zaghloul, Aurelio Ravarini, and Alessio Maria Braccini. *STPIS 2021: Socio-Technical Perspective in IS Development 2021, CEUR Workshop Proceedings*, 3016 (October): 216–231. https://stpis.org/.

Lin, Cecilia I.C., Feng-Yang Kuo, and Michael D. Myers. 2015. "Extending ICT4D Studies." *MIS Quarterly* 39 (3): 697–712.

McEvoy, Thomas Richard, and Stewart James Kowalski. 2019. "Deriving Cybersecurity Risks from Human and Organizational Factors – A Socio-Technical Approach." *Complex Systems Informatics and Modeling Quarterly*, no. 18 (April): 47–64. https://doi.org/10.7250/csimq.2019-18.03.

Orehek, Špela, and Gregor Petrič. 2021. "A Systematic Review of Scales for Measuring Information Security Culture." *Information & Computer Security* 29 (1): 133–158. https://doi.org/10.1108/ICS-12-2019-0140.

Parsons, Kathryn Marie, Elise Young, Marcus Antanas Butavicius, Agata McCormac, Malcolm Robert Pattinson, and Cate Jerram. 2015. "The Influence of Organizational Information Security Culture on Information Security Decision Making." *Journal of Cognitive Engineering and Decision Making* 9 (2): 117–129. https://doi.org/10.1177/1555343415575152.

Pătrașcu, Petrișor. 2019. "Promoting Cybersecurity Culture through Education." *Conference Proceedings of ELearning and Software for Education (ELSE)* 15 (2): 273–279. www.ceeol.com/search/article-detail?id=782853.

Patriotta, Gerardo. 2003. *Organizational Knowledge in the Making: How Firms Create, Use, and Institutionalize Knowledge*. Oxford and New York: Oxford University Press.

Pham, Hiep Cong, Linda Brennan, Lukas Parker, Nhat Tram Phan-Le, Irfan Ulhaq, Mathews Zanda Nkhoma, and Minh Nhat Nguyen. 2019. "Enhancing Cybersecurity Behavior: An Internal Social Marketing Approach." *Information & Computer Security* 28 (2): 133–159. https://doi.org/10.1108/ICS-01-2019-0023.

Pollini, Alessandro, Tiziana C. Callari, Alessandra Tedeschi, Daniele Ruscio, Luca Save, Franco Chiarugi, and Davide Guerri. 2021. "Leveraging Human Factors in Cybersecurity: An Integrated Methodological Approach." *Cognition, Technology & Work* 24: 371–390. https://doi.org/10.1007/s10111-021-00683-y.

Reeves, A., P. Delfabbro, and D. Calic. 2021. "Encouraging Employee Engagement with Cybersecurity: How to Tackle Cyber Fatigue." *SAGE Open* 11 (1): 1–18. https://doi.org/10.1177/21582440211000049.

Sallos, Mark Paul, Alexeis Garcia-Perez, Denise Bedford, and Beatrice Orlando. 2019. "Strategy and Organisational Cybersecurity: A Knowledge-Problem Perspective." *Journal of Intellectual Capital* 20 (4): 581–597. https://doi.org/10.1108/JIC-03-2019-0041.

Siponen, Mikko, and Anthony Vance. 2010. "Neutralization: New Insights into the Problem of Employee Information Systems Security Policy Violations." *MIS Quarterly* 34 (3): 487. https://doi.org/10.2307/25750688.

Steen, Tommy van, Emma Norris, Kirsty Atha, and Adam Joinson. 2020. "What (If Any) Behaviour Change Techniques Do Government-Led Cybersecurity Awareness Campaigns Use?" *Journal of Cybersecurity* 6 (1): 1–8. https://doi.org/10.1093/cybsec/tyaa019.

Tankard, Colin. 2015. "Data Classification – The Foundation of Information Security." *Network Security* 2015 (5): 8–11. https://doi.org/10.1016/S1353-4858(15)30038-6.

Vance, Anthony, Mikko T. Siponen, and Detmar W. Straub. 2020. "Effects of Sanctions, Moral Beliefs, and Neutralization on Information Security Policy Violations across Cultures." *Information & Management* 57 (4): 103212. https://doi.org/10.1016/j.im.2019.103212.

Wiafe, Isaac, Felix Nti Koranteng, Abigail Wiafe, Emmanuel Nyarko Obeng, and Winfred Yaokumah. 2020. "The Role of Norms in Information Security Policy Compliance." *Information & Computer Security* 28 (5): 743–761. https://doi.org/10.1108/ICS-08-2019-0095.

Zwilling, Moti, Galit Klien, Dušan Lesjak, Łukasz Wiechetek, Fatih Cetin, and Hamdullah Nejat Basim. 2020. "Cybersecurity Awareness, Knowledge and Behavior: A Comparative Study." *Journal of Computer Information Systems* 62 (1): 82–97. https://doi.org/10.1080/08874417.2020.1712269.

19 Ethical Aspects of Cybersecurity in E-Commerce

Tanya Kumar and Satveer Kaur

CONTENTS

INTRODUCTION

In today's scenario, business is executed through digital mechanisms, and technological tools play a major role in handling networking and operational activities. With an increasing level of technology, the data related to business are stored through digital mechanisms. Data are a source of information stored in the form of files or other virtual tools. Data protection is one of the major aspects of today's business world. This all increases the need to protect data from being hacked and take strategic action to manage data safely using cybersecurity. Moreover, some businesses are adopting unfair means to provide better protection to their data. It is the responsibility of technical experts to handle cybersecurity ethically. Ethics is one of the branches of philosophy which is concerned with what is right or wrong. In the case of e-commerce, while dealing with ethical cybersecurity, it is important to determine what is right or wrong for users of information (Kavitha and Preetha 2019). Ethical cybersecurity a major concern for everyone.

Ethical aspects of cybersecurity deal with security, privacy policy, risk management, and so on (Tronnier et al. 2022). E-commerce platforms deal with the exchange of goods, services, and information through a digital mechanism. Emphasis is given to estimate the ethical issues related to cybersecurity and faced by the researchers. It was determined that the current scenario of ethical cybersecurity is not adequate, and issues related to privacy concerns, bias in digital norms, and data control need to be addressed. Ethical conduct includes avoidance of harm to others, honesty, and trustworthiness, maintaining confidentiality, privacy concerns, fair policy and non-discrimination, credentials for intellectual property, respect towards copyrights and patents, and contribution towards human beings and society in general. The e-commerce ecosystem is facing financial as well as reputational damage while handling its relevant business data. Ethical issues manifest in the business of e-commerce while handling the processing or storage of data. Data storage can be an area of concern for big companies in managing their data through information systems (Tronnier et al. 2022). Data processing includes the conversion of raw data into a useful form.

Cybersecurity is a strategic process that can be used in the critical protection of business systems from data breaches. With the evolution in technology, there are inherent risks in the business world

DOI: 10.1201/9781003319887-19

in the form of cyber threats or cyberattacks, and security can be attained by adopting the right means through multi-layered protection using cybersecurity. Cybersecurity is one of the necessities of today's business world, as systems consist of valuable and sensitive information, and it is used by businesses to protect their relevant data from theft or damage. The purpose of the chapter is to determine the ethical issues regarding cybersecurity in e-commerce and those required to manage cybersecurity as a relevant matter of ethics in today's digital world. Cybersecurity is a necessity in a fast-paced and emerging digital world. In today's digital scenario, it is necessary to follow ethical standards to securely enjoy the privacy of data in the e-commerce framework (Macnish and Ham 2020). Ethics is a need in today's business world and helps to manage business operations in a significant manner.

Cybersecurity can be a source to analyze market trends by gathering and assessing manifold data to evaluate the results and retain a better position in the market. Ethical standards are fixed in business contexts per the work performed by them as well as the resources used to execute business processes in many aspects. Cybersecurity can also be known by its alternative name, information technology security (Banik 2021). Emerging trends as well as recent developments were also discussed in the study. The focus was given to highlighting the fundamental concepts related to the study. The sources of cyber threats are also discussed, including foreign countries, hackers, organized hackers, terrorists, internal dissatisfied factors, and sabotage groups. The types of cyberattacks were also highlighted: spyware, frequent counting, viruses, Trojan horses, sniffers, abuse tools, logic bomb, denial of service, and so on (Tunggal 2022). The types of cybersecurity were also discussed, such as cloud security, data security prevention, end-user training, information security, application security, network security, infrastructure security, and cloud security.

The study also determined that information security can be maintained through confidentiality, integrity, and availability. It can be concluded that theoretical aspects play a major role in contributing to cybersecurity. The study focused on determining the challenges faced by cybersecurity along with analyzing the emerging trends of cybersecurity as the latest technology (Tunggal 2022). The challenges included spam, cyber harassment, fraud, intrusion, content-related issue, and vulnerability. The trends changing in cybersecurity included web servers, cloud computing, mobile networks, and encryption. The role of social media in cybersecurity was also discussed in the study, along with cybersecurity techniques related to access control and password security, authentication of data, malware scanners, firewalls, and anti-virus software (Macnish and Ham 2020). The study also highlighted the concept of cyber ethics. Moreover, it was concluded that cyber threats increased on a regular basis, and there was no hard and fast rule to manage them. Companies made great efforts to handle them, but there is no hard and fast rule to minimize cybercrime. In other words, there is no perfect solution developed yet for cybercrime. The study revealed that cybercrime rose during the coronavirus pandemic, and these attacks affected the economy in many ways (Ashford 2020). Cyberattacks affected the world at a great pace.

NEED FOR AND SIGNIFICANCE OF STUDY

With the rising threat to data, it is important to conduct a study on it. Cybersecurity is an emerging topic which can be studied from various perspectives. The focus is on studying the ethical aspects of cybersecurity by developing objectives related to it. Technological upgrades can be seen in every corner of our lives. These all form an overall view of ethical cybersecurity in e-commerce. The execution of the right strategy is the need to operate e-commerce platforms that enable customers to make their purchase-related decisions wisely. Cybersecurity is one of the necessities of today's business world, as systems consist of valuable as well as sensitive information, and cybersecurity is used by businesses to protect relevant data from theft (Ashford 2020). The goals and objectives of the businesses can also be attained if they follow the path of ethics.

Ethical standards are developed for attaining possible better returns. The objectives of the study are developed in such a way that could enable in-depth knowledge regarding business strategies and procedures of cybersecurity.

Focus is also given to studying future trends taking place in e-commerce businesses. Various business opportunities can be analyzed through research, and data are the basis for research. Hackers make use of unethical strategies to gather the data of their competitors as well as to capture the large target base of the market. Ethical standards can be a tool to measure the performance of e-commerce operations and further help provide wide protection to business operations under ethical as well as legal constraints.

RESEARCH METHODOLOGY

The study is conducted to achieve the following objectives:

- To determine the ethical issues regarding cybersecurity in e-commerce.
- To study the ethical measures to manage cybersecurity in the online environment.
- To assess cybersecurity as relevant matter of ethics in today's digital world.
- To analyze updated trends in e-commerce operations.

The study is based on analytical research design, as the data are collected from secondary sources to derive conclusions. The secondary data were collected from different sources such as websites, blogs, journal articles, and conference proceedings. The study is conceptual in nature and considers theoretical aspects to achieve results.

ETHICAL ISSUES IN E-COMMERCE RELATED TO CYBERSECURITY

Data and information are the major ingredients that lead to the creation of new digital products and services. These processes of e-commerce networks are connected to create major insights from data stored in information systems (Boles 2017). Cyberattacks are increasing at a great pace as everyone in the e-commerce world wants to secure a better position among customers, and due to this, they opt for unethical means to raise their position in the competitive digital market. Various ethical barriers affect the standards of cybersecurity. With rising ethical issues, appropriate protection is required for users of e-commerce. E-commerce platforms enable electronic data interchange over the internet. The e-commerce framework offers convenience to both consumers as well as producers in conducting buying and selling processes (Boles 2017). The connection is between both parties over the internet. The flexibility in carrying out business transactions might lead to some ethical issues directly or indirectly linked to cybersecurity such as web tracking, web spoofing, privacy invasion, cyber-squatting, phishing, theft related to intellectual property, copyright trolling, and online privacy.

Cybercrime has become quite sophisticated these days, and various solutions can be used in securing business-related data. There are various modes of recovery from a data breach even if it is hacked. Cybersecurity plays a major role in protecting business information by keeping it digitally secure and safe (Hamburg and Grosch 2017). These issues affect the ethical cybersecurity structure of e-commerce platforms. Businesses rely on security systems that can be implemented to address business risks related to cybersecurity. Cybersecurity is important for operational efficiency, which helps protect customers' and business-related information. Cybercriminals focus on finding personally identifiable information of customers.

Phishing is one of the mechanisms used to steal sensitive data by sending fraudulent emails, and it is one of the most famous forms of cyberattack taking place currently. Cybersecurity aims to protect data from breach, which could be an expensive procedure for businesses due to which they have to incur huge losses in the form of lost revenue, long-term reputational damage, downtime, and effect on brand image (Hamburg and Grosch 2017). The risk of cyberattacks is increasing continuously in the case of e-commerce operations (Willis 2021). This further results in a loss of sensitive information due to data exposure and can lead to the disruption of digital operations.

Cyber terrorism is politically based information technology that creates a widespread disruption socially. Criminal activities are growing at their own pace and are a threat to businesses in managing their information. These crimes also hinder the growth and development of businesses. Businesses are unable to properly configure their cloud security, which can lead to the passing of confidential information regarding internal plans and policies to hackers (Burg et al. 2021). Hackers misuse business information for their benefit, and data collection is a complex tasks which is expensive in terms of cost as well as time in general. Once the data are collected, they can be analyzed by hackers for their benefit, and the company has to suffer because of it. Businesses rely on digital marketing, which is convenient for businesses as well as customers.

ETHICAL MEASURES FOR MANAGEMENT OF CYBERSECURITY IN ONLINE ENVIRONMENTS

Ethical cybersecurity aims to ensure privacy regarding information stored in systems by conservation of data integrity and ensuring the information can be provided to approved users only. There are varieties of ethical approaches toward cybersecurity that exist in the market. Cybersecurity ethics needs to be focused on, as there are major principles for the management of cybersecurity. The principles are explicability, beneficence, autonomy, justice, and non-maleficence (Yaghmaei et al. 2017). Cybersecurity practices and policies secure information by using employee education, email or web filtering, firewalls, network access control and monitoring, application security patches, and multifunction printer security. Explicability includes accountability as well as responsibility for the protection of data and systems, betterment in the use of artificial intelligence, transparency, development, and diligence in terms of professionalism (Willis 2021). The applicability of this principle could enable users to practice accountability as well as responsibility in general. The other principle is beneficence, as it would help to strengthen trust among parties by promoting well-being. Privacy protection can also be beneficial for e-commerce users in terms of finance, connectivity, and reputation in return.

Autonomy is another principle that helps to balance relationships by respecting the people who are involved. Informed consent as well as data control can be systematically regulated through this principle. Privacy settings can also be balanced through autonomy. Justice is another ethical area of concern and involves avoidance of bias, adoption of democracy, accessibility, fairness, and self-defense. The fifth principle is non-maleficence, which involves the prevention of various harm in terms of physical, financial, system, data, psychological, and so on. There is a need to adopt consistency in the adoption of ethical cybersecurity practices by removing the barriers in the field. The ethical measures taken to manage issues in cybersecurity faced by e-commerce platforms includes implementing ethical principles to ensure the protection of data by adopting multi-factor authentication by introducing justice, autonomy, integrity, confidentiality, and professionalism in management of business data and keeping business records safe and secure from the access of third parties.

Moreover, confidentiality can be maintained in data through security by encryption of data and ensuring multifactor verification. Confirmation using biometrics can be another tool of protection using ethical cybersecurity (Yaghmaei et al. 2017). The following ethical norms could be a great source of improvement in business operations and could raise the image of the business among interested parties. These healthier relations could ensure long-run survival as well as increased profitability in working operations. The costs can be minimized with optimization of data and analyzing opportunities to a maximum extent. Passwords are to be strong, along with regular backups to protect data from cyberattack. There are several tactics employed by cybersecurity experts such as securing of passwords, adopting two-way authentication, initializing regular updates of security systems, introducing antivirus software, avoidance of phishing scams, employing encryption, and securing domain names to ensure the safety of computer systems (Yaghmaei et al. 2017).

Employees are to be trained and developed in such a way that they can make better choices of steps to be taken to protect data from being hacked. They must be able to tell the difference between the original and a fake data interface. Policies are to be developed after conducting in-depth research regarding the protection of data from all aspects. Plans and actions are initiated after considering the records of the company, which is a way of providing it with a competitive edge. Cybersecurity is a necessity in a fast-paced and emerging digital world. In today's digital scenario, it is necessary to follow ethical standards to securely enjoy privacy in data in the e-commerce framework (Unni 2022). The aim behind data management should be ethical, which could be a source of survival, and pre-defined norms can be an effective measure to handle cybersecurity in a digital environment.

IMPORTANCE OF ETHICAL CYBERSECURITY IN THE DIGITAL WORLD

Companies operate through cloud security, and these data can be accessible to employees via any digital device. Cybersecurity helps protect that data through firewalls or password protection. System security is important for the central flow of data in order to keep it protected from cyberattacks (Unni 2022). This will help keep employee and customer personal information safe and secure from being hacked by criminals. Cybersecurity provides a safe working environment for employees to collaborate by having quick access to apps, files, or websites. IT infrastructure provides options for automated detection of fraud. It ensures centralized and systematic management of data. It also integrates other security options by deploying additional services. Businesses are making use of artificial intelligence and other machine learning tools and techniques to detect attacks by adopting the right cybersecurity strategies.

Cybersecurity plays a major role in protecting business information by keeping it digitally secure and safe. Cybersecurity must be a part of business culture (Subramoni and Singh, n.d.). Security is the responsibility of everyone in the organization. Today's business world is based on technology, and cybersecurity defends connected devices from cyberattacks using artificial intelligence, the Internet of Things, robotics, and so on. Data sharing is increasing at a fast pace, which is the reason for the introduction of cybersecurity as a major concern to protect shared data from breach. Cybersecurity initiatives are important to protect necessary information as well as the working operations of e-commerce businesses. Ethics is needed in today's business world to help manage business operations in a significant manner. Cybersecurity provides online protection of data and the most valuable business assets of e-commerce business owners. Cybersecurity helps make customers feel safe and secure by protecting their confidential information. It also ensures effective management of IT services, which leads to the growth and development of e-commerce businesses in the long run. Precautionary actions are to be taken, which could help to keep businesses and customers safe and secure now and in the future. Cybersecurity can help analyze market trends by gathering and assessing manifold data to evaluate results and reach a better position in the market (Subramoni and Singh, n.d.). Ethical standards are fixed in business contexts per the work performed by them as well as the resources used to execute business processes in many aspects.

E-commerce regulators can execute business operations by managing their chain of operations and maintaining their confidentiality, which could be a source of survival in a competitive world. Protection and security can be handled through cybersecurity, which could be a widely used tool, but its usage varies from business to business. Along with this, the working and execution of data can be ethical or unethical. On the other hand, intellectual property is a reason to protect data that can be a major advantage to manage privacy in general.

Digital data consist of personal information of customers. It is one of the major responsibilities of the experts to protect their interests by maintaining long-lasting healthy relationships with them and protect their information from being leaked to criminals in a digital environment. In today's world, the trust of the customer is one of the most powerful assets to survive. This all can be possible by maintaining privacy in business concerns through cybersecurity to safeguard customer data. Ethical concerns play a major role in handling the security of data, which could be advantageous for e-commerce industries in many ways and enable them to implement business strategies to grow and survive in a competitive business world. Experts stress defending databases and other assets from cyberattack. Moreover, the identification of threats plays a major role in using digital tools and weapons by maintaining cloud security. The effective management of network security protects software and hardware from unauthorized excess or abuse. Business data can be controlled through virtual as well as physical access using strong passwords and multi-factor authentication. There is a need for a comprehensive approach to determine better solutions for security (Gade and Reddy 2014).

TRENDS IN MANAGING THE CYBERSECURITY OF E-COMMERCE

Focus is also given to protecting personal data, which could be a strategic tool for business operations. Various modes can be employed in handling business operations, ensuring strong and technical passwords which ensure effective security of the data. Cybersecurity is a strategic process that can be used in the critical protection of business systems from data breaches (Gade and Reddy 2014). With the evolution in technology, there are inherent risks in the business world in the form of cyber threats or attacks, and security can be attained by adopting the right means through multi-layered protection using cybersecurity. Two-factor authentication is a must that protects data from being hacked. The details regarding traffic are also assessed, which enables e-commerce operators to ensure information security to large extent. Data should be regularly backed up, and regulatory policies should be explained to employees to practically execute business policies regarding cybersecurity.

Companies need to provide information to their employees to at least make them aware of the tools and practices, which could be the source of survival in a competitive world. Employee performance can also be improved by enhancing their motivation level by providing them with the necessary information regarding business operations. The protection can be granted in business from various aspects of cybersecurity implementation can be an automated tool that also makes use of robotics, artificial intelligence, and the Internet of Things. These sources can be the tools to regulate business operations in an effective and efficient manner. Information technology support also plays a major role in the practice of cybersecurity in the business world.

With rapid digitalization, crimes are also rising quickly, which is a reason to create an effective protection policy by introducing cybersecurity in the business world. The confidence of customers can also be increased, as their personal information is secured in business records and the experts are also protecting their data from being hacked. These processes can further lead to making long-term healthy relationships with customers as well as retaining them in the market for a longer period. Cybersecurity is one of the necessities of today's business world, as systems consist of valuable as well as sensitive information, and it is used by businesses to protect their data from theft or damage. Cybersecurity requires a secure flow of transactions through an electronic mechanism that aims to secure the interest of the relevant parties. Protection of privacy is one of the major areas of concern in e-commerce, and it could be made possible by the adoption of ethical norms related to cybersecurity in the best possible manner (Cremer et al. 2022).

Emerging practices need to be developed in the management of risk through cybersecurity (Gade and Reddy 2014). Technological improvements are taking place in the areas of finance in cryptocurrency, which is dealing in digital cash, and it runs on blockchain technology, which is a secure mechanism that can be operated between individuals without making use of any intermediary. The results can be obtained by maintaining a higher level of confidentiality in many aspects and offering a higher security level in return. The right implementation of cyber policies can offer recovery solutions to cyber threats. It is a technical solution that is both adaptable and resilient in nature, which helps in the identification of risks and taking strategic action to handle them.

FINDINGS AND DISCUSSION

The major aim to implement cybersecurity is to reduce data from unauthorized exploitation. Cybersecurity is important because the cost of breaches is rising, and sophisticated cyberattacks are increasing day by day. Cybersecurity is a critical issue, and strategic action must be taken to protect data from cyberattackers. There may be common cyber threats which could affect the performance of e-commerce platforms, such as backdoors, malware, form jacking, crypto jacking, domain name systems, poisoning attacks, or distributed denial of service attacks. In e-commerce, there might be issues such as hacking; misuse of data of businesses and customers; theft of monetary data; attacks related to phishing; fraud related to credit cards; unprotected provision of e-commerce services; or attacks related to blockchain, cryptocurrency, or artificial intelligence.

When we discuss ethical measures taken to manage issues in cybersecurity faced by e-commerce platforms, it includes implementing ethical principles to ensure the protection of data by adopting multi-factor authentication by introducing justice, autonomy, integrity, confidentiality, and professionalism in the management of business data and keeping business records safe and secure from the access of third parties. The three security measures needed are management, operational, and physical controls. There are various updated market trends which could affect e-commerce industries in managing their cybersecurity, such as cloud vulnerability, data centers, logical security, behavioral analytics, and zero trust models. Cybersecurity is the need of e-commerce, as cybercrime could result in lost revenue or data (Cremer et al. 2022). There are various cyber criminals who make use of tactics to steal the business data of e-commerce industries. In today's scenario, cyber threats are one of the major concerns of e-commerce businesses and could be a barrier to the success of e-commerce operators. Cybersecurity provides online protection of data as well as most valuable business assets of e-commerce business owners.

Cybersecurity helps make customers feel safe and secure by protecting their confidential information (Day, 2021). It also ensures effective management of IT services, which leads to the growth and development of e-commerce business in the long run. Precautionary actions are to be taken that could help to keep businesses and customers safe and secure in the present and future. Effective management of cybersecurity could help to improve the user experience using strategic navigation and convenient mechanisms of data. It also helps to boost the confidence of employees by providing them with better training opportunities to prevent cyber threats in e-commerce business.

CONCLUSION

E-commerce is one of the fastest-growing businesses in the world. With the evolution in technology, the internet offers many solutions to carry out business transactions worldwide. When we look from an ethical point of view, it is the responsibility of businesses to look out for threats to data by handling security concerns as well as protecting confidential information in multiple ways. There are various issues apart from those discussed in this chapter, such as electronic payment threats in the form of fraud, tax evasion, payment conflicts, and eavesdropping. There are various other threats, such as personal information threats such as scraping, spamming, bots, SQL injections, brute force attacks, cross-site scripting, Trojan horses, hacktivism, and so on. Along with these, there might be other threats related to debit or credit cards, such as skimming, unwanted presences, POS theft, and issues in handling online transactions.

To handle these issues, there is a need to manage them by adopting the right solutions in security by ensuring secure payment gateways to best protect data; following well-defined rules by introducing block security using a firewall; and adopting a standard protocol, which helps to protect encrypted data. Encryption is a tool used to protect data from being hacked. Ethical concerns are necessary to carry on e-commerce or other businesses by showing the right path to take necessary action for the betterment of working in a commercial and digital world. The right path and direction can be adopted by businesses to manage their business operations at a larger scale by maintaining their required level of confidentiality (Day, 2021). Security concerns can be dealt with by management of server security. In today's online world, it is important to opt for multi-layered security, which also includes data back-up for benefit of e-commerce operators. The systematic update of software is another mechanism that helps to safeguard the interest of e-commerce users by performing security audits on a regular basis. With the introduction of hybrid working, databases are designed to be used by different people on the team, which brings the necessity to protect data from being leaked, as the software has access to different members of organizations.

Organizations need to treat their employees in the best possible manner, which makes them feel committed, as they will also take further steps to protect data from a breach. The level of security can be ensured if employees contribute their best to handling business-related information. Ethical conduct includes avoidance of harm to others, honesty, trustworthiness, maintaining confidentiality, privacy concerns, fair policy and non-discrimination, credentials for intellectual property, respect towards copyrights and patents, and contribution to human beings and society in general. The approach of cybersecurity is to provide multi-layered protection across programs, systems, computers, and networks to keep data in a safe and secure manner.

Cyber ethics is the code of the internet. Various online startups are being created, and the factors discussed here can be advantageous for managing data in an effective manner, which further results in growth and development in the economy from an ethical as well as legal perspective. These ethical codes and standards regulate the proper usage of the internet and keep data safe over internet systems. In today's digital scenario, it is necessary to follow ethical standards to securely enjoy the privacy of data in an e-commerce framework. E-commerce operators can increase their production capacity by developing their regulatory policies by considering ethical standards along with introducing cybersecurity into businesses to keep their data safe and secure.

Cybersecurity hygiene is not as good as expected in today's business world due to complexities in the digital ecosystem. These complexities are difficult for businesses to deal with, as there are various people involved in handling working operations, which require regular training and development for survival in a competitive world. Businesses can compete if their employees are up to date and aware of current technological advancements taking place in the modern business environment. The right security measures help protect data from breaches, which could be beneficial for businesses in protecting their personal information.

REFERENCES

Ashford, W. (2020). *Time to rethink business continuity and cybersecurity*. Retrieved from ComputerWeekly.com: https://www.computerweekly.com/opinion/Time-to-rethink-business-continuity-and-cyber-security.

Banik, A. (2021). *Why is prevention better than recovery in cybersecurity?* Retrieved from Analytical Insight: https://www.analyticsinsight.net/why-is-prevention-better-than-recovery-in-cybersecurity/.

Boles, J. (2017). *Five cybersecurity issues that private businesses should address now.* Retrieved from pwc: https://www.pwc.com/gx/en/services/entrepreneurial-private-business/five-cyber-security-issues.html.

Burg, D., Maddison, M., & Watson, R. (2021). *Cybersecurity: How do you rise above the waves of a perfect storm?* Retrieved from EY: Building a Better World: www.ey.com/en_gl/cybersecurity/cybersecurity-how-do-you-rise-above-the-waves-of-a-perfect-storm.

Cremer, F., Sheehan, B., Fortmann, M., Kia, A. N., Mullins, M., Murphy, F., Materne, S. (2022). *Cyber risk and cybersecurity: A systematic review of data availability* (The Geneva [20] Papers on Risk and Insurance – Issues and Practice). Retrieved from Springer: https://link.springer.com/article/10.1057/s41288-022-00266-6.

Day, J. (2021). *9 cybersecurity practices to ensure business continuity.* Retrieved from Vmblog.com: https://vmblog.com/archive/2021/06/07/9-cybersecurity-practices-to-ensure-business-continuity.aspx#.Ys_Eg3ZBzIU.

Gade, N. R., & Reddy, U. G. (2014). *A study of cybersecurity challenges and its emerging trends on latest technologies.* Retrieved from ResearchGate: https://www.researchgate.net/publication/260126665_A_Study_Of_Cyber_Security_Challenges_And_Its_Emerging_Trends_On_Latest_Technologies.

Hamburg, I., & Grosch, K. R. (2017). Ethical aspects in cybersecurity. *Archives of Business Research*, 5(10), 199–206.

Kavitha, D. V., & Preetha, D. S. (2019). Cybersecurity issues and challenges: A review. *International Journal of Computer Science and Mobile Computing*, 8(11), 1–6.

Macnish, K., & Ham, J. V. (2020). Ethics in cybersecurity research and practice. *Technology in Society*, 63(101382), 1–10.

Subramoni, S., & Singh, T. (n.d.). *How modernizing cybersecurity empowers business growth.* Retrieved from TATA Consultancy Services Perspectives: www.tcs.com/perspectives/articles/cybersecurity-modernization-iot-implementation.

Tronnier, F., Pape, S., Löbner, S., & Rannenberg, K. (2022). A Discussion on Ethical Cybersecurity Issues in Digital Service Chains. In: Kołodziej, J., Repetto, M., & Duzha, A. (eds) *Cybersecurity of Digital Service Chains. Lecture Notes in Computer Science, vol. 13300.* Springer, Cham. https://doi.org/10.1007/978-3-031-04036-8_10.

Tunggal, A. T. (2022). *Why is cybersecurity important?* Retrieved from UpGuard: https://www.upguard.com/blog/cybersecurity-important.

Unni, A. (2022). *Why cybersecurity is important for business.* Retrieved from Cybersecurity Insights: https://www.stickmancyber.com/cybersecurity-blog/why-cyber-security-is-important-for-business?hs_amp=true.

Willis, B. (2021). *Three categories of security controls.* LBMC Family of Companies. Retrieved from https://www.lbmc.com/blog/three-categories-of-security-controls/#:~:text=These%20include%20management%20security%2C%20operational%20security%2C%20and%20physical%20security%20controls.

Yaghmaei, E., van de Poel, I., Christen, M., Gordijn, B., Kleine, N., Loi, M., Morgan, G., & Weber, K. (2017, October 4). *Canvas white paper 1 – cybersecurity and ethics.* Retrieved from SSRN: https://ssrn.com/abstract=3091909 or http://dx.doi.org/10.2139/ssrn.3091909.

20 Cybersecurity in Healthcare

Arijita Banerjee and Sumit Kumar

CONTENTS

INTRODUCTION

Cybersecurity attacks are significantly increasing in healthcare organizations (Haukilehto and Hautamäki 2019). This leads to disruptions in clinical settings due to accidental disclosure of private protected health data, thus having adverse effects on healthcare systems. Effective measures should be used in healthcare organizations to avoid damage to health records and accessibility. Currently, the focus should not be on healthcare systems but rather on prevention and detection capabilities (Hyla and Fabisiak 2020). Cybersecurity hygiene or resilience is an important element which needs to be established before a cyberattack. The US National Institute of Standards and Technology has already put an emphasis on incident handling as violations of security policies have been increasing. This callous attitude is more evident in healthcare organizations.

If we talk about the wide variety of healthcare technologies, then it must swing from the massive electronic health records (EHRs) to various wearable, portable and embedded devices with advanced technology associated with machine learning algorithms. With the vast evolution in medical technology, interconnection between devices and hospitals has also increased to reduce error, enhance efficiency and remote monitoring, and improve patient care. Thus, health information is widely available, making it vulnerable to cyber threats. Breaches to health records, getting access to them, and even data theft through stolen machines or misplaced records have affected millions of peoples' lives and raised the question of the integrity of machine learning across the world. Celebrity health data could be a prize to many such hackers, and today it could be easily accessed remotely through electronic health records. Hacking or unauthorized access to any system and the use of malicious software such as malware are deliberate actions to extract login credentials, security settings, and passwords to gain access to confidential data (Haukilehto and Hautamäki 2019).

The World Health Organization (WHO) has recently published that with the advent of digital technology in forms of smart phones, tablets, iPads etc., the cybercrimes are increasing (Hyla and Fabisiak 2020). One may wonder why the health industry attracts so many cyber criminals. It is because the health industry is a reservoir for sensitive health documents which contain both personal and financial information (see Figure 20.1). For example, the personal information about persons

DOI: 10.1201/9781003319887-20

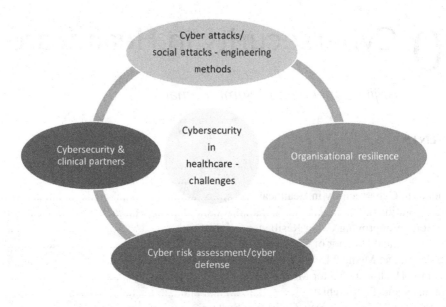

FIGURE 20.1 Overview of cybersecurity in healthcare.

with rare blood groups can be misused by the cyber criminals in lieu of money. Thus, it is very important to generate awareness programs for healthcare professionals and organizations dealing with patient safety.

The main aim of this chapter is to review the literature regarding issues in cybersecurity, developments in cybersecurity, and the role of human behavior in addressing cybersecurity for strengthening cyber defense within the healthcare industry. The chapter includes the following:

- A substantial review of various cyberattacks seen in the healthcare industry.
- Assessing defense methods undertaken by healthcare organizations against cyber threats.
- Evaluating cybersecurity policies and their applicability.
- The role of clinical partners.

CYBER THREATS

Healthcare organizations encounter cyber threats mainly in the following forms: ransomware attacks against the industry, which can cripple the healthcare sector for the sake of economic gains; attacks on IT infrastructure, leading to network disabilities like overflooding of server requests; denial of service (DoS); software bugs and structured query language (SQL) injections; and cryptographic attacks (see Figures 20.2 and 20.3). Back in 1982, the first computer virus, Elk Cloner, was introduced against IT systems by a high school student. Though the former was a harmless program, over time, with the development of technology, the nature of cyberattacks against healthcare and clinical settings also evolved immensely. Cyber threats inspired the US government to develop the US National Institute of Standards and Technology (NIST), which has claimed that approximately 94% of healthcare sectors across the world have suffered from data loss, data breaches, or hacking incidents (Hyla and Fabisiak 2020). Hacking was made familiar and accessible to cyberattackers because during these periods most healthcare sectors had acclimatized themselves to digital technologies by maintaining electronic health records. Also, there was a lack of awareness among healthcare providers that resulted in callousness and mishandling of security policies (Millard 2017).

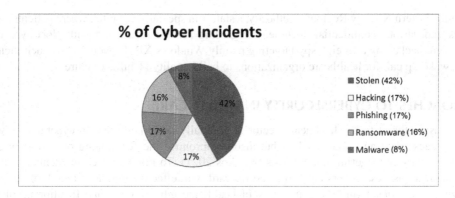

FIGURE 20.2   Cyber incident breakdown in the healthcare sector.

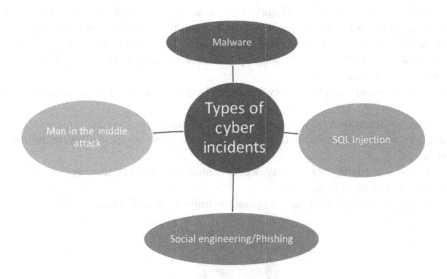

FIGURE 20.3   Types of cyberattacks in healthcare, structured query language.

In 2016, a terrible ransomware attack was reported where a very well-known medical center in Los Angeles, Hollywood Presbyterian Medical Center, had to pay a hefty sum to hackers, resulting in disruption of the smooth functioning of the hospital (Howell 2020). Another form of cyberattack reported in healthcare is social engineering methods; the most common form is phishing, where attackers exploit large amounts of public information posted on social media platforms. There are even insider attacks to perform deliberate actions that include responding to phishing mail links, misuse of passwords, and loss of laptops with confidential data. In 2017 there was a worldwide cyberattack named Wannacry targeting the Microsoft operating system by encrypting data, misconfiguring programs, and demanding ransom payments (Howell 2020).

There were various other malware attacks, including those which affected medical devices like Medjack ("medical device hijack"). Due to crippled and hacked medical devices, diagnostic equipment failed to function for almost four to five days. MRI machines, ventilators, and infusion pumps all work with the principles of artificial intelligence and thus are considered a huge platform for big data. Various simulated attacks have been discussed, like attacks on pacemakers, defibrillators, and drug infusion pumps, which are usually remote operated. Another incident was in January 2018 at the South-Eastern Norway Regional Authority, a state-run specialist hospital, where patients' health records and various confidential documents regarding service interaction with Norway's armed forces were hacked by a foreign spy targeting mainly Windows XP (Howell 2020). Such incidents were a wake-up call for healthcare organizations to build quality IT infrastructure.

APPROACHES TO CYBERSECURITY IN HEALTHCARE

An increasing threat to the healthcare sector is gradually developing due to cyberattacks which not only cause data and financial loss but also compromise the functioning of various medical equipment, thus endangering human lives (Nifakos 2021). To mitigate such incidents in near-future organizations, researchers need to come forward with effective measures and develop quality IT environment considering the complexity of healthcare infrastructure and functioning of these complex systems. The healthcare industry is unique by comprising many departments and branches of medicine, along with super specialties requiring specific degrees and human power, plus the coordination of administrative departments like finance, human resources, establishment, and civil. Also, there are separate legal and regulatory policies defining the healthcare industry. What is of utmost importance here is the protection of personally identifiable information (PII) unique to every individual such as full name, phone number, bank account number, and email address. It is recommended to create a well-planned cybersecurity taskforce to promote regulatory compliance and counter hackers (see Figure 20.4).

Various solutions within the cybersecurity framework have been identified as follows (Nifakos 2021):

i. Recover – responsibility is to recover secure IT systems.
ii. Identify – whose responsibility it is to assess the risks, and oversee and govern the defense strategies.
iii. Protection – to enable data security, access control, and network security.
iv. Detect – detection of cybercrimes.
v. Respond – analysis, collection and operation, mitigation, and planning.

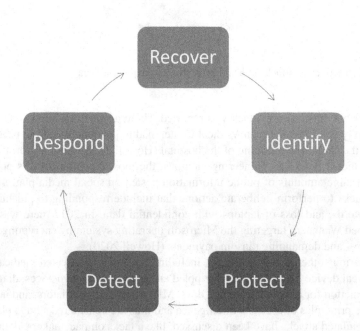

FIGURE 20.4 Integrated measures against cyber threats in healthcare.

TECHNICAL SOLUTIONS

The following technical mitigation measures must be executed to enable cyber-resilience (see Figure 20.5):

- Regular backups: The European Union Agency for Network and Information Security (ENISA) encourages implementing regular backups to avoid cyber incidents such as ransomware. In addition, securing backups in the cloud or offline could make hospitals resilient to such attacks (Gioulekas et al. 2022). Hospitals are recommended to implement mock system recovery tasks regularly to check restore capabilities.
- Firewalls and network segmentation: Per ENISA, it is very much recommended to apply firewalls and separate critical and non-critical parts of network, which could protect medical devices from a wide range of attacks. Use of data diodes following unidirectional communication, micro-segmentation, and zero-trust networks have always been recommended by security agencies to provide protective coverage to medical devices (Millard 2017).
- Disabling unused physical ports: It is always recommended to disable USB ports to prevent malicious access to the devices.
- User authentication and access rights: User authentication or access rights is the basic security element because it does not allow any user activities to happen if access is denied at the preliminary stage. Such security measures will also help reduce data encryption. Various healthcare departments like pediatrics, surgery, radiology, and dermatology use sensitive images, and unauthorized access to such images is crime. To reduce such incidents, user administrator account implementation is necessary, which could reduce the chances hackers have to gain access to administrator privileges in a single attack.
- Regular updates and patches: ENISA favors regular patching and updating antivirus software to ensure proper protection of medical devices, health informatics, electronic data, and cloud-based data against cyber threats.
- Encryption: Encryption of data is only possible while the data are "at rest" or "in transit" either using a network or storage medium. ENISA states that hospitals should "ensure a proper and effective use of cryptography to protect the confidentiality, authenticity and/or integrity of data and information (including control messages), in transit and in rest. Ensure the proper selection of standard and strong encryption algorithms and strong keys and disable insecure protocols. Verify the robustness of the implementation" (Nifakos 2021).

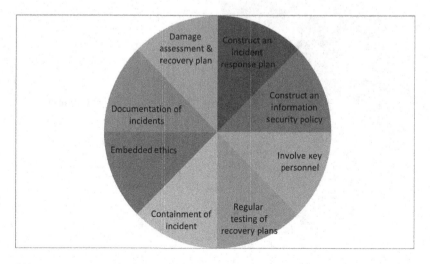

FIGURE 20.5   Integrated strategies for cyber incidents.

- Network monitoring and intrusion detection: This is an important strategy to protect healthcare system from malware, malicious websites, encrypted emails, and other fraudulent sources.
- Protection of mobile devices: It is highly recommended by ENISA that hospital patients or employees not connect their own personal mobile devices to hospital systems via Wi-Fi or virtual private network (VPN) to protect sensitive data stored in mobiles.

HUMAN ROLE IN IMPROVING CYBER RESILIENCE

Human factors play an important role in uplifting cyber-resilience in healthcare organizations (see Figure 20.6). The activities necessary for protection against cyber incidents are classified into three main categories: a) training on social engineering attacks, b) promoting general awareness against cyberattacks, and c) promoting cyber hygiene. The primary focus of the study was to strengthen organizational defense against cyberattacks. It was revealed that though there are an increasing number of policies and regulations against cybercrimes, the casual attitude of healthcare employees resulted in various attacks, leading to loss of big data. Proper training should be delivered to healthcare staff to avoid common cyberattacks like phishing (Gioulekas et al. 2022). Several strategies need to be developed for creating a balanced workload for employees to improve cyber resilience and prevent leakage of information. Phishing attacks could be office related, personal, or information technology related. Though there are many ongoing training programs, one in every six phishing links was clicked by hospital employees. Various social factors influence behaviors like workload, stress, and vigilance. Awareness-raising activities should be done for individuals who are able to identify the security risks, while training exercises are mainly meant for developing skills in cybersecurity measures.

The use of open data sets, such as linked open data databases, when offering training to healthcare professionals has been proposed by many authors who had worked previously on cybersecurity measures.

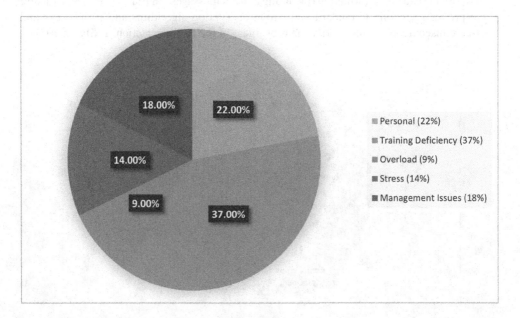

FIGURE 20.6 Human factors resulting in cyber incidents.

TABLE 20.1

Role of Clinical Director of Cybersecurity

1.	Establishment of clinically relevant education programs for clinician understanding of cybersecurity
2.	Cybersecurity rounds for demonstrating effectiveness
3.	Tool development for reporting cyber incidents
4.	Engagement with other cybersecurity professionals as required
5.	Security governance
6.	Patient advisory
7.	Cyber incident response
8.	Leadership

ROLE OF THE CLINICAL DIRECTOR OF CYBERSECURITY

From the previous section, it is evident that adequate training and awareness programs for healthcare professionals are mandatory to prevent cyber incidents. An educated clinical director of cybersecurity specially trained in informatics can be an asset to a healthcare organization. The main function of clinical director is to create a balance between IT security and clinical engineering. He or she should be able to work on the main streams of cybersecurity programs like awareness, management, cyber hygiene, and incident response. The role of the clinical director is specified in Table 20.1.

One example of a clinical director as a partner is in San Diego, where an emergency medicine expert was appointed as clinical director of cybersecurity and became a key member of the organization's security committee, thus contributing to development of various policies.

MOBILE HEALTH AND MEDICAL DEVICE–RELATED POLICIES

The policies and regulations for the protection of patients' health data has unfolded into a few acts passed by the United States (see Figure 20.7 and Table 20.2). In 1996, the Health Insurance Portability & Accountability Act (HIPAA) came about, which demanded protection of health information,

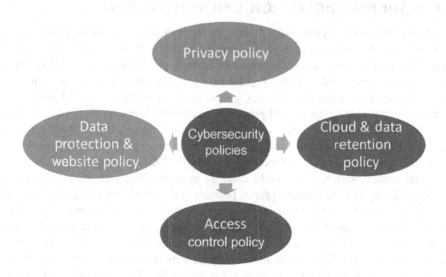

FIGURE 20.7 Cybersecurity policies.

TABLE 20.2

Various Aspects of Different Policies in the Healthcare Sector

Cybersecurity Policies	Healthcare Sector
Privacy policy	• Regulations to enhance secure patient information from unauthorized collection, disclosure, processing, or transmission. • Act in accordance with HIPAA. • High level of privacy required in health cloud, personal wearable healthcare monitors.
Website security policy	• Rules to avoid any cross-site scripting and clickjacking. • Provide secure health services. • Authentication and authorization procedures claim that resources on websites are safely accessible.
Cloud computing security policy	• High security level for the healthcare cloud. • Encryption of data before storage in the health cloud should be supplied.
Email security policy	• The Health Information Technology for Economic and Clinical Health Act ensures the protection of personal health information in email or data transfer. • Emails should contain secure marking based on the sensitivity of information enclosed.
Access control policy and data retention policy	• Rules to protect patient privacy and prevent unwanted and unexpected parties from accessing and using sensitive datasets. • Regulations to ensure preservation of personal patients' data for a specific period of time.

storage, and disclosure (Giasanti 2021). Further, in 2009, the United States passed the Health Information Technology for Economic and Clinical Health (HITECH) Act, which raised penalties for violations of HIPAA. The European Union (EU) replaced its existing regulations with the General Data Protection Regulation (GDPR) in 2016 (Razaque et al. 2019). This mainly laid emphasis on penalties and improving technical and organizational challenges for cybersecurity.

HOW CAN THE HEALTHCARE SECTOR MOVE FORWARD?

From the literature discussed previously, there is no 100% effective way to avoid all cybersecurity breaches, but cybersecurity must be implemented, especially in the healthcare sector, with a holistic approach keeping in view culture, people, and technology (Razaque et al. 2019). Basic cyber hygiene needs to be practiced by doing regular backups, updating software, maintaining proper authentication process, and limiting access. Cybersecurity should be considered an important part of patient care culture, and unprotected processes need to be immediately replaced with secure ones by proper regulations and timely inspections from accredited bodies. With the occurrence of cyber breaches, more companies are turning towards insurance. Security improvements are needed through appropriate insurance incentives (Giasanti 2021). To implement cyber-resilience, clinicians and administration staff should undergo basic training and practice cyber hygiene, and decision makers need to demand proper policies and consider cybersecurity in purchasing decisions, while manufacturers should supply products with appropriate cybersecurity measures. Information security teams should provide various measures for users to respond to social engineering methods, like filtering e-mail content and suspicious URLs in e-mails for linked malicious code, as well as blocking Flash and pop-up advertisements when required. A collective, collaborative, state-of-the-art approach is needed to ensure better and secure patient care and data (Giasanti 2021).

CYBERSECURITY AND TELEPSYCHIATRY

Before the dawn of the 21st century, the term "Internet of Things" (IoT) came into existence when Kevin Ashton was working with Procter & Gamble. Since then there has been a great rise of this sophisticated technology which has been ever growing from its inception (Arain et al. 2019). According to the Oxford Dictionary, the IoT is "the interconnection via the Internet of computing devices embedded in everyday objects, enabling them to send and receive data." IoTs contribute to host of our day-to-day life activities and make them easier and more comfortable, which includes transportation, phones, televisions, home appliances, factories, wearables, automation, home monitoring, and healthcare – which includes mental health. Time and again, technology has empowered people with ways to improve their present state and move into the future, but bringing some adversities with it. With modern-day healthcare transforming in the digital era, psychiatry and psychological services are not immune to these advancements. Telepsychiatry, also termed tele-mental health or e-mental health, is broadly defined as the use of information and communication technology to provide or support psychiatric services across distances.

PITFALLS: SOURCES OF ERROR IN DATA COLLECTION SYSTEMS

The potential ways telepsychiatry/e-mental health could be vulnerable to cybercriminals are various electronic data taken at the time of interviews for patient assessment, innumerable wrist bands, smart devices, insurance claims, medication papers, cloud computing software, and others. Psychiatrists, psychologists, and various mental health professionals who organize appointments through email, text messages, tele-services, digital assessments such as the Weschler Adult Intelligence Scale (WAIS-IV), and Weschler Intelligence Scale for Children (WISC), are mainly vulnerable to cybercriminals (Coventry and Branley 2018). Persons becoming victims of cybercrime in relation to technology always have an associated psychological factor attached to it. Young people fall prey to romantic scams, and young men and women in their 30s fall for situations which has more chance of decision making mistakes. So it is the technology which unknowingly paves its way and brings about dissatisfaction and sorrows which in the contrary was invented for making our lives easier.

Likewise, social networking sites like Facebook, WhatsApp, Instagram, and Telegram have made inroads into our houses efficiently and in a manner such that they form an important part of our daily lives, resulting in dissociation from our families. The bond between family members is affected, and so are communities, via this mode of communication. Owing to these social media platforms, psychiatric illness is on the rise, resulting in emotional turmoil, decreased self-esteem, humiliation, disgust, shame, depression, post-traumatic stress disorder, psychotic episodes, and anxiety disorders like panic and phobia (Ghazvini and Shukur 2016).

Interventions required to circumvent the problems:

- The storage medium must be ascertained beforehand: the use of pen drives should be stopped, as they can be a source for cybercriminals to gain unauthorized access.
- Encryption of patient data is of the utmost importance, as they might be utilized for unethical means.
- Who can have access: data access should be given to certain personnel: only those who are an integral part of the team.
- Automated logout systems: whenever there is no activity for a certain time, the user should be logged out.

Steps taken to strengthen shortcomings in protected healthcare information by mental health professionals:

1. Personnel dealing with highly sensitive protected health information should be very cautious regarding privacy and confidentiality of the data.
2. Data to be collected should be standardized beforehand and prioritized so specific unnecessary data accumulation is avoided.

3. Personnel who will be accessing the data should be trained according to the standards and have proper login IDs so that the protocols are followed.
4. Encrypted data should always be utilized for storage as well as performing various tasks.
5. Data to be utilized in research should be kept anonymous to maintain confidentiality and privacy.
6. Data transfer should always be done through electronic monitoring to have detailed proof of the transfer.

LAW ENFORCEMENT AGENCIES

In accordance with the Information Technology Act 2000 and the Indian Medical Council Professional Conduct, Etiquette, and Ethics Regulations 2002, there are various punishments laid out by the government of India, including for those who are involved in the misuse of protected health information.

The Mental Health Act 2017 lays down that if confidentiality is compromised, the accused must be punished for a term which may extend to six months, a fine of 10,000 rupees, or both, and if contravention is found, then the fine will be 50,000 rupees, which maybe extended to 5 lakh, imprisonment of two years, or both.

CONCLUSION

Steps should be taken to improve protocols as to how data collected for mental healthcare should be stored and retrieved to maintain patients privacy and confidentiality. Proper decisive efforts culminate into safe and efficient pool of data generation free from the reach of cybercriminals. Mental health professionals, including psychiatrists, psychologists, psychiatric social workers, and staff associated with data collection processes, in synchronization with law enforcement agencies need to develop and work on a system of secure pool of protected healthcare information.

REFERENCES

Arain, M.A., Tarraf, R., Ahmad, A. Assessing Staff Awareness and Effectiveness of Educational Training on IT Security and Privacy in a Large Healthcare Organization. *J. Multidiscip. Heal.* 2019, 12, 73–81.

Coventry, L., Branley, D. Cyber Security in Health Care: A Narrative Review of Trends, Threats and Ways Forward. *Maturitas.* 2018, 113, 48–52.

Ghazvini, A., Shukur, Z. Awareness Training Transfer and Information Security Content Development for Healthcare Industry. *Int. J. Adv. Comput. Sci. Appl.* 2016, 7, 361–370. https://doi.org/10.14569/IJACSA.2016.070549.

Giansanti, D. Cyber Security and the Digital-Health: The Challenge of This Millennium. *Healthcare.* 2021, 9, 62. https://doi.org/10.3390/healthcare9010062.

Gioulekas, F., Stamatiadis, E., Tzikas, A., Gounaris, K., Georgiadou, A., Michalitsi-Psarrou, A., Doukas, G., Kontoulis, M., Nikoloudakis, Y., Marin, S., Cabecinha, R., Ntanos, C. A Cybersecurity Culture Survey Targeting Healthcare Critical Infrastructures. *Healthcare.* 2022, 10, 327. https://doi.org/10.3390/healthcare10020327.

Haukilehto, T., Hautamäki, J. Survey of Cybersecurity Awareness in Health, Social Services and Regional Government in South Ostrobothnia, Finland. In *Internet of Things, Smart Spaces, and Next Generation Networks and Systems.* Cham, Switzerland: Springer, 2019, pp. 455–466. Available online: https://link.springer.com/chapter/10.1007/978-3-030-30859-9_39.

Howell, P. *A Patient Has Died after Ransomware Hackers Hit a German Hospital.* Available online: www.technologyreview.com/2020/09/18/1008582/a-patient-has-died-after-ransomware-hackers-hit-a-german-hospital.

Hyla, T., Fabisiak, L. Measuring Cybersecurity Awareness within Groups of Medical Professionals in Poland. In *Proceedings of the 53rd Hawaii International Conference on System Sciences*, Maui, HI, 7–10 January 2020. https://doi.org/10.24251/hicss.2020.473.

Millard, W.B. Where Bits and Bytes Meet Flesh and Blood. *Ann Emerg Med.* 2017. https://doi.org/10.1016/j.annemergmed.2017.07.008.

Nifakos, S., Chandramouli, K., Nikolaou, C.K., Papachristou, P., Koch, S., Panaousis, E., Bonacina, S. Influence of Human Factors on Cybersecurity Within Healthcare Organisations: A Systematic Review. *Sensors.* 2021, 21, 5119. https://doi.org/10.3390/s21155119.

Razaque, A., Amsaad, F., Khan, M.J., Hariri, S., Chen, S., Siting, C., Ji, X. Survey: Cybersecurity Vulnerabilities, Attacks and Solutions in the Medical Domain. *IEEE Access.* 2019, 7, 168774–168797.

21 Business Continuity and Disaster Recovery Strategies as Resilience Tools after Cyberattacks in Toxic Entrepreneurship Ecosystems

Lukman Raimi

CONTENTS

INTRODUCTION

In the global entrepreneurship ecosystem, business operations and industrial activities of corporate organizations and entrepreneurs are routinely disrupted by the growing incidence of cyberattacks. Ugly incidents of cyberattacks have been widely reported in the United Kingdom, United States, Europe, and other developed countries (Hunker & Probst, 2011; Rudner, 2013). The abuse of cyberspace through cyberattacks, cyber wars, cybercrime, and cyber harms negative externalities that are not constrained by geography, time, and space. The surge in the incidence of cyberattacks, the international community, the comity of nations, policymakers, IT professionals and corporate organizations requires cybersecurity awareness and culture to avert cybercrime and foster cyber resilience. According to Calif (2020), Warren Buffet, a billionaire businessman and philanthropist, described cybercrime as the topmost problem with mankind, and cyberattacks pose a larger threat to humanity than nuclear weapons. Therefore, stakeholders in the global entrepreneurship ecosystem must give cyberattacks the necessary attention because national infrastructural systems such as water, electricity, healthcare, finance, food, and transportation are largely and increasingly being driven by interconnected computer systems and digital backbones, and when attacked, they could pose serious national security problems (Gandhi et al., 2011). Generally, cyberattacks on corporate organizations (at the macro level) and countries (at the macro level) have been linked to insiders and outsiders who seek to gain financial, reputation, and political benefits by inflicting cyber harms on others, thereby causing disruption to their computer systems and digital infrastructural backbones (Hunker & Probst, 2011; Agrafiotis et al., 2018). When viewed in terms of social, economic, and political implications, the issue of cyberattacks poses an existential threat to people, organizations, and national security because it is impossible to predict the nature of an attack, the timing and extent of disruption, and the harms that could arise. Moreover, human lives and the national security of the state and businesses are critical; hence, sound knowledge of cybersecurity must be given serious attention to curb cyberattacks and punish offenders (Rid & Buchanan, 2015). A cyberattack is so serious and devastating that it could potentially disable the economy of a city, state, or nation. Ted Koppel warned that a major cyberattack on America's power grid is possible and would be devastating if the US government does not raise the level of preparedness (Calif, 2020). The most effective and efficient way of embedding cybersecurity in organizational space is through business continuity and disaster recovery plans (BCDRPs).

A BCDRP is an amalgam of a business continuity plan (BCP) and a disaster recovery plan (DRP). While a business continuity plan (BCP) refers to a structured document with detailed contingencies on how business operations will be carried out by managers and employees during a period of unforeseen events or unplanned disruptions to commercial activities (IBM Services, 2020), a disaster recovery plan, on the other hand, is a strategic document that describes how an organization can quickly resume operations after a disruption by an unplanned incident. However, unlike a BCP, a DRP strictly focuses on the reactivation of an organization's computer systems and functioning information technology (IT) infrastructure, especially the resolution of data loss and the recovery of system functionality in the aftermath of cyberattacks and related incidents (Brush & Crocetti, 2022). Both nuances are pervasively and widely being discussed in the fields of economics, strategic management, and environmental management to boost the capabilities and abilities of entrepreneurs and corporate organizations to cope with adverse events and economic turbulence (Elliott Swartz & Herbane, 2010; Kuckertz et al., 2020). The BCDRP has become expedient because the globalization wave, especially interconnectedness, through trade openness on the internet, transportation, e-commerce platforms, and different social media, has exposed countries and companies to new types of threats, reputational crises, cyberattacks, and pandemic diseases with far-reaching consequences (Glenn & Gordon, 2002; Păunescu & Argatu, 2020; Sawalha, 2021).

It has also been argued that the adoption of disruptive technologies for managing human affairs and society by organizations and nations comes with mixed effects. On a positive note, digitalization and disruptive technologies such as 3D, 4D, and 5D printers; AI; drones; blockchain; automated reality; robotics; big data and data analytics; cloud computing; and the Internet of Things (IoT) are revolutionizing the business landscape for agriculture, commerce, healthcare, social media, and manufacturing (Dharmaraj & Vijayanand, 2018; Frizzo-Barker et al., 2020; Borah et al., 2022). On the negative side, digitalization and disruptive technologies have escalated incidents of cyberattacks, threats to cybersecurity, violations of users' privacy, cyber wars, and global polarization of technology-rich and technology-poor countries (Smith et al., 2020; Yaacoub et al., 2020; Feldstein, 2021).

To cope with a plethora of threats from cyberattacks on digitalization and disruptive technologies, experts recommend business continuity and disaster recovery strategies (BCRS) as the most effective and efficient means of stabilizing production, marketing, and sales in the face of cyberattacks. A BCRS is a combination of two concepts, business continuity plan (BCP) and disaster recovery plan (DRP). Both have emerged as effective tools for the actualization of organizational objectives, especially the delivery of products, services, and business solutions, even during turbulence and market disruptions (Gibb & Buchanan, 2006). The former proactive process or preventive measure assists organizations in planning ahead for likely internal and external threats, and the latter is a complementary process or supplementary measure deployed during and after the actual occurrence of critical incidents put in place to forestall and mitigate business interruptions (Sawalha, 2021).

This chapter is apt and necessary because the threat posed by cyberattacks to the global business landscape is causing serious uncertainty in the face of a lack of effective metrics, tools, and frameworks for quantifying and estimating the financial implications and operational harms arising from surging cyberattacks (Agrafiotis et al., 2018). Additionally, understanding cyberattacks and the associated cyber-harm is helpful for organizations and entrepreneurs in gaining effective controls for preventing attacks and mitigating business risks in the case of cyberattacks.

In bridging these gaps, this chapter discusses the diverse business continuity and disaster recovery strategies that entrepreneurs and corporate organizations can use to forestall cyberattacks in toxic entrepreneurship ecosystems. In specific terms, the study provides answers to three questions: (a) What are the definitions of cyberattacks, cyber harm, and cybersecurity? (b) What are the effects of cyberattacks and associated cyber harm on entrepreneurs and corporate organizations using digital infrastructural facilities? (c) What are the diverse business continuity and disaster recovery strategies that entrepreneurs and corporate organizations can use to forestall cyberattacks in toxic entrepreneurship ecosystems? There are seven sections in this chapter. The introduction section focuses on the introduction and methods/analysis, and the literature review section reviews the extant literature to provide clarity on the definitions of cyberattacks, cyber harm, and cybersecurity. The methods and analysis section discusses supportive cases of cyberattacks in global entrepreneurship ecosystems. This section also explains different business continuity and disaster recovery strategies. The discussion and results section presents empirical views on cyberattacks and performance. This section also examines the legal and regulatory environment for cybersecurity in global entrepreneurship ecosystems. The conclusion and recommendations section concludes with a summary of the insights and recommendations.

LITERATURE REVIEW

CYBERATTACKS

Attempts to secure information by individuals, organizations, and nations has made cybersecurity an important issue in policy and academic circles. Cybersecurity entails safeguarding computer systems, and the integrity, confidentiality, and availability of the data kept inside the IT infrastructure is critical to national security because of a surge in cyberattacks (Cashell et al., 2004). The meaning of cybersecurity extends to the deployment of people, processes, and technology for protecting an organization's IT-related assets, network installations, databases, and computer systems from planned digital attacks with the intent of accessing, destroying, or changing sensitive information and ultimately halting business operations (Kim & Solomon, 2016; Hasan et al., 2021).

The term cyberattack has several interesting definitions. According to Unisys (2022), cyberattack simply refers to an attempt by mischievous groups and cybercriminals to disable computer systems, steal valuable business data through identity theft, breach of access, password sniffing, system infiltration, instant messaging abuse, website defacement, or using a breached computer system to launch attacks on business organizations. The different forms of cyberattacks leave organizations with devastating consequences. However, IBM (2022) defines a cyberattack as an unwelcome attempt criminally motivated attackers to steal, expose, alter, disable, or destroy information of individuals, organizations, and nations through unauthorized access to computer systems and IT infrastructural facilities for the purpose of securing financial gain and enjoying an unfair advantage by newcomers over competitors, revenge by disgruntled current or former employees, and attention seeking by hacktivists. Furthermore, IBM (2022) and Unisys (2022), as cybersecurity experts, identified the following as the prevalent types of cyberattacks on businesses.

a) **Malware attack:** This describes an attack that breaches a vulnerable network although malicious software such as spyware, ransomware, viruses, and worms. The attack occurs when users click on dangerous links or email attachments that trigger attacks and install risky software.

b) **Phishing attack:** This type of cyberattack occurs by sending fraudulent communications via emails that appear genuine or emanating from reputable organizations. The purpose of phishing is to steal, compromise, and access sensitive data such as credit card information and login details and at times install malware on the victim's computer systems and IT infrastructure.

c) **Man-in-the-middle (MitM) attack:** The MitM attack is also called the eavesdropping attack because it occurs when cyberattackers strategically plant themselves in the middle of two parties involved in transactional relationships because of unsecure public Wi-Fi and malware attacks. By virtue of this strategic implant, the attacker can interrupt, filter, and steal data in the traffic.

d) **Denial-of-service attack:** This type of cyberattack is critical because attackers use multiple devices to launch attacks and flood computer systems, servers, and networks with heavy traffic that exhausts resources and bandwidth. This attack therefore denies the victims access to service. It is also called a distributed-denial-of-service (DDoS) attack.

e) **Structured Query Language (SQL) injection:** SQL injection is a type of cyberattack that occurs when malicious code is inserted into a server with SQL and a vulnerable website search box, and this dangerous act forces the server to disclose confidential information and private data that have been kept secret.

f) **Zero-day exploit:** The type of cyberattack is launched against an organization that announces a network vulnerability at a point in time. This attack is made quickly before a solution is implemented to correct the network vulnerability.

g) **Domain Name System (DNS) Tunneling:** DNS tunneling is another pervasive cyberattack that deliberately exploits the DNS protocol to send HTTP and other protocol traffic over DNS to disguise outbound traffic as DNS with evil intentions, exfiltrate data from a victim's computer system to the attacker's infrastructure, and control callbacks from the attacker's infrastructure to the compromised system of the victim.

BUSINESS CONTINUITY PLAN

Several scholars have stated that a business continuity plan refers to a proactive, planned, and deliberate effort of a business organization to continue operating business activities in the likelihood of disruption by unplanned events, environmental risk, sociopolitical threat, and economic turbulence (Sawalha, 2021). A BCP is also viewed as a preventive measure and a proactive process put in place to reduce the probability of occurrence of critical incidents (Hiles, 2010). From these definitions, the BCP is expedient in contemporary organizations because of the inevitability of unplanned incidents within the volatile business environment. Apparently, a BCP offers a resilient approach to critical incidents that aligns with the view of the International Organization for Standardization (ISO) that business continuity is an organization's capability to continue the delivery of products or services at acceptable predefined levels during the period of a disruptive incident or happening (Somasekaram, 2017). The extant literature on BCP explains that organizations must be proactive, future oriented, and responsive by adjusting to business risks and environmental threats and matching their conditions to fit a set of circumstances (Fani & Subriadi, 2019). Cerullo and Cerullo (2004) noted that BCP has three organizational elements: (a) business impact analysis (BIA), (b) disaster contingency recovery plan, and (c) test and training. However, Karim (2011) explained that BCP has six organizational elements: strategic management, business risk analysis, BCP resources, training and awareness, BCP documentation, and information life cycle management.

DISASTER RECOVERY PLAN

The term disaster recovery plan has also received significant discussion in the literature. Sawalha (2021) defines DRP as the strategic process of looking at the immediate actions needed during critical incidents and after the incident had ceased purposely to ensure that the organization that suffered the disaster is empowered to function and mitigate business interruptions. DRP has also been described as the process, policies, and procedures deployed by organizations to prepare for immediate recovery or continuation of technology infrastructure, systems, and applications. In other words, the intent of DRP is the restoration of vital IT applications and data recovery after a catastrophe (Myers, 1993; Cervone, 2017; Unitrends, 2022). Unlike BCP, DRP is a more technically oriented approach that addresses managing the technical aspects of an organization's operations that support business recovery and continuity in the context of a disaster. Therefore, the DR focuses more on minimizing downtime as well as the impact of a disaster by ensuring vital support systems are up and running as quickly as possible with minimal loss of data. Furthermore, the disaster recovery plan is a strategic document that describes how an organization can quickly resume operations after the disruption of operations by an unplanned incident. It strictly focuses on the reactivation of an organization's computer systems and functioning information technology infrastructure, especially the resolution of data loss and the recovery of system functionality after the aftermath of cyberattacks and related incidents (Brush & Crocetti, 2022). Irrespective of the industrial sector, a well-designed DRP must have the following essential elements to be effective and efficient: a statement of intent and a DR policy statement; plan goals; authentication tools, such as passwords; geographical risks and factors; tips for dealing with media; financial and legal information and action steps; and plan history (Brush & Crocetti, 2022).

BUSINESS CONTINUITY AND DISASTER RECOVERY STRATEGIES

In the literature, there seems to be a definitional controversy between business continuity planning and disaster recovery planning. At times, both concepts are used interchangeably to explicate organizations' plans before, during, and after a socioeconomic and environmental occurrence that disrupts business operations (Sawalha, 2021). Broadly, a BCDR refers to a set of processes and techniques designed and implemented by organizations to help them recover from socioeconomic and environmental disasters and by providing capabilities to continue their routine business operations (Cervone, 2017; Unitrends, 2022). The BCDR is inevitable in the current era of surge in cyberattacks on IT infrastructure of organizations across the globe by dissidents, hackers, and disgruntled internal and external stakeholders. Any organization that fails to take BCDR seriously risks the possibility of going out of business, because reliable statistics affirm that 40% of vulnerable organizations that suffered critical incidents or natural disasters do not recover because of repercussions such as damaged reputation, loss of data, loss of revenue, operational instability, and reduced employee productivity (Carroll, 2022). Vulnerabilities that are associated with critical events such as hurricanes, war, floods, fires, tornadoes, earthquakes, and emerging trends of sabotage and cyberattacks are threats to business operations. BCP and DRP are complementary measures targeted at neutralizing disastrous events (Walleit, 2021).

More importantly, Unitrends (2022) explains that purposeful BCDR plans have five goals. First, the BCDR plan assesses the current state of a vulnerable organization by identifying the threats and deploying appropriate priorities for quick mitigation and remediation efforts. Second, the BCDR plan evaluates operational risks within the organization by looking for inherent weaknesses, lapses, and gaps that may disrupt business operations with a view to providing solutions that would not jeopardize BCDR strategies. Third, the BCDR plan reviews and tests the existing plan periodically through simulation to ensure it is up to date, effective, and comprehensive enough to cover all aspects of the business operations for rapid recovery in the likelihood of business disruption. Fourth, the BCDR plan identifies suitable locations for the storage of business data and assets to assist disaster recovery personnel and IT professionals in speeding the recovery process. Fifth, the BCDR plan allows top management and other organizational members to know the disaster recovery teams, their roles, and how they could be contacted during a critical incident or an emergency. For cybersecurity specialists and informaticians, Cervone (2017) advised that there are three critical technology infrastructure areas and thematic questions that the DRP aspect of the BCDR should focus on: (a) network infrastructure (How do vulnerable organizations recover from a network disaster?), (b) data storage infrastructure (What data storage medium is required to precipitate recovery as quickly as possible?); and (c) application infrastructure (How do vulnerable organizations bring applications back online for business continuity? How should organizations manage application switchover to prevent a failover situation?).

SUPPORTIVE CASES OF CYBERATTACKS

Threats posed by cyberattacks and cybercrime in general are real and financially costly to corporate organizations, entrepreneurs, and countries. A reliable report from the International Data Corporation (IDC), a premier global provider of market intelligence, indicated that on average, an infrastructure failure due to cyberattacks costs USD $100,000 an hour, while a critical application failure from cyberspace attacks can cost USD $500,000 to USD $1 million per hour (IBM Services, 2020). The financial and economic costs of cyberattacks are huge. These costs include damage and destruction of data, stolen money, lost productivity, theft of intellectual property, theft of personal and financial data, embezzlement, fraud, postattack disruption to routine business activities, cost of paying for forensic investigation, payment for restoration and deletion of hacked data and systems, and irreparable reputational harm (Calif, 2020). The United States Federal Bureau of Investigation (FBI) reported that there are more than 4000 daily ransomware attacks on different organizations (Chang & Ho, 2006), and worse still, more than 330,000 dangerous malware applications are created daily by cybercriminals (Hasan et al., 2021).

Regrettably, small businesses are largely prone to risk from different types of cyberattacks because of the misconception that they are too small to be targeted by cybercriminals as well as poor exposure to cybersecurity. Reliable reports revealed that 71% of ransomware attacks target vulnerable small businesses whose valuable business and customer data are not supported. To resume business operations as quickly, these small businesses succumb to paying ransoms that have been estimated to have cost them an average of $116,000 (Witts, 2022). These worrisome incidents of cyberattacks are launched for different reasons. Chang and Ho (2006) explained that the problems posed by cyberattacks on information security in terms of percentages are malicious code (31%), securing authorized users (23%), threats to IT and telecom (15%), unauthenticated users (11%), and threats to organizational management (9%). Let us explore a few cases of cyberattacks and their implications.

The first case is the dreadful incident of a well-planned and perfectly executed cyberattack that caused a blackout for six hours in Ukraine's capital city of Kiev. The attack on the national power grid brought business operations to a sudden halt and inflicted serious hardship on hundreds of thousands of customers in the city of Kiev (Sullivan & Kamensky, 2017).

The second case affected Kaseya, a US-based remote management software solution company that experienced a ransomware attack in its supply chain reported to have been carried out by the Russian-based REvil cybercrime group. Specifically, the attackers developed a sophisticated capability to use the Kaseya VSA product to infect customer machines (especially customers using a fake software update labeled Kaseya VSA Agent Hot Fix) with ransomware, thereby damaging the reputation of Kaseya. The attackers also chained together other new vulnerabilities discovered in the Kaseya product, such as credential leaks, business logic flaws, and two-factor authentication flaws. Official reports indicated that between 800–1500 small and medium-sized enterprises (SMEs) were infected by REvil ransomware because of the Kaseya cyberattack (Imperva, 2021).

The third case of cyberattack is the business email compromise (BEC) alleged to have been committed by Ramon Olorunwa Abbas, popularly called Ray Hushpuppi, a Nigerian national based in

Dubai. The business email compromise is a well-coordinated fraud and large-scale financial scam and computer hack aimed at exploiting the international financial system; it also targeted private individuals, businesses, foreign banks, and celebrities. The BEC schemes involve hacking computer systems, gaining unauthorized access to a business's email account, blocking or redirecting electronic communications to and/or from that email account, and then using the compromised email account or a separate fraudulent email account to communicate with personnel from a victim company, thereby tricking them into making an unauthorized wire transfer. Financial gains from cyberattacks running into hundreds of millions of dollars were used to finance his opulent lifestyle, often displayed on social media (US Department of Justice, 2020).

The fourth case is the cyberattack that compromised the supply chain of SolarWinds, an Austin-based IT management company. The attack is viewed as one of the most devastating cyber espionage attacks carried out by the APT 29 cybercrime group, which has links to the Russian government, in the United States. The attack injected the Sunburst or Solorigate malware into Orion's updates. SolarWinds breached the data of most Fortune 500 organizations, the US military, and several US-based federal agencies responsible for nuclear weapons and management of critical infrastructure services (Imperva, 2021).

METHODS AND ANALYSIS

This chapter adopts a systematic literature review (an interpretivist paradigm of qualitative research) to provide deeper insight into two issues that are critical in the entrepreneurship and cybersecurity literature. These are cyberattacks and different business continuity and disaster recovery strategies. We conducted a systematic literature review on both issues by sourcing relevant academic resources from Google Scholar, ProQuest, Semantic Scholar, EBISCO, cybersecurity newspapers, and professional websites in the period 2007–2022 following purposive sampling techniques (Palinkas et al., 2015). Preference for purposive sampling is justified because academic resources on the focused issues in the database (population) are very large and hence subjectively selected based on relevance. After purposive selection of these resources, a systematic literature review (SLR) was used to review, integrate, and synthesize the extracted textual information. To avoid doubt and encourage clarity, SLR is the processing of sourcing different academic resources to describe the dynamic relations between two or more phenomena, particularly when insights and facts about such relationships are fragmented in the literature (Pittaway et al., 2004). At the end of the SLR, 55 papers were identified as the most relevant and representative of the available literature that provides the needed insights on cyberattacks and different business continuity and disaster recovery strategies. The SLR used as explained is consistent with and follows the methodological approach of Hasan et al. (2021).

DISCUSSION AND RESULTS

DIFFERENT BUSINESS CONTINUITY AND DISASTER RECOVERY STRATEGIES

In toxic entrepreneurship ecosystems, it is compulsory for corporate organizations and entrepreneurs to have business continuity and disaster recovery strategies, as safety plans assist in protecting physical assets, IT infrastructural facilities, and the lives of employees, as stipulated by the Occupational Safety and Health Administration (OSHA), and the BCRS are required to conform with Regulation 1910.38 Emergency Action Plans (Walleit, 2021). The essence of the BCRS is to detect and mitigate disruption and deter future occurrence (Carlin, 2015). The following BCRS were discussed by scholars and industry professionals in the extant literature (see Figure 21.1).

a) **Readiness Assessment Strategy:** This is a deliberate, planned, and thorough diagnostic investigation into an organization's readiness and risk for a planned change that may be forced on organizations by disastrous events (Pellettiere, 2006). The strategy underscores

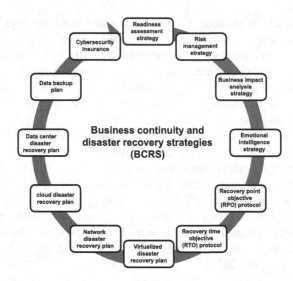

FIGURE 21.1 Proposed business continuity and post-disaster recovery strategies by author.

the need for business organizations to accept the reality that operational disasters, critical events, and cyberattacks are a reality of life; hence, management must pragmatically assess the capability and risk readiness of the organization to continue cloud computing operations as quickly as possible after disruptive events (Alharbi et al., 2017).

b) **Risk Management Strategy:** This entails carrying out a risk assessment on core business activities to identify organizational risk factors and prioritize observed risk factors, with a view to mitigating and controlling the risk factors that may cause future business interruptions (Mu et al., 2009). Risk control measures implemented after risk assessment lower the exposure to any potential risk, lessen the effect of threats and business disruption, and improve organizational resilience.

c) **Business Impact Analysis Strategy:** The BIA strategy for business continuity examines the impact of disasters and critical events on business and other operational activities when they occur. The BIA strategy starts with evaluating the consequences of hazardous events on the employee and community, financial damages, reputation, and quality of services (Păunescu et al., 2018). Proactive entrepreneurs conduct a business impact analysis as a mitigation measure to identify which parts of business operations have been critically affected, and they develop business continuity plans to move on.

d) **Emotional Intelligence (EI) Strategy:** The EI strategy is a crisis leadership competency that helps the recovery process, especially in facility management. Deploying an EI strategy underscores the fact that critical disasters or crises that truncate business operations are a test of the emotional intelligence and social operating system of an organization (Wisittigars & Siengthai, 2019). It is the responsibility of top leadership during crises to motivate and encourage all other members to leverage the four domains of EI as key drivers of the business recovery process. The four domains of EI are self-awareness, self-management, social awareness, and relationship management (Md-Nawi et al., 2017).

e) **Recovery Point Objective (RPO) Protocol:** This is an important strategy required for implementing a disaster recovery plan in organizations whose IT infrastructural facilities are halted by disasters caused by human and ecological factors. The RPO is concerned with determining prior to the occurrence of a disaster how much operational data an organization can afford to lose in the interim (including the maximum amount of time) before the event hurts financially or disrupts business continuity (Kirby, 2021).

f) **Recovery Time Objective (RTO) Protocol:** In implementing DRP in organizations, the RTO is concerned with estimating the impact that downtime will have on business operations in relation to a specified timeframe or length of time it would take for the IT systems to be restored after the disaster for business continuity. From a strategic lens, the RTO should commence in organizations immediately when operational disruption occurs until when business operations resume (Kirby, 2021).

g) **Virtualized disaster recovery plan (VDRP).** The VDRP strategy, often described as virtualization, systematically provides organizations with opportunities to implement DRP in a simple, methodical, structured, and efficient manner. When IT infrastructural facilities are halted by disasters in a virtualized environment, the VDRP spins up new virtual machines instantly within minutes, thereby averting operational disruption and prompting the recovery process. Testing the validity of a VDRP is strongly dependent on the RPO and RTO (Brush & Crocetti, 2022).

h) **Network disaster recovery plan (NDRP):** The NDRP strategy is a resilient plan specifically developed for recovering a network when business operations become more complicated as the network becomes more complex. To ensure business continuity and avert disruption to IT networks, the IT department is expected to develop a tested and trusted document that provides detailed information on network disasters, including a step-by-step recovery procedure to be followed by networking staff and other professionals during network disruption (Brush & Crocetti, 2022).

i) **Cloud disaster recovery plan (CDRP):** As the name suggests, the CDRP, or cloud DR, is an efficient and cost-effective cloud-based disaster recovery strategy. Functionally, the CDRP ranges from routine file backup procedures in the cloud to a complete replication of data and valuable information, and all the CDRP options require effective management of secured physical and virtual servers (Brush & Crocetti, 2022).

j) **Data center disaster recovery plan (DCDRP):** Beyond the procedural and ad hoc approach to disaster recovery, the cybersecurity literature recommends the DCDRP. This strategy creates a dedicated data center charged with the exclusive responsibility of focusing on the IT facility and infrastructure in the data center that support business operations. The data center preempts disaster by conducting operational risk assessment under different possible scenarios on components of the organizations, such as building location, power systems and protection, security, and office space, to know the vulnerability and resilience of the data center to respond effectively to disasters that may disrupt IT systems and business operations (Brush & Crocetti, 2022).

k) **Data backup plan:** The data backup plan is a proactive step of ensuring the safety of business data and avoiding the loss of the data when a disaster occurs or there are attacks on the computer systems and IT infrastructure. Procedurally, data backup, especially for databases, financial data, vital information on spreadsheets, customers' data, word processing documents, and human resources records, is carried out by regularly maintaining and storing additional copies of all processed information and updated data to always ensure easy retrieval and availability. There are two types of data backup plans: full backup and differential backup. The full backup overloads storage space and takes a longer time to backup, but it is the most comprehensive because it entails deliberately cloning all operational data such as files, folders, SaaS applications, hard drives, and other business databases. The differential backup is simply the process of updating a full backup done initially by including recent changes made to former files, folders, SaaS applications, hard drives, and other business databases. It is handy and preferred because it reduces the burden on the storage space and increases backup speed (Wallen, 2020).

l) **Cybersecurity Insurance:** Because cybersecurity risks and resulting breaches are realities of contemporary entrepreneurship ecosystems, the use of cybersecurity insurance for business continuity and disaster recovery plans is highly desirable (Xu & Hua, 2019).

Cybersecurity insurance is simply a sustainable means of transferring part of the cybersecurity risks associated with potential cyberattacks and future breaches to insurance companies at a cost or premium (Bodin et al., 2018. Cybersecurity investments are very costly compared to the benefits derived from incremental security (Gordon et al., 2015); hence, cybersecurity insurance premiums to be collected by insurance companies are determined based on the degree of cybersecurity risks and potential breaches they assume to manage and compensate in writing insurance policies (Xu & Hua, 2019).

EMPIRICAL VIEWS ON CYBERSECURITY AND BUSINESS PERFORMANCE

Operational information and data are valuable assets that support the process of value creation and distribution; hence, they are carefully protected, safeguarded, and secured by business organizations for strategic reasons (Loonam et al., 2020). The escalation of data breaches and cyberattacks across global entrepreneurial ecosystems poses a serious threat to information and data management and may negatively impact the performance of business organizations. To what extent is this presumption supported by previous empirical studies? Considering the foregoing, what is the relationship between cyberattacks and performance on one hand and cybersecurity and performance on the other? Answers to this important question are provided by previous empirical studies.

In the United States, Angst et al. (2017) investigated the relationship between cyberattacks and performance using panel data from over 5000 US hospitals and 938 reported data breaches spanning the period 2005–2013. The study found that an organization can achieve superior security performance and consequently reduce the number of data breaches over time if it increases its readiness to combat cyberattacks by investing well in IT security. In Bahrain, Hasan et al. (2021) found that the cybersecurity readiness of IT professionals positively impacts organizational security performance, which also positively affects the financial and nonfinancial performance of businesses. Another study by Loonam et al. (2020) found that risks associated with cyberattacks increase, and vulnerable organizations that were attacked also suffered significant reputational damage and loss of valuable information and knowledge with serious implications on their operational and financial performance. Furthermore, interviews conducted for IT leaders indicated that effective leadership with sound security thinking and cyber-security strategy is required in organizations to create a new cultural mindset on cyber-resiliency and the development of an ecosystem that would mitigate cyberattacks and avert reputational damage.

All the empirical studies discussed affirmed directly and indirectly that cyberattacks negatively impact the financial and nonfinancial performance of business organizations and that the negative impacts on performance could be mitigated and averted through (a) effective leadership with sound security thinking, (b) cybersecurity strategy, (c) a cultural mindset on cyber resiliency among employees and managers, (d) organizational readiness to combat cyberattacks, and (e) investment in IT security.

LEGAL AND REGULATORY ENVIRONMENT FOR CYBERSECURITY

The threats that may arise from cyberattacks and cybercrime call for regional, national, and international cybersecurity laws because victims of cyberattacks suffer financial losses and reputational damages (Melnyk et al., 2019; Sineviciene et al., 2021; Taeihagh et al., 2021). The legal and regulatory environment for cybersecurity is expedient to protect citizens' safety, business livelihood, and emotional and physical health in the face of existential risks and threats associated with disruptive technologies (Li et al., 2020; Taeihagh et al., 2021). The need for strong cybersecurity laws became a topical issue after the privacy scandals involving Facebook and Google. Facebook was accused of inappropriately sharing the electronic information of 87 million users with Cambridge Analytica, and the latter subsequently deleted the improperly acquired data (Bruns, 2019; Yue et al., 2020). If these data had been acquired by hackers, cybercriminals, and cyberattackers, they could have been used to unleash financial and economic mayhem on individuals and corporations. Criminal networks, fraudsters, terrorist organizations, and organized crime groups (OCGs) launch cyberattacks to steal sensitive information on payment cards, large-scale data breaches, and high incidents of e-fraud (Blanco Hache & Ryder, 2011; Dasaklis & Arakelian, 2021). A good example is the arrested Hushpuppy and Woodberry cybercriminals, who defrauded individuals and corporate organizations in the United States and other parts of the world through coordinated cyberattacks on computer systems and IT infrastructural facilities. The cybercriminals launched e-fraud by deceptively using the physical card or cardholder data (CHD) to make cashless payments without the knowledge of the real cardholder (Ryman-Tubb and Krause, 2011; Ryman-Tubb et al., 2018; Dasaklis & Arakelian, 2021).

For illegally sharing the information of 87 million users with Cambridge Analytica and failure to provide users with transparent and understandable information on its data use policies, Google was fined €50 m (£44 m) in Europe (Rossi et al., 2019; Ramos & Blind, 2020).

Considering several warnings that the United States faces imminent danger from cyberattacks and threats to its power grids from cyber terrorists (Sullivan & Kamensky, 2017), the United States has therefore developed a very strong legal and regulatory environment when measured in terms of number, quality, and specificity. According to Law Business Research (2020), the following are general and specific acts that strengthen cybersecurity governance in the United States:

- The Federal Information Security Management Act (FISM) establishes cybersecurity standards for federal government agencies and their contractors.
- The Federal Risk and Authorization Management Program (FedRAMP) is a public program that provides a standardized approach to security assessments, authorization and continuous monitoring for all corporate bodies in the United States, providing cloud services to federal civilian agencies.
- Key Provisions of the Department of Defense (DOD) Defense Federal Acquisition Regulations Systems (DFARS) mandate the use of cybersecurity-related contract clauses (particularly security controls and cyber incident reporting) in all DOD contracts and subcontracts made with vendors and contractors.
- The Federal Acquisition Regulations (FAR) Council developed a rule that prescribes a set of safeguards for acquisitions by US federal executive agencies on when contractors' information systems may key federal contract information.
- The Federal Trade Commission (FTC) enforces the FTC Act prohibition that stipulates the minimum-security requirements with respect to entities collecting, maintaining, or storing consumers' personal information.
- The Sarbanes–Oxley Act of 2002 requires publicly traded companies in the United States to maintain a system of internal controls over financial reporting, management evaluation of the risk of misstatement in financial reports, and consideration of the vulnerability of the entity to fraudulent activity by maintaining a series of IT "general controls" on systems for financial reporting.
- The Veterans Affairs Information Security Enhancement Act 2006 requires the Department of Veterans Affairs (VA) to implement information security procedures to protect sensitive personal information held by the department.
- The Food and Drug Administration (FDA) has developed guidance procedures for medical companies that address cybersecurity vulnerabilities during the design and development of medical devices and after medical devices have entered the market.
- The Massachusetts Standards for the Protection of Personal Information of Residents of the Commonwealth (MSPPIRC) requires corporate entities to collect personal information from Massachusetts residents to provide formal written documents on their commitment to safeguard residents' personal information.

• The Computer Fraud and Abuse Act (CFAA) clearly outlaws intrusions and interference with the security of a government computer network and other computers connected to the internet. The Electronic Communications and Privacy Act (ECPA) prohibits unauthorized electronic eavesdropping on electronic communications. The Wiretap Act prohibits the deliberate interception of information, use or disclosure of wire, oral, or electronic communication. The Stored Communications Act (SCA) prohibits access and storage of electronic communication without authorization.

Like the United States, India has strict cyber laws. Sharma (2022) explained that the Information Technology Act 2000 ("the IT Act") is the main law that provides legal recognition for electronic commerce and electronic record filing and management, but the three other acts that provide strict governance over cybercrime and cyber abuses are (a) Information Technology (Certifying Authority) Rules, 2000, (b) Information Technology (Security Procedure) Rules, 2004, and (c) Information Technology (Certifying Authority) Regulations, 2001. In line with deterrence theory, all the supporting cases and insights from previous empirical studies as well as the robust pieces of legislation in the United States justified the urgency for policymakers to legislate cybersecurity rules and regulations and industry standards, including compliance, enforcement, and sanctions by relevant government bodies. Thus, deterrence theory provides a lens through which to examine external forces that affect an organization's cybersecurity, such as government regulations and industry standards.

CONCLUSIONS AND RECOMMENDATIONS

This chapter enriched the literature by discussing business continuity and disaster recovery strategies as resilience tools for coping with the vulnerability of cyberattacks in toxic entrepreneurship ecosystems. The growing cyberattacks in developed and developing countries have far-reaching negative impacts on financial and nonfinancial performance. This chapter discusses the key impacts of cyberattacks, such as business disruption, network disconnection, damage to computer systems and IT infrastructural facilities, monumental data theft, financial losses, reputational damage, sudden bankruptcy, and threats to entrepreneurialism. More importantly, the deployment of cybersecurity measures and the adoption of 11 business continuity and disaster recovery strategies by entrepreneurs and corporate organizations are proposed as transitional and transformational support measures for forestalling cyberattacks in toxic entrepreneurship ecosystems. In view of the importance of cyberattacks and their negative impact on financial and nonfinancial performance, the following recommendations are provided for policymakers:

a) Entrepreneurs and corporate organizations operating in toxic ecosystems require comprehensive policy documents outlining their business continuity and disaster recovery strategies to forestall cyberattacks in fast-emerging toxic entrepreneurship ecosystems.

b) There is an urgent need for entrepreneurs and corporate organizations to promote cybersecurity awareness and culture among managers and employees because it is impossible to predict the nature of cyberattacks and the timing and extent of disruptions and harms that could arise from such attacks. Periodic in-house training and sensitization on diverse business continuity and disaster recovery strategies are expedient.

c) Policymakers in entrepreneurship ecosystems must invest heavily in cybersecurity and deploy sustainable BCRS because national infrastructural systems in the areas of water, electricity, healthcare, finance, food, and transportation are largely driven by interconnected computer systems and digital backbones and, when attacked, could pose serious national security problems.

d) A policy becomes efficient and effective when supported by top management; hence, entrepreneurs and corporate organizations are to put in place transitional and transformational support measures because cyberattacks pose existential threats to people, organizations, and national security. Transition measures focus on improving cybersecurity governance and the integration of business continuity and disaster recovery strategies into business operations, while transformational support measures focus on fostering a mindset for cyber-resiliency and security thinking in organizations.

Overall, this theoretical discourse provides rich qualitative insights into cyberattacks and the importance of business continuity and disaster recovery strategies for fostering cyber resilience and cybersecurity. Future research should provide richer empirical findings that can be generalized.

REFERENCES

Agrafiotis, Ioannis, Jason R. C. Nurse, Michael Goldsmith, Sadie Creese, and David Upton. 2018. A taxonomy of cyber-harms: Defining the impacts of cyberattacks and understanding how they propagate. *Journal of Cybersecurity*, 4(1), tyy006.

Alharbi, Fawaz, Anthony Atkins, and Clare Stanier. 2017. Cloud computing adoption readiness assessment in Saudi healthcare organizations: A strategic view. In *Proceedings of the second international conference on Internet of things, data and cloud computing* (pp. 1–8). Cambridge, UK: Association for Computer Machinery.

Angst, Corey M., Emily S. Block, John D'arcy, and Ken Kelley. 2017. When do IT security investments matter? Accounting for the influence of institutional factors in the context of healthcare data breaches. *MIS Quarterly*, 41, 893–916.

Blanco Hache, Ana Carolina, and Nicholas Ryder. 2011. 'Tis the season to (be jolly?) wise-up to online fraudsters. Criminals on the Web lurking to scam shoppers this Christmas: 1 a critical analysis of the United Kingdom's legislative provisions and policies to tackle online fraud. *Information & Communications Technology Law*, 20(1), 35–56.

Bodin, Lawrence D., Lawrence A. Gordon, Martin P. Loeb, and Aluna Wang. 2018. Cybersecurity insurance and risk-sharing. *Journal of Accounting and Public Policy*, 37(6), 527–544.

Borah, Prasad Siba, Shuja Iqbal, and Shamim Akhtar. 2022. Linking social media usage and SME's sustainable performance: The role of digital leadership and innovation capabilities. *Technology in Society*, 68, 101900.

Bruns, Axel. 2019. After the 'APIcalypse': Social media platforms and their fight against critical scholarly research. *Information, Communication & Society*, 22(11), 1544–1566.

Brush, Kate and Paul Crocetti. 2022. *Disaster recovery plan (DRP)*. www.techtarget.com/searchdisasterrecovery/definition/disaster-recovery-plan

Calif, Sausalito. 2020. Cybercrime to cost the world $10.5 trillion annually by 2025. In *Special report: Cyberwarfare in the C-Suite*. https://cybersecurityventures.com/cybercrime-damage-costs-10-trillion-by-2025/

Carlin, John P. 2015. Detect, disrupt, deter: A whole-of-government approach to national security cyber threats. *Harvard National Security Journal*, 7, 391.

Carroll, Lisa. 2022. *10-step disaster recovery plan for your IT department*. Kelser Corporation. www.kelsercorp.com/blog/10-step-disaster-recovery-plan-it-department

Cashell, Brian, William D. Jackson, Mark Jickling, and Baird Webel. 2004. The economic impact of cyberattacks. In *Congressional research service documents, CRS RL32331* (p. 2). Washington, DC: Congressional Research Service. https://sgp.fas.org/crs/misc/RL32331.pdf

Cerullo, Virginia, and Michael J. Cerullo. 2004. Business continuity planning: A comprehensive approach. *Information Systems Management*, 21(3), 70–78.

Cervone, H. Frank. 2017. Disaster recovery planning and business continuity for informaticians. *Digital Library Perspectives*, 33(2), 78–81. https://doi.org/10.1108/DLP-02-2017-0007

Chang, Shuchih Ernest, and Chienta Bruce Ho. 2006. Organizational factors to the effectiveness of implementing information security management. *Industrial Management & Data Systems*, 106(3), 345–361.

Dasaklis, Thomas K., and Veni Arakelian. 2021. Special issue on financial forensics and fraud investigation in the era of industry 4.0. *Digital Finance*, 3(3), 299–300.

Dharmaraj, V., and C. Vijayanand. 2018. Artificial intelligence (AI) in agriculture. *International Journal of Current Microbiology and Applied Sciences*, 7(12), 2122–2128.

Elliott, Dominic, Ethné Swartz, and Brahim Herbane. 2010. *Business continuity management: A crisis management approach*. Oxfordshire, UK: Routledge.

Fani, Silmie Vidiya, and Apol Pribadi Subriadi. 2019. Business continuity plan: Examining of multiusable framework. *Procedia Computer Science*, 161, 275–282.

Feldstein, Steven. 2021. *The rise of digital repression: How technology is reshaping power, politics, and resistance*. Oxford: Oxford University Press.

Frizzo-Barker, Julie, Peter A. Chow-White, Philippa R. Adams, Jennifer Mentanko, Dung Ha, and Sandy Green. 2020. Blockchain as a disruptive technology for business: A systematic review. *International Journal of Information Management*, 51, 102029.

Gandhi, Robin, Anup Sharma, William Mahoney, William Sousan, Qiuming Zhu, and Phillip Laplante. 2011. Dimensions of cyberattacks: Cultural, social, economic, and political. *IEEE Technology and Society Magazine*, 30(1), 28–38.

Gibb, Forbes, and Steven Buchanan. 2006. A framework for business continuity management. *International Journal of Information Management*, 26(2), 128–141.

Glenn, Jerome C., and Theodore J. Gordon. 2002. Creating a better world: 15 global challenges. *Foresight*, 4(5), 15–37.

Gordon, Lawrence A., Martin P. Loeb, William Lucyshyn, and Lei Zhou. 2015. The impact of information sharing on cybersecurity underinvestment: A real options perspective. *Journal of Accounting and Public Policy*, 34(5), 509–519.

Hasan, Shaikha, Mazen Ali, Sherah Kurnia, and Ramayah Thurasamy. 2021. Evaluating the cybersecurity readiness of organizations and its influence on performance. *Journal of Information Security and Applications*, 58, 102726.

Hiles, Andrew. 2010. *The definitive handbook of business continuity management*. Hoboken: John Wiley & Sons.

Hunker, Jeffrey, and Christian W. Probst. 2011. Insiders and Insider Threats-An Overview of Definitions and Mitigation Techniques. *Journal of Wireless Mobile Networks, Ubiquitous Computing, and Dependable Applications*, 2(1), 4–27.

IBM. 2022. *What is a cyberattack?* www.ibm.com/topics/cyberattack

IBM Services. 2020. *Adapt and respond to risks with a business continuity plan (BCP)*. www.ibm.com/au-en/services/business-continuity/plan

Imperva. 2021. *What is a cyber attack?* www.imperva.com/learn/application-security/cyberattack/

Karim, Akram Jalal. 2011. Business disaster preparedness: An empirical study for measuring the factors of business continuity to face business disaster. *International Journal of Business and Social Science*, 2(18), 183–192.

Kim, David, and Michael G. Solomon. 2016. *Fundamentals of information systems security: Print bundle*. Burlington, MA: Jones & Bartlett Learning.

Kirby, James. 2021. Understanding RPO and RTO for disaster recovery. *Micro Pro Article*, May 21. https://micropro.com/blog/understanding-rpo-and-rto-for-disaster-recovery/

Kuckertz, Andreas, Leif Brändle, Anja Gaudig, Sebastian Hinderer, Carlos Arturo Morales Reyes, Alicia Prochotta, Kathrin M. Steinbrink, and Elisabeth S. C. Berger. 2020. Startups in times of crisis – a rapid response to the COVID-19 pandemic. *Journal of Business Venturing Insights*, 13, e00169.

Law Business Research. 2020. *Cybersecurity in USA*. Wilmer Cutler Pickering Hale and Dorr LLP. www.lexology.com/library/detail.aspx?g=14512a9f-9886-453d-b441-cad42d8992b1

Li, Yanwei, Araz Taeihagh, Martin de Jong, and Andreas Klinke. 2020. Toward a commonly shared public policy perspective for analyzing risk coping strategies. *Risk Analysis*. https://doi.org/10.1111/risa.13505.

Loonam, John, Jeremy Zwiegelaar, Vikas Kumar, and Charles Booth. 2020. Cyber-resiliency for digital enterprises: A strategic leadership perspective. *IEEE Transactions on Engineering Management*. https://doi.org/10.1109/TEM.2020.2996175.

Md-Nawi, Nurul H., Marof Redzuan, Hanina Hamsan, and Noor H. Md-Nawi. 2017. Emotional intelligence (self-awareness, self-management, social awareness and relationship management) and leadership behavior (transformational and transactional) among school educator leaders. *International Journal of Educational Studies*, 4(2), 37–47.

Melnyk, Leonid Hryhorovych, Iryna Borysivna Dehtyarova, Iryna Borysivna Dehtiarova, Oleksandr Vasylovych Kubatko, and Mykola Oleksiiovych Kharchenko. 2019. *Economic and social challenges of disruptive technologies in conditions of industries 4.0 and 5.0: the EU experience*. https://doi.org/10.21272/mer.2019.86.04.

Mu, Jifeng, Gang Peng, and Douglas L. MacLachlan. 2009. Effect of risk management strategy on NPD performance. *Technovation*, 29(3), 170–180.

Myers, Kenneth N. T. 1993. *Total contingency planning for disasters: Managing risk, minimizing loss, ensuring business continuity*. New York: John Wiley & Sons.

Palinkas, Lawrence A., Sarah M. Horwitz, Carla A. Green, Jennifer P. Wisdom, Naihua Duan, and Kimberly Hoagwood. 2015. Purposeful sampling for qualitative data collection and analysis in mixed method implementation research. *Administration and Policy in Mental Health and Mental Health Services Research*, 42(5), 533–544.

Păunescu, Carmen, and Ruxandra Argatu. 2020. Critical functions in ensuring effective business continuity management: Evidence from Romanian companies. *Journal of Business Economics and Management*, 21(2), 497–520.

Păunescu, Carmen, Mihaela Cornelia Popescu, and Laura Blid. 2018. Business impact analysis for business continuity: Evidence from Romanian enterprises on critical functions. *Management & Marketing*, 13(3), 1035–1050.

Pellettiere, Vincent. 2006. Organization self-assessment to determine the readiness and risk for a planned change. *Organization Development Journal*, 24(4), 38–43.

Pittaway, Luke, Maxine Robertson, Kamal Munir, David Denyer, and Andy Neely. 2004. Networking and innovation: A systematic review of the evidence. *International Journal of Management Reviews*, 5(3–4), 137–168.

Ramos, Esmeralda Florez, and Knut Blind. 2020. Data portability effects on data-driven innovation of online platforms: Analyzing Spotify. Telecommunications Policy, 44(9), 102026.

Rid, Thomas, and Ben Buchanan. 2015. Attributing cyberattacks. *Journal of Strategic Studies*, 38(1–2), 4–37.

Rossi, Arianna, Rossana Ducato, Helena Haapio, and Stefania Passera. 2019. When design met law: design patterns for information transparency. *Droit de la consommation*, (1), 79–121.

Rudner, Martin. 2013. Cyber-threats to critical national infrastructure: An intelligence challenge. *International Journal of Intelligence and Counter Intelligence*, 26(3), 453–481.

Ryman-Tubb, Nick F., and Paul Krause. 2011. Neural network rule extraction to detect credit card fraud. In *Engineering applications of neural networks* (pp. 101–110). Berlin and Heidelberg: Springer.

Ryman-Tubb, Nick F., Paul Krause, and Wolfgang Garn. 2018. How Artificial Intelligence and machine learning research impacts payment card fraud detection: A survey and industry benchmark. *Engineering Applications of Artificial Intelligence*, 76, 130–157.

Sawalha, Ihab Hanna. 2021. Views on business continuity and disaster recovery. *International Journal of Emergency Services*, 10(3), 351–365. https://doi.org/10.1108/IJES-12-2020-0074.

Sharma, Animesh. 2022. Cyber security, cyber laws and preventive actions. *Publication of Times of India*. https://timesofindia.indiatimes.com/readersblog/digitalwala/cyber-security-cyber-laws-and-preventive-actions-42793/

Sineviciene, Lina, Luc Hens, Oleksandr Kubatko, Leonid Melnyk, Iryna Dehtyarova, and Svitlana Fedyna. 2021. Socioeconomic and cultural effects of disruptive industrial technologies for sustainable development. *International Journal of Global Energy Issues*, 43(2–3), 284–305.

Smith, Catherine, Helen Dickinson, Nicole Carey, and Gemma Carey. 2020. The challenges and benefits of stewarding disruptive technology. In *The Palgrave handbook of the public servant* (pp. 1–17). Dissertation published by Uppsala University Press, Uppsala, Sweden.

Somasekaram, Premathas. 2017. *A component-based business continuity and disaster recovery framework*. Department of Information Technology, Uppsala Universitet. www.diva-portal.org/smash/get/diva2:1108197/FULLTEXT01.pdf

Sullivan, Julia E., and Dmitriy Kamensky. 2017. How cyberattacks in Ukraine show the vulnerability of the US power grid. *The Electricity Journal*, 30(3), 30–35.

Taeihagh, Araz, M. Ramesh, and Michael Howlett. 2021. Assessing the regulatory challenges of emerging disruptive technologies. *Regulation & Governance*, 15(4), 1009–1019.

Unisys. 2022. Cyber attacks – what you need to know. *Glossary of terms by Unisys*. www.unisys.com/glossary/cyberattack/

Unitrends. 2022. *BCDR: How business continuity and disaster recovery can improve business resilience*. www.unitrends.com/blog/bcdr-business-continuity-disaster-recovery

US Department of Justice. 2020. *Nigerian national brought to US to face charges of conspiring to launder hundreds of millions of dollars from cybercrime schemes*. Press Release of the US Attorney's Office, Central District of California. www.justice.gov/usao-cdca/pr/nigerian-national-brought-us-face-charges-conspiring-launder-hundreds-millions-dollars

Walleit, Sina. 2021. Business continuity plan vs disaster recovery plan: How do they differ? *Parallels International GmbH*. www.parallels.com/blogs/ras/disaster-recovery-plan-vs-business-continuity-plan/

Wallen, Dave. 2020. *Types of backup: Understanding full, differential, and incremental backup*. Published by Spanning Cloud Apps, LLC. https://spanning.com/blog/types-of-backup-understanding-full-differential-incremental-backup/

Wisittigars, Boonkiat, and Sununta Siengthai. 2019. Crisis leadership competencies: The facility management sector in Thailand. *Facilities*, 37(13/14), 881–896. https://doi.org/10.1108/F-10-2017-0100.

Witts, Joel. 2022. The top 5 biggest cyber security threats that small businesses face and how to stop them. *Expert Insights Article.* https://expertinsights.com/insights/the-top-5-biggest-cyber-security-threats-that-small-businesses-face-and-how-to-stop-them/

Xu, Maochao, and Lei Hua. 2019. Cybersecurity insurance: Modeling and pricing. *North American Actuarial Journal*, 23(2), 220–249.

Yaacoub, Jean-Paul, Hassan Noura, Ola Salman, and Ali Chehab. 2020. Security analysis of drones' systems: Attacks, limitations, and recommendations. *Internet of Things*, 11, 100218.

Yue, Tao, Raminta Beraite, and Vidhi Chaudhri. 2020. *Facebook's reputation: Trials and tribulations.* RSM Case Development Centre. http://hdl.handle.net/1765/131568

22 Building Cybersecurity Capacity Through Education, Awareness, and Training

Ruth Shillair, Patricia Esteve-González,
William H. Dutton, Sadie Creese, and Basie Von Solms

Funding for this research has been provided by: The UK Foreign, Commonwealth and Development Office and the State Government of Victoria, Australia with in-kind support from the Organization of American States and the Inter-American Development Bank.

CONTENTS

INTRODUCTION

Despite the ubiquity of internet-connected devices and the use of technology for essential functions, many users have limited knowledge or awareness of the security risks of being online and have never been involved in educational or training programs on cybersecurity (Aiken, 2019). Yet all globally recognized standards for managing cybersecurity of organizations include risk control related to the training and education of people in the organization, for example, ISO27001 (ISO, 2022), UK Cyber Essentials (NCSC, 2022), and the NIST Cybersecurity Framework (NIST, 2018). This relative lack of education, awareness, and training could be contributing to increased problems with cybersecurity, including rising levels of cybercrime targeted at both individual users of cyberspace and organizations operating online. By one estimate, the global costs of cybercrime (including the damage and destruction of data) are in the trillions of dollars per year (Morgan, 2020). For such reasons, initiatives to improve cybersecurity education, awareness and remediation of threats, and training to mitigate these harms have risen in priority worldwide.

The potential value of these initiatives might be taken for granted, given that safe, reliable, and accessible information and communication technologies (ICTs) are at the heart of local and global economic growth. This growth is not without risks, as new connections can turn into new security vulnerabilities. Security problems, even as common as compromised passwords and weak authentication processes can result in exposure to ransomware attacks or stolen databases with the potential for considerable loss of reputation, money, and worker time (Morgan, 2020). The threats to critical societal infrastructure are too broad and serious to be handled by piecemeal responses to problems as they arise. Instead, national level efforts are needed to guide building capacity to proactively avoid threats and minimize harms that do occur. Enhancing security through building cybersecurity capacity at the national level is seen to minimize potential risks while at the same time still benefitting from utilizing technological affordances (Creese et al., 2021). These efforts include advances in cybersecurity education, awareness raising, and training at multiple levels, from nations to organizations to households and individuals.

Many individuals online are sufficiently informed and motivated to protect themselves and help protect others (Shillair et al., 2015), but many others do not understand how these attacks occur or how to protect themselves. For example, a survey of US households found that three-quarters (75%) of respondents could recognize a strong password, but less than a quarter (13%) knew what a virtual private network (VPN) does and even fewer (10%) could recognize an example of multi-factor authentication (Olmstead & Smith, 2017). As a result, people are very often the attack vector targeted by threats seeking to establish a foothold on victim organizations' systems. Given such low awareness of even basic security precautions, it is likely that improving educational offerings, raising awareness, and providing opportunities for training in cybersecurity would be of value around the world. For such reasons, there have been several long-term national efforts, including initiatives of the US Computer Science and Telecommunications Board (CSTB) and the UK's National Cybersecurity Centre to model the potential of what can be done at the national scale (Clark, Berson & Lin, 2014; Coventry et al., 2014).

Nevertheless, cybersecurity policy largely assumes, but has not yet developed, systematic empirical evidence on such basic questions as: what are the impacts of policies at the national level for cybersecurity education, awareness, and training programs? Furthermore, leaders of organizations and businesses face challenges as they must decide how to best utilize limited resources. Do these programs help improve internet use and commerce? Alternatively, would a deeper awareness of online threats have a chilling effect, even causing a decline in use of the internet for commerce, communications, and governmental functions?

The present research provides empirical support that national level efforts to improve cybersecurity education, awareness raising, and training (CEAT) have not put a brake on use but have made a positive impact.[1] This research is based on evidence of CEAT initiatives in 80 nations that were analyzed using the Cybersecurity Capacity Maturity Model for Nations (CMM).[2] The CMM framework was used to estimate the maturity stage of different national cybersecurity capacities (GCSCC, 2021). The framework was developed with input from over 200 experts from technological, academic, and policy sectors.[3] Over multiple iterations and data collections by international teams, these assessments probed into key aspects of cybersecurity capacity at the national level.

The CMM entails five dimensions of cybersecurity capacity: cybersecurity policy and strategy, cybersecurity culture and society, building cybersecurity knowledge and capabilities, legal and regulatory frameworks, and standards and technologies. Each dimension is evaluated using a mix of factors that were determined by rounds of discussion and input from CMM experts as essential to that dimension. Factors are further segmented by measurable aspects that are further operationalized by observable indicators. These indicators are used to gauge the maturity stages across all five dimensions of capacity building and the factors that make up each dimension. Stages of maturity range across five levels, from start-up to formative, established, strategic, and a dynamic stage. More details about the CMM and measures are in the data and analysis section. The CMM allows researchers to take a broad and rather abstract concept and break it into more concrete measurable indicators. The CMM review process produces content-rich qualitative evaluations and transforms it into quantitative measures that allow analysis and evaluation of cybersecurity capacity building efforts.

Based on the CMM dimension focused on building cybersecurity knowledge and capabilities, CEAT – the focus of the present analysis – is evidenced by three factors (see Table 22.1). The first, education, is focused on the provision and administration of educational programs on cybersecurity. Second, awareness raising, which includes programs aimed at the internet user community at large but also initiatives in executive awareness raising. Third, training is indicated by the provision and uptake of training programs. More details and the operationalization of these concepts are described in GCSCC (2016) and summarized in Table 22.1. In our analysis, factors of cybersecurity education, awareness raising, and training are combined for an overall indication of the maturity of CEAT in each nation. Empirical analysis demonstrates that CEAT makes a positive difference, but this impact might be limited in that many nations have low maturity levels on CEAT. As our research found, levels and approaches to cybersecurity education, awareness raising, and training are too often only at the initial maturity levels of start-up or formative, given a preponderance of low-income nations in the sample. Therefore, to better understand this problem, we complemented the quantitative

TABLE 22.1

Brief Description of the CEAT Indicators in the CMM

Factor	Aspect	Summary of Indicators
Education	Provision of education	Availability of cybersecurity education offerings and educator qualification programs.
	Administration of education	Coordination and resources for developing cybersecurity education frameworks based on national demand.
Awareness	Awareness-raising programs	Existence of a national program for cybersecurity awareness raising; range of demographics and issues covered; engagement of different stakeholders.
	Executive awareness raising	Efforts to raise the executive's awareness of cybersecurity issues in different sectors.
Training	Provision of training	Availability of cybersecurity professional training programs for enhancing skills and capabilities.
	Uptake of training	Certified employees trained in cybersecurity through cybersecurity training programs and knowledge transfer within organizations.

Source: Adapted from "Cybersecurity Education, Awareness Raising, and Training Initiatives: National Level Evidence-Based Results, Challenges, and Promise," by Shillair et al., 2022, *Computers & Security*, 119, p. 3.

research with a qualitative analysis of the full CMM reports of 23 selected nations, as described in a later section. This yielded descriptions of what each of these nations were and were not doing for CEAT, enabling us to show the ways more concretely in which cybersecurity education, awareness, and training were being deployed. These CEAT efforts at national levels can be replicated at all levels of organizations, thus further improving cybersecurity capacity.

THEORETICAL FRAMEWORK AND RELATED LITERATURE

Nearly every credible cybersecurity capacity building model that is supported by nations and NGOs, such as the World Bank, includes aspects of what we have defined as CEAT (Azmi, Tibben & Win, 2018). It might seem obvious that increasing user skills would reduce the gap between what users need to do to protect themselves and what they do (Shillair, 2018). However, there is a serious lack of empirical evidence over the value of investing in cybersecurity education, awareness raising, and training – which we have summarized as CEAT investments. Often this results in uncertainty that leads to under-investment in these efforts, particularly in low-income countries (Nagyfejeo & Solms, 2020). However, underinvestment in CEAT is seen globally and could help explain the shortage of cybersecurity skills worldwide. In addition, approaches to mitigating such deficiencies are not easy to study because governments do not use metrics or any consistent systems to evaluate the impact of such policies (De Zan, 2019; De Zan & Di Franco, 2019).

Experts in cybersecurity capacity building are divided over the efficacy of putting substantial resources into CEAT. For example, cybersecurity involves legal, technical, and societal protections that require broader and deeper educational initiatives than can be easily packaged and offered to a wide range of individuals. Moreover, awareness raising has had a history of challenges in discovering how to raise awareness across a broad public without instilling fear and undermining use. In addition, awareness raising often fails to guide people on what to do in situations involving specific software and problems. Finally, the most effective training programs are those that can reach all users, not just the technologically savvy. They also need to entail a significant range of material and interaction with trainers and learning materials, such as practice with confronting and identifying phishing emails or problematic attachments.

Given these challenges, top cybersecurity executives and policy communities might aspire to delivering effective education, awareness raising, and training but also be unable to resource these activities at the levels required for them to be truly effective. In addition, there is a more basic confrontation between experts arguing that solutions should focus on technology, since people are the problem, and those who posit that we need to see people as the key to solutions.

The people are the problem position maintains the need to place more resources into technical advances that obviate the need for human awareness at the level of internet users. Advances in spam filters and antivirus protection software illustrate the potential for such an approach. The people are the solution position maintains that every technical fix is a partial solution, requiring humans to identify and respond to problems, and that most, if not all, "technical fixes" create new problems, such as shifting attacks to new targets (Kassner, 2020). The nature of how cyberattacks are conducted, whereby threat actors can orchestrate campaigns that exploit weakness in both humans and technology, is further evidence that defensive measures are likely to require similar capability – placing people firmly at the center of protective measures (across prevention, detection, response, and recovery).

DATA AND ANALYSIS

The present study sought to establish whether those countries that have more mature levels of capacity building in CEAT will see demonstrable gains accruing to users, such as in the vitality of internet-enabled governmental and business services and growing commercial use of the internet. We examined this by analyzing cross-national data from up to 80 countries that have been reviewed through the lens of the Cybersecurity Capacity Maturity Model for Nations of the Global Cybersecurity Capacity

Centre (GCSCC) at the University of Oxford. Using the indicators on CEAT, we compare nations at different levels of maturity, controlling for their context, such as national wealth, which enables us to determine what impact – if any – is achieved through greater maturity in CEAT.

INDICATORS OF CYBERSECURITY

The CMM (GCSCC, 2021) is a theoretical framework that help nations to estimate their level of maturity in five *dimensions* of cybersecurity: cybersecurity policy and strategy, cybersecurity culture and society, building cybersecurity knowledge and capabilities, legal and regulatory frameworks, and standards and technologies. Each dimension contains different *aspects* that are grouped by topic or *factor*. Aspects are the units of study whose maturity is benchmarked in the CMM. The model considers five maturity stages that define different actions in capacity building for each aspect. To move from one maturity stage to another, there is an evaluation of indicators (specific operationalizations) of aspects which build together to form the factors. The *start-up* maturity stage indicates no observable evidence of cybersecurity capacity in that aspect, the *formative* maturity stage shows evidence of ad hoc activity, the *established* maturity stage has evidence of indicators in place with little decision-making on their choices, the *strategic* maturity stage shows evidenced mechanisms with choices according to the needs of the nation or organizations, and the *dynamic* maturity stage indicates that such mechanisms can be altered depending on the changing environment with rapid decision-making.

SAMPLE OF COUNTRIES

Since the CMM launch in 2014, the GCSCC and its implementation partners have used this model to review the cybersecurity capacity in more than 80 nations.[4] Table 22.2 summarizes some key characteristics of the nations studied in this chapter. The sample has representative nations from all the regions in the world and different income groups as defined by the World Bank (2021c). However, some regions are particularly overrepresented (for example, Latin America and the Caribbean), while others are underrepresented (for example, Middle East and North Africa). Similarly, high-income countries are underrepresented compared to the other income groups. The reason behind this is that the countries in the sample are not selected randomly. A review is only started when a government organization in a nation interested in implementing the CMM contacts the GCSCC to start the review process. Moreover, for all the sample countries in the Latin America and the Caribbean region, we considered the data in IDB and OAS (2020) secondary data.

TABLE 22.2
Descriptive Information on the Nations in the Sample

Year of CMM[5]	N	Region (WB, 2021c)	N	Income (WB, 2021c)	N
2015:	6	East and Pacific:	10	High:	14
2016:	4	Europe and Central Asia:	14	Upper middle:	31
2017:	5	Latin America and the Car.:	32	Lower middle:	26
2018:	10	Middle East and North Afr.:	1	Low:	9
2019:	18	South Asia:	3		
2020:	37	Sub-Saharan Africa:	20		
Total:	*80*	*Total:*	*80*	*Total:*	*80*

Source: Adapted from "Cybersecurity Education, Awareness Raising, and Training Initiatives: National Level Evidence-Based Results, Challenges, and Promise," by Shillair et al., 2022, Computers & Security, 119, p. 4

THE PROCESS OF A NATIONAL CMM REVIEW

The process of a CMM review involves field data-gathering from consultations with national stake-holders and desk research, collecting direct information on cybersecurity capacity in the nation, and having a national CMM report the evidence-based outcome of such review. To prepare a national report, researchers from the GCSCC or implementation partner arrange focus group meetings with teams of up to a dozen people from ten different stakeholder groups. These stakeholder clusters are from academia, civil society, and government representatives; criminal justice and law enforcement, defense, and intelligence communities; legislators and policy makers; CSIRT and IT leaders; critical national infrastructure workers; the private sector; cyber task forces; and international non-government agencies.

These modified-focus groups[6] meet and discuss the dimensions of the CMM, giving their eval-uations as insiders of what steps the nation is taking. Their responses enable the team to look for evidence of the indicators that rank the maturity of the aspects and factors of each CMM dimension. The modified-focus group feedback is coded by the research team, supported by evidence, and the team produces a national CMM report using the CMM framework. This report is submitted to the host government for further evidence and inputs if needed, and the final national CMM report is published at the discretion of the government.[7]

While conducting the many national reviews, the research team discovered that bringing many indi-viduals across sectors of the nation together to discuss areas of cybersecurity capacity was a major contribution to awareness raising. Many attested to have never been in the same room together and felt that they had learned much from the diversity of participants in the focus groups. Often this is because the pressures of daily work force a narrow focus on immediate responsibility and operations, incen-tivizing people to remain in traditional siloes and limiting the potential advantages of collaboration and resulting broadening of knowledge and understanding. Such a tight focus might be preventing an appreciation of how cyberattacks and resulting risk can propagate through and across organizations and supply chains – which may be further limiting the effectiveness of cyber defensive measures and harm mitigation controls.

A national CMM report contains qualitative information on the cybersecurity capacities of the nation in the CMM framework, expanding on the cybersecurity indicators found when the CMM review was done. While the researchers write the CMM report, they synthesize this qualitative infor-mation into the maturity stage of each aspect. Once the report is finished, the maturity stages of all aspects are joined to the dataset, allowing to consider each aspect in the CMM as an ordinal variable that can take a value between 1 (start-up maturity stage) and 5 (dynamic maturity stage). For more detailed information about the data collection and the CMM review processes, see Creese et al. (2021) and Creese, Dutton and Esteve-Gonzalez (2021).

THE EVOLUTION OF THE CMM

This chapter focuses on the CMM dimension related to building cybersecurity education, aware-ness, and training. This dimension was particularly modified from the first edition of the CMM in 2014 to the second edition in 2016 (GCSCC, 2016) to incorporate lessons learnt from the deploy-ment of the model. With the aim of incorporating all the nations feasible in the analysis, the data of the seven countries reviewed under the 2014 CMM edition were converted to the 2016 edition;[8] the remaining 73 countries were reviewed under the 2016 CMM edition. As shown in Table 22.1, the 2016 CMM edition considers that the CEAT dimension contains three factors, and each factor con-tains two aspects. The aspects are formed from multiple indicators that are specific operationaliza-tions of the aspect as determined by the teams of experts developing the scales. More details about cybersecurity indicators that define the maturity stages of each aspect can be found in GCSCC (2016, pp. 32–38).

CHALLENGES TO CEAT BASED ON QUALITATIVE INSIGHTS FROM COUNTRY REVIEWS

To gain a concrete understanding the challenges to addressing CEAT, the team reviewed the reviews of cybersecurity capacity of a sample of nations. The reports were informed by in-depth expert analyses, desk research, and discussions with country experts within each nation, particularly through the modified focus groups. All this information can be found in the national evidence-based reports produced after reviewing countries through the CMM. These reviews incorporate the perspectives of individuals from multiple stakeholder clusters, including academia, civil society, government representatives; criminal justice and law enforcement, defense, and intelligence communities: legislators and policy makers; CSIRT and IT leaders; critical national infrastructure workers; the private sector; cyber task forces; and international non-government agencies. To ensure comparability of responses, we selected those nations where at least one member of the GCSCC participated in the national CMM review (conducting desk research, consultations with representatives of national stakeholders, and writing the national report). Steps were taken to improve internal validity and the rigor of the observations (Miles, Huberman & Saldaña, 2018). For confidentiality reasons, our subsample of countries only selected nations with published CMM reports, although we included five additional countries with non-published reports to make sure we were not biasing the analysis by our selection criteria.

This resulted in reviewing a subset of 23 countries' CMM reviews conducted in 23 country CMM reviews spanning nations throughout Europe, Africa, and the Oceania region. The following challenges to the development of CEAT were observed: 1) the lack of a coordinated cybersecurity awareness program at the national level, 2) a limited level of awareness at the executive or board level, 3) inadequate national budgetary allocations for cybersecurity education, 4) a limited number of qualified educators in cybersecurity, 5) the migration of skilled cybersecurity professionals, 6) the high-cost of professional cybersecurity certificates, 7) a lack of knowledge transfer across nations, 8) language barriers, and 9) a limited role of community leaders. These areas are discussed in the following sections in more detail.

NATIONAL AWARENESS RAISING PROGRAMS

In several countries, some ad-hoc initiatives in cybersecurity awareness-raising from public and private entities were available. However, these campaigns were not coordinated and were often run without a government-led agency that would have the sufficient authority and resources to develop and implement a national cybersecurity awareness raising program. In addition, many countries lacked a national online cybersecurity awareness portal that would serve as a single point of contact on awareness and disseminate all possible programs. These results are in line with the findings of Nagyfejeo and Solms (2020).

BOARD-LEVEL CYBERSECURITY AWARENESS

Ensuring that cybersecurity is a top management, board-level concern is critical, as they play a vital role in determining the response to cyber threats in the organization. Leadership is crucial in setting the tone and culture for organizations, as well as providing effective oversight and governance in the face of cybersecurity incidents. Results from the CMM reports indicate that board-level understanding of cybersecurity is relatively limited and reactive rather than pro-active. The participants of focus group discussions suggested the need for more targeted awareness campaigns for executives regarding how cybersecurity risks affect their organizations. However, executives of multinational companies and from the finance sector, such as in banking, appeared to be more aware of cybersecurity risks. Another challenge raised was that IT staff lacked the ability to demonstrate the value of cybersecurity to the management and the boards, such as not speaking the same "business language."

In addition, CEOs worry of the financial burdens of cybersecurity for the organization. Such a focus on quantification of returns on investments, combined with a low awareness on cybersecurity at the board level, we hypothesize, might in turn result in a lack of foresight when conceptualizing future risk scenarios that might require budget to prepare effectively for.

CYBERSECURITY TRAINING AND EDUCATION BUDGETS

Even though integrating cybersecurity on the national curriculum is seen as essential to develop cybersecurity skills and awareness-raising throughout the formal education systems (ITU, 2018), it is a struggle to get budgetary support to achieve those goals. The CMM reports noted that many countries allocated no or limited budgets for cybersecurity education and the national curriculum due to resourcing and capacity constraints. As a result, there is often no resourced formal national curriculum for cybersecurity training or degree. In exceptional cases, the government, schools, and industry collaborated in an ad-hoc manner to supply the resources necessary for CEAT. Given the rapid transformation and expansion of the cyber domain, academic institutions are struggling to keep their curricula up to date.

QUALIFIED EDUCATORS IN CYBERSECURITY

The demand for cybersecurity skills far exceeding the current supply of traditionally qualified individuals was widely discussed by the focus groups. Comments included that the market requires technical and professional cybersecurity skills that are often not obtained through rigorous theoretical programs offered by universities and other institutions. Given a shortage of qualified cybersecurity educators/staff and limited expertise to teach cybersecurity, university-level supply is limited. Also, these assessments highlighted that women were dramatically underrepresented in cybersecurity, a problem that might need university-level recruitment, outreach, and retention initiatives.

THE CYBERSECURITY BRAIN DRAIN

Generally, government representatives discussed the struggle to find and keep skilled cybersecurity talent due to strict budgetary concerns, working with legacy technologies, and often the inability to pay as well as the private sector, which was also found by another study (e.g., Crumpler & Lewis, 2019). We found that qualified IT staff often leave the country and go abroad to seek better opportunities in the European Union or North America. Graduates are often recruited by international companies directly at the university. Also, some organizations are not allowed by law to hire new IT staff due to some budget restrictions. Those ICT professionals who remain in the country usually move into the private sector to earn higher salaries and find jobs for more specialized staff. Many companies opt for outsourcing ICT work.

CYBERSECURITY CERTIFICATIONS

Cybersecurity job responsibilities are complicated and span all organizations, requiring continuous learning and on-the-job training. The CMM reports revealed that professional training certificates were often prohibitively expensive and often available only abroad; therefore many experts were self-educated or gained their expertise on the job. Another challenge mentioned was the lack of transparency concerning qualifications, resulting in many job holders not having the training and professional qualifications to meet the demands of their roles. Also, training initiatives within the public and private sector are still largely focused on IT professionals.

BARRIERS TO KNOWLEDGE TRANSFER

The CMM reports highlighted the need to have more knowledge transfer within both the public and private sector. In some countries, private enterprises usually train their own staff internally.

One major challenge that came out of the reviews was that due to the high rate of staff turnovers, government agencies and companies do not spend enough time on introducing knowledge and properly sharing it, resulting in new employees being not fully briefed on their tasks. This is a concern for future economic growth as organizations can benefit greatly from knowledge and skills acquired by their employees after completing previous cybersecurity training (Kroll, Mäkiö & Assaad, 2016).

LANGUAGE BARRIERS

Overcoming cybersecurity communications barriers between cybersecurity professionals and non-technical users (e.g., government officials, company's senior executives, average citizen) remains a challenge and creates a disconnect. Moreover, some CMM reports highlighted the lack of appropriate local language options to explain new technological concepts for the citizens therefore creating another language barrier in the effectiveness of cybersecurity awareness raising programs.

ROLE OF COMMUNITY LEADERS

Participants from some regions in Africa and Oceania highlighted the vital role that community leaders, such as chiefs of local village councils and religious leaders, play within society. They could play a crucial role in shaping citizens' perspectives on cybersecurity and awareness on cyber risks but are seldom enrolled in this effort (Nagyfejeo & Solms, 2020).

QUANTITATIVE INSIGHTS FROM COUNTRY REVIEWS

In this section we discuss the quantitative analysis in Shillair et al. (2022) that studies the impact of having mature capacities in CEAT on the national internet use for 80 countries where the CMM was deployed.

CEAT DATA

After careful review of the modified-focus group data, the levels of maturity for the six aspects or variables in the CEAT dimension for the sample of countries are summarized in Table 22.3. Taking all the countries together, the average maturity stage did not achieve the formative maturity stage (corresponding to a value of 2) for any of the CEAT aspects because there were many countries in the sample with a start-up maturity stage (corresponding to a value of 1) when they were reviewed. For example, the awareness raising of executives was the most mature aspect on average but with only an average value of 1.90. The least mature aspect on average for our sample of countries corresponded to the administration of education, with an average maturity stage of 1.52. However, some nations achieved maturity stages above the established level (corresponding to a value of 3) on all the aspects of this dimension, illustrating the variability within the sample. Details of these measures are in Table 22.3.

The relationships among the six aspects within the CEAT dimension were positive and strong, indicating that these six variables were likely to be positively and linearly related. While all the relations between aspects were positive, some were stronger than others. For example, the provision and uptake of training were the two aspects with the strongest correlation (Pearson's coefficient 0.75), highlighting the dependency between having a supply of cybersecurity professional training programs at the national level and the ability of corporations in that nation to invest in training their workers.

After calculating the average maturity stage at the factor level, taking the average maturity stage of the two aspects within each factor, we obtained a value that was not categorical and had more variance than the single variables. On average, the countries in the sample showed a lower

TABLE 22.3

Average Maturity Scores on Indicators and Factors Related to CEAT for the Full Sample of 80 Countries

Variable	Obs.	Mean	S. D.	Min	Max
CEAT	80	1.79	0.55	1.00	3.33
Education	80	1.67	0.61	1.00	3.80
Provision of education	80	1.82	0.76	1.00	3.80
Administration of education	80	1.52	0.61	1.00	3.80
Awareness	80	1.84	0.61	1.00	3.50
Awareness raising programs	80	1.77	0.74	1.00	4.00
Executive awareness raising	80	1.90	0.67	1.00	3.00
Training	80	1.85	0.64	1.00	4.00
Provision of training	80	1.87	0.71	1.00	4.00
Uptake of training	80	1.84	0.65	1.00	4.00

Adapted from "Cybersecurity Education, Awareness Raising, and Training Initiatives: National Level Evidence-Based Results, Challenges, and Promise," by Shillair et al., 2022, *Computers & Security*, 119, p. 4.

maturity in the education framework than in the other two factors (awareness and training). One reason behind this is because education was the factor with the highest proportion of countries with lower maturity stages. Fully 50% of the countries in our sample had an average maturity stage below 1.50 for education. Also, 50% of the countries fell below 1.71 for awareness and 2.0 for training. To have a single variable capturing the maturity of the sample countries in the CEAT dimension, we used the average of the three factors that constituted this dimension. Table 22.3 displays the descriptive statistics of this variable. Most of the countries in the sample had maturity scores near the start-up and formative maturity stages for this new variable, with the mean value for this variable below 2 (representing a formative maturity stage). Concretely, only 24 nations out of 80 had an average maturity stage equal or above formative, accounting for the 30% of the sample. Similarly, only 5 nations out of 80 had an average maturity stage equal or above established (6.25% of the sample).

SECONDARY DATA

The literature has shown that the wealth of countries has a relevant role in determining the cybersecurity capacity of nations, jointly with the scale and centrality of internet (Creese et al., 2021; Creese, Dutton & Esteve-Gonzalez, 2021; Dutton et al., 2019). We included these determinants to explain the level of maturity in the CEAT indicator. National *wealth* was measured as the GDP per capita, *centrality* by the percentage of internet users, and *scale* as the number of internet users in the nation. We considered the *size* of the country as an indirect determinant of CEAT, measuring it by the nation's total population. Given that GDP per capita, number of internet users, and total population have a different scale to CEAT and a highly skewed distribution given our country sample, we applied the natural logarithm of the value for these three variables.

As explained earlier in the chapter, the level of maturity in CEAT may have an impact on the vitality of individual's use of the internet and social media. We expect that countries with more maturity of CEAT have more digitalized societies, with digital technologies incorporated more centrally into daily business and social activities. We looked at seven outcome variables related to the digitalization of countries. The variable *access account* captures how many users in a country access

TABLE 22.4

Descriptive Statistics and Sources of the Secondary Variables

Variable	Description and Source	Obs.
Centrality	Individuals using the internet as a percentage of population (World Bank, 2021c)	80
Scale	Natural logarithm of the number of users calculated with the total population of each country and centrality, both variables from World Bank (2021c)	80
Wealth	Natural logarithm of the gross domestic product (GDP) per capita in constant 2010 US$ (World Bank, 2021c)	80
Size	Natural logarithm of total population (World Bank, 2021c)	80
Firms with web	Percentage of firms with their own website (World Bank, 2021a)	78
Access account	Percentage of respondents who used a mobile phone or the internet to access a financial institution account in the past year (World Bank, 2021b)	55
Secure servers	Natural logarithm of the number of secure internet servers (World Bank, 2021c)	79
E-Government	E-Government Development Index (from 0 to 1) including the provision of online services, telecommunication connectivity, and human capacity; index multiplied by 100 (UN DESA, 2021)	79
E-Participation	E-Participation Index (from 0 to 1) including the use of online services to facilitate information by governments to citizens, interaction with stakeholders, and engagement in decision-making processes; index multiplied by 100 (UN DESA, 2021)	79
Gig economy	Normalized score (between 0 and 100) included as an indicator of the Inclusion sub-pillar (Network Readiness Index, 2020)	52
Business use of digital tools	Normalized score (between 0 and 100) included as an indicator of the businesses sub-pillar (Network Readiness Index, 2020)	52
Internet use	Composite variable made up of seven secondary variables	47

Source: Adapted from "Cybersecurity Education, Awareness Raising, and Training Initiatives: National Level Evidence-Based Results, Challenges, and Promise," by Shillair et al., 2022, *Computers & Security*, 119, p. 5.

financial accounts through their mobile phone or the internet. The variables *firms with web* and *business use of digital tools* capture how businesses use digital tools for their internal and external activities. The variable *gig economy* considers the prevalence of jobs related to online platforms in a country, usually freelance jobs or flexible jobs that strictly depend on the demand of the online platforms. The variables *e-government* and *e-participation* are more related to the online services provided by governments and their quality. The last outcome variable we consider is the number of *secure servers* that countries have, as countries more mature in CEAT would use and request more secure connections to the internet.[9] The sources of these variables and the descriptive statistics for the countries in our sample are described in Table 22.4.

The seven outcome variables were all positively correlated, and a factor analysis confirmed that the seven outcome variables could be combined in a composite variable, which we simply called *internet use*.[10] Notice that our sample of 80 countries was highly affected by the availability of secondary data, reducing the number of observations to 47.

REGRESSIONS

Table 22.5 displays the regression results of testing our first hypotheses that wealth, scale, and centrality are determinants of the maturity of countries in CEAT. When we have the three variables in the model, only wealth and scale have a significant positive impact on CEAT. A 1% increment of the number of users is estimated to have an impact on the average maturity stage of CEAT by 0.14 units,

TABLE 22.5

Regression to Explain CEAT Capacity

	CEAT	CEAT	CEAT
Centrality	0.01***	0.01***	0.00
	(0.00)	(0.00)	(0.00)
Scale		0.13***	0.14***
		(0.02)	(0.02)
Wealth			0.22**
			(0.08)
Constant	1.17***	-1.16**	-2.81***
	(0.09)	(0.39)	(0.73)
N	80	80	80
R-sq	0.33	0.55	0.60

Source: Robust standard errors in parenthesis below the corresponding coefficient.

Notes: $^*p < 0.05$, $^{**}p < 0.01$, $^{***}p < 0.001$

Adapted from "Cybersecurity Education, Awareness Raising, and Training Initiatives: National Level Evidence-Based Results, Challenges, and Promise," by Shillair et al., 2022, Computers & Security, 119, p. 6.

TABLE 22.6

Regressions to Explain Internet Use

	Internet Use	Internet Use	Internet Use	Internet Use	Internet Use
CEAT	1.31***	0.74***	0.53***	0.43*	0.38*
	(0.17)	(0.15)	(0.20)	(0.19)	(0.17)
Centrality		0.02***	0.02***		0.01**
		(0.00)	(0.00)		(0.00)
Scale			0.18***	0.16**	0.18***
			(0.05)	(0.05)	(0.05)
Wealth				0.57***	0.37**
				(0.10)	(0.13)
Constant	-2.65***	-2.59***	-6.00***	-8.98***	-8.09***
	(0.34)	(0.31)	(0.97)	(1.16)	(1.17)
N	47	47	47	47	47
R-sq	0.57	0.74	0.80	0.82	0.84

Source: Robust standard errors in parenthesis below the corresponding coefficient.

Notes: $+ p < 0.10$, $^*p < 0.05$, $^{**}p < 0.01$, $p < 0.001$.

Adapted from "Cybersecurity Education, Awareness Raising, and Training Initiatives: National Level Evidence-Based Results, Challenges, and Promise," by Shillair et al., 2022, Computers & Security, 119, p. 7.

and a 1% increment of the GDP per capita would increase CEAT by 0.22 units. Centrality does not have a significant impact on CEAT; this is partially explained by the strong correlation between the variables centrality and wealth.[11]

Table 22.6 displays the results of testing the second hypothesis that CEAT has a positive impact on internet use. The results show that CEAT does have a significant and positive impact on internet

TABLE 22.7
Regressions to Explain Outcome Variables

	Firms with Web	Access Account	Secure Servers	E-Government	E-Participation	Gig Economy	Business Usage
CEAT	7.20+	5.75+	0.16	3.85	14.49**	5.13	6.70
	(4.25)	(3.23)	(0.42)	(2.66)	(5.38)	(7.43)	(4.76)
Centrality	0.38*	−0.25**	0.01	0.33***	0.39**	−0.29	−0.23
	(0.16)	(0.08)	(0.01)	(0.07)	(0.13)	(0.20)	(0.14)
Scale	2.05+	−1.59+	0.87***	1.15+	2.53+	0.24	2.29+
	(1.10)	(0.86)	(0.12)	(0.62)	(1.42)	(1.93)	(1.32)
Wealth	1.18	10.24***	1.02**	5.42**	−1.65	8.87	11.66**
	(3.53)	(2.45)	(0.30)	(1.81)	(3.60)	(5.70)	(3.97)
Constant	−36.74	−41.11*	−18.94***	−35.80*	−26.50	−38.95	−92.69*
	(32.29)	(18.55)	(3.27)	(16.44)	(37.50)	(55.35)	(34.91)
N	78	55	79	79	79	52	52
R-sq	0.47	0.56	0.75	0.85	0.62	0.16	0.54

Source: Robust standard errors in parenthesis below the corresponding coefficient.

Notes: $+ p < 0.10$, $^* p < 0.05$, $^{**} p < 0.01$, $^{***} p < 0.001$.

Adapted from "Cybersecurity Education, Awareness Raising, and Training Initiatives: National Level Evidence-Based Results, Challenges, and Promise," by Shillair et al., 2022, *Computers & Security*, 119, p. 7

use even when we use control variables that are the same variables that determine CEAT (centrality, scale, and wealth). However, a close analysis shows that the relation between CEAT and internet use is relatively weak and mainly explained by the outcome variable e-participation.

Table 22.7 displays the estimation of the same model as in Table 22.6, but it explains each individual outcome variable used to construct internet use. While the results show that CEAT would have a positive impact on these outcomes, these results are not statistically significant except for e-participation. Increasing one maturity stage in CEAT would increase e-participation (variable that ranges from 0 to 100) around 14.5 units. To illustrate the size of this impact, consider, for example, the country with the lowest e-participation index in our sample with a value 11.86. An identical country, but with an average maturity stage in CEAT one unit larger, would have an estimated value in its e-participation index of 26.35 (more than double). Centrality was the other explanatory variable in our model that had a significant and positive impact on e-participation, although the size of this impact was smaller.

Our model explains particularly well the outcome variables e-government, secure servers, and e-participation, explaining 85%, 75%, and 63% of the variance of these three variables, respectively. Notice that, for these three outcome variables, there was availability of data for almost all the countries in our sample (our initial sample had 80 countries reviewed under the CMM). While the number of observations for explaining the percentage of firms with web was close to 80, the model did not explain this variable very well. Only centrality seems to have a positive impact on the percentage of firms on the web. The model did not explain well the remaining three outcome variables, gig economy, business usage, and access account, with R-squares 0.16, 0.54, and 0.56, respectively. Moreover, the number of observations was particularly low for these three last estimations.

PATH ANALYSIS

A latent variable structural model was used to test the dimension of education, awareness, and training and how it is associated with our indicators of the centrality and scale of internet use, given the other external variables of scale, scope, and wealth. By using this model, it allows us to better understand the construct of CEAT and how it impacted internet use, given the other external variables that also affect internet use. This model of key factors shaping cybersecurity capacity building impacts evolved over a series of studies (Dutton et al., 2019; Creese et al., 2021). The data were analyzed using SmartPLS software (Ringle, Wende & Becker, 2015). The model fit measures were good, with a standardized root mean square residual (SRMR) of 0.046 in the saturated model and 0.048 in the estimated model. Acceptable models are conservatively less than 0.080 (Bentler & Bonett, 1980). The normed fit index (NFI) also indicated a good fit, with .951 for the saturated model, measures over 0.90 being considered acceptable when considering incremental fit (Bentler & Bonett, 1980). All items were tested for collinearity, and all measures had a VIF of less than 5.0. The results of the analysis are in Figure 21.1.

The CEAT construct was overall significant for internet use. The construct of wealth, while having a strong beta ($b = 0.336$), had a high standard deviation (st. dev. 0.245), which is not surprising since our sample has a large proportion of lower-income countries. The significance of wealth to CEAT ($b = 0.455$, $p < 0.01$) demonstrates how having greater financial resources for education, awareness, and training led to more use of the internet for commercial purposes. The scale of use to CEAT ($b = 0.288$, $p < 0.001$) indicates that perhaps the sheer numbers of users would lead governments to increase CEAT if possible. These quantitative analyses left questions about why the levels of CEAT were so low across so many of the nations and why the relationship between CEAT and internet use was not more prominent. For this purpose, we turned to a more qualitative look at the indicators of CEAT within each nation in our sample, which is discussed in the next section.

DISCUSSION

Common sense might support the value of cybersecurity education, awareness, and training; however, up to this point, there has been little systematic empirical evidence to support its impact, especially in developing nations. This research demonstrates the importance of CEAT to the increased use of the Internet for economic purposes. Current levels of CEAT reflect the knowledge gaps between the relatively poor and wealthy nations and the resulting impacts on potential economic gains that countries could experience. This empirical analysis demonstrates the close ties to scale of Internet access and growth in CEAT. This would suggest that as the digital divide is reduced, CEAT should also increase in developing nations. However, this prospect is offered with the caveat that an increase of cybersecurity education, awareness, and training will not necessarily happen organically. Just deciding on what should be included in basic cybersecurity education is often a multi-year, multi-stakeholder effort (Newhouse et al., 2017). This relatively slow process contrasts with the rapidly evolving changes in the cyberthreat landscape. At the same time, incorporating "cybersecurity training" that is not evidence based can lead to poor results (de Bruijn & Janssen, 2017). The level of CEAT required to make a difference for individuals and organizations require multi-stakeholder commitment and resources to implement effective and culturally aware programs to meet increasingly sophisticated threats. The qualitative findings in this research provide detailed examples of the problems created by a lack of the economic and financial resources to provide CEAT.

The empirical findings of this research add support to conventional wisdom about the need for cybersecurity education, awareness raising, and training. However, the findings also document the relatively low levels of CEAT initiatives across the nations of our sample. In short, CEAT can make a positive impact, but such initiatives are being underutilized in developing the cybersecurity capacity of nations. This research adds empirical support to demonstrate the need for investment in CEAT at all levels in organizations, even as they invest in engaging more fully in utilizing technology is critical functions. The implications of this analysis for decision makers are critical. It is not simply a few case studies of CEAT that underscore the problematic levels at which these initiatives are currently pursued. In fact, this may be a far broader problem with most implementations of education, awareness raising, and training in cybersecurity requiring more investment and higher levels of maturity.

The qualitative analysis underscored the multiple factors undermining CEAT across our nations. That said, one key problem is that building community awareness of online risks was not always a priority. For several decades, governments and multi-stakeholder organizations in many countries have focused on getting internet access to as much of their population as possible, especially in developing countries (Hargittai, 1999; Viard & Economides, 2014). Internet access was shown to increase multiple economic indicators, with a robust telecommunications policy being crucial to national connectivity (Hargittai, 1999). National policies often supported distribution and efforts to get internet access to marginalized groups (Cullen, 2001) as the internet allowed access to educational materials, health information (Cline & Haynes, 2001), economic opportunities (Manyika & Roxburgh, 2011), and governmental services (Rice, 2002). Efforts were often focused on getting individuals engaged online, even for sensitive transactions like banking, as these had many advantages for consumers and businesses alike (Jiang et al., 2022). Furthermore, the internet opened up opportunities for individuals to become more than just consumers of information; it was a medium that was allowed individuals to creatively participate in issues of importance (Dutton, 2009). Despite the focus on positive impacts of engaging populations online, the awareness of a need for CEAT is long standing.

Some notable national level efforts to improve cybersecurity education include the US National Initiative for Cybersecurity Education (NICE) that lays out a structure for formal cybersecurity educational efforts (Newhouse et al., 2017). Businesses and organizations also work to build effective cybersecurity awareness programs (Bada & Nurse, 2019). And those OECD countries that are more mature in cybersecurity combine policies led by governments and partnerships between universities and private corporations interested in strengthening local expertise (Radunović & Rüfenacht, 2016). Despite these laudable efforts to improve cybersecurity resilience, as this research shows, there are many challenges ahead, especially for developing nations.

The responsibility to enhance cybersecurity is principally lodged at the executive level of public and private organizations (Von Solms, 2022). Board directors are routinely responsible for overseeing the risk management of their companies, including online risks (Price, 2018). Governments and stakeholders are demanding greater accountability for security issues, and board members may be held personally accountable for a breach (Fortium, 2017). However, as explained in the same article, many executives assume that cybersecurity is the responsibility of IT staff. Typically, board responsibility will sit with the CIO or CTO function for large publicly listed organizations, and assuming appropriate reporting is in place, this may deliver oversight – yet our research suggests such practices are not yet commonplace globally. Further, lack of awareness and education at the board level more widely can mean that oversight is not as effective as it might in this space. A single member of the board or a committee should be assigned responsibility for learning the company's security needs and status (Ottolenghi, 2012) and prioritize cybersecurity as a company-wide responsibility, from the board down to every single worker, as workers can become cybercrime fighters with their practices and can help to protect the company from online threats. Therefore, cybersecurity is not only a technical measure. It has human-oriented aspects that require investment in cybersecurity knowledge, and this is as important as the technical aspects of cybersecurity.

SUMMARY AND CONCLUSIONS

The quantitative findings of this research provide added empirical support for the effectiveness of CEAT initiatives across a sample of 80 of countries. This is in line with related research that shows that overall cybersecurity capacity building has had an independent impact on key outcomes (Dutton et al., 2019; Creese et al., 2021). This suggests that CEAT programs, as developed across our population of 80 nations, have demonstrated an independent impact on key outcomes of internet use, as detailed in the previous sections. However, the countries in our sample showed a low maturity in CEAT. The results of a qualitative analysis related this finding showed a weak coordination of cybersecurity awareness programs, a limited level of awareness among executives, insufficient budgetary allocations for CEAT, and a cybersecurity brain drain, among other reasons. Thus, the utility of this research that is focused on CEAT empirically demonstrates the value of efforts to improve education, awareness, and training, as there are measurable returns on internet use and its associated economic growth.

That said, there are limitations of the present study. While we have reviews relevant to CEAT for 80 nations, we lack adequate secondary data to incorporate of all these nations in our multivariate analyses. Second, while we have a statistically significant relationship between CEAT and internet use, it is largely driven by one or another component of the combined index, such as e-participation. Third, and more importantly, the low level of CEAT across the low-income nations and the limited range of CEAT even among wealthier nations suggest that the adequacy of CEAT is a basic problem globally. The development of more precise indicators of CEAT, which is being developed using "structured field coding" (Dutton, Axon & Harris, 2021), and the expansion of our sample through additional reviews and better secondary data sources need to move forward to examine the validity of our findings more definitely.

NOTES

1. This chapter builds on and updates Shillair et al. (2022).
2. The concept of a maturity framework follows the seminal work of Humphrey (1988) on software maturity, on which many maturity models have subsequently been based.
3. The development and evolution of the CMM are at https://gcscc.ox.ac.uk/development-and-evolution-of-the-cmm.
4. The implementation partners of the GCSCC that have conducted CMM reviews are the World Bank, Organization of American States, Oceania Cybersecurity Centre, NRD Cybersecurity, the International Telecommunication Union, the Commonwealth Telecommunications Organisation, and Cybersecurity Capacity Centre for Southern Africa.
5. This information is available at the website of the Global Cybersecurity Capacity Centre. https://gcscc.ox.ac.uk/https://gcscc.ox.ac.uk/cmm-reviews, accessed on 4 November, 2020.
6. Focus groups most often are facilitated to generate a wide range of ideas and observations. Our use of focus groups is to identify activities, attitudes, and other behavior of relevance to cybersecurity in a context that enables colleagues to raise questions with observations as well as to define areas of clear agreement.
7. The published national CMM reports are available at https://gcscc.ox.ac.uk/cmm-reviews, accessed on 28 June, 2022.
8. The newest edition of the CMM (GCSCC, 2021) has been used to review two nations. However, at the moment Shillair et al. (2022) was written, these national CMM reports were in a preliminary phase, and these data could not be included in this study.
9. We considered the natural logarithm of the number of secure servers in each country to mitigate the problems related to its skewed distribution and the different scale compared to the rest of variables in the model.
10. "National-Level Evidence-Based Results, Challenges, and Promise," by Shillair et al., 2022, *Computers & Security*, 119, p. 3.
    This factor analysis is available under request.
11. This result was already found in Creese, Dutton and Esteve-Gonzalez (2021).

REFERENCES

Aiken, Mary. 2019. 'Life in Cyberspace'. European Investment Bank. www.eib.org/attachments/eib_big_ideas_life_in_cyberspace_en.pdf

Azmi, Riza, William Tibben, and Khin Than Win. 2018. 'Review of Cybersecurity Frameworks: Context and Shared Concepts.' *Journal of Cyber Policy*, 3, no. 2: 258–283. https://doi.org/10.1080/23738871.2018.1520271

Bada, Maria, and Jason R. C. Nurse. 2019. 'Developing Cybersecurity Education and Awareness Programmes for Small-and Medium-Sized Enterprises (SMEs).' *Information & Computer Security*, 27, no. 3: 393–410. https://doi.org/10.1108/ICS-07–2018–0080

Bentler, Peter M., and Douglas G. Bonett. 1980. 'Significance Tests and Goodness-of-Fit in the Analysis of Covariance Structures'. *Psychological Bulletin*, 88, no. 3: 588–606. https://doi.org/10.1037/0033-2909.88.3.588

Clark, David, Thomas Berson, and Herbert S. Lin. 2014. 'At the Nexus of Cybersecurity and Public Policy: Some Basic Concepts and Issues'. In *Computer science and telecommunications board* (p. 150). National Research Council. www.anagram.com/berson/nrccsp.pdf

Cline, Rebecca J., and Katie M. Haynes. 2001. 'Consumer Health Information Seeking on the Internet: The State of the Art'. *Health Education Research*, 16, no. 6: 671–692. https://doi.org/10.1093/her/16.6.671

Coventry, Lynne, Pam Briggs, John Blythe, and Minh Tran. 2014. 'Using Behavioural Insights to Improve the Public's Use of Cybersecurity Best Practices (p. 20).' UK Government Office for Science. http://nrl.northumbria.ac.uk/id/eprint/23903/1/14-835-cyber-security-behavioural-insights.pdf

Creese, Sadie, William H. Dutton, and Patricia Esteve-Gonzalez. 2021. 'The Social and Cultural Shaping of Cybersecurity Capacity Building: A Comparative Study of Nations and Regions'. *Personal and Ubiquitous Computing*, 25: 941–955. https://doi.org/10.1007/s00779-021-01569-6

Creese, Sadie, William H. Dutton, Patricia Esteve-González, and Ruth Shillair. 2021. 'Cybersecurity Capacity Building: Cross-National Benefits and International Divides'. *Journal of Cyber Policy*, 6, no. 2: 214–235. https://doi.org/10.1080/23738871.2021.1979617

Crumpler, William, and James Andrew Lewis. 2019. 'The Cybersecurity Workforce Gap'. Washington, DC: Centre for Strategic and International Studies (CSIS). www.csis.org/analysis/cybersecurity-workforce-gap

Cullen, Rowena. 2001. 'Addressing the Digital Divide'. *Online Information Review*, 25, no. 5: 311–320. https://doi.org/10.1108/14684520110410517

de Bruijn, Hans, and Marijn Janssen. 2017. 'Building Cybersecurity Awareness: The Need for Evidence-Based Framing Strategies'. *Government Information Quarterly*, 34, no. 1: 1–7. https://doi.org/10.1016/j.giq.2017.02.007

De Zan, Tommaso. 2019. 'Mind the Gap: The Cybersecurity Skills Shortage and Public Policy Interventions'. Global Cybersecurity Centre. https://gcsec.org/wp-content/uploads/2019/02/cyber-ebook-definitivo.pdf

De Zan, Tommaso, and Fabio Di Franco. 2019. 'Cybersecurity Skills Development in the EU'. European Union Agency for Cybersecurity (ENISA). https://op.europa.eu/en/publication-detail/-/publication/f28aaf4c-7550-11ea-a07e-01aa75ed71a1

Dutton, William H. 2009. 'The Fifth Estate Emerging through the Network of Networks'. *Prometheus*, 27, no. 1: 1–15. https://doi.org/10.1080/08109020802657453

Dutton, William H., Louise Axon, and Caroline Weisser Harris. 2021. 'Structured Field Coding and It Application to National Assessments'. Global Centre for Cybersecurity Capacity Building (GCSCC), January. https://papers.ssrn.com/sol3/papers.cfm?abstract_id=3781600

Dutton, William H., Sadie Creese, Ruth Shillair, and Maria Bada. 2019. 'Cybersecurity Capacity: Does It Matter?' *Journal of Information Policy*, 9: 280–306. https://doi.org/10.5325/jinfopoli.9.2019.0280

Fortium. 2017. Cybersecurity: The Buck Stops in the Boardroom. www.fortiumtech.com/news/cyber-security-the-buck-stops-in-the-boardroom

GCSCC, Global Cybersecurity Capacity Centre. 2016. 'Cybersecurity Capacity Maturity Model for Nations (CMM)'. Revised Edition. https://doi.org/10.2139/ssrn.3657116

GCSCC, Global Cybersecurity Capacity Centre. 2021. 'Cybersecurity Capacity Maturity Model for Nations (CMM)'. 2021 Edition. https://gcscc.ox.ac.uk/files/cmm2021editiondocpdf

Hargittai, Eszter. 1999. 'Weaving the Western Web: Explaining Differences in Internet Connectivity among OECD Countries'. *Telecommunications Policy*, 23, no. 10: 701–718. https://doi.org/10.1016/S0308-5961(99)00050-6

Humphrey, Watts S. 1988. 'Characterizing the Software Process: A Maturity Framework'. *IEEE Software*, 5, no. 2: 73–79.

IDB and OAS, Inter-American Development Bank and Organization of American States. 2020. 'Cybersecurity. Risks, Progress and the Way Forward in Latin America and the Caribbean'. 2020 Cybersecurity Report. https://publications.iadb.org/publications/english/document/2020-Cybersecurity-Report-Risks-Progress-and-the-Way-Forward-in-Latin-America-and-the-Caribbean.pdf

ISO, International Organization for Standardization. 2022. 'Popular Standards. ISO/IEC 27001 Information Security Management'. www.iso.org/isoiec-27001-information-security.html

ITU, International Telecommunication Union. 2018. 'Guide to Developing a National Cybersecurity Strategy', www.itu.int/dms_pub/itu-d/opb/str/D-STR-CYB_GUIDE.01-2018-PDF-E.pdf

Jiang, Mengtian, Nora J. Rifon, Sheila R. Cotten, Saleem Alhabash, Hsin-Yi Sandy Tsai, Ruth Shillair, and Robert LaRose. 2022. 'Bringing Older Consumers Onboard to Online Banking: A Generational Cohort Comparison'. *Educational Gerontology*, 48, no. 3: 1–18. https://doi.org/10.1080/03601277.2021.2021730

Kassner, Michael. 2020. 'Cybersecurity Pros: Are Humans Really the Weakest Link?'. *TechRepublic*, 21 December. www.techrepublic.com/article/cybersecurity-pros-are-humans-really-the-weakest-link/

Kroll, Josiane, Juho Mäkiö, and Manal Assaad. 2016. 'Challenges and Practices for Effective Knowledge Transfer in Globally Distributed Teams'. In *Proceedings of the 14th International Joint Conference on Knowledge Discovery, Knowledge Engineering and Knowledge Management* (pp. 156–164). https://doi.org/10.5220/0006046001560164

Manyika, James, and Charles Roxburgh. 2011. 'The Great Transformer: The Impact of the Internet on Economic Growth and Prosperity' (pp. 0360–8581) [1]. McKinsey Global Institute. http://ict-industry-reports.com.au/wp-content/uploads/sites/4/2011/11/2011-the-great-transformer-McKinsey-Oct2011.pdf

Miles, Mathew B., A. Michael Huberman, and Johnny Saldaña. 2018. 'Qualitative Data Analysis: A Methods Sourcebook'. Thousand Oaks, CA: SAGE. 4th Edition. https://us.sagepub.com/en-us/nam/qualitative-data-analysis/book246128.

Morgan, Steve. 2020. 'Cybercrime to Cost the World $10.5 Trillion Annually by 2025'. *Cybercrime Magazine*, November 18, 2020, 13. https://www.globenewswire.com/news-release/2020/11/18/2129432/0/en/Cybercrime-To-Cost-The-World-10-5-Trillion-Annually-By-2025.html.

Nagyfejeo, Eva, and Basie von Solms. 2020. 'Why Do National Cybersecurity Awareness Programmes Often Fail?'. *International Journal of Information Security and Cybercrime*, 9, no. 2: 18–27. www.ceeol.com/search/article-detail?id=938012

NCSC, National Cybersecurity Centre. 2022. "Cyber Essentials". www.ncsc.gov.uk/cyberessentials/overview.

Network Readiness Index. 2020. 'Network Readiness Index 2020'. https://networkreadinessindex.org/

Newhouse, Bill, Stephanie Keith, Benjamin Scribner, and Greg Witte. 2017. 'National Initiative for Cybersecurity Education (NICE) Cybersecurity Workforce Framework'. *NIST Special Publication*, 800, 181.

NIST, National Institute of Standards and Technology. 2018. 'Framework for Improving Critical Infrastructure Cybersecurity'. https://nvlpubs.nist.gov/nistpubs/CSWP/NIST.CSWP.04162018.pdf

Olmstead, Kenneth, and Aaron Smith. 2017. 'What the Public Knows about Cybersecurity'. *Pew Research* (p. 18). www.pewinternet.org/2017/03/22/what-the-public-knows-about-cybersecurity/

Ottolenghi, Les. 2012. 'Cybersecurity, Governance, and the Implications of Oversight: How Your Board of Directors Could Be at Risk'. *CXO Revolutionaries*. https://revolutionaries.zscaler.com/insights/cybersecurity-governance-and-implications-oversight-how-your-board-directors-could-be-risk

Price, Nicholas J. 2018. 'The Relationship Between Cybersecurity and Corporate Governance'. *Diligent*. www.diligent.com/insights/cyber-risk/the-relationship-between-cybersecurity-and-corporate-governance/

Radunović, Vladimir, and David Rüfenacht. 2016. 'Cybersecurity Competence Building Trends'. *DiPLO*. www.rcc.int/p-'cve/download/docs/Cybersecurity%20Competence%20Building%20Trends%20in%20OECD.pdf/9be68dfd9a803a0bcfcf76347d894916.pdf

Rice, Ronald E. 2002. 'Primary Issues in Internet Use: Access, Civic and Community Involvement, and Social Interaction and Expression'. In *Handbook of New Media: Social Shaping and Consequences of ICTs* (pp. 105–129). http://rrice.faculty.comm.ucsb.edu/C36Rice2002.pdf

Ringle, Christian M., Sven Wende, and Jan-Michael Becker. 2015. 'SmartPLS 3'. Boenningstedt: SmartPLS GmbH. www.smartpls.com

Shillair, Ruth. 2018. 'Mind the Gap: Perceived Self-Efficacy, Domain Knowledge and Their Effects on Responses to a Cybersecurity Compliance Message'. (Doctoral dissertation, Michigan State University).

Shillair, Ruth, Shelia R. Cotten, Hsin-Yi Sandi Tsai, Saleem Alhabash, Robert Larose, and Nora J. Rifon. 2015. 'Online Safety Begins with You and Me: Convincing Internet Users to Protect Themselves'. *Computers in Human Behavior*, 48, 199–207. https://doi.org/10.1016/j.chb.2015.01.046

Shillair, Ruth, Patricia Esteve-González, William H. Dutton, Sadie Creese, Eva Nagyfejeo, and Basie von Solms. 2022. 'Cybersecurity Education, Awareness Raising, and Training Initiatives: National Level Evidence-Based Results, Challenges, and Promise'. *Computers & Security*, 119. https://doi.org/10.1016/j.cose.2022.102756

UNDESA, United Nations Department of Economic and Social Affairs. 2021. 'Division for Public Institutions and Digital Government'. https://publicadministration.un.org/egovkb/en-us/Data-Center

Viard, V. Brian, and Nicholas Economides. 2014. 'The Effect of Content on Global Internet Adoption and the Global Digital Divide'. *Management Science*, 61, no. 3: 665–687. https://doi.org/10.1287/mnsc.2013.1875

World Bank. 2021a. 'Global Findex Database'. https://globalfindex.worldbank.org/

World Bank. 2021b. 'World Bank Country and Lending Groups. Historical Classification by Income'. https://datahelpdesk.worldbank.org/knowledgebase/articles/906519-world-bank-country-and-lending-groups

World Bank. 2021c. 'World Development Indicators'. https://datacatalog.worldbank.org/dataset/world-development-indicators

23 Cybersecurity Awareness
Prerequisites for Strategic Decision Makers

Sadiq Nasir

CONTENTS

INTRODUCTION

The internet remains the foundation of modern-day development; various organizations depend on the internet for essential business operations. Technology and internet innovations in the last decade have increased significantly, bringing several new challenges and opportunities (Nasir and Vajjhala 2020). Rising cyberattacks are threatening business development with the aid of the internet, and breaches amount to about $3.62 million in loss globally per breach (Tang, Li, and Zhang 2016). Breaches are a big challenge that can result in revenue leakage and damage the organization's reputation. In any organization, there needs to be an alignment of the business objectives with cybersecurity; cybersecurity helps organizations stay safe and away from any data breach. The decision makers of any organization curate and manage the vision and mission of the organization as well as maintaining measures to prevent cybersecurity breaches. People are any company's greatest assets, posing the most significant vulnerability. As much money is invested in the ICT to set up and maintain the technological set up (cybersecurity setup), much attention should be paid to the human factor of cybersecurity, especially decision makers. The increased use of ICTs in today's business environment has brought about new possibilities, expanding an organization's cyber risks. However,

DOI: 10.1201/9781003319887-23

organizations must be better protected to ensure their information systems and data conform to the confidentiality, integrity, and availability (CIA) triad. The CIA triad is the foundation corner stone of cybersecurity.

Cybersecurity leadership needs to understand that cybersecurity is vital to any business. Cybersecurity happens to be an operational task, which is a component of any business. It is the decision maker's responsibility to know as much as possible and develop with keen interest; cybersecurity isn't just for ICT experts. Every decision maker is required to have an excellent working knowledge of cybersecurity. Cybersecurity is as strong as its weakest link: the human being. It can serve to prevent revenue losses to the organization and reputational damage. ICTs have become even more robust and dynamic in their use and operations. In this context, these ICTs refer to devices such as computers, systems, and servers, though there is not any standard definition of what ICT means. Threat actors have also become even more complex and advanced, as have the hacking tools used to conduct such operations. The IT team and decision makers in these organizations are responsible for securing computer systems from threat actors due to the increased requirement for this. In addition, other forms of data breaches exist that exploit human vulnerability through social engineering.

Sometimes the victims of these attacks have no idea they were attacked, depending on the threat methods used. Some organizations only discover a breach when someone finds stolen data on the dark web marketplace. A data breach tends to have long- and short-term effects on the organization. One of the best methods of mitigating cybersecurity risk remains increasing the organization's level of cybersecurity awareness; this has always been the most significant threat domain, as humans remain the weakest link. More importantly, the organizational leader needs to have continuous cybersecurity awareness. With their increased understanding, they can better create policies and procedures for other users in the organizations to protect the information systems. As a result, users can take responsibility for their actions as they do their jobs.

Cybersecurity awareness should be a push to even the homes and families of the organization's leadership. For instance, an organization's network and computer systems are well protected. However, a threat actor can breach an organization's network at home through the family of the organization's decision makers. Outside regular cybersecurity is training and awareness; platforms should also be available to encourage continuous learning to gain awareness. The organization must regularly visit its country's national cybersecurity strategies every five years to keep up with trends and changes. Decision makers outside should learn to better protect office information assets and equipment; they must provide the budget and policy direction to prevent data breaches. This chapter attempted to answer the following research question:

Why should decision makers be aware of cybersecurity, what should this awareness include, and who should be informed?

REVIEW OF LITERATURE

DEFINITION OF CYBERSECURITY

Cybersecurity is a composition of technologies and processes designed to protect data, networks, and systems from unauthorized access (AlKalbani, Deng, and Kam 2015). When cybersecurity is effective, it lowers the likelihood of unauthorized access. Further, it ensures that organizations and individuals remain protected from the threat of unauthorized exploitation of their technologies, systems, or networks (Garba et al. 2015). There must be multiple protection layers that spread across the information system for cybersecurity to be effective. Cybersecurity is a multidisciplinary field by nature (Cains et al. 2020), and its application involves all sectors, industries and stakeholders. The most significant of these layers is the human factor. The human factor is the weakest layer in the cybersecurity setup (Chamkar, Maleh, and Gherabi 2022). Though the human element is essential, it must complement the other, which is the technical layer, to have a robust structure.

CYBERSECURITY CONCEPTS: CIA TRIAD

There are many cybersecurity models brought forward by research and practice. This research work follows the most popular model in the space of cybersecurity. The model referred to here is the CIA triad. The CIA stands for confidentiality, integrity, and availability. The CIA model highlights the three most critical areas in cybersecurity. Several conceptual models have been presented to define and capture essential constructs of cybersecurity. The most popular is the CIA triad. The relevance of the CIA triad as a cybersecurity model speaks for itself, each of the three letters signifying a core premise in cybersecurity. The model highlights the three most critical notions in this domain. Taking note of these three concepts in the context of the triad can help create organizational security policies. The trinity assists companies in asking focused questions about how value is given in those three major areas when analyzing requirements and use cases from prospective new goods and technology. Decision makers can better understand the links between the three CIA triad concepts if they consider integrated systems rather than separate independent images.

The following explains the three concepts.

Confidentiality: Confidentiality safeguards are in place to protect sensitive data from unauthorized access. Data are frequently rated according to perceived value and risk level when in the wrong hands.

Integrity entails ensuring that data are consistent, accurate, and trustworthy throughout their existence. Data must not be intercepted when in transit, and precautions must be taken to ensure that unauthorized parties cannot change data stored in transit.

Availability implies that authorized parties should have constant and easy access to information when required. It entails correctly maintaining the hardware, technological infrastructure, and information-holding and display systems.

RELATED WORK

Nobles (2019) suggests that a human factors program can provide a framework for addressing and reducing human-centric concerns; this can be done by offering workers hands-on training. This research also suggests that business organizations are constantly plagued by human mistakes in cybersecurity, resulting in data breaches, cyberattacks, and long-term reputational harm, resulting in lower revenues. The study reached the following conclusions:

- Good human factor programs can help business organizations address cybersecurity risks.
- Without psychology-based specialists in cybersecurity, most corporate organizations will struggle to get it right; this is important in tackling the human factor-based difficulties in cybersecurity.
- There needs to be an open collaboration with psychologists, cognitive scientists, and human factors specialists to get it right.
- Human factor risks in cybersecurity are costly and almost always preventable.
- Cybersecurity and technology workers require human factor training continuously.
- Organizations' cybersecurity risk assessments are inconclusive without human factor evaluation.

(Pienta, Tams, and Thatcher 2020)

This work emphasizes that the human factor in cybersecurity is a recurring issue for businesses. Advances in theoretical understanding of the adverse effects of trust formed between individuals and the cybersecurity function (i.e., those responsible for protection), cybersecurity system, and organization (i.e., those verifying the cybersecurity department) lead to suboptimal compliance behaviors.

By creating a concept of "dark side trust" and a model, this research contributes to the study of information system trust in cybersecurity. The study included 87 participants from a southeastern United States university. By creating this conceptualization of dark side trust and model, this study contributes to the study of trust in information systems research outside the cybersecurity domain.

According to the findings of one of the studies, cybersecurity is an essential component in combating cybercrime and cyber terrorism (Rowland, Podhradsky, and Plucker 2018). Regarding cybercrime, including cyber terrorism, the research suggests that cybersecurity breaches will cost the global economy $6 trillion per year by 2021. According to the study, the cybersecurity industry expanded from $3.5 billion in 2004 to $75 billion in 2015 and is estimated to be $170 billion in 2020. And as cyberattacks become more complex, the demand for cybersecurity personnel rises. Yet, according to this research, there is a shortage of cybersecurity experts worldwide. Moreover, initiatives to promote awareness have yielded limited results during the previous decade.

Prabhu and Thompson (2020) demonstrated how the advent of new technologies, network-enabled devices, and enhanced connectivity enabled organizations to be internationally linked and improve their business operation. While the increasing integration of outsourcing, offshore labor, and remote offices provides numerous benefits, it also exposes information systems to cybersecurity threats and dangers. These hazards emerge due to weakening organizational security barriers and increasing the number of persons with insider access privileges from a remote location. The study emphasizes that some threats might originate from inside an organization. For example, an insider works for or was formerly employed by the organization (Prabhu and Thompson 2020). According to the research, understanding the dangers people might pose is critical, as this knowledge can help organizations apply the correct methods to safeguard their information systems. Several scholars have proposed categorization approaches for insider threats. The work made three conclusions. First, we notice that academics have categorized insider threats based on variables such as purpose, motive, technical competence, or combinations of these. The paper classifies an insider threat to cybersecurity as:

- Accidental: inadvertent, non-malicious
- Negligent: purposeful, non-malevolent, owing to inactivity
- Mischievous: intended, non-malicious, due to acts via the misuse of privileges
- Malicious: intentional, negative

FOCUS OF THE CHAPTER

There is a disconnect between decision makers of cybersecurity and the quantity of cybersecurity awareness to make educated cybersecurity-related decisions. While cybersecurity helps us protect our digital lives, leadership faces issues that their predecessors did not due to more dependence on ICT to conduct business operations. The top leadership team in any organization must work together to care for the organization's cybersecurity needs. Responsibilities of the decision makers include formulating policies to develop and providing budgets to attain standard best practices. Cybersecurity is traditionally perceived to be the responsibility of the IT teams. However, this is a technical as well as a non-technical concept. Cybersecurity is a shared responsibility. Before leadership makes critical decisions, decision makers must have a clear understanding and awareness of cybersecurity. When a decision maker lacks working knowledge, this never gets the attention it needs, which can be allocating resources. They should be able to identify the risk area and make critical decisions to better the organization.

In 2012, Saudi Aramco, the largest company globally, was hit by the worst cybersecurity breach of its kind ever. The threat actors temporarily halted Saudi Aramco's activities because over 30,000 computers had been affected by the Shamoon virus (Alelyani and Kumar 2018). The company had a flat network; the network was not segmented. Not segmenting the network made it easy for various threat actors to move on and around the web quickly. The problem was that the company never took cybersecurity as a core function, so it exposed its vulnerabilities when attacked.

The company then did not have to request leadership to mitigate this data breach. As a result, it reached out to Chris Kebeck to help respond to the connection and get the hard drive back to order. She was reluctant at first but requested a salary she thought was relatively high; the company reverted a week later with a 25% increase in her proposed fee. The restoration took two weeks, but the entire saga lasted three months; they could restore the company's network to its total capacity and be better prepared to arrest any data breach. This case study teaches that cybersecurity is everybody's responsibility, not just technical managers. An active post form waits for a data breach before being set up in a secure environment. Cybersecurity should be a proactive approach with an emphasis on resilience. Although it is impossible to protect an organization 100%, it is advised to follow standard best practices.

SOCIAL ENGINEERING

In cybersecurity, social engineering refers to the psychological manipulation of persons (Fan, Lwakatare, and Rong 2017), individuals doing a task or disclosing their private information. Threat actors utilize social engineering tactics to trick unsuspecting individuals into providing sensitive information (Aldawood and Skinner 2019). This can be done by infecting their systems with malware or clicking on links to compromised websites. Furthermore, hackers may exploit a user's lack of essential cybersecurity awareness. Due to the fast development of ICTs, many customers and workers are unaware of the actual value of their personal data identifier (PDI). As a result, they cannot relate to the standard best practices in keeping information safe and inaccessible from threat actors.

Cybersecurity awareness and education are the first steps in protecting employees from cybersecurity risk. Decision makers need to know what web links to click and what not to click. Identifying malicious links can be the difference between staying safe and clicking on a link that enables the attacker to access login credentials. This applies to office environments as well as at home. A typical scenario of a social engineering attack is when you get an email that requires you to a click to track a transfer or a payment to a service. Typically, this type of email comes with a sense of urgency to reply from the user. Hovering over the email address to display it is a simple technique to avoid this. The conduct and way decision makers conduct it can easily influence the organization's cybersecurity culture.

SOCIAL ENGINEERING METHODS FOR ATTACK

Social engineering attacks can be carried out anywhere there is a chance of human interaction. The five most typical types of digital social engineering attacks are listed in the following.

Baiting

As the term suggests, baiting attacks use a fictitious promise to spark a victim's curiosity or sense of avarice. Then, to steal their personal information or infect their systems with malware, they trick users into falling into a trap.

Scareware

Scareware taunts victims with bogus threats and misleading alarms. Users are tricked into believing their computer is infected with malware, which results in them installing software that serves only to benefit the executor or is malware in and of itself. Other names for scareware include fraudware, deception software, and rogue scanner software.

Pretexting

A threat actor gains knowledge by telling a string of cleverly fake narratives. The con is frequently started by a threat actor who poses as someone who requires the victim's private information to fulfil a crucial task.

Threat actors typically start by gaining the victim's trust by pretense as a coworker, police officer, bank, or any person with authority to know something. Then, through allegedly necessary queries to confirm the victim's identification, the pretext collects sensitive, personally identifiable information.

Phishing

Phishing scams, one of the most popular forms of social engineering attack, are email and text message campaigns designed to make victims feel rushed, curious, or afraid. Then it prompts people to divulge private data, click on links to malicious websites, or open attachments polluted with malware.

An illustration would be an email sent to subscribers of an online service informing them of a policy violation that necessitates quick action, like a necessary password change. Instead, it contains a link to a malicious website (attack vector) that looks almost exactly like its legitimate counterpart and asks the unwary user to click on the link.

Spear Phishing

The threat actor picks specific individuals or companies to target in this more focused phishing scam. Then, to make their attack less noticeable, they modify their communications based on their victims' traits, positions, and contacts. Spear phishing is challenging and might take weeks or even months. However, if done expertly, it's significantly more difficult to detect and has higher success rates.

Avoiding Social Engineering

Social engineers use human emotions like curiosity and terror to their advantage to carry out their plans and lure victims into their traps. Therefore, exercise caution if you receive a worrying email, find an offer on a website, or come across errant digital media. You can defend yourself against most online social engineering attempts by being vigilant. The following advice can also help you become more vigilant about social engineering scams.

Avoid opening attachments and emails from unknown senders. You don't need to respond to emails from senders you don't know. Instead, cross-check and confirm the news from other sources, such as over the phone or a service provider's website, even if you know them and have doubts about their message. Keep in mind that email addresses are frequently spoofs; an attacker could have sent email that appears to be from a reliable source. Multifactor authentication should be used; user credentials are among the most valuable pieces of data that attackers look for. Additionally, if the system is compromised, using multifactor authentication helps to ensure no harm is committed.

Be skeptical of tempting offers – if an offer sounds too good to be true, consider it carefully before taking it. You can immediately tell if you're dealing with a genuine offer or a snare by Googling the subject. Keep your antivirus/antimalware software up to date. Either make it a routine to download the newest updates first thing every day or ensure automatic updates are turned on. Regularly verify that updates have been installed and run a system scan to look for potential infections.

CYBERSECURITY RISKS

Cybersecurity risks are sometimes hidden by covering the truth from the supposed victim to gain an undue advantage. While this applies to ethical and immoral hackers, ethical hackers might gain moral support for their deceit by saying they must stay hidden to safeguard a network from cyber assault. As a result, from the standpoint of ethical hackers, deceit may be a terrific tool for a much-needed hassle-free environment. From this perspective, all ICT personnel must assume the position of an ethical hacker and master cybersecurity risk. As a result, ICT personnel can obtain intelligence from any cyberattackers, as intelligence generated by such approaches generates more reliable data as the sources are domains held by attackers.

Some cybersecurity risk entails impersonation and concealment, which may be actualized through multiple means. The tactics described previously can benefit both ethical and unethical hackers. For example, a threat actor may produce a phony webpage to entice innocent visitors to gain money and influence. However, an ethical hacker may use the same tricks to fool an attacker into defending their network. When ethical hackers utilize the strategies, information about attackers can be collected, allowing the defense to understand the goal and reason behind the cyber assault.

One could argue that it is difficult to deceive Internet users in the Information Age, given the resources available for spotting and avoiding cyber fraud. However, cybersecurity has become a global problem owing to two factors: first, computer users tend to accept what they see in front of their eyes, making them susceptible to well-planned cyber traps. Thus, hackers profit from such human vulnerabilities. As a result, websites that seek to do business are constantly subjected to cyber assaults, as they are the preferred targets of hackers because many websites have flaws in one or more of their layers. Hacking tools are generally accessible online or on the dark web. As a result, many individuals engage in hacking, which is why cyber breach incidents worldwide have increased.

Unethical hackers also use many methods to develop their skills, since that is all they need to invest in. But, on the other hand, ethical hackers are frantically looking for ways to conduct rigorous tests to assess the efficiency of all the protective technologies used in cybersecurity management. It is worth noting that human mistake has been one of the significant causes of vulnerability in any information system. Many security breaches were caused by human errors by security managers and other information professionals. Ordinary individuals reliant on internet activity for financial or other information exchange faced a nightmare. Complaints about Internet fraud are on the rise. Thus, such a situation completely legitimizes the fraudulent activities of ethical hackers, who try to expose immoral hackers and prevent them from defrauding organizations and individuals. However, the power dynamic favors evil hackers primarily concerned with technology's destructive element. Although they have yet to be successful, decoys, honeypots, and other anti-hacking systems are being deployed to fight hackers' constant counter-research. Websites that use deception methods, such as tar traps, to fool attackers and prevent unauthorized access to their websites are also included.

Computer systems, too, are subject to assaults, which necessitates the expanded application of cybersecurity for defense. However, at least in the broad cyber realm, defensive deception is still in its early phases. There are requests to seek aid from the military sector, which deploys various cybersecurity tactics to safeguard its networks successfully. Nonetheless, not all measures and tactics have online counterparts. Some of the most relevant examples are honeypots. Cyber security situational awareness (Cyber-SA) lets decision makers throughout an organization have the knowledge and understanding accessible to make informed judgments. These fake computer systems promote assaults to collect data and information about the attackers and their attack tactics to better cyber-SA and cybersecurity.

As previously stated, it is difficult to defend against cyberattacks and crimes because the practice is asymmetric, with the advantage in the hands of the attacker, who usually retains the ability to decide on the location, time, and method of attack, about which the defender has no prior knowledge. Naturally, this increases the attacker's chances of committing the crime. As a result of this, there is an urgent need to develop a multi-layered defense system capable of detecting and dealing with threats effectively. There should be a concentrated effort to fight cyberattackers, and with this in mind, operators should examine all feasible options to beat them effectively.

Although it varies significantly from one network expert to the next, the attack procedure typically consists of the following steps: reconnaissance, scanning, acquiring access, keeping access, concealing traces, and hiding. Furthermore, legal support is vital in combating cybercrime; hence, legal cooperation among nations regarding the enforcement of agreed-upon rules of cyber behavior is required. All states should agree on the types of conduct considered cybercrime within national borders. That agreement should then be interpreted into a legal regime in which those states strictly prohibit the identified forms of destructive cyber behavior and, at some point, establish a framework for sharing cyber incident intelligence so that all states benefit.

Since unethical hackers always exploit easy access to information, there should also be an effective defensive architecture to identify the real intention of each cyber visitor to filter the cybercriminals from ordinary people. This research found that cyber deception is an essential component of cybersecurity for gathering intelligence about cyberattacks to help build a strong cyber SA; thus, cyber deception is required for active cyber SA. A plethora of literature deals with the art of cyber deception in cybersecurity, the topic of this study, which will be covered in the discussion section.

Much may be learned about the topic of study via research and evaluation of the literature from various writers and researchers. First, however, this section requires that some fundamental facts be provided regarding the efficiency of ethical deception (deception used by an ethical hacker) in securing networks in the form of active defenses that applies such a dynamic measurement for cybersecurity. For example, moral deception may be a tool for cyber operators to collect information necessary for security agents, who can use better techniques to arrest cyber criminals. At this point, one key issue emerges. There should be a clear guideline for seizing trans-continental cybercriminals, and it is time for the governments of various states to begin a clear discourse in this respect. The lack of a common strategy to govern cyberspace gives cybercriminals a significant edge. Cybersecurity may also be a marvelous shield to secure an organization's essential data and information. As a result, from a commercial standpoint, cybersecurity may be a competitive advantage for the corporate organization, as it can promote efficient operations.

CYBERSECURITY INCIDENT LANDSCAPE

Cybersecurity incidents can be devastating to companies, mainly when they result in the loss of millions of dollars. But unfortunately, many organizations do not consider cybersecurity incidents when doing their organizational risk matrix. For instance, one of the most significant cybersecurity incidents is the theft of millions of credit cards. It occurred in 2012 when cyber criminals gained unauthorized access to credit card processors. This resulted in the stealing of millions of credit card numbers. The theft caused a worldwide reduction in the use of credit cards, resulting in massive financial losses for companies. Companies that were affected by this incident include Target, Home Depot, JC Penney, and over a dozen others. Although credit card information is encrypted, this incident serves as a reminder of the importance of cybersecurity. Companies should invest the resources necessary to prevent breaches and respond quickly. Companies can only make effective decisions when decision makers fully appreciate cybersecurity as they should (Smith and Mulrain 2018). Another significant incident is the theft of millions of payment card numbers from Target. This occurred in 2016 when hackers accessed Target's payment systems and stole customer data (Pigni et al. 2018). The hackers then used this data to make fraudulent purchases and steal money from the accounts of unsuspecting customers. The hack affected over 40 million credit and debit cardholders, resulting in company losses. Although the payment system was protected by encryption, this incident warns companies to invest in cybersecurity.

Companies that weren't as concerned with cybersecurity may have also been hacked, resulting in the theft of billions of dollars. In 2017, hackers gained unauthorized access to Equifax, one of the world's largest providers of credit information. The hackers accessed the information of nearly 145 million people and caused massive monetary losses for companies (Smith and Mulrain 2018). They also accessed the data of people employed by the US government and businesses, causing similarly devastating effects. Although companies are dealing with lawsuits and negative publicity over these incidents, companies must deal with them and address the security issues that caused them. Companies that ignore their cybersecurity are risking the safety of their assets and employees.

Due to how difficult they can be to detect and protect against; businesses often do not consider cybersecurity risks. While accurate, some techniques identify cybersecurity problems and lessen their effects. These problems can be seen with a thorough cybersecurity strategy incorporating physical, technical, and, most importantly, human measures. Companies should invest the necessary funds and resources to implement a comprehensive cybersecurity strategy. Ransomware is the latest threat to businesses; ransomware is a sort of malware that encodes a victim's documents and media and then requests payment for their decryption (Huang et al. 2018); the request for this payment is usually in bitcoin (Richardson 2017). Cybercriminals use ransomware to cause financial damage to organizations that do not pay the ransom. Cybercriminals create ransomware by exploiting vulnerabilities in computer systems. They use this to extort money from organizations that have data that they want. More potent than previously assumed, ransomware is a developing issue. The decision makers of any organization must understand how to handle it for this reason.

Organizations can lose data and even their operations if they cannot get rid of ransomware (Luo and Liao 2007). This happens when they can't access their systems or payment systems. Some businesses cannot pay the ransom because they don't have the budget. Some companies have experienced temporary closures or reduced staff due to ransomware. There's no way for them to pay the ransom and restore their systems. Instead, they must pay the ransom to fix their systems. Losing these options is why some businesses choose to pay the ransom. They don't want to start over; they want their systems back. However, payment of the ransom does not guarantee complete data recovery.

Since ransomware is a lucrative source of income for thieves, experts expect it will become much more potent. It's easy for them to create new ransomware strains that are more powerful than the previous ones; this means that cybercriminals will have even more ways to make money. As a result, they'll create new tensions that are more powerful than the ones that exist today, allowing them to generate more money and cause more damage. Even after the creation of new anti-ransomware software, the problem still exists. Because there are numerous misconceptions, many experts think ransomware is being over-hyped as a threat. For example, many people believe that it only affects large companies. Unfortunately, this couldn't be further from the truth. Even small companies can be affected by ransomware. It's just much more profitable for cybercriminals if they target large businesses.

THE PROBLEMS AND ISSUES

This section identifies the principal issues contributing to the lack of cybersecurity. A discussion on cybersecurity awareness usually revolves around specific individuals or organizations that lack the necessary skills and knowledge to protect their systems from cyberattacks. Various factors contribute to this problem, including educational institutions not adequately training students in information security, businesses failing to properly implement best practices for data protection, and employees using personal devices at work without taking appropriate precautions.

Cybersecurity has turned out to be a critical issue in today's world. Cyberattacks have become much more familiar with the increasing use of technology (Eian et al. 2020). Cybercrime has now become one of the world's top leading criminal activities. (Anderson et al. n.d.) There are various reasons lack of cybersecurity awareness for decision makers is a problem. Some of the main issues contributing to this lack of understanding are:

- The increasing use of technology has led to widespread cyberattacks.
- Poor education on cybersecurity.
- Difficulty in recognizing cyber threats.
- Ineffective strategies to prevent cyberattacks.

A model to show the main issues contributing to this lack of cybersecurity awareness for decision makers is presented in this chapter.

We need to increase cybersecurity awareness among decision makers to address the lack of cybersecurity awareness. Creating awareness-raising campaigns is a workable alternative; instructional resources, like e-books, can be very beneficial. Another effective strategy for raising public awareness of cybersecurity is social media. There is no single answer to how best to deal with cyberattacks. Instead, there are many possible solutions, and it is essential that each organization evaluate its unique situation and select the most appropriate solution for itself. Cybersecurity is a huge issue nowadays, with many people becoming increasingly aware of the dangers. Cybersecurity awareness means understanding the risks of online activities and taking steps to defend organizations from potential consequences (Zwilling et al. 2022).

Cybersecurity is not a simple issue to understand, but with effort and focus, it can be easier to understand and protect oneself and the organization. Decision makers can do a few things to be more aware of their online activities. First, they should always be mindful of the devices that they are using. For example, decision makers should ensure that their computer is always up to date with the latest security patches and that they use a secure browser. They should also be careful about what information they share online and the links they click on. Finally, they should also ensure that their online activities are kept confidential and that they do not distribute or disseminate any illegally obtained information. Protecting oneself from cybercrime is essential, as protecting oneself is the same as watching the entire organization. Decision makers can take a few simple steps to reduce the chances of becoming a victim.

CONCLUSION

Cybersecurity is an ongoing battle that requires everyone involved to adopt safe practices and be proactive about stopping potential attacks before they happen. Those steps can secure their organization and build a bright future. The decision makers in any organization have the responsibility to champion cybersecurity; they will only be dependable if they have a good understanding and appreciation of cybersecurity awareness. Cybersecurity is a top priority for any organization. Many businesses have been affected by cyberattacks in recent years. Many organizations have also invested a lot of money and effort in protecting their networks from hackers. However, many companies still fall victim to cyberattacks. To protect themselves from these attacks, organizations must take steps to stay safe, and decision makers need to be involved in the process; cybersecurity is not only for the technical team A cybersecurity decision maker must ensure the company is secure from attacks. For example, a threat actor could gain access to sensitive information or launch a destructive cyberattack against the organization's systems. To keep the company safe, the person responsible for cybersecurity must remain vigilant and monitor all network activity closely. They should also set up systems that can detect potential hacker attempts and take necessary actions to stop them before it gets out of hand. There is a need to have a significant focus on research into the relationship between cybersecurity and business continuity. However, this should be done with a clear plan for how decision makers in businesses can most effectively comprehend the value of cybersecurity and the connection to business continuity and risk management strategies for their organizations and that of other stakeholders, such as customers, suppliers, and regulators. It should also encompass the interaction between the two areas as well as the role played by third-party vendors.

REFERENCES

Aldawood, Hussain, and Geoffrey Skinner. 2019. 'Contemporary Cybersecurity Social Engineering Solutions, Measures, Policies, Tools and Applications: A Critical Appraisal'. *International Journal of Security* 10 (1): 1–15.

Alelyani, Salem, and Harish Kumar G. R. 2018. 'Overview of Cyberattack on Saudi Organizations'. *Journal of Information Security and Cybercrimes Research* 1 (1): 32–39. https://doi.org/10.26735/16587790.2018.004.

AlKalbani, Ahmed, Hepu Deng, and Booi Kam. 2015. 'Investigating the Role of Socio-Organizational Factors in the Information Security Compliance in Organizations', *Proceedings of Australasian Conference on Information Systems*, Adelaide, Australia, 12 (1), pp. 1–11.

Anderson, Ross, Chris Barton, Rainer Boehme, Richard Clayton, Carlos Ganan, Tom Grasso, Michael Levi, Tyler Moore, Stefan Savage, and Marie Vasek. 2013. 'Measuring the Cost of Cybercrime'. In R. Böhme (Ed.), *The Economics of Information Security and Privacy* (pp. 265–300). Heidelberg, BE: Springer.

Cains, Mariana G., Liberty Flora, Danica Taber, Zoe King, and Diane S. Henshel. 2020. 'Defining Cybersecurity and Cybersecurity Risk within a Multidisciplinary Context Using Expert Elicitation'. *Risk Analysis* 42. https://doi.org/10.1111/risa.13687.

Chamkar, Samir Achraf, Yassine Maleh, and Noreddine Gherabi. 2022. 'The Human Factor Capabilities in Security Operation Center (SOC)'. *EDPACS* 66 (1): 1–14. https://doi.org/10.1080/07366981.2021.19770 26.

Eian, Isaac Chin, Lim Ka Yong, Majesty Yeap Xiao Li, Yeo Hui Qi, and Fatima Z. 2020. 'Cyberattacks in the Era of COVID-19 and Possible Solution Domains'. *Preprint* 12 (1): 1–15. https://doi.org/10.20944/preprints202009.0630.v1.

Fan, Wenjun, Kevin Lwakatare, and Rong Rong. 2017. 'Social Engineering: I-E Based Model of Human Weakness for Attack and Defense Investigations'. *International Journal of Computer Network and Information Security* 9 (1): 1–11. https://doi.org/10.5815/ijcnis.2017.01.01.

Garba, Abubakar Bello, Jocelyn Armarego, David Murray, and William Kenworthy. 2015. 'Review of the Information Security and Privacy Challenges in Bring Your Own Device (BYOD) Environments'. *Journal of Information Privacy and Security* 11 (1): 38–54. https://doi.org/10.1080/15536548.2015.10 10985.

Huang, Danny Yuxing, Maxwell Matthaios Aliapoulios, Vector Guo Li, Luca Invernizzi, Elie Bursztein, Kylie McRoberts, Jonathan Levin, Kirill Levchenko, Alex C. Snoeren, and Damon McCoy. 2018. 'Tracking Ransomware End-to-End'. In *2018 IEEE Symposium on Security and Privacy (SP)*, 618–631. San Francisco, CA: IEEE. https://doi.org/10.1109/SP.2018.00047.

Luo, Xin, and Qinyu Liao. 2007. 'Awareness Education as the Key to Ransomware Prevention'. *Information Systems Security* 16 (4): 195–202. https://doi.org/10.1080/10658980701576412.

Nasir, Sadiq, and Narasimha Vajjhala. 2020. 'Evaluating Information Security Awareness and Compliance in Sub-Saharan Africa: An Interpretivist Perspective'. In *Proceedings of the 13 Th IADIS International Conference Information Systems 2020*, 187–190. IADIS Publications. https://doi.org/10.33965/is2020_202006R025.

Nobles, Calvin. 2019. 'Establishing Human Factors Programs to Mitigate Blind Spots in Cybersecurity', *Proceedings of 14th Midwest Association for Information Systems*, 1–6. Wisonsin.

Pienta, Daniel, Stefan Tams, and Jason Bennet Thatcher. 2020. 'Can Trust Be Trusted in Cybersecurity?', *Proceedings of the 53rd Hawaii International Conference on System Sciences*, 4264–4273.

Pigni, Federico, Marcin Bartosiak, Gabriele Piccoli, and Blake Ives. 2018. 'Targeting Target with a 100 Million Dollar Data Breach'. *Journal of Information Technology Teaching Cases* 8 (1): 9–23. https://doi.org/10.1057/s41266-017-0028-0.

Politou, Eugenia, Efthimios Alepis, and Constantinos Patsakis. 2018. 'Forgetting Personal Data and Revoking Consent under the GDPR: Challenges and Proposed Solutions'. *Journal of Cybersecurity* 4 (1). https://doi.org/10.1093/cybsec/tyy001.

Prabhu, Sunitha, and Nik Thompson. 2020. 'A Unified Classification Model of Insider Threats to Information Security'. *Proceedings of 31st Australasian Conference on Information Systems*, 1–12. Wellington, Australia.

Richardson, Ronny. 2017. 'Ransomware: Evolution, Mitigation and Prevention'. *International Management Review* 13 (1): 10–21.

Rowland, Pam, Ashley Podhradsky, and Stephanie Plucker. 2018. 'CybHER: A Method for Empowering, Motivating, Educating and Anchoring Girls to a Cybersecurity Career Path'. *Proceedings of the 51st Hawaii International Conference on System Sciences*, 3727–3735. Hawaii, USA.

Smith, McKay, and Garrett Mulrain. 2018. 'Equi-Failure: The National Security Implications of the Equifax Hack and a Critical Proposal for Reform'. *Journal of Natural Security Law & Policy* 9 (1): 549–588.

Tang, Mincong, Meng'gang Li, and Tao Zhang. 2016. 'The Impacts of Organizational Culture on Information Security Culture: A Case Study'. *Information Technology and Management* 17 (2): 179–186. https://doi.org/10.1007/s10799-015-0252-2.

Zwilling, Moti, Galit Klien, Dušan Lesjak, Łukasz Wiechetek, Fatih Cetin, and Hamdullah Nejat Basim. 2022. 'Cybersecurity Awareness, Knowledge and Behavior: A Comparative Study'. *Journal of Computer Information Systems* 62 (1): 82–97. https://doi.org/10.1080/08874417.2020.1712269.

Printed in the United States
by Baker & Taylor Publisher Services